SCIENCE ANNUAL

A Modern Science Anthology for the Family

1988

ACKNOWLEDGMENTS

Sources of articles appear below, including those reprinted with the kind permission of publications and organizations.

WHAT WE'VE LEARNED FROM COMET HALLEY, Page 8: Reprinted with permission from *Astronomy* magazine.

MARS, EARTH, AND ICE, Page 15: From *Sky & Telescope* magazine, © 1986 Sky Publishing Corp. All rights reserved.

THE LIMITS OF MANNED SPACE FLIGHT, Page 22: Reprinted from *The Sciences,* September/October 1986 © by The New York Academy of Sciences.

THE UNGENTLE DEATH OF A GIANT STAR, Page 30: Reprinted by permission from the January/February 1986 issue of SCIENCE 86. Copyright © 1986 by the American Association for the Advancement of Science.

EVENING THE SCORE, Page 40: Reprinted with permission from PSYCHOLOGY TODAY MAGAZINE. Copyright © 1987 American Psychological Association.

CALLS OF THE WILD, Page 46: Copyright © 1986 by Doug Starr and reprinted with permission of Omni Publications International Ltd.

THE MYSTERY OF MASTERY, Page 55: Reprinted with permission from PSYCHOLOGY TODAY MAGAZINE. Copyright © 1986 American Psychological Association.

BRAIN SCANS FOR DRUG TESTING, Page 62: Reprinted with permission from *American Health* © 1986.

GENETIC ENGINEERING DOWN ON THE FARM, Page 72: Reprinted with permission from TECHNOLOGY REVIEW, M.I.T. Alumni Association, copyright 1987.

THE MAGIC OF METAMORPHOSIS, Page 80: Reprinted with permission of the author; article first appeared in *Smithsonian,* May 1986.

THE STRATEGIC ARTISTRY OF BIRD EGGS, Page 89: Reprinted with permission of the author; article first appeared in *Audubon,* the magazine of the National Audubon Society.

KRILL: FOOD OF THE FUTURE?, Page 95: Reprinted by permission from *Sea Frontiers,* © 1987 by the International Oceanographic Foundation, 3979 Rickenbacker Causeway, Virginia Key, Miami, Florida 33149.

COMPUTERS THAT ALMOST THINK, Page 106: Reprinted from June 2, 1986, issue of *Business Week* by special permission, © 1986 by McGraw Hill, Inc.

FACTORING FERMAT NUMBERS, Page 112: Article first appeared in *New Scientist,* London, the weekly review of science and technology.

MAKING COMPUTERS WORK FOR DISABLED PEOPLE, Page 118: Reprinted with permission from TECHNOLOGY REVIEW, M.I.T. Alumni Association, copyright 1987.

WARNING: THIS SOFTWARE MAY BE UNSAFE, Page 126: Reprinted with permission from SCIENCE NEWS, the weekly magazine of science, copyright © 1986 by Science Service, Inc.

GIANTS THAT SHAPE THE EARTH, Page 136: Copyright 1986 by the National Wildlife Federation. Reprinted from the December 1985–January 1986 issue of *National Wildlife* magazine.

STORM WARNINGS, Page 140: First appeared in the January 1986 issue of OCEANS.

THE MYSTERIOUS OZONE HOLE, Page 148: Reprinted by permission of the authors; article first appeared in *Space World* magazine.

THE PUZZLE OF EL NIÑO, Page 154: Reprinted from *Popular Science* with permission © 1986, Times Mirror Magazines, Inc.

ROLLING WITH COAL, Page 166: Reprinted with permission from SCIENCE NEWS, the weekly magazine of science, copyright 1986 by Science Service, Inc.

PAPYRUS AS FUEL, Page 173: Reprinted with permission from *Aramco World Magazine,* May/June 1986.

A BRIGHT FUTURE FOR SOLAR ENERGY, Page 178: Copyright © 1986 by The New York Times Company. Reprinted by permission.

THE AFTERMATH OF CHERNOBYL, Page 182: Copyright © 1986 by The New York Times Company. Reprinted by permission.

VIRGIN FORESTS UNDER FIRE, Page 194: Copyright 1986 by the National Wildlife Federation. Reprinted from the February–March 1986 issue of *National Wildlife* magazine.

STAFF

EDITORIAL

Editorial Director
Bernard S. Cayne

Executive Editor
Joseph M. Castagno

Managing Editor
Doris E. Lechner

Copy Editors
David M. Buskus
Ronald B. Roth

Proofreaders
Ruth J. Lofgren
Meghan O'Reilly

Chief Indexer
Jill Schuler

Manuscript Typist
Joan Michael Calley

Art Assistant
Elizabeth Farrington

Art Director
Eric E. Akerman

Production Editor
Diane L. George

Staff Assistant
Jennifer Pickett Vogt

Manager, Picture Library
Jane H. Carruth

Chief, Photo Research
Ann Eriksen

Photo Researcher
Paula J. Kobylarz

Photo Assistant
Renee L. Sturges

MANUFACTURING

Director of Manufacturing
Joseph J. Corlett

Production Manager
Teresa Kluk

Production Assistant
Barbara L. Persan

CONTRIBUTORS

LAWRENCE K. ALTMAN, M.D., *The New York Times*
REVIEW OF THE YEAR: HEALTH AND DISEASE

DEAN BAKER, Journalist
VIRGIN FORESTS UNDER FIRE

EMIL J. BARDANA, JR., Vice chairman, Department of Medicine; head of the Division of Allergy and Clinical Immunology, Oregon Health Services University, Portland, Oregon
WORKPLACE EPIDEMICS

MAURY BATES, JR., Director of publications, Conoco
A 20TH CENTURY NOAH'S ARK

RICHARD BERRY, Editor-in-chief, *Astronomy*
WHAT WE'VE LEARNED FROM COMET HALLEY

FRANK BOWE, Former executive director, American Coalition of Citizens with Disabilities; author of *Personal Computers and Special Needs* and *Changing the Rules*
MAKING COMPUTERS WORK FOR THE DISABLED

BRUCE BOWER, Staff writer, *Science News*
REVIEW OF THE YEAR: BEHAVIORAL SCIENCES

GENE BYLINSKY, Board of editors, *Fortune*
THE 10,000 MPH AIRLINER

JAMES R. CHILES, Lawyer and writer
STANDING UP TO EARTHQUAKES

ARTHUR CLARK, Contributor, *Aramco World Magazine*
PAPYRUS AS FUEL

BRUCE M. CORDELL, Planetary scientist, writer, and consultant
MARS, EARTH, AND ICE

TONY DAVIS, Environmental writer
KEEPING RIVERS WILD

WILLIAM M. DeCAMPLI, M.D., Ph.D., consultant to NASA and the Aeronautics and Space Engineering Board of the National Academy of Engineers
THE LIMITS OF MANNED SPACE FLIGHT

VINCENT G. DETHIER, Professor of zoology and director of the Neuroscience and Behavior Program, University of Massachusetts, Amherst, Massachusetts
THE MAGIC OF METAMORPHOSIS

KEITH DEVLIN, Reader in mathematics, University of Lancaster, England
FACTORING FERMAT NUMBERS

STUART DIAMOND, *The New York Times*
THE AFTERMATH OF CHERNOBYL

ROBERT S. DORNEY, Chairman of the board, Ecoplans Limited; professor, School of Urban and Regional Planning, University of Waterloo, Waterloo, Ontario, Canada
BRINGING WILDLIFE BACK TO THE CITY

JOHN FREE, Senior editor, *Popular Science*
CHUNNEL FOR THE CHANNEL

ELLEN FRIED, Free-lance writer
THE UNGENTLE DEATH OF A GIANT STAR

ROBERT GANNON, Consulting science editor, *Popular Science*
THE PUZZLE OF EL NIÑO

JERALD GREENBURG, Associate professor of management and human resources, Ohio State University
Coauthor, EVENING THE SCORE

KATHERINE HARAMUNDANIS, Free-lance writer formerly with Smithsonian Astrophysical Laboratory, Cambridge, Massachusetts; coauthor, *An Introduction to Astronomy*
REVIEW OF THE YEAR: ASTRONOMY

KIM HEACOX, Free-lance writer
GIANTS THAT SHAPE THE EARTH

BERND HEINRICH, Department of Zoology, University of Vermont
THE STRATEGIC ARTISTRY OF BIRD EGGS

JOHN HERZFELD, Free-lance writer and copy editor for *American Health*
BRAIN SCANS FOR DRUG TESTING

MIKE HIGGINS, Former editor of *Personal Robot News;* author, *A Robot in Every Home: An Introduction to Personal Robots & Brand-Name Buyer's Guide*
PERSONAL ROBOTS OF TOMORROW

GLADWIN HILL, Free-lance writer; former environment editor, *The New York Times*
REVIEW OF THE YEAR: THE ENVIRONMENT

LAURA HOFSTADTER, Science writer, Stanford University Medical Center News Bureau
SEEKING AN ANTIDOTE FOR AIDS

ROBERT F. JONES, Special contributor, *Sports Illustrated*
TEXOTIC WILDLIFE

MARC KUSINITZ, Editor, *New Medical Science*
REVIEW OF THE YEAR: PHYSICAL SCIENCES

BILL LAWREN, Writer; author of *General Groves and the A-Bomb*
UNDERSEA CITIES

THOMAS LEAHY, Free-lance writer; director of communications and publications for the Florida Sea Grant College Program at the University of Florida
STORM WARNINGS

BENEDICT A. LEERBURGER, Free-lance science writer and editorial consultant; author, *The Complete Consumer's Guide to the Latest Telephones*
MEASURING: AN ANCIENT ART REFINED
REVIEW OF THE YEAR: TECHNOLOGY

DENNIS L. MAMMANA, Free-lance science writer
REVIEW OF THE YEAR: SPACE SCIENCE

MELVIN M. MARK, Associate professor of psychology, Pennsylvania State University
Coauthor, EVENING THE SCORE

WILLIAM H. MATTHEWS III, Regents' professor of geology emeritus, Lamar University, Beaumont, Texas
REVIEW OF THE YEAR: EARTH SCIENCE

MARTIN M. McLAUGHLIN, Free-lance consultant; former vice president for education, Overseas Development Council, Washington, D.C.
Coauthor, REVIEW OF THE YEAR: PAST, PRESENT, AND FUTURE

DIANE MOSER, Writer specializing in space and technology
Coauthor, THE MYSTERIOUS OZONE HOLE

MARK NELSON, Contributing editor, *Chevron World*
STALKING THE GREAT GRAY OWL

STEPHEN NICOL, Formerly with the Institute of Marine Biology, University of Cape Town, South Africa
KRILL: FOOD OF THE FUTURE?

ELAINE PASCOE, Free-lance writer
THE 1986 NOBEL PRIZE FOR PHYSIOLOGY OR MEDICINE
THE 1986 NOBEL PRIZES FOR PHYSICS AND CHEMISTRY
IN MEMORIAM

IVARS PETERSON, Technology editor, *Science News*
WARNING: THIS SOFTWARE MAY BE UNSAFE

DAVID PIMENTEL, Professor of insect ecology and agricultural sciences, Cornell University
GENETIC ENGINEERING DOWN ON THE FARM

ALAN PISTORIUS, Writer and lecturer on natural history
THE BIG SLEEP

OTIS PORT, Associate editor, *Business Week*
COMPUTERS THAT ALMOST THINK

JANET RALOFF, Policy/technology editor, *Science News*
REVIEW OF THE YEAR: ENERGY

JIM SCHEFTER, West Coast editor, *Popular Science*
REVIEW OF THE YEAR: COMPUTERS AND MATHEMATICS

ELLEN RUPPEL SHELL, Senior writer, WGBH-TV, Boston; free-lance writer
FLAVORS: MORE THAN A MATTER OF TASTE

NANCY SHUTE, Free-lance writer on science and the environment
THE OTHER KIND OF RADIATION

JOANNE SILBERNER, Biomedicine editor, *Science News*
REVIEW OF THE YEAR: BIOLOGY

RAYMOND SPANGENBURG, Writer specializing in space and technology
Coauthor, THE MYSTERIOUS OZONE HOLE

DOUG STARR, Free-lance writer
CALLS OF THE WILD

F. RICHARD STEPHENSON, Astronomer and senior research fellow, Department of Physics, University of Durham, Durham, England
CELESTIAL DATING

BOB STROHM, Executive editor, *National Wildlife* magazine
REVIEW OF THE YEAR: WILDLIFE

ANTHONY STUART, Castle Museum, Norwich, England
WHAT HAPPENED TO THE GIANT MAMMALS?

WALTER SULLIVAN, *The New York Times*
A BRIGHT FUTURE FOR SOLAR ENERGY

RICHARD TALCOTT, Associate editor, *Astronomy*
WHAT WE'VE LEARNED FROM COMET HALLEY

JENNY TESAR, Free-lance science writer; author, *Parents as Teachers* and *Introduction to Animals*
CRACK: CHEAP, DEADLY COCAINE

DIETRICK E. THOMSEN, Senior editor/physical sciences, *Science News*
ROLLING WITH COAL

ROBERT J. TROTTER, Senior editor, *Psychology Today*
THE MYSTERY OF MASTERY

ROB WECHSLER, Reporter, *Discover* magazine
UNSHACKLED FROM DIABETES

PETER S. WELLS, Director, Center for Ancient Studies, University of Minnesota
Coauthor, REVIEW OF THE YEAR: PAST, PRESENT, AND FUTURE

ROBERT WILBUR, Pharmacologist and research consultant
A DRUG TO FIGHT COCAINE

ROBERT W. WILLETT, JR., Corporate communications specialist in Houston, Texas
THE RIDDLE OF THE RIDLEYS

CAROL WILLIS, Architectural historian; curator of the touring exhibition "Hugh Ferriss: Metropolis"
THE TITAN CITY

DENISE ALLEN ZWICKER, Free-lance writer
NICE NEWS ABOUT NOISE

CONTENTS

ASTRONOMY AND

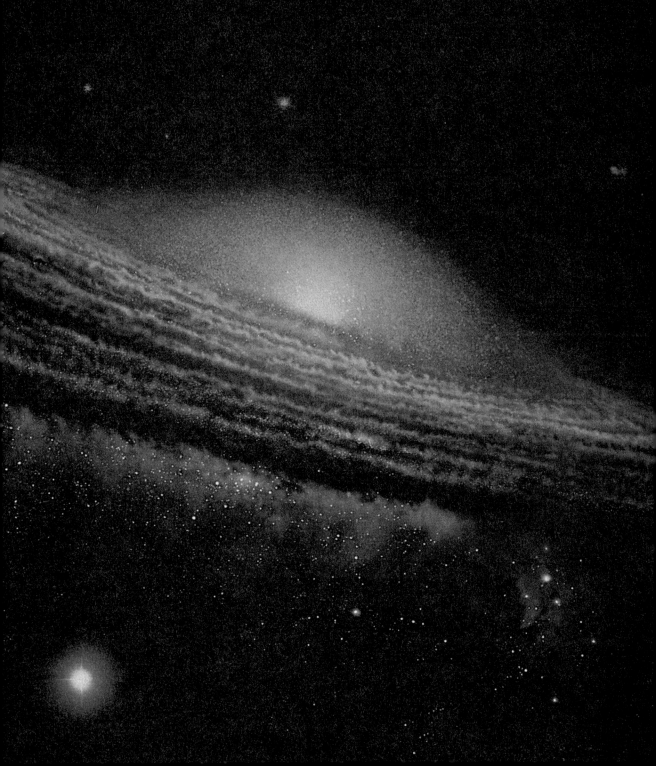

SPACE SCIENCE

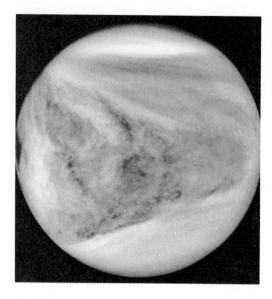

The thick atmosphere of Venus obscures its surface (left), as photographed by the Pioneer Venus orbiter. At right, the radar altimeter of the orbiter sees through the cloud cover to allow mapping of the planet's terrain.

REVIEW
OF THE
YEAR

ASTRONOMY AND SPACE SCIENCE

The year 1986 began in an exciting fashion. In early January, the robot spacecraft Voyager 2 flew past the planet Uranus and returned to waiting scientists on Earth remarkable photos and information about the mysterious Uranian clouds, moons, and rings.

But as scientists anticipated their fullest and most rewarding year of space exploration since a human first walked the dusty soil of the Moon in 1969, a string of disasters rocked the American space program and changed the complexion of space exploration and commercialization forever.

THE SOLAR SYSTEM

Voyager 2 passed Uranus in January 1986, providing discoveries of at least 10 new moons, many rings, a surprising magnetic field, unexpected atmospheric winds, a new emission in the atmosphere called electroglow, and the amazingly complex geology of its moon Miranda.

Electric field observations from the Pioneer Venus orbiter have established that, although Venus has huge volcanic cones on its surface,

today it is volcanically dead. ■ Spherical grains have been discovered that are similar to granules from meteorites in the oldest Earth rocks. These grains may indicate that large impacts played a more important role in the history of the solar system than had previously been thought.

Scientists at the Jet Propulsion Laboratory (JPL) suggest that, based on Viking orbiter pictures, Mars may have had ancient lakes or seas covering up to 15 percent of the planet. ■ The Sun, as described by the "solar constant" observed by various means, appears to be fading by 0.02 percent per year. This phenomenon seems linked to a solar cycle, such as the 11-year sunspot or 22-year magnetic cycles. If the trend continues over decades, our climate could be affected.

A new theory suggests that the Moon may have been formed from the solar nebula when a roughly Mars-sized object smashed into the proto-Earth. Debris ejected as a result of the collision formed a prelunar disk from which the Moon later formed. More work is needed before the hypothesis can be confirmed. ■ Comet Halley, well studied by an international team of satellites, was found to have a two-lobed velvet-black nucleus subject to bright outbursts. (See page 8.) ■ Comet Wilson, discovered August 5, may be the first known visitor from the Oort Cloud. The Oort Cloud is a theoretical ring of comets that circles the solar system outside the orbit of Pluto. The comet, discovered by Christine Wilson of the California Institute of Technology (Cal Tech), made its closest approach to the Sun in April 1987.

THE MILKY WAY GALAXY

A star about to become a planetary nebula was discovered that has already passed the giant/supergiant stage. It is rapidly passing through the phase that will make it a planetary nebula: a star surrounded by a vast, thin shell. ■ The X-ray source 4U1820-30, located in the globular cluster NGC 6624, appears to be a binary system: two stars rotating around each other in the incredibly short period of less than 11 minutes. This is the shortest period for any binary system found and the first binary system ever found in a globular cluster (a large, densely packed group of stars). The same X-ray source also emits unexplained quasi-periodic oscillations. ■ The search continues for brown dwarfs, thought to be the missing mass in the universe. So far, no brown dwarfs have been found, but the search continues nonetheless. ■ Three obscured globular clusters have been found in the Galactic Bulge, using advanced Charge-Coupled Device (CCD) instrumentation. ■ A new kind of light analyzer—an amplitude interferometer—was used to measure the angular diameter of the star Sirius for the first time. This measurement (5.63 arc-milliseconds) will enable astronomers to determine the actual size of Sirius with great accuracy. ■ A massive shell found around the variable star R Coronae Borealis is unexplained by current theories. The shell is so huge that, if centered on the Sun, it would hold not only the entire solar system but the 50 nearest star systems as well. ■ Scientists have found, in an infrared object IRAS 1629A, a molecular cloud that is rapidly infalling to form a protostar. Oddly, the inside is falling inward while the outside remains stable, as predicted by theory. ■ Observations strongly suggest a massive black hole at the center of our galaxy. The object—dubbed Sgr A*—is as small as a star but with all the properties of a black hole, that is, a compact, nonthermal radio source.

THE UNIVERSE

The nucleus of nearby Seyfert galaxy NGC 2992 was identified as hourglass-shaped with a disk of gas and dust at the center from which the observed radio emissions are flowing. ■ Spectroscopic evidence has been gathered that indicates a star falling into a black hole in the center of the galaxy NGC 5548. The black hole is 30 million times more massive than the Sun. This observation is the first of accretion going on in the center of the nucleus of an external galaxy. The galactic center of this galaxy is thought to be a black hole.

Motion studies of galaxies suggest that the universe is inhomogeneous (nonuniform), and that galaxies tend to lie along sheets like the surfaces of bubbles. Galaxies also tend to participate in galactic drifting that proceeds at the speed of 1,250 miles (2,000 kilometers) per second. Galactic drift may be caused by the gravitational attraction of large, invisible concentrations of matter. ■ The largest structures in the universe—great glowing arcs resembling

The Greater Magellanic Cloud, a nearby galaxy, as it appeared before February 25, 1987 (left). On that date, Supernova 1987A blazed into view over the southern sky (right)—the closest such occurrence since 1604.

Both photos: NOAO

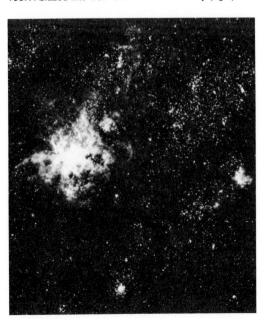

strings of pearls trillions of miles long—have been discovered. They are associated with clusters of galaxies engaged in massive collisions. ■ There is more clumping of clusters of galaxies, and the clumps are larger than previously expected, astronomers have determined. The superclusters can be up to 500 million light-years across, extending over perhaps 1 percent of the known universe. These findings suggest that the universe is not expanding smoothly and uniformly and may be subject to forces other than the Big Bang—the explosion theorists believe began the expansion of the universe.

A team of U.S. and U.K. astronomers has found a quasar, 1208+1011—90 percent of the way to the edge of the universe, or 73 billion trillion miles from Earth, making it the most distant object known. Its red shift of 3.8 places 1208+1011 near to other quasars with red shifts of about 3.5. Quasars prompted Wallace Sargent of Palomar Observatory to remark that "light expands as the universe expands." This quasar's light takes over 12 billion years to reach us. ■ Observations made by radio telescopes both in California and in Central Europe have found superluminal quasars that astronomers calculate are moving faster than the speed of light relative to us. So far, 14 such quasars have been found. According to the theory of special relativity, in its own frame of reference, no quasar is going faster than the speed of light, so the cosmic speed limit is not violated. ■ The first infrared quasar, 13349+2438, has been found with IRAS (InfraRed Astronomical Satellite). Scientists believe this IR quasar represents a very early stage in quasar evolution.

Observations made from Chile toward the South Galactic Pole using a supersensitive CCD have obtained a picture of the distant regions of the universe that are increasingly filled with the images of galaxies. The picture is not yet completely filled with images (a visual whiteout) because we look out not only into space but back in time. The faintest galaxies seen in the picture may be only 1 billion to 2 billion years old—younger than Earth.

KATHERINE HARAMUNDANIS

A STRING OF DISASTERS

It began on January 28 with the worst disaster in spacefaring history. On that day the space shuttle Challenger exploded 73 seconds into its mission, killing all seven astronauts on board. All scheduled shuttle flights were immediately postponed until the cause of the accident was pinpointed and corrected.

The troubles continued throughout the spring as Titan and Delta vehicles failed during launches that sent them and their payloads plunging back to Earth. And as if that weren't enough, two

planetary missions were scrubbed during the summer when the National Aeronautics and Space Administration (NASA) decided their liquid-fueled boosters were too risky to carry on board the shuttle.

SHUTTLE MODIFICATIONS

Perhaps the most profound and furthest-reaching of the problems was the Challenger disaster. To get the shuttle fleet flying again, engineers have begun redesigning the faulty joints on the solid-fuel rocket that are believed to have caused the explosion. A third O-ring has been added, and engineers have installed a "capture feature" to keep the joint from opening again.

But changes in the shuttle system are going far beyond these corrections. Modifications to the external tank valves, installation of heavy-duty landing brakes, and a new steering system are all being planned for the revamped shuttle fleet, together with a crude but effective escape system for the crew. Long-term overhauls to about half a dozen major subsystems are expected to be completed by the mid-1990's. After the accident, NASA began carrying out the most extensive managerial and technical review in its history. Nearly all agree that these changes will result in a significantly safer shuttle when flights resume.

CONSEQUENCES

The setbacks of the U.S. space program during 1986 may damage the nation's leadership in space exploration. Major research missions including the Galileo atmospheric probe of Jupiter, the Ulysses flight through the polar regions of the Sun, and the Hubble Space Telescope may not fly now until the end of this decade.

Some feel that these problems could have economic and strategic implications well into the next century. The inaugural launching from the new launch pad at Vandenberg Air Force Base has been delayed until at least 1992. And with more than three dozen commercial and military satellites backed up, industry officials are turning to French, Japanese, or Chinese vehicles to get their payloads into orbit.

An encouraging sign for the shuttle program occurred on the morning of October 9, when the space shuttle Atlantis underwent several successful tests and a practice countdown atop launch pad 39-B. In mid-November, officials conducted a highly successful disaster drill in which they found at least 50 safety improvements to make before the next launch.

OTHER NATIONS' SPACE PROGRAMS

Even with a staff and budget dwarfed by that of NASA or the Soviets, the multinational European Space Agency (ESA) has made a substantial

The manned space station now under development will incorporate numerous space- and Earth-viewing devices.

impact in space research, exploration, and commercialization.

The French Centre National d'Etudes Spatiales (CNES) has continued its design of Hermes, a delta-winged reusable spaceplane. In October, 10 countries made formal commitments to participate in the $35 million Hermes development. When operational in the mid-1990's, the craft will perform a number of missions, including assembly and servicing of space stations or orbital platforms, and flights for a variety of science and commercial requirements.

Eastern countries have made huge inroads in the commercialization of space as well, particularly because of their lower launch costs. In August a new Japanese H-1 test rocket launched two satellites into orbit. During the year, companies in Sweden and the U.S. agreed to launch communications satellites on Chinese vehicles. China also plans to build an orbiting space station in the late 1990's and a shuttle sometime later.

Meanwhile, the U.S.S.R. continues its work on a reusable shuttle as well as the development of a productive space station. On February 20 a station named Mir—a third-generation space laboratory—was launched into Earth orbit. Designed to become the hub of a permanently manned space research complex, its six docking ports allow it to link up simultaneously with expansion modules and a variety of ships.

A few weeks after Mir's launch, two cosmonauts linked up with it and began their work of testing and debugging the station. In May the cosmonauts left Mir behind and docked with an older Salyut 7 station some 1,900 miles (3,050 kilometers) away.

AMERICAN SPACE STATION

As the Soviets performed this history-making mission, NASA unveiled blueprints for its own manned station. The model is a scaled-down version of an earlier concept, yet will be more spacious than the Soviet facility.

Plans call for it to have five major pressurized modules capable of housing six to nine people. These modules will be built by the U.S., Japan, and ESA for the scientific and technological research. Canada will also contribute a satellite-servicing and -repair center.

The football-field-sized station will cost between $8 billion and $13 billion, and will be among the most complex and visible technological achievements in history and serve as the centerpiece for future international space activities.

DENNIS L. MAMMANA

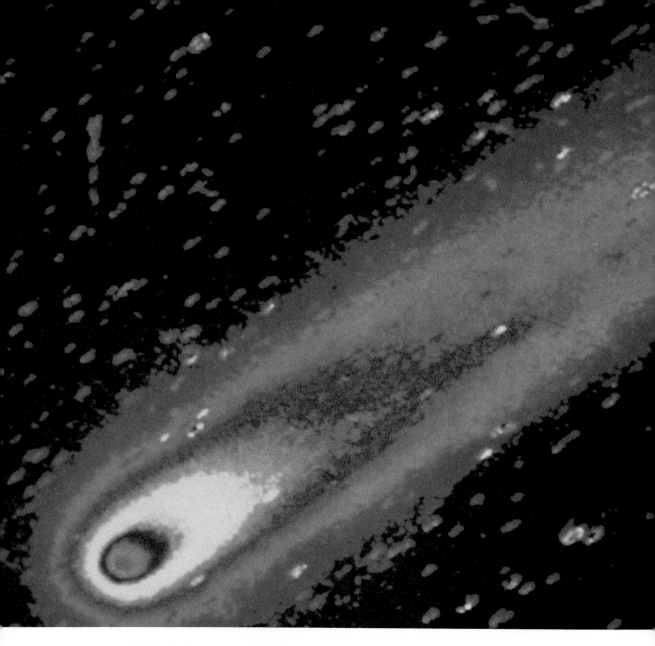

What We've Learned From COMET HALLEY

by Richard Berry and Richard Talcott

As the huckster's call—"Step right up, folks; it's a once-in-a-lifetime experience"—fades into astronomical memory, you may wonder: What was it all about? Why the hoopla and why the hype, why the excitement and why the pronouncements? Was it all worth it? If we take at face value that we set out to learn something about comets from Comet Halley, then what exactly did we learn from Comet Halley?

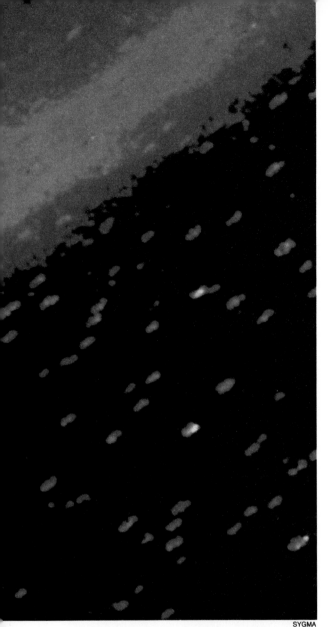

Well, it turns out that we've learned a lot. Although it will be years before all the data collected have been thoroughly analyzed, astronomers have already begun announcing their findings.

An International Effort

Oddly enough, it's results from the highly complex experiments aboard the Soviet, European, and Japanese spacecraft that have been reported, rather than simpler ground-based studies. From an astronomer's point of view, Halley is only one comet among many, and photographs and spectra can be studied at leisure long

after the comet has vanished. Results from space experiments come quickly because they are narrowly focused on answering one or two specific scientific questions, and also because national prestige demands that results, any results, be announced as soon as possible.

Although the long tails, the bright coma (head), and the enigmatic jets of a comet provoke astronomers' curiosity, it's the nucleus they really want to know about. But, sad to say, it is the nucleus that we know least about.

Halley's Nucleus

From Earth, comet nuclei are too small to show any detail whatsoever; they appear as starlike specks of light embedded in the glowing coma of the comet. Astronomers had deduced, from the gas and dust thrown into space, that comet nuclei are composed of water ice mixed with other frozen gases, stony meteoritic material, and fine dust, and that the comet nucleus is a body between 0.6 and 6 miles (1 and 10 kilometers) in diameter. Pre-flyby estimates for the size of Halley's nucleus put it at about 4 miles (6 kilometers) in diameter with a reflectivity of about 25 percent—a big "dirty snowball" in space. These estimates were wrong.

In early March 1986, three spacecraft—two Soviet Vegas and the European Giotto—flew through Halley and photographed the nucleus. The Vega 1 and Vega 2 spacecraft passed some 5,525 and 5,000 miles (8,890 and 8,030 kilometers) from the nucleus, respectively; the Giotto spacecraft passed only 375 miles (605 kilometers) from the nucleus.

The Soviet images, which in their raw form appear unsharp, reveal the nucleus as an irregular, potato-shaped body some 10 miles (16 kilometers) long and 5 miles (8 kilometers) thick by 5.6 miles (9 kilometers) wide. In those images the nucleus appears to be very dark, reflecting roughly 4 percent of the light falling on it. This is as dark as finely ground charcoal or carbon black. The images show this dark body enveloped in a cloud of dust and sometimes obscured by it. Of the several thousand images obtained, the 70 best will be extensively processed, and from these the Soviet investigators expect to be able to reconstruct the complete three-dimensional shape of the nucleus.

The Giotto images suggest a somewhat different shape for the nucleus, though Giotto did not have as good a viewing angle as the Vegas. In the images the nucleus appears "as a solid object of irregular shape visible as a dark silhouette against background light scattered by dust," according to the Giotto imaging team scientists. The profile of the nucleus is 9.3 miles (15 kilometers) long by 5 miles (8 kilometers) wide. Dust surrounding the nucleus makes finding the sunlit edge of the nucleus difficult, so the width of the nucleus cannot be determined with any precision. The net result is that, although they are considerably sharper than the Vega pictures, the Giotto images are difficult to interpret.

The Vega images reveal almost nothing of the surface of the nucleus. In the Giotto images, very little can be seen on the dark side of the nucleus, although the profile of the nucleus suggests a fairly rugged terrain of craterlike depressions, fumaroles (volcanic holes), or rolling hills ranging in size from about 300 feet (90 meters) to 3,000 feet (915 meters) across.

A Dirty Snowball?

Both the Vega and the Giotto images show something not entirely unexpected: jets coming from the nucleus. In the classic "dirty snowball" model for comet nuclei, the comet's coma and tail are composed of gas that has evaporated and dust that has been blown away from the surface of the nucleus. Before the flybys, most astronomers assumed that the gas would evaporate from the surface uniformly, carrying dust particles with it as they were uncovered in a process informally known as an "inverse snowstorm." Although ground-based observations showed local brightenings in the inner coma, these jets were generally passed off as minor anomalies (irregularities) in the smooth outflow of gas and dust from the nucleus to the coma.

Even before the flybys, it was becoming apparent that the "dirty snowball" model didn't really work. A study of the night-to-night variations of features in the coma, based on photographs taken in 1910, led astronomers Steve Larson and Zdenek Sekanina to predict jets of gas and dust from Halley's nucleus. They even prepared a map showing where the jets had been in 1910.

The spacecraft showed virtually all of the gas and dust vents from six or seven small areas on the surface as narrow jets. One of the jets is much larger than any of the others, and it and the second largest jet account for the bulk of Comet Halley's gas and dust emission. The rest of the surface appears to be completely inactive.

All the jets appear on the sunward side of the nucleus, and, as best as can be determined, none are found on the dark side. The jets cover

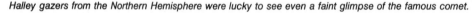

Halley gazers from the Northern Hemisphere were lucky to see even a faint glimpse of the famous comet.

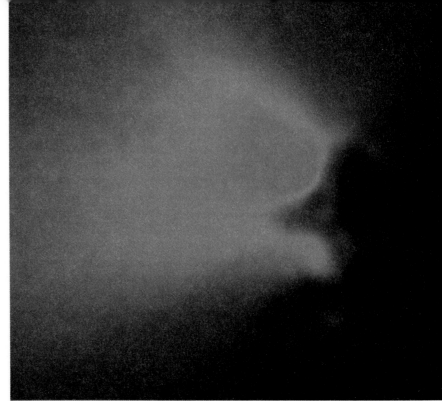

Nucleus of Comet Halley. The green jets are thought by astronomers to represent the emission of gas and dust from the comet.

Max Planck Institut für Aeronomie, Lindau Harz, FRG

roughly 10 percent of the surface of the nucleus. The two Vega spacecraft viewed Halley's nucleus from a wide range of angles and detected at least five jets. Both the Soviet and the European images show that the largest jet and possibly several smaller jets have internal structure, suggesting that the jets are clusters of smaller jets or that they come from multiple sources.

When the nucleus heats up as Halley approaches the Sun, water and volatile organic materials evaporate out, leaving a skeleton of nonvolatile organic materials and silicate dust holes where volatiles had been. Such porous structures absorb light very well and could explain why the nucleus appears jet black. Because its surface is black, the nucleus should absorb sunlight and be quite warm. Infrared spectra of the nucleus obtained by Vega 1's infrared spectrometer show that the temperature of the nucleus and the dusty cocoon that surrounds it is between 80° F and 260° F (27° C and 127° C)—much too hot for a surface of bare ice. If the surface were ice, it could not be that hot because it would be cooled by evaporation. But according to the Soviet scientists, the high temperature is entirely explained if Halley's surface is mantled with what they call a "porous dark substance of low thermal conductivity" that keeps the interior cool.

Given this high surface temperature, there is further reason to think that loss of material from Halley is confined to the jets. The observed rate of mass loss—5×10^{29} water molecules per second—is one-tenth of what a hot, bare icy nucleus should generate at the temperatures observed by Vega. This implies that the crust protects the interior of the nucleus from heating and evaporating, and that the crust is not dirty ice but some kind of residue that does not evaporate. The Giotto investigators conclude that the surface of Halley is covered with a "nonvolatile, insulating crust of dark material."

Nucleus Rotation

Like most celestial bodies, comet nuclei rotate. The same 1910 study that had mapped the location of the nuclear jets showed that the features in the inner coma vary with a 53-hour period. More recently, the Japanese Sakigake and Suisei spacecraft showed that the hydrogen gas coma surrounding the comet "breathes" (expands and contracts) in a similar time period, and the Vega spacecraft images are consistent with the 53-hour rotation period, give or take a few hours.

The rotation, coupled with the lack of any active jets on the dark side of the nucleus, may eventually give us clues about the unseen inte-

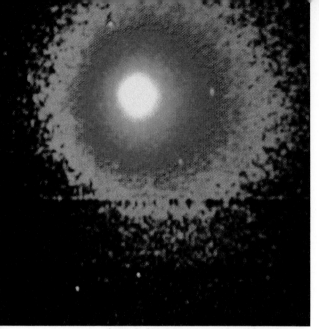

Courtesy Dr. Edwin Barker, University of Texas McDonald Observatory

Halley's coma is actually a cloud of gas and dust formed when the comet's nucleus is heated by the Sun.

rior and overall structure of Halley's nucleus. As the nucleus rotates, new areas enter the "daytime" side, heat up, and presumably become active. Active areas rotate into darkness and turn off. The speed of turn-on and turn-off will depend strongly on the insulating and heat-absorbing properties of the crust, giving astronomers an idea of its thickness and composition.

To the Giotto imaging team, the irregularity of the shape of the nucleus and the jets suggest that the interior is not uniform or that the crust varies considerably in thickness. Over successive appearances, the most volatile regions of the nucleus evaporate more rapidly than nonvolatile parts, leaving cracks, honeycomb structures, or even gaping caverns in the interior. As the interior is depleted, the crust may crack and collapse inward under the force of gravity or sections may blow off into space, depending on the strength and thickness of the crust. Any or all of these processes may play roles in forming the irregular surface that the spacecraft images hint is there.

Halley's Coma
Surrounding a comet's nucleus is its coma, or "atmosphere," an expanding, roughly spherical cloud of gas and dust that has evaporated from the Sun-heated nucleus. Traditional visual observations show that a typical comet's coma extends some 60,000 miles (100,000 kilometers) into space from the nucleus, but space-based imagery shows a much larger halo of hydrogen gas that extends much further.

The coma is of interest to astronomers for two reasons. First, the composition of the gases in the coma must reflect the composition of the nucleus, since that is where the gas comes from. Second, the interaction of the coma with sunlight, the solar wind (the stream of atomic and subatomic particles constantly being emitted by the Sun), and the magnetic fields around the comet allows us to learn about both comets and the conditions in interplanetary space and to test our understanding of the chemistry and physics involved.

The Giotto probe flew deep into Halley's coma, measuring the amount of gas and its composition at distances down to a few thousand miles (kilometers) from the nucleus. Roughly 80 percent of the molecules in the coma turned out to be water; and most of the remaining 20 percent, molecules of carbon dioxide. At a distance of about 600 miles (1,000 kilometers) from the nucleus, the instruments reported the coma to be quite thin. At sea level the atmosphere of Earth is, in fact, 300 billion times as dense as Halley's coma.

Since dust is released as the nuclear ices sublimate (change from solid to gas without an intermediate liquid state), the amount of dust produced should vary proportionally to the gas production. Giotto flew through this cloud of dust, colliding with dust particles, counting the numbers of impacts, and directly sampling the composition of the dust particles. Altogether, the dust instrument team found that Giotto collided with upward of 0.005 ounce (150 milligrams) of dust in its passage through the coma, and they determined that Halley's rate of dust ejection was 3 tons per second. This means that Halley ejects one-eighth as much dust by mass as it does gas (i.e., water and carbon dioxide), which is consistent with Halley's generally accepted classification as a moderately dusty comet.

The bulk of dust particles—roughly 80 percent of them—contain abundant hydrogen, carbon, nitrogen, and oxygen, with some sulfur, and they appear to have a low-density, or "fluffy," structure. These have been tentatively identified as radiation-damaged ice by the dust team scientists. The remaining particles were rich in sodium, magnesium, silicon, calcium, and iron.

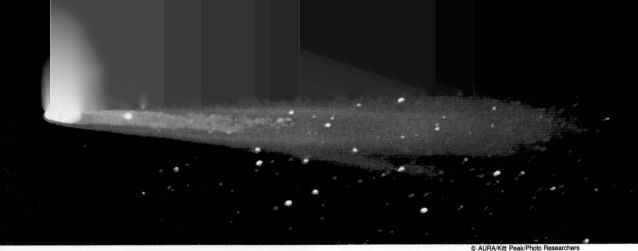

In 1910, Comet Halley (shown above in a computer-reconstructed image) provided a much more spectacular display than during its 1986 visit (left). Our scientific knowledge of comets was nonetheless greatly expanded by data from numerous spacecraft rendezvous with Halley.

NOAO

Molecules Incognito

As gas molecules travel away from the nucleus, they are subjected to a variety of processes that mask their original identity. In the inner coma, which is generally considered to be the inner 6,000 miles (10,000 kilometers) of the atmosphere, collisions between molecules and photodissociation (the breakup of a molecule caused by intense ultraviolet radiation from the Sun) destroy many of the original, or parent, molecules. Throughout the coma, solar radiation is strong enough to ionize (strip an electron from) both atoms and molecules. The net result is that the gases found in the outer coma are not usually the same as the ones released from the nucleus. Reconstructing the original composition requires detailed models of the chemical and physical processes taking place.

The dust coma is more straightforward, and the Vega and Giotto probes added much new information about it. Both detected the outer boundary of the dust coma at between 155,000 and 185,000 miles (250,000 and 300,000 kilometers) from the nucleus. From there the density of particles increased as the probes moved closer to the nucleus. Vega's instruments noted rapid fluctuations in the number of impacting particles as it came to closest approach, again presumably in response to nuclear jets.

The Japanese Suisei probe detected the hydrogen coma to be "breathing"—rhythmically changing in brightness—with a period of 2.2 days, reflecting the nucleus's rotation rate. This was an early indication that the nucleus was largely covered by a hard substance with sublimation occurring in concentrated jets.

One of the most unusual findings about Halley was the recording of radio emission by the Japanese spacecraft Sakigake. Passing through the outer part of the coma, the spacecraft picked up emission in the 30- to 195-kilohertz range. These emissions have been dubbed Cometary Kilometric Radiation and may arise from shock waves in the coma region resulting from turbulence in the solar wind.

Halley's Tail

The solar wind plays a more significant role in the life of a comet than just creating radio emissions. Halley's Comet has now provided us with numerous insights into the relationship between comets and the solar wind.

The solar wind is a stream of charged particles (mostly protons and electrons) that flow away from the Sun because of the corona's high temperature and carry the sun's magnetic field with it. Because charged particles cannot move easily across magnetic field lines, any ion (charged particle) that the solar wind encounters, such as those in the gas around a comet, will be swept up in the flow.

The solar wind normally travels outward at about 250 miles (400 kilometers) per second at 1 AU (astronomical unit, which equals 93

In one of its final flybys, Comet Halley streaks across the Arkansas night sky above a waning crescent moon.

© Greg Polus

million miles) from the Sun, Halley's approximate distance during the Giotto flyby.

The solar wind does not move unimpeded through the comet's atmosphere. Because many of the atoms in the coma are ionized, they are not free to travel across the magnetic field lines carried by the solar wind, and so are caught up in the flow of the solar wind. Because ions are continually produced in the coma, the wind is forced to carry more material along with it and must therefore slow to conserve momentum. The process continues as more ions are added, and the flow slows down until the inward pressure exerted by the solar wind is balanced by the outward pressure from the gases of the coma. This boundary is known as the contact surface. Since the solar wind cannot penetrate beyond this surface, a magnetic cavity is created that contains no magnetic field. The width of this cavity was about 13,700 miles (8,500 kilometers) along Giotto's path. Neither of the Vega spacecraft flew inside the contact surface.

Since none of the space probes passed on the tail side of the nucleus, most of our knowledge on tail structures will come from Earth-based images, taken mostly with big Schmidt cameras. The analysis of rays, streamers, kinks, and disconnection events will come when the images are correlated to measurements of the solar wind taken over the entire apparition. This is done to ensure that an observed tail feature regularly results from a specific change in the solar wind and is not an isolated, random occurrence. With past comets, only isolated instances were recorded, making a cause-and-effect relationship difficult to discern. Once such an analysis is complete, researchers will have a much better idea just what effect irregularities and sector boundaries in the solar wind have on a comet's gas tail.

The Final Analysis

Learning about Comet Halley had nothing to do with the hoopla and hype. The process began with the recognition of an impending astronomical event and continued with painstaking planning to ensure the cooperation of astronomers around the world. The true story of Comet Halley is one of contained scientific excitement, of space missions proposed and budget requests denied, of long nights in cold observatory domes, of years spent building instruments to collect five minutes worth of data, of spacecraft telemetry streaming back, and weeks, months, and even years of data analysis.

The Susitna Glacier on Alaska's Mt. Hayes demonstrates that ice still dominates some parts of the Earth's surface.

MARS, EARTH, and ICE

by Bruce M. Cordell

Twenty thousand years ago, sheets of glacial ice a mile (1 to 2 kilometers) thick covered parts of Canada and extended across the United States as far south as the Missouri and Ohio river valleys. Sea level fell by hundreds of feet, and temperatures plummeted, as our planet succumbed to one of the devastating ice ages that have plagued it for millions of years.

Someday the Earth may again become enveloped in global ice—but when? Unfortu-

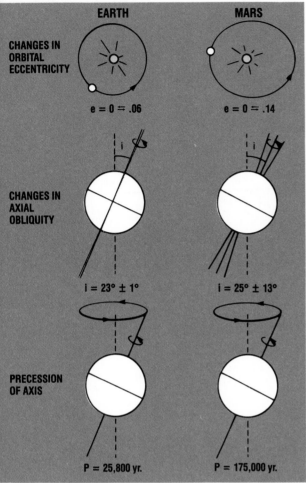

	EARTH	MARS
CHANGES IN ORBITAL ECCENTRICITY	e = 0 = .06	e = 0 = .14
CHANGES IN AXIAL OBLIQUITY	i = 23° ± 1°	i = 25° ± 13°
PRECESSION OF AXIS	P = 25,800 yr.	P = 175,000 yr.

Sky & Telescope

The orbital eccentricity and the axial characteristics of Mars vary more widely than do those of Earth.

changes we call seasons; other factors, some quite subtle, also are at work. For example, changes in a planet's orientation or the shape of its orbit affect both the seasonal and latitudinal distribution of sunlight. Continents reflect solar energy, modify atmospheric circulation and humidity, and drastically alter the transport of heat between the equator and the poles. And the Sun itself has experienced a considerable increase in brightness since the solar system's birth 4.6 billion years ago, as well as short-term variations that we are only now beginning to measure.

The complexity of our climate, together with the obvious practical implications for civilization, add excitement—even urgency—to the research for an understanding of these phenomena. It is a classic exercise in comparative planetology: insights gained from the exploration of Mars's somewhat simpler environment have increased our understanding of Earth; conversely, Earth's more complete climatic record suggests fruitful new questions to investigate on Mars.

The only demonstrably periodic climatic fluctuations on Earth are associated with predictable changes in the shape of its orbit and in the orientation of our globe with respect to the Sun. These mechanisms were originally suggested by Milutin Milankovitch over 50 years ago.

Milankovitch Orbit Cycles

First, the gravitational influences of the Sun and planets cause Earth's spin axis to wobble like a top, or *precess,* tracing out a cone in space every 25,800 years. Second, they force its orbit to oscillate between circular and more elliptical *(eccentric)* shapes every 100,000 years. Finally, besides causing the seasons, Earth's *obliquity,* or axial tilt, varies over a 4-degree range during yet another cycle of 41,000 years. Changes in orbital eccentricity cause the strength of sunlight to vary throughout the year, while changes in axial tilt alter the amount of solar energy absorbed at different latitudes.

Important evidence for the consequences of these orbital effects, at least during the most recent round of terrestrial ice ages, came in 1976. James Hayes of Columbia University and his collaborators showed the close correspondence of Earth's past climatic cycles with its orbital variations, as recorded principally in ocean sediments. However, the British astronomer Fred Hoyle has recently challenged the quality and reality of their statistical fit.

nately, theoretical models alone cannot predict our climatic destiny. But in Mars, a neighboring world much like ours, we have the potential to help determine the answer. There, as here, sunlight, wind, gas, and dust interact in an ongoing "global experiment" that can be observed and analyzed. Thanks in part to the perspectives afforded by spacecraft, our research efforts are beginning to reveal the forces that have shaped the histories—and will govern the futures—of both worlds.

The Complexity of Climate

To a large degree, the climates of Mars and Earth are determined by solar radiation and its interactions with these planets. Yet there is more to this energy balance than the cycle of

Hoyle argues that the Earth's oceans, which store roughly a 30-year supply of solar energy—some 1,000 times more potent than the variations due to Milankovitch cycles—should smooth out the orbital effects. Instead, he suggests, major changes occur after the collision of large objects with the Earth, a frequent occurrence on geological time scales. Such impacts should create huge clouds of tiny airborne particles, which reduce the sunlight reaching the oceans and thus trigger ice ages.

Nevertheless, it is generally accepted that Milankovitch cycles do affect climate. Then how, specifically, do these cycles induce periods of global cold?

Carbon dioxide may be the culprit. During Earth's last glacial episode, atmospheric carbon dioxide was at least 25 percent less abundant than now. Carbon dioxide in the air traps infrared radiation and causes elevated temperatures, a process termed the greenhouse effect; reducing it should therefore promote global cooling. Knowing that the atmosphere's carbon dioxide content has varied over time, Hayes and others have deduced that orbital variations seem to precede these fluctuations, which in turn trigger climatic changes. Hoyle's objections aside, the problem, then, is to find how the atmospheric abundance of this gas is regulated by orbital cycles.

Clues from Mars

The effects described by Milankovitch also seem to affect Mars. Evidence for recent climatic cycles there is found mainly in a series of conspicuous layered deposits surrounding each pole. The layers are typically a few tens of meters thick and probably consist of a dust-ice mixture. In general they are devoid of impact craters (indicating geologic youth) and occupy most of the area above 80 degrees in latitude. Their smooth, laminated appearance suggests that these are wind-related features created during the alternating episodes of deposition and erosion. Although it seems likely Milankovitch cycles are responsible for polar layering on Mars, the ages of its individual laminations are uncertain. Obviously, the most accurate determination would come from samples scooped out of these areas by a spacecraft and returned to Earth.

Gravitational tugs from the Sun and other planets affects Mars's axial tilt and its orbit significantly more than Earth's. The Martian obliquity, now at its mean value of 25 degrees, varies

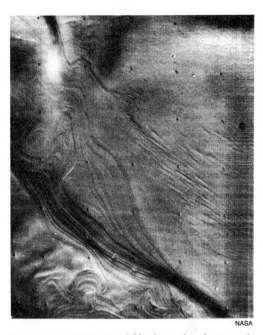

NASA

The layered terrain around Mars's south pole suggests that the planet once underwent wide swings in climate.

by ±13 degrees over 120,000 years—about ten times what Earth experiences. William Ward of the National Aeronautics and Space Administration's (NASA's) Jet Propulsion Laboratory (JPL) in Pasadena, California, has shown that, prior to the formation of a huge volcanic bulge called Tharsis, Mars's mean obliquity was much larger (32 degrees) than at present and oscillated between extremes of 45 and 25 degrees. Tharsis' formation then redistributed the planet's mass in such a way that such large oscillations were precluded, thus damping the Milankovitch cycles.

What about Mars's orbital eccentricity? It also fluctuates over a broad range, about 2½ times more than Earth's. When the orbital eccentricity is high, one polar region can receive considerably more solar radiation than the other, especially if summer solstice coincides with perihelion (the point in a planet's orbit closest to the Sun). The planet's 51,000-year-long precession cycle, however, tips each polar region alternately toward the Sun and away from it at perihelion, thus producing a potent climate-driving cycle. (At present, Mars reaches perihelion during summer in the southern hemisphere. Scientists believe this stirs up the atmosphere and triggers the planet's famous dust storms.)

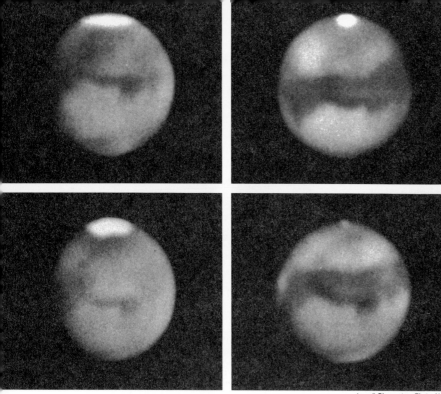

The polar cap of Mars, which expands and contracts according to the season, is composed largely of frozen carbon dioxide. Carbon dioxide gas is the chief constituent of the Martian atmosphere.

Modeling the Martian Atmosphere

Fortunately for theorists, the Martian atmosphere is easier to simulate accurately than ours—its capacity for storing heat is negligible, and Mars has no oceans to serve as heat reservoirs. James Pollack, Owen Toon (both at NASA's Ames Research Center), and others have developed a theory relating orbital cycles to recent climatic oscillations on Mars. The researchers mathematically modeled the Martian surface and the physical properties of its atmosphere utilizing data obtained by the Viking spacecraft. Based on several lines of evidence, they conclude that a vast reservoir of carbon dioxide has escaped from the Martian interior over its history, enough to create a surface pressure of 1 to 3 bars (1 bar of atmosphere nearly equals Earth's sea-level pressure). Yet today Mars is veiled by only 0.006 bar of atmosphere, so what happened to it all?

If Pollack and Toon are correct, Mars has probably stashed this huge volume of carbon dioxide in the form of carbonate rocks—as Earth has. Interestingly, Robert Singer (University of Hawaii) and his colleagues have analyzed the red planet with near-infrared spectroscopy, and they recently reported the first detection of clay minerals. These probably formed in and around Mars' now-vanished ancient rivers. But rather surprisingly, they found no evidence for carbonates.

Pollack's team finds that at maximum axial tilt, the Martian poles should receive enough solar energy to vaporize the frozen carbon dioxide in its permanent polar caps. Some water would be driven from the caps, too, along with other volatile compounds stored in the soil. The result would be the activation of a greenhouse effect on Mars. Conversely, at low obliquity the atmospheric pressure drops, permanent carbon dioxide caps form, water is trapped as ice in the polar areas and as permafrost elsewhere, and dust storms cease.

Other recent work suggests that during periods of low obliquity, almost all of the water left in Mars's thin atmosphere precipitates onto the poles, with important consequences. Sunlight dissociates water vapor into hydrogen and oxygen, and carbon dioxide into carbon monoxide and oxygen. But with all Mars's water "out of circulation," hydrogen would not be available to assist in the recombination of carbon monoxide and oxygen into carbon dioxide; up to 0.1 millibar of free oxygen could then exist in the atmosphere, which could become captured irreversibly by the surface through oxidation. Potentially, the long-term composition of the entire atmosphere could be affected.

Continents and Climate Change

Many geologists have emphasized the importance of continents and their shifting positions to climatic change on Earth. Continents and their mountain ranges modify the flow of wind, and the resulting uplift of air currents, cloud formation, and precipitation essentially determine the broad aspects of regional climate. Large continental areas also experience the greatest seasonal extremes of temperature. Indeed, a continent's poleward drift is reason enough for glaciation to begin.

Furthermore, since the oceans provide most of the Earth's equator-to-pole heat transfer, the obstruction of oceanic currents by continents—especially by a polar continent (such as Antarctica)—can apparently trigger polar and then global cooling. Current evidence suggests that continental blockage of Earth's poles is necessary, but not sufficient, to trigger an ice age. Northern continents certainly make large ice sheets easier, but glacial and interglacial periods are nonetheless dictated by Milankovitch orbital oscillations.

No Continental Drift on Mars

Unlike Earth, Mars is not scarred by the remains of ancient horizontal continental motions. Nor has it, with the exception of the Tharsis region, created large volcanic constructs such as the Hawaiian Islands. Thus, Mars's static, "one-plate" tectonic style has moderated its climatic history in a profound way, while Earth's mobile continents have made it extremely sensitive to the climatic ups and downs induced by Milankovitch effects.

Planetary geologists have long suspected that Mars had a very different climate long ago, as evidenced by numerous channels crossing its surface that were apparently carved by running water. Notably, complex systems of small, interconnected channels are confined to ancient terrains on Mars. Perhaps the planet once possessed a thick atmosphere and a more clement environment; then rainfall and the formation of these rivulets could have been common.

But what if Mars's red soil never experienced the refreshing splash of rainwater? Could rivers still have formed? Bruce Jakosky (University of Colorado, Boulder) and Michael Carr

(U.S. Geological Survey) say the answer may well be "yes," based on careful scrutiny of Viking imagery. They find that channels are sometimes located where other signs of erosion by water (such as degraded craters) are absent, which suggests that precipitation and, by inference, a dense atmosphere were not factors in their formation.

"Until recently," observes Carr, "we thought Earthlike conditions were necessary to form the small channels." But within the past year that attitude has changed. Jakosky and Carr analyzed the wide swings in obliquity that existed early in Martian history. With Mars's axis tipped 45 degrees to the Sun, polar ice would have evaporated during local summer and migrated toward the opposite pole.

But once near the equator, Carr and Jakosky point out, this poleward journey would be interrupted as the water vapor condensed during each frigid Martian night. Over time it would accumulate as huge equatorial snowpacks. At their base, isolated from both the atmosphere and sunlight, enough runoff would flow from beneath the ice pack to produce the channels we see today.

The channels of Mars, which strongly resemble Earth's river beds, may have been formed by running water.

NASA

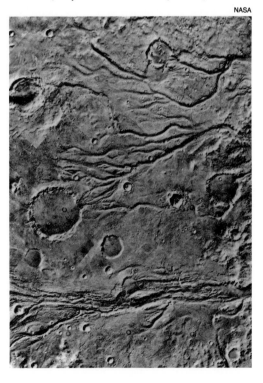

Viking 2's view of the bleak Martian landscape. Some astronomers think liquid water is present beneath the surface.

The Faint Young Sun

Milankovitch cycles have not been the only factors determining our climate, for astrophysicists are convinced that the Sun is now 30 percent brighter than it was when the Earth formed 4.6 billion years ago. This is a consequence of the irreversible effects of thermonuclear fusion in its core. But if the young Sun was so faint, Earth and Mars must have been much colder than at present.

Geologists disagree. Their analyses of radioactive isotopes found in ancient sediments suggest that a few billion years ago, Earth was at least as warm as it has been during the past half billion years—and probably warmer. Networks of channels already imply that Mars was warmer and wetter a few billion years ago. Thus, if the Sun gradually grew hotter, it appears both planets responded by either cooling or, at least, preserving the thermal status quo.

But two nagging questions remain. First, if the Sun was so faint, how did the infant Earth and Mars get so warm? Second, what caused this heating mechanism to cease?

Early on, some combination of volcanoes, atmospheric greenhouses, and climate-moderating oceans probably helped the Earth avoid a frigid fate. However, had the Earth ever been completely covered with ice, it probably would have remained so indefinitely. Ice reflects sunlight so well that the Sun's luminosity would have had to flare by 50 percent to trigger a global thaw. In theory, therefore, any worldwide coating of ice created long ago should have survived to the present—an assertion we can quickly reject by looking out a window.

Origin of the Atmosphere

An atmospheric greenhouse could also have kept the planet warm, but this requires healthy abundances of water vapor and carbon dioxide. (Ammonia and methane have also been proposed, but they are destroyed too rapidly by photochemical processes to be effective.) Unfortunately, deducing the abundance of water on Mars and Earth is enmeshed in the still larger issue of the origin of planetary atmospheres.

Shortly after they formed, the planets captured hydrogen and other gases available locally in what remained of the solar nebula. However, these primitive envelopes did not endure—apparently, intense solar winds swept them away soon thereafter.

The present-day atmospheres of Earth and its neighbors arose from volcanic exhalations that occurred long after the original envelopes left. Carbon dioxide, water vapor, and a few other dominant gases accumulated over time. Unlike Venus, however, Earth was distant enough from the Sun so that its water liquified and formed the oceans. Carbon dioxide was absorbed by the oceans, where it was ultimately converted to carbonate rocks and withdrawn from atmospheric circulation. Endahl and Schatten estimate that 30 times the present carbon dioxide abundance would be needed to counteract the Sun's diminished output 2 billion years ago, even more for earlier epochs.

Martian Moisture?

For Mars, the past moisture and carbon dioxide inventory of the planet's atmosphere can only be estimated, and this complicates attempts to understand why the planet cooled over time

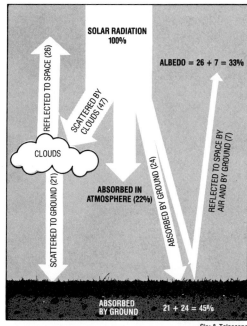

Of the solar energy that interacts with Earth and its atmosphere, about one-third is reflected back to space.

even though the Sun became more luminous. However, a "flood" of new data continues to argue that water is—and has been—abundant there, perhaps even equivalent to a layer 300 feet (100 meters) deep over the entire planet. For example, Baerbel Lucchitta of the U.S. Geological Survey has recently identified three fresh water-bearing landslides in a prominent canyon, Ophir Chasma. Similar slides appear elsewhere in Mars's vast Valles Marineris canyon system, suggesting that subsurface water or ice must have been widespread in that region in geologically recent times. Also, certain layered deposits in Valles Marineris can best be explained if they were deposited in standing liquid water, perhaps in ice-covered lakes.

Yet no compelling evidence exists that large bodies of water ever existed on Mars. And without oceans, carbon dioxide driven out of the interior should have remained in the atmosphere and created an appreciable greenhouse. Early theoretical models of the Martian atmosphere indicated that 1 bar of carbon dioxide could have maintained the global mean temperature above freezing; more recent studies, however, favor larger values closer to 3 bars. Perhaps this huge outpouring of carbon dioxide was eventually removed by chemical reactions that permeated deep into the Martian surface layers. However, Peter Schultz (Brown University) and two colleagues feel much of Mars's early atmosphere could have been thrown irretrievably into space during the enormous impact that formed the Argyre basin.

A question of special interest to planetary scientists (and thirsty Martian explorers of the future) is: Where did all the water go? Only a relatively small fraction of the total reservoir can now be residing in the atmosphere and polar caps. One major storage site of the Martian "oceans" is probably its surface rocks, such as certain clays, which can bind water chemically; other likely hiding places lie still deeper, in widespread ice deposits (permafrost) and perhaps reservoirs roughly 1 mile (1.6 kilometers) down, where Mars's internal warmth can maintain water in its liquid state. When the Martian explorers land, they'll have to dig deeply.

What's Ahead

More of the puzzle may be solved in the coming years. Both the Soviet Union and NASA plan return visits to Mars, to be launched in 1988 and 1991, respectively. These missions will focus on where the planet is now storing its water, but there are other ways to get meaningful answers. For example, if water once covered part of Valles Marineris, perhaps carbonate rocks now lie exposed on the canyon floors and could be discerned from orbiting spacecraft. Maybe we will find active volcanoes, or at least evidence that their outpourings occurred recently. And the greatest scientific rationale for actually exploring Mars ourselves may ultimately be to gain a better understanding of the Earth's climatic future.

THE LIMITS OF MANNED SPACE FLIGHT

by William DeCampli

Photos: NASA

When the Soviet cosmonauts Vladimir Lyakhov and Valeriy Ryumin emerged from the Soyuz 34 spacecraft on August 18, 1979, touching solid ground for the first time in 175 days, they looked far less triumphant than one might expect of two men who had just made history. A record-breaking six-month stay aboard the Salyut 6 space station had so disrupted the cosmonauts' basic bodily functions—so weakened their muscles, upset their circulation, and distorted their perception—that the return to Earth had left them virtually paralyzed.

For the first few days, Lyakhov and Ryumin were unable even to stand; when they tried, their hearts raced, their heads swam, their muscles trembled, and they sweated profusely. Only after four days of massage, heat treatments, and breathing exercises did they gain the strength and coordination to stand up unassisted. On the fifth day, they started walking, and after eight days managed to amble six miles at a time, stopping periodically for back and leg massages.

But only after a month of rest and therapy in a sanatorium could they endure normal physical exertion. And it was six weeks before their physicians declared them fully recovered.

Planning a Journey to Mars

More than 250 human beings have ventured into space during the past 25 years. But fewer than 30, Lyakhov and Ryumin among them, have stayed for durations of more than a month. The Soviets set the current record for time aloft, in 1984, when cosmonauts Leonid Kizim, Vladimir Soloviov, and Oleg Atkov spent 237 days—nearly eight months—aboard Salyut 7. That is fully three times the duration of any U.S. mission to date, yet it is a mere fraction of the time future space voyages may require. A Mars mission, including the return to Earth, could last as long as three years. And the creation of a working colony on another planet could require that people spend large portions of their lives beyond Earth's atmosphere.

Sending astronauts to Mars, a vision once

propagated mainly by cranks and science fiction writers, is no longer just an idle fantasy. On the contrary, it is an acknowledged goal of the Soviet space program and a cause célèbre among a growing number of American scientists and public officials. It is widely accepted among aerospace engineers that we could, within decades, put human beings on the surface of the Red Planet. The 110,000-member Planetary Society and the presidentially appointed National Commission on Space, to name but two prominent examples, have embraced the idea—the commission calling recently for the launch of a manned Mars mission by 2010, the creation of a permanent Mars base by 2025, and the eventual placement of several spacecraft in continuous Earth-to-Mars service.

Senator Spark Matsunaga of Hawaii, meanwhile, is proposing that the United States and the Soviet Union declare 1992 International Space Year and celebrate it by starting a collaborative Mars program. And President Reagan has called for the establishment of a permanent space station—a prerequisite for a manned Mars mission—by 1994.

But even if we manage within the next few decades, despite the National Aeronautics and Space Administration's (NASA's) current state of disarray, to build a vessel that can carry astronauts to Mars, a fundamental question—not an engineering question but a medical one—will remain: Could a crew of human beings survive the journey?

Weightlessness

Of all the health effects of long-term space travel, those resulting from microgravity, or weightlessness, are the best understood. Many of our basic physiological systems are governed to some degree by the force of gravity, and, as the experience of cosmonauts Lyakhov and Ryumin demonstrates, to deprive them of that force is to disrupt them. The cardiovascular system (heart and blood vessels), for example, has evolved to ensure a steady blood supply to all regions of the body even as their positions change in relation to Earth's inward pull. Unresisted, gravity would pull our blood to our feet when we moved from a lying to a standing position, leaving other organs, notably the brain, high and dry. Luckily, the arteries are equipped with baroreceptors—biological gauges that anticipate and counteract any drop in blood pressure in the head and neck. Alerted by the baroreceptors, the heart speeds up and the vessels in

the lower regions of the body constrict, to maintain blood pressure to the brain.

In the weightless environment of outer space, the same reflex causes an imbalance. First, as the cardiovascular system automatically continues to compensate for gravity, 1 to 4 pints (½ to 2 liters) of blood surges headward, causing nasal stuffiness, facial swelling, and a loss of circulation in the legs. Then, in a few hours' time, the increase in upper-body blood pressure triggers a release of the hormone ANF (atrial natriuretic factor), which reduces the body's overall fluid volume through diuresis—the increased output of urine.

During the early years of space travel, fluid shift and diuresis were thought to be the only effects of microgravity on the cardiovascular system. Then, upon the launch of Skylab in 1973, and the advent of 28- to 84-day missions, a new issue arose. It became evident that after prolonged weightlessness, the circulatory mechanisms that normally counteract gravity were shutting down, making the journey more tolerable but forcing the astronauts to make yet another adjustment on their arrival home. Space voyagers returning from long-term missions have all experienced this cardiovascular deconditioning, despite attempts to alleviate it through increased fluid intake (to counter the effects of diuresis) and vigorous exercise (to increase the demand for oxygen in the tissues and thus stimulate cardiac output).

No one knows just how microgravity shuts down our circulatory reflexes; the leading theory is that it somehow desensitizes the baroreceptors in the aorta and the carotid artery. In a future Spacelab mission—SLS1, probably to be launched before 1990—astronauts will test that hypothesis by wearing collars designed to gauge baroreceptor activity after varying exposures to microgravity. How far cardiovascular deconditioning would progress during a three-year mission to Mars and back—and whether the cardiovascular system might eventually lose the ability to regain normal function—remain pressing questions.

Heart Shrinkage

Sensitivity to gravity may not be all the cardiovascular system loses after prolonged weightlessness; experiments suggest a concurrent shrinkage of the heart muscle itself. Using a technique called echocardiography, Soviet and American investigators have measured 8- to 20-percent decreases in the volume of the myocardial muscle of returning astronauts. This is not really surprising; given the relative inactivity of astronauts during flight, and the fact that even vigorous movement provides little exercise in a gravity-free environment, one might predict it. Still, the finding is controversial, because echocardiography, which uses sound waves to create crude images of the heart, produces only indirect evidence of the changes taking place. If heart muscle is in fact being lost, the problem

are equally affected by the absence of gravity. The symptoms, like those of cardiovascular deconditioning, are usually short-lived but can be dangerous. They include not only nausea (NASA officials reportedly considered scrubbing the 1968 Apollo 8 mission to the Moon when, after leaving Earth orbit, astronaut Frank Borman started vomiting), but also an array of odd bodily perceptions. An astronaut climbing a ladder may have the unsettling feeling that he

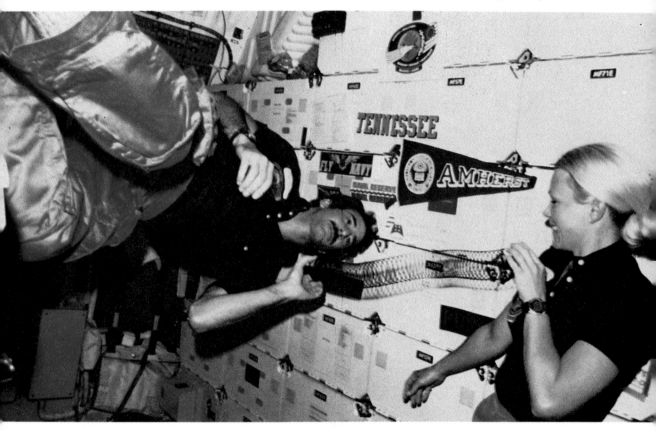

may reflect more than a simple lack of exercise, for in-flight workouts lasting up to three hours a day have done nothing to stop it. Does the presence of gravity make that great a difference in the benefits derived from physical activity, or does microgravity somehow affect the heart directly? Before subjecting astronauts to three-year periods of weightlessness, we will have to solve this basic mystery.

Balance and Orientation

Cardiovascular disturbances are not the only result of prolonged weightlessness; the mechanisms responsible for balance and orientation

is descending headfirst, and a mere turn of the head may produce sensations of falling, floating, or spinning.

The reason is that the neurovestibular system—the basis of balance—involves not only the eyes and the extremities but also the gravity-sensitive otolith organs: tiny calcium particles, far smaller than grains of sand, that sit in pockets of fluid above highly sensitive hair cells in the inner ears. Normally, gravity controls the movement of the particles, so they bear down against different hair cells as the body changes position. This contact generates neural signals that converge with visual images and other sen-

Zero gravity—demonstrated during a space shuttle flight using a slinky toy (left)—can, if prolonged, lead to bone degeneration, cardiovascular upset, and loss of balance. Side effects of weightlessness can be reduced if the astronauts exercise regularly in flight (above).

ment to microgravity? No one knows. It is possible that an astronaut's ability to perform sophisticated tasks remains impaired long after the acute space sickness recedes.

Breakdown of Bones

Still another effect of microgravity, perhaps the most serious and enduring, is the rapid breakdown it causes in bones. Bones, like muscles, deteriorate in the absence of stress; a group of researchers led by John E. Deitrick, formerly of the New York Hospital–Cornell Medical Center, demonstrated this nearly 40 years ago by placing healthy young men in body casts for six to seven weeks and documenting a dramatic increase in the calcium content of their urine (as bone dissolves, its calcium is eliminated as waste). Experiments in space have shown that astronauts experience the same syndrome: the amount of calcium in the urine of Skylab astronauts increased by 60 to 100 percent, reflecting an overall bone loss of nearly half a percent a month—even when the astronauts exercised vigorously.

The mechanism by which microgravity causes skeletal breakdown is still not fully understood. Bones are maintained through the complementary activity of cells known as osteoblasts, which produce new bone matter, and osteoclasts, which break it down. The absence of stress on the bones somehow tips the balance in favor of osteoclastic activity. But how these cells sense stress remains a fascinating mystery.

The critical question is whether skeletal breakdown would level off or continue unabated throughout a long mission. If it persisted, the consequences would soon become serious. Once an astronaut's skeleton had lost 20 to 25 percent of its mineral content, individual bones (particularly those in the legs, which experience disproportionate mineral loss) would become extremely fragile. And if fractures occurred, the lack of gravity could impede proper healing. (Bones tend to mend at the angle of maximum stress. In the absence of gravity, it is not clear whether healing would take place properly.) Moreover, the constant breakdown of skeletal matter inside the body could produce kidney stones: solid masses that precipitate out of calcium-rich urine and may pass painfully from the body. (It is rumored that the 1982 Salyut 7 mission had to be cut short after 211 days, when a crew member developed an impacted renal stone.) The possible complications from this

sory data to produce an overall sense of orientation. In the absence of gravity, a given head motion still produces the same visual sensation, of course, but it has a radically different effect on the otoliths. The result is a conflict of messages.

For the first few days, this sensory conflict causes clumsiness, dizziness, and nausea. Like the cardiovascular system, however, the neurovestibular system soon adjusts: the brain comes to expect, and rely on, a new set of signals from the otoliths, and the symptoms recede, only to return with the reimposition of gravity. But does the absence of nausea reflect a complete adjust-

condition include kidney infection, blockage of the ureter, and, in extreme cases, kidney failure.

Counteracting the Effects of Microgravity

Until we understand the mechanisms by which microgravity affects the bones, any attempt to mitigate the damage would be a shot in the dark. Dietary calcium supplements have been as fruitless as exercise for stopping resorption. Soviet cosmonauts have also tried traveling in "penguin load suits," which distribute continuous stress through a system of elastic straps. Such outfits are cumbersome, to say the least, and would be highly impractical for a three-year journey. Drugs may thus hold more promise. Diphosphonate compounds, for example, which percolate into the bone matrix and create a sort of shield against the activity of osteoclasts, might prove useful in space.

Probably the most effective countermeasure to microgravity is simply to equip the entire spacecraft with artificial gravity—to rotate it at such a rate that the centripetal force inside the cabin approximates the force of gravity on Earth. NASA engineers have suggested, for instance, building a craft composed of modules on opposite ends of a tether. If the modules were 1,000 feet (300 meters) apart, then rotating the entire structure once a minute would create roughly the equivalent of Earth's gravity. A revolving tethered spacecraft could go a long way toward alleviating the cardiovascular, neurovestibular, and musculoskeletal problems associated with microgravity—if its many engineering hazards could be worked out. The trouble is, it would provide no relief on a lunar base or in a Mars settlement.

Radiation Exposure

Microgravity is by no means the only obstacle to long-distance space travel. Another major health hazard is the radiation that exists beyond Earth's atmosphere. The Sun constantly ejects protons—the nuclei of hydrogen atoms shattered in its fiery interior—that whirl about the solar system as a sort of radioactive wind. Here on Earth, thanks to the shielding effects of the atmosphere and the planet's magnetic field, the average person receives no more than 200 millirems of radiation a year. (A rem, or roentgen equivalent man, is a unit of biological effect and consists of different absolute doses of various radiation types. Official estimates by U.S. government agencies define a single dose of 600

rems as invariably fatal; half of those exposed to 450 rems would likely die within 60 days.) But, beginning at 180 miles (290 kilometers) above Earth's surface, where a spacecraft enters low Earth orbit (the orbit of the space shuttle), astronauts are bombarded by increasing numbers of protons and electrons as the craft's altitude increases. Crew members may receive 100 millirems—one-tenth of a rem—a day while thus situated, despite the dense protective shielding that encases any spacecraft. Most of this exposure results from proton bombardment and from secondary particles, mainly X-radiation.

The levels of proton and electron flux increase sharply in the inner Van Allen belt, a region extending 3,000 miles (4,800 kilometers) beyond low Earth orbit. Spending any length of time at this altitude would be dangerous, causing daily exposure levels of many rems. Luckily, most spacecraft manage to pass through it in just a few hours, as did all the lunar Apollo missions.

Solar Flares

At a distance of about 24,000 miles (38,000 kilometers), a craft enters geosynchronous orbit (travels above the equator at the same speed as the Earth rotates), the possible location of future space platforms. Electron flux remains high here, causing significant secondary particle radiation. But the greatest hazard in geosynchronous orbit, and everywhere beyond it, is that Earth's magnetosphere becomes too weak to confer protection against solar flares and galactic cosmic rays.

Solar flares are intense, erratic bursts of proton radiation that tend to occur at 11-year intervals and may last anywhere from 12 to 24 hours. A recent one, in August of 1972, pushed radiation in the geosynchronous zone to a million times the level we experience on Earth. Had a spacecraft encountered that flare, armed only with a shuttle-type radiation shield, the entire crew would have received lethal doses of radiation. Even with five such shields surrounding them, crew members would have received skin doses or roughly 135 rems—more than enough to cause acute radiation sickness.

The most likely solution to the problem of solar flares would be to equip any long-range spacecraft or extraterrestrial colony with a storm shelter. Encased in ten times as much shielding as a shuttle vehicle, such a shelter would protect anyone who remained inside it for the duration of a flare; the only problem would be getting

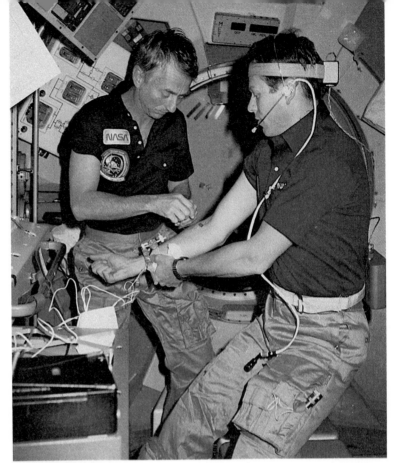

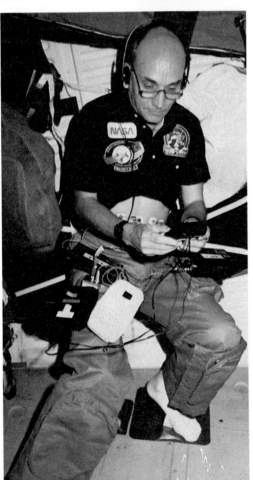

Astronauts on extended space missions will be closely monitored for any change in their medical conditions. Even now, astronauts on short-term flights are almost constantly subjected to medical tests. Blood is drawn at periodic intervals for later testing on Earth (right). Below, U.S. senator Jake Garn performs a medical experiment on himself aboard a Discovery flight in April 1985. The senator's role in the space shuttle program was essentially that of a guinea pig for medical tests.

everyone into it quickly enough to avoid exposure, since the blast of radio waves that precedes a flare would give only an hour's warning. If an astronaut who had been working outside the craft were stranded there for the first few hours of a flare, the effects would be serious and irreversible. Within 24 hours he would suffer nausea and diarrhea as the cells lining his intestinal walls were destroyed, and the resultant dehydration might cause further problems, including hemorrhage and cardiovascular instability. These symptoms might recede after a few days, but others—including anemia, infections, and bleeding—would set in three to six weeks later, as his radiation-damaged bone marrow stopped producing new blood cells. Were the astronaut to survive this assault, the possibility of longer-term effects—including infertility, eye cataracts, and cancer—would haunt him for the rest of his life.

Cosmic Rays

Galactic cosmic rays, the second pervasive radiation danger in and beyond geosynchronous orbit, are composed of protons, alpha particles, and HZEs (the energetic nuclei of heavy particles). Cosmic rays are very difficult to protect against, but they are often disregarded because astronauts receive them in such low doses. Unfortunately, the effects are not determined entirely by the level of exposure. Particle-accelerator experiments have shown that HZEs operate by single-hit kinetics: each particle creates a sort of microscopic stab wound, whose severity is determined by its position on the body and the angle at which the particle strikes the target cell. Thus, it is the geometry, not the intensity, of exposure that determines the biological effect of a cosmic particle.

Alan Nelson of the Massachusetts Institute of Technology (MIT) and Cornelius Tobias of the Lawrence Berkeley Laboratory in California have shown in experiments on rats that even a single HZE particle can cause irreparable lesions in a corneal cell. This finding implies that unlike other kinds of radiation (which damage a cell's genetic material, and thus its offspring, but leave the cell itself unharmed), galactic cosmic rays destroy existing cells, including, possibly, the irreplaceable, nondividing cells of the central nervous system. Unless somehow mitigated, the effects of cosmic rays on long-distance space travelers could eventually resemble those of Creutzfeld-Jacob disease or Alzheimer's disease: a subtle but progressive loss of judgment, memory, and coordination, leading to outright dementia. Obviously, we will need to know a great deal more about HZE exposure before placing astronauts in space for several years at a time.

The Spacecraft Environment

If the hazards of the external environment did not dissuade the prospective voyager to Mars, the hardships of the internal environment might. Cosmonaut Valeriy Ryumin succinctly portrayed the difficulty of living in a closed container when, paraphrasing O. Henry, he wrote in his diary that "if you want to encourage the craft of murder, all you have to do is lock up two men for two months in an 18- by 20-foot [5.5- by 6-meter] room." Imagine, then, being locked in such a cabin for three years. Such seemingly minor annoyances as noise, odors, or a lack of work space could place serious strains on the crew's mental health. And a small mechanical malfunction, if it affected the availability of food, the discharge of toxins, or the regulation of temperature or atmospheric composition, could be lethal.

It was just such a glitch that foiled the Apollo 13 lunar mission in 1970. Three days into the journey, an externally mounted oxygen tank exploded, knocking out the electronic panel responsible for water, electricity, and air inside the cabin. The crew survived the 36-hour journey back to Earth by crawling into their lunar module and turning down its heaters to conserve electricity. But it was a narrow escape. If the same mishap were to occur eight months, or even two weeks, into a Mars mission, the crew would freeze to death. And the monetary cost of a failed mission might reach $100 billion—some 50 times that of losing a space shuttle.

Just as any mechanical emergency would have ample time to run its course during a long-range space mission, so would many of the medical and surgical problems that might arise. In any group of four men and three women aged 30 to 55—a plausible profile of a Mars-bound crew—medical statistics suggest that at least one member would get sick enough during a three-year period to require hospitalization or surgery. Obviously, astronauts are screened for conditions that might make space travel risky, but there is simply no way to foresee some of the medical problems that might crop up during a Mars mission. Coronary artery disease, for example, though undetectable before takeoff, might cause a heart attack while the mission was under way. And NASA, despite its increasing interest in long-duration missions, has so far devoted little attention to designing a space-based critical-care facility. Space shuttle medical kits contain such emergency drugs as atropine and Adrenalin, which can stimulate an arrested heart, and procainamide, which can help restore a regular heartbeat. But they include none of the technology—a defibrillator, for example—that a hospital would use if drugs failed.

Various cancers, though unlikely, could also pose problems. Suppose an astronaut noticed a swollen lymph node in his neck or armpit eight months into a three-year mission, and a biopsy by the surgeon on board revealed Stage I Hodgkin's disease. Unable to administer radiation therapy, the surgeon would begin chemotherapy; lacking the facilities to treat its toxic side effects, however, he would limit the dosage. Twelve months later the astronaut might begin to suffer fatigue, fevers, and abdominal pain; further diagnosis would reveal that the disease had progressed to Stage IV. Finally, just

Crew members of a 1985 space shuttle Discovery flight are all smiles during their one-week mission. In a multiyear voyage to Mars, however, the cramped conditions and prolonged togetherness might create a less happy picture.

three months before reentering Earth's atmosphere, he would die. A disease that on Earth is 90 percent curable with early and proper treatment would have turned the Mars mission into an agonizing deathwatch.

Injuries, too, could prove far more difficult to treat in space than they are on Earth. A severe head, chest, or abdominal injury can require not only sophisticated facilities, including an operating room, but also weeks of around-the-clock care by trained specialists and a large staff. Donald Trunkey, the chairman of the department of surgery at the Oregon Health Sciences University in Portland, has argued that before embarking on construction of its proposed space station, NASA will need to develop policies—and adequate facilities—for dealing with outer space emergencies.

Getting Ready for Mars

Manned space travel is never without risks. The explosion of the shuttle Challenger in January 1986 brought to four the number of fatal accidents that have marred mankind's exploration of the cosmos. In 1967 cosmonaut Vladimir Komarov was killed when a parachute recovery system apparently failed during the landing of Soyuz 1. Three American astronauts perished the same year, when Apollo 1 burned on the launching pad during a countdown rehearsal. And three cosmonauts died in 1971 when, during their return from a 23-day mission, the failure of an air valve depressurized the Soyuz 11 command module and asphyxiated them. But such accidents are not the only danger facing future space travelers. Even in the best possible vessel, and under the best of all conditions, microgravity, atomic radiation, the psychological stress of confinement, and the lack of medical facilities would remain major problems for a Mars-bound crew.

There is every reason to believe we will soon be capable of launching a manned Mars mission. And there is little doubt that, when a Mars-worthy vessel is ready, there will be qualified and courageous people eager to occupy it. The mission is an important one, and we should pursue it tirelessly. The point is not that human beings are too fragile ever to colonize the universe, but that creating conditions under which they can survive the journey will be—must be—at the very heart of our efforts.

The Ungentle Death of a
GIANT STAR

by Ellen Fried

W hen the most massive stars die, they explode, releasing as much light as an entire galaxy of stars. The explosion, called a supernova, can catapult a star from obscurity to spectacular prominence in the night sky. One supernova in 1006 shone so brightly that objects could be seen by its light for weeks. Another in 1054 was visible even during the day. Astronomers believe that one in 1,000 stars becomes a supernova; a star probably blows up in the Milky Way every 100 years or so.

Yet not a single supernova has been seen in our galaxy since 1604. Astronomers blame that on the blinding effect of intergalactic dust. Hoping to learn more about what happens before and during an explosion, researchers are eager to catch the next one visible in our galaxy. More than just spectacular light shows, supernovas have probably created some of the most exotic objects in the universe—neutron stars and black holes. And most of the elements that make up our world have been released by the explosions.

What Causes a Supernova?

Astronomers believe that a supernova occurs when a star at least eight times the mass of the Sun runs out of the nuclear fuel that keeps it shining. At birth, all stars, the most massive powerhouse included, are merely balls of simple hydrogen atoms mixed with a dash of other

Stansbury, Ronsaville, & Wood Inc.

elements from interstellar gas. Each star lives for as long as it can resist the weight of its mass, which continually compels it to collapse. Under the heat and pressure created in the core of the star by the pull of gravity, the hydrogen atoms fuse to form helium. The energy generated by these nuclear fusion reactions gives the star enough outward thrust to balance gravity's inward pull.

When the hydrogen fuel is exhausted, the nuclear reactions die out, and gravitational contraction takes over. The core grows hotter and denser, and the star's outer layers redden and expand. The internal pressure becomes enough to ignite the core's accumulated helium. Helium is converted into carbon, a yet heavier element,

releasing enough energy to once again resist the pull of gravity.

But for a star of average mass like our Sun, helium burning is the last stage of life; internal pressure and heat never rise high enough to ignite the newly created carbon. When the star reaches an age of about 10 billion years, all fusion ceases and gravity triumphs. The star shrinks into a small, dense, burned-out corpse known as a white dwarf.

A massive star, however, leads an extravagant life, careening through time toward a violent death. The weight of such a star creates so much internal pressure and heat that the star burns its fuel at a breakneck speed, coming to the end of its life in perhaps only 10 million years. The heat and pressure also produce a whole series of successively heavier elements, from helium all the way to iron. For example, carbon is ignited and converted into oxygen, releasing enough energy to again resist gravity. The oxygen atoms then fuse to form silicon and sulfur; the process repeats itself over and over until, in a very massive star, the core is pure iron. At that point, reactions can proceed no further. The iron absorbs rather than releases energy, and the stellar fire dies out.

The star's tremendous mass does not allow for a graceful collapse. Through a process not yet completely understood, the star explodes. According to a popular theory, the iron ore first shrinks, creating intense pressure. Within a split second a shock wave begins to move outward from the core toward the surface, blasting the star's middle and outer layers into space at more than 6,000 miles (9,656 kilometers) per second. The collapsed core becomes a neutron star—an object even denser than a white dwarf, so dense a pinhead of its matter weighs more than 1 million tons (900,000 metric tons). Or it may even shrink into a black hole, an object from whose gravity not even light can escape. And in the intense heat of the explosion, the heaviest elements in the universe, such as gold and lead, are thought to be born. The elements created during the life and death of a star may eventually be incorporated into new stars, and into planets orbiting those stars, and, on at least one planet, into living beings.

Studying Remnants

Unfortunately the dearth of nearby supernovas to study has prevented astrophysicists from confirming such theories. The little they know has been gleaned from supernovas in distant galaxies and supernova remnants scattered across the Milky Way galaxy. Clues in one such remnant, however, have recently pointed to two stars likely to explode in the future, raising hopes that we may be able to watch such a spectacle at close range.

The remnant that has caught scientists' attention is a gas cloud called Cassiopeia A, or Cas A for short. When a star explodes as a supernova, it leaves an expanding cloud of gas. By measuring the rate of expansion, astronomers can calculate backward to estimate the remnant's age. Of the more than 100 remnants that have been detected in our galaxy, most date back thousands of years. Not so the youngest, which lies in the constellation Cassiopeia.

Though apparently unobserved at the time, the Cas A supernova seems to have occurred around 1680. Astronomers are interested in the remaining cloud because its chemical composition has not yet been diluted with other material in space. From the remnant's composition as well as its structure, astronomers have deduced likely characteristics of the Cas A progenitor— the star that exploded to create the shell of debris.

The cloud consists of two very different kinds of gaseous clumps. The first are shooting outward at about 5,000 miles (8,050 kilometers) per second; the second at only one-twentieth that speed. The faster clumps are clearly the debris of the supernova itself, accelerated to tremendous velocities by the force of the explosion. The slower ones seem to have been ejected by the star near the time of its death.

By studying the wavelengths of light coming from Cas A, scientists have identified the chemicals in the glowing gases. In 1971 such spectral analysis of the slow clumps revealed an enormous amount of nitrogen. It was the first known instance of nitrogen being ejected from a star. To produce such a large amount of nitrogen, a star must be very mature. Apparently the Cas A progenitor was coughing up the nitrogen-rich gas shortly before it exploded. Finding other massive stars expelling gas rich in nitrogen might help astronomers identify the stars most likely to explode in the future.

Potential Supernova?

A star in the Southern Hemisphere named Eta Carinae is probably our most extraordinary supernova candidate. Perhaps as much as 150 times the mass of the Sun, it is one of the most massive stars known. Its peculiar nature kept astronomers puzzling for most of the past century. It was cataloged as a star of ordinary brightness by Edmund Halley in 1677, but during the 1800's it dramatically increased and decreased in brightness several times, becoming at one point the second brightest star in the sky, and ultimately fading almost entirely from view without a telescope. For more than a century, scientists argued the age and nature of the star. By the early 1970's it was still unclear whether it was young, old, or just a freak.

In 1975 Nolan Walborn, an expert on massive stars at the Cerro Tololo Inter-American Observatory in Chile, turned a powerful 13-foot (4-meter) telescope on Eta. To his surprise, sur-

IRON **SILICON AND SULFUR** **OXYGEN AND MAGNESIUM** **OXYGEN AND NEON** **CARBON AND OXYGEN** **HELIUM** **HYDROGEN**

The heart of a heavyweight. A giant star begins as a sphere of mostly hydrogen atoms. For most of the star's 10-million-year life, the hydrogen atoms fuse to form helium, releasing energy that makes the star shine. In its dying stages, the star builds up layers of other elements. Helium in the core is converted to carbon and oxygen; further conversions produce still heavier elements until at the very end, the core is pure iron. Since iron cannot produce energy, the stellar fires in the core die out—the last stage before the star explodes as a supernova.

Stansbury, Ronsaville, & Wood Inc.

rounding the star he saw a faint ring of clumps or condensations of gas.

"Not many people were aware that those condensations existed," says Walborn, now at the Space Telescope Science Institute in Baltimore, Maryland. "With a small telescope, you can't see them." And because the clumps were much dimmer than the main body, most photographs of the star had been taken at exposures that didn't reveal them. Searching the literature, however, Walborn found one group of photographs, taken in 1950 by South African astronomer A. D. Thackeray, that did show the condensations. Comparing those pictures with his, Walborn discovered that the condensations had moved outward in the intervening quarter century, an indication they had been shot out from the body of the star.

Walborn thought of the supernova remnant Cas A, whose slow-moving clumps were believed to have been ejected from the progenitor star shortly before it exploded. Perhaps, he suggested, the clumps around Eta Carinae came from a similar pre-explosion ejection.

To confirm his theory, Walborn measured their velocities and analyzed the spectra of their lightwaves, a technique that would help determine the chemical composition. The clumps were moving about 250 to 870 miles (400 to 1,400 kilometers) per second, comparable to the speeds of the Cas A clumps. And while the spectrum of Eta Carinae itself has always been difficult for astronomers to interpret, the spectra

of the outlying gas clumps turned out to be remarkably easy to read. They seemed to show a great deal of nitrogen.

Walborn was aware, however, that shock waves from past supernovas could have produced the appearance of excess nitrogen. So in 1981 he showed his results to Kris Davidson of the University of Minnesota. Davidson, an expert on the spectra of gas clouds, was stunned by the apparent high level of nitrogen. "With his background," says Walborn, "he appreciated how remarkably unusual those spectra were. More deeply than I had, I think." That much nitrogen—if it was nitrogen—could come only from inside a very mature star.

"When he showed me his evidence," says Davidson, "I realized instantly that we had to get a spectrum of those clumps with the IUE satellite."

Satellite Analysis

The IUE, or International Ultraviolet Explorer, is a satellite that detects a whole different set of wavelengths—the ultraviolet rays, which are just shorter than those the eye can perceive. Being in space, the IUE is not hampered by the atmosphere, which prevents most ultraviolet rays from reaching the Earth. Ultraviolet wavelengths are especially reliable in determining the composition of nebulas.

Joining forces with Ted Gull, an astrophysicist who had worked with the IUE at the National Aeronautics and Space Administration

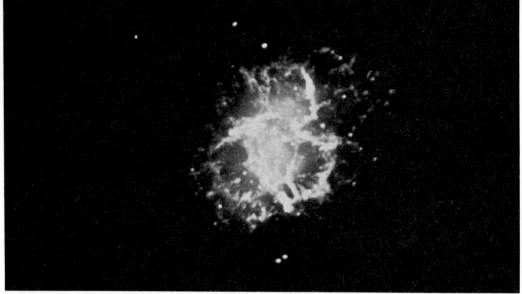

The Crab Nebula in the constellation Taurus—the remnant of a violent supernova explosion that occurred in AD 1054.

(NASA), the astronomers looked at one of the condensations. "It was just remarkable," says Davidson of their analysis. "There'd hardly ever been anything like it. There were these terrifically bright lines" indicating the presence of nitrogen. And other lines indicating carbon and oxygen, which normally appear in the ultraviolet spectrum of less developed stars, didn't show up at all.

"That's really extremely peculiar," says Walborn. "It's probably impossible to come up with any alternative explanation given something so extreme as that. The material must be almost pure processed material from the nuclear reactions inside the star." It seems that this massive star has lived through most of its life. It must now be poised on the brink of a supernova explosion.

Supergiants

A star as extremely massive as Eta is thought to be so unstable that it bypasses one of the life stages typical of a smaller star. Before exploding, stars between about eight and 50 solar masses develop into what are called red supergiants. As this more typical supernova candidate ages and nuclear reactions proceed from one level to the next, the soaring temperature of its core heats the star's outer layers. These layers expand, cool, and redden, transforming the star into the supergiant. Several such aged, massive stars are known in our galaxy, and each is a supernova candidate. But the red supergiant stage may last for 100,000 years before an

explosion, and it is hard to tell just how far along any given star is.

There may be one exception: the well-studied red supergiant Betelgeuse, right shoulder of the constellation Orion. At somewhere between 15 and 30 solar masses, it is much less hefty than Eta Carinae, but because it is much closer to us, it is one of the brightest stars in the sky. Like Eta, Betelgeuse is losing matter into space. In addition, the chemical composition of Betelgeuse, like that of Eta, is difficult to analyze; though various researchers have tried, they come up with conflicting results.

In 1980 astronomers Michael Jura and Mark Morris, now both at the University of California at Los Angeles, took an indirect approach by studying data from two other groups of astronomers interested in Betelgeuse. One group had detected radio waves emitted by carbon monoxide in the star's ejected gas; another group, studying visible wavelengths, had discovered particular effects produced by potassium. Jura and Morris took into account conditions believed to prevail in the gas stream and developed mathematical models that seemed to fit both sets of observations. They could then calculate the ratio of potassium to carbon—a ratio that seemed to be 25 times greater than in average stars.

This could mean one of two things: either the carbon was unusually low or the potassium high. Potassium is thought to be created only at the high temperatures typical of a supernova explosion. The potassium currently in Betelgeuse was probably not created by the star but picked up in its infancy from the debris of earlier generations of supernovas. Carbon, however, is more easily affected by the nuclear reactions that take place in a massive star. In fact, the same cycle of reactions that increases a massive star's nitrogen should cause a corresponding decrease in carbon. Jura and Morris concluded that a low level of carbon implied an extraordinary amount of nitrogen—indirect evidence that the composition of Betelgeuse was similar to that of the Cas A progenitor.

Jura and Morris's calculations pointed to other similarities as well. For example, the rate at which gas was flowing from the star seemed even greater than the already high rate of the Cas A progenitor. "The parallels between Betelgeuse and the likely progenitor of Cas A," the two astronomers concluded in a 1981 paper, "are sufficiently striking that it seems reasonable to imagine that Betelgeuse will become a supernova similar to the one that produced Cas A."

Since then, new measurements suggest that there is actually less potassium and more carbon than previously thought. "The evidence is still pretty good, though," says Jura, "that the abundances are unusual in Betelgeuse—just not as extremely unusual as we said four years ago." However, some astronomers are not yet convinced the chemical makeup of the star's outer layers is all that different from that of an average star like the Sun.

Some recently collected data may reveal more about Betelgeuse's evolutionary state. In 1983 the InfraRed Astronomical Satellite (IRAS) detected a series of faint dust shells extending out to a distance of about 4½ light-years from the star. The dust was apparently ejected from the star 50,000 to 100,000 years ago as the star evolved into a red supergiant. Since the supergiant stage probably lasts only about 100,000 years, Betelgeuse may be quite close to the supernova explosion that will ultimately end its life.

So either Betelgeuse or Eta could explode at any moment. "What we're observing right now is the warning," Nolan Walborn says of Eta Carinae. Its mass is so tremendous that Eta must be evolving very quickly and should explode soon—although "soon," on a cosmic time scale, may mean anytime in the next 10,000 years. Michael Jura figures Betelgeuse may have 50,000 years left to go. "But it could happen tomorrow," he adds.

Astronomers Are Ready

These stars are only two of a number in our galaxy that could blow up next. But no matter which explodes first, all major astronomical instruments will turn toward it in a hurry. Astronomers hope to catch a nearby supernova in its earliest, and least understood, stages. Perhaps the most perplexing problem to solve is how the energy of an inward-falling core is transformed into the explosion that blows off the star's middle and outer layers. According to one model, the collapsing core emits neutrinos—elusive, probably massless, particles that move at the speed of light. The neutrinos are then trapped just outside the core, providing enough pressure to blast away the star's outer layers, while the core continues to collapse. There are several neutrino detectors on Earth that might catch a burst from a nearby supernova, helping to confirm the model.

With a supernova in our galaxy, astronomers may also be able to tell what exotic object is left behind—perhaps a neutron star or black hole. A neutron star is thought to manifest itself as a pulsar, a rapidly pulsing source of radio waves. But of the many known pulsars in the Milky Way, only three have been found within supernova remnants. Though it might be more difficult to prove the existence of a black hole, gases spiraling into one might heat up and emit X rays that our instruments could detect.

No matter what scientists learn, a supernova close to Earth could create quite a spectacle in the sky. The closest remnant discovered lies just 1,500 light-years away. The explosion that created it 5,000 to 11,000 years ago may have been the brightest celestial event ever seen by humans. Betelgeuse is perhaps only 520 light-years distant, so its explosion could look even more extraordinary. And though Eta Carinae lies about 9,000 light-years away, it is so massive that when it blows up, it may outshine every other star and be visible during the day. Astronomers are not the only ones who should expect to enjoy our galaxy's next supernova.

SELECTED READINGS

"New class of supernovae confirmed." *Astronomy,* October 1986.

"Supernova of a different kind." *Sky and Telescope,* August 1986.

"Supernova patrol makes its first score" by D. E. Thomsen. *Science News,* May 31, 1986.

"Radio studies of extragalactic supernova" by K. W. Weiler et al. *Science,* March 14, 1986.

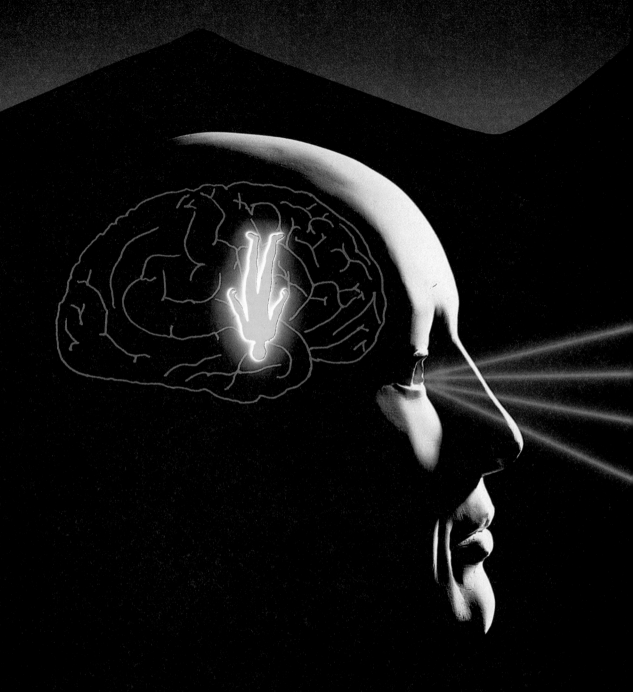

BEHAVIORAL
SCIENCES

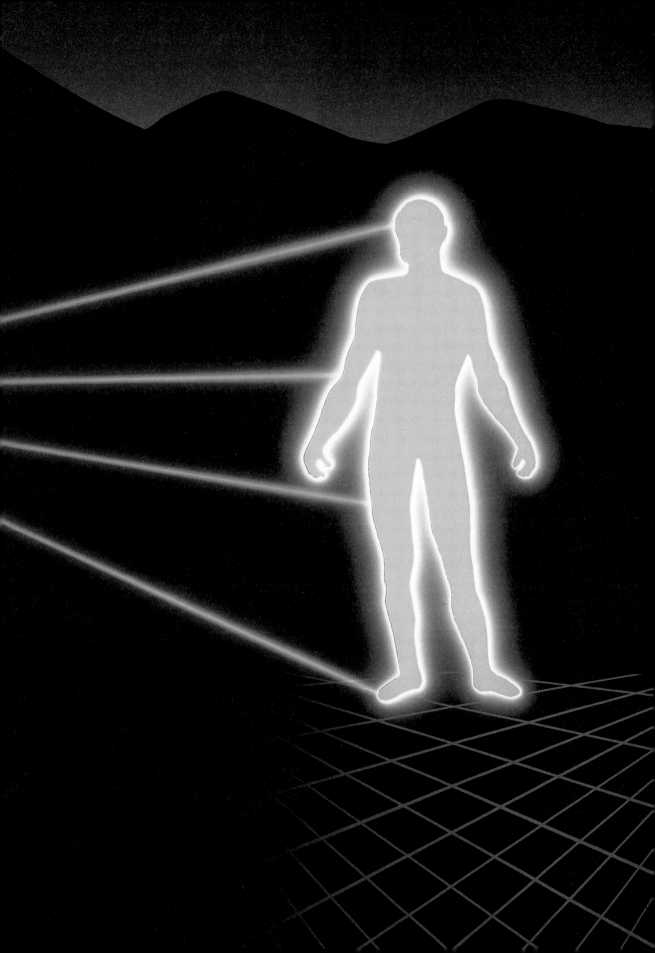

Card playing is one way that elderly people can keep their reasoning and spatial abilities well tuned.

© Erika Stone

REVIEW OF THE YEAR

BEHAVIORAL SCIENCES

The value of talk therapies in the treatment of depression, methods of reversing the deterioration of inductive reasoning and spatial orientation in the elderly, and the apparent discovery of where sign language is controlled in the brain were among 1986's breakthroughs in the behavioral sciences.

TREATMENTS FOR DEPRESSION

Preliminary findings of an extensive study of depressed patients indicated that two short-term forms of "talk" therapy ease symptoms of depression just as well as a commonly prescribed antidepressant drug, and better than an inactive "placebo" pill. Patients were treated in weekly one-hour sessions for 12 to 16 weeks; psychologist Irene Elkin and her colleagues at the National Institute of Mental Health (NIMH) have yet to analyze improvement over the 18 months after treatment ended.

The two talk therapies in the study are known as cognitive behavior therapy and interpersonal therapy. The former approach attempts to correct distorted thinking and overly negative views held by depressed persons about themselves, the world, and the future. Interpersonal therapy focuses on developing better ways to relate to family members, coworkers, and others.

Drug and pill placebo treatments were dispensed weekly by experienced psychiatrists, who also provided about one-half hour of support and encouragement per week.

The 236 moderately to severely depressed patients recruited by the researchers were treated in one of three major university medical centers. Although both talk therapies worked just as well overall, their effectiveness varied markedly across the three sites. A closer look at the data, said Elkin, will examine site-specific effects, such as the relationship between patients and therapists and the skill of therapists in carrying out the assigned treatment.

When taken as a whole, however, more than half of all patients in both therapy and drug groups recovered with no serious symptoms after 16 weeks, compared with 29 percent of the placebo group. The least depressed patients in the sample responded surprisingly well to placebos, according to Elkin, indicating that this approach may significantly help many moderately depressed people. Severely depressed patients, on the other hand, responded far better to the "active" treatments.

Although this is the most exhaustive study of psychotherapy to date, it has its limitations, added Elkin. Only two of the many available psychotherapies were offered, and only one of a number of antidepressant drugs was administered to subjects.

Depression researchers familiar with the project said further studies will need to concentrate on the outcome of talk-therapy/antidepressant-drug combinations, now being touted as superior to either treatment alone. They also noted that a depressed patient's support from friends and family should be considered over the course of recovery.

INTELLECT AND AGING

It is often assumed that with aging comes the inevitable dwindling of the ability to think and reason. But declines in two important types of intellectual function among the elderly are largely avoidable and, in many cases, quickly counteracted by supervised training, according to psychologists at Pennsylvania State University. The same training, reported K. Warner Schaie and Sherry L. Willis, boosts the performance of a substantial number of older adults whose intellectual abilities remain stable.

The researchers tested 229 healthy adult volunteers in 1970 and again in 1984. Subjects ranged in age from 64 to 95 years by the end of the study. "Inductive reasoning" was assessed by showing individuals several series of letters, numbers, and words; they were asked to find the pattern in a series and select the next element from among five choices. "Spatial orientation" involved the ability to mentally rotate two- and three-dimensional objects.

A significant decline on one or both of the measures occurred among 122 subjects; the other 47 percent remained stable. Five-hour training sessions in reasoning or spatial orientation were then held. Those declining in one ability took training in that area. Individuals who declined in both skills or who remained stable were randomly assigned to training.

The results: more than 60 percent of subjects whose performance had declined in one or both areas since 1970 achieved markedly higher scores after training. In addition, more than half of the subjects whose scores remained stable over the 14 years significantly improved after training.

According to the researchers, many older adults suffer the kind of intellectual declines observed in this study because they simply do not use reasoning and spatial abilities as much as they used to. These skills, they said, relate to everyday tasks such as understanding instructions on medicine bottles and finding one's way in neighborhoods and buildings. A big question remains, however: What distinguishes the older adults who responded well to training?

LANGUAGE IN THE BRAIN

The traditional notion of a "split brain" in which the left hemisphere controls spoken language while the right hemisphere regulates visual and spatial skills is being revised as a result of recent studies. Antonio Damasio of the University of Iowa College of Medicine and his coworkers found that the ability to use and understand sign language, which depends on hand movements and spatial judgments and has been considered a right-hemisphere function by many researchers, is rooted in the left hemisphere. Thus, the right hemisphere is not involved in all visual and

American School for the Deaf

The use and understanding of sign language is now thought to be controlled by the left side of the brain.

spatial tasks, said Damasio; the left side of the brain appears to transform both the spoken and signed labels of a language into meanings.

His conclusion is based on the rare opportunity to study a hearing individual who is also proficient in sign language, before and after damage to a critical portion of her right hemisphere. The 27-year-old woman, an interpreter for deaf people, sought surgical treatment after drug therapy failed to quell her persistent seizures. When a barbiturate (sedative) was injected into an artery leading into her left hemisphere, both her spoken and sign language abilities were temporarily shut down. Surgical removal of part of her right hemisphere was then performed, and seizures stopped. A year later the woman showed no changes from before surgery on tests of language, memory, and perception. In videotaped interviews, she confirmed her ability to sign and understand signing as well as ever.

This finding agrees with several recent studies of deaf individuals fluent in sign language who suffered brain damage due to strokes. Those with left-hemisphere lesions had marked problems signing; lesions to the right hemisphere created difficulty with several spatial skills, but sign language was unaffected.

It is possible, said Damasio, that parts of the right hemisphere would regulate the learning of sign language. Once learned, the use and compre-hension of signs are predominantly controlled by the left side. Noted Damasio: "The lingering idea that the right hemisphere is involved in all visual and spatial tasks is changing."

BRUCE BOWER

39

Evening The Score

by Melvin M. Mark and
Jerald Greenberg

T hey had the hammer; they enforced it. I'll have the hammer in my hand next year, and I'll use it. . . . I'll have more drive to have a good year.'' New York Yankee first baseman Don Mattingly was bitterly describing what he saw as an injustice when he talked about the hammer shortly before the 1985

In baseball, one means by which the umpire disciplines team members who violate the rules is by ejecting them from the game. Some transgressors are also fined.

season. Although he had won the American League batting championship in 1984, the Yankees refused to pay what he thought he was worth the next year, and instead renewed his contract for 1985 at a salary of $325,000.

The hammer that Mattingly expected to hold was the salary arbitration he became eligible for the next year. After he led the league in runs batted in in 1985, he used it to restore his sense of justice by winning a salary of $1,375,000 in 1986.

In sports, as in the rest of life, justice comes in three distinct forms: distributive justice, which deals with how resources are fairly allocated—the subject about which Mattingly was concerned; retributive justice, which involves the mechanisms by which the victims of rule violations are given fair redress; and procedural justice, which is concerned with the fairness of the mechanisms themselves.

When we think about justice, we usually picture courts and judges, but it makes just as much sense to visualize playing fields and referees. Umpires and referees enforce the rules and penalize violators in sports just as police officers and judges do in society at large. Examining sports and games from this perspective not only helps us understand them better, it can help us appreciate the significance of justice in our everyday lives.

Getting What's Deserved

According to predominant theories of distributive justice, people should be rewarded in proportion to their contributions. Equity theorists such as the late J. Stacey Adams and Elaine Hatfield (previously Elaine Walster) have hypothesized that when people feel they aren't getting the rewards they deserve, they try to restore equity, often by lowering their performance level.

Many studies have confirmed these predictions, including one in which psychologist Robert Lord and graduate student Jeffrey Hohenfeld of the University of Akron examined the performance of 23 big-league baseball players who played out their options in 1976, the first year of free agency. These men had their 1976 salaries cut by about 20 percent, on the average, compared to what they had earned in 1975. As predicted by equity theory, these players overall had lower batting averages, hit fewer home runs, and had fewer runs batted in during 1976 than in 1975.

Perceived underpayment can lead to good performance rather than bad if the player sees future rewards as directly related to performance, as Mattingly did. Other people who feel underrewarded use another approach: they try to restore equity by getting bigger rewards immediately. Quarterback Dan Marino of the Miami Dolphins took this approach in 1985. In an attempt to have his salary increased to match his record-breaking performance of the previous year, he stayed away from the preseason camp. Other holdouts and strikes, such as the short-lived 1985 baseball strike in which players sought what they felt was a fair portion of greatly increased television revenues, may be seen as similar attempts to achieve distributive justice.

Award Allocation

In addition to studying how people react to rewards they consider unfair, equity researchers examine how awards are allocated. Usually, as you might expect, we give larger rewards to people who produce more. But in sports, rewards are rarely distributed in direct proportion to contributions. Instead, the desire for equity is usually satisfied by an ordinal allocation of rewards. The first-place finisher receives more than the second-place finisher, who receives more than the third-place finisher, and so on, but the rewards are not directly proportional to the magnitude of differences among them. In the Super Bowl, for example, the winning and losing teams receive predetermined awards whether the game is a one-sided rout or an overtime squeaker.

Fairness in Perspective

To many fans, the six- or seven-figure salaries of professional athletes seem outrageous and certainly not "fair." But as research and theory on social comparison indicate, people tend to compare themselves with others like themselves and to compare "upward," to people doing somewhat better than they are. Not surprisingly, then, professional athletes usually contrast their salaries with those of teammates and competitors of seemingly comparable ability who are better paid.

Different perspectives also enter into salary negotiations such as baseball's arbitration, in which the team and the player each propose a salary, and, after testimony from each side, the arbitrator decides which of the two salaries the player should receive. Not surprisingly, players and management focus on different types of performance. One agent who has worked with players in arbitration explains, ''When I represent a power player, the other side wants to talk about how many bases he steals. When I have a player who scores runs, the other side wants to talk about slugging percentage.''

Providing Incentive

In recent years, many teams have changed their compensation practices to add incentive clauses to contracts. Players receive additional money for achieving particular goals, such as a certain number of home runs, wins, or touchdowns, or being elected to an all-star team. These incentives connect players' rewards more directly to their actual performance.

Team sports provide team rewards as well as individual salaries. For example, for winning the Super Bowl in 1986, each Chicago Bear received $36,000, while each of the losing New England Patriots received $18,000. These amounts were in addition to the $28,000 and $34,000, respectively, that each member of the Bears and Patriots received for winning earlier play-off games.

Individual performance has no effect on these bonuses. The game's outstanding star receives the same bonus as a player who has a terrible game. There are sound reasons for this seeming flouting of distributive justice. An equal division facilitates group cohesiveness and cooperation, otherwise known as team spirit. In addition, games such as baseball and football require a great deal of coordination. It is impossible to determine precisely how much each player contributes to the outcome of a particular game. So giving equal team bonuses may be the fairest method as well as the least disruptive to team morale.

Meting Out Penalties

The second type of justice, retributive, deals with the assignment of penalties to rule violators. It means, to use a sports metaphor, ''evening the score.'' The late Philip Brickman pointed out that in sports, penalties are of two types: equity-based, ones intended to restore parity between opponents, such as the loss of yardage in football, the loss of strokes in golf, and the awarding of free throws in basketball; and deterrent-based penalties chiefly designed to deter rule violations, such as disqualification or forfeiture for playing an ineligible player in college football, moving one's ball in golf, or hitting an official in virtually all sports. (For the sake of simplicity, we will call them equity or deterrent penalties from here on.)

Equity penalties are applied to actions that are perfectly expectable in the course of normal play, such as fouls in basketball, or that differ only in degree from acceptable practices, such as holding in football, an extension of legal blocking. In contrast, deterrent penalties are assessed for actions that violate basic assumptions of the game, such as the use of ineligible players or deliberate fouling.

Because equity and deterrent penalties have different objectives, they also differ in severity. Equity penalties are meant to correspond approximately to the benefit denied by

Flag down on the play. Punishments for gridiron infractions range from yardage penalties to player evictions.

the violation: when basketball players are fouled in the act of shooting, they are awarded two free throws, giving them the chance to make the two points they might have scored if they hadn't been fouled. In contrast, deterrent penalties such as disqualification and large fines are deliberately more severe, administered in hopes of preventing future misconduct.

The National Collegiate Athletic Association (NCAA) and various professional sports leagues modify their rules nearly every year, frequently in an attempt to improve the equity-restoring or deterrent quality of penalties. For example, three years ago college football changed the rule for pass interference. Now, if the defender interferes on a long pass, the penalty is 15 yards from the line of scrimmage rather than advancement of the ball to the spot of the infraction. This change was made because it was believed that the stiff older penalty too often favored the offensive team rather than simply restoring equity.

Due Process

The third kind of justice, procedural justice, deals with due process, the fairness of the methods involved in playing the game. Who gets to make the decisions? Who makes the rules about reward and punishment? Who administers the rules? How well? Are the procedures unbiased? These are fundamental questions of procedural justice.

Among social scientists, interest in procedural justice is far more recent than interest in distributive and retributive justice. The topic was popularized by two researchers then at the University of North Carolina, the late psychologist John Thibaut and law professor Laurens Walker, and their colleagues. They conducted a series of studies that compared people's reactions to various systems of legal dispute resolution that differed in how much control they gave judges and litigants over the resolution of the case and the legal process itself.

American and British courts use an adversary system in which judges have control over the verdicts but not over such crucial matters as the type of evidence to be presented. These decisions are left to litigants and attorneys. Legal systems in continental Western Europe rely on the inquisitorial system: judges control not only the verdicts but also the way evidence is collected and presented. Which system is perceived as better?

In general, Thibaut and Walker found that

© Paul J. Sutton/duomo

Restoring equity. A referee awards two free throws to a basketball player fouled in the act of shooting.

people believed the adversary procedure was both more effective and fairer. The key factor appeared to be control over the process of developing evidence. More recent research in areas as diverse as endorsement of political leaders, police-community relations, acceptance of personnel administration systems, and classroom grading policies underscore this point: procedures are seen as being fairer when the people affected by them have some say in them.

When a football game begins with a coin toss, the winner decides whether to kick or receive. Later on, teams have the option of accepting or declining penalties, whichever is better for them. In less formal games, players sometimes help set up the rules. When we play the board game Monopoly, for example, we are more satisfied if we are consulted about what variations, or "house rules," are used. This desire to have a say in matters that affect them is one reason players' associations are becoming more vocal about rule changes and want to be consulted about them.

Appealing for justice? Tennis ace John McEnroe's frequent outbursts on the court sparked debate among sports fans on whether an umpire's judgment should continue to be considered infallible.

© Paul J. Sutton/duomo

Fair Application

Another aspect of procedural justice is the fairness with which rules are applied. A growing body of research demonstrates how important this perception of fairness is. For example, social psychologist Tom R. Tyler of Northwestern University and his colleagues have shown that when people feel that teachers, politicians, or those in the criminal-justice system are using unfair procedures to reach decisions, they are less satisfied with these decisions. Other research, including our own, has found that perceptions of unfair procedures make people feel hostile and resentful. This suggests that seemingly unfair applications of the rules in sports lead to dissatisfied participants and fans and may provoke violence on and off the field.

The importance of impartial, consistent officiating was demonstrated by the National Basketball Association (NBA) referees' strike in 1983. The replacement referees were inadequate, particularly in their failure to control fighting for position away from the ball. The poorer quality of play and many fights led some sportswriters to dub the NBA the "National Boxing Association." The most equitable rules do not result in justice or in control of the game if they are not applied fairly and well.

Improving officiating on the field primarily affects equity penalties, but procedural justice may be even more important for deterrent penalties. Brickman noted that while equity penalties for offenses such as holding are applied immediately, deciding on deterrent penalties usually takes a long time. Sanctions for recruiting violations often involve investigations that span several years.

The loss of TV and bowl-game revenues through NCAA sanctions against universities can run into millions of dollars. Likewise, in an age of millionaire athletes, suspension without pay can produce more severe fines than are likely in a criminal court.

Consider the case of Tom Lysiak, who in 1983 was a center for the Chicago Black Hawks of the National Hockey League (NHL). In a game with the Hartford Whalers, Lysiak flagrantly tripped an official. He was suspended for 20 games, based on a then-new NHL rule designed to deter violence against officials. The suspension would have cost Lysiak about $50,000, so he won a restraining order in court. He later dropped the suit when the NHL Board of Governors amended the rule to give penalized players the right to appeal.

Equity Penalties in Real Life

In short, the microcosm of sports and games clearly reveals a good deal about our society's ideas of justice. Brickman took this idea a step further by arguing that society could profit by replacing many of its deterrent penalties with the kinds of equity penalties common in sports. This would mean substituting restitution for prison sentences in many cases, setting up systems through which offenders would provide fair compensation to their victims. Doing so, Brickman maintained, would have several long-term benefits.

First, conflict and illegality in the pursuit of gain would be realistically accepted as inevitable, rather than unrealistically seen as preventable. Second, if restoring fairness were acknowledged as the primary goal of the justice system, then both victims and criminals might see the punishment as just and reasonable. Brickman also argued that restitution systems would be more likely to treat offenders with different backgrounds alike and to minimize the stigmatizing effect of the present system.

There are, however, differences between sports and society in general that might make equity penalties less acceptable in society. In sports, for example, participants must continue to interact after a rule violation. Society must deal with infractions involving strangers or others with no continuing contact. In sports, imperfect and imperfectly administered equity penalties may be acceptable because people feel that errors will even out over the course of the game or season. For criminal acts in society, people have no reason to believe in such evening out, and victims want justice in their particular case, not the long run. In sports, equality of opportunity is guaranteed. Contests begin with the score tied. In society, individuals come from vastly different circumstances, making equity penalties less practical.

Sports as a Microcosm

Despite these differences, sports and games do have something to teach us about justice in the nonsports world. Examining the differences may suggest when restitution programs in society are likely to be most useful. For example, restitution might be more successfully applied in cases that involve continuing relationships rather than among strangers.

Sports may also suggest alternative systems of penalization. In basketball, foul shots serve to restore equity (with the shooter's skill determining the outcome), but a player who commits too many fouls is ejected from the game. That is, multiple violations of an equity rule lead to a deterrent penalty. Demerit systems in schools also have such a cumulative effect, as do laws that provide more severe penalties for repeat offenders.

Other sports have penalties of a different structure. Hockey has its penalty box, which bears a considerable resemblance to the "time-out" practices popular with parents. For nearly all offenses, football applies only the equity-oriented penalty of assessing yardage or loss of down. By examining these and other sports penalization schemes, society may discover more workable alternatives, more ways of making the punishment fit the crime.

In a policelike role, a hockey official separates quarreling players. Disobedience could mean time in the penalty box.

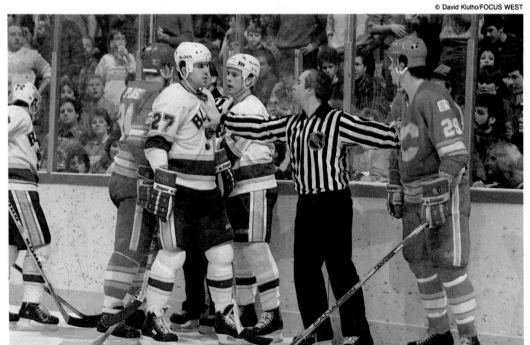

© Anthony Bannister/Animals Animals

Elephants apparently communicate with each other through sounds made below the frequency audible to humans.

CALLS of the WILD

by Doug Starr

"Want corn." Alex seems annoyed. At the moment he wants some corn on the cob. But the woman keeps taunting him with painted wooden shapes.

"Want corn," he insists as she waves the shapes in his face.

"Come on, Alex. What's the same about these? What's the same?" She holds up two wooden hexagons. One is green; the other is red.

"Want corn," he says clearly. "I . . . WANT . . . CORN!"

He shifts jerkily from one foot to the other,

flexing his claws around the wooden perch. He puffs out his gray chest feathers. He clicks his black beak. He cocks his head so that one eye points straight up and the other straight down.

"I'm gonna go away," says the parrot. He turns and walks away.

"Come on, Alex," says Irene Pepperberg, an ethologist at Northwestern University. "Don't be a bore. Now tell me: What's the same?"

He stops and squawks, "Shape."

She holds out a red square and a green square.

"Good! What's different?"

"Color."

"Good parrot!" She gives him one of the squares. He chews it to splinters. "Want corn," he reminds her.

"Sure," says Pepperberg, holding up a cob. "And what color is this?" She speaks in the same singsong style people use when talking to a small child.

"Yel-low!" he says, in the same tone.

"Good parrot! Good birdie!"

"You tickle me?"

"Sure." Pepperberg scratches his head, perhaps a bit too roughly.

"Gen-tle," he reminds her.

"Okay, I'll be gentle."

It's a typical day in the life of Alex the parrot, who in many ways is just a typical bird. Pepperberg bought him in a pet store. But in some ways Alex is unique. For during the past nine years, he has demonstrated abilities that most scientists had relegated to the realm of man. He labels objects. He perceives quantities. He requests specific foods. Alex also generalizes concepts—like color and shape—and applies them to objects he's never been shown before.

In short, Alex doesn't just mimic, like other parrots. He communicates.

New Generation of Communicators

You probably haven't heard about Alex and Pepperberg. That's because the field of interspecies communication has been quiet of late.

The research was big news in the 1960's, when scientists taught chimpanzees to communicate using human sign language and even suggested that dolphins, with their ultralarge brains, might one day speak English. But by the time the late 1970's rolled around, the work had been branded a bust.

While the original researchers had tried to measure even the most subtle reactions of their animals, the critics said, they failed to study themselves. Just as cell biologists couldn't understand the cell without calibrating the microscope, many critics said, interspecies communicators couldn't possibly comprehend animal thoughts and feelings without calibrating their own measuring instrument—the human animal. The result of this omission, they added, was painfully clear: Scientists like John Lilly imposed their own bias on experiments, insisting that dolphins were not only smarter than people but also able to see into the future and past. And because some chimp researchers were either too close or too cruel to their subjects, they couldn't prove that they weren't unconsciously coaching the animals to do languagelike "tricks."

© Bill Boyle

She's talking to the animals. Ethologist Irene Pepperberg partakes in interspecies communication with her remarkable parrot Alex.

By the early 1980's the field of interspecies communication lay in ruins. Critics blitzkrieged the studies, calling them "self-deception" and even "outright fraud." Many of the scientists involved in the experiments lost their funding. Most of their animals were sent to wildlife preserves and zoos. As far as the public knew, the work had stopped.

But today a new generation of interspecies communicators has arrived on the scene. In less than a decade, they have rendered the outback of animal consciousness increasingly clear. Not only is the new work scientifically solid; it also possesses a grandeur and beauty that eclipse the work of a generation before. For the first time, a parrot can use, really use, English labels. A pygmy chimp understands dozens of spoken words, something it was assumed nonhumans could never do. And dolphins and sea lions have gone further still, grasping not only words but also some basic rules of grammar.

"Animals have much more complex communication abilities than we ever imagined," Pepperberg says.

The extraordinary new findings have emerged from a potent array of experimental techniques. Today's primate biologists use remote cameras and moment-by-moment video playback to check and recheck each gesture the chimps make. Dolphin experts have also become increasingly precise, wearing goggles and controlling body language to eliminate subtle cues. As a result we may someday be forced to recast our notion of what it means to be human. Most of us accept the idea that man evolved from the apes. We know we share certain physical characteristics with our evolutionary ancestors, from the backbone of the crocodile to the almost human facial structure of the baby chimp. Now it seems we may share some intellectual characteristics as well. And that gives rise to troubling questions: Are humans alone in their ability to use language? Will there be no bastion left for the uniqueness of man?

A Controversial Legacy

Interspecies communication has a long and controversial history, but its modern era began when Dr. John C. Lilly pioneered human-dolphin communication. Dissecting the creatures, he found that they had among the world's largest brains when compared with their body size. He explored their intelligence with simple tests, rewarding them with food when they correctly completed such tasks as flipping a switch.

Later on he found a more powerful motivator than food: he inserted electrodes into their brains, stimulating their pleasure centers when they were successful and their pain centers when they were not. Using this method, Lilly says, he'd caused dolphins to learn faster than any other creature he'd seen.

Even as Lilly was speculating about communication with dolphins, others were trying to talk to the apes. In the mid-1960's the husband-and-wife team of R. Allen and Beatrix Gardner raised a chimp named Washoe in a house trailer at their Reno, Nevada, home. They treated her like a child, providing toys, good food, and plenty of friends. She eventually acquired the signs of American Sign Language (ASL), the gestural language of the deaf. Within a few years, Washoe had mastered 170 word signs, from "want drink" to "dirty."

Soon Washoe was joined by other pioneers. At the University of Pennsylvania, a chimp named Sarah learned to arrange in logical sequences colored shapes that represented words. At the Yerkes Regional Primate Center in Atlanta, Georgia, a chimp named Lana could "speak" with her human trainers by punching a computerlike keyboard.

Then, in the late 1970's, Columbia University psychologist Herbert Terrace did some fateful sign work with a chimp called Nim Chimpsky (in honor of Noam Chomsky, the linguist who said language was intrinsically human). Terrace thought Nim had mastered the signs, until he looked at videotapes of the training sessions. Rarely did Nim sign when not asking for food. Rarely did Nim initiate conversations. He frequently interrupted his teachers, not realizing that in language one takes turns.

Soon after publication of Terrace's paper, the New York Academy of Sciences sponsored a conference whose sole purpose, it seemed, was to discredit the original experiments. One critic compared the ape-language work to "the most rudimentary, circuslike performances." The scientific establishment seemed to agree.

Those under attack, meanwhile, launched a defense of their own. Home rearing, they said, had been a key part of their work. But Nim was raised as if in a prison. He lived in an 8- by 8-foot (2.5- by 2.5-meter) room and was drilled several hours a day by any of 60 trainers. Under those circumstances, they argued, he could scarcely be expected to sign like a human. His tendency to interrupt, they added, was very human—just like the babble of a toddler.

Chimpanzees are at the forefront of studies on interspecies communication. The chimpanzee at left responds to questions posed by its trainer by pressing the appropriate buttons on a keyboard labeled with lexigrams (picture representations of words). Above, Tatu—a chimp adept at sign language—communicates the word "black."

The Human Factor

As it turned out, both sides had a valid point. Whether or not the scientists had been cuing the chimps, the human part of the dialogue had simply been imposed on the experiment—without ever being taken into account.

The danger of this phenomenon was documented recently by Lawrence D. Wieder, associate professor of communications, sociology, and philosophy at the University of Oklahoma. Wieder did something that had never been done before: he studied the chimper, the person who studies the chimps. He found that many ape researchers set up a dominant-submissive relationship with their charges. Some of them, Wieder states, set up their dominance with "yells, bluffs, choke chains, cattle prods, BB guns, and blank-loaded guns." As a result, he concludes, the chimp talk seemed mechanical. The work would have profited if the scientists had either analyzed their own effect on communication, Wieder says, or, better yet, taught sign language and then just stepped back and watched the animals.

That's just what the new brand of researcher has begun to do. Some of the most significant results have come from the husband-and-wife team of Roger and Debbi Fouts, who now work with Washoe and several other chimps at the University of Central Washington in Ellensburg.

At first glance, Ellensburg seems an unlikely place for signing chimps. It's about 15 square blocks of the Old West, where the biggest tourist attraction is the sprawling Black Angus Ranch. But when you're there for a while, the location makes sense. As the only real stopover between Seattle and Spokane, Ellensburg is an oasis for ex-hippies, liberals, and offbeat academics. It's a place where longhairs and cowboys stroll the same streets, where art galleries and gun shops peacefully coexist, and where a restored old saloon serves nouvelle cuisine. It's just the sort of place to have welcomed the chimps.

"You can look at the chimps," Roger said when I arrived, "but try not to stare. I don't want them to feel like they're on display."

He led the way through the second floor of the psychology building, to several interconnecting, room-size cages. Inside were Tatu and Moja, Loulis and Dar. And there in the corner sat Washoe, the matriarch herself. Fouts says the chimps get plenty of human contact. But when it's time for observation, the humans go away.

Dolphins have long been considered among the most intelligent mammals. In Hawaii, dolphins have been trained to answer yes or no questions by poking the appropriate paddle.

© Louis Herman

Once a year the Foutses set up three remote cameras just outside the cages. Then at random intervals they make 20-minute tapes. They do this until they have 15 hours, then go back and analyze the tapes. So careful is the analysis of gestures, activities, and postures that studying one minute of tape takes three hours.

That care has paid off. Like field biologists watching a little-known species, the Foutses have made important new findings, refuting their critics on several fronts. They've shown that the chimps do not imitate their trainers; after all, they communicate when no one's around. Nor do the chimps use signs just to beg for food. After viewing more than 5,000 signings, the Foutses found that 88 percent of the chimps' "conversations" involved play, reassurance, or social interaction. Only 5 percent involved food. They've also shown that a chimp will sign to itself when it's alone. Sometimes Loulis signs "drink, drink" before he gets himself some water. Washoe used to sign "hurry" as she ran to the toilet. This private signing, as it's called, means the chimps may even be thinking in symbols.

The Foutses' most significant finding involves Loulis. When Loulis arrived in 1979, they agreed not to teach him to sign. It was part of their strategy to see what the chimps could do on their own. Yet eight days after he moved in with Washoe, Loulis made a sign. Several months later he started making two-sign combinations, like "come tickle."

Loulis was signing an average of 37.75 times a month. When the Foutses obtained two more signing apes, his signing increased more than tenfold. It was the first time that one nonhuman had ever learned a human language from another.

Self-taught Chimps

Loulis isn't unique. Last year, E. Sue Savage-Rumbaugh of the Yerkes Primate Center at Emory University in Atlanta, Georgia, reported that a pygmy chimp named Kanzi had taught himself a human language as well. Kanzi lived in the laboratory with his mother, who was being taught to use geometric symbols called lexigrams. The chimp sits in front of a computerized keyboard with dozens of buttons. Each button is labeled with a lexigram representing such words as "apple," "get," "please," or "give." Each time the chimp presses a button, the symbol flashes on a screen for the trainer to see. So by pressing buttons, the chimps and trainers can converse.

Kanzi would watch his mother's lesson, although he did not take part. Then one day he started using the keyboard. He punched the "ball" key, for example, and kept pointing to a ball until the attendant brought one. Soon Kanzi started signaling fluently—often, it seemed, just for the pleasure of communicating.

But where Kanzi really excels is in understanding English. If asked, "Kanzi, can't you find apple?" he'll immediately touch the "apple'' button on the keyboard. At one point a trainer called out the names of 35 items in English, and Kanzi responded by choosing the correct photographs, lexigrams, or objects 95 percent of the time. Kanzi's vocabulary currently consists of about 200 symbols for English words.

"Kanzi actually understands English," says Savage-Rumbaugh, "something it had been concluded apes just could not do."

If apes can learn English, meanwhile, sea mammals seem to have gone further still. Not only do dolphins and sea lions comprehend human words, they also understand syntax—the link between word order and meaning. Syntax, after all, allows us to take a limited number of words and combine them into a near infinite number of meanings. It's the reason why the phrase "dog bites man" means something different from "man bites dog."

Schooling Sea Mammals

The task of teaching grammar to dolphins was recently taken up by marine specialist and psychologist Louis M. Herman of the University of Hawaii. By using standard reward techniques, he trained dolphins to associate symbols, or names, with objects and actions. He then taught them how the object names and action names could be combined to form meaningful sentences. For instance, the dolphins understood that "Frisbee fetch surfboard" meant take the Frisbee to the surfboard. "Surfboard fetch Frisbee" meant take the surfboard to the Frisbee. "We discovered that dolphins could comprehend not only the meanings of words," Herman says, "but also how they were ordered in a sentence." It was the first convincing evidence that animals could grasp some fundamental grammatical rules.

Scientists at the University of California at Santa Cruz have recently shown that even sea lions (who are far less intelligent than dolphins) can master the grammatical complexity of multiword commands. The star of the show is a sea lion named Rocky, who lives in a pool overlooking the Pacific Ocean.

Poolside at the U. of C. at Santa Cruz, grad student Michelle Jeffreys explains that part of the success comes from increased awareness of ourselves. To avoid influencing Rocky by repeating unconscious patterns, Jeffreys doesn't decide what tasks Rocky will perform; instead, another student reads the tasks from a randomized list. Jeffreys simply listens to the directions

through headphones, then communicates with Rocky by motioning with her arms.

Jeffreys makes the symbols for "ball car fetch." Suddenly Rocky turns. She swims past six toys floating in the pool, then uses her nose to push a plastic car over to a ball. On the next trial, Jeffreys makes some more motions. This time Rocky nose-butts the ball to the car.

"There's a lot more going on here than simple circus tricks," says Ronald Schusterman, the psychologist in charge of the lab. Rocky understands the rules in the sentences as well as the words. This holds true even when Schusterman adds modifiers—words describing color and size. Rocky now has a vocabulary of some two dozen words and has responded to thousands of new commands.

Back in Hawaii, Herman has expanded his studies as well. Each of the two dolphins he trained knows 40 to 50 words and has a repertoire of thousands of different commands. One dolphin responds to hand signals; the other, to computer-generated sounds.

Using this technique, Herman has demonstrated new levels of dolphin cognition. His dolphins know right from left. When given the command "mimic," they imitate the next sound they hear. They understand the concept of "erase," in which a sign from Herman tells them to disregard one message and obey another.

"I place them in the same intellectual ballpark as the chimpanzees," Herman says. "They're cognitive cousins—which is amazing when you consider that in terms of evolution, they separated from land mammals about 60 million years ago."

Referential Reporting

Recently Herman took another step toward human-dolphin communication. He installed two paddles in the dolphins' pool: one paddle was for "yes," and the other for "no." Now when asked if a certain object is in the water, the dolphin pokes a paddle to answer. The answers, while limited, open a window on the dolphin's mind. For when a dolphin pokes "no," it means it understands the sign, forms a mental image, and deduces that the item isn't there. This ability—which is called referential reporting—has previously been documented only in apes and man.

Another scientist has pushed human-dolphin communication even further. At Marineworld/Africa USA, north of San Francisco,

California, ethologist Diana Reiss has built a submersible keyboard. It's about 2 feet (0.6 meter) square and consists of nine keys. Each time a dolphin pushes a key with its beak, a computer records the action and produces a sound specific to that symbol. Then the dolphin gets what it asked for, be it a ball, fish, or back scratch. Just as in human language, the animal links the label with the object, action, or reward.

Reiss is a small, dark-haired woman who speaks with great intensity about dolphins. She doesn't mythologize; when Reiss tells you something, she backs it up with a videotape and a computer analysis.

She recalls that soon after she installed the keyboard, the dolphins taught themselves to use it. Then they started to imitate the sounds. They'd push a button, hear the computer whistle, and within milliseconds, match the sound. Sometimes they'd make the sound even before pushing the button.

According to Reiss, the computer represents a middle ground, "a shared code that animals and humans can both understand." But to be truly powerful, any such system must incorporate a knowledge of the vocal and nonvocal symbols that the animals use among themselves.

Playback Decoding

The foundation of such knowledge—the ability to give specific meanings to animal sounds—has begun to emerge. A breakthrough came in 1980, when Robert Seyfarth, Dorothy Cheney, and Peter Marler were observing vervet monkeys in the jungles of Kenya. They knew that vervets, like other primates, are very vocal creatures. They're also rather small, which means they have many natural predators and a variety of alarm calls. Seyfarth and Cheney wanted to know if the different alarm calls had different meanings or if they just portrayed the level of the vervet monkeys' fright.

They used a simple but little-tried technique. They recorded three kinds of alarm calls and played them back to see how the monkeys would react. When they played back one call— a bark—several of the monkeys scurried up trees. A grunting call made them dive for cover. A rapid series of coughs caused them to jump up on tiptoes. Those vastly different reactions showed that the differences between the calls were related to the messages they carried. The bark warned that a leopard was on the prowl.

The grunts said that an eagle was overhead. And the coughs meant that a snake was underfoot.

Subsequently Cheney and Seyfarth expanded their dictionary of monkey sounds. They now know of six alarm calls (the other three are for jackals, baboons, and humans), at least four grunts, and three or more chattering sounds, each with its own meaning. The messages range from cries of alarm and territoriality to expressions of kinship and social standing. What they all have in common is their symbolic nature—something that was thought to be exclusive to human communication.

"We firmly established that animals in the wild can use their own calls to represent things in the external world," says Cheney, now at the University of Pennsylvania. "It's a little like what the signing chimps do—only humans haven't taught them."

Not only did Cheney and Seyfarth's work reverse old notions of how animals communicate, but it established a powerful new research tool. Now several other researchers are using playback to decode animal messages as well. A team from the University of Minnesota is currently in Tanzania's Serengeti National Park, recording and playing back the roars of lions. The goal: to learn the social function of a variety of specific sounds. At the University of Washington, ornithologist Philip Stoddard is using playback to learn how some birds identify their young and define their territory. And at the University of Florida, biologist Harry Hollien is planning to use playback to analyze tiger calls. So far he's compiled a brief tiger dictionary by presenting caged tigers with a wide range of stimuli and recording the responses.

After running hundreds of such trials, Hollien has categorized a number of tiger sounds. A prousten—a pulsing kind of purr—means "I recognize you; don't attack me; let's check each other out," says Hollien. A prousten followed by a moan means the tiger wants to be friends. "I've never had one turn on me after that," he adds.

Herman did an even more extensive form of playback with humpback whales. Members of his team tracked a pod of humpbacks off the coast of Alaska and then recorded their calls. Then they played back the calls to whales in Hawaii. Though the results are preliminary, they found that feeding sounds could stop whales in their tracks a kilometer away, turn them around, and cause them to follow the vessel.

Stranded Humphrey the humpback whale was led safely back to the Pacific Ocean using tape-recorded whale calls.

The Humphrey Experience

That discovery found a practical use not long ago when a humpback named Humphrey was stranded in the Sacramento River. Nothing could remove him—until Herman mailed a tape to California authorities. When they broadcast the trumpet sound through an underwater speaker, Humphrey charged the boat. He kept following, all the way to the Golden Gate Bridge—53 miles (85 kilometers) and seven hours later.

But the most precise work with playback may someday emerge from a small medical lab in downtown Seattle, Washington. Here Richard Ferraro, a nationally known expert in medical electronics at the Institute of Applied Physiology and Medicine, recently unveiled a new invention: a computer that can pick up animal calls, digitize them, display them graphically, and create sounds in reply. In short it's the closest thing we've got to a human-animal translation machine.

With Ferraro's device you can punch up any of dozens of presynthesized calls, play them to animals in the wild, and see how they react. Or you can use a joystick to create novel sounds of your own.

Such a machine could be used with any animal sound, but Ferraro has focused on the orca, or killer whale. By following whales off the coast of Washington, he has gathered and analyzed hundreds of calls. He's grouped them into more than 50 categories according to their sonic character, which he can display on a screen.

He's also begun to use the machine to interact with the orca. In a recent pilot study, he took the machine into Puget Sound on a small boat. Motoring to within 50 yards of a pod of orcas, he broadcast the computer's version of an orca call consisting of two descending notes. After several tries, a few orcas called back. Then Ferraro modified the call by adding a third note at the end. Again some of the orcas responded—only this time with a new call. Finally he broadcast what he calls his "signature"—a unique, custom-designed call that announces Ferraro is around. It's a creaky, two-note glissando that sounds like a wolf whistle. It's not part of the normal orca repertoire. Yet just as before, a few orcas responded with an imitation.

Ferraro concedes that his results are preliminary. But they do show that killer whales may respond to a strange call. "I think they have the desire to interact," Ferraro says. The next step is to play back small pieces of whale calls and see which sounds provoke which response. "We're trying to isolate areas of the orca call and find out what aspects are important," Ferraro explains. Someday work like Ferraro's may yield human-animal dictionaries that are relatively complete.

Inaudible Frequencies

Some human-animal dictionaries may involve voices we can't even hear. Recently Katherine Payne of Cornell University stunned the zoological world when she found that elephants may communicate with calls beyond the range of human hearing. Payne is the world-renowned whale expert who discovered that humpback songs change from year to year, like Top 40 tunes. Thinking that elephants might also have songs, she sat in a zoo and observed an elephant family for hours—only to go home after not hearing a thing. She suspected that there may have been more than met her ear, so she returned with a high-speed tape recorder. She recorded the elephants at normal speed and played the tape back at high, raising the pitch of their calls enough to hear them.

She uncovered a hidden world of sound. Elephants were already known to call one another with assorted rumbles, roars, trumpets, and barks. But here was a whole new component to their calls—a repertoire of infrasonic sounds.

By correlating the high-speed tapes and her hours of observation, Payne learned that the elephants use the calls in a variety of situations, from caressing their calves to seeing the zookeeper arrive with food. To get a better idea of what the calls mean, she took the recordings to Kenya, where she and elephant expert Joyce Poole played them back to wild elephants. She found that elephant herds often move in parallel tracks, even though they're out of sight of one another. By using infrasonic calls, which travel for miles, the herds may be keeping tabs on one another. It's also known that bull elephants, which live apart from females, travel great distances to find them during mating season. Again, long-distance infrasonic calls may play a role.

"A lot of people think there is a very big line between humans and animals," says Poole. When they learn how much elephants have to say to one another, they'll realize just how intelligent and how communicative some animals are—even the parrot, thought to be just a bit more intelligent than a cat or a dog.

Social Modeling

The key to that extraordinary accomplishment is a new teaching method based on the way parrots learn in the wild. These birds are not born with the ability to make complex calls, Northwestern's Pepperberg says; instead they learn from parents and peers. Pepperberg adapted that knowledge into what she calls "social modeling." Essentially, it's a form of role playing with two human teachers involved: One person plays the parrot; and the other, the instructor. The "parrot" asks the instructor for a particular object, which it gets if it has applied the label correctly. To make sure Alex focuses on the words and not the people, the trainers switch roles. Then Alex tries. Pepperberg gives him only what he asks for, reinforcing the meaning of labels.

First Alex learned to label objects. Then he learned to request them by inserting the word "want" into his speech. He learned to refuse by saying "no." He also learned colors, shapes, and quantities. He grasped the meaning of such concepts as "different" and "same." "I'm not suggesting Alex says abstract things," Pepperberg states. "But when he's put in his cage at night, he'll say, 'Want a nut, tickle me.' It's like a child who doesn't want to go to bed. We've shown that even with a creature as distant from us as the parrot, true interspecies communication can exist."

From English-speaking parrots to singing whales to signing apes—in the past few years, researchers have made a compelling case that animals can learn language. Of course, we'll probably never chat with chimps about politics or philosophy. The gap between animal and human language is just too great. But interspecies communication has opened a window on animals' minds. By observing that chimps "talk" about social interactions (hug, tickle, you chase me), scientists have learned what's important to the species. By finding that a parrot can classify shapes and colors, they have learned more about what humans and birds cognitively share.

"We have to be open to the possibility of true animal consciousness," Diana Reiss states. "Assuming that only humans can give voice to complex thoughts just isn't scientifically sound."

Nigel Eddis

A chess master can recognize up to 100,000 board positions, and instinctively make the best response to each.

The MYSTERY of MASTERY

by Robert J. Trotter

The grand master chess player, the Olympic swimmer, the Nobel-prizewinning physicist, the concert pianist. They're all experts—people who do a skilled job effortlessly, fluidly, intuitively, and almost never make a mistake.

The taxi driver who breaks just enough laws to get you to the airport on time. The 4-year-old who walks through a crowded room without spilling his milk. They're experts, too. In fact, almost everybody has some expertise in numerous day-to-day activities. Recognizing faces, riding a bicycle, carrying on a conversation—with practice, these activities are mastered to the point at which they're done easily, almost naturally.

How do experts in a particular field achieve their high levels of performance? How do they differ from those of us who are merely competent or proficient? The answer to these questions may change the way teachers teach and learners learn, and may eventually help us all become better thinkers and doers.

Pioneering Research

With these goals in mind, cognitive psychologists are trying to become experts on expertise, primarily by comparing the performance of novices (beginners) and experts. Pioneering work in this area was conducted 20 years ago with expert chess players. It had been assumed that the ability to think many moves ahead and consider the implications of each move was what separated the expert from the novice chess player. But in the mid-1960's, psychologist Adriaan de Groot showed that neither experts nor novices think more than a few moves ahead. What separates the two is the expert's ability to temporarily remember board positions. Master chess players, de Groot found, were much better at remembering any real game board after seeing it for only five seconds. This ability, it appears, is related to superior knowledge of the game, not to superior memory. The experts were no better than the novices at remembering random arrangements of pieces.

The late William Chase and his fellow psychologist Herbert Simon, of Carnegie-Mellon University in Pittsburgh, followed up on this research in the early 1970's and, after extensive experimentation with chess players, changed the way we think about how experts think. Their findings suggest that a chess master is someone who, after years of experience, can recognize as many as 100,000 meaningful board positions and make the best response to each. So instead of being a deep thinker who can see many moves ahead, the master chess player is now seen as someone with a superior ability to take in large chunks of information, recognize problem situations, and respond appropriately. This explains how a chess master is able to defeat dozens of weaker players in simultaneous play. For the most part, the master relies on pattern-recognition abilities, or so-called "chess intuition," to generate potentially good moves, according to Chase and Michelene Chi of the University of Pittsburgh's Learning Research and Development Center (LRDC).

Practice Makes Perfect

This particular hypothesis about how the thinking of experts and novices differs has been elaborated upon in numerous experiments, many of them conducted at the LRDC. One aim of the research being done there is to discover general principles of expertise that apply to a variety of areas. Studies of the spatial skills of expert cabdrivers in Pittsburgh and the cognitive skills of experts at solving physics problems, for example, suggest that spatial skills involve the same general principles as do more cognitive skills. "The most important principle of skill performance is that skill depends on the knowledge base," say Chi and Robert Glaser, director of the LRDC. "In general," they say, "the more practice one has had in some domain, the better the performance, and from all indications, this increase in expertise is due to improvements in the knowledge base."

Summing up the results of recent research on expertise, Glaser notes, first, that expertise seems to be very specific. That is, expertise in one domain is no guarantee of expertise in others. However, some types of knowledge may be more readily generalized than others, so that adults who are experts in applied mathematics or aesthetic design, or children who have learned measurement and number concepts, have forms of expertise that can be transferred to other areas.

Experts develop the ability to perceive large meaningful patterns, and do so with such speed that it appears almost intuitive. This extraordinary ability, Glaser explains, seems to depend on the nature and organization of knowledge. Expert cabdrivers, for example, seem to have their knowledge of the city organized by ranks, from larger geographic areas (such as the North Side) down to smaller neighborhoods and specific locations within neighborhoods. To get from a location in one neighborhood to a location in another neighborhood, the cabbies first select a route that connects the two neighborhoods, and follow it until they encounter cues from the environment that trigger specific choices along the route. Decisions made along a well-traveled route, Chi and Glaser say, usually are accomplished smoothly, automatically, and unconsciously.

One reason expert cabbies can do this is because they have better visual knowledge of the city, as the researchers found when they showed pictures of secondary intersections (nonmajor streets) to expert and novice drivers.

Expert drivers could also name more streets and generate shorter and better routes between two locations.

While some researchers are focusing on how experts organize their knowledge and use it, others are examining the long and sometimes difficult journey from novice to expert. Twin brothers Hubert L. Dreyfus and Stuart E. Dreyfus of the University of California, Berkeley, have studied how people learn to become airline pilots, chess players, automobile drivers, and masters of a second language. In their recent book *Mind Over Machine*, they report that in all cases the learners go through five stages from novice to expert.

Stage 1: Novice

During the first stage of acquiring a new skill, the novice learns to recognize various objective facts and features relevant to the skill, as well as rules for deciding how to act on these facts and features. At this stage the facts and rules are "context free." That is, they are clearly and objectively defined so the novice can recognize and apply them regardless of the situation or context in which they occur. Someone learning to drive a stick-shift car, for example, is told at what speed to shift the gears and, at any given speed, how far to stay behind the preceding car. These basic rules ignore context by ignoring such things as traffic density or anticipated stops. A beginning chess player is taught how to evaluate pieces and told to exchange pieces only

if the value of those captured is greater than that of those lost. The beginner generally is not told that there are certain situations in which this rule should be violated.

Novices are usually so caught up in following the rules that they have no coherent sense of the overall task. "Like the training wheels on a child's first bicycle," explain the Dreyfus brothers, "these rules allow the accumulation of experience, but soon they must be put aside to proceed."

Stage 2: Advanced Beginner

As the novice gains experience in real situations, performance improves to a marginally acceptable level. This encourages the learner to consider more than context-free facts and fosters an enlarged vision of the world of the skill. Through practical experience in concrete situations, and by noting the similarities between novel situations, the advanced beginner learns to recognize and deal with previously undefined facts and elements. The person also learns to apply more sophisticated rules, to both context-free and situational factors.

As experience accumulates, the advanced beginner learns such things as how to use engine sounds as well as speed to decide when to shift gears, and how to distinguish between a drunken driver and one who is impatient but alert. Similarly, as beginning chess players progress, they learn to avoid certain dangerous situations, despite the lack of well-defined rules

The road to expertise is a long one. In East Germany promising young gymnasts begin training at a very young age.

or verbal descriptions of such situations. "In all these cases," say the Dreyfuses, "experience seems immeasurably more important than any form of verbal description."

Stage 3: Competence

With experience, the learner begins to recognize more and more context-free and situational elements. To avoid being overwhelmed by this information explosion, the future expert is taught to adopt a hierarchical view of decision making. By choosing a plan to organize the situation and then concentrating on only the most important elements, the person both simplifies and improves performance and gradually grows in competence.

A competent driver who wants to get across town in a hurry no longer merely follows rules and may at times even choose to break the law. Traffic, distance, and other important elements are considered, while such things as scenery and driver courtesy are ignored. A competent chess player, someone in the top 20 percent of tournament players, who decides to attack an opponent's king may do so despite certain recognized vulnerabilities and risks. Removing the pieces protecting the enemy's king becomes the overriding objective.

At this stage of the game, objectivity often goes out the door. The novice relies on certain context-free elements and specific rules. The advanced beginner learns to deal with situational elements but still applies learned rules and procedures. By contrast, the competent person appraises the situation, sets a goal, and then chooses a plan, which may or may not involve following the rules. But choosing a plan is no simple matter. In running a red light or weakening one's board position to attack an enemy king, one takes a calculated risk. Whether the plan succeeds or fails, the situation and its outcome are likely to be vividly recalled—an important resource for future expertise.

Stage 4: Proficiency

In the earlier stages, rules are applied and goals and plans are consciously chosen in a deliberate, rational manner. But proficiency brings with it a new style: rapid, fluid action that does not always stem from detached reasoning. For the proficient performer, usually deeply involved in the task, important elements of the task will stand out clearly and others will recede into the background and be ignored. As the situation changes, different features may take on

importance and different plans may evolve. "No detached choice or deliberation occurs," explain the Dreyfuses. "It just happens, apparently because the proficient performer has experienced similar situations in the past, and memories of them trigger plans similar to those that worked in the past."

The Dreyfuses call this phenomenon "holistic similarity recognition," and use as an example a boxer who seems to recognize the exact moment to begin an attack. The boxer doesn't apply rules about the position of his body and that of his opponent. Instead, the scene in front of him and sensations within him trigger the memory of earlier similar situations in which an attack was successful, and he acts.

Proficient performers still think analytically, but at times they seem to have an intuitive grasp of the situation, an understanding that occurs effortlessly because they see similarities to previous experiences. A proficient driver, for example, intuitively slows down when approaching a curve on a rainy day, then consciously decides whether to reduce pressure on the accelerator or put on the brakes. A chess master (in the top 1 percent of all serious players) will recognize a certain type of position and intuitively produce a plan for dealing with it, rationally calculating a move that best achieves the plan.

Stage 5: Expertise

Experts don't apply rules, make decisions, or solve problems. They do what comes naturally, and it almost always works. When they fail, it often is because they are pitted against another expert, as in a world-title chess match.

Experience-based holistic recognition of similarity, the Dreyfus brothers explain, produces the deep situational understanding that leads to the expert's fluid performance. We seldom choose our words or place our feet; we simply talk and walk. The same goes for experts: Their skill has become so much a part of them that they are no more aware of it than they are of their own bodies. An expert driver has become one with the car, knowing when an action such as slowing is required and how to do it without comparing alternatives. A grand master chess player (one of about two dozen in the United States) can recognize tens of thousands of types of positions for which the most desirable tactic or move immediately comes to mind.

The mental processes of the expert driver or chess player, the Dreyfuses say, are the same

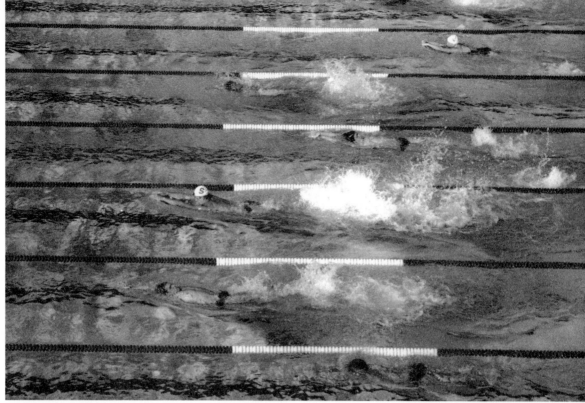

© David Madison/Bruce Coleman Inc.

Practice makes perfect. Olympic swimming contenders dedicate many hours per day to perfect their performance.

as those of the expert business manager, surgeon, nurse, lawyer, or teacher who is totally engaged in a skillful performance.

Nurturing Expertise

The five steps from novice to expert described by the Dreyfus brothers give us some idea of the types of thinking involved in becoming an expert. A study by educational researcher Benjamin S. Bloom and his colleagues at the University of Chicago suggests how expertise can be nurtured.

Bloom and his colleagues identified 120 immensely talented young people who had become world-class experts in their respective fields before the age of 40. Among them were concert pianists, accomplished sculptors, Olympic swimmers, world-class tennis players, and exceptional research mathematicians and neurologists. Each was acknowledged by other experts to be among the top 25 performers in the nation in his or her field.

In their book *Developing Talent in Young People,* Bloom and his colleagues use case studies and interviews with the young experts, their parents, and teachers to help describe the long road to the top. And although each road taken

was slightly different, the researchers found common signposts along the way. In a concluding chapter, Bloom sets out, in three stages, the continuous learning process that ultimately leads to expertise.

In the early years the family and home environment were especially important in fostering a particular talent. Most swimmers, pianists, and mathematicians, for example, came from families interested in sports, music, or intellectual activity, respectively. This gave the youngsters a head start in learning something about their future field. They began instruction in the field more by circumstance than by personal choice. But in each case, Bloom also notes, there was a relatively good fit between the child's physical and personal characteristics and the chosen field.

The choice of a first teacher was very important. Most were almost perfect for young children, Bloom explains. They rewarded their students with praise, encouraged them, and were enthusiastic about the field and what they had to teach. But most important, Bloom says, they made learning fun. The children were introduced to the field as a playful activity, and learning at this stage was like a game.

AP/Wide World

© Diego Goldberg/SYGMA

Some people achieve mastery while still quite young. Steve Baccus (above) studied college-level data processing as a 12-year-old. Midori Gotoh (left), a 14-year-old violinist, has already taken a concert tour of Japan.

With good teachers and approving, helpful parents, these youngsters made relatively rapid progress. Within two to five years, most of them began to see themselves in terms of their field. They saw themselves as "pianists" and "swimmers" before the age of 11 or 12 and as "mathematicians" before the age of 16 or 17.

The Perfectionist Teacher

The middle years are the years of growing commitment to the chosen field. A significant step forward at this stage is the selection of a new teacher. A parent, an expert in the field, or even the original teacher suggests that the budding talent will blossom only if a new, more expert teacher is found. And for most of those in the study, the new teacher was a perfectionist, someone who worked only with outstanding students. These teachers insisted that the student reach his or her highest possible level of achievement, and demanded a great deal of practice—as much as five hours a day. The emphasis during these years was on precision and accuracy in all areas of the field. "Only

Master musicians, such as concert pianist Earl Wild, frequently come from families that foster an interest in music.

individuals almost fully committed to the talent field could make the progress expected of these students," Bloom says.

The final years, the years of mastery, begin with the selection of yet another teacher, a master teacher who emphasizes the perfection of talent to its highest level, the development of a personal style, and an understanding of the larger purpose and meaning of the talent. During these years the students devote all of their time to the talent or skill, much of it in preparation for sessions with the master.

"It typically takes these individuals 10 to 15 years to move from the relatively simple beginnings to the complex and difficult processes that characterize the later learning in each of the fields," explains Bloom. And as long as they remain in the field, he says, learning is never complete—even when they no longer have designated teachers or coaches.

The Road Is Long

The journey from novice to expert, Bloom and his colleagues conclude, requires "enormous motivation, much support from family, the best teachers and role models possible, much time,

and a singleness of purpose and dedication that is relatively rare in the United States at present."

The road, of course, is long, but that does not mean that it is impassable—as the exceptional people Bloom studied show. In fact, after 40 years of intensive research on school learning, Bloom's major conclusion is this: "What any person in the world can learn, almost all persons can learn if provided with appropriate prior and current conditions of learning."

Discovering the conditions of learning that enable people to think like experts, of course, is among the primary goals of research on expertise. And it is a goal that is being achieved. Or, as Glaser puts it, "Teaching thinking has been a long-term aspiration, and now progress has occurred that brings it into reach."

SELECTED READINGS

"Smart kids" by B. Kirsch. *Omni*, March 1986.

"Skills for adolescence: a new program for young teenagers" by E. R. Gerler. *Phi Delta Kappan*, February 1986.

"Education for gifts and talents: a change in emphasis" by B. L. Bull. *Education Digest*, January 1986.

© Charles Waller Design

BRAIN SCANS FOR DRUG TESTING
by John Herzfeld

The time is Monday morning, the year . . . . soon. You arrive for work late, bleary-eyed and disheveled from a bout of insomnia. In water-cooler small talk, you seem a bit disoriented. Back at your desk, you make a series of small mistakes, then a big one. Suddenly your supervisor's standing over you:

"Come on, we're going down to the medical department for a brain-wave scan to see if you're on drugs. Don't get upset—if you're clean, that machine will let you go."

Sound farfetched? Maybe not, to judge by the clamor over workplace drug abuse, and the push for new testing technology.

Brain-wave scans for drug and alcohol intoxication are a reality—a portable scan, the Veritas 100 Analyzer, was unveiled recently at the annual meeting of the American Chemical Society in New York City. Devised by an ear, nose, and throat specialist from Shrewsbury, New Jersey, the computerized monitor is supposed to solve some of the problems raised by controversial urine tests. And if the early interest in the Veritas 100 is a sign, on-the-job drug testing, for all its failings, is an idea that's not about to go away.

Drug testing began in prisons and treatment programs, moved on to the military and sports, and only recently spread into the American workplace. Advocates of on-the-job testing for drug abuse claim it makes economic sense. The Research Triangle (North Carolina) Institute estimates U.S. companies lost $33 billion in 1983 to the havoc wreaked by employees high on drugs. Carlton Turner, Ph.D., President Reagan's top drug adviser, has called drugs and alcohol "probably the biggest problem industry faces today." And the White House Commission on Organized Crime set off a storm of controversy when it urged drug testing at work. Civil liberties groups and some labor unions admit the drug abuse problem, but see testing as a real invasion of privacy.

Today nearly 30 percent of Fortune 500 companies test employees or job applicants for drugs—10 times as many as four years ago. In a special report by The Bureau of National Affairs, Inc., a business information service, Turner predicts that within the next three years, every major U.S. corporation will screen job applicants. In five years, he says, every annual corporate physical will use a drug screen.

Screening by Urinalysis

You might think the worst problem in using urine samples for drug testing is—well, getting the samples. And it's true, no one likes being given a choice between urinating into a beaker (while someone is watching) and losing a job. But it's when a company has a urine sample and sends it to a lab that the real confusion begins. What's really in that beaker—and how does the lab find out?

Urinalysis is only one tool, experts say; it should never be the sole reason for accusing a person of drug abuse. But even getting a credible result from a urine test can be a lot less scientific, and a lot more expensive, than most employers expect.

First, they need to set a threshold (minimum level)—measured in nanograms (billionths of a gram) per milliliter—for the amount of chemical traces that will be considered a sign of guilt.

A company may want to launch a testing program as a deterrent—spread the word that drug use is forbidden—without risking lawsuits from employees who claim the test fingered them unfairly. So they'll set the cutoff at 1 billionth of a pound per fluid ounce, low enough to catch a few chronic marijuana users but probably high enough to let weekend partiers off the hook.

Or the lab itself may insist on a 4 ten-billionth of a pound cutoff as a matter of economics. They don't want lawsuits, either—they'd have to provide expert-witness testimony, documentary evidence, and more time and energy than their budgets might allow. And

A technician double-checks the results of a urinalysis. Samples testing positive for drugs are rechecked.

© Rick Browne/Picture Group

The aftermath of a rail crash. Train engineers may soon join airline pilots and air-traffic controllers as being classified in jobs upon which the public safety depends—and therefore subject to mandatory spot drug tests.

© J. L. Atlan/SYGMA

every positive sample should be confirmed by a second test, which can cost the lab money. So it's to their benefit to limit the number of positive results—even if it means missing a portion of the drug users the tests were designed to uncover in the first place.

Samples have to be retested because no single kind of test is completely accurate. The most popular method, the enzyme immunoassay test, is inexpensive and widely used: the U.S. Army and Navy even administer it in the field. But it's costly to confirm this test with a second method: radioimmunoassay, thin-layer chromatography (TLC), gas chromatography (GC), or—best of all—GC/mass spectrometry.

Although employers may balk at the expense of retesting, experts warn that it's necessary. Says Ted F. Shults, a lawyer and toxicologist affiliated with CompuChem, a North Carolina testing lab: "When we test racehorses

for doping, we always confirm with GC/mass spectrometry. I expect no less when someone's job or reputation is on the line."

Some labs do offer low fees, but you might get what you pay for. Shoddy handling and inadequate record keeping can plague even the best operations. And since drug-testing labs do not need to be licensed—though many experts think they should be—the customer needs to double-check the lab's proficiency with decoy samples. This, too, costs more money.

Finally, even when all the tests show proof positive, an employee can claim he didn't knowingly use the drug. Studies show only negligible residues from the kind of secondhand smoke you might breathe at a party. But the so-called brownie defense—"I didn't know it was spiked"—can work if you have credibility. Some military officers beat a cocaine rap by claiming the stuff had been sprinkled on potato chips at a party; the court believed them because they all had top-notch service records.

The fallout from all this: Some companies are giving up plans for random screening of all employees, and just testing "probable cause" cases. That means, except for accident investigations, the tests may be reserved for obvious druggies—or perhaps the office troublemaker the boss never liked in the first place.

Scientific Obstacles

Many scientists and drug counselors want to put the brakes on the bandwagon. Civil liberties concerns aside, they argue, biological testing—at least as it's generally practiced today—is fundamentally a bad way to fight drug abuse. They cite real scientific obstacles. Multiple chemical tests are required to tell anything definitive from a urine sample. But that's too expensive to do—unless the boss already suspects an employee because of poor job performance.

And even if someone's urine sample is "hot," it may not mean what the company thinks. Urine tests show only whether people have recently used drugs—not whether drug use is hurting their job performance, or even whether they use drugs at work. Breakdown products of marijuana can show up in urine four to 10 days after a single joint and up to 36 days after chronic smokers quit. Weekend smokers, people who try a toke at a party, or those who indulge with friends once in a while for old times' sake could all get caught in the net—and perhaps sue their employers if they're fired for on-the-job intoxication.

The military was one of the first organizations to institute drug testing. All new recruits (above) are screened for drug use. Thereafter, military personnel of all ranks randomly are required to submit urine samples for testing (right).

Enter the Brain Scan

The Veritas 100 scanner, its inventors say, could help solve this problem: By checking for drug effects—brain waves called drug-evoked potentials—the machine can point to on-the-job intoxication. Don a disposable headband containing two electrical leads, go through a series of eye movements while sitting and then lying down, wait for a computer printout—and, presto, the machine tells you whether drugs are present, suspected, or not present in your system. No prying into your private life, no collection of body fluids.

Developed by otolaryngologist S. Thomas Westerman and researcher Liane Gilbert, the Veritas 100 was adapted from an established medical test for dizziness. The test, called an electronystagmograph (ENG), has long been known to show altered patterns in the presence of drugs or alcohol. Westerman and his colleagues have worked to correlate specific brain-wave patterns with specific chemicals—alcohol, marijuana, cocaine, tranquilizers, amphetamines, opiates, hallucinogens, and others, as well as 75 combinations of drugs.

Although the device is being used now in a handful of locations, scientists are a long way from accepting it. Westerman and his colleagues claim almost 100 percent accuracy in detecting the presence of drugs. But they've only begun the kind of validation needed for full scientific credibility, with small-scale tests under way at Johns Hopkins University in Baltimore, at the Cleveland Clinic, and at the Medical College of Philadelphia. "I have to remain open until they produce a whole lot more data," says Richard L. Hawks, Ph.D., chief of the research technology branch of the National Institute on Drug Abuse (NIDA). "It's an untried

device as far as the forensic-science community is concerned."

Westerman sees a future for the Veritas 100—not only in workplace drug testing, but in law enforcement and medical settings. It could even help doctors tailor prescription drugs to the tolerance of each patient. But without Food and Drug Administration (FDA) approval, it can now be used only for preliminary screening to see if more tests are needed.

The brain-wave monitor also cannot solve a basic problem in drug testing: There's no clear connection between the amount of a drug in the body and its effect. In an issue of the *Journal of the American Medical Association (JAMA)* published in 1985, a group of experts gathered by NIDA concluded there are not enough data to correlate drug concentrations with driving impairment, as has been done for alcohol. That will take more research—needed especially for marijuana and Valium, the two most widely used drugs in the U.S.

Despite these problems, drug testing might give some extra assurance in high-risk fields like construction, transportation, utility-line repair, and nuclear power. But for other jobs, many counselors urge "constructive confrontation": Simply present an employee with the evidence of poor performance. Any number of problems can make employees slow, sloppy, or accident-prone—including fatigue, emotional turmoil, and on-the-job distractions. "Drug testing is no substitute for a supervisor exercising reasonable judgment and powers of observation," argues labor arbitrator Tia Schneider Denenberg. "Why enter into all these arcane scientific disputes over what a test can and cannot prove?"

On-the-job drug testing may ultimately be extended to occupations where the principal danger is to oneself.

Fire Speeders Instead?

Even if an employer believes a drug test is clearly positive, the next question is how to use the results. Dismissal is one option. But critics say this unfairly singles out illegal drug use as a problem. It can become more punishable than abuse of alcohol, prescription drugs, and over-the-counter medications (though the best programs do deal with these), or other types of lawbreaking. "I'd sooner fire an employee for getting a speeding ticket than for smoking marijuana," says Arthur J. McBay, Ph.D., chief toxicologist for North Carolina's medical examiner. "There's more data that speeding kills people on the highway than there is for marijuana."

Another option is referring the drug user to

HOW PEOPLE FIGHT BACK

When people are faced with a urine test for drugs, they resort to any number of steps to beat it. Some defenses are legitimate maneuvers to protect the innocent; some are unscrupulous. First the valid ones:

An expert on forensic toxicology, Arthur J. McBay writes that anyone being tested at work has a right to certain guarantees. The employer "should be prepared to demonstrate the need for the program and to ensure that testing will be properly conducted and the significance of the results properly interpreted."

Without that safeguard, his advice—if you're clean—is to insist on a split sample, with one half sent to the company's testing lab and the other kept refrigerated or frozen. If the lab says you've been using drugs and you haven't, split your sample again: half to the company's lab for retesting, half to a knowledgeable lawyer to arrange for testing at a lab of your choosing. That way you have legal evidence if you are unfairly accused.

Another option, if you have a good lawyer or a union, is to object to the testing formally. In Newark, New Jersey, one cop allowed himself to be tested only after he was threatened with suspension for refusing to go along with a general screen of the narcotics bureau. His union began legal proceedings that have stopped the testing while the union and city try to work out a fair way to do it.

In San Francisco, California, a woman sued her boss for firing her after she refused to give a urine sample. But her case hasn't yet been settled, and some lawyers warn that the very act of refusing a test can still cost you your job.

People who are using drugs have their own devious ways of beating the system. Some try to substitute clean urine samples for their own. This might work in a poorly monitored testing program; before the U.S. military improved its screening effort, selling clean urine was big business around Navy bases. Another ploy: hydration. But experts say a user would have to drink almost more water than humanly possible to dilute a urine sample.

It gets worse. Some people have smuggled in clean urine in a hospital catheter bag hidden under a shirt; squeeze a tube running down the sleeve, and out flows the bogus sample. One female addict even filled a condom with someone else's urine, put it inside her body, and punctured it when it came time to deliver a sample. But most labs are on to such desperate tricks. Says consultant Ted Shults: "Unfortunately, part of drug addiction is this kind of devious behavior."

---

a treatment center. "We feel the goal should be to identify people who need help, not to fire them," says Robert T. Angarola, former general counsel to the White House Office of Drug Abuse Policy. "No company I've counseled wants to fire people. They might move them to a less sensitive job, but they don't want to lose all the training and experience an employee represents—and then maybe end up replacing him with someone else that has a drug problem."

But some counselors balk at the prospect of admitting patients solely on the basis of a drug test. "Any facility that takes someone with only a 'hot' urine in the absence of a well-documented substance abuse problem, in my opinion, is not an ethical institution," argues Steve Fineman, M.S.W., until recently director of clinical services for Eagleville (Pennsylvania) Hospital, a major treatment center. "You shouldn't take up bed space—or take people's money—unless someone's really sick. And a casual user is not suffering from an addictive disease."

High-tech advances like the Veritas 100 may improve the science of drug testing. But better science can't answer all the questions the practice raises. Some critics believe employee rights in drug tests will not be safe until we have laws to protect them.

That may happen soon. An ordinance in San Francisco, California, already bars random urine screening for drugs. And laws to regulate drug testing are beginning to make their way through a few state legislatures. If these and other measures take hold, the time could arrive when we can be sure that machines like the brain-wave monitor will be used as a helpful tool—and not as a weapon.

BIOLOGY

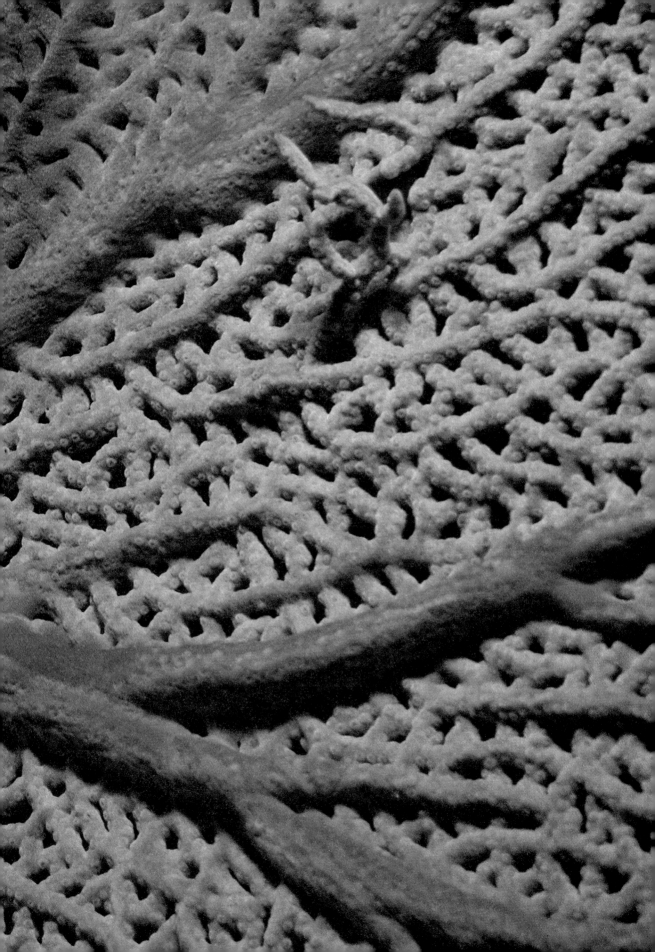

The poor health of these and other sugar maple trees in the United States and Canada has been attributed to acid rain.

© Budd Titlow/F/Stop Pictures

REVIEW OF THE YEAR

BIOLOGY

In 1986 important developments in biology were played out in federal agencies, courtrooms, and open fields, as well as in the laboratory.

BIOTECHNOLOGY—THE SCIENCE . . .

In the more conventional scientific arena—the laboratory—researchers from Washington University and the Monsanto Company implanted genes that confer disease resistance into tobacco and tomato plants. It was reportedly the first time scientists have been able to imbue plant lines with resistance to viral infection.

Animals also got some new genes. Mice that would have been infertile because they lacked a gene for producing a hormone were made fertile by gene transplantation at the fertilized-egg stage. As in the plant studies, the change was inheritable.

Stanford University researchers developed a way to electrically shock plant cells into accepting new genetic material, a process expected to make genetic manipulation of plants easier. Meanwhile, University of California at San Diego researchers have given tobacco plants a gene that makes them glow. The gene, from fireflies, produces a luminescing protein. The gene has the potential to be a visible marker for activation of nearby genes.

On the level of basic research, life may become easier for some biologists. California Institute of Technology researchers built a machine that can determine the order of subunits in strands of DNA; Applied Biosystems Inc., the same company that markets a DNA synthesizer, plans to market the new device.

. . . AND THE APPLICATION

On the government front, the congressional Office of Technology Assessment warned that biotechnology could seriously harm the family farm. Advances are most likely to benefit wealthy farms that can afford the new technology, the report claimed.

Out in the fields, Advanced Genetic Sciences of Oakland, California, became the first company to get government approval to field-test genetically altered bacteria. The company engineered the bacteria that act as a seed for frost formation on plants; without a key gene snipped out in the engineered version, the bacteria "protect" the plants on which they sit from frost.

But the project has been marked by troubles. First the Environmental Protection Agency (EPA) began investigating outdoor tests done by the company in 1985, without EPA approval, on a rooftop in Oakland. Then the company put its own hold on the testing in order to repeat some safety studies. The EPA, claiming the company had falsified data, suspended its permit and fined the company $20,000. It later reduced the charge to $13,000, and changed its charge from falsification of data to failure to report data.

Meanwhile, the EPA approved small-scale testing of a similar frost-resistant bacteria developed by plant pathologists at the University of California at Berkeley.

The EPA also delayed a Monsanto application to test a bacterially produced cutworm toxin because data submitted by the company weren't enough to convince the agency that the product wouldn't damage the environment.

The Department of Agriculture approved the marketing of a genetically altered virus for use against pseudorabies, a costly and rapidly spreading swine disease. It was the first government approval for marketing a live, altered virus. But after objection by a citizen's group, the department pulled its approval, only to regrant it a couple of weeks later.

A genetically engineered product did make it out into the open air. Agracetus, a Middleton, Wisconsin, biotechnology company, planted genetically engineered tobacco. The plants were made resistant to crown gall, a bacterial disease, via inclusion of a protective gene from yeast.

Ecogen Inc., a Langhorne, Pennsylvania, biotechnology company, got approval from the EPA to field-test a product of bacteria altered by heating different strains so that they exchanged genetic material. The bacteria are already used against some species of pests; the offspring of the new product produce a toxin that kills two cotton pests, bollworms and budworms.

There was also activity at the animal level. Oregon State University researchers went to New Zealand to test a gene-altered virus as a vaccine against a common animal virus. They said they conducted the trial in New Zealand in order to avoid the cumbersome regulatory process in the United States.

And Wistar Institute researchers also went out of the country. They tested a new rabies vaccine on cows in Argentina.

To establish order on the applications of biotechnology, the White House released regulatory guidelines for biotechnology, assigning duties to various government divisions. But some legislators claimed that loopholes in the regulations could lead to trouble.

BY THE SEA

Commercial development has already begun on an aquaculture system devised by Smithsonian Institution scientists. They have raised Caribbean king crabs in cages in the ocean. The crabs eat blue-green algae grown on floating glass-fiber screens.

National Oceanic and Atmospheric Administration (NOAA) scientists found a new shrimp and a member of what had been thought to be an extinct species on a trip to the Atlantic Ocean floor. The shrimp lives on bacteria growing in 660° F (350° C) water that streams from cracks in the ocean floor. The "extinct" creature is a six-sided animal about the size of a silver dollar and covered with rows of black dots. While 70

Dr. Peter A. Rona/NOAA

Shrimp of a species long thought extinct by scientists was discovered thriving on the Atlantic Ocean floor.

million-year-old rock fossils show similar animals, they had been thought to be extinct.

And Oregon State University fish biologists trained baby salmon to be afraid of cod. They put the fish in a Plexiglas tank within a tank of cod. In the wild, cod eat salmon; the idea is startle the young salmon, which are otherwise released into the environment without ever getting the chance to see and run from cod.

An animal species that apparently relies on methane was found at oil and natural gas seeps in the ocean floor off Louisiana. ■ Bacteria in the gills of the mussel are suspected to produce something the mussels use for energy.

WILDLIFE

Cornell University researchers discovered that elephants are talking behind our backs. After noticing strange vibrations in the air while observing elephants at a zoo, Katharine Payne and her colleagues measured subaudible sounds. The sounds were found to occur at the same time part of the elephants' foreheads fluttered, leading the researchers to suggest that forehead fluttering is how elephants make the sounds.

Acid rain was blamed for a precipitous decline in sugar maple trees. In Quebec, 82 percent of sugar maples observed in an aerial survey were in evident bad health. And a possible mechanism for acid rain's effect on Atlantic salmon was identified by University of New Hampshire scientists, who discovered that acidic water disturbs salmon's sense of smell.

And while elephants may be busy with private conversations, certain Peruvian birds are busy lying. The New York Zoological Society's Charles A. Munn found that some birds in Peruvian rain forests let out an alarm warning of an impending predator when there was none around, in order to distract other nearby birds momentarily. The sentinel birds thus get the edge on grabbing food.

JOANNE SILBERNER

© Grant Heilman

GENETIC ENGINEERING
DOWN ON THE FARM by David Pimentel

For thousands of years, farmers have benefited from what might loosely be called genetic engineering. By patiently selecting and crossing plants, farmers and breeders have developed crop lines that produce larger yields of vegetables, grains, and fruits; that survive in harsh environments; and that resist pests.

From this perspective, modern genetic engineering might seem to offer farmers little that is substantively different. The new techniques, however, offer the opportunity to transfer genes from one kind of organism to another, such as from a bacterium to a tobacco plant, and therefore open up significant opportunities for creating new agricultural products. Biotechnology can also be used to develop new strains far more rapidly. Whereas it used to take up to 12 generations, or about six years, to produce an insect-resistant strain of tomatoes, gene splicing can cut the time to four generations, or two years.

Pros and Cons

The agricultural benefits from gene splicing and other genetic-engineering techniques could be enormous. Scientists will develop products that

One of the first genetic engineering breakthroughs was a vaccine to control outbreaks of pseudorabies in swine.

will increase food production, reduce fertilizer use, and decrease the need for costly, environmentally dangerous pesticides. But genetically engineered agricultural products could also cause sobering ecological, social, and economic problems. Although the risk is slight, if sound regulations are not developed, engineered organisms released into the environment could create new kinds of pests. And some engineered products will probably only add to a saturated market, putting more small farmers out of business. As we enter the era when the products of genetic engineering leave the lab for the fields, we must head off the potential liabilities with thorough testing and careful decision making.

Genetically engineered farm products will almost surely have a broad range of uses in coming decades. Consider the benefits that will result when organisms such as bacteria, viruses, fungi, nematodes, and insects are engineered to control insect pests, weeds, and plant diseases. The savings could be enormous, since more than one-third of all U.S. crops—worth about $50 billion—are annually lost to pests. Pesticide costs could also drop by as much as $500 million. In addition, some pest outbreaks would decrease if fewer chemicals were used. This is because pesticides now destroy many natural enemies of insect pests, allowing their populations to rebound to alarming sizes.

By increasing crop yields, genetic engineering could also reduce the amount of land needed for agriculture. Geneticists expect to be able to use biotechnology to increase the proportion of the crop that can be harvested—usually the fruit—while reducing the proportion of stems, roots, and male sex parts, which are usually not used as food. Thus, the same amounts of land, fertilizer, and pesticide would yield more food. These results would be especially advantageous in areas of the world where arable land is limited.

Biologists have recently shown that they can use genetic engineering to reduce the susceptibility of certain crops to frost. Scientists have eliminated from the bacterium *Pseudomonas syringae*, which inhabits most plants, the genes that produce the protein that serves as a nucleus for ice to form. Spraying enormous numbers of the altered bacteria—known as the ''ice-minus'' strain—on potatoes, tomatoes, strawberries, corn, and other crops allows the bacteria to outproduce and replace the wild form of *Pseudomonas*. This could extend crops' growing seasons and increase yields.

Fixing Nitrogen

Geneticists expect that in 20 to 40 years, they will also be able to enable basic food grains such as corn and wheat to ''fix'' their own nitrogen. That is, these plants will be able to transform the nitrogen in the air into a form they can use. This would save farmers $3 billion to $4 billion each year in nitrogen fertilizer costs. Nature has extended this property to only a few kinds of plants, such as peas and other legumes. The task

Spraying crops to protect them during freezes may be unnecessary once scientists develop frost-resistant plants.

Exhaustive testing is required to determine the effect of bioengineered organisms on beneficial plants and animals. Particularly at risk is the honeybee, which pollinates billions of dollars' worth of crops annually. If bees were to become diseased by a genetically engineered bacterium, the effect on U.S. agriculture could be devastating.

© Grant Heilman

of engineering other plants to fix nitrogen will be enormous, since these plants are genetically far more complex than the bacteria involved in most of today's biotechnology work.

Biotechnology is also being used to develop vaccines and drugs to improve livestock production. The genetically engineered pseudorabies vaccine—developed to control deadly pseudorabies outbreaks in swine—is already on the market.

Genetic engineering will be used to increase the quantities of products such as ethanol that are derived from grain. About 625 million gallons (2.4 billion liters) of ethanol, which can be used as motor fuel, are produced by fermenting grain. Through genetic-engineering techniques, it should be possible to at least double that yield.

Possibilities also exist for using microbes to produce valuable new products. For example,

John E. Kinsella of Cornell University is trying to determine whether microbes could be engineered to produce a cocoa extract from carbohydrates. Perhaps in the future, similar research could yield coffee, tea, and other foods.

Environmental Risks

While genetic engineering promises great advances for agriculture, it also carries with it environmental risks. Experience with one of the first genetically engineered organisms, the ice-minus bacterium, illustrates the potential environmental effects that must be studied before releasing an engineered organism. Last spring a sharp controversy arose after Advanced Genetic Sciences, developer of the frost-resistant *Pseudomonas syringae* strain, injected it into trees on the roof of a building before receiving the approval of the Environmental Protection Agency (EPA).

Wild *Pseudomonas syringae* reduces productivity in many of the crop families on which the ice-minus type may be used. These include the rose family, which contains a number of fruit trees; the pea family, which includes wheat and other major grains; and the nightshade family, which includes potatoes and tomatoes. Productivity suffers after a frost. But what might happen if the modified *Pseudomonas* lowered plant productivity regardless of frosts? There is a slight chance that this could occur.

Some evidence also suggests that the ice-minus bacterium makes some insects more resistant to freezing, which could hurt crops if the insects are pests. Furthermore, when Advanced Genetic Sciences tested the bacterium outdoors, it did not have enough evidence from laboratory and greenhouse tests to determine how the engineered organism would affect beneficial plants and animals. For example, consider what would happen if the genetically engineered bacterium caused disease in honeybees. In the United States alone, the honeybee pollinates about $20 billion worth of crops annually and is a major pollinator of wild plants.

Another furor arose this past year when the U.S. Department of Agriculture (USDA) approved the use of a genetically engineered live-virus swine vaccine without going through its established procedure of consulting its Recombinant DNA Committee. Fortunately, all tests indicate that pseudorabies vaccine is unable to threaten other mammals. But in the future, thorough tests will be needed to certify that altered live-virus vaccines do not have the potential for causing the very diseases they are supposed to prevent, threatening animals and even humans. Such problems have occurred from the use of some polio and rabies vaccines.

Monsanto is now submitting another species of genetically engineered *Pseudomonas* bacteria to extensive laboratory and greenhouse tests. The product is the combination of a *Pseudomonas* organism that lives in the soil, and a toxic element from *Bacillus thuringiensis* (B.t.). B.t., a bacterium that is sprayed on many crops to control caterpillars, normally cannot live for more than a short time in soil. However, the genetically engineered organism can survive there and might control such major soil insects as the black cutworm, a corn pest that causes $10 million to $50 million in damages each year. But it is critical to ensure that the engineered bacterium cannot also kill earthworms and beneficial soil insects.

Inheriting Traits

Scientists know, largely from laboratory studies, that engineered microorganisms can transfer genes to plants. Therefore, some of the genetic characters added to crop plants could possibly be transferred to weeds. If a gene added to a cereal grain to enable it to resist a plant pathogen were transferred to a weed species of the same family, the weed would resist the pathogen and be able to spread faster. The odds of this happening are extremely small, but such an occurrence could alter the ecosystems of both natural lands and farms.

Clearly, there is always room for another organism in an ecological system. Communities of plants and animals are tremendously flexible in accommodating new genetic variations and species. After all, about 1,500 insect species have been introduced and become established in the United States since 1640. Several of these, like the gypsy moth, have become serious pests.

Some scientists, including Nobel laureate David Baltimore, claim that genetically engineered organisms will likely be weaker than natural organisms in the environment, and will therefore not survive long enough to cause ecological problems. But other biologists such as

The voracious gypsy moth ranks high on the list of insect pests that bioengineers hope to eliminate someday.

© Grant Heilman

Steven Lindow, who works at the University of California at Berkeley and has consulted with Advanced Genetic Sciences, claim that modified organisms will survive well in nature because they have been changed only slightly from their natural form. The actual outcome will depend on the particular organism and the specifics of the genetic engineering. The soundest policy is to thoroughly study the ecological interactions of each engineered organism in the lab and greenhouse before releasing it into the environment.

The Problems of Herbicide Resistance

Herbicide-resistant crops are an example of a genetically engineered agricultural product that could have a complicated effect on both the environment and the business of agriculture. If a crop can be developed that is not affected by an herbicide that normally kills a broad range of plants, the chemical can be used to eliminate weeds without damaging the crop. This could enable farmers to grow certain crops in regions that now are troubled by burdensome weeds.

However, weeds that can resist the herbicides would become more numerous. Ever more herbicides would be needed to kill the resistant weeds, creating a treadmill effect. In addition, the problem of herbicides drifting onto adjacent fields planted with nonresistant crops would grow worse as more herbicides were applied. This phenomenon already destroys more than $70 million worth of crops every year.

Most resistant crop lines are being developed to withstand herbicides with active ingredients that break down rapidly into harmless components, or that cannot leach appreciably into groundwater. However, some crop lines are being developed to resist the more dangerous herbicides. If these were marketed, soil and water pollution would increase, since more of those herbicides would then be used.

Similarly, greater use of persistent herbicides would prevent crop rotations of herbicide-sensitive plants in soil, contaminated by the compounds. This could intensify soil erosion and problems with pest populations that thrive on crops that are grown in the same place annually. Even now, some crops cannot be seasonally rotated if certain herbicides are used. For example, soybeans cannot be planted after a corn crop is grown if residues of the herbicide atrazine remain in the soil. For these reasons, it is doubtful that crop lines resistant to persistent herbicides will be marketed.

But the increased use of any herbicide—whether persistent or not—might make some crops more susceptible to certain diseases and insect pests by altering the plants' physiologies. When corn was treated with the recommended

Various crops are being altered genetically to increase their resistance to herbicides used to eliminate weeds.

dosages of the popular herbicide 2, 4-D, which breaks down within several weeks, it became infested with three times as many corn leaf aphids. The corn also became much more susceptible to European corn borers, corn smut disease, and southern corn leaf blight. Those crop lines resistant to herbicides could end up requiring more insecticides and fungicides if more herbicides were used, intensifying environmental problems.

Seed/Herbicide Packages

An unanticipated economic side effect of the effort to engineer herbicide-resistant plants has been the move by a few herbicide producers, including Monsanto and CIBA-Geigy Corporation, to buy seed companies. The chemical companies' goal is to sell farmers packages of the modified seed and the herbicide. Farmers using the seed would have no choice but to use the companies' corresponding herbicides.

Herbicide-resistant crop lines will probably be popular only in areas that have special weed problems. If the companies that produce the crop lines succeed in selling them widely in those regions, farmers may face problems because genetic diversity will be reduced. A narrow genetic base has caused serious damage to crop yields before. In the early 1970's, American corn farmers relied on varieties that all had one set of genes that, in part, made the crops resistant to the fungus southern corn leaf blight. A fungal permutation allowed the blight to cause a loss of about 15 percent of the U.S. corn crop. The loss would have been much smaller if there had been greater genetic diversity. Similarly, the lack of genetic diversity in some rice planted in the Philippines, Thailand, and India has led to a cycle of pest outbreaks, increased pesticide use and pest resistance, and more pollution of farmers' fields.

Social and Economic Liabilities

In addition to creating environmental risks, genetic engineering of agricultural products will create economic and social problems. For example, genetically modified organisms that control pests and diseases will increase food supplies and therefore reduce prices in the marketplace, speeding the demise of small farms.

Consider the mixed blessings associated with bovine growth hormone (BGH), which increases milk production in cattle as much as 30 percent and can be produced using genetically engineered organisms. The USDA and the Food

© Runk/Schoenberger from Grant Heilman

Regulatory repetition. To stay on the safe side, a USDA researcher subcultures cloned shoots of apple trees.

and Drug Administration (FDA) are expected to approve the hormone for general use in about a year. Because farmers will need fewer cows and therefore perhaps 10 percent less food to produce the same amount of milk, their production costs and the amount of land needed for forage crops will drop. But this advance comes at a time when milk production is at an all-time high and diet-conscious Americans are consuming less. The USDA is already paying some farmers to eliminate their herds of dairy cattle. Other nations that can afford to buy more dairy products also have a surplus, so there is little likelihood that the market can absorb even more milk products.

This means that the use of BGH will reduce the number of dairy farms even further, continuing the trend of the past two decades. This outcome will entail both financial disaster and great emotional cost to those whose farms fail, and will exacerbate the already severe problems of communities, banks, and state treasuries in farming regions.

Greater milk production by cows given a bioengineered hormone will come at a time when highly automated dairy operations (left) are already producing more milk than they can sell. Below, tomato plants previously subjected to stress tests are evaluated to determine which strain will thrive under the most adverse conditions.

Above: © Grant Heilman; below: © Runk Schoenberger from Grant Heilman

By helping to eliminate small farmers, genetic engineering will speed the increase in the size and industrialization of farms that is already occurring throughout the world. From 1954 to 1985, the number of U.S. farms dropped by more than half, from 4.8 million to 2.3 million. At the same time the average farm size almost doubled, from 242 to about 445 acres (100 to 180 hectares). Losing small U.S. farmers is unfortunate, since they contribute to the social diversity of an increasingly urban society.

Ensuring the Success of Engineered Crops

There are a number of ways to address the many problems that the engineering of agricultural products could create. For example, scientists working in temperate zones should engineer only tropical organisms, which would die out during the cold weather. U.S. growers must already contend with several thousand pest species; we do not need genetic engineering to add more to this list. U.S. manufacturers might want to sell some of their engineered products in the tropics, but that should be allowed only if thorough analysis indicates that this would not create environmental problems.

Setting up regulatory procedures is a much-needed first step in controlling such activities. In June of 1986, the federal government approved rules and guidelines for regulating the biotechnology industry. Responsibility for weighing the safety of new products was divided among five federal agencies:

- The USDA is responsible for engineered organisms used with crop plants and animals.
- The FDA is responsible for genetically engineered organisms in foods and drugs.
- The National Institutes of Health (NIH) are responsible for engineered organisms that could affect public health.
- The Occupational Safety and Health Administration (OSHA) is responsible for engineered organisms that may affect the workplace.
- The EPA is responsible for engineered organisms released into the environment for pest and pollution control and related activities.

However, many scientists believe that these divisions of authority are cumbersome and inadequate. Agencies such as the USDA both promote and regulate the new technology. That combination did not work when the USDA was responsible for the use of pesticides, so control of those substances was transferred to the EPA in 1970. Perhaps biotechnology should be regulated primarily by the EPA and OSHA—agencies that are set up to regulate rather than promote industries. The other agencies could contribute representatives to the EPA and OSHA committees that would review the release of engineered organisms.

Ecological Protocols

These agencies should ensure that sound ecological protocols are followed before any genetically engineered organism is released into the environment. Although there is only a small chance that such an organism could cause an environmental problem, a single mistake could lead to a major disaster. To reduce risks, the government should require companies to thoroughly test engineered plants and organisms in the laboratory and the greenhouse to determine their potential for surviving and reproducing in nature. Such efforts would require teams of microbiologists, ecologists, plant breeders, agronomists, wildlife specialists, public health specialists, and botanists to work together.

As part of this process, the developer of an engineered product should have to identify every potential plant and animal that an engineered organism could attack, and the possible interactions. For example, the ice-minus bacterium should be tested on all major crops in which it could lower productivity. It should also be exposed to several important species of wild plants and beneficial insects to determine its effects. (Advanced Genetic Sciences has taken most of these steps.) And geneticists should document the potential of an engineered organism for transferring genetic material to other species.

After conducting indoor tests, the developer of a modified product should conduct field tests on islands and similarly isolated areas. This has been done before with the screwworm fly, which in its maggot stage infests cattle and other mammals. In 1954 sterilized screwworm flies (not genetically engineered) were dropped on the island of Curaçao to see whether they could control infestation.

Impact on Employment

It is also essential that government take into account the economic and social impacts of genetic engineering when deciding whether to approve these products. For example, if some farmers and farm laborers who are forced out of agriculture because of bovine growth hormone turn to welfare, any benefits associated with lower food costs could be eliminated by increased taxes to support welfare. On the other hand, economic problems would be minimized if displaced farmers were assisted in finding other gainful employment. Unfortunately, other jobs may not be available or may be low-paying service positions. Given the current lack of social policies to aid the untold numbers of steel and textile workers whose jobs have been eliminated by automation, the odds are that another poor, disillusioned sector of American society will develop.

Granted, it is costly and time-consuming to protect society and the environment from possible problems related to genetic engineering. But that could ensure the success of the industry. Surely we have learned from our past mistakes with pesticides that it takes many years to regain public confidence in the safety of new technologies once that assurance has been lost.

SELECTED READINGS

"Brave new world of superplants" by J. Carey. *International Wildlife*, November–December 1986.
"Engineering crops to resist herbicides" by C. M. Benbrook and P. B. Moses. *Technology Review*, November–December 1986.
"The coming push on biotechnology" by J. Dineen. *Environment*, November 1986.

The Magic Of
METAMORPHOSIS

by Vincent G. Dethier

A small child watched in wide-eyed wonder as a monarch butterfly struggled from its chrysalid skin. The emergence of the butterfly was as magical to the child as the appearance of a rabbit from the hat of a magician. For those of us who are older, the magic has vanished, but the wonderment remains. We who are born in the image of our parents, who grow, develop, and mature with measured grace and predictability, tend to assume that all creatures grow with a comparable gradual, ordered cadence. We expect no abrupt changes in form. We ourselves look human from the moment the egg completes the early developmental stages that are common to all animal eggs. At birth we are very well developed little people, and from that time on we pass through infancy, childhood, puberty, adolescence, maturity, and old age with few visible changes other than those wrought by hormones, accident, and the ravages of time.

Yet we are fascinated by the idea of metamorphosis. It permeates our mythologies, theologies, fiction, and art. We find it in Ovid's *Metamorphoses,* Stevenson's *Dr. Jekyll and Mr. Hyde,* and Kafka's *Metamorphosis.* We need not, however, turn to imagination and dreams. In nature, metamorphosis is real. The world around us teems with animals that undergo such drastic changes in form that skilled scientists have on occasion descibed the young as one species and the adults as another.

A Special Kind of Change

Literally speaking, metamorphosis is a change in form, usually but not necessarily abrupt. It is accompanied by an alteration of style of life, biochemistry, and behavior. Often the metamorphosed animal occupies a different habitat from that of its larval days. These changes are strikingly represented by moths and butterflies, aerial creatures borne aloft on colorful gossamer wings, feeding delicately on nectar and epitomizing the ideal carefree existence. Without

foreknowledge no one would ever guess that a caterpillar would come to this.

Butterflies and day-flying moths are designed to survive the dangers of sunny days during which they are prey to insectivorous (insect-eating) birds, crab spiders lying in ambush among the petals of flowers, mantids camouflaged in the foliage, and hosts of other rapacious predators. Night-flying moths are fair game for sonar-tracking bats and other nocturnal hunters. Over the millions of years that the species have been in existence, they have evolved clever ruses to avoid violent death, and intricate rituals of courtship to perpetuate their kind—but their kind also includes caterpillars.

At a propitious moment, females seek places to lay their eggs. Some species are remarkably cavalier, laying their eggs with abandon on stick, stone, or lamppost. One of the keys to the gypsy moth's success is its propensity for laying eggs on camping vehicles that carry them to far places. Other females are more fastidious. It is at this point in their lives that the first intimation of a double life is revealed. The meticulous female whose lifetime association with plants has centered on flowers and nectar develops an interest in leaves. She seeks out plants that she may never before have visited and with which she has had no behavioral or metabolic association. On selected leaves and twigs, she lays her eggs.

Hatching a Caterpillar

The first surprise for those who do not know is the emergence from the egg of a small caterpillar instead of a miniature butterfly. After all, hens' eggs produce chicks; turtles' eggs produce small turtles; grasshoppers' eggs produce small grasshoppers. Only in stories like E. B. White's

Mexican bean beetle, seen here in all stages of metamorphosis. The adult at bottom lays eggs. Larval stages are "spiked"; pupae are smooth with old skin crumpled at one end.

Stuart Little, in which the offspring of a surprised couple was a small mouse, does one expect to find organisms not replicating their kind at birth or hatching.

If butterflies could think, imagine their astonishment and dismay at viewing their first-born. The actions of the caterpillar appear to defy the laws of genetics. The newly hatched one begins its life by consuming the eggshell; thereafter, it embarks on a gourmet vegetarian life. It has its own particular enemies: birds that did not attack its parents; hordes of predatory ants and carnivorous bugs; legions of parasitic flies and wasps; and infections by viruses, bacteria, and fungi. Just as the butterflies evolved over time to become successful butterflies, so did the caterpillars evolve during the same period to become successful caterpillars.

The collection of genes that the butterfly bequeathed to the caterpillar must program the structure and behavior of the caterpillar and at the same time carry in trust the traits of the adult that the caterpillar will one day become. Just as the adult harbors within its body the germinal tissue that is to become the caterpillar, the caterpillar from the day of hatching carries within its body small pockets of cells destined to form a butterfly.

Obviously, however, the relationship of two directing forces within one body cannot continue harmoniously forever. Such a course would lead eventually to a chimera: half caterpillar, half butterfly. Chimeras populated mythology, but they could never survive the vicissitudes of a hostile world. At some point an intermission in growth must occur to reset the stage, and the intermission must not expose the animal to attack. The solution is a pupal stage.

Acrobatics Before the Great Transition

In preparation for this momentous transition, different species of caterpillars perform acrobatics that are marvelous to behold. Swallowtail caterpillars perform right side up, monarch caterpillars upside down. The swallowtail caterpillar spins a small silk pad on a plant stem and fastens the hooks of its last pair of prolegs into it. Secure on this end, it reaches up the stem and builds itself a safety belt by fastening a strand of silk to the stem where its left shoulder would be if it had one. Spinning out the strand, it produces a long loop reaching over its head and fastens the end to a spot near its imaginary right shoulder. Repeated spinning back and forth produces a many-stranded belt. The caterpillar then must wriggle this belt down over its back until at the completion of the maneuver it resembles a window washer leaning back against his safety belt. There is a practical way to appreciate the difficulty in accomplishing this feat. Take a 4-foot (1.2-meter) length of twine and attach a bit of adhesive to each end. Stand facing a wall. With most of the twine in your mouth, attach one end to the wall at shoulder height. Next, by moving your head, pay out the twine from your mouth, bending your head as far back as possible and twisting to produce a long loop. Attach the second sticky end to the wall near your other shoulder. Now, wriggle yourself underneath the loop until it fits snugly around your shoulders.

If you conquer this challenge, try to emulate the monarch caterpillar that fastens its last pair of prolegs to a pad of silk on the underside of a milkweed stem, hangs head down, splits its caterpillar skin along the back, wriggles free, and at the last moment attaches its pupal hooks into the silk pad without falling to the ground. You can best appreciate the problem by hanging from a tree branch with both hands gloved, removing your hands from both gloves simultaneously, and grasping the branch with bare hands before falling.

The pupa (known as the chrysalis in butterflies) is a strange, mummylike creature. The animal that was the caterpillar seems to have fallen asleep. It will wiggle restlessly if poked, but otherwise shows no sign of life. There are traces in bas-relief of the adult to be—indications of adult eyes, stubby wing pads, and outlines of antennae and mouthparts.

The quiet exterior is no indicator of the turmoil that is going on internally. Most caterpillar tissues and organs are being broken down and recycled. Genes of adult tissue that had been quiescent are now released from suppression by a complex interplay of hormones. As caterpillar organs are dismantled by programmed cell death, their raw materials are built into adult organs. Within a few days—or, for some, two weeks (unless the pupa is overwintering)—a complete adult has been constructed. At the appointed moment the pupal skin splits and a bedraggled but complete adult appears. The magic that the child has seen in the emergence of the butterfly seems even more magical when one understands the biochemical and physiological events that had to be coordinated to make the trick work.

The caterpillar of a spice-bush swallowtail butterfly (upper left) hangs from a twig on a silken "safety belt" it has spun. The caterpillar skin is shed without losing or tearing the belt (upper right), revealing the pupa inside. The wing patterns are clearly visible (lower left) within the metamorphosing pupa. Metamorphosis now complete (lower right), the new swallowtail fans its wings dry before embarking on a new life as a butterfly.

Strategic Advantages

Why did such complicated transformations evolve, and what advantages do they confer? One could imagine, for example, that a more direct method would be a disadvantage in some cases because it would produce moths, butterflies, flowerflies, and bees so small that their tongues could not reach down into the corollas of flowers. This argument would not apply to leaf-feeding beetles, however, because little beetles chew leaves as well as big ones.

Some scientists have suggested that complete metamorphosis is a splendid way of life because it allows a species to exploit more of the environment. Because nectar-feeding adults do not compete with leaf-feeding caterpillars, denser populations of the species can exist in a given area. This argument is less compelling when one considers Mexican bean beetles, Colorado potato beetles, and ladybird beetles, species in which young and adults dine on the same menu at the same table.

Probably we should look at metamorphosis with an evolutionary perspective. Its common occurrence in nature, the many forms that it takes, and its appearance in numerous unrelated species suggest that it was designed very early in geologic time and reappeared independently many times. It may have been part of such steps as ventures into fresh water, emergence onto

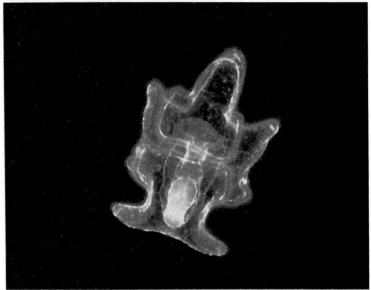

For some creatures, the various stages of metamorphosis bear no apparent resemblance to one another. A starfish larva (top) displays a side-to-side symmetry more characteristic of humans and other mammals. But in its adult form (bottom), the starfish assumes its totally different—although more familiar—radial symmetry.

land, and the establishment of mutualistic relations—for example, pollination—with land plants.

Different crises and different opportunities would call forth different designs for metamorphosis. Not all insects go to the extremes shown by moths, butterflies, beetles, and others. Eggs of crickets, for example, hatch insects that are undeniably miniature crickets. They lack wings; hence they are unable to chirp and serenade one another—and have little need to anyway because they are sexually immature. But they are crickets. Unlike caterpillars, which keep adding caterpillar tissue, most of which never becomes directly part of the adult, the cricket,

like you and I, grows and develops adult tissue from the day it hatches. In manner of growth it differs from us principally in shedding its skin periodically. The final shedding to adult marks its maturation and ends its metamorphosis.

Oceanic Origins

Fresh water, however, is not the place to search for memories of ancient customs. One must turn to the ocean, where life began, because here there are still creatures whose lineage stretches farther back in time than that of insects. The ocean provides a more continuous record of what has been. It harbors a bewildering collection of monstrous larvae saddled with a correspondingly bewildering array of complex names. Perhaps here one can find some clues to the meaning of metamorphosis.

One can conceive of an advantage to an organism in restricting the amount of yolk packaged in an egg. Some starfish seem to do this. The yolk supply is limited; the egg ''hatches'' an animal that is still an embryo with a lot of development still ahead of it. It is, however, well equipped to fend for itself. What hatches from a starfish egg is little more than a ball of cells covered with motile cilia (hairlike structures) providing propulsion. As a ball, it swims around continuing the development that in other animals occurs within the safe confines of an eggshell or in the nourishing protection of a uterus. It then becomes a larva, the bipinnaria, a weird, lobed little monster with looped bands of cilia. Eventually, after a succession of odd changes, it attaches itself to some handy bit of substrate, where it metamorphoses into a recognizable starfish.

A different kind of metamorphosis characterizes a beautiful, iridescent, segmented creature with the mundane name of clam worm. Its scientific name, *Nereis*, is much more romantic. *Nereis* was named after the Nereids of Greek mythology, who were graceful sea nymphs. The

adult worm can lay legitimate claim to this name because it is the most elegant of creatures when it deserts its burrow to undulate smoothly through the clear green seawater. Upon hatching from the egg, however, it is a dull larva with the technical name of trochophore. Trochophore larvae resemble two opposed bowls, one capping the other. A belt of cilia wraps around the middle, and a ridiculous-looking tuft of cilia extends from the top. Gradually this larva transforms into a worm by elongating and adding segments to its lower part.

Dragonflies, damselflies, kissing bugs, assassin bugs, stinkbugs, squash bugs, and scores of others have settled on a strategy intermediate between butterflies and crickets. The slender, graceful, metallic green or blue damselflies fly in tandem while mating. The females are clasped around the ''neck'' by claspers at the end of the male's abdomen. The male alights on a water plant; the female bends her abdomen into the water and lays her eggs on the submerged stem. The insect that hatches from that egg is a naiad, named for the mythological nymphs who frequented streams and waterfalls. The insect naiad is a slim aquatic creature with large eyes, three leaflike anal gills for respiration and propulsion, and a most remarkable

Aquatic turns airborne. A damselfly pulls itself from the exoskeleton of the swimming naiad it had been—until now.

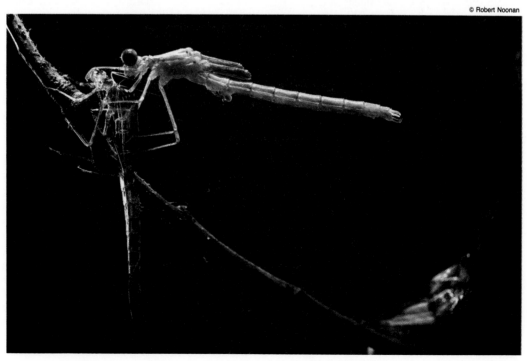

mouth. This mouth is equipped with strong, serrated mandibles and maxillae, but both are masked by a long lower lip that at rest is folded over them. The end of this lip is armed with sharp hooks. When small aquatic animals stray within reach, the naiad thrusts out the lip in a lightning stroke, seizes the hapless victim, and transfers it to the mandibles.

From Aquatic Naiad to Airborne Damselfly

The naiad is a compromise between the complete metamorphosis of the caterpillar and the imperceptible metamorphosis of the cricket. It is a fierce, formidable underwater predator growing stronger with each molt, attacking larger prey while at the same time preparing to be a damselfly. It has large, efficient compound eyes that will also be the eyes of the adult. It has stubby wing pads growing externally as wings should, but they are no hindrance to aquatic living.

Finally, when it reaches full naiad size, some inner urges impel it to crawl up the stump of a plant or up a stick or rock projecting above water. For a truly aquatic animal to desert water for air would have been unpardonable at any other time. It would have meant a slow, desiccating death. But now the inner damselfly asserts itself. The naiad skin splits along the back; legs are withdrawn as though from stockings; the gills peel off; wings are unpacked from wing pads and, almost like an inflatable life raft, are pumped to full size by pulses of blood. When all is finally taut and dry, the new insect is ready to launch itself on its maiden aerial voyage.

Everywhere in the quiet pond from which it emerged, other exciting metamorphoses are taking place. Beneath the placid surface, voracious larvae are becoming diving beetles and whirligig beetles; wriggling mosquito larvae are forgoing a diet of microorganisms, becoming pupae and metamorphosing into bloodthirsty adults; young giant water bugs, water boatmen, back swimmers, and water scorpions are becoming sexually mature, winged adults; grubs and maggots in bottom mud and decaying vegetation are turning into crane flies, midges, and beetles.

The most complicated life histories known are those of parasitic worms. Blood flukes, which cause the disease schistosomiasis, and liver flukes undergo an extravagant series of changes. Consider the life history of the Chinese liver fluke. This flatworm is a hermaphrodite that lives in the liver of human beings. Here it produces fertilized eggs that pass into the host's intestine and from there into canals and irrigation ditches. The released eggs are eaten by snails, where they hatch in the intestine. Each emerging larva, the miracidium, finds its way into the snail's tissues, where it loses its cilia and becomes a sac called a sporocyst. Eventually the sporocysts produce new forms (rediae) that in turn develop into tadpolelike forms called cercariae. These, liberated from the snail, swim freely in the water until they encounter a freshwater fish. They bore into the muscle and are encapsulated. When a human being eats the fish raw or half-cooked, the cysts are digested in the stomach. Young flatworms emerge and journey up the bile duct to the liver, where they may live happily for many years, to the distress of their host.

All these last cases of metamorphosis have evolved independently at different times, presumably in response to change or as adaptations enhancing survival and competition. All share one feature, larvae that can disperse widely in ocean currents (or fresh water, in the case of parasites). The survival and propagation of the species benefits by separating two basic functions. Dispersal is relegated to the larvae, which occupy one habitat, the unbounded space of the sea, while reproduction is the task of the adult, which is most often a stay-at-home bottom dweller. What a contrast to the insects, where the unfettered flying adults are the agents both of dispersal and reproduction, while larvae are the sedentary ones carrying on the metabolic housekeeping for the species.

Vertebrate Metamorphosis

Recourse to a metamorphic way of life is not by any means restricted to invertebrates. Living representatives of some of our earliest ancestors, unlikely looking marine animals commonly called sea squirts, undergo remarkable metamorphoses. Sea squirts, more formally tunicates, are small, saclike animals; most live attached to rocks, coral reefs, and wharf piles. They are members of the phylum Chordata, however, the same phylum to which humans belong. Tunicates are characterized by having early in life a long, cartilaginous rod (the notochord) extending from head to tail. Tunicates and other primitive chordates such as acorn worms and lancelets have two other vertebrate characteristics, a dorsal tubular nerve cord (our spinal cord) and gill slits as in fishes. But one can look in vain for a notochord in adult tuni-

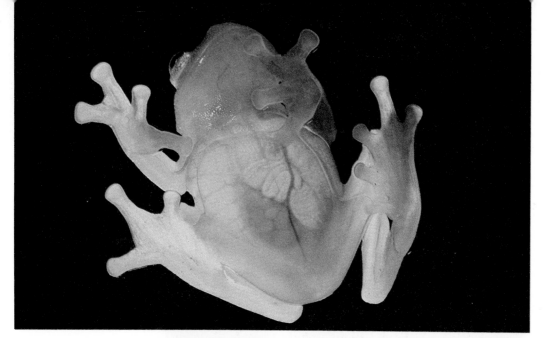

Frogs provide one of the most familiar examples of metamorphosis in the animal kingdom. Eggs can be seen inside the Fleischmann's glass frog (above), viewed from underneath through a clear panel. At the first sign of spring, the eggs will be laid. At right, a male glass frog stands guard over the gelatinous egg mass, which is attached to a leaf overhanging a pond. Tadpoles can be seen in the clear jelly. Once they are completely hatched from the eggs, the tadpoles will drop off the leaf into the water.

Both photos: Richard K. La Val/Animals Animals

cates. The fact that there is none caused scientists for the longest time to misclassify these animals. Only when the larvae were discovered was the true nature of the animals revealed.

A tunicate larva is a small, tadpolelike animal up to 0.08 inch (2 millimeters) long. It possesses a perfectly normal notochord, but for a short time only. After swimming as a free animal for a few minutes, or a few days at the most, it heads down for a hard surface, where it stands on its head. In this position it glues itself permanently upside down by means of three papillae on its chin. It then proceeds to metamorphose. The tail is absorbed; the larval nervous system and notochord are reabsorbed; other larval organs are broken down to be replaced by a set of adult organs suited to a sessile, or sedentary, life. It is an entirely new animal.

While complex life cycles must have enjoyed some adaptive value when they originally evolved, it is clear that their continuing value depends on a neat balance between the various metamorphic stages being maintained. The more complex they are and the more dependent on a stable environment, the greater the chance of something going wrong. Over the long haul, metamorphosis leads to inherent instability. It is not surprising, therefore, to discover instances in which a particular phase of a metamorphic life cycle that may have been advantageous at one time is subsequently discarded. In tsetse flies, for example, the free-living larval stage is lost; that is, the larva develops completely within the adult, and is laid as a mature larva that never functions as such and that immediately becomes a pupa.

It is in the amphibia, however, that the loss of stages is among the most diverse. Some salamanders are perpetual larvae, no adults ever being produced. In other salamanders and in frogs, the reverse may be the case, there being no free-swimming larval stage. But many of our common species of toads and frogs still retain the Jurassic ways: they metamorphose completely.

Spring is the time to observe them, when they congregate in grand choruses to beget not frogs but tadpoles. In nature's world of music, late spring and summer belong to the birds; midsummer and fall to the crickets and singing grasshoppers; spring belongs to the frogs and toads. The ice has hardly left the swamps when the frogs bestir themselves in the mud, the toads in their winter dens, and together crawl into shallow water and swamp grasses to serenade their mates. True love knows no greater sacrifice than to sit up to one's chin in freezing water and sing the night through.

From the moment it emerges from the gelatinous egg similar to pearl tapioca, the tadpole is a creature of the water. It is a swimming vegetarian breathing with gills. Its organ systems are perfectly designed for this way of life. As spring gives way to summer, however, strange things begin to happen. Little hind legs, like Pinocchio's nose, grow longer and longer. The tail begins to shrink. Soon front legs appear. Inside, even more drastic changes are in progress. Lungs are getting ready to replace gills; the long-coiled vegetarian digestive system is rebuilt to the shorter system of carnivores; the sense of smell, which was most efficient for detecting watery chemicals, is reorganized to detect scents in the air. There is now an urge to catch flies; sit on lily pads in the sun; and, especially in the spring, sing, or at least "chuggarium," on still nights.

The tadpole has become a frog. The metamorphosis is complete. The frog will never become a prince.

Struggling for survival: tadpoles are unlikely to see adulthood unless they develop front legs before the pond dries up.

The Strategic Artistry of Bird Eggs

by Bernd Heinrich

© Arthur Singer

The four tiny eggs that were cradled on feathers in a nest of moss, lichens, and spiderwebs were decorated more beautifully than any I had ever seen before. They were greenish blue, marked with purple and lavender blotches and black scratchy squiggles.

I was then eight years old, and in the following years I became obsessed with collecting the nests and eggs of other species. The more I found, the greater the obsession became. Each find rewarded me with revelations about the species's intricacies and its individualities.

Later, while in grammar school and high school in central Maine, I continued to collect songbird nests and eggs. I did not dare let the authorities at my boarding school know, in part perhaps because my pleasure was so great that it did not seem it could be morally right. I spent endless days in the woods watching birds and hunting for nests. I kept my carefully tended illicit collection hidden under the floorboards of an abandoned shed. (At that time I did not know anything about wildlife laws.) Now, 35 years later, this collection of 96 species of Maine land-bird eggs with their nests is still in excellent condition, in the museum and teaching collections of the University of Vermont. Although

I long ago stopped collecting wild bird eggs, my fascination and enthusiasm have not been erased. I still collect these jewels, but only on film. The main excitement now is in trying to find a coherent system of filing it all in the mind. And as I am a biologist, the filing system I use is based on evolution.

Color Variations Abound

First one sees the diversity. The four eggs of the scarlet tanager, in a cup of loose twigs lined with dark rootlets, are sky blue and spotted with light brown in a ring at the larger end. The four eggs of the eastern pewee are a light cream, with a wreath of reddish-brown and lavender spots about the larger end. These colors are set against a perfectly round nest-cup decorated with gray-green lichens. Woodpecker and kingfisher eggs, from holes excavated in trees and sandbanks, respectively, are translucent white without any trace of markings. The different colors, or lack of them, are products of evolution. What were the selective pressures that produced them?

The hermit thrush above apparently fails to recognize that the dissimilar cowbird egg is not one of its own.

© Arthur Singer

Eggs of a broad-winged hawk. Hawk eggs often differ more within the same nest than between species.

Although the eggs of many species of songbirds have characteristic colors that are fairly uniform within a clutch, I noticed that those of most hawks differed radically within the same nest, even more than they differed between species. One egg of a broad-winged hawk, for example, had distinct dark brown or purple splotches. Another in the same clutch had chocolate brown spots and squiggles. A third had purple or brown washes, and still another might be almost colorless. The same variety of colors—but in greens, blues, grays, and browns—was present in any one clutch of common raven's and common crow's eggs.

These combinations of markings and colors on bird eggs seemed like creativity gone berserk. Why should the color of an eggshell matter to a bird? Why, indeed, have any color at all?

The Pigmentation Process

Bird eggs are marked by pigments secreted from the walls of the oviduct. The egg remains uncolored until just before being laid, when it traverses the region of the uterus. The pressure of the egg squeezes the pigment out of the uterine glands onto the eggshell, and the motion of the egg affects the color patterns. It is as if innumerable brushes hold still while the canvas moves. If the egg remains still, there are spots; and if it moves while the glands continue secreting, then lines and scrawls result.

Egg color is under genetic control, and there is considerable genetic plasticity. Strains of domestic chickens have been developed that lay eggs tinted blue, green, and olive, as well as the more familiar white and brown.

It is not surprising that Charles Darwin, with his wide-ranging interests, also thought about the adaptive significance of the coloration of bird eggs. Since coloration is generally absent in hole-nesters such as woodpeckers, parrots, kingfishers, barbets, and honey guides, he supposed that the pigmentation on the eggs of open-nesters acts as a sunscreen to protect the embryo. The British ornithologist David Lack, in turn, believed the white coloration of eggs of hole-nesters allowed the birds to see their eggs in the dark. Even if it is advantageous for birds to see their eggs in the dark (which I doubt), we are still left to explain the tremendous differences in colors and patterns found, especially in the species that do not nest in holes.

Protective Coloration

Experiments confirm that the color of some bird eggs conceals them from predators. In a famous experiment, Niko Tinbergen distributed equal numbers of naturally spotted eggs of black-headed gulls, uniformly khaki-colored eggs, and white eggs near a gull colony and then recorded the predation by carrion crows and herring gulls on these unguarded eggs. The natural eggs suffered the least predation.

We might reasonably assume that the color of snipe, killdeer, and gull eggs is adaptive for camouflage, and that it evolved under selective pressure from visually oriented egg predators. But why, then, do other ground-nesting birds—most ducks and many grouse—have unmarked eggs that cannot be considered camouflaged by any stretch of the imagination? Perhaps part of the answer is that most of these birds hide their nests in dense vegetation, and the incubating female's own body is a camouflage blanket.

Many birds with nests that have no loose material with which to cover the eggs also have unmarked, uncamouflaged eggs. They include hummingbirds, pigeons, and doves. But these birds lay only two eggs per clutch, and they incubate as soon as the first egg is laid. Perhaps because none of their eggs are normally left uncovered, there has been no need to color them for camouflage.

The best explanation for the lack of coloring and markings on hole-nesters' eggs and those of birds that lay small clutches is probably simply that there was no need for color, so none evolved. Yet, as already mentioned, there are birds that nest in holes and also lay spotted eggs.

From BIRDS OF THE WORLD illustrated by Arthur Singer
© 1961 Western Publishing Co., Inc. Reprinted by permission.

K-BELLIED PLOVER

ELEGANT CRESTED-TINAMOU

GUANAY CORMORANT

PEREGRINE FALCON

COMMON NIGHTHAWK

NORTHERN JACANA

BLACK SKIMMER

AMERICAN SWALLOW-TAILED KITE

WY EGRET

GREAT HORNED OWL

NORTH ISLAND KIWI

EARED GREBE

AMERICAN ROBIN

CTUS WREN

BELTED KINGFISHER

RUFF

SLATY-BACKED GULL

RAZORBILL

CANADA GOOSE

INCA TERN

SCARLET IBIS

RA CUCKOO

GREAT CRESTED FLYCATCHER

EURASIAN BITTERN

MADAGASCAR BULBUL

RED-BREASTED MERGANSER

PRITCHARD'S MEGAPODE

LONG-TAILED JAEGER

HOUSE WREN

TURKEY VULTURE

BROWN BOOBY

OW PTARMIGAN

SCARLET MACAW

EURASIAN BLACKBIRD

ROSEATE TERN

REDDISH PLANTCUTTER

OOD THRUSH

RED-TAILED TROPICBIRD

WATER PIPIT

ST SANDPIPER

THICK-BILLED MURRE

NORTHERN FLICKER

CHUCK-WILL'S- WIDOW

COMMON PAURAQUE

The parasitic European cuckoo (top), having removed an egg from a host nest, will replace it with its own egg. When hatched, the cuckoo fledgling destroys any other eggs in the nest. Below, the young cuckoo is fed by its host, a much smaller lesser whitethroat.

All of these birds, however, build nests inside the holes. (True hole-nesters excavate their own holes and lay white eggs without adding any nest material.) I suspect, therefore, that the spots are evolutionary baggage. They tell us that these birds had previously been open-nesters who switched to hole nesting. But they retained the habit of building nests, as well as the coloration of their eggs, because there was no great selective pressure for change.

Role in Recognition

While coloring and markings of bird eggs are primarily for camouflage, they can also function to make something stand out like a red flag. On our Atlantic and Pacific coasts, on adjacent islands, and in Europe, birds called murres nest on the ledges and sea cliffs in colonies of hundreds of thousands. Several species of colonial cliff-nesting murres (as well as the extinct great auk) have eggs that vary endlessly in colors and markings. The ground color of the eggs varies from creamy to white, reddish, warm ocher, pale bluish, or even deep greenish blue. The markings upon this ground color, in turn, may be blotches, spots, or intricate interlacing lines of yellowish brown, bright red, dark brown, or black. Some eggs are totally unmarked. (When a murre loses the one egg—its entire clutch—it lays another, and this one is colored like the first.) In contrast, the eggs of the closely related auklets, which nest in burrows or rock crevices, have few or no markings.

Chester A. Reed, one of the early oologists (scientists who study bird eggs) during the heyday of egg collecting in the past century, says of the murres: "The eggs are laid as closely as possible on the ledges where the incubating birds sit upright, in long rows like an army on guard. As long as each bird succeeds in finding an egg to cover on its return home, it is doubtful if the bird either knows, or cares, whether it is its own or not." Thanks to experiments some 25 years ago by Beat Tschantz of the Zoological Institute of the University of Bern, Switzerland, we know that Reed was wrong. The murres no more incubate each other's eggs than do lobstermen tend each other's traps. Both use color and markings to identify their property. Tschantz switched eggs in nests and found that if an egg of a different color or marking pattern was substituted for the bird's own egg, that egg was rejected, but another egg with a similar pattern was accepted. The birds don't have innate recognition of their own eggs. For example, if a murre's egg is marked with white feces in small increments, the bird learns the new color pattern and will reject eggs of its own pattern. This fine discrimination by murres stands in contrast to the behavior of some birds—herring gulls, for example—which accept almost anything of any color even remotely resembling an egg.

Brood Parasitism

Recognition of eggs by their color pattern has evolved in some other birds under an entirely different set of selective pressures: the need to detect and destroy the eggs of parasites.

Reproductive success in murres is enhanced if the females can pick out their own uniquely colored eggs. In contrast, under the

ATLANTIC PUFFIN

NORTHERN MOCKINGBIRD

CRESTED CARACARA

WHITE WAGTAIL

KING PENGUIN

...SHLAND TINAMOU

COMMON GRACKLE

GREAT-TAILED GRACKLE

WHITE-TAILED EAGLE

SCISSOR-TAILED FLYCATCHER

BRITISH STORM-PETREL

...MMON RAVEN

GREAT TINAMOU

EURASIAN SKYLARK

MACGREGOR'S BIRD OF PARADISE

BLUE-GRAY GNATCATCHER

ARCTIC LOON

AMERICAN WOODCOCK

GOLDEN EAGLE

AMERICAN CROW

...ELLOW-BILLED CUCKOO

ANHINGA

LIMPKIN

EASTERN BLUEBIRD

SMALL-BILLED TINAMOU

SAGE GROUSE

SANDHILL CRANE

HOOPOE

BARN SWALLOW

EUROPEAN BEE-EATER

BROWN PELICAN

SPRUCE GROUSE

GENTOO PENGUIN

MALLARD

SHARP-TAILED GROUSE

RED-BREASTED PITTA

DWARF CASSOWARY

WHITE-WINGED TRILLER

BROAD-BILLED HUMMINGBIRD

GREAT ANTSHRIKE

OLIVE-SIDED FLYCATCHER

RATTLING CISTICOLA

selective pressure of brood parasitism (the laying of eggs by one species in the nest of another), a bird's reproductive success is enhanced if it can recognize the eggs of other birds in its clutch and discard them. The possibility of parasitism would place selective pressure on the host bird to detect the odd-colored eggs. This would, in turn, put pressure on the parasite to produce eggs resembling those of its host.

In European passerine birds heavily parasitized by cuckoos, for example, there has been potent selective pressure to foil the parasitism. Hosts have developed a strong attention to egg color code, abandoning many nests with cuckoo eggs or throwing the cuckoo eggs out. This puts stronger pressure on the cuckoos to produce even better egg mimicry. Only the well-matched eggs are accepted.

Parasitism in North America is no less severe, but the principal parasite of songbirds, the brown-headed cowbird, thus far has not evolved egg-color mimicry. Nevertheless, the cowbird is a highly successful parasite. It is one of the most common of our native passerine birds, and it is also one of the most widely distributed. According to Herbert Friedmann, a longtime student of avian brood parasitism, it parasitizes more than 350 species and subspecies of birds. Some species suffer heavily. Up to 78 percent of all song sparrow nests in some areas have been victimized by this parasite. The cowbird, however, also lays eggs occasionally in the nests of such unlikely potential hosts as the spotted sandpiper and ruby-crowned kinglet, as well as in many other nests where its eggs regularly get damaged or evicted. In short, it wastes many eggs. The cowbird is partial to open habitat, having spread east from the shortgrass prairies in the Midwest only in the past two or three centuries.

At this point in the evolutionary race, only some of the potential victims of the brown-headed cowbird have evolved appropriate egg-rejection responses. Stephen I. Rothstein of the University of California at Santa Barbara determined this by making plaster of paris eggs and painting them to mimic cowbird eggs. He deposited these in a total of 640 nests of 43 species. He found that two-thirds of the passerine birds accepted the parasite eggs, while only one-fourth consistently rejected them. Some birds—like the red-winged blackbird, yellow warbler, phoebe, and barn swallow—consistently accepted both fake and real parasite eggs, while others—like the catbird, robin, and kingbird—consistently rejected them. Since the birds were either consistent "acceptors" or "rejectors," he speculated that once the rejection behavior was genetic, it was of such advantage that it spread rapidly and became fixed.

Why don't more birds practice the art of parasitism? As with many historical questions, we don't have an ironclad answer, but we may identify some of the selective processes at work. One possibility is that after a parasite has become established, and through millions of years improved its strategy, the hosts will have such good methods of egg detection that another bird just starting out would have no success. For example, I doubt that the brown-headed cowbird could become established in Europe, because the European birds, under the selective pressure of the cuckoo, have already evolved such a sophisticated egg-recognition system that they would not be fooled by the crude tactics of the cowbird.

There are other implications. For example, a parasite would have a great advantage if it could utilize a variety of hosts. And multiple parasitism would be easy if all the parasite's victims had similar eggs. Any bird lucky enough to have distinctively marked eggs should most easily spot and reject a parasite's eggs. In other words, to avoid parasitism, a bird should have eggs that are different from those whose nests the parasite already uses. This would make for variety among different species but uniformity within clutches. And in general these are the patterns we see in nature.

The Tendency Toward Diversity

Perhaps there is, after all, an evolutionary reason for the "general tendency of birds toward diversity." Perhaps catbirds' eggs, by being blue, are less camouflaged, but they gain instead by providing a sharp contrast so cowbirds' eggs can be detected and evicted.

It will likely not be possible ever to say with any degree of precision why a robin's egg is blue or a kingbird's egg is white and splotched with dark brown and purple. However, the diversity of patterns shows that there are different selective pressures at work. The coloration of bird eggs reflects a long interplay of forces, in the face of randomness and chance, to produce organization in many parallel evolutionary paths that we now see in different stages. This, in turn, "colors" the mind as well as the eye, and gives eggs an additional beauty that no person's brush could ever impart.

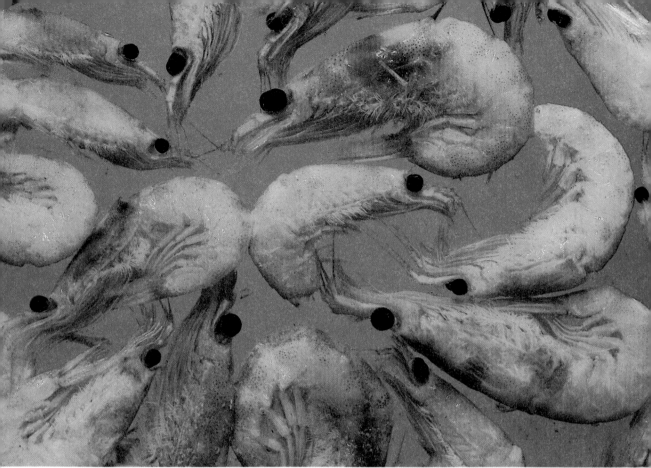

KRILL: Food of the future?

by Stephen Nicol

Can the millions of shrimplike krill that once fed hundreds of thousands of whales now feed humans?

Since the number of great whales has been drastically reduced, it has been argued that there must now be a surplus of krill. Based upon simple calculations concerning the pre-whaling population of whales, a surplus krill population of up to 150 million tons was estimated. But recent evidence has shown these original projections were much too large.

Krill have been found to have a longer life expectancy than originally thought, and the schools are very widely dispersed. This appears to indicate a much lower feasible harvest. In fact, the Soviets are now harvesting only one-quarter of their 1983 catch, which may indicate that krill populations are declining. In addition,

other predators—such as crabeater seals, penguins, and minke whales—appear to have increased in numbers, and this may be because they are consuming the "surplus." Indeed, any fishery based on Antarctic krill must take into account the pivotal role that krill play in the southern ecosystem.

What Are Krill?

The word *kril* means "tiny fish" or "small fry of fish" in Norwegian. During the passage of time, however, whalers adopted the word (with a second *l*) to refer to the shrimplike crustaceans found in the stomachs of baleen whales. The scientific name for krill is euphausiid, and they are a small taxonomic order with about 85 exclusively marine species.

Although, in appearance, krill resemble

© Stephen Nicol

Thousands of krill (above) make up a school. Below, a roughly life-size schematic of the North Atlantic variety.

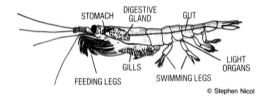

STOMACH   DIGESTIVE GLAND   GUT

LIGHT ORGANS

GILLS

FEEDING LEGS   SWIMMING LEGS

© Stephen Nicol

prawns and shrimps, they are thought to be distinct from these groups. Krill are mostly transparent, but have patches of bright red over their bodies. Most possess large eyes and a row of downward-pointing, light-producing organs called photophores. Deep-dwelling species approach the sea surface at night and remain at depth during the day, although there are occasional reports of huge swarms of euphausiids at the surface during daylight.

The biology of these delicate creatures is difficult to study in the laboratory. They rapidly damage themselves on the walls of aquariums and, being open-ocean animals, are sensitive to water quality and temperature. The largest euphausiids are deep-living, open-ocean forms that may reach 6 inches (15 centimeters) in length; however, most are about 1 inch (2.5 centimeters) long.

Krill reproduce sexually and lay several thousand large eggs, which most species shed into the water, although some do brood their eggs until they hatch. The first post-hatching stage is the nauplius, which is completely dissimilar to the adult and may be 100 times smaller. A bewildering variety of larval forms are passed through before the adult form is reached. Some of the larvae are so different from the adults that they were once classified as separate species.

Feeding begins after the nauplius stage. All subsequent stages, including the adult, feed upon microscopic plants and animals that make up the plankton on the surface of the ocean. Food is captured by the spiny legs of the thorax. The legs appear to act as a filter or trap for food particles. The food itself is presumably detected by the large eyes and antennae.

In the Far South

Although euphausiids are found throughout the world's oceans, it is in the Antarctic regions that they have reached their dominance. Probably the best-known species is the antarctic krill (*Euphausia superba*), which grows to 2 inches (5.1 centimeters) in length and is found exclusively in the Antarctic Ocean (which includes the southern parts of the Atlantic, Pacific, and Indian Oceans). It has been estimated that 150,000 giant blue whales used to spend the austral (Southern Hemisphere) summer in the Antarctic Ocean, each of them consuming up to 3 tons of krill a day before their decimation by the whaling fleets.

Because of their overwhelming importance in the diet of the great whales, krill have become the focus of much of the research in the Antarctic Ocean since the late 1960's. Scientists and fishery technologists are keen to examine the pivotal role that these crustaceans play in the productive Antarctic marine ecosystem.

One behavior pattern of several species of euphausiids, including Antarctic krill, that is of great interest to both pure and applied scientists is their aggregation in huge swarms. One such swarm of Antarctic krill was discovered off Elephant Island, near the Antarctic Peninsula, in 1981, and was estimated to contain between 2 million and 10 million tons, supposedly the largest single aggregation of one species ever measured. The animals in these swarms are packed tightly, with as many as 600,000 per cubic yard (785,000 per cubic meter). It is in such dense aggregations that krill are an attractive food source for the great whales, which need such high densities to economically feed. The aggregating habit that makes krill the favored prey of whales also makes them possible targets for a commercial fishery.

Nutritious Food

Krill are an attractive food source, for they are high in protein, low in fat, and a good source of vitamins A, D, and the B group. Three major problems exist in producing a marketable food product from krill, however. First, they spoil easily, turning black and becoming unusable soon after capture, and this problem is exacerbated by crushing during and after capture.

Second, several studies have shown that krill are naturally rich in fluoride, containing many times what is recognized as a safe dose per unit weight of flesh. The majority of the fluoride load is, however, carried in the shell. If the flesh is rapidly peeled from the shell following capture, the fluoride does not move into the flesh, and the levels of fluoride in the edible portion remain at acceptably low levels.

Peeling Krill

Third, krill are small relative to other commercially exploited crustaceans, and it is difficult to separate the edible flesh from the horny shell, or exoskeleton. Several mechanisms have been used to remove the shell: roller peeling, centrifugal peeling, mechanical peeling, and peeling by water jets; each method produces a slightly different product. The shells are composed of a chemical called chitin, which itself has many commercial uses (for example, in water purification, wound dressings, and drug encapsulation). So, if the separation can be accomplished efficiently, two marketable products will emerge.

Several foodstuffs have been produced from krill. The USSR has produced a krill paste that is formed by the squeezing of raw krill to release liquid protein that is then coagulated. The paste is used as a food additive in sausages, soups, and other processed-food products. In Chile, krill are sold as breaded fish sticks; in West Germany and Sweden, as artificial crabmeat; and in Japan, krill-tail meats are eaten both raw and cooked.

A krill fishing fleet works the waters off Japan. The Japanese enjoy the tail meat of krill whether raw or cooked.

How Much Is Caught?

The exact size of the present fishery on Antarctic krill is unknown. Some of the last reported statistics reveal that in 1979–80, Japanese boats took 40,000 tons, and boats from the USSR caught 400,000 tons. Additionally, there is a coastal fishery off Japan for the smaller euphausiid *Euphausia pacifica*, although most of the catch of around 40,000 tons (1978) is directed to fish farms or is used as a feed supplement for domestic animals.

Despite the potential of the fishery for Antarctic krill, there are still many problems to be worked out both from the biological and from the economic standpoint. Even though krill have been intensively studied for several decades, much of their basic biology remains a mystery. There is at present much debate regarding the longevity of these animals, and current estimates range from three to ten years. No one knows where they go during the long, dark Antarctic winters or what they eat then, if indeed they do. One study demonstrated that krill can survive for over 200 days without food, a remarkable feat since they are heavier than water and must swim continuously to avoid sinking. The krill in this study shrank as starvation progressed, and this behavior is being investigated as a possible overwintering strategy.

Also of concern is that a fishery would depend on krill being in large swarms, but there is little information as to where and when or even why they form such aggregations.

At What Cost?

Economic problems are largely centered on the immense distance that separates the Antarctic Ocean from most of the nations that might exploit this resource. This has led to an upsurge in interest in Antarctic research by nations from the Southern Hemisphere. For a Northern Hemisphere nation to maintain a fishing fleet in the Antarctic Ocean, which can be used only from December to April, is prohibitively expensive. As a consequence, krill would have to fetch a premium price and would have to be sold as a luxury food. The fishery is in an unusual position at present; far more krill can be caught than can be processed in the time necessary, and far more can be caught and processed than can be marketed. So the potential supply of krill at present far outruns the demand, and, until a palatable product is produced at a reasonable price, it is unlikely that the krill resource will be utilized by any but the most heavily government-subsidized fishing industries.

To protect the Antarctic ecosystem as a whole, the Convention on the Conservation of Antarctic Marine Living Resources was formed in 1980. The convention was mindful of the destructive exploitation of the seals and whales in the Antarctic region in the past, and sought to avoid similar disasters in the harvesting of fish and krill. Under the terms of the convention, conservation includes rational use of the resources; however, it is unique among fisheries treaties, as it concerns itself with the ecosystem rather than with individual species.

It is hoped that such measures, implemented before the exploitation of krill becomes widespread, will help to avert the disastrous effects of overfishing, which has decimated so many of the world's major fish stocks. These conservation measures, coupled with the inhibitions of the fishing industries of the world when faced with a vast financial outlay for an uncertain reward, indicate that krill and the krill-based ecosystem of the Antarctic Ocean have a temporary reprieve. The long-term future of this resource—in a world where a growing population demands increasing supplies of protein—is, however, less certain.

Krill is especially abundant in Antarctic waters, where six species thrive in the virtual absence of predators.

© Nicklin & Associates

THE 1986 NOBEL PRIZE
Physiology or Medicine

by Elaine Pascoe

The 1986 Nobel Prize in Physiology or Medicine was shared by two scientists—Dr. Stanley Cohen, an American biochemist, and Dr. Rita Levi-Montalcini, a biologist who holds both Italian and American citizenship—for their separate research into growth factors: substances that influence the orderly development of tissues. Their research, besides its value in unlocking the secrets of human growth, has had important implications for cancer and other health problems.

In the 1950's Cohen and Levi-Montalcini worked together at Washington University, St. Louis, Missouri, but subsequently pursued their projects separately. In a discovery that the Nobel committee called a "fascinating example of how a skilled observer can create a concept out of apparent chaos," Levi-Montalcini identified nerve growth factor, a substance that plays a crucial role in the development of nerve cells. She also recognized the fact that growth factors of various kinds influence the development of different cell types within the body.

Cohen identified epidermal growth factor, a substance central to the development of many tissue types, including skin and the cornea of the eye. He also identified the protein on cell surfaces that acts as a receptor for the growth factor. As a result, the Nobel committee noted, "For the first time, scientists had a factor available [that] . . . allowed study of the growth process." The two scientists split a cash award of approximately $290,000.

Creating a Network of Nerves

The identification of nerve growth factor provided the first clue to understanding how embryonic nerve cells develop into a network that permeates the body. Levi-Montalcini made her discovery in the 1950's while collaborating with Dr. Viktor Hamburger, a pioneer in the study of nerve development, at Washington University.

AP/Wide World

Pioneers in the study of chemicals that govern the growth of cells shared the 1986 Nobel Prize for Physiology or Medicine. Dr. Rita Levi-Montalcini (left) identified nerve growth factor; Dr. Stanley Cohen (below) discovered epidermal growth factor.

© Clark Thomas/Picture Group

Early research showed that mouse tumors stimulated nerve development in chicken embryos, even when the tumors were not in direct contact with the embryos. Levi-Montalcini, postulating that the tumor must emit some chemical that prompted the accelerated nerve growth, devised a test that identified the substance responsible, a substance she called nerve growth factor. Cohen, who joined the project in the mid-1950's, succeeded in purifying the substance, and showed it to be a protein.

In the human body, nerve growth factor is produced by "target" cells in a wide variety of tissues. When it reaches a nerve cell, nerve growth factor binds to a receptor on the cell surface and is carried to the nerve cell nucleus. The chemical message it delivers prompts the cell to grow projections, or axons, that reach out toward the target cells and ultimately connect with them, forming networks called synapses. In this way—by the growth of nerve cells toward the target cells—an orderly network of nerves is created throughout the body.

Although the early research demonstrated the factor's effect on sensory and sympathetic nerve cells, subsequent work has indicated that nerve growth factor also helps maintain certain brain cells, including those that degenerate in Alzheimer's disease and Huntington's disease. It remains for future research to demonstrate a relationship between lack of nerve growth factor and these diseases; it may well be that more than one factor is involved. Levi-Montalcini's work also holds promise for new methods of treating Parkinson's disease and a better understanding of birth defects.

Stimulating Tissue Development

Cohen's discovery of epidermal growth factor came as an outgrowth of his work with nerve growth factor. He observed that newborn mice, injected with a substance containing nerve growth factor extracted from the saliva of adult mice, opened their eyes six to seven days ahead of schedule, and their teeth erupted early. He immediately suspected that a separate chemical stimulant was at work, since these effects were not seen with pure nerve growth factor.

Pursuing his studies, Cohen discovered the cause of the early opening of the eyes: the skin cells of the lids had been stimulated to differentiate and grow more rapidly. By 1962 he had succeeded in isolating epidermal growth factor as the substance that prompted this change. He later purified the substance and determined the types and sequence of the 53 amino acids that make up its protein molecule.

Subsequent work showed that epidermal growth factor influences a wide range of cells. Besides its research value, the substance has been used to grow human skin tissue in the laboratory for use in treating severe burns. Its

WHAT NERVE GROWTH FACTOR DOES

Nerve growth factor (NGF) performs a dual role: it stimulates the growth of nerve cells and it figures prominently in the organization of the nervous system. Target cells secrete NGF (top), inducing the axon of an immature nerve cell to grow toward them (middle). The axon then forms synapses to serve as connectors to the target cells (bottom)—a process vital to the proper development of the nervous system.

TARGET CELLS SECRETE NGF

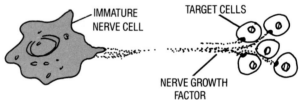

IMMATURE NERVE CELL

TARGET CELLS

NERVE GROWTH FACTOR

AXON GROWS TOWARD TARGET CELLS IN RESPONSE

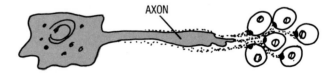

AXON

AXON FORMS SYNAPSES THAT CONNECT WITH TARGET CELLS

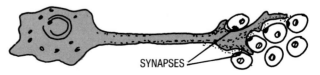

SYNAPSES

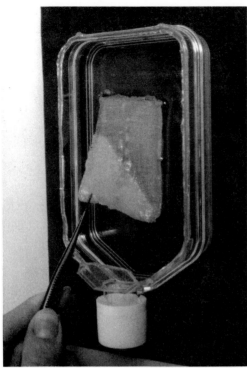

Skin tissue grown in the laboratory using epidermal growth factor has been used to treat severe burns.

© Ira Wyman/SYGMA

inhibition of acid production in the stomach (it is identical to the hormone urogastrone) may well mean use in the treatment of ulcers as well.

Since the discovery of nerve growth factor and epidermal growth factor, a number of other growth factors have been identified. But, while Cohen's identification of the cell receptor that receives epidermal growth factor was an important step in understanding how such factors work, a central question that remains unanswered is precisely how this and other growth factors deliver their messages that turn cells "on," so that they begin to multiply.

This question is thought to be crucial to cancer research, since disturbances in cell growth can lead to the development of the disease. Some recent research has suggested that links may exist between growth factor receptors and oncogenes, genes that appear to contribute to the formation of cancerous tumors under certain conditions.

Dr. Rita Levi-Montalcini, born in 1909 in Turin, Italy, graduated from the medical school of the University of Turin in 1936. She was working at a research institute at the university in 1939 when the enactment of anti-Semitic laws forced her to leave her position. With a microscope and a few other pieces of equipment, she set up a small laboratory in a bedroom of her family home and continued her research, expanding her knowledge of cellular biology.

When the Nazis occupied Italy, Levi-Montalcini fled with her family to Florence, where she lived underground for the remainder of the war. After the liberation of Italy, she volunteered her services as a physician to the Allies and helped fight a series of epidemics that raged through the civilian population. After the war she returned to the University of Turin and, in 1947, moved to the United States. There she obtained a position on the faculty at Washington University and began her work with Hamburger on nerve-cell growth. She became an American citizen in 1956.

In the 1960's Levi-Montalcini began to divide her time between the United States and Rome, where she holds a position as a senior scientist at the Institute of Cell Biology. Although she retired from Washington University in 1977 and now lives with her twin sister, Paola, in Rome, she has also retained her position as professor emeritus at that school. Besides the Nobel Prize, her work has brought her many other awards, including a 1986 Lasker Award shared with Cohen.

Dr. Stanley Cohen was born in the Flatbush section of Brooklyn, New York, on November 17, 1922. The son of a Russian immigrant tailor, he attended Brooklyn College and earned a doctorate in biochemistry at the University of Michigan in 1948. In 1953 he joined Levi-Montalcini at Washington University and became involved in the nerve growth factor research project.

As a researcher, Cohen soon developed a reputation as a highly focused individual who pursued his goal intently, often with little help and well before the importance of growth factor research was widely recognized in the scientific community. In 1959 he joined the faculty of Vanderbilt University in Nashville, Tennessee, as a professor of biochemistry, a position he still holds. It was there that he accomplished much of his work on epidermal growth factor.

Like Levi-Montalcini, Cohen has been the recipient of many awards for his work, including the 1986 Koch Award of the Endocrine Society, which termed him "the father of growth-factor research." He is married and the father of three children.

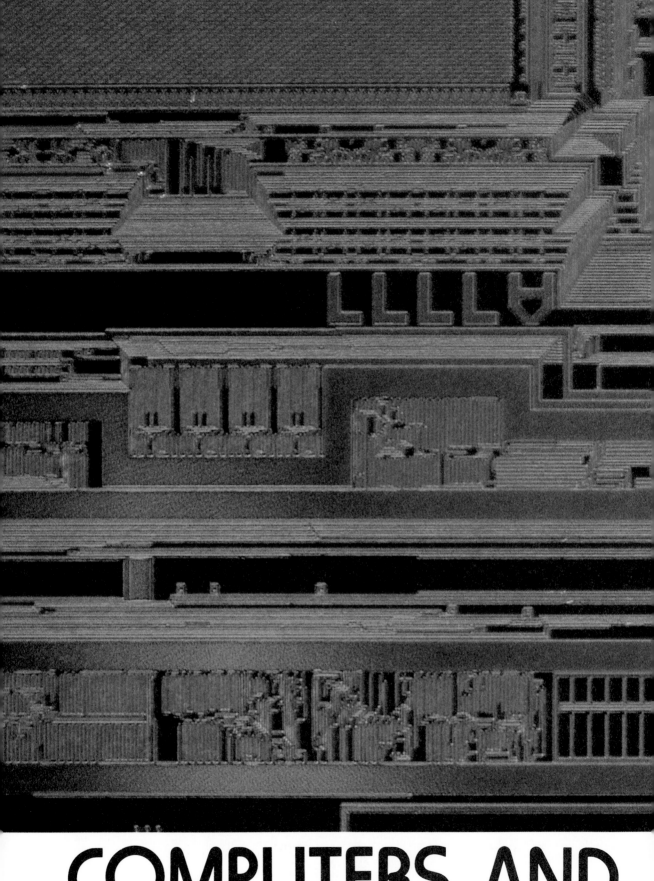

COMPUTERS AND

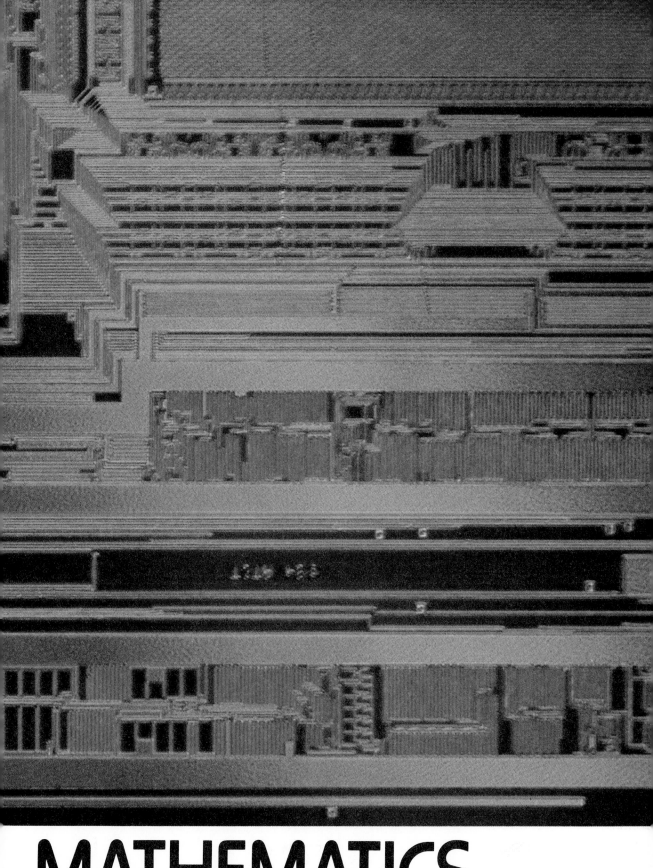

MATHEMATICS

TRW's Fast Data Finder can scan huge databases simultaneously for responses to nearly 600 different search requests.

TRW

REVIEW OF THE YEAR

COMPUTERS AND MATHEMATICS

After stalling briefly in the industry's shakeout of 1985, computer technology regained forward momentum in 1986, though at a slower pace than earlier in the decade. Desktop publishing systems using personal computers and laser printers brought new capabilities to thousands of U.S. businesses, and a new high-speed microprocessor chip led to yet another generation of small computers. But only a handful of new personal computers were revealed by major companies. In mathematics, computer experiments led to discovery of new families of geometric shapes that may have practical applications in other fields.

DATABASE SEARCH MADE EASIER

Computer databases are massive collections of information, usually stored on high-speed hard disk drives. For personal computers, the hard disk holds anywhere from 10 million to 80 million characters. (This article has about 8,000 characters.) Corporate or information service databases—which may include employee records for thousands of people, back issues of hundreds of newspapers or magazines, or a complete encyclopedia—use hard disks capable of storing billions of characters.

Finding exactly the information you want can be time-consuming and tedious, even when up to 10 percent of the hard disk is used for an extensively cross-referenced index. Now a new system developed by a scientist at TRW, Inc., in Redondo Beach, California, cuts search time to a handful of seconds and eliminates the need for indexing.

Called the Fast Data Finder (FDF), the system reads every word in a database to locate exactly the text—number or letter sequences, words, phrases, full sentences, or any combination of all four—that you need. Its developer, Dr. Kwang-I Yu, demonstrated the system in late 1986 by storing four months of Associated Press news stories, about 100 million characters, on a hard disk. He typed in commands to ask FDF to find every story that mentioned rockets failing or exploding, but which did not mention the words "shuttle" or "Challenger." The purpose was to find information on space mission failures other than the Challenger.

In less than 15 seconds, FDF scanned the entire database, located 67 separate news stories, and marked them for quick retrieval on a desktop computer screen. The system's speed was limited by the fact that the large industrial hard disk could provide data at only 7 million characters per second.

Personal computer hard disks operate at 1 million characters per second or less. At that rate, FDF would need 20 seconds to scan a fully packed 20-megabyte hard disk and isolate files containing the requested text. That's considerably faster than possible with current indexing techniques.

The Fast Data Finder is a combination of hardware—specially designed chips that each contain 37,000 separate devices—and the software that makes it work. It was developed for highly specialized Department of Defense (DOD) applications in military command, communications, and control, and then made available for commercial use. The system is particularly useful in sorting databases of random information, such as newspaper or magazine stories.

But it also would allow new databases, even traditional alphabetical listings, to be entered and stored randomly. The current FDF system is sized for commercial users. But a version fitting into a package smaller than a shoe box could be available for personal computer systems by 1990.

MEGABIT CHIPS

The race to produce 1-megabit memory chips, a single chip capable of storing 1 million bits of information, went to a U.S. company in 1986, when IBM announced full-scale production of the high-density devices and said that it would use them first in its new Sierra series of mainframe computers.

One-megabit chips hold 16 times as much data as the 64K chips standard in most early personal computers, and four times as much as the 256K chips found in late-model mini- or mainframe computers, or such advanced desktop machines as the Macintosh Plus. IBM beat major Japanese electronics companies, and competing U.S. companies, to the market with the chips, which have been in development at least three years. By significantly increasing the memory available in a computer, the new chips will drive costs down while allowing computers to be both smaller and more productive.

IBM will produce the chips only for its own computers. One-megabit chips from Japanese and other American manufacturers are expected to be widely available during 1987 and find their way quickly into new desktop computers. At least one U.S. computer company, Apple, said that advanced versions of its machines would be able to use the new chips.

DESKTOP PUBLISHING SCORES

For more than 50,000 computer users, ranging from mom-and-pop printshops to magazine publishers to major U.S. corporations, 1986 was the year of desktop publishing. That's how many Macintosh desktop publishing systems were reported sold by Apple Computer, Inc. Smaller numbers of systems based on the IBM PC, or its look-alikes, also were installed, to drive the total even higher.

Desktop publishing systems allow users to change typefaces and sizes, manipulate graphics, and lay out full pages of magazines, books, reports, or other documents on a computer screen. Software with names such as PageMaker, ReadySetGo, and others reduces both the complexity and expense of publishing. For medium-quality output, pages are printed on a desktop laser printer with 300 dots per inch (DPI) resolution, then reproduced with copy machines or photo-offset presses. For high-quality

documents, such as magazines or annual reports, a larger laser printer with 1,200-DPI resolution is used for the intermediate step.

Only three significant new personal computers reached U.S. consumers in 1986. IBM introduced a laptop version of its popular PC weighing just 12 pounds (5.5 kilograms). The battery-powered machine has two built-in disk drives and a flip-up liquid crystal display screen. The screen can be removed and replaced by a full-size monitor for office or home use.

Continuing its pledge to make the Apple II an ongoing standard, Apple unveiled a high-speed "GS" model with significantly improved high-resolution graphics and stereo sound capability. Standard memory in the II-GS is 256K, with expansion potential to 8 megabytes. The computer is based on a new 16-bit microprocessor that triples operating speed and allows development of larger and more complex software. At the same time, the machine runs almost all software written for earlier Apple II computers based on an 8-bit microprocessor.

Compaq Computers Inc., chief rival to IBM with its look-alike machines, introduced a new computer late in 1986 based on Intel's 80386 microprocessor chip. The 16-bit processor combines normal operations and high-speed math functions, previously requiring separate chips, into a single package. It operates at higher speeds than earlier versions of the chip, allowing more rapid calculations and data manipulation.

Industry observers expect the 80386 processor to become a standard in new computers using the MS-DOS operating system favored by IBM and its clones.

SHAPES, CURVES, AND OTHER MATHEMATICAL MYSTERIES

Until 1986, mathematical wisdom held that geometrical shapes called "infinite minimal surfaces" came in just three forms—flat planes; helicoids, or spirals; and catenoids, or hourglass shapes. Minimal surfaces are defined by mathematical equations and represent the smallest area over which a surface can be stretched. In the practical world, the equations help solve problems such as fluid flows.

But using computers to analyze equations and graph the results on a screen, mathematicians David A. Hoffman and James T. Hoffman of the University of Massachusetts and William H. Meeks of Rice University discovered varieties of new shapes, including surfaces with holes, that were previously unsuspected. The work could impact fields as diverse as architecture, in designing new structures, and chemistry, in solving the riddles of molecule chains that create polymers.

JIM SCHEFTER

COMPUTERS THAT ALMOST THINK

by Otis Port

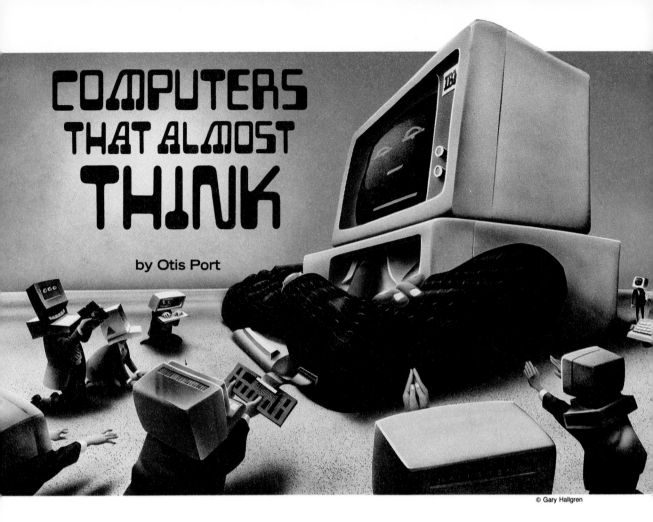

© Gary Hallgren

"Ahh-nu-no-nunu-ru-unn." It sounds like baby babble, and in a sense it is. It's a radically new type of computer learning to read—on its own. Nobody programs it, except to tell it when it makes a mistake. Yet after an hour or so of trial and error, that babble starts to become coherent. The system gradually figures out which speech sounds are associated with what letters and syllables, that certain collections of sounds are words, and that strings of words are sentences. Left overnight, the machine will acquire the language skills of a 6-year-old.

The proud father of this eerily precocious little machine is Terrence J. Sejnowski, associate professor of biophysics at Johns Hopkins University. In 1983 Sejnowski became intrigued with a new approach in designing computers based on the latest theories about how the human brain processes information. To construct a so-called neural-network computer, with circuits patterned after the complex interconnections among nerve cells in the brain, Sej-

nowski teamed up with Scott E. Fahlman and Geoffrey E. Hinton, computer scientists at Carnegie-Mellon University, and Scott E. Kirkpatrick, a researcher at International Business Machines Corp. (IBM).

What they cooked up has only a tiny fraction of the power of a snail's brain—just 200 processing elements, or simulated "neurons." Yet it can teach itself to read aloud. And Sejnowski says the system could just as readily learn to interpret images or convert speech into text. This system's astonishing performance—and similar results with a dozen or so variations in other university and corporate laboratories—is convincing researchers that it may soon be possible to build truly intelligent machines.

Deaf and Blind

While scientists working in the field of artificial intelligence (AI) have produced computer programs that capture some reasoning ability in narrow slices of knowledge, AI has long been bedeviled by a paradox: Conventional computers easily cope with adult skills, such as playing chess, solving differential equations, or balancing financial records, but they freeze when it comes to the things that even infants quickly learn—to recognize their mother's face and the sound of their own names. "There are no machines today that can really see or understand speech," declares Robert Hecht-Nielsen, head of TRW Inc.'s Rancho Carmel Artificial Intelligence Center near San Diego, California.

Hecht-Nielsen and a small group of researchers are betting that neural-net computers will soon change that. TRW recently introduced a commercial version of a neural-net machine developed for the Pentagon's Defense Advanced Research Projects Agency (DARPA). This special-purpose computer is designed to work alongside a conventional computer and help with such tasks as recognizing images. TRW expects it will be snapped up for making visual equality checks in factories.

This summer the company will unveil what is probably the most sophisticated neural computer ever built. Expected to carry a price tag in the mid-six-figure range, it will outperform a $20 million supercomputer at certain jobs. In addition, Texas Instruments, American Telephone & Telegraph (AT&T), and IBM have their own development projects under way.

What distinguishes neural-net systems from regular computers is a radical departure in architecture—how a computer's electronic innards are organized. The design for virtually all of today's computers was laid down by mathematician John von Neumann in the 1940's. It calls for physical separation of the computer's memory and its processor, with a communications link in between. While this arrangement provides for tight control over the computer's operations, it also slows down the machine because the processor spends most of its time waiting for data to be plucked out of storage or sent back. So it seems unlikely that von Neumann computers will ever attain the hyperfast speeds needed to attack some of the thorniest problems that now confront science and engineering.

Strange Behavior

The neural-net approach avoids that bottleneck by mimicking the brain's vast web of interconnected neurons. When a neuron "fires" in the brain, it broadcasts a signal to thousands of other neurons, which in turn alert millions more. In a split second, entire regions of the brain become involved, and processing seems to happen everywhere at once. Neural-net computers do something similar, though on a much smaller scale. The brain has an estimated 10 bil-

---

HOW DIGITAL AND NEURAL COMPUTERS DIFFER

DIGITAL COMPUTERS	NEURAL NETWORKS
● Process digital data that are written in the 1s and 0s that constitute the binary code for mathematical precision	● Process analog signals that fluctuate continuously, providing a range from, say, black through all shades of gray to white
● Make yes/no decisions, using mathematical and logical functions	● Make weighted decisions on the basis of fuzzy, incomplete, and contradictory data
● Handle data in a rigidly structured sequence so that operations are always under control and results are predictable	● Independently formulate methods of processing data, often with surprising results
● Find precise answers to any problem, given enough time	● Find good, quick—but approximate—answers to highly complex problems
● Sort through large data bases to find exact matches	● Sort through large data bases to find close matches
● Store information so that specific data can be retrieved easily	● Store information so that retrieving any piece of information automatically calls up all related facts

© Max Aguilera-Hellweg

Robert Hecht-Nielsen of TRW's Artificial Intelligence Center builds computers to mimic human brain response.

lion neurons and more than 1,000 times that many interconnections. TRW's new machine will have a "mere" 250,000 processors and 5.5 million connections. But this is just for starters, says Hecht-Nielsen: "We have already designed systems that have 100 million processing elements."

Even the midget neural-net systems built so far exhibit strange but exciting behavior that comes suspiciously close to thinking. Surprisingly, the key lies in the scope of the interconnections among the processors, not the number of processors. If each processor has multiple links to many others, even a lattice with fewer than 100 "neurons" will exhibit what scientists term "emergent behavior"—teaching itself to read, for example.

The One About the Traveling Salesman

Some problems in computer science are so notoriously hard that a solution guarantees newspaper headlines and instant fame. A network de-

signed by California Institute of Technology (Cal Tech) and AT&T Bell Laboratories can solve the very complicated "traveling-salesman problem" in a fraction of the time required by ordinary computers. The problem is a classic: Given a list of cities, what is the shortest route a salesman can take and still make a sales call in every city?

At first glance, the solution seems easy: Just tell a computer to arrange the cities in every possible combination, add up the distances between all of the cities in each combination, and pick the smallest number. The rub is that the possible combinations rapidly escalate out of sight. A list of 10 cities can be combined in 181,440 routes. For a large mainframe computer, that's a breeze—a few seconds of computing. But with 30 cities, there are an astronomical 1 trillion billion billion (1 followed by 30 zeros) possible combinations. That's an hour-long job.

By comparison, a neural-network computer finds the answer to both problems in less than one-tenth of a second. The trade-off is that the neural network doesn't always find the best answer—just a good one. However, in many situations "a good solution obtained very quickly is better than waiting for the perfect solution," says David W. Tank, a researcher at AT&T Bell Laboratories. That's certainly the case in routing telephone calls, or scheduling the use of a fleet of aircraft or trucks.

Tank and John J. Hopfield, a biophysicist at Cal Tech, put a neural network to the test. For a list of 10 cities, it usually selected one of the two best routes. For 30 cities, the network's solutions were among the best 100 million choices. That may not seem very accurate, but those answers all fall in the top 0.000000000000000000001 percent.

At the University of California's San Diego campus, David E. Rumelhart, director of the Institute of Cognitive Science, once asked a neural net to determine if pairs of positive and negative numbers were symmetrical, or equal to zero. The network fashioned a special pattern for linking a few of its processors that did the job. A computer called Wisard seems to learn to recognize images in much the same way that people do. If it's shown different pictures of Igor Aleksander, head of the team at Imperial College in London, England, that developed the machine, Wisard gradually pieces together a sort of universal image. After that, it can recognize Aleksander from any perspective.

Cal Tech's John J. Hopfield. His long-standing support of brainlike computers has earned him the title "guru of neural computers."

Incredible Ensemble

No one can fully explain how a network creates seemingly organized behavior itself. "It's something that just emerges from the local interactions among this incredible ensemble of interconnected components," says John Seely Brown of the Intelligent Systems Lab at Xerox Corp.'s Palo Alto Research Center. Somehow, "important computational properties arise spontaneously," says Cal Tech's Hopfield.

Hopfield is largely responsible for the current surge of interest in brainlike computers, but—ironically—the idea can be traced all the way back to von Neumann. A thriving research effort to build so-called cybernetic systems was actually under way in the 1960's, spurred by the work of Frank Rosenblatt, a neurobiologist at Cornell University who invented a neuronlike device called the perceptron in 1957. "But the problems turned out to be tougher than ex-

To find the best route for a salesman traveling to 10 cities, scientists used a neural network with 100 processors arranged in a grid (left). Each column of processors was allowed to pick one city, with the first city on the route in column 1, the second in column 2, and so forth. Column 2 at first wanted both Cleveland and Indianapolis (center). But the grid settled down, and in the final solution (right), Richmond was the first stop and Winston-Salem the last.

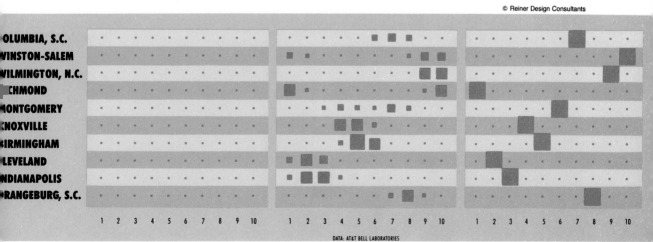

DATA: AT&T BELL LABORATORIES

pected,'' recalls A. Harry Klopf, manager for network-architecture research at Wright-Patterson Air Force Base. And then Marvin L. Minsky, a professor of computer science at Massachusetts Institute of Technology (MIT), wrote a book in 1969 that criticized perceptrons as next to useless. Funding soon dried up.

Nevertheless, a band of about two dozen diehards, including Hecht-Nielsen, continued their work in relative obscurity and on shoe-string budgets. Hopfield changes all that in 1982. Already a famous biophysicist and a member of the prestigious National Academy of Sciences, he published a landmark paper on neural networks that triggered a landslide of new interest. ''About 80 percent of the full-time researchers in this field have been brought in by Hopfield,'' says Hecht-Nielsen. Until recently, when DARPA held neural-net meetings, says Craig I. Fields, DARPA's chief scientist, about 50 people would show up. In April 1986, a meeting in Utah drew more than 150 research-ers—and nearly 100 more had to be turned away for lack of hotel space.

MIT's Minsky remains skeptical of neural-net research, however. He and other critics argue that so little is known about how the brain works that it's pointless to use it as an architec-tural model. There is no way for neural-net pro-ponents to know whether their creations bear even a faint functional likeness to actual brain networks.

Crazy and Simple

TRW's Hecht-Nielsen retorts that whether the machines actually resemble the brain really doesn't matter. ''What matters,'' he says, ''is that these theoretical models can be proven mathematically to have interesting information-processing capabilities.'' Even though most of the new research is still in the laboratory, the neural-net researchers insist that tantalizing glimpses of a new age in computer science are already emerging.

Future machines will be far more facile at handling enormous volumes of data. Suppose, for example, that you wanted to find the one person on earth whose height and weight comes closest to your own. A conventional supercom-puter would take about seven minutes to slog through the statistics for 5 billion people, one by one. But with TRW's neural network, the an-swer would pop out in roughly 75 thousandths of a second.

The reason is the way the computer's memory is ''mapped'' onto the network. Imag-ine a hugh graph: along one axis is an ounce scale; on the other, inches. Each person is rep-resented by a dot, so as soon as the system plots the location for your height and weight, it immediately knows which other dot is the near-est. It doesn't have to make 5 billion separate comparisons. ''This system, as crazy and sim-ple as it looks, has the net effect of matching your height and weight against those of every-

Unmanned space probes will benefit from the ability of neural computers to function even when heavily damaged.

NASA

one else on earth almost instantaneously,'' says Hecht-Nielsen. That capability could finally throw open the door to the childlike things that computers have never been able to do. ''The ability to quickly match many, many situations is the core of vision and speech understanding,'' says Fahlman of Carnegie-Mellon.

Such systems would pave the way for real-time processing of radar, sonar, and video signals. If each of the 250,000 pixels in a video picture were assigned its own ''neurons,'' images could be analyzed as fast as video cameras can transmit them. That capability is vital to a host of Pentagon programs, including computerized battle-management systems and a missile shield for the Strategic Defense Initiative (SDI), or ''Star Wars'' defense.

Floppy Ears

The ability of neural-net systems to learn also points to a host of new applications. Learning seems to happen when one memory pattern in a neural network is repeatedly reinforced. Present a picture of an elephant to a conventional computer, and no matter how many elephants it has seen, it will not recognize the image unless it can find an exact match or has been told explicitly to relate certain features, such as a very long nose or big floppy ears, with elephants. But show several pictures of elephants to a neural-net computer, and it will develop its own sense of the animal's distinguishing features. Then it can recognize an elephant from only a glimpse of its trunk or ears. In other words, given just a snippet of information, the network can retrieve all pertinent related data. This is the key to a so-called free-association memory—something that has so far eluded computer researchers.

To show that neural networks don't choke on fuzzy or inconsistent data, Cal Tech's Hopfield has used his system to recall strings of words by giving it just a hint—a few letters—of what he wanted. And when he intentionally inserts spurious letters or switches their order, the network corrects the error and returns the proper string. Similarly, Kunihiko Fukushima, a scientist at NHK Science & Technology Laboratories in Japan, has designed a system that can recognize characters (letters or numbers) in any typeface, even when they are distorted or smudged. Brown University's James A. Anderson, a professor of cognitive science, has a neural net that stores information on the diagnosis and treatment of various illnesses in an associative memory. Presented with an unfamiliar diagnosis, the system comes back with suggested treatments based on diagnoses that correspond closely to the one in question.

Silicon Brains?

Moreover, because of the cooperative nature of neural networks, they continue to function even after a number of processors—up to 15 percent—are damaged or become defective. Hopfield believes this ''robustness'' will make neural networks invaluable for unmanned space probes. Inspired by Hopfield's work, a team of scientists at Cal Tech's Jet Propulsion Laboratory (JPL), led by Senior Scientist John L. Lambe, is already working on such applications.

While no one suggests that neural-network research is even remotely close to replicating the human brain, neither do the researchers discount that possibility by the middle of the next century. Indeed, to Allen Newell, professor of computer science at Carnegie-Mellon, some form of silicon intelligence is inevitable. Already, researchers are building neural-net microchips of increasing complexity. A Cal Tech group led by Professor Carver A. Mead has one that contains 22 processors and 484 interconnections. At Bell Labs, where Hopfield also keeps an office, researchers have designed a chip with 512 processors and 256,000 connections—the densest yet.

Still, neural networks will not replace traditional computers. They have just as much trouble doing arithmetic as today's computers have in handling sights and sounds. But together, the two technologies promise a new age in computers, one that will return computing to the real world of human experience, where information doesn't have to be either black or white but can come in a rich variety of grays as well. Such computers will be able to deal with phenomena in the same terms that people perceive them. With neural networks serving as eyes and ears, tomorrow's machines will not only be able to watch, listen, and talk back, they'll also tolerate human foibles and idiosyncrasies.

SELECTED READINGS

''Representing Knowledge.'' *Byte,* November 1986.
''Etching neural systems in silicon'' by T. A. Heppenheimer. *Popular Science,* October 1986.
''Surrogate brains'' by G. Fjermedal. *Omni,* October 1986.
''Computing with neural circuits: a model'' by J. J. Hopfield and D. W. Tank. *Science,* August 8, 1986.

Factoring Fermat Numbers

by Keith Devlin

The ancient Greek mathematician Euclid knew, around 350 B.C., that every positive whole number other than 1 is either prime or a product of a unique collection of primes. This simple result is so important that it fully justifies its name—the fundamental theorem of arithmetic. It means that the prime numbers occupy a role in the theory of all whole numbers similar to the chemist's elements or the physicist's fundamental particles. Prime num-

bers can be exactly divided only by 1 and by themselves: some examples are 2, 3, 5, 7, 11, 13, 17, and 19. Knowledge of the prime decomposition of a given number (how to express that number as a product of primes) tells a great deal about the number. Examples of prime decompositions are:

$$3 = 3; 15 = 3 \times 5; 120 = 2 \times 2 \times 2 \times 3 \times 5.$$

On the face of it, the task of checking a given number to see if it is prime is closely related to the determination of some or all of the prime factors of that number. Given a number N, the most obvious way to determine if N is prime or not is to make a systematic search for any smaller number that divides it. First try 2, then 3, then 4, then 5, and so on all the way up to $N-1$. If one of these exactly divides N, then N cannot be prime; and what is more, you have discovered one of its factors. The first factor found will always be a prime factor. Can you

Without a computer, prime factors of a multidigit number can be determined only through tedious calculations.

see why? By dividing N by the factor and starting the process over again with the quotient, it is possible to go on until you obtain the entire prime decomposition—in theory.

Speeding Up the Process

If you stop and think about it, you will find that there are several ways of speeding up this process of trial division (as it is known). For one thing, once you have found that 2 does not divide N, there is no need ever again to trial-divide by an even number. Similarly, if 3 does not divide N, there is no need to trial-divide by any multiple of 3. Generalizing these observations, you see that you really need to trial-divide only by primes. And what is more, there is no need to trial-divide by primes greater than $\sqrt{N}$. If N has no divisor less than or equal to $\sqrt{N}$, then N has to be prime.

On a computer, this method of trial division works very well with moderately sized numbers, those that have 10 digits or so. (Rather than store a long list of primes to trial-divide, it is usually better to store, say, the first 20 or so primes and then trial-divide by all odd numbers that are not multiples of any of these primes. There are various ways of improving on this idea.) But even on a very fast computer, the method of trial division becomes impractical for numbers that have more than 20 digits. For larger numbers, say between 20 and 1,000 digits, there are several efficient tests to determine whether a number is prime—called primality tests—that produce a result in a fraction of the time that trial division takes.

Primality Tests

These more efficient methods use mathematical properties of prime numbers other than the mere definition of a prime. But their speed is obtained at a cost. If such a test shows that a number N is not prime, it does not provide any information about the factors of N. All you get is the straight fact that N is not prime—nothing more. If you want to know the factors, you have to start again using a different approach. And this can be quite hard. For whereas there are efficient tests for primality, there is no known way to factorize numbers of more than about 80 digits. What is at issue here is a method that will work on any number. A large number that is just a product of many small primes, such as $2^{100} \times 3^{50}$, can be factored by trial division. But a 200-digit number that is a product of two 100-digit primes is beyond any known method of attack.

This fact is used in the design of a very secure form of encryption, called the RSA Public Key System. (The RSA stands for Rivest, Shamir, and Adleman, after the three mathematicians who invented the method.) Roughly speaking, coding a message in the RSA system corresponds to multiplying two large primes—which is easy. Decoding corresponds to factoring that big product—a task that can be accomplished only if the two prime factors are known in advance. What makes this method particularly useful is that encoding a message does not require knowledge of the two primes, only their product, so there is no need for anyone other than the message's receiver ever to know the prime factors critical to the decoding. This characteristic makes the system practical for use on a public communications network.

We can factorize a number that has more than around 80 digits only if it has a special form upon which we can play extra mathematical tricks. The Fermat numbers are a case in point. A Fermat number has the formula:

$$F_n = 2^{2^n} + 1.$$

Fermat numbers take their name from the great French amateur mathematician Pierre Fermat, who was a jurist in Toulouse. In 1640 Fermat wrote a letter to his countryman the monk Marin Mersenne, in which he claimed that all the numbers F_n are primes. We do not know on what evidence Fermat based this conclusion. Certainly the first few Fermat numbers are prime. It is possible to check "by hand" the primality of each of:

$$F_0 = 2^{2^0} + 1 = 2^1 + 1 = 3,$$
$$F_1 = 2^{2^1} + 1 = 2^2 + 1 = 5,$$
$$F_2 = 2^{2^2} + 1 = 2^4 + 1 = 17,$$
$$F_3 = 2^8 + 1 = 257, \text{ and}$$
$$F_4 = 2^{16} + 1 = 65,537.$$

But most people would balk at trying to test the next Fermat number for primality.

$$F_5 = 2^{2^5} + 1 = 2^{32} + 1 = 4,294,967,297.$$

And this indicates the problem that Fermat numbers raise from the very start. The double exponentiation means that such numbers become extremely large very quickly. To the computational mathematician, this is like a red cape to a bull. Balanced against their size, there is, of course, a great deal of ordered structure to such numbers.

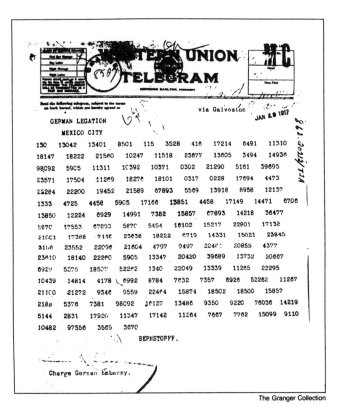

The Granger Collection

MARS

During both world wars, prime numbers were used to encode classified dispatches. The Zimmerman Telegram (left), an encoded message in which Germany expressed its intention to conduct unrestricted submarine warfare, led the U.S. into World War I. At right is a German Enigma machine, used by the Nazis to encode messages during World War II.

For instance, there is a highly efficient primality test for Fermat numbers, known as Proth's test. This says that a Fermat number F_n will be prime if, and only if:

$$3^{(F_n - 1)/2} \bmod F_n = -1.$$

To get back to Fermat's claim, though the size of F_5 might well frighten off most people not armed with a good computer, it did not deter the great Swiss mathematician Leonhard Euler. In 1732 he discovered that F_5 is divisible by the prime number 641:

$$F_5 = 641 \times 6,700,417.$$

So Fermat was wrong. But by then it was too late. The problem of testing Fermat numbers for primality and of finding their prime factors was already established.

Primes and Polygons

The first real significance of Fermat numbers (other than the fact that they represent one of the very few occasions when Fermat was wrong)

was provided by a remarkable result derived by the German mathematical child prodigy Karl Friedrich Gauss. In 1801, at the age of 24, Gauss produced a monumental work, *Disquisitiones Arithmeticae*, that laid the foundations of modern number theory. In the book, Gauss proved that the Fermat primes are intimately connected with the classical ancient Greek problem of constructing regular polygons with ruler and compasses only. (Technically, the ruler may be used only for drawing straight lines, not for measuring, and the compasses may be used only for drawing circles, or arcs of circles, not as dividers for transferring lengths.) Gauss's result was that you can construct with ruler and compasses a regular polygon of n sides if, and only if, either n is a power of 2, or else n is of the form:

$$n = 2^k \times p_1 \times p_2 \times \ldots \times p_r$$

where k > 0 and $p_1, p_2 \ldots p_r$ are distinct Fermat primes.

Mathematicians have known since the time of the Greeks that they could construct regular polygons of 2^k, $2^k \times 3$, $2^k \times 5$, and $2^k \times 15$ sides. In particular, they could construct regular n-sided polygons where n = 3, 4, 5, 6, 8, 10, 12, 15, or 16. But until Gauss's discovery, no one had even suspected that it was possible to construct a regular "17-gon" using ruler and compasses (as the primality of $17 = F_2$ implies). Gauss himself was so proud of his discovery that he requested that a regular "17-gon" be engraved on his tombstone. This wish was not fulfilled, but such a polygon is inscribed on a monument to him erected in his birthplace of Brunswick, Germany.

Start with Trial Division

Gauss's result aside, however, the principal interest in Fermat numbers in recent times has been the problem of finding their factorization. We know that F_n is composite (in other words, not prime) for all values of n from 5 to 16, and for various other values of n. The current "guess" is that they are all composite except for the first five, which Fermat had observed to be prime. (The evidence for this guess is no better than Fermat's evidence for the opposite conjecture.)

Landry discovered the composite nature of F_6 in 1880. He obtained a prime factor, namely 274,177.

F_7 is a number with 39 digits. In 1905 Morehead and Western used Proth's test (mentioned earlier) to show that it is composite. Then, in 1909, the same pair used the same method to show that the 78-digit F_8 is also composite. F_7 and F_8 proved to be the two Fermat numbers out of the first few that were the hardest to factorize—or rather, to find the first prime factor. Each of F_9 through to F_{13} turned out to have a fairly small prime factor, the largest being a 13-digit factor of F_{13}, though the sheer size of these numbers has precluded complete factorizations. For instance, we know that F_9 is a product of the prime 2,424,833 and a 148-digit composite number, but no one so far has factorized that into primes.

Only when mathematicians had developed two new and extremely powerful methods could they factorize F_7 and F_8. In 1971 Brillhart and Morrison used a method introduced by Lehmer and Powers some years previously in order to factor F_7. The computation took an hour and a half on an IBM 360-91 computer. The prime factors have 17 and 22 digits, respectively. Then, in 1981, Brent and Pollard used an ingenious method of Pollard's to factorize F_8 on a Univac 1100/42 computer. The calculation took two hours to find the 16-digit first prime factor. But Brent and Pollard were unable to verify that the other, 62-digit, factor was prime. H. C. Williams managed this feat shortly afterward.

So just how do you set about trying to factor a number once you have ruled out trial division? For a start, do not rule out trial division altogether. It is prudent to start any factorization process by trial division by the first few thousand (or even million) primes (or some sequence containing them all.) A computer can carry out this process quickly, and the odds are heavily in favor of finding a factor in this way. (Half of all numbers are even, another third are multiples of 3, and so on.) If trial division fails, then you know that the number is either prime or the product of "large" prime factors. Since testing for primality is now an "easy" matter, you might check at this stage to see if your number is in fact prime. If it is not, then you have to start looking for large prime factors.

Identify the Perfect Square

Fermat himself discovered a particularly simple way of doing this. The idea is to make use of algebraic identity:

$$x^2 - y^2 = (x + y)(x - y).$$

If N is the number you are trying to factorize (which, by this time, you will already know

Secret messages encoded using prime numbers are decipherable only if the prime factors are known.

Illustrations: The Bettmann Archive

About 350 B.C., Euclid, an ancient Greek mathematician, defined the fundamental concept of prime numbers.

Pierre Fermat, a French mathematician, claimed that all numbers of the form $2^{2n} + 1$ were prime numbers.

to be composite, odd, and without any small prime factors), you try to find numbers x and y such that:

$$N = x^2 - y^2.$$

The first identity will then give you the two factors $(x + y)$ and $(x - y)$ of N. Of course, it may be that neither of these is prime, but you can then repeat the procedure for each of them, and continue until you do get down to primes.

To find x and y, you rewrite the second equation as:

$$y^2 = x^2 - N.$$

Starting with x, the smallest number whose square exceeds N, you keep on increasing x by 1 at a time, checking at each stage to see if $x^2 - N$ is a perfect square. If it is, then the factorization is complete; otherwise, keep going.

A good example to carry out for yourself is the factorization of 119,143. The smallest number whose square exceeds 119,143 is 346, so you start out by looking at:

$$346^2 - 119{,}143 = 119{,}716 - 119{,}143 = 573.$$

Since 573 is not a perfect square, you keep

going, looking next at 347. In relatively few steps, this process leads to a factorization.

Obviously, Fermat's method is particularly (and only) suited to numbers that are the product of two roughly equal primes, both of which will then be fairly close to the square root of the number, which is where Fermat's method of searching begins.

The method used by Morrison and Brillhart to factorize F_7 has as its starting point a variant of the Fermat method. Instead of looking for solutions to $N = x^2 - y^2$, they looked for (unequal) numbers x and y (less than N) such that:

$$x^2 \bmod N = y^2 \bmod N.$$

(This is a shorthand way of saying that you get the same remainder when you divide x^2 by N as when you divide y^2 by N. For example, 14 mod 3 = 17 mod 3, because $14 \div 3 = 4$ with remainder 2; and $17 \div 3 = 5$ with remainder 2. If $x \bmod N = 0$, then N exactly divides z.) There will be many more solutions to this equation that do not satisfy the earlier equation. Accordingly, there is a much greater chance of finding a solution to this one.

Swiss mathematician Leonhard Euler found that the "prime" when Fermat's n = 5 is divisible by 641.

German mathematician Karl Freidrich Gauss linked Fermat primes with ancient Greek theories about polygons.

A solution to this equation will give a factorization, since it implies that N divides $x^2 - y^2$, or, in other words, N divides $(x + y)(x - y)$. So the highest common factor of N and $(x + y)$ will be a nontrivial factor of N. Since the algorithm gives a very efficient method of calculating highest common factors, once you have found x and y, the hard work is over.

There are various ways of making a systematic search for solutions to the equation. The method adopted by Brillhart and Morrison involved looking at the continued fraction expansion of $\sqrt{N}$. In effect, their approach replaced the problem of finding the factors of the large number N by the problem of trying to factorize several much smaller numbers. More recent modifications of this method achieve a great deal of their speed by performing these smaller factorizations in parallel, thereby making use of current computer technology.

Relying on Probability

Pollard's method, used to factorize F_8, is an example of a "Monte Carlo method." As the name suggests, such methods rely on the rules of probability to "ensure" their success. The idea is ridiculously simple, and it is easy to implement on a home microcomputer. To factorize N, you start by choosing some simple polynomial, say $x^2 + 1$, and a number x_0 less than N. Then you repeatedly calculate a whole sequence, x_0, x_1, x_2, and so on, of numbers below N by (in the case of the polynomial $x^2 + 1$) the following procedure:

$$x_{n+1} = (x_n{}^2 + 1) \bmod N.$$

As you proceed, you look at each of the numbers $x_k - x_h$ for $h = 2^i - 1$ and $2^i \le k < 2^{i+1} - 1$ (for increasing values of i.). The theory behind the method says that there is a very high probability that you will soon find values k, h such that the highest common factor of $x_k - x_h$ and N is greater than 1 (and is thus a proper factor of N), which is easily calculated using the Euclidean algorithm. The probability depends on the choice of polynomial and starting value x_0. The polynomial $x^2 + 1$ works well on numbers that microcomputers can handle. To factorize F_8, Brent and Pollard used $x^{2^{10}} + 1$. A "bad" choice of polynomial would lead to the repetition continuing indefinitely without producing a factorization.

Graham Cook, a quadraplegic unable to speak or hear, communicates with the outside world by means of a computer that he operates by remote control through head movements.

MAKING COMPUTERS WORK FOR THE DISABLED

by Frank Bowe

In Fairfax, Virginia, Rick Pilgrim, who has a spinal-cord injury that prevents him from moving even his head, works as a systems analyst for the National Institutes of Health (NIH). Thirty miles (48 kilometers) away, Kevin Riley, who has a similar injury, works as a programmer for International Business Machines Corporation (IBM). Telecommuting— using a modem-equipped personal computer in the home to receive, process, and send information back to the workplace—promises to allow severely disabled individuals to work at demanding jobs. These same technologies can permit severely disabled children to "go to school" without leaving their homes. Speech synthesizers that read print and instantly transform it to speech now give people who are blind or have dyslexia access to worlds of information previously unavailable.

The Accessibility Hurdle

However, a major problem remains before computer technology can fulfill its promise of allowing people to overcome the limitations of severe physical handicaps and learning disabilities. The technology must be designed to be fully accessible to—that is, easily usable by—people who are handicapped. Today computers are not set up to accommodate the input and output devices that many disabled people require. This means that special keyboards and other aids often require custom solutions for use with each computer, making the devices expensive and limiting their availability. If options for different users were incorporated into the design of all computers, the lives of millions of disabled individuals could be greatly enhanced.

The concept of accessibility is most familiar in the design of buildings. We see accessible architecture in the form of automatic doors and entrances level with exterior landscaping in airports, at hotels, on college campuses, and in libraries. These designs seem natural to us: they do not look as though they were created specifically for individuals who are handicapped. Most people do recognize ramps and lifts, lowered public telephones and drinking fountains, Brailled elevator buttons, and bathroom grab bars as designs with a special purpose. But whether striking or unobtrusive, architectural accessibility has opened up hundreds of thousands of buildings to use by people with disabilities.

Efforts to make information technologies more usable by and affordable to people who are disabled would not only allow a major segment of our society to communicate more easily and participate fully in productive work, but would also benefit all other users as well.

The Retrofit Solution

The architects who built America's cities were not concerned about making them accessible, since disabled people would not be living in and using the facilities. Similarly, there was no apparent reason for engineers to extend the concept of accessibility to sophisticated machinery in the mid-1970's, when high technology remained the preserve of the few. So in technology we have repeated the pattern we followed in architecture: we have designed for people with full possession of their faculties, only to discover later that we had inadvertently excluded large numbers of disabled individuals. Indeed, some 36 million Americans—15 percent of the population—have disabilities.

When Congress first passed the Rehabilitation Act, computers were still obscure and frightening machines for most Americans. These room-sized contraptions were kept in locked areas, attended by professional programmers, and intolerant of even slight errors on data-entry cards. The Apple II personal computer appeared just about the time handicapped activists stormed the U.S. Department of Health, Education, and Welfare (HEW) in April 1977 to demand enforcement of the act passed four years earlier. Yet not until 1980 and 1981, when the Apple IIe and the IBM PC were introduced, did the idea that the computer could become a commodity for the masses take hold. Dramatically lowered costs were largely the reason for the change, but so was the blossoming idea of "user friendliness": that computer hardware and software could be designed specifically for nonprogrammers.

People with disabilities were quick to grasp the potential of the personal computer to help them surmount the obstacles of everyday life. In Fort Wayne, Indiana, after a motorcycle accident left him blind, Bill Grimm wrote special software that linked an Apple IIe to a small speech synthesizer that read aloud the text on his computer screen. In Shreve, Ohio, Barry Romich built extralarge keyboards so friends with

Computer technology is proving to be an invaluable aid to the blind. Below, a computerized reading machine scans a book and reads it aloud to a blind library patron.

© Dan McCoy/Rainbow

cerebral palsy could use IBM PCs to write. And in Rockville, Maryland, John Yeh wrote machine codes allowing him to use the telephone despite his deafness.

These were all retrofit solutions, or "patches" in computer jargon—analogous to placing wooden ramps beside stairs. Custom-designed alterations were expensive, and the number of people who could afford the technologies was limited.

Special Needs

Some computer technologies designed to help people who are disabled have since become more affordable and therefore have come into more common use. For example, speech synthesizers, some now selling for as little as $100, can convert many kinds of text to artificial speech. Personal computers can also be equipped with software that translates from English to Braille for printing. But even these advances have their limitations. Most popular word-processing and business software uses the PC operating system in a way that prevents a speech synthesizer from capturing the output. Thus, many blind and dyslexic individuals are restricted to software designed specifically to be used with a speech synthesizer, reducing the choice from tens of thousands of programs to a

A Parkinson's disease victim (above) unable to write or type dictates into a headset microphone. His spoken commands are translated into computer code, virtually eliminating the need for a keyboard. Below, blind people can read computer screens using a special probe.

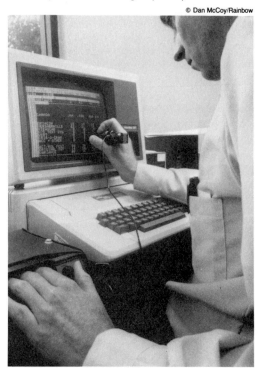

few dozen. Moreover, most synthesizers cannot read pictorial symbols (or icons) and graphics.

People with conditions that limit finger mobility, such as cerebral palsy, quadriplegia (paralysis of all four limbs), and severe arthritis, can use a light pen, joystick, or large keyboard to give the computer commands. Again, however, such keyboard substitutes work with very few commercial programs. Moreover, to make the computer think that input is coming from the standard keyboard, an "emulator" must be attached between the keyboard and the operating system. The emulator has to be custom-designed for each of the many PC models, including those produced by the same company, because there is no standard configuration now in use. The situation is similar to that of a remote-control device for a TV. Viewers can change channels by touching keys or using the remote control; an emulator in the TV allows it to respond to both kinds of input. Yet the remote-control unit cannot be used with a set of a different model. The retrofit solution helps, but it doesn't help enough.

Furthermore, because computers are not now designed to accommodate special needs, adaptations such as those allowing someone with cerebral palsy to use a PC can cost as much as $20,000. That cost could drop significantly if the problems of fitting different components together did not require custom solutions.

One-Dimensional Changes

In some cases, educators have created problems by needlessly designing software to teach some disabled children at the expense of others. Some of this software is excellent, and most is readily affordable by schools. For example, talking software teaches blind children to count, and touchpads enable children with cerebral palsy to answer questions posed on the screen. But these one-dimensional changes create barriers for other disabled students: deaf children cannot hear the talking programs. The new aids also sometimes help keep handicapped children segregated from other children. That effect runs counter to the mandate of federal law, which requires schools to integrate disabled children into regular classrooms whenever possible.

Some problems with inaccessible technology occur because decision makers don't understand the consequences of their decisions. When Drexel University in Philadelphia required all its freshmen to purchase Macintosh computers, the school apparently did not realize it was send-

Both photos: Kurzweil/Schneider

The prototype voice-controlled robot above responds to quadriplegic Bob Yee's request for a coffee mug (below). When the three-wheel, omnidirectional robot is sent to a nearby room to fetch an item, Yee can monitor the robot's movements on the screen in front of him.

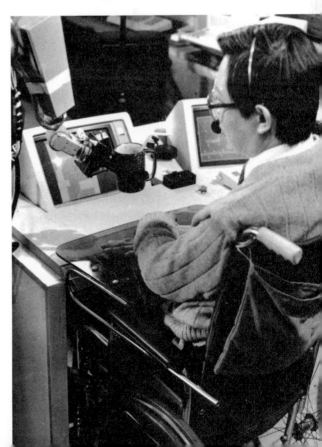

ing the message that "no blind person need apply here"—a move of questionable legality. The original Macintosh required the use of icons, which voice synthesizers cannot read. The Macintosh also used a mouse input device, which blind people cannot point effectively. Had the university chosen another machine without those restrictions, such as the IBM PC or a compatible, these problems would not have arisen. Apple has redesigned the Mac to permit keyboard entry of commands previously available only by mouse, and is doing research on the problem of enabling voice synthesizers to read icons. But such products are not yet on the market, and Drexel's action erected barriers to the disabled that need never have existed.

Designing for Access

How does one design hardware and software to be more easily usable by people with disabilities? The key concept is "transparency"— designing the parts of the PC to work together smoothly without the need for artificial aids. For example, the operating system of a transparent PC might not need an emulator because it would not distinguish between input from a keyboard and that from a joystick or other device. Users could therefore adopt whatever format for the machine that most suited their needs. Nor would the PC and its software "know" that the output was going to a voice synthesizer instead of a screen. This capacity would allow people needing a synthesizer to choose any software on the market.

The second critical idea is "redundancy"—designing hardware and software to provide output simultaneously to both the screen and synthetic speech at the user's option. If a software package throws up icons onto the screen, it should provide text as well. The text might be hidden until someone blind or dyslexic asks for it, but it would be available. Redundancy would allow users to choose how they want to use a system, while transparency would allow the hardware and software to work together smoothly with any option.

The third requirement is to ease physical access to machines. There is no good reason, for example, for locating on/off switches at the rear of a PC. There is no excuse for requiring users to press two keys simultaneously to activate a command when the keyboard and software can just as easily be designed to accept sequential keying.

These three concepts apply not only to PCs but to copiers, printers, telephones, and other technologies as well. The idea is to acknowledge the fact that different people have different needs. IBM and Xerox discovered the importance of this concept when they tried selling their big copiers in Japan: few companies wanted to buy them because they were too high and their controls were located toward the back. Like Americans using wheelchairs, Japanese of short stature couldn't reach the controls. The retrofit solution? The U.S. companies suggested that the Japanese use stools. Of course, the better solution would have been to lower the control panel.

American Telephone and Telegraph Company (AT&T) has offered redundancy as a solution to disabled people who are not dexterous enough to use coin telephones. An individual dials "O," says the word "special," and is connected to an operator who charges the call to the person's credit card. Newer phones are more obviously redundant: users can insert their credit cards directly, bypassing the coin slots altogether. Extrex Electronics even introduced a special telephone in 1984 that permits users to "answer" simply by saying "phone": the unit behaves exactly as if the user had lifted the receiver.

In California, Steven Wozniak, cofounder of Apple Computer and now president of a company called Cloud Nine, is trying to build transparency into remote-control devices so they will function with any TV, stereo, or compact disc player. It's an exciting and potentially far-reaching advance in making technologies accessible.

Legal Mandates

What are the chances that we will make our technologies as accessible as our buildings? In architecture, nothing much happened until the government made accessibility a requirement in state- and federally-assisted projects.

The Rehabilitation Act of 1973 could be used to mandate that government-assisted employers provide accessible technology. Section 504 requires any program or activity that receives federal grants to provide access for disabled people that is "equally effective" to that offered to nondisabled individuals. Section 504 also requires programs receiving federal aid to supply "auxiliary aids" so that individuals who are disabled may participate. Some lawyers argue that Congress did not intend to include personal computers, which had not even been invented in 1973, in the law's purview. Litiga-

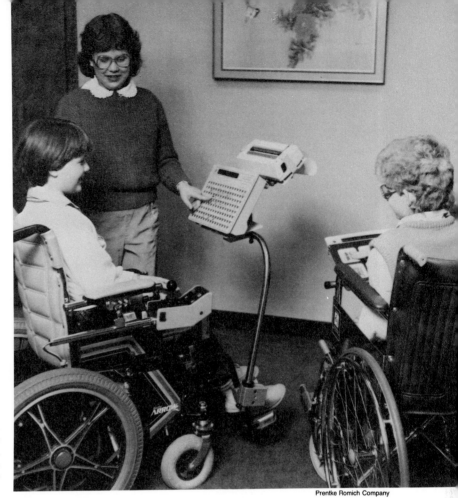

The girl at the left is learning to communicate using a light talker. She first directs an optical headpointer (or a variety of other devices according to the disability) at a square on the grid programmed to mean a certain word or phrase. The light signal is then transferred to a voice synthesizer which "speaks" the words; the words can also be printed out. The girl at right, who has touch capabilities, presses the appropriate square to activate the voice synthesizer.

Prentke Romich Company

tion will be needed to resolve that question, but none is now pending.

Section 501 of the same act requires federal agencies to make "reasonable accommodations," including providing equipment and other assistance to disabled employees so they can perform work for which they are qualified. And in Section 503, Congress mandated that the federal government's 30,000 prime contractors and 75,000 subcontractors take affirmative action and make reasonable accommodations in hiring disabled employees. But it is unclear whether these provisions mean that agencies and private employers must purchase technology that is specifically designed to accommodate the needs of handicapped workers.

When Congress reauthorized the Rehabilitation Act in October 1986, it did call upon the General Services Administration (GSA) to develop guidelines for all federal agencies in purchasing accessible PCs and other office automation equipment. The act requires the GSA to work with electronics companies and representatives of disabled consumers in writing the guidelines. Unfortunately, federal agencies often are free to accept or reject the GSA's suggestions. The agency has until October 1988 to develop the guidelines for fiscal year 1989, so the effect of the new law will be unclear for some time.

The Prognosis

If federal agencies do comply with GSA-issued requirements, the effect on making technology more accessible to disabled consumers would be dramatic. The U.S. government is the world's largest buyer of office automation equipment. In 1986 agencies purchased $845 million in hardware, software, and related products. By 1991, according to one market-research firm, government agencies will spend $1.3 billion on office automation. Virtually every computer manufacturer would want to respond by making its products more accessible.

Some disabled consumers are working through large organizations such as the Boston

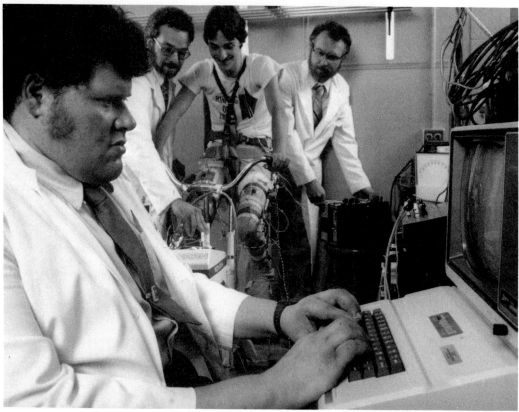

Dr. Jerrold Petrofsky at the controls of a system he developed in which a computer is programmed to generate the same pattern of electrical signals as that emitted by the brain of a person wanting to move. Here, the electrical signals are being transmitted to the legs of a young paraplegic, Greg Kramer, allowing him to pedal a stationary bicycle.

Computer Society to pressure computer manufacturers to modify their equipment. These groups could extend the pressure to manufacturers of all kinds of commodity electronics. Such consumer activism could prove to be an important supplement to government regulation, and there have been some encouraging early results. IBM hastily redesigned one of its products after shipping the first units when it realized that the device could not be used by some blind people. Xerox has added sharp contrast to the lettering on its Marathon copiers to help people with poor vision read the controls. The company also designed paper trays so that people with severely limited hand dexterity can use them easily.

Another hopeful sign is the emerging dialogue among representatives of government, industry, and disabled consumers. In February of 1984, representatives of these groups met in the Indian Treaty Room in the White House to discuss what could and should be done to make computer hardware and software more accessible. Many of the companies that attended this meeting, including Apple, Honeywell, AT&T, and Digital, are examining their product lines to determine how to redesign the next generation. These companies will have to make such concerns an ongoing part of their work, since the pace of change in electronics is so rapid that efforts to make one product more accessible would have little permanent effect.

Better for Everyone

The costs of such efforts will vary widely but need not be severe. Programming a keyboard to accept sequential keying costs nothing. A chip that allows a computer to give voice output costs only about $5. Writing code to instruct hardware and software to send information to that chip may be a lengthy and costly procedure, but possibly only the first time each manufacturer makes the effort.

Yet industry has begun to realize that equipment developed to meet the special needs of disabled consumers is more attractive and practical for everyone. Companies are working to develop computers that understand human speech not in response to the needs of people who are deaf and blind: they are doing it because many executives are reluctant to use keyboards. Workers who use their hands for other tasks, such as quality inspectors on factory assembly lines, will also find computers that recognize the human voice invaluable.

Similarly, the idea of transparency is attractive to many nondisabled users who want to be able to link hardware and software from different vendors. For example, companies are now trying to develop transparency for "local area networks": office systems in which a series of computers, printers, and other devices work together.

The idea of redundancy also appeals to many nondisabled users. Some people prefer to listen to information rather than to read it. Some like to use a mouse, while others shun the rodent. Some people prefer the mouse for

A language-disabled six-year-old gestures triumphantly after a talking word processor repeats aloud what he has typed. Speech-equipped word processors benefit millions of handicapped children and adults.

© Enrico Ferorelli

spreadsheets but find it awkward for word processing. Redundancy allows users to choose different options in different situations. The concept is simply an extension of user friendliness: it permits users to "do it their way."

The Promises

Designing electronics to accommodate diverse needs will allow tens of millions of disabled Americans to participate fully in community life. The personal computer will be able to see for blind people, remember for those who are retarded, hear for those who are deaf, and move for individuals with physical limitations.

Computers that can recognize the speech of different people—the next major advance in making this technology accessible—will revolutionize the lives of many disabled people. These machines will probably use the new Intel 80386 chips, which partition vast amounts of memory so that the computer can run several software programs at once (called "multitasking"). These chips are expected to allow programmers to design software that understands tens of thousands of words, allowing desktop computers to print what they hear as they hear it. This will enable deaf individuals to talk on the telephone, participate in meetings, even overhear gossip. The machines will also enable blind and physically disabled people to enter words and data without keying.

Such speaker-independent systems are probably still five to ten years away. IBM's experimental Tangora system now recognizes thousands of words and displays them instantly on the screen, but it and other such systems can understand only the voice that trains them. Commercial speech-recognition systems now cost about $7,000 to $9,000, but, as with all other electronics, the cost will probably drop by about 20 percent a year as they are mass-produced.

There will always be a need for special computer components and software, just as accessible buildings do not meet the needs of all disabled people. Individuals who are both blind and deaf and many who are retarded, for example, will need extraordinary measures to permit them to use electronics in everyday life. But these exceptions will be few. When society makes a commitment to making new technologies accessible to everyone, the focus will no longer be on what people cannot do, but rather on what skills and interests they bring to their work. That will be as it always should have been.

WARNING
THIS SOFTWARE MAY BE UNSAFE

by Ivars Peterson

At first glance the problem seemed minor. The Bank of New York's computer program for handling sales of government securities was supposedly designed to cope with up to 36,000 different issues. But a burst of activity on one November day uncovered a software glitch. Too little computer storage space had been allocated for keeping track of that many securities.

This error sparked a series of computer problems that damaged thousands of transaction records. Because the computer could not promptly pass on transaction data to the New York Federal Reserve Bank, the Bank of New York ended up owing as much as $32 billion. At the end of the day, it was forced to borrow about $24 billion—pledging all of its assets—to balance its accounts overnight.

This incident, which took two days to clear up, cost the Bank of New York millions of dollars in interest payments. The securities market was disrupted, and some investors lost money because of processing delays. But its greatest impact may have been on federal banking officials worried about the fragility of computer systems that handle financial transactions.

Disruptions Are Commonplace

While the Bank of New York case was the most serious problem yet caused by a banking computer malfunction, less serious disruptions occur frequently. In 1985 software and equipment problems delayed end-of-day account settlements more than 70 times, says E. Gerald Corrigan, president of the New York Federal Re-

Software snafu—the logo for a recent conference on software safety illustrates one possible consequence of a computer program gone amiss.

IEEE

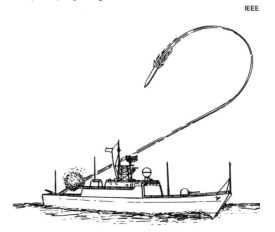

serve Bank. "It is unrealistic to expect that we will ever achieve a fail-safe payments system," he says. Yet without computers, the system couldn't work as efficiently and economically as it does.

"Like it or not," says Paul A. Volcker, Federal Reserve Board chairman, "computers and their software systems—with the possibility of mechanical or human failure—are an integral part of the payments mechanism. The scale and speed of transactions permit no other approach." Volcker and Corrigan made their remarks last December to a banking subcommittee of the U.S. House of Representatives investigating the computer failure.

Errors Are Inevitable

The U.S. banking system is not the only place where a computer failure would have disastrous consequences. Air traffic control systems, nuclear reactors and chemical plants, medical technology, defense and aerospace systems all depend heavily on computer software to function properly. The software reliability issue has also starred in the debate over the feasibility of the proposed Strategic Defense Initiative (SDI), or "Star Wars" defense.

"Our health and welfare as individuals and as a nation are increasingly dependent on the proper functioning of computer systems," says Herman O. Lubbes, Jr., of the navy's Space and

Naval Warfare Systems Command in Washington, D.C. "We have spent little time or effort to assure ourselves that we are taking proper care in the computer use." Lubbes organized and chaired a recent conference on "Computer Assurance" held in Washington, D.C.

"How can we be sure," asks Lubbes, "that vague or incomplete specifications, design flaws, or implementation errors won't result in systems [that] fail to perform when needed or perform incorrectly, . . . threatening human life and welfare?"

The problem is that errors in large, complicated computer programs are practically inevitable. John Shore, a research scientist at the Naval Research Laboratory (NRL) in Washington, D.C., writes in *The Sachertorte Algorithm* (Viking, 1985): ". . . the typical large computer program is considerably more likely to have a major, crash-resulting flaw than is the typical car, airplane, or elevator. The computer may be the ultimate machine, but today it's less trustworthy than many of its predecessors."

When designing systems and writing the computer software, says David L. Parnas, a computer scientist at NRL and Queen's University in Kingston, Ontario, "we need to know what we can and can't do."

Quality Control

Software engineers try to measure the quality of software in several ways. A computer program is considered "correct" if it always does exactly what it's supposed to do; that is, it meets specifications. Except in simple cases and by

Avionics awry. The software for the F-16 jet fighter instructed the plane to flip over whenever it crossed the equator. Fortunately, a flight simulation uncovered the error before it happened on an actual mission.

© Chris Harris/Gamma Liaison

The computer-controlled operation of a nuclear power plant makes it particularly vulnerable to software flaws.

using, for instance, formal mathematical proofs, such perfection is practically impossible to achieve. Furthermore, although extensive testing may uncover errors, it doesn't guarantee that all of them have been found. And the initial specifications may themselves be incomplete, poorly stated, or wrong.

"Reliability" expresses the probability of an error cropping up when a program is in use. High reliability means that the program is unlikely to contain many errors. Again, testing, simulations, and long experience with a program help weed out defects. Nevertheless, there is always a chance that something won't work properly.

"We often accept systems that are unreliable," says Parnas. But they should be used only if no possible system failure can lead to a disaster. A writer, for instance, could occasionally afford to lose an article because of a defect in a word processing program. It would be inconvenient, but rarely, if ever, life-threatening. The same could not be said for software that controls the firing of a ballistic missile.

Given that perfection is all but impossible to achieve, measures of "trustworthiness" try to distinguish between errors that are minor and those that could lead to catastrophic results. The idea is to find and eliminate the errors that could cause the greatest harm. In this way, "debugging" efforts are concentrated where they are most needed.

"Even if all failures cannot be prevented," says computer scientist Nancy G. Leveson of the University of California at Irvine, "it may be possible to ensure that the failures that do occur are of minor consequence."

But it's still a formidable task.

Errors Abound

Several years ago an error in the avionics software for the F-16 jet fighter instructed the aircraft to flip upside down whenever it crossed the equator. Luckily, a simulation uncovered the problem before it happened to a pilot on a mission.

More recently, an F-18's computer, which controlled the firing of a wing-mounted missile, performed the functions it was supposed to—opening the missile rack, firing the missile, and then closing the rack. Unfortunately, the rack was closed too soon, and the pilot had to contend with a "live" missile attached to his aircraft. The plane dropped about 20,000 feet (6,100 meters) before the pilot regained control.

In separate incidents, software bugs were responsible for the death of one patient and injuries to two others when an irradiation unit for cancer therapy generated "inappropriate" doses.

An error in software for evaluating the effects of earthquakes on nuclear reactors forced the temporary closing of five power plants that had been constructed according to the original, flawed computer model.

And the list goes on and on. "Experience shows that even the most carefully designed systems may have serious flaws," says Peter G. Neumann of SRI International in Menlo Park, California. "In addition, human misuse can compromise even the best systems. We must be extremely careful in doing anything at all." Neumann has documented many "computer-related disasters and other egregious horrors," as he puts it, including the ones described above, in publications of the Association for Computing Machinery in New York City.

What can be done to avoid the possibility of catastrophic software errors?

"One option is not to build these systems or not to use computers to control them," suggests Leveson. Alternatives should be looked at. Designs should include backup systems. And a given system shouldn't rely entirely on software to control critical functions.

"For the most part, however, this option is unrealistic," she admits. "There are too many good reasons why computers should be used and too few alternatives."

The experimental X-29 aircraft, for example, with its novel swept-forward wing design, is aerodynamically unstable. Only a computer can make adjustments quickly enough to fly the airplane. This new jet fighter is now being tested.

Working Backward

Leveson herself is developing a set of techniques and tools that can be used to enhance software "safety." These attempt to eliminate errors that could lead to failures resulting in death, injury, environmental harm, or loss of equipment and property.

Only a computer can make adjustments fast enough to fly the experimental X-29. A software error could prove deadly.

Courtesy the Grumman Corporation

One key element involves imagining the worst possible consequences of a system failure, then working backward to ensure that no possible path through the software leads to those results. Another approach is to examine carefully how well a software package fits in with the rest of the system it controls. Many, if not most, serious accidents are caused by multiple failures, says Leveson, and by complex, unplanned, and unfortunate interactions between components of a system.

In one famous example, the first space shuttle flight was delayed because two different computer programs, both designed to ensure that the orbiter could be flown reliably, were not synchronized. Considered separately, the programs worked, but an interface bug prevented the backup flight software from starting up at the right time.

Donald I. Good of the University of Texas at Austin argues that it may be possible mathematically to prove that computer programs—or at least significant parts of them—are completely free of logical errors. But this would be feasible only if the time it takes, for instance, to prove that a piece of software performs exactly as required for every possible input is short. That means developing automatic or mechanical theorem provers so that much less human labor is required.

Most of the elements that would go into such methods are now available, says Good. Among them is the use of "functional" programming languages, which make a logical and mathematical approach easier to implement.

Good and his colleagues have developed several schemes for mechanizing logic. These schemes have already successfully proved the correctness of some simple systems, including one 4,211-line program. "We believe that it is quite possible that the final technology will be able to produce proved systems with less human labor than is required to produce comparable, unproved systems today," says Good.

Testing of some kind, however, would still be needed. What's missing, says Good, is a basis for formulating precise statements of what the programmer is trying to do in the first place. Too often, software engineers start writing computer "code" before they really understand the problem they are trying to solve.

"We begin building systems without really understanding what we're building," says the navy's Lubbes. "We do a very poor job of expressing our intentions."

The first space shuttle flight was delayed when two otherwise correct computer programs did not interface properly.

NASA

Expert Systems

For some software developers and users, the magic words are now "artificial intelligence" or "expert systems." They suggest that computer programs that attempt to mimic the way human experts analyze and solve problems would also be useful for ensuring that programs are written correctly or for testing completed software.

The difficulty, says NRL's Shore, is that expert systems are themselves computer programs, which may contain flaws. In fact, trial-and-error methods now used to build many such systems are extremely difficult to analyze. Adding a new rule, for instance, can have quite unpredictable effects on the way the program responds. Often, the "correct" behavior itself is a matter of opinion.

"While expert systems may be more glamorous than other software," says Shore, "they are not more reliable. Like other large computer programs, expert systems suffer from the inadequacy of testing, the curse of flexibility, the existence of invisible interfaces, and other problems." The best systems, he says, are based on precise mathematical methods that impose consistency and logic.

Good expert systems may turn out to be helpful for special software-writing purposes. One such system could be used as an assistant to make sure that specifications are complete. Another could generate suitable tests. Other expert systems could perform the inspections required by the tests—a tedious, error-filled task for humans.

"But there is no guarantee of total coverage," says Stan Letovsky of Yale University. "It just provides a systematic approach."

"Human fallibility is a given," says Shore. "We must recognize this in software engineering." This means writing computer programs more carefully so that they are easier to check and easier to alter when necessary. It means testing programs again and again in many different ways. It means using the programs and watching for flaws.

Future Technology

Unfortunately, cautious approaches are often overlooked in the rush to bring software products to market or by low-bid contractors cutting corners to meet a deadline or to keep costs down in military projects. Moreover, although there are many computer programmers, too few have the skills or knowledge to develop truly reliable and trusted software. Perhaps, says computer scientist Parnas, people who call themselves software engineers ought to meet some kind of standard.

"There are a lot of good ideas around," says Lubbes. "But research and practice are still far apart."

Furthermore, the need to ensure that software is safe is growing steadily. The Food and Drug Administration (FDA) is searching for a way to inspect and regulate medical instruments that are run by computer programs. "We want safety built into consumer products," says FDA's M. Frank Houston. "But checking for safety must be made less expensive."

The National Aeronautics and Space Administration (NASA) faces a massive task in preparing to resume space shuttle flights. Somehow, NASA engineers must check millions of lines of computer software to make sure that there is no "O-ring problem smoldering in that mountain of software."

No one even knows how much shuttle software is in use. The problem is made more difficult, says Wilson, because much of the software was hurriedly patched together to meet deadlines. It was not designed for ease of testing. "We may also end up with new software if the shuttle is modified significantly," says Wilson. "That would have to be certified too."

What about the future? The next decade may see machines with a million or more processors working in parallel instead of the single processor that sits at the heart of most of today's computers. Individual computer chips may bear as many as a billion electronic devices. Light pulses rather than electronic signals may carry messages. "These new technologies present new problems," says Alfred W. Friend of the Space and Naval Warfare Systems Command. Ensuring safety will not get any easier.

"The good news is that computer system technology is advancing," says SRI's Neumann. "Given well-defined and reasonably modest requirements, good people, adequate resources, and suitably reliable hardware, systems can be built that satisfy their requirements most of the time.

"The bad news," he says, "is that completely guaranteed behavior is intrinsically impossible to achieve."

He concludes that " . . . even if we are extremely cautious and lucky, we must anticipate the occurrence of serious catastrophes in the future."

EARTH SCIENCES

Cameroon's Lake Nios, from which erupted a deadly cloud of poisonous gas that killed nearly 2,000 people.

© Orban/SYGMA

REVIEW OF THE YEAR

EARTH SCIENCE

Significant fossil discoveries, continued debate about causes of mass extinctions, unusual volcanic and earthquake activities, and new findings in the earth's core were the major earth science developments of 1986.

FOSSILS AND PALEONTOLOGY

A fossil find in Iowa shed new light as to the time when marine animals first invaded the land. Consisting of more than 500 specimens, these 340 million-year-old, salamanderlike creatures are the oldest tetrapods (four-footed animals) yet discovered. ■ And a possible ancestor of the horned dinosaurs was described from bones collected in Montana. The 7½-foot (2.3-meter) specimen—a plant-eating reptile—was a juvenile that weighed about 400 pounds (181 kilograms). The world's largest known dinosaur was found in 150 million-year-old Jurassic rocks in New Mexico. Named *Seismosaurus,* or "earth shaker," this gigantic beast measured 18 feet (5.5 meters) at the shoulder, 15 feet (4.5 meters) at the hip, was as much as 120 feet (37 meters) long, and weighed 80 to 100 tons.

Bones believed to be those of the oldest known bird were recovered from a quarry in Texas. The primitive, crow-sized bird—dubbed *Protoavis* ("first bird")—has characteristics of both birds and reptiles. It is about 75 million years older than *Archaeopteryx,* the famous fossil bird discovered in Bavaria in 1861. ■ New plant species resembling slimy green algae, discovered among the oldest known Precambrian fossils, suggest that photosynthesis began some 700 million years earlier than previously believed. These fossils offer further proof that life was present on our planet more than 3.5 billion years ago.

VOLCANOES AND VOLCANOLOGY

The floor of Lake Nios in the Cameroon was the site of a deadly eruption on August 21, 1986. The lake partially fills the crater of one of Cameroon's many extinct volcanoes. A cloud of poisonous gas burst through the lake's bottom sediments and swept over the land. This deadly mixture of carbon dioxide and hydrogen sulfide devastated herds of livestock and killed almost 2,000 people. The exact cause of this catastrophic eruption has not yet been determined, but some geologists think that an earthquake-triggered landslide disturbed the bottom sediment, thereby releasing the gas. It has also been suggested that renewed subterranean volcanic activity may have caused toxic gases trapped in the rocks below the lake to break through the lake waters and be released in the air. Another theory assumes that the gas was produced by the decay of organic matter on the lake's floor. A giant bubble formed and eventually exploded. Winds and temperature changes associated with the normal change of seasons may have also been involved.

Hawaii's Kilauea volcano continued its outpourings of lava, destroying homes and highways. Volcanologists report that Kilauea's behavior has changed radically, apparently as the result of alterations in the underground pipelines that feed its crater. The lack of towering lava fountains, more or less continual outpourings of lava, and a lake at the summit of its most recently formed cone all suggest changes in the volcano's "plumbing."

EARTHQUAKES AND SEISMOLOGY

Sporadic seismic activity in the eastern United States has led to speculation on the likelihood of stronger earthquakes such as the killer quake of 1866 that killed more than 100 people and destroyed much of Charleston, South Carolina. Attention is also being directed to the New Madrid fault. This great subsurface crustal break extends 120 miles (193 kilometers) from southern Illinois to northeast Arkansas. Three great earthquakes were spawned by this fault in December 1811 and February 1812. Felt over an area of 2.5 million square miles (762,000 square kilometers), the temblors caused the land to sink and formed present-day Reelfoot Lake. A similar quake in this area, now densely populated, would cause very heavy property damage and many casualties.

A quake measuring 6.1 on the Richter scale hit parts of California, Utah, and Nevada on July 21, 1986. Its epicenter was 12 miles (3.7 kilometers) northwest of Palm Springs. Activity along California's San Andreas fault system generated other earthquakes in April and July. In October an earthquake of magnitude 3.9 rattled south-central New Hampshire.

Also in October, an earthquake of magnitude 5.4 shook San Salvador, capital of El Salvador. Several hundred were killed, and thousands more were injured and left homeless. Two strong earthquakes, measuring 7.7 and 6.3, hit Taipei, Taiwan, in mid-November, killing 14 people and injuring 41.

TECTONICS AND EARTH STRUCTURE

Information derived from the study of earthquake waves has enabled seismologists to probe the earth's interior and make the first maps of its core, once thought to be a smooth sphere of molten metal. Instead, the maps reveal mountains higher than the Alps and canyons deeper than the Grand Canyon. Made by the new technique of seismic tomography, the maps are similar to the maps of the human brain that are produced by X rays in computerized axial tomography, or CAT scans. The core's bumpy surface is believed to develop when hot magma rises through the overlying mantle, cools, and sinks again. Geophysicists hope to interpret data from seismic tomography to discover clues as to how the mantle moves and how these movements may

© L. Boyd/Gamma Liaison

The clean-up job was almost overwhelming after San Salvador, El Salvador, was struck by a powerful earthquake.

produce energy to move Earth's great crustal plates.

A study recently completed by National Aeronautics and Space Administration (NASA) scientists suggests that tectonic movements associated with strong earthquakes along the San Andreas fault have rotated the northwest Mojave Desert about 25 degrees clockwise. The movement apparently occurred when the Pacific plate slid in a northwesterly direction along the San Andreas fault and past the North American plate. The rotation is believed to have occurred about 20 million to 16 million years ago.

By means of radio signals from the edge of the observable universe, scientists have, for the first time, been able to measure directly the amount of movement of the continental plates. As a result, it is estimated that Miami, Florida, is creeping away from Europe at the rate of four-tenths of an inch (1 centimeter) per year; Hawaii and Japan are being separated by as much as 5 inches (12.7 centimeters) per year.

WILLIAM H. MATTHEWS III

GIANTS *THAT SHAPE THE EARTH*

by Kim Heacox

Captain George Vancouver sailed the H.M.S. *Discovery* into the cold, uncharted waters of southeastern Alaska in 1794 and found what he thought was the entrance to the fabled Northwest Passage to Asia. Unfortunately, it was blocked by a 300-foot (90-meter)-high wall of ice, "extending," he said, "from shore to shore and connected with a range of lofty mountains." Vancouver, of course, was wrong about the Northwest Passage. Behind the wall was more ice—hundreds of square miles of glacier, a frozen river flowing to the sea.

Eighty-five years later, a bearded, blue-eyed naturalist from California paddled a canoe to the same place. Captain Vancouver would have been shocked. Where ice thousands of feet thick had once buried the land, a new world had unfolded with valleys, ridges and fjords. The massive glacier had split in two and retreated 50 miles (48 kilometers)—and the ecstatic canoeist, John Muir, had discovered Glacier Bay.

It is difficult to think of huge masses of ice as being restless and even mysterious. But these throwbacks to the Ice Age can be frighteningly unpredictable, causing dramatic changes in the shape of the land and threatening to wreak havoc in Alaskan sea lanes. They remain a mystery to scientists, who are using increasingly sophisticated techniques in an attempt to gain some understanding of glaciers' "behavior."

Alaska has more than 100,000 glaciers covering some 29,000 square miles (75,000 square kilometers), an area almost the size of South Carolina. Originating in vast ice fields thousands of feet thick, the smallest glaciers are scattered throughout isolated basins and valleys. The largest, the Bering Complex, measures some 2,250 square miles (5,825 square kilometers)—ten times larger than all the glaciers in the lower 48 states combined.

How Does a Glacier Form?

Snow that accumulates and survives a summer without melting compacts into solid granules called firn. Beneath the pressure of successive layers of snow, the firn crystallizes into glacial ice. This isn't the same stuff that forms in your refrigerator; glacial ice is similar to metamor-

phic rock, having hardened under extreme pressure for hundreds of years. It is denser and less porous than standard ice. When hit by light, it absorbs the red end of the spectrum, giving the glacier's walls a pristine blue color. But the ice is not pure; trapped within it are pollen, algae, sediment, gravel, boulders, and meltwater.

Meltwater? Shouldn't water freeze inside glaciers? Yes, if the ice is cold enough. But apparently, the summer temperature of most Alaskan glaciers is exactly freezing: 32° F (0° C). Only at that temperature can flowing water come in contact with ice without either changing into the other. The flowing water forms ice caves with ceilings that sometimes soar 30 feet (9 meters). Geologists say this is typical of "warm" glaciers—as opposed to the "cold" glaciers of Greenland and Antarctica, which are below freezing throughout the year and have no meltwater flowing within them.

Glacial Retreat

Warm temperatures, along with a lack of snow, can cause glaciers to retreat—leaving behind spectacular formations like Glacier Bay. But glaciers usually flow downhill. Thus, how can they "retreat"? A glacier's position is determined by its leading face, or terminus.

Although some glaciers terminate in a flat sheet of ice, many others do so with ice walls that can rise hundreds of feet above the sea. Towers of ice lean precariously from these walls, groaning and teetering as the tides rise and fall beneath them. These towers often break off, or "calve," into the sea with a thundering crash. Hundreds of icebergs are born by such glacial sacrifice. If calving of the ice—along with melting at lower elevations—exceeds the rate of snow accumulation at higher elevations, the terminus will fall back, thus putting the glacier in retreat. When snow accumulation is heavy, the ice face inches forward and the glacier is considered to be advancing.

Most of Alaska's glaciers have been retreating steadily since the Ice Age, or about 10,000 years. One of the most spectacular of those now in retreat is the 40-mile (64-kilometer)-long Columbia Glacier, which empties into Prince William Sound. To glaciologists, it offers a look at a phenomenon rarely witnessed: the collapse of a glacier. Last year the Columbia discharged about 1.2 cubic miles (5 cubic kilometers) of ice into the sea and retreated two-thirds of a mile (1 kilometer). "The icebergs were so thick," recalls Carolyn Driedger, a

Glacier spectating and spelunking. Tourists in an Alaskan fjord (top) take a close-up look at an iceberg, which formed when a large chunk of ice broke off, or calved, from a glacier. Below, an explorer checks the icy walls of a cave in the heart of Alaska's Muir glacier.

hydrologist with the U.S. Geological Survey (USGS), "that we could no longer maneuver our vessels up to the face of the glacier."

Galloping Glaciers

The scientists were coming face-to-face with the glacier in an attempt to probe the water's depth. This is crucial to the stability of all tidewater glaciers—those, like the Columbia, that flow into the sea. When the terminus moves into deep water, the glacier becomes unstable and may start to retreat. Throughout the past decade, the Columbia's terminus rested securely on a muddy shoal. Last year, though, the glacier receded completely off the shoal and into water ten times deeper. The glacier's calving rate suddenly accelerated. "The Columbia is on the run," says Driedger. In the next few decades, it could retreat 25 miles (40 kilometers), open a new fjord, and discharge 50 cubic miles (208 cubic kilometers) of ice into Prince William Sound.

This gives shipping officials pause. Just east of Prince William Sound lies Port Valdez, terminus of the Trans-Alaska Oil Pipeline. Tankers carry oil south from Valdez to refineries in the lower 48 states. Large icebergs have drifted into shipping lanes, creating a nightmare for sailors. "We're taking no chances," says one oil company spokesman. "When the sun goes down, our tankers stop running."

There may be a solution, albeit an expensive one. The U.S. Coast Guard has proposed stretching a cable or nylon net from Glacier Island to mainland Alaska to trap the drifting icebergs.

Advancing glaciers can be equally worrisome to people, especially when they suddenly lunge forward, or "surge." One of the most spectacular surges in modern times took place in Alaska during the winter of 1936–37, when the Black Rapids Glacier advanced 3 miles (4.8 kilometers) in six months, threatening to overrun a highway near the Delta River. Alaskans nicknamed it the "Galloping Glacier."

Measuring Surge

Today scientists are still not sure what causes the phenomenon. They have discovered, to their puzzlement, that a glacier that surges has its own internal clock, thrusting forward with astonishing regularity. Some accelerate every 10 years, others every 100. The most plausible explanation is meltwater, which pools beneath the glacier, spreading out and lubricating the interface between ice and rock. Meltwater accumulates for a certain number of decades until it finally reaches a threshold, and then the glacier suddenly slides downhill as much as 100 times faster than normal.

Researchers can now measure such surges with greater accuracy than ever before. "Glacial movements used to be determined by comparisons of photographs over time," says Bruce Molnia, a USGS glaciologist who has conducted extensive studies in Alaska. "Now new techniques using lasers can measure movements of one-millionth of an inch from a mile away."

One Alaskan glacier, the Variegated, has been studied more intimately: scientists have camped right on top of it. Located in a valley near the head of Yakutat Bay in the southeastern corner of the state, Variegated surged 8,000 feet (2,400 meters) between November 1982 and July 1983. It eventually reached a velocity of 200 feet (61 meters) per day.

Another Ice Age Coming?

Glaciologist Barclay Kamb of the California Institute of Technology (Cal Tech) says the movement of the ice, its "continuous snapping, cracking, and thudding," kept the researchers awake at night. "It was unbelievable," agrees a colleague. "We could hear a meltwater river rumbling deep beneath the glacier. The ice was alive."

During the Ice Age, great continental glaciers were even livelier. They flowed and ebbed over much of North America, creating the Great Lakes, Puget Sound, Manhattan Island, and Cape Cod.

Some scientists believe that we are currently experiencing a warm respite of an ongoing Ice Age, and that once again the glaciers will march down from the north. Other glaciologists think that rising levels of carbon dioxide in the atmosphere will trap the sun's energy, warm the Earth, and keep the glaciers at bay.

The scientists' uncertainty is excusable. After all, it's difficult enough to know what a single glacier will do next—let alone a whole continent of the capricious giants.

SELECTED READINGS

"Glacier turns a fjord into a lake" by H. E. McLean. *Oceans*, November–December 1986.
"High time on a glacier." *National Geographic World*, July 1985.
"Glaciers on the run" by J. Beard. *Science 85*, January–February 1985.

In June 1986 the towering walls of Alaska's Hubbard Glacier began to crumble (above), dropping tons of icy debris into the mouth of Russell Fjord. Dozens of seals, cut off from their normal saltwater environment, began to turn an unhealthy shade of muddy brown (left). Racing against time, animal-rescue volunteers airlifted to the scene began returning the trapped seals to the sea on stretchers (below). The problem finally solved itself when the ice dam plugging the fjord suddenly collapsed, allowing the remaining animals to escape on their own.

High winds from Hurricane Frederic whip the beaches of the Alabama Gulf coast in advance of the storm's landfall.

STORM WARNINGS

by Thomas Leahy

For the National Hurricane Center, 1985 was a busy year, and the most frenetic month was September. Hurricane Elena had just finished its devastation of the Mississippi coast when the weather system that became Hurricane Gloria began forming off the coast of Africa. Feeding on moist air and warm tropical waters, Gloria quickly matured into one of the most powerful hurricanes ever recorded in the open Atlantic, carrying winds of 150 miles (240 kilometers) per hour.

Activity at the Hurricane Center

The National Hurricane Center is on the sixth floor of the IRE Financial Building in Coral Gables, Florida. During the life of Gloria, the Center's lights burned all night. Every 30 minutes the video terminals displayed a new satellite image of the hurricane's movements as the staff tracked her course toward the Carolinas. As Gloria's winds swirled around the eye of the storm, the action in the operations center revolved around the National Hurricane Center's director, Dr. Neil Frank.

When Frank was not talking on one of the telephones clustered on a table, he was checking the latest charts, studying the satellite view of the storm on one of the video terminals, consulting with his staff members, and making decisions. He held brief press conferences, and, from time to time, he would be wired for sound, the television lights would come on, cameras would roll, and Neil Frank would explain in his down-home drawl just what Gloria was doing and what she might do.

"The electronic media," Frank says, "have become essential to the warning process." And warning is what the National Hurricane Center does. Before Hurricane Gloria died, Frank gave over 250 briefings.

Gloria had been ranked a borderline Category Five storm, the strongest rating on the Saffir-Simpson scale used to rank hurricanes in much the same way as the Richter scale ranks earthquakes. The storm had weakened after bypassing the Bahamas, but with winds up to 130 miles (210 kilometers) per hour, it still posed a substantial threat to the East Coast. Frank's hurricane specialists knew that if Gloria hit the Carolinas at that strength, she could cause major destruction.

But she didn't. After giving North Carolina's Outer Banks a strong brush with her peripheral winds, Gloria weakened. She skipped along the northeast coastal areas and crossed Long Island and Connecticut—spawning strong winds that knocked down trees and knocked out electrical power—and touched Rhode Island and Massachusetts before passing Maine and dying out at sea.

During a hurricane, Neil Frank has no time for in-depth interviews or backgrounders on the post he has held since 1974, or on the mission of the National Hurricane Center. When a hurricane is on the way, Frank and his staff of 35 work shifts around the clock, monitoring the storm and issuing information, including—if necessary—warnings.

When no hurricane is threatening, Frank talks: he gives speeches and interviews, moving along the Gulf and Atlantic coasts regaling audiences with stories of past major hurricanes and describing what can happen when a major storm arrives at a highly developed coastal area.

"We have a people problem" is the way Frank puts it. So many people are concentrated on waterfront property and offshore islands that they can't reach high ground within the lead times of the Center's warnings. He says, "I'm not sure we can evacuate places where we have such large groups of people."

Local governments—not Neil Frank—are legally responsible for evacuating the populace from the path of an oncoming hurricane. Frank and the National Hurricane Center are responsible for finding and tracking hurricanes, for forecasting their behavior, and for issuing the appropriate warnings.

From June 1 to November 30 each year, the Center usually tracks as many as 100 tropi-

Satellite photo shows the distinct eye of a Gulf Coast hurricane and the tightly wound cloud circulation around it.

NOAA

cal waves (atmospheric waves, not ocean waves). Typically, 10 of these waves develop into storms—of which six grow into hurricanes.

Life Cycle of a Hurricane

A hurricane "scenario," according to Bob Sheets, acting deputy director of the Center, usually begins with pictures from a geostationary weather satellite 22,300 miles (35,887 kilometers) above the equator, which are received every 30 minutes by an antenna at Wallops Island, Virginia. The pictures, relayed to the National Hurricane Center through a facility at Suitland, Maryland, show about one-third of the globe and give the first hint of any weather disturbances, usually in the form of tropical "waves"—which are vast movements of air, not water. If one of these waves begins to spiral into a closed circle, it then forms a low-pressure center and is classified as a "tropical depression."

When a depression or other system moves within range, special weather observation aircraft, from either the U.S. Air Force or from the National Oceanic and Atmospheric Administration (NOAA), are ordered into the area. They fly into the eye of the storm and report by radio on the velocity of the winds and the exact location. At the Center, this information is then plotted on a map. If the tropical depression continues to gather strength and if the sustained winds reach 39 miles per hour (63 kilometers per hour), the depression is designated a "tropical storm" and given a name. When the winds reach 74 miles per hour (119 kilometers per hour), the storm becomes a hurricane.

As the hurricane builds strength, the National Hurricane Center issues advisories every six hours, increasing this frequency up to every three hours—or even more frequently—as the storm approaches land.

Charting Its Progress

In the chart room at the Center, six Teletypes continually receive numerical data on weather conditions over North America, Central America, the northern part of South America, the Caribbean, and the Atlantic Ocean across to Africa. Frank assembles information for an advisory from these data and the information plotted on maps that show the storm's progress, from firsthand reports of storm-traversing aircraft on wind velocity and location, and from time-lapse pictures of the storm based on the

satellite images on the video terminal. At this point, Frank must decide whether to issue a "hurricane warning," which might trigger mass evacuations in the target coastal areas. If the meteorological data indicate that a hurricane warning should be issued, local officials in the affected areas are the first consulted about the wording of the warning—to make it as effective as possible.

Neil Frank admits that he and his staff do a very effective job of observing a storm. With radar, a satellite picture every 30 minutes that they can manipulate to show the cloud actions, and special observation aircraft they can send right inside a storm, they have every meteorological tool available to do the job, and the expertise to use the tools.

The same technology permits people sitting at home to see satellite pictures of the storm on television. Frank believes this has a tendency to make people feel lees vulnerable, to feel that with all the wonderful technology available to observe the weather, the National Hurricane Center must be doing a great job of forecasting. Frank does not agree.

"In the past 10 years," he says, "weather data collection has become so efficient that it has far outdistanced the expertise of our hurricane forecasters. Our forecasting skills have improved perhaps only 10 or 15 percent over the past 25 years, despite satellites and sophisticated computers."

Rivers of Air

To do a good job of forecasting a storm, you must know what is going on in the environment around it. The problem is, Frank adds, the Center does not get meteorological reports from over the vast regions of the Atlantic. There is an occasional ship report during the daytime, but not at night. ("Radio operators on ships don't like to stay up until midnight.") And they receive a few reports from airplanes flying across the top of the atmosphere: reports from up top and down on the surface, but nothing in the middle. "We don't have direct observations in this area in the middle part of the atmosphere where the steering currents are generated," Frank says.

Tracking storms, on the ground and in the air. At the National Hurricane Center (top), meteorologists monitor storms around the clock. Once one becomes threatening, weather observation aircraft (bottom) fly into its eye and take readings.

Photos: Paul Chelsey/Photographers Aspen

Hurricanes actually move along in rivers of air, Frank explains, just as a block of wood moves along a river of water. But with one basic difference: in the atmosphere, there are no riverbanks to contain the rivers of air—so they move around. The problem is to identify those "rivers" and then to try to predict where they are going to eventually move. They are generated over the middle of the ocean by large high-pressure areas; but the Center doesn't have any observers out there to determine what those rivers of air look like or where they might carry a storm. There is another complication: when one river of air on which a storm is moving encounters another river that comes wandering along from the top of the atmosphere, there is an interaction.

"It is this interaction that we don't evaluate very well sometimes," Frank says. "It's almost like trying to forecast where a novice bowler is going to throw a bowling ball. It might end up in the left gutter, or right gutter, or it might go right down the middle of the alley. What we're talking about is an alley, but it's 200 miles [320 kilometers] wide. We don't know if the hurricane is going to be on the left side or the right side or down the middle."

Populous Coasts

It sounds bleak to say that little more could be done from a meteorological standpoint to improve warnings. But Frank indicates that warnings could be made more effective. He and his staff have been concentrating for the past few years on education programs for coastal residents and for county commissioners, emergency management officials, and other decision makers to help them develop a clearer understanding of the uncertainties of the warning process.

Reflecting on the evolution of the Center's warning process, Neil Frank says, "When I took over in 1974, I asked, 'What is the hurricane problem?'

"My staff said, 'What do you mean? Here's our accuracy and here are the techniques we use to forecast.'

Dr. Neil Frank (left), director of the National Hurricane Center, reviews charts with an associate before issuing an updated forecast.

© Thomas Leahy

Getting out: residents of beach communities often ignore evacuation warnings until the storm has already struck.

"I asked again, 'What's the hurricane problem? How many people living along our coastline have ever experienced a major hurricane?' Well, nobody knew."

By 1980 they had gotten the census data for every coastal county from Texas to Maine to see how the population had grown from 1970 to 1980. Then they checked the date of the last great hurricane to see how many people lived in the affected counties at that time. They learned that among 40 million people living in the coastal counties from Texas to Maine, 32 million had never experienced a major hurricane.

Evacuation Lead Times

Next, Frank began to wonder how long it would take to evacuate these people. Historically, the Center had been giving a 12-hour lead time, although he didn't know why it was 12 hours. ("It was probably within the framework of their skills at that time.") They did know, however, that with the 12-hour warning time, half the evacuation orders later proved unnecessary. In 1978 Lee County in southwest Florida did the first comprehensive study of the evacuation problem. They found that they could evacuate

Sanibel, an offshore barrier island, in less than 10 hours. But when residents of Fort Myers Beach, Cape Coral, and other nearby areas in Florida were included, the time nearly doubled—to 18 hours.

"A six-county study after that, from Sarasota to Naples, disclosed that evacuation time for some of those communities goes to 27 hours," Frank continues. "In other areas where there have been studies, the results are frightening. It takes between 25 and 30 hours to evacuate the Galveston Bay area, the Florida Keys, and the southwest Florida coast. It takes 20 to 25 hours to evacuate the Miami–Fort Lauderdale area and the Tampa Bay area, and the time is increasing one hour a year. In every place where we've done a study, there is not one where the evacuation time is under 12 hours.

"We haven't even completed studies in the northeastern states. In places like Delaware, Virginia, Maryland, and New Jersey, the studies haven't even been started. We are trying to get the New Orleans and southeastern Louisiana study completed. But in the middle of the 1985 hurricane season and in over half of our coastal areas, we don't even know how long it takes to

Beached by a hurricane. These three oceangoing freighters bear grim testimony to the storm's awesome power.

evacuate. And we're trying to provide warnings!"

One point of the Center's information, and of the warnings, is improved preparation, at sea as well as on shore. Hurricanes can pose a threat not only to coastal lands but to vessels on the ocean. During a tropical storm or hurricane, advisories go out to all ships (U.S. and international) on the entire Atlantic Ocean every six hours. Center staff people work closely with private meteorological organizations, providing advisories and exchanging information. Many oil companies have their own meteorologists who receive information from the Center and modify it so their companies can make decisions necessary to safeguard their interests. AMOCO meteorologists, for example, call the Center daily to check on storms because of their concerns for oil rigs in the Gulf of Mexico and for their tankers moving along the eastern seaboard.

Issuing a Warning

If possible, we want to encourage governments, lawmakers, and elected officials to adopt better codes and more realistic building practices, Frank says. "I don't have that as a direct mission, but I am certainly sympathetic to it, and if I have an opportunity to speak to it, I certainly speak to it. I think there are things we could do to help minimize the dollar loss. Maybe not permit any building within 100 yards [90 meters] of the waterfront, for example. I have never made a statement against development on barrier islands or on waterfront property, but I am certainly concerned about them being death traps.

"When we found out that the lead time of 12 hours was not sufficient for most locations, we made adjustments, but these adjustments have just come in the past five years. What we try to do now is to issue a hurricane watch with 24- to 30-hour lead time. This means that there is a storm out there, but it may not pose a threat; however, be prepared to evacuate in the event the storm does come your way. We try to give an 18- to 24-hour lead time on a hurricane warning for evacuation. What we are trying to do is make our warnings consistent with the lead time local officials require."

But Neil Frank knows that even with sufficient lead time, there remains the critical problem of just how well people understand the hazard of great hurricanes, and how well they will respond to warnings. That's why he puts so much emphasis on public awareness.

"Now, as for the reaction of people who receive the warnings, that becomes a matter of a behavioral response. But with a warning where there is lead time before the event arrives, most persons will ask themselves three questions. 'Is there a threat?' We can show there is, through

event of a hurricane that you have about auto insurance? I've paid automobile insurance all my life, and at the end of a year I've never written the company or cussed at it because I didn't have a major accident. I'm very happy if I didn't have an accident and didn't have to collect. So when we post a hurricane warning, what I tell people along the coastline is this: I pledge to you never to post a hurricane warning if there isn't a threat. I won't always guarantee that when we put a warning up, the storm is going to come over you. What I would like you to do, in terms of attitude, is to say: 'O.K. Neil, you tell me when there's a threat, and then I'm going to take my action.'

"Anytime we post a hurricane warning with 24-hour lead time, probably 80 percent of the people will be evacuated unnecessarily," Frank points out. "In other words, only once in about five times will it be necessary. If we reduce the lead time to 12 hours, we're only going to be wrong maybe 50 percent of the time. If we stretch it to 24 hours, those coastal residents are going to have to pay the price of being overevacuated and overwarned. I don't consider that too high a price to pay."

An Active Season

The 1985 hurricane season officially ended on November 30 of that year, but not before Hurricane Juan formed in the Gulf of Mexico and came ashore in Louisiana, causing widespread damage during the last days of October. And not before Hurricane Kate emerged from the Caribbean via Cuba and the Florida Keys to hit the Gulf Coast (where some 100,000 did evacuate). It was an extraordinary season. Not since 1933 had two hurricanes hit the U.S. coast in the same month, as had Elena and Gloria in September. Hurricane Bob had earlier come ashore in South Carolina, and Danny in Louisiana. When Kate came ashore in Florida, it marked only the second time in this century that six or more hurricanes had made landfall in the U.S. in one season. For Neil Frank, another kind of season was beginning. During the "off-season," he will speak to thousands of people in the coastal areas about the hazards of hurricanes, of hurricane forecasting, and how to understand and respond to hurricane warnings.

"Hurricanes are relatively rare events," Frank says. "People may live for a long time on the waterfront and never be threatened. But if they do live there, they need to prepare for the worst."

the electronic media. There's the satellite picture on television. The threat is indeed real. The next question is, 'Is that meteorological danger out there going to threaten me where I live?' And the last question—'Can I do something to minimize my risk?' "

Frank responds: "How about taking the same attitude toward protecting your life in

Emil Schulthess

THE MYSTERIOUS OZONE HOLE

by Ray Spangenburg and Diane Moser

It could be a science fiction movie of the 1950's. All the elements are there. A gigantic hole suddenly appears in the atmosphere over cold and isolated Antarctica—a breach in the ozone layer that leaves the Earth vulnerable to dangerous rays from outer space. A team of top scientists is put together in a hurry to fly a special "spy plane" into the area and investigate.

You might still catch the whole thing on the late show, maybe showing back-to-back with *The Thing from Outer Space* or *The Giant Spider Invasion*. Only it's not a movie. It's what's happening today, and the danger is not imaginary but very real.

The "hole" is a new character in a drama that has been playing out since the 1970's, when scientists first focused on the problem of ozone depletion in the atmosphere. Opinions about the severity of the ozone depletion problem have zigzagged ever since, and no one yet has come up with conclusive evidence about the causes— or what we can expect for the future.

In the early 1970's, F. Sherwood Rowland and Marlo J. Molina, both at the University of California at Irvine, threw the spotlight of suspicion on chlorofluorocarbons (CFCs), often referred to by the trade name Freon, and in 1978 the Environmental Protection Agency (EPA) banned the use of CFCs in aerosol cans in the United States. Judging by new evidence, however, it now looks as if that move wasn't far-reaching enough, or that the problem is really more complex, or both.

In the mid-1980's the drama has come to a sudden and unexpected head: high in the skies over Antarctica, near the fringes of outer space, scientists have discovered in the ozone layer a huge, gaping hole that develops each year in September and October, then closes up again. This has been going on, it turns out, since 1973. First reported by British scientists, the discovery sent National Aeronautics and Space Administration (NASA) scientists scurrying back through data collected by the Total Ozone Mapping Spectrometer (TOMS) instrument on board the Nimbus 7 weather satellite. From their research came more alarming news: from 1978 to 1985, a period for which data are available, the size and depth of the hole have steadily increased. Then, in November 1986, the ozone hole disappeared entirely.

"Nontrivial" Destruction

As Joe Pinto, a Harvard atmospheric chemist visiting at NASA's Ames Research Center, puts it, "It's important as an indication of what could be in store for the future. The actual amounts of ozone that are being destroyed in this hole are really nontrivial." Pinto sees the "hole" as an indicator of what might be going on in the rest of the atmosphere, a kind of concentration of the worldwide problem.

Ozone has been an essential part of Earth's ecology for a billion years or more. Early in the planet's history, once plants began to contribute oxygen to the atmosphere, ozone also began to form through the interaction of solar energy and oxygen. As a result, an ozone (or, in chemistry

Images created by the Total Ozone Mapping Spectrometer (TOMS) over a period of six weeks in 1986. On August 22 the outline of the ozone hole is indicated by bands of light and dark blue. By September 2 the ozone hole has deepened and expanded. One month later the region of very low ozone (violet color) covers an area the size of the U.S. The depth of the ozone hole reached its maximum on October 10. By mid-November (not shown) the hole had disappeared entirely.

Illustrations: NASA

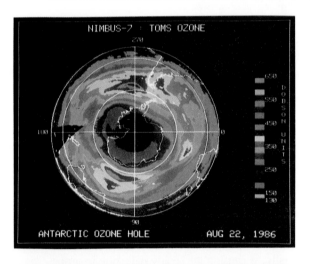

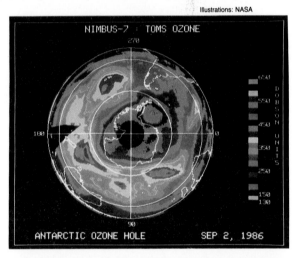

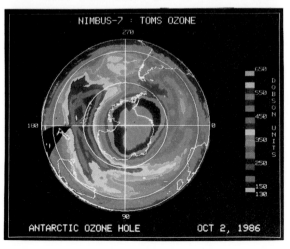

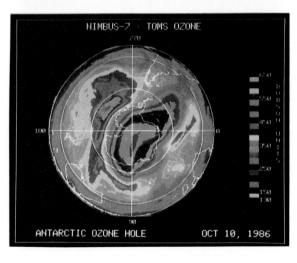

Scientists prepare to launch a balloon to measure ozone levels in the stratosphere over Antarctica. Such balloon studies—called soundings—are performed three times per week.

National Science Foundation

shorthand, O_3) layer formed—a vast shield centered about 20 miles (32 kilometers) above the planet that protects terrestrial life from ultraviolet radiation that can be harmful, even lethal.

Without the ozone layer, life as we know it would never have developed, and the layer's relatively sudden destruction high in the stratosphere poses a very real problem. It is estimated that the amount of ultraviolet light reaching the Earth's surface increases by 1 to 3 percent for each 1 percent loss in ozone. Damaging effects on crops, farm animals, plankton, and human life could be serious, with estimated increases in the number of human skin cancer cases running into the hundreds of thousands.

According to Susan Solomon, a research scientist at the National Oceanic and Atmospheric Administration (NOAA) Aeronomy Laboratory, the change in ozone in Antarctica "has increased systematically over the last 10 to 15 years, so that every year in the spring there is a little bit less ozone than there was the year before." Now, judging from satellite data and from ground-based instruments, she says there is "only about 50 percent of what there used to

be in the late 1960's and early '70's, so the ozone layer has depleted by half. That is just a totally unprecedented change in the total column."

Expeditions Under Way

But why Antarctica? Why does the hole develop and then disappear? Will it spread? And what, finally, is causing the steady reduction in ozone worldwide? The questions have multiplied, along with the theories to answer them, and specialists in atmospheric research have begun a rapid marshaling of forces to go to the Antarctic and gather hard new evidence.

A ground expedition of 13 researchers, led by Solomon, set off into the frigid winter night of the American base at McMurdo Sound. Organized by the National Science Foundation and composed of groups from NOAA, NASA's Jet Propulsion Laboratory (JPL), the University of Wyoming at Laramie, and the State University of New York at Stony Brook, the expedition is using advanced instrumentation to fill in some of the gaps in our knowledge. "Right now," says Solomon, "all we know is what ozone is doing. We don't really know anything about any of the other molecular species."

The Laramie group is using balloons to measure ozone in the stratosphere, doing about three soundings a week. At the same time, they are measuring the particle size distributions inside polar stratospheric clouds. The other three groups are running ground-based measurements in different regions of the spectrum. The Stony Brook crew is working in the microwave region and is measuring chlorine monoxide and ozone. The NOAA group is measuring NO_2, ozone, NO_3, and $OClO$ in the visible region of the spectrum, and JPL is looking at a wide range of molecules in the infrared. If successful, Solomon expects the teams to come home in early November with new results that will help weed out or refine some of the several competing theories intended to explain the hole.

Meanwhile, NASA Ames scientist Estelle Condon has begun putting together yet another expedition to Antarctica—this one airborne—that could yield even firmer results, if it gets off the ground.

High-Altitude Research

Condon's researchers hope to use NASA's ER-2 ("Earth Resource-2") plane, a special high-altitude atmospheric research aircraft that operates at 65,000 to 70,000 feet (20,000 to 21,350 kilometers)—exactly the same altitude, according to Pinto and Phil Russell, head of the NASA Ames Atmospheric Experiments Branch, where

the ozone problem has developed in the stratosphere. The ER-2—carrying sensors that can measure nitrogen oxides, CFCs, ozone, and other chemicals—provides the only opportunity for making the needed chemical and meteorological measurements at the actual site of the problem.

Basically a larger, civilian version of the U-2 spy plane, with sophisticated atmospheric testing instruments on board, the ER-2 was originally outfitted for a related study, the Stratosphere-Troposphere Exchange Project (STEP), which will investigate the chemistry and dynamics of clouds over Australia. That study may also cast some light on the ozone question, according to Pinto, since STEP will take a close look at the very strong vertical mixing that goes on in that area, which may contribute to the rise of CFCs into the stratosphere.

After completing the STEP mission and making some minor instrument changes, according to current plans, the NASA ER-2 will head for Antarctica toward the end of the Antarctic winter, in September 1987. But, while its high-altitude capacity makes it the ideal researcher for the Antarctic hole, several other factors about the flight worry Condon and her colleagues.

According to Russell, "It looks like a very difficult flight for the ER-2. There's a real safety question about the feasibility of the expedition, and NASA's going to be taking a very hard look at that." The airplane, explains Condon, is

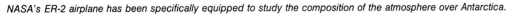

NASA's ER-2 airplane has been specifically equipped to study the composition of the atmosphere over Antarctica.

NASA

essentially a one-engine glider operated by a single pilot. Operation over the cold waters of the Antarctic could prove hazardous, especially after considering possible landing complications like crosswinds and icy runways.

"The potential for problems is large," says Condon. "The aircraft people will do a complete hazards analysis for this mission before the decision is made about whether we can in fact take our ER-2 down there." Political and budgetary problems also plague plans for the $1.5 million mission, and Condon says, "It's going to be a real challenge to pull it together in less than a year." But if it flies, the ER-2 could be crucial to resolving the ozone question.

A DC-8 jet, also now set up with instrumentation for the STEP program, may fly the Antarctic mission, too, supplying valuable data from lower altitudes.

Are CFCs the Culprits?

Exactly what do Solomon and Condon and their teams expect to find out? The possibilities are complex, much more so than originally thought. Some 200 chemical reactions in the stratosphere alone may play a role.

Lead suspects for the cause of ozone depletion are still the now-infamous CFCs. They were first developed between 1928 and 1931 by industry giants General Motors and Du Pont, and they caught on fast with manufacturers and consumers. Commonly used as propellants in spray cans, as refrigerants in air-conditioning and refrigeration, and as a foaming agent in the manufacture of polyurethane foam, they seemed ideal for a number of reasons. They were inert, they were nontoxic, and they did the job. Since that time, it is estimated that we have poured several million tons of CFCs into the atmosphere.

But the same properties that made CFCs so useful also made them prime suspects in the ozone depletion mystery. Solomon, whose theory naming CFCs as the culprit was recently published in *Nature,* says that, unlike other man-made pollutants, chlorofluorocarbons do not break up or rain out of the lower atmosphere. "There's no way to get rid of them," she says. "Once you put them in, they just last forever in the troposphere [the atmospheric layer where weather occurs], and they eventually sort of percolate up to the stratosphere.

"So when the chlorofluorocarbons get just above the ozone layer, they start hitting all that ultraviolet light and they start photolyzing—

they get dissociated by the light they encounter. And that produces chlorine atoms." The free chlorine then combines with ozone, according to several theorists, in a complex catalytic reaction that destroys the ozone and produces yet more chlorine. "So the more inert a chlorofluorocarbon is, the more dangerous it is," Solomon concludes.

There's also a correlation that casts further suspicion on CFCs, Philip Russell explains. "The ozone depletion increased just at the time that Freons were increasing in the atmosphere. It's very suggestive because theories predict that Freon should deplete ozone."

"But the picture is very clouded," Russell adds, "because the models that we use to predict stratospheric ozone depletions by Freons did not predict this Antarctic ozone hole. The models have to have something else added to them in order to predict it."

Unique Antarctic Environment

For this reason, both Solomon's and Condon's expeditions are looking carefully at other trace elements in conjunction with ozone. They're also looking for unique factors about the Antarctic that might explain why the hole has appeared there and not, say, in the Arctic or elsewhere in the Northern Hemisphere.

"What is unique about Antarctica is that it really is the coldest place on Earth," says Solomon. "The temperatures in Antarctic winter and spring are about 15 to 20 degrees colder than the corresponding temperatures in the Arctic winter and spring, and that makes all the difference between clouds and no clouds."

The clouds, Solomon believes, may provide a special environment for chemical reactions, so that "the presence of the clouds makes the chlorine come out of an inert form and turns it into a form that is potentially very damaging to the ozone layer." There's no more chlorine present in the Antarctic than anywhere else, she thinks, but, as chlorine's presence in the stratosphere rises worldwide, the special conditions are accentuating the results. Furthermore, she suggests, there has been no increase in naturally formed sources of chlorine: "It's the man-made, the industrial chlorofluorocarbons that are increased."

So pressure is building fast for more controls on these industrial products. But unless controls are imposed at the international level, asserts Gordon Duffy, editor of *Air Conditioning, Heating, and Refrigeration News,* then reg-

Du Pont Co.

© David & Linda Phillips

The use of chlorofluorocarbons, or CFCs, are thought to be the main cause of ozone depletion. CFCs enter the atmosphere through such seemingly harmless uses as refrigerants for air conditioners (left) and refrigerators, and as propellants in spray cans (above).

ulation of refrigerant use in the U.S. makes no sense. As of now, he says, 30 percent of the CFCs used in Europe are due to aerosol cans, even though other viable, economical propellants exist.

Action Must Be Taken

"Just about everything in modern life is dependent in some stage of its production on refrigeration," says Duffy, and the alternatives to use of CFCs all have serious drawbacks. Further, some kinds of CFCs, he says, break down in the troposphere and would be safer environmentally, although their universal use would require redesign of most refrigeration systems. "Obviously," he concludes, "if these refrigerants are harming the atmosphere, something has got to be done. The only thing is, the search has been on for more than a decade now, and we really haven't come up with any alternatives."

Whatever we do, the worst news is that the damage cannot be undone. "We can't go up there with vacuum cleaners, or pump up more ozone," says Harvard's Pinto. If CFCs prove to be a major cause of the problem and if we could put an absolute stop to their use today, such large quantities still dwell in the troposphere that, Solomon says, "Even if we stop today, the amount of time it will take for all the junk that we've put into the troposphere to work its way up and get destroyed is on the order of 50 to 100 years."

So the stakes in understanding the problem as soon as possible are high. "I think it's imperative that we get more data," asserts Solomon. "Right now," she adds, "all the theories, including my own, frankly should be considered as little more than pie in the sky. We know so little. All we know is that ozone has gone down dramatically."

The Puzzle of
EL NIÑO

by Robert Gannon

J ulia Weinthal, manager of The Marine Room, a 40-year-old seaside restaurant in La Jolla, California, stood on the balcony and watched the dining room as it was slowly destroyed. "I couldn't believe that it was really happening," she says. "I couldn't believe the waves. The size!" She saw the plate-glass windows pop in one by one, saw the dining room fill with water as waves came crashing through, watched a floating refrigerator bob gently among the drifting tables and chairs.

She may be surprised when she learns the cause of the destruction: a rise of 10.8° F (6° C) in the temperature of the Pacific Ocean's surface waters off the coast of Ecuador.

It was December 2, 1982, and Weinthal wasn't the only one suffering. On virtually every continent, 1982 and 1983 were replete with weather-related disasters. Australia, Africa, and Indonesia were plagued with droughts, dust storms, and brush fires. Tahiti hadn't been hit by a typhoon in half a century, but it was lashed by six that season. Peru was hit with the heaviest rain in recorded history: areas with a normal rainfall of 6 inches (15 centimeters) received 11 feet (3.35 meters). Some rivers carried 1,000 times their normal flow.

The reason: El Niño. Its signature: a cold tongue of water, lying along the equator off the coast of South America, that had become relatively warm. The event was blamed for between 1,300 and 2,000 deaths and up to $8 billion in damage to property and livelihoods.

A Repeat Performance?

While you are reading this, El Niño may be arriving again. In the early summer of 1986, oceanographers and meteorologists were predicting another one—albeit a milder event than in 1982–83. A few years ago no forecaster would have been so bold. But new models and data have raised confidence. Says Mark Cane, a meteorologist at Columbia University's Lamont-Doherty Geological Observatory, in Palisades, N.Y.: "There's not a doubt at all in my mind that we can now predict an El Niño event at least six months in advance, probably a year."

If he's right, the models developed during the past two or three years represent major advances toward the elusive goal of long-range

In 1982–1983, California beachside residents were battered by storms blamed on El Niño weather patterns.

forecasting. Stephen Zebiak, also of Lamont-Doherty, says that the new theories "finally make long-range climatic prediction a realistic goal."

El Niño events appear every few years, and they have been recorded as far back as 1541. Years ago, El Niño was considered only a local event—a slight annual warming of a current in Ecuadorian waters, usually in late December. Spanish-speaking fishermen named that disturbance El Niño, "The Little One," after the Christ Child.

Occasionally—at least nine times in the past 40 years—the warming has intensified and penetrated farther south to Peru, where anchovy fishermen awaited it fearfully. They knew it would be a bad year for fishing. Fish can't survive without the cold, nutrient-rich water that sustains the plankton on which they feed. They either die or migrate to deep water.

Climatic Seesaw

Today scientists know El Niño as a colossal shift in the waters and winds of the tropical Pacific. And they know El Niño doesn't act alone, but in conjunction with the Southern Oscillation (SO), a periodic seesaw in climate around Earth's middle. The SO results from pressure variations (which cause wind changes) that take place over several years, and it usually stretches over the equatorial Pacific and Indian Oceans. (Meteorologists often use the difference in pressure between Darwin, Australia, and Tahiti as an index of the SO's amplitude and phase.) Scientists call the merged air and water patterns ENSO, for El Niño–Southern Oscillation. The ENSO combination can trigger momentous weather changes that stretch over at least two-thirds of the globe.

In the normal state, the trade winds nudge surface water toward the western Pacific. The warm, upper water along the South American coast is continually replaced by upwelling, icy water—the coldest to be found anywhere in the low latitudes. It sometimes dips to 68° F (20° C) or even lower. By the time the winds reach Micronesia, a third of the way around the earth, the sea level has risen about 3 feet (1 meter) and the water has warmed about 7° F (3.8° C).

In the east the thermocline (the interface between warm surface water and frigid deep water) rises to just below the surface, but the warmer water in the west pushes it down to a depth of perhaps 660 feet (200 meters). At the thermocline in the central ocean, the eastward-

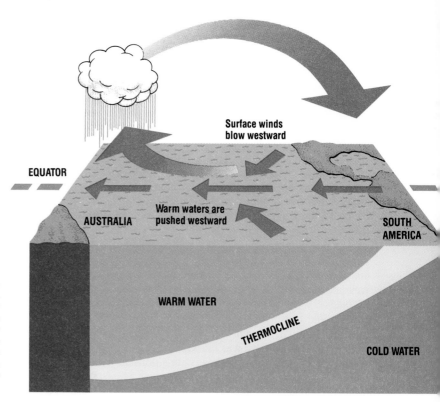

NORMAL CONDITIONS

Trade winds driven by high atmospheric pressure in the eastern Pacific and low pressure in the west first blow northwest along the South American coast and then westward along the equator, dragging surface water with them. The warm water is continually replenished by cold, nutrient-rich water upwelling from below the thermocline—the buffer zone between the upper layer of water and the frigid waters from the ocean floor. Meanwhile, steamy water in the western Pacific feeds torrential rainfalls. High above, the air slowly returns to the east, closing a loop meteorologists call the Walker Circulation.

Surface winds blow westward

EQUATOR

AUSTRALIA

Warm waters are pushed westward

SOUTH AMERICA

WARM WATER

THERMOCLINE

COLD WATER

flowing Cromwell Current, or Equatorial Undercurrent, the most powerful of the subsurface flows, streams toward South America at about 2½ miles (4 kilometers) per hour.

Oregon State's Robert Smith, a specialist in subsurface currents, measured the thermocline off the South American coast during the 1982 El Niño, and found that it had descended to about 500 feet (150 meters). About the same time, the University of Hawaii's Eric Firing, studying western Pacific currents with a Pegasus sonar system, was astonished to discover that the enormous Cromwell Current had virtually disappeared.

Ripple Effect

No one knows what upsets the normally balanced elegant cycle of wind and water, but every few years something triggers a change—perhaps snow on the Himalayas affecting a wandering jet stream just enough to prod the SO into oscillation. Whatever it is, something pushes the annual warm current too far south. And Peru gets drenched while Australia is parched.

Major weather changes in one part of the planet have a ripple effect. "Jiggle the tropical ocean," says Pennsylvania State University meteorologist Peter Webster, chairman of the Scientific Steering Group of the international Tropical Ocean & Global Atmosphere (TOGA) Programme, "and the world's atmosphere responds. Small changes in the warm ocean cause major shifts in the atmosphere and in global heating. And heating is what drives the whole weather apparatus."

Although ENSO seems to be a self-perpetuating cycle like the Pacific weather loop called the Walker Circulation, it eventually spends itself. Cane and Zebiak explain that ENSO deteriorates after 14 to 22 months because poleward flows empty the warm-water equatorial basin. "After a time there's no longer enough warm water to sustain above-normal surface temperatures in the east," says Zebiak. "Then El Niño begins to decay."

Soon the winds begin to blow from the east again. Warm water returns to the equator and the Walker Circulation starts anew.

Fooled by Mother Nature

The 1982–83 event was an aberration, even for an El Niño. It was the most destructive El Niño in at least a century, perhaps the worst in recorded history. (Nobody has yet figured out

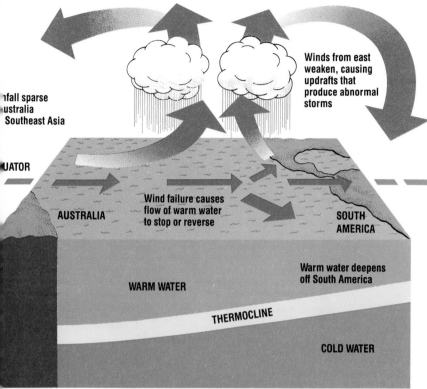

Winds from east weaken, causing updrafts that produce abnormal storms

ᵢfall sparse ₐustralia Southeast Asia

ᵤATOR

AUSTRALIA

Wind failure causes flow of warm water to stop or reverse

SOUTH AMERICA

WARM WATER

Warm water deepens off South America

THERMOCLINE

COLD WATER

EL NIÑO CONDITIONS

The annual warm current that churns southward until it reaches the coast of Ecuador thrusts further south to the waters off Peru. There it mixes with upwelling cold water, warming it slightly and depressing the thermocline. Being warmer, the water no longer effectively cools the air above it. Without the cross-ocean temperature difference, winds stop or even reverse, bringing rain and more warm water eastward. When it reaches the coast the warm water splits into two currents that move poleward and empty the basin of warm water. Once the warm water supply is depleted, the El Niño cycle decays.

Reprinted from Popular Science with permission © 1986 Times Mirror Magazines, Inc.

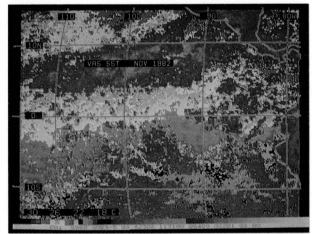

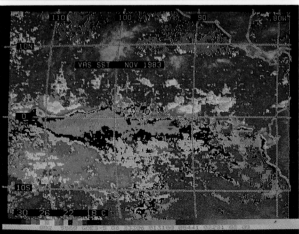

why it was so powerful.) And it didn't develop in an expected way.

Ordinarily, an El Niño first shows itself in the early spring as a slight coastal-water warming along northwestern South America. In 1982, though, temperatures were stable as summer arrived. Other signs, however, were emerging across the sea: atmospheric pressures over the Indian Ocean had been rising since July 1981—a strong sign of change. Indonesia, Australia, and the Philippines—normally well into the rainy season by then—were dry. Most important, in late June and early July, along the equator in the sparsely populated western Pacific, data were being collected that showed that the wind had reversed itself. That should have been the clincher.

Yet nobody was chancing a prediction because Peruvian coastal-water temperatures held constant. In September 1982, a United Nations-sponsored committee appointed to discuss El

Digital satellite images of the tropical Pacific under El Niño (top) and normal conditions record surface water temperatures by different colors. The warmer sea during El Niño registers yellow and orange; the cooler temperatures of a normal year (bottom) show brown and blue.

THE CATASTROPHIC CONSEQUENCES OF EL NIÑO

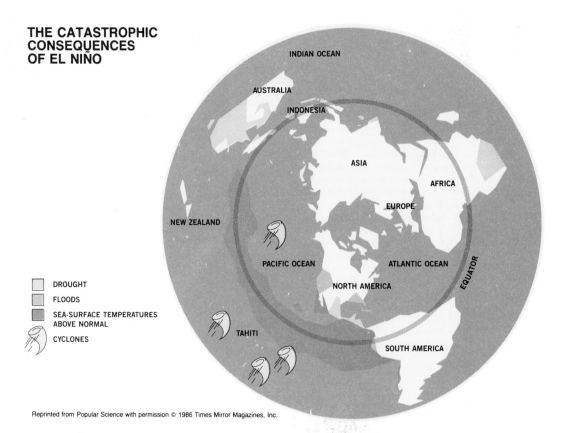

DROUGHT
FLOODS
SEA-SURFACE TEMPERATURES ABOVE NORMAL
CYCLONES

Niño forecasting spent much of one conference arguing about whether or not El Niño was coming. Meteorologist Jerome Namias of the Scripps Institute of Oceanography, best known for his annual fall forecasts of the severity of forthcoming winters, was at that meeting. Says Namias: "As far as I know, at that time no categorical prediction was made about an El Niño emerging, let alone the greatest episode in history." Then he adds, "It's humbling."

All doubt dissolved that September 25. Along the seacoast near the village of Paita, Peru, sea-surface temperatures shot up 7.2° F (4° C) in 24 hours. By the end of November, they had risen another 4.5° F (2.5° C).

For climatologists who had been working on mathematical models designed to predict El Niño, the experience was both disappointing and illuminating. They had failed to foresee the mammoth 1982–83 event, but the failure jarred loose old conventions and made the experts look anew at their models.

Statistical Modeling

The most common modeling approach is statistical. It is similar to the way economists predict changes in the stock market: they draw associa-

tions statistically between current observations and past events. Established patterns are applied to current data to show where the weather is heading.

Scripps oceanographer Tim Barnett is one of the best of the statistical modelers. His fourth-floor corner office—decorated with pictures of game fish—overlooks the Pacific, and from his window he can gaze across La Jolla Bay to the spot where Weinthal's restaurant was demolished by waves in 1982.

Barnett uses large-scale pressure patterns, mostly over the Pacific and Asia, to attempt to spot a developing ENSO. In particular, he looks for unusually high pressures moving eastward along the equator. He recently assembled readings from the western and central Pacific gathered over 31 years—up to 1982—and ran them through his model. The readout clearly projected an El Niño for 1982. "We could have said a big event was under way," he claims, "months before anyone else would have said so."

Barnett's forecast for the 1986 season: "A weak El Niño event is likely." But he adds a qualifier: "The probability of that forecast being correct is 60 percent."

Physical Modeling

While Barnett watches wet-suited surfers skirting the Scripps wharf, Mark Cane and Stephen Zebiak, from their Lamont-Doherty offices perched high on New York's Palisades, watch sailboats glide by on the Hudson River.

The Cane-Zebiak team, the forecasting fraternity agrees, has developed the best mathematical model based on physical principles. Unlike virtually all other models, this one used no statistics derived from past El Niños. Instead, the researchers have worked out the basic processes that go into an El Niño event to describe couplings between ocean and atmosphere. They plug in surface-water temperatures and wind data, and come up with a prediction.

The crucial set of data needed for the model is the variation in depth of the tropical Pacific thermocline over time. Unfortunately, such measurements are almost nonexistent. But the team overcame this problem by developing a computer program that uses information about surface winds to estimate thermocline depth.

To check the model, Cane and Zebiak made hindcasts for each of the past 15 years, using only data available at the time. The results: three-quarters of the projections were correct, and the rest weren't wrong, only cloudy. When projected two years ahead, 45 percent of the forecasts were correct, 27 percent "gave strong correct indications," 15 percent were wrong, and the rest were "problematic."

Could the model have foreseen the 1982–83 El Niño? "Absolutely," says Zebiak. "We could have predicted it by the end of 1980," adds Cane.

What was predicted for 1986–87? "An El Niño event of some sort," prophesied the researchers at a press conference in March. "It will reach its peak in the winter of 1986–87," they said. But by mid-May they were hedging; winds had unexpectedly begun blowing from the east. But by the end of that month, Cane saw "a new development that is sending some fairly strong westerly bursts of wind along the equator." He was still calling for an event, but one of only moderate strength.

The real beauty of the Cane-Zebiak model is its simplicity, say those in the field. It doesn't require long-range statistics or figures from weather events outside the tropical Pacific region—no need to worry about such mystical entities as anticyclone anomalies, convergence zones, and vague currents and eddies.

Some meteorologists suspect that the Cane-Zebiak model is too neat; they say one can't simply ignore the rest of the world. A few, in fact, believe that such a large event as an ENSO is so dominated by random factors that accurate prediction is close to impossible.

Klaus Wyrtki, an oceanographer at the University of Hawaii, for instance, says "progress in understanding short-term climate variation will come in decades, not years." And Oswaldo Garcia, a meteorologist at the National Oceanic and Atmospheric Administration

During the most recent El Niño cycle, fishing boats lay idle in port as the Peruvian offshore waters grew too warm to support the schools of anchovies on which scores of local fishermen depend for their livelihood.

(NOAA) in Silver Spring, Maryland, cautions that "nature always takes exception to itself; there's no guarantee a pattern will remain the same."

Cane answers with a nod and a shrug: "Yes—it's surprising to us, too, that it works as well as it does."

It does seem significant that both the Barnett and the Cane-Zebiak models call for a 1986–87 El Niño event. "That's a remarkable thing," says Barnett, "because our methods are completely different, using very different information, and yet they say the same thing."

Others are also on the lookout for an El Niño. Eugene Rasmusson of NOAA's Climate Analysis Center issued an El Niño "advisory" in March 1986. Warren White and Jerome Namias of Scripps; Wang Zongshan, a Chinese scientist specializing in the sea/atmosphere interface; and others agreed that some kind of El Niño would develop around the end of 1986.

Westerly Winds

By mid-June, it seemed that all the predictions would fail to materialize. The vigorous westerly winds observed in May had weakened. "The odds are getting longer all the time," Rasmusson remarked, but he added that it was still too early to rule out an El Niño. Judging from wind and rainfall patterns, though, it looked like a better year for fishing than for forecasting.

"We're still waiting for that wonderful day when a model forecasts something before it occurs," Rasmusson admitted. The new models have made successful retroactive predictions, but they are not yet reliable enough to be used for economic decision making about future events. "There'll always be misses," Rasmusson said. Even daily forecasts, which have improved tremendously in recent years, sometimes give bum steers. In the end, each model is just a caricature of the real weather system.

If everyone is wrong, it won't necessarily be because their theories are faulty, but because the data are insufficient. Because all the forecasters survey the same conditions, it is likely they will hit or miss as a group, Rasmusson explained. Much more information is available than in the past. But measurements still come from a haphazard collection of ships that happen to cross the Pacific, as well as from weather stations dotted randomly across thousands of square miles, deep-sea probes dropped occasionally from research planes, sensors on a few drifting and anchored buoys, and tide gauges on remote islands. Says Barnett: "The lack of information is terrible right now. It's amazing that we can get out of it the things we do."

The problem should be rectified in the early 1990's. Two research satellites—one to measure wind fields, the other to monitor sea levels—are scheduled to go into orbit. "That will be a quantum jump in oceanography in general, and in solving the ENSO problem in particular," says Barnett. Forecasters should then be able to warn Pacific countries close to the equator of El Niño–caused weather calamities at least six months in advance, probably more.

Ocean Acoustics

Meanwhile, a group of researchers at NOAA's Atlantic Oceanographic and Meteorological Laboratory in Miami, Florida, is designing an experiment to test a third technique for monitoring El Niños. Physicist David Palmer and his associates still study ocean acoustics for clues. They believe that a layer of water 160 to 920 feet (50 to 280 meters) deep becomes very quiet during an El Niño, because low-frequency sound waves are deflected at steeper angles when the upper layer of the ocean warms. The waves crash quickly into the bottom rather than traveling underwater for long distances, as they do under normal conditions.

Palmer's group developed a computer model that uses temperature and salinity data to calculate El Niño's impact on sound propagation. They say the sound level in the Pacific's upper layers may have decreased by up to 1,000 times during the 1982–83 El Niño. Unlike other scientists, Palmer and his colleagues have not been able to test their model by making hindcasts; they will have to wait for new data from their sound probes. If their experiment works, they, too, may someday predict arrivals of "The Little One."

Early-Warning System

El Niño is the most dynamic and best-defined disturbance in the ocean-atmosphere system, so if there is a key to long-range weather forecasting, El Niño is it. If researchers' models of it prove reliable, they should make long-range climate prediction routine for the tropics, and forecasts for North America should follow.

Fine-tuned models of the ENSO complex may also put health-care officials on the lookout for El Niño's less conspicuous effects. Michael Glantz of the National Center for Atmospheric Research in Boulder, Colorado, reported some

El Niño's far-flung effects. Halfway around the world from El Niño's origins in the Pacific, a young man in Botswana, Africa, ponders the drought that has decimated herds of cattle. In Australia's Great Barrier Reef (right), unusually warm water devastated the picturesque coral population.

secondary problems caused by the 1982–83 event: encephalitis outbreaks on the East Coast of the United States (a warm, wet spring provided ideal mosquito environments); increased snakebites in Montana (hot, dry weather caused mice living at high elevations to migrate downward in their search for food and water, and rattlesnakes followed); a rise in bubonic plague in New Mexico (a cool, wet spring created favorable conditions for flea-bearing rodents); an increase in shark attacks off the Oregon coast (owing to unseasonably warm sea temperatures); and a rash of spine injuries in California (weather-altered coastal seafloors fooled surfers).

Some meteorologists have tied El Niño to the above-normal temperatures recorded in Alaska and northwestern Canada, and it may have reduced the salmon harvest. In the eastern United States, 1982–83 was the warmest winter in 25 years.

The 1982–83 El Niño even slowed down the earth. David Salstein and Richard Rosen of Atmospheric and Environmental Research Inc., in Cambridge, Massachusetts, calculated that the angular momentum of the earth shifted slightly as a result of changes in the normal pattern of the jet stream and trade winds. In late January, at El Niño's peak, the day length stretched by 0.2 millisecond.

El Paso's solar pond power system—the first to go on line in the United States—doubles as a desalination unit.

REVIEW OF THE YEAR

ENERGY

Two topics dominated the energy picture for most of 1986: the catastrophic destruction of the Chernobyl nuclear power plant and the declining price of oil. Ironically, while fallout from the Soviet nuclear disaster garnered more public attention, it was the price of oil that had the most pervasive effect on investments in energy conservation, new production, and new technologies.

CHERNOBYL

At 1:23 on the morning of April 26, 1986, a massive explosion ripped apart a reactor at the Chernobyl nuclear power station, initiating the worst nuclear plant accident in history. Extensive fallout from the Ukrainian accident may eventually cause as many as 40,000 excess cancer deaths inside the Soviet Union—and more throughout the rest of the world.

"While the Chernobyl accident was very serious, it will have no effect . . . on the further development and growth of nuclear power generating capacity in the USSR," according to A. Petrosyants, chairman of the Soviet State Committee on the Utilization of Atomic Energy. In fact, the Soviet government reported in August that for environmental reasons, coal-generated electric power is being phased out—and all major future Soviet electric-generating stations will be nuclear powered. (See also page 182.)

OTHER NUCLEAR ADVANCES

In the United States, nuclear fission was the second largest—and fastest-growing—source of electricity, with a major new commercial nuclear plant approved by the Nuclear Regulatory Commission (NRC) an average of once every seven weeks. By year-end a total of 105 were licensed to operate, and capable of generating 16 percent of the nation's electricity. Despite three cancellations for nuclear plants in the U.S. last year, U.S. reactor manufacturers received their first new nuclear plant order in eight years—for a pair of reactors to be built in Korea.

For engineering commercial fusion power, there are two basic approaches under development: imploding small, individual fusion-fuel pellets with lasers or particle beams; and confining a more diffuse, ionized gas in a magnetic field until the gas's nuclei fuse. Substantial progress on both fronts was achieved in 1986.

An X-ray burst from the Nova laser during spring tests at the Lawrence Livermore National Laboratory compressed a pellet of hydrogen, deuterium, and tritium fuel to a density of 2×10^{24} ions and a temperature of 17,000,000°C—roughly one-twentieth the density and one-third to one-fifth the temperature needed to pass the "break-even" point—the point at which a fusion reaction creates more energy than is needed to initiate it.

OIL AND GAS

"There is a serious devastation in the oil and gas industry," said Energy Secretary John S. Herrington in an address December 4, 1986. Exploration for new supplies is not only down, he said, but production from existing wells is also falling. In fact, U.S. drilling hit a 46-year low in July 1986, and overall was down 50 percent from the year before. By year-end, Herrington said, "it is estimated that this industry will have lost a quarter of a million jobs." The fact that U.S. oil and gas consumption is rising at the same time domestic production is falling constitutes "a national problem with potential long-term consequences," Herrington said. The worst of those consequences could be renewed dependence on the Mideast for 50 percent or more of U.S. oil, and another "out-of-control" spiraling in energy prices, he said. Just during 1986, the share of the world's oil produced by members of the Organization of Petroleum Exporting Countries (OPEC) increased from about 15 percent to almost 40 percent.

Fueling the oil and gas industry's problems was a continuing glut of oil in world markets—particularly from the world's largest Eastern Hemisphere producers—those with fields in the North Sea, the Mideast, and Africa. The resulting decline in the price of oil during 1986—from an average per-barrel price of $23.64 to a low of just $11.51—discouraged conservation measures and encouraged consumption.

Since 1977 the U.S. has been stockpiling oil in underground caverns against the next oil emergency. Known as the Strategic Petroleum Reserve (SPR), its 500 millionth barrel of crude oil arrived on June 1, 1986. Though the Reagan administration had intended to end SPR filling when the stockpile reached 502 million barrels (roughly two months later), Congress objected and ordered the Department of Energy (DOE) to keep adding oil. By year-end, DOE had actually increased the stockpile's fill rate by 50 percent—to 75,000 barrels per day.

ALTERNATIVE ENERGY SOURCES

On June 18, 1986, scientists from Los Alamos National Laboratory in New Mexico completed the first successful monthlong test of what they described as "the world's largest man-made geothermal-energy system." They used hydraulic pressure to fracture a hot, dry-rock formation to a depth of two miles. Water pumped through the rock rubble can extract some of its geothermal heat.

During the test, water was circulated through the system's 4 billion-cubic-foot (113-cubic-meter) rock reservoir at a rate of 290 gallons (1,100 liters) per minute. Heated to 375° F (190° C), this water carried about 10 megawatts of thermal power. The hot water can either be used directly for industrial processes or be run through turbines to generate electricity.

In April, Stanford University researchers announced they had achieved a record 27.5 percent efficiency in converting sunlight to electricity using their novel "point-contact" silicon solar cell. The silicon in each cell is about one-quarter the size of a postage stamp and only 0.004 inch (0.1 millimeter) thick. Its textured upper surface diffuses the incoming light, and its mirrored lower surface helps trap it. A polka-dotted pattern of impurities is scattered across the silicon crystal's lower surface. Tiny aluminum threads penetrating down to them collect the generated current and carry it out of the cell.

The first U.S. solar-pond power system began generating electricity on September 19 at a test site near El Paso, Texas. The 0.8-acre (0.32-hectare) pond has three layers: an insulating low-salt upper layer into which cool water is continuously pumped; a warm and moderately salty intermediate layer; and a hot, extremely briny bottom layer. Sunlight-heated brine at the bottom is pumped out and over a system of pipes holding Freon, causing the Freon to boil. The boiling Freon drives a generator to produce up to 100 kilowatts of electricity. The system, which can also be used to desalinate otherwise useless saline reservoirs, is a cooperative project among the University of Texas, El Paso Electric Company, Bruce Foods Corporation, and the Interior Department's Bureau of Reclamation. Designed by the Israeli Ormat Systems, Inc., it is similar to an even larger project that has operated at the Dead Sea in Israel for three years.

JANET RALOFF

The lowest oil prices in years slowed research into other energy sources. Prices began to rise again in 1987.

© Paula Kobylarz

The Bettmann Archive

ROLLING WITH COAL

by Dietrick E. Thomsen

Railroads and coal went together for a long time. The first railroads were tramways in coal mines. The first railway in the world to use steam locomotives, England's Stockton and Darlington, was built to carry coal in the Tees River Valley. Coal was and is a major component of the traffic of many railroads, and for more than 100 years it was the major fuel for railroads. Railroads in the United States today still haul a lot of coal, but, with very rare exceptions, they no longer burn it.

Diesel Oil Alternatives

What railroads burn today is diesel oil. The United States is largely dependent on imports for supplies of this commodity. On the other hand, the United States has large reserves of coal. Other countries with large coal reserves and little oil, such as Poland, China, and some in Latin America and Africa, have retained the steam locomotive. Lately a number of people and organizations, both in the U.S. government and out of it, have started to look at the possibility of a return to coal-fueled locomotives in the United States. In addition, the Chinese have recently shown some interest in selling their coal-fired locomotive technology in the United States.

Recently the Morgantown, West Virginia, Energy Technology Center of the Department of Energy (DOE), which oversees such things for the federal government, published a report, "Assessment of Coal-Fueled Locomotives," on the state of such efforts. The report is one result of renewed attention to the subject that began in earnest about two years ago and gained the support of some members of Congress, including particularly Senators Robert C. Byrd (D-W.Va.), Paul Simon (D-Ill.), and John Warner (R-Va.). The report describes seven projects in fair detail, including a reciprocating steam engine, gas turbines, and what are essentially coal-burning diesels. The organizations that are working on them range from the two largest U.S. manufacturers of the diesel-electric locomotives now used, General Motors (GM) and General Electric (GE), to fairly small design and engineering organizations.

However, the president of the railroad that says it runs the last steam locomotive in regular revenue service in the United States feels the report is not as comprehensive as it might have been. Hugh W. Crane of the Crab Orchard and Egyptian Railroad (CO&E) in Marion, Illinois, says the report omits important information about his locomotive that he submitted regarding the CO&E's proposal. (The report was compiled from responses to a solicitation published by DOE in the *Commerce Business Daily* of November 6, 1985.)

The CO&E Perseveres

The Crab Orchard and Egyptian is an 8-mile (12.8-kilometer) line operated by four persons—"If I weren't sitting here talking to you, I might be out running a train," Crane says. The railroad maintains a steam locomotive of wheel arrangement 2-8-0 (two pilot wheels in front, eight drive wheels, no trailing wheels under the firebox), known in the trade as a consolidation type. It was built in Canada in 1940, and came to the CO&E secondhand from the Roberval Saguenay Railway in Quebec province. The 46-year-old steamer operates competitively with the line's diesels (of model SW 12), Crane says.

Other traditional steam locomotives operate in the United States and Canada, but are either found in museums or used primarily for excursions or tourist attractions. The CO&E's consolidation pulls regular freight trains, some of them coal cars, in fact. Crane says he once "ran off" a television reporter who wanted to do a cute story. "We're not in it for 'cute,'" Crane says. "If it didn't pull our train, we wouldn't want it." The steamer runs competitively with the diesels as long as the price of diesel oil is above 50 cents a gallon, he says.

The price of diesel oil right now, as the DOE report points out, is about 40 cents a gallon. The renewed interest in coal fuel began when the price of oil was much higher. However, few believe the price of oil will stay that low for long. Martin J. Hapeman of General Electric says GE calculations relating to its project of a coal-fired diesel locomotive indicate that interest in alternate fuels might return and the coal-fired diesel be profitable to both manufacturer and purchaser when diesel oil hits 85 cents a gallon.

The factors that determine the price of oil are mostly out of U.S. control. "This country is getting like the bears of Yellowstone," says Richard Wolfe, vice president and director of coal research for the United Coal Company of Bristol, Virginia. "We're losing our capability to develop our own energy resources." Coal forms a large part of American domestic energy resources, and Wolfe complains that this is a very depressed time for the coal industry, with coal selling at $20 a ton. The coal industry would like to open new markets. Wolfe estimates the locomotive market as representing 50 million to 75 million additional tons a year, or about 10 percent of present production.

Slow Starters

There are two basic approaches to the problem of coal as a locomotive fuel (and also as a fuel for marine and stationary engines), Wolfe points out. You can try to make a fuel from coal that will operate existing diesel engines with more or less—preferably less—modification. Or you can burn the coal in a reciprocating steam engine, a steam turbine, or a gas turbine and mount that in place of the diesel. Most of the proposals DOE has reviewed want to retain the electric drive of the present diesels.

The standard locomotive of today is actually a diesel-electric. A diesel engine drives a generator that powers electric motors connected to the driving axles. These electric traction motors, as they are called, give advantages in control and pickup that most designers prefer to

Hugh W. Crane (left), president of the Crab Orchard and Egyptian (CO&E) Railroad in Illinois, engineers the last steam locomotive still in regular service in the United States. Below, one of the CO&E's four employees performs one of railroad's grittiest jobs: hand-firing a steam locomotive.

maintain. Crane, who works with both, describes the difference as one of how the horsepower of the motor relates to its tractive effort, which is how well it pulls cars.

A steam locomotive is relatively hard to start—Crane cites the old saying about steam locomotives: "If you can start a load, you'll pull it along." Steam locomotives work best at fairly high speeds over 20 miles (32 kilometers) per hour, he says. Electric traction is easier to start and accelerate and works well at low speeds. Locomotives do much of their most complicated work at low speeds with frequent stopping, starting, and reversing, and most designers want to preserve the advantages presented by the electric drive in these operations.

Coal-Water Slurries

Among the proposals to DOE, the closest to present technology are those of the two large locomotive manufacturers, GM and GE. Each of these companies is working on a modified diesel engine that would use a coal-water slurry instead of oil as fuel. In describing the GM projects, the report notes, "Modification of an existing engine to operate on coal slurry fuel appears to be more feasible than the complete R&D (research and development) effort required to manufacture a new engine."

The parts of the engine that come in contact with the fuel would have to be modified. Coal does not burn as cleanly as oil, and the engine must resist corrosion by chemicals released in the burning of coal. The DOE report does indicate that more R&D is needed on both the formation of the slurry and coal-resistant materials for the engine. It also points out that for the system to come into widespread use, means for

manufacturing, transporting, and loading the slurry would have to be developed.

GE's Hapeman points out that his company's calculations allow for these factors. His figure of 85 cents a gallon as the competitive level takes into account construction of their own slurry plants by the railroads. The slurry can be made economically, he says, and adds that a company in Syracuse, New York, can process the coal to the 5-micron size they need. GE, he says, has actually run a test diesel engine with the slurry.

Nevertheless, in Wolfe's opinion, a coal-water slurry is not the way to go. It depends, he says, on whether one approaches the problem from the point of view of the locomotive manufacturer, who wants to build locomotives, or of the coal company, which wants to compete with oil fuel. According to Wolfe, United Coal decided to try to produce a liquid fuel from coal that would work in current internal combustion engines. By a process called "mild gasification," he says, United Coal has run diesel and gasoline engines on the liquid coal fuel, although not yet a locomotive. At present the company has only a very small plant for producing it, he says. United Coal has made presentations at the Morgantown Energy Technology Center, trying to interest DOE. The report states, "In one project, mild gasification fuels were produced and successfully burned for short times in a diesel engine and a small residential furnace. The key unknown that remains is the cost of these coal-derived liquids."

Gas Turbine Locomotives

General Electric and General Motors are also working on gas turbine locomotives fueled by coal-water slurry. In this arrangement, hot gases produced in combustion would power a turbine that powers the electrical generator, and so forth. Back in the 1940's, several railroads experimented with gas turbines, including the Union Pacific, the former Chesapeake and Ohio, and the former Norfolk and Western. Those experiments were not successful. The Norfolk and Western's reason for dropping the gas turbine then was that it made too big a locomotive, according to Robert Fort, a spokesman for the Norfolk and Western's successor, Norfolk Southern. Lately, Fort says, Norfolk Southern has been studying gas turbines again, but it has turned over whatever it had to GE.

A gas turbine, or possibly a gas reciprocating engine, fueled by run-of-the-mine coal (coal not specially treated), is proposed by Brobeck Corporation of Berkeley, California. The locomotive would carry a coal gasifier, and the gasified coal would be fed to the turbine. This manner of fueling is preferable, says Kenneth M. Thomas of Brobeck, because "it's not clear that producing the slurry is going to be done on any cost-effective basis."

Stepping Out with Steam

Other proposals reviewed by DOE use more of the traditional steam technology, and therein lies a psychological stumbling block for present-day railroad managements. As Frederick Prahl of National Steam Propulsion Company, a subsidiary of Skinner Engine Company of Erie, Pennsylvania, puts it, "They think going to steam is a step backward." Nevertheless, several organizations propose just that step.

In something approximating a traditional steam engine, coal can be burned in a firebox, thus lessening corrosion problems (a firebox has no moving parts). The different proposals use various methods of controlled combustion to minimize unwanted emissions and increase efficiency. Furthermore, they are none of them choochoos. That sound comes from exhaust

High-speed, diesel-powered trains like the streamlined Zephyr, shown at right at the 1934 World's Fair in Chicago, drew passengers away from the slower steam trains of the era.

American Coal Enterprises

A prototype coal-burning locomotive—the ACE 3000—is being tested for its competitiveness with diesel engines.

steam from the cylinders going up the stack. All these steam engines would capture the exhaust, condense and recycle it. Thus, the locomotive doesn't have to stop every 30 to 40 miles (50 to 65 kilometers) for water as the old ones did.

National Steam Propulsion Company proposes a reciprocating steam engine to power the standard electric motors. It would burn pelletized coal in a fluid-bed combustor. They chose not to connect the reciprocating engine to the wheels in the style of old-fashioned steamers, Prahl says, because railroad managements want to keep the diesel-electric drive.

Another proposal that would use a steam engine to power the electric drive comes from the Crab Orchard and Egyptian Railroad. According to the CO&E's Crane, this would be a booster for the existing steam engine to help it in starting and in low-speed operations. The engine would be mounted on the frame of the tender that carries the steam locomotive's fuel and water.

A particular steam engine that might be used for this booster is one made by the Daytong Locomotive Works in China. People from Daytong came to visit the CO&E, Crane says, because they had heard it had the last steam locomotive in revenue service in the U.S., and they want to sell their steam engines here.

Dropping the Electric Drive

There have been at least two proposals for a straight steam reciprocating locomotive without the electric drive. The report mentions the North American Locomotive Company of Monument, Colorado, which had proposed a modernized version of a traditional steam locomotive, but it notes: "However, this developer is no longer located in the Monument, Colorado, area, and, if it still exists as a corporate entity, its new offices could not be located."

North American Locomotive Company is no longer a corporate entity, but its former marketing manager, Asa C. Putnam of Santa Rosa,

Schematic diagram of a gas-turbine locomotive being developed by General Electric to run on a coal-water slurry.

GE/DOE

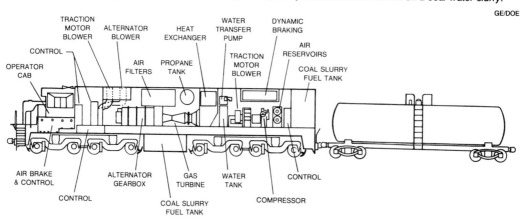

ELEGY IN AN ABANDONED TRAIN STATION

Among my earliest memories is one of sitting on the windowsill in the house where I was born, watching a locomotive move cars on a coal-dumping trestle. I have been fascinated by trains ever since. It's an emotion that affects quite a number of people. I don't know whether it has ever been scientifically analyzed, but one longtime writer about railroads, John H. Armstrong, suggests it has to do with the way trains move.

Trains have a special place in the history of North America. In the United States and Canada, railroads not only held each nation together, but in many cases preceded and enabled settlement of the West—a quite different function from what railroads had in Europe and Asia. In the American equivalent of the Icelandic saga or the German Nibelungen cycle, namely the Western, there are usually trains around somewhere. For the pious, for those who prefer their trains not carrying gamblers, gunmen, and painted ladies, there's the gospel train, which "don't carry no gamblers. . . ." (I have never heard of a gospel airplane.) Those departing this mortal existence left on the midnight train.

Trains in the night. "From Memphis to Mobile, from Natchez to St. Joe," those who sang the blues in the night could always "hear that lonesome whistle blow." Richard Nixon hated the shrill music of a languorous locomotive; I have always loved it.

There's a certain expansiveness, a Vicki Baum–ish, Grand Hotel–ish sense of impending adventure about rolling across the landscape in a train. Those whose idea of travel is being confined claustrophobically in a flying tin can can't imagine it. It has affected a number of writers. Particularly it brought forth the rather baroque prose of Lucius Beebe, chronicler of the luxe that used to be.

Some of the luxe managed to last even down to the days of Amtrak. Just before Amtrak, I remember entering the first-class diner on the Florida Special and getting a menu listing 15 dishes, plus a complimentary glass of champagne. Even after Amtrak, on the Southwest Limited, there was steak Chateaubriand on the menu. Take that, you microwaved cheeseburger!

But romance prints no bank statements. Nevertheless, we ought to remember that what was true in 1869 is still true today: Steel wheels on steel rails are still the most efficient way of moving people and goods overland, most efficient in terms of energy consumed, of environmental impact, and of psychological impact on the rest of the citizenry. On the day that ultimate gridlock occurs, we may remember this.

California, says the company fell apart, not because of defects in the product, but because of internal disagreements. They were working with the Burlington Northern Railroad, Putnam says, to develop a reciprocating steam locomotive that would be analogous to one of the biggest of the traditional steamers. The wheel arrangement for this was to have been 2-8-8-4, with two separately powered sets of eight drivers. It would have produced up to 14,000 indicated horsepower, or a tractive effort of 190,000 pounds (8,600 kilograms). This is three times that of the standard diesel. It would have had a steam turbine electric booster on the tender, adding another 40,000 pounds' (1,800 kilograms') tractive effort.

This model 190, as Putnam calls it, would have been fueled by coal chemically treated and pelletized according to the Lurgie process under a German patent. Putnam says he was negotiating for $3 million needed to build a prototype, when the company folded.

The ACE 3000 of American Coal Enterprises of Lebanon, New Jersey, is also a modernized reciprocating engine, but somewhat smaller, at 3,000 horsepower. Fueled with run-of-the-mine coal, it uses a special double combustion process to increase efficiency and lower unwanted emissions. ACE has been pushing development. Recently, according to Lloyd Lewis, a spokesman for the transportation company CSX, ACE used tracks of a CSX subsidiary, the Chesapeake and Ohio Railroad, for tests involving an old steam locomotive. DOE rates it as a ''low-risk near-term technology choice.'' Some think it could be the first on the rails.

When the Price Is Right

Coal may come back as a fuel. According to James Swisher, director of the Coal Research Center at Southern Illinois University at Carbondale, ''on paper the railroad industry could save by a shift back to coal if oil prices were higher.'' Supposing oil prices go up, he foresees the modified steam engines as being most useful in the near term, with the more efficient diesels and turbines coming in later. ''Steam engines are inherently inefficient,'' he says.

It would take development money. Several million dollars is estimated for each of the examples in the DOE report. GE's Hapeman suggests a total figure between $30 million and $50 million, and says the money is unlikely to come from the customers.

Railroad managements have usually been reluctant to spend for technological development. Their attitude, as Thomas puts it, is, ''Show me one I can ride on and pull some cars, and I'll buy it.'' As Hapeman suggests, that leaves foundations or the federal government as the likely suppliers of development funds.

In India and elsewhere, steam locomotives continue to play a primary role in the transportation of people and goods.

© B. Gysenbergh/Gamma Liaison

© Michael Jones

The luxuriant stands of papyrus found in swamps throughout central Africa may be an untapped energy source.

PAPYRUS as FUEL

by Arthur Clark

Papyrus, the plant used by the pharaohs' scribes, by Rome's bureaucrats, and by Charlemagne's bookkeepers, may soon become an important source of fuel for central African nations, according to engineers and botanists studying the tall, tufted reed in the far reaches of the Nile.

Dr. Michael Jones inspects papyrus plants growing in a greenhouse at the University of Dublin from seeds brought from Rwanda. Much of the briquette-forming technology is derived from the age-old techniques used by the Irish and other northern Europeans to transform sedge plants into a bricklike fuel.

© Arthur Clark

Using "briquetting" techniques developed in Ireland and northern Europe to turn sedge plants into a fuel, those engineers and botanists—specialists assigned to Rwanda by the United Nations—have already developed a sample of salable papyrus "bricks" that, they say, could be developed into a valuable fuel—at least in central Africa, where forests are being destroyed in a frantic search for firewood.

The papyrus is harvested by hand—much as depicted on ancient Egyptian papyrus documents. Then, in a $100,000 briquetting factory funded by the Irish government, the papyrus can be chopped into strawlike pieces, compressed some 25 times, and extruded in (formed into) sausage-shaped briquettes for home cooking or heating purposes.

A Rich History

Though its use as a fuel is new, papyrus in other ages was once a vital substance. Papyrus was, in fact, the sole writing material in much of the world for more than 5,000 years; the Romans used papyrus so extensively that the failure of the Egyptian crop once brought imperial Roman commerce to a halt.

Papyrus was also used for shipbuilding in both Egypt and the Persian Gulf region. As Thor Heyerdahl wrote in *The Tigris Expedition,* reed ships were depicted on the walls of caves in Palestine and on Hittite seals at Gaziantep on the Turkish-Syrian border. Heyerdahl himself, in 1970, crossed the South Atlantic in the wholly papyrus-built vessel *Ra,* made of 12 tons (11 metric tons) of the plant from Ethiopia's Lake Tana. Heyerdahl believes that cultivation of the plant was brought to the Canary Islands, off the Atlantic coast of Morocco, and some botanists think the papyruslike giant sedge along the shore of the Gulf of Mexico may be evidence that the plant was introduced to the Americas by Mediterranean-based explorers.

© Michael Jones

The harvesting of papyrus is strictly controlled to prevent damaging the delicately balanced African ecosystem.

As a writing material, papyrus, along with parchment and vellum, was replaced almost as soon as the Islamic forces reached the Chinese border in the year 751 and learned the secret of making paper; as a consequence, papyrus plants along the Nile were eventually uprooted and replaced by other still useful crops. For over 1,000 years, papyrus was virtually unused by man.

Papyrus still grows on millions of hectares of swampland in the Sudd in the Sudan, along the edge of Lake Victoria, and in the swamps and river valleys of Rwanda, Burundi, Uganda, Ethiopia, Kenya, and Tanzania, but has had no commercial use for centuries. Though the techniques of processing papyrus were "rediscovered" by Egyptian Hassan Ragab in the early 1960's, the "paper" made from the reed has been sold mainly as conversation pieces, and more often than not, the papyrus plant is considered a nuisance; large chunks of papyrus still break off Lake Victoria's shores and form floating islands that hinder navigation.

Fuel for Rwanda

In the late 1970's, however, James Martin, an engineer with Ireland's Peat Board, was dispatched to Rwanda by the U.N. to survey the potential for peat production in the country's vast swamps and wide river valleys; partly carbonized vegetable matter similar to coal, peat is an important fuel in places like Ireland and the Soviet Union, and was reported to be plentiful in Rwanda.

Few better specialists could have been found for the job: Martin, now retired, calls himself the Peat Board's "idea man"—and peat itself generates a full quarter of Ireland's electricity.

With 5.1 million people, Rwanda, Africa's most densely populated country, was especially interested in peat because, Martin said in an interview in Dublin, "the government had been told in Rwanda they were resting on a treasure chest of peat." It was when Martin arrived in Rwanda's capital, Kigali, in 1978 that he found that the peat was "by and large unrecoverable in any modern, mechanical way because the land was always flooded." On the other hand, Martin found that there were great quantities of papyrus available. "And when I chopped them up, I turned out a darned fine briquette." To be sure his theory was practical, Martin sent half a ton (0.45 metric ton) of papyrus to Europe to be tested under factory briquetting conditions. In 1980, satisfied with the results, Martin suggested an alternative to the Rwanda government: instead of destroying the papyrus to dig out the peat, why not utilize the papyrus?

In 1981, unfortunately, Martin, still investigating, ran into a snag. Dr. Michael Jones, professor of plant physiology at Dublin's Trinity College, who had already studied papyrus in Uganda and Kenya, warned that extensive use of payrus required caution. "Overharvesting the papyrus . . . could mean the destruction of an entire plant culture," Jones said in an interview. "Papyrus is a natural resource that needs to be protected as much as trees."

As a result, he said, the decision was made that while developing papyrus briquetting, botanical studies should be carried out as well. Jones brought papyrus seeds to Dublin, Ireland, where, in the Botanical Gardens at Trinity College, they grow 5 feet (1.5 meters) tall—pygmy size compared to their wild cousins, but not so bad in Ireland's cool climate. They also recorded that in its natural environment, papyrus can shoot up 2 inches (5 centimeters) a day, reaching its 15-foot (4.5-meter) maturity in 50 days. The plant has a 150-day life cycle, meaning the natural community grows two "crops" a year. Furthermore, papyrus cultivation yields abundant harvests; per hectare, they can reap as much as 32 tons (29 metric tons).

More to the point, the specialists decided that a papyrus-based fuel could become a paying proposition—not least in spots like heavily populated Kigali (90,000 residents), where, with proper development, briquetted papyrus might provide virtually the same amount of heat per kilogram as wood. Indeed, according to a study undertaken for the United States Agency for International Development (AID), briquetted papyrus "burns like charcoal" within 15 minutes of lighting, "with a steady, clean heat up to three hours without replenishment . . . outperforming both charcoal and wood."

Papyrus Instead of Wood

The fuel does have drawbacks: papyrus briquettes take longer to light than traditional fuels and cannot be extinguished with water and then relit. Sales therefore have been lower than had been originally hoped for. But in places like Rwanda, as in many other African countries, charcoal and wood-fuel dealers are having to travel farther and farther in search of marketable material; around Rwanda's capital of Kigali, for example, there is virtually "nothing left" of once large forests, says Jones.

Papyrus, in fact, could turn out to be an important addition to the world's fuel resources. Last July, Edouard Saouma, director general of the Food and Agriculture Organization (FAO), told the Ninth World Forestry Congress in Mexico City, Mexico, that 2 billion people depend on wood for fuel, and 1 billion of them are cutting down trees faster than the trees can be replanted and replaced. As a result, said FAO officials, some 27 million acres (1 million hectares) of tropical forests disappear every year. The forestry congress also called for the establishment of a world fund to safeguard and foster forest resources.

In Rwanda, such warnings are taken seriously—as is Jones's warning on overharvesting the papyrus plants. A 30-acre (12-hectare) river valley some 25 miles (40 kilometers) away from the capital is now being harvested in planned biannual cuttings—a less-than-maximum harvest to ensure that the plant community will not be environmentally harmed. The field is part of an estimated 50,000-acre (20,000-hectare) papyrus forest, and the annual harvest of papyrus is expected to measure 10 tons per acre (25 tons per hectare) per year. Since Kigali's requirement for domestic fuel is estimated at 5,000 to 6,000 tons per year, the amount of fuel available should be "more than needed in the foreseeable future," notes Martin.

In fact, plans have already been drawn up to establish a second briquetting factory to supplement the initial half-ton-per-hour output of the first, and though the pilot plant went up on the industrial outskirts of the capital, the second is targeted to be built adjacent to the papyrus valley itself.

A Host of Other Uses

Meanwhile, Martin and Jones note, research is under way at Zaza, 50 miles (80 kilometers) from Kigali, into the possibility of again making paper from papyrus. More work may make it economically feasible to truck briquetted papyrus from Rwanda or the Sudan to mills to produce a paper similar to recycled paper, possibly at a lower cost than imports from Europe.

Other uses for the chopped and pressed reed are to make softboard, hardboard (with the addition of necessary resins), and fuel for tin smelting. A long-term vision is to use the plant

Photos: © Michael Jones

Bundled papyrus (above) ready to be made into briquettes. The briquetted papyrus (left) reportedly burns like charcoal, providing heat for up to three hours.

as a gasified alternative to petroleum products to power vehicles.

What's critically important about papyrus is that it's a "renewable source of energy," notes Jones. "You can compare that with peat or oil or coal, which are nonrenewable."

Thousands of years have passed since papyrus was a highly valued commodity. But it may not be long before the tufted giant will make a name for itself once more. This time, though, it won't be in the throne rooms and libraries of potentates; it will be in the kitchens and modest homes of those who might otherwise be without fuel to cook their food and warm themselves.

The 1,818 sun-tracking mirrors of the Solar One plant near Barstow, California, concentrate light on a central receiving tower, where it is used to convert water into steam that, in turn, creates electricity in a conventional turbine generator.

A Bright Future for
SOLAR ENERGY
by Walter Sullivan

Several intriguing developments in the design of photovoltaic cells—devices that convert sunlight directly to electricity—are helping to reawaken interest in solar energy. Many of the most significant advances in solar technology have occurred so recently that energy specialists say there has not yet been time to evaluate their long-term reliability or to develop their full potential. Nevertheless, these specialists say, sunlight is expected to emerge as an important source of the nation's energy when oil and gas prices inevitably rise again.

The most recent development, announced this month by researchers at Stanford University in California, is a novel solar cell that has reached 27.5 percent conversion efficiency. With modifications, its efficiency is expected to reach 30 percent. Until now, the best silicon-based solar cell efficiency was 21 percent.

Other advances have come in designs that use computer-guided sun-tracking mirrors or dishes to focus sunlight on central "power towers" or containers of liquid or gas, producing vapor that in turn drives engines or turbines.

These advances could also reduce the cost of generating solar energy to the point that it will rival conventional fuels by the end of the century, according to an assessment by the Electric Power Research Institute, an organization sponsored by more than 450 utility companies nationwide.

Although many utility companies are already experimenting with large-scale solar power plants, it is the photovoltaic cells that are exciting the most interest. The cell developed at Stanford uses a parabolic mirror to concentrate sunlight to 500 times its normal intensity. After entering the cell, this concentrated light is then reflected back and forth between thin layers of silicon, dislodging electrons to form an electric current.

The Stanford device is known as a "point-contact" cell because the electric current is collected at small metallic contact points on the back of the cell. The use of the tiny points as collectors, instead of the full surface used in previous designs, allows most of the surface area of the back layer to serve as a reflector. Photons (solar energy) reflected off the back in turn are trapped by the texturized surface of the top layer, further increasing the cell's electrical efficiency.

Multilayer Designs Tested

While the point-contact cell is considered a breakthrough, the energy industry also has bright hopes for other cell designs that use multiple layers of semiconductors and respond to different parts of the solar spectrum. A special appeal of these multilayer cells is their ability to produce electricity from diffuse sunlight, making them applicable in regions where hazy or cloudy days are common.

Scientists have discovered that extremely thin and light semiconductor layers can be produced by spraying silicon gas onto supporting layers of steel or glass.

The resulting films of amorphous silicon—so called because its atoms are arranged at random, instead of symmetrically as in the crystalline form—should be less expensive to produce and more optically absorptive than wafers of silicon crystals. However, the films tend to degrade after long exposure to sunlight, a problem many laboratories are trying to overcome.

A variety of other substances are being tested for multilayered solar-energy cells, including amorphous silicon-germanium, copper indium diselenide, and cadmium telluride.

Vast Power Plants Built

In addition to the research in photovoltaic cells, utility companies are investing hundreds of millions of dollars in the construction of vast solar power plants that use sun-tracking panels, dishes, or mirrors to produce electricity indirectly through heat.

One such solar dish design, built by the McDonnell Douglas Corporation of Huntington Beach, California, is now being tested at the experimental site of the Southern California Edison Company at Daggett, 70 miles (113 kilo-

At the Solar Energy Generating System Two (SEGS II)—the world's largest solar generating plant—85,000 mirrors focus sunlight on oil-filled troughs. The heated oil is used to create steam, which drives a turbine generator to make electricity.

Solar energy continues to find wider application, especially in areas having predominantly sunny climates. Above, a laundromat in California uses solar energy to produce its heat. At left, the Steinhart Auditorium in San Francisco relies on solar energy to heat its water.

meters) northeast of Los Angeles in the Mojave Desert.

Its mirrors are assembled to form a dish 36 feet (11 meters) wide that, guided by computers, follows the path of the sun across the sky and focuses sunlight on a tank of hydrogen. As the hydrogen expands, it drives a four-piston engine, generating 25 kilowatts of electricity, enough to supply the power needs of about 15 houses. A field of 2,000 such dishes would produce 50 megawatts, enough to supply 30,000 homes.

While 30 percent efficiencies have been forecast for the solar dish, the operating lifetime of its engine remains uncertain.

Oil Heated in Troughs

Nearby in Daggett is the 30-megawatt SEGS II (Solar Energy Generating System Two) plant. Built in nine months at a cost of $95 million, it is described by its designers as the world's largest generating plant powered primarily by sunlight. Its 85,000 mirrors, covering an area of 135 acres (55 hectares), are aligned to form east-west troughs that focus sunlight onto oil-filled tubing. Computers adjust the tilt of the troughs during the day to match the changing elevation of the sun.

As the oil passes through the tubing, it is heated to 590° F (310° C). This heat is then transferred to water, producing steam that is

How a Solar Cell Works

In 1839 the French physicist Edmund Becquerel discovered that light falling on certain materials can generate a weak electric current. Intensive exploitation of this property was initiated in the 1950's by the Bell Telephone Laboratories as a possible source of power for remote telephone systems. This led to the development of the first solar cells, including those used to power early spacecraft.

The cells were formed of two layers of silicon crystal. One, the "n"-layer, was "doped" with traces of a substance that enabled negatively charged electrons to escape from the crystal lattice and move freely. The other, the "p"-layer, was doped with material that allowed positive charges, or "holes," to move through the lattice.

Light falling on the cell liberated electrons in the n-layer and holes in the p-layer. If the layers were linked by a wire, the electrons flowed through it to join holes, producing an electric current.

then superheated to 780° F (415° C) by gas and drives a turbine generator.

SEGS II was built by Blount International of Montgomery, Alabama, using technology of Luz International of Encino, California, with financing by a number of banks and other private investors. Ownership is shared by a subsidiary of CP National Corporation of Concord, California.

Three more 30-megawatt plants similar to SEGS II are projected, probably at Kramer Junction, 40 miles (64 kilometers) away.

Silent, Efficient, and Nonpolluting

It is, however, on photovoltaic plants—those plants whose arrays of solar cells convert sunlight directly into electricity—that the utilities are focusing much of their attention. Because photovoltaic plants have no turbines or other moving parts, they are nonpolluting, silent, and can be operated unattended. A computer "awakens" them after dawn and shuts them down as the sun sets or goes behind clouds.

Plants of this type capable of substantial power production are beginning to appear, particularly in California, where industry analysts

say no further construction of atomic or fossil-fuel plants is envisioned.

In view of curtailed federal support for research on solar cells, researchers become more dependent on revenue from the increasing use of such cells in small-scale applications. These include powering lighthouses, buoys, mountaintop radio relays, and, particularly in developing countries, irrigation pumps and refrigerators that store vaccines and drugs.

Flat, immobile panels of solar cells are providing electricity to housing subdivisions in Arizona and are mounted on the roofs of McDonald's fast-food restaurants in California. They are cheaper than flatbed arrays that follow the sun, but less efficient.

The high cost of preparing, cutting, polishing, and mounting single-crystal silicon wafers for photovoltaic cells has made it difficult to finance the vast arrays, reckoned in hundreds of acres, needed for bulk production of electricity. At least two companies are moving into the mass production of polycrystalline silicon, which, like amorphous silicon, has advantages in low-cost production and a high optical absorption.

According to Robert H. Annan, director of the Department of Energy's (DOE's) solar cell program, most of the government's future support will go to research on thin-film and multi-layer technologies. Thin films are of special interest to industry, he said, because they have applications in other areas, such as photocopying and thin-film transistors.

Limitations of Solar One

None of the approaches to large-scale power generation from solar energy has operated long enough to assess its relative merits. One of the oldest projects, Solar One, has been on-line for only four years.

Modeled after a smaller prototype at Sandia National Laboratories in Albuquerque, New Mexico, Solar One consists of 1,818 independently controlled mirrors that focus sunlight onto a single boiler atop a 298-foot (91-meter) tower. It currently produces 10 megawatts, and plans are being studied for a 100-megawatt plant.

The final evaluation of its performance will come after its test period ends next year, but currently its prospects as the first choice of the industry appear dim. According to industry sources, Solar One's operating costs have exceeded revenues.

The AFTERMATH of CHERNOBYL

by Stuart Diamond

On April 26, 1986, an explosion at the Chernobyl nuclear power plant 70 miles (112 kilometers) north of Kiev in the Ukraine touched off what would ultimately be a disaster unprecedented in the history of nuclear power. In its wake the Chernobyl nuclear disaster is leading to major reappraisals of reactor safety and emergency planning around the world, even for nuclear plants far different from the ruined Soviet unit, nuclear experts say.

Despite statements soon after the April 26 accident that it involved a reactor design different from Western units, experts are now concluding that Chernobyl in fact has important lessons for all nuclear power plants.

This conclusion is evident in a flurry of recent international conferences and local meetings, in a variety of reports on the accident, and in dozens of interviews with reactor safety experts. Governments, the nuclear industry, and other groups are assessing the accident.

Deadly Potential Realized

It has long been agreed that nearly all reactors have the theoretical potential, albeit a very low one, for a disaster on the scale of Chernobyl. Now that this potential has been realized in one case, the experts have more solid ground for worry that such an event could be repeated.

"This is the first time there has been a nuclear accident of the severity we have all feared," says Dr. Richard Wilson, a Harvard physicist who last year led an American Physical Society study on severe reactor accidents. "No one concerned with nuclear power, in the United States or elsewhere, can pretend that the Chernobyl accident makes no difference."

Moreover, the Chernobyl disaster revealed weaknesses in emergency planning and accident response that could be repeated outside the Soviet Union, experts said. Evacuation and significant radioactive contamination occurred up to 100 miles (160 kilometers) from the Chernobyl plant—a distance 10 times the emergency zone in the United States.

Demographics of Disaster

There are 374 operating nuclear power plants in the world, 102 of them in the United States. Another 157 are being built, 24 in the United

States. More than 700 million people live within 100 miles (160 kilometers) of a nuclear plant. About 3 billion people—three-fifths of the world's population—live within 1,000 miles (1,600 kilometers), the maximum distance at which food consumption was restricted due to Chernobyl contamination.

Nations that did not pay much attention to nuclear power in other countries are for the first time asking questions about safety programs everywhere, mindful of the worldwide radioactive fallout from the Soviet disaster.

"The Chernobyl accident demonstrates vividly that nuclear safety is truly a global issue," says James K. Asselstine of the U.S. Nuclear Regulatory Commission (NRC). "We would be remiss if we ignored some of the accident's broader issues that transcend the design differences. In a very real sense, we are all hostage to each other's performance."

The extent to which the lessons can be fully understood and acted upon, however, is uncertain. Some depend on detailed numerical and physical data from the Soviet Union, but the Russians have so far declined to answer more than 600 questions posed by Western scientists and officials. International cooperation on follow-up studies of radiation victims, urged by the West, has been agreed to only on a limited basis by the Soviet Union.

It is also uncertain how widely all the important lessons will be acted upon, given the extra cost involved and the need in some cases for an exchange of information that is politically or commercially sensitive.

Nonetheless, experts say the accident will advance knowledge and safety on a wide range of nuclear power issues. They include:

• *Overall safety planning.* Chernobyl ended the debate over whether a "worst case" accident could actually happen. Now, instead of arguing over whether catastrophes could occur, experts are studying how to prevent them.

• *Design.* The accident showed the importance of the many safety devices used in Western reactors, but suggested, too, that more such devices may be needed. New questions arise now about the adequacy of containment structures designed to trap radiation.

• *Operation.* Chernobyl, with its major operator violations, proved again that humans are the weak link in reactor safety. Some experts say many operators and managers are still insufficiently trained or careful to prevent another major mishap.

The damaged Chernobyl reactor (left, top) was sealed in concrete (left, bottom). This method of radiation containment is less costly than others, but allows higher levels of radiation into the environment.

• *Accident response.* Chernobyl showed major gaps in procedures for fighting radioactive fires and treating victims, and highlighted the fact that no local emergency plan now in existence is designed to handle an accident as large as Chernobyl.

• *Recovery programs.* Much can be learned from the Soviet experience in entombing reactors, resettling tens of thousands of people, decontaminating and monitoring a vast area, reducing exposure to residual radiation, and managing workers who regularly enter a radioactive area.

• *International relations.* Concerns over the timely issuance of accident warnings to other countries have been settled since Chernobyl, but there is no wide agreement on economic liability, radiation standards, and the sharing of accident data. International inspection of nuclear reactors remains voluntary.

The accident also stirred many old nuclear controversies, including nuclear waste disposal, insurance for nuclear disasters, investments in solar energy, and whether nuclear power is unfairly criticized in a civilization that seems to tolerate tens of thousands of fatal car accidents each year.

The International Nuclear Safety Advisory Group, a team of experts from 12 countries that reviewed the Soviet report on Chernobyl, says, "An opportunity now exists for the world's safety experts to learn from this tragic event to greatly improve our understanding of nuclear safety." Whether that will occur remains to be seen, experts say.

The Debate Is Over on Worst-Case Disaster

The most important lesson, experts agree, is that the Chernobyl accident seems to have settled the debate over whether a worst-case disaster could actually occur.

"Those who claim that Chernobyl can't happen here tell a dangerously misleading half-truth," says Robert D. Pollard, a nuclear engineer at the Union of Concerned Scientists, a Washington group critical of the overall performance of nuclear industry.

"Differences in design between U.S. and Soviet plants mean that the accident could not happen in precisely the same way here," Pollard explains. "What they do not tell the public is that an accident with as large a release as Chernobyl, or worse, could happen."

At a recent Harvard symposium, Dr. James MacKenzie of the World Resources Institute in Washington said studies in West Germany and Sweden indicated that an accident destroying a reactor somewhere in the world has a 70 percent chance of happening in five years and an 86 percent chance of happening in 10 years. He noted there have been two core destructions in 4,000 reactor-years of operating experience: Three Mile Island and Chernobyl. Each year, 400 years of reactor operation are added.

"There are too many ways these plants can go wrong," Dr. MacKenzie said. "And our reactors continue to suffer from control problems."

Some nuclear industry experts, who once agreed that Western reactors presented a risk of disaster so small as to warrant no serious consideration, now issue cautions. Bernard J. O'Keefe, the chairman of the executive committee of EG&G, Inc., a company that supplies nuclear services, says "Nuclear core melts are likely to happen again. The set of circumstances will be new, so one can almost guarantee that people will not be prepared for them."

But other experts say the risk of a disaster will decrease because of safety improvements that are going to be adopted as a result of Chernobyl. "After every major accident, modifications are made," says Dr. Anthony R. Buhl, a nuclear engineer who heads the American nuclear industry's severe accident study group.

A Central Issue: The Containment

The most disputed design issue, experts say, involves the containment, the steel and concrete structure around a reactor to trap escaping radiation. After Chernobyl, American nuclear proponents took out newspaper advertisements saying a Chernobyl-type accident could not happen here because Western containments are much stronger than Chernobyl's.

This remains the view of many. "Our containments are good enough," says Dr. Buhl.

But the assessment is being increasingly challenged even within the nuclear establishment. Dr. Morris Rosen, who oversees nuclear safety programs at the International Atomic Energy Agency (IAEA) in Vienna and is the top American staff member there, says the Chernobyl and Western containments were designed to withstand pressures caused by certain types of accidents. But the lesson driven home by Chernobyl, he says, is that there can be other kinds of accidents in nuclear power plants that will trigger explosions that no current containment vessel may be able to withstand.

All traffic leaving the contaminated zone around the damaged Chernobyl plant was checked for radiation exposure.

Marshall Berman, head of severe accident containment analysis at Sandia National Laboratories in New Mexico, says some steam explosions could breach the containment of some American reactors. A steam explosion occurred at Chernobyl.

With that uncertainty, the West is reexamining the ability of its designs to withstand a wider variety of possible accidents, including steam explosions and runaway reactions, as well as phenomena, such as rapid fuel breakup instead of slow meltdown, that had been only postulated theoretically before Chernobyl.

The mechanics of radiation releases are also being studied. The release did not occur all at once. Only 25 percent escaped the first day; the rest escaped over the next eight days, traveled far from the plant, and included more long-lived plutonium than expected. Experts say current models of radiation releases may be wrong or incomplete.

Chernobyl Units 1, 2, and 3 were contaminated by the ruined Unit 4, partly through ventilation systems. Changes to the ventilation and methods to quickly decontaminate control rooms are being discussed, particularly for multireactor sites.

The Chernobyl accident, as at Three Mile Island, began with a nonnuclear task: water filter cleaning at the Pennsylvania plant, a turbine

test at the Ukrainian one. The Soviet accident again raised the controversial issue of treating all equipment in a nuclear plant as safety-related, even if it means more rigorous design, testing, and cost.

Chernobyl also renewed the notion of building reactors that, by their design alone, cannot produce a disaster. Such inherently safe reactors could operate at lower temperatures, pressures, and power densities than existing plants. Some could be small and modular, others underground.

The Human Role in Stemming Disaster

Even more than design, Chernobyl underscored problems in human error and management quality. Although some design flaws existed at Chernobyl, the accident would not have occurred without six separate operating violations.

Experts said Chernobyl showed the need for evaluations based not just on power output but also on safety excellence: small maintenance backlogs, few emergency shutdowns. The experts stressed the need for a "safety culture" among plant staff: the ingrained philosophy that safety comes first.

Chernobyl exposed the biggest weaknesses in accident response. "The general field of accident management techniques is still in its in-

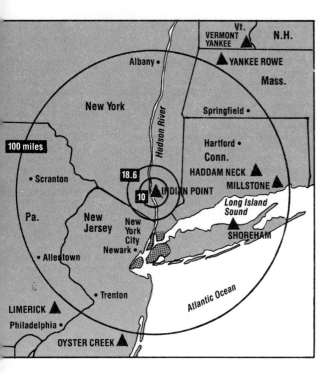

The 10-mile circle shows the emergency planning zone around the Indian Point plant. At Chernobyl, an 18.6-mile radius was completely evacuated, and children living within 100 miles of the damaged plant were removed.

Evacuation Plans: A Renewed Concern

Evacuation planning has been the most debated aspect of American nuclear power in recent years. The evacuation zone mandated by the United States government has a 10-mile (16-kilometer) radius, but the U.S. nuclear industry before Chernobyl was urging a smaller zone.

The Chernobyl evacuation, however, challenged some American assumptions. All residents within 18 miles (29 kilometers) of the Soviet plant were evacuated, but not until two days after the accident, because the radiation at first soared farther away. But children were evacuated from villages as much as 100 miles (160 kilometers) from the plant.

"Under a really major accident, you may have to go out several tens of miles," Dr. Mac-Kenzie says. Other disagree; the subject is being debated vigorously.

The stakes are high: Lying within a 100-mile (160-kilometer) radius of the Indian Point, New York, reactor, for example, are New York City; Albany, New York; Trenton, New Jersey; and Hartford, Connecticut—in all, more than 20 million people. Indian Point officials say their plans, based on a 10-mile (16-kilometer) zone, are adequate.

American emergency planners, however, admit that they have no contingencies for some of the recovery programs that could be needed in the aftermath of a major nuclear disaster, programs that at Chernobyl meant resettling 135,000 people and building thousands of new homes; erecting 12 miles (19 kilometers) of dikes to prevent radiation from running into a river; sealing thousands of wells and digging 58 new deep wells to supply the city of Kiev, 80 miles (130 kilometers) from the reactor; and building new aqueducts.

In the Ukrainian village of Bragin, 25 miles (40 kilometers) from the plant, where most of the roads were unpaved, every street had to be paved to keep down radioactive dust. Trees and shrubs were pulled up and buried as radioactive debris. Buildings are being washed in an area of thousands of square miles. Food hundreds of miles away was destroyed.

"We obviously do not have plans in place to do that sort of thing," says Peter Slocum of the New York State Health Department. He adds, however, that "we have an increased concern for looking outside the 10-mile (16-kilometer) area." He says the state plans talks with other states in handling radiation that might cross borders.

fancy," the IAEA said. "People who are responsible for this type of work should study this case and learn from it."

Fighting fires amid high levels of radiation was one new experience. The Chernobyl disaster showed the need for lightweight protective clothing to shield workers from high temperature and radiation, as well as for fire-fighting robots, less flammable turbine oils, and dosimeters with alarms for emergency workers. The dosimeters, which measure radiation, are used at some Western nuclear plants. All 31 Chernobyl deaths were workers unaware they were getting a lethal dose of radiation.

The Russians eventually dropped 5,000 tons (4,540 metric tons) of lead, limestone, sand, and boron from helicopters into the open reactor, curbing the fire and radiation. Experts said the innovative technique deserves more study because it is not clear that the Russians used the proper mixture. At first they tried water, the traditional material, but it produced radioactive effluent that leaked from the reactor and flowed toward Units 1 and 2, contaminating the ground and threatening the other units.

Much More to Learn in Medical Response

The medical needs created by Chernobyl exposed many gaps in Western plans. The Russians gave potassium iodide tablets to tens of thousands of people to prevent the buildup of radioactive iodine in their thyroids. The treatment was deemed successful, without serious side effects. American nuclear plants generally do not stock such tablets in amounts sufficient to treat the general public.

After Chernobyl, 500 people were hospitalized, many with serious burns. Bone marrow transplants, which had been regarded as a major treatment for radiation sickness, were tried after Chernobyl, but were largely ineffective.

Dr. Robert Peter Gale, an American bone marrow specialist who treated Chernobyl victims, said the United States could not handle hundreds of radiation victims from one accident, and urged more research on treating such victims.

The number of people who will die of cancer over the next 70 years from radiation released by Chernobyl is estimated to range from 5,000 to 500,000, with estimates of 6,000

© SYGMA

Potassium iodide was administered to thousands of people to prevent thyroid damage due to radiation (right). Below, American doctor Robert Gale, who specializes in the transplantation of bone marrow tissue, helped the Soviets treat radiation victims.

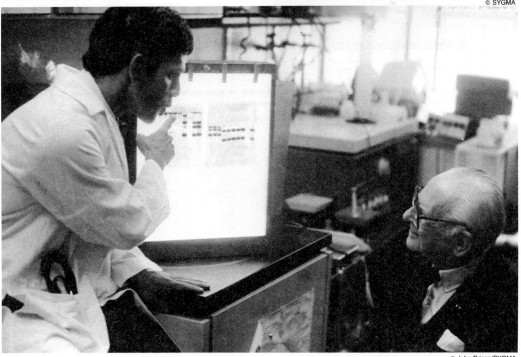

© John Brison/SYGMA

to 24,000 predominating. There is also uncertainty about radiation-induced genetic abnormalities, which usually run 20 to 40 percent of the cancer cases.

"Nobody really knows the correct answer," says Dr. Roger E. Linnemann, a Philadelphia radiation consultant.

Coping with Long-Term Radiation

The long-term response to Chernobyl also holds important lessons, experts say. There are more than 100,000 evacuees now being resettled; for many of them, new work must be found and psychological problems must be addressed. Forests, buildings, and land as far as 36 miles (58 kilometers) from the plant must be cleaned of radiation.

The Russians say it could be years before the public can reenter the 18.6-mile (30-kilometer) evacuation zone. Methods are being explored to keep unauthorized people out.

Radiation monitoring also presents a challenge. It includes tracking contaminated water supplies and studying the radiation's effect on plants, animals, and people.

The entombment of Chernobyl Unit 4 is of great interest to reactor operators. No large power reactors have ever been retired, but all will be. The Russians said last month that they had finished pouring 3 feet (1 meter) of concrete around Chernobyl 4, and are devising ways to prevent the inside from overheating. They are also planning decades of monitoring.

The technology is in its infancy; there have already been problems with the special heat-resistant concrete. There is additional concern about possible leakage of radiation into the groundwater and about the foundation strength. The Russians are building a second foundation under the reactor.

The entombed reactor has a continuing radiation leak rate estimated at up to 500 times the natural "background" levels. This radiation is expected to continue for many years, but is not expected to pose additional health problems to the public. But it is uncertain whether the rate can be kept from growing, because there is some question whether the structure can remain intact for more than 50 years.

Reducing the long-lived radioactive cesium and strontium that fell to the ground in the Soviet Union and Europe will also reduce cancer, experts say. It would be too costly to scrape up the soil, so scientists plan to experiment with cheaper means. The soil can be treated with calcium compounds that capture strontium and carry it below the topsoil, or with potassium fertilizers that limit plants' cesium uptake.

Many of the victims of the Chernobyl disaster were unaware that they had received lethal doses of radiation.

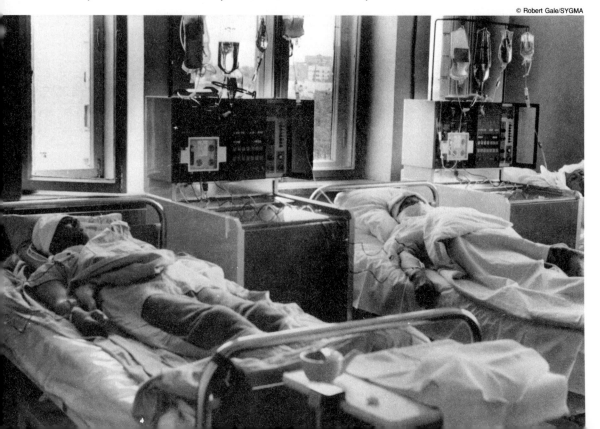

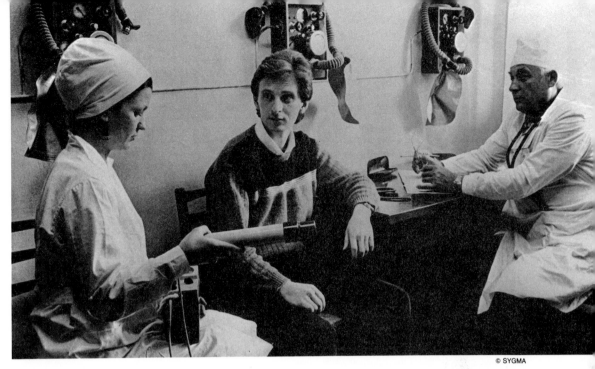

© SYGMA

An engineer at one of the three undamaged Chernobyl reactors is examined by Soviet doctors for radiation exposure.

Hopes for Improving Global Cooperation

The Chernobyl accident also highlighted the need for international sharing of fallout data and for international standards on radiation treatment and food restrictions.

Chernobyl showed that reactor accidents, which can be very costly, lack clear lines of liability among countries. The Soviet Union said in September that its direct costs for the accident were nearly $3 billion, including $885 million for new housing and the $590 million reactor loss.

Hundreds of millions of dollars in contaminated food was destroyed in Europe. The Russians have refused to compensate Western countries for these losses.

Most scientists hope cooperation on the long list of items will improve safety as never before. Says Dr. Rudolf Rometsch, a Swiss nuclear expert who chaired the August symposium on Chernobyl: "It will be difficult, but it's worth a try."

SELECTED READINGS

"Chernobyl: errors and design flaws" by C. Norman. *Science,* September 5, 1986.

"Soviets unveil lessons from Chernobyl" by J. Raloff. *Science News,* August 30, 1986.

"Witness to disaster: an American doctor at Chernobyl" by R. P. Gale. *Life,* August 1986.

"After Chernobyl." *Nation,* May 10, 1986.

In Western Europe, tons of fresh produce and dairy products were dumped after being tainted with radiation.

© Gamma Liaison

THE ENVIRONMENT

© dpa/Photoreporters

Fish life in the Rhine River was nearly decimated by the discharge of toxic chemicals from a Swiss plant.

REVIEW OF THE YEAR

THE ENVIRONMENT

Problems of poisonous wastes from the myriad activities of mankind continued to dominate the environmental landscape, nationally and internationally, in 1986. Measures for coping with air pollution, water pollution, and soil pollution preoccupied scientists, public officials, and citizens around the globe. But easy solutions remained elusive. Scientific concern mounted over three international problems: depletion of the earth's protective stratospheric ozone layer, worrisome growth of the globe's shroud of carbon dioxide, and acid rain—the precipitation of corrosive airborne pollutants.

THE ATMOSPHERE

The atmospheric layer of naturally formed carbon dioxide helps maintain the earth's accustomed temperature levels by blocking the escape of heat: the "greenhouse effect." But many scientists are apprehensive that man's proliferating combustion processes within the next generation or two may produce so much carbon dioxide, trapping more heat, as to raise global temperatures to calamitous levels. An increase of only a few degrees, it is believed, might melt ice sheets, raising ocean levels and flooding shorelines and important land areas, and disrupt agricultural and botanical patterns. A United Nations task force recommended that nations seek alternatives to fossil fuels, reduce industrial emissions, and curb widespread destruction of forests, which absorb carbon dioxide. A basic concern was whether collective global action could be mobilized before inordinate "greenhouse effects" become irreversible.

Combustion processes—chiefly coal-burning power plants emitting sulfur compounds—also are blamed primarily for acid rain, whose deleterious impacts on waterways, forests, and crops in the United States, Canada, and Europe gathered documentation during the year. Corrective regulations including Clean Air Act amendments were bogged down in Congress. But the Reagan administration, after parleys with Canada, endorsed in principle the outlay of $5 billion over the next five years for studies aimed at pinpointing critical details of the problem.

The notion that atomic warfare could so cloud global skies with smoke as to block out solar heating and bring on a catastrophic "nuclear winter" continued to be a focus of animated scientific debate. The theory, broached by a group of scientists in 1983, was based on computer studies, and critics have suggested that the assumptions used were implausibly extreme. To get some practical data, scientists from a dozen governmental agencies made elaborate observations of a man-made brush fire covering nearly 1 square mile (2.6 square kilometers) that was touched off in California's San Gabriel Mountains in December.

RHINE TOXIC SPILL

The international implications of pollution were dramatically underscored when a fire at a chemical plant in Basel, Switzerland, November 1, 1986, released a large volume of toxic chemicals into the Rhine River, which in its 500-mile (800-kilometer) course to the North Sea traverses three other nations—Germany, France, and the Netherlands.

The discharge, estimated as high as 27 tons (30 metric tons), included mercury and some 30 other chemicals. It created a 30-mile (50-kilometer) plume in the 10 days it moved downstream, contaminating many drinking water sources and untold quantities of fish and other aquatic life, and jeopardizing two decades of biologists' work to revivify the oft-polluted Rhine's biota. Experts conjectured that toxic effects from deposited chemicals might linger for a decade. At Basel, 10,000 people demonstrated in protest against inadequate precautions. The Swiss government and the chemical company, Sandoz, acknowledged its responsibility.

WATER

In the United States the Environmental Protection Agency (EPA) reported finding that some 40 million Americans were drinking water containing toxic amounts of lead, due mainly to deterioration of lead pipe in plumbing, which the agency banned in 1985. The EPA, which has had a safety standard of 50 parts per billion of lead in drinking water, moved to reduce this drastically to 20 parts; some scientists said the limit should be 10 parts. Drinking water is considered a major source of ingested lead, with the rest coming from auto fumes, paints, and other substances. Excessive levels of lead in the body can cause pregnancy problems, mental retardation in children, and other ailments.

Increased concern about drinking water moved Congress to enact amendments to the Safe Drinking Water Act of 1974 directing the EPA to set new safety limits on 82 other contaminants, and authorizing the expenditure of $800 million over the next five years (nearly double the previous rate) on federal programs and grants to states to assure water purity.

Congress also passed unanimously renewal of the Clean Water Act, containing measures to abate nationwide pollution, but President Reagan vetoed the bill, saying the $18 billion it provided for community sewerage improvements was excessive. (The act was passed over the president's veto in early 1987.) To date, the federal government has given $37 billion to states and communities for improved sewerage. Eliminating waterway pollution from sewage discharges by the year 2000 would cost $109 billion.

RADON

A new environmental poison, unattributable to human activities, came to the fore in the form of radon. It is a colorless, odorless, radioactive gas that seeps out of the earth—the product of the natural nuclear disintegration of uranium and its offspring radium. Radon can make its way into inadequately ventilated buildings and accumulate in harmful concentrations. The EPA, after the latest studies of the problem, estimated that this hazard might be present in as many as 8 million homes, and could be causing from 5,000 to 20,000 of the 130,000 lung cancer deaths each year. Radon occurs in all 50 states, but to date has been observed in abnormal amounts chiefly in a geological belt comprising parts of Pennsylvania, New Jersey, New York, and Connecticut. The EPA said that concentrations of more than 4 picocuries (one trillionth of the standard radiation unit, and the equivalent of 20 chest X rays in a year) called for correction through sealing of structural apertures at ground level, and improved ventilation.

SUPERFUND

After two years of strenuous debate, Congress achieved enactment of an impressive enlargement of the federal "Superfund" program for cleaning up the thousands of hazardous waste dumps that pock the nation. In contrast to the initial 1981–85 $1.6 billion appropriation for the program, the new legislation provided for the expenditure of $9 billion in the next five years. The law set a schedule for EPA action, including 375 new cleanup starts. The EPA has listed 25,000 toxic dump sites. Of these, some 6,300 have been inspected and 888 listed for priority action. The EPA said "cleanup work" had begun on more than 450, but that includes preliminary analyses, which in themselves may take as much as two years. Congress in 1984 mandated an end to land disposal of hazardous wastes by 1990. Most of the $9 billion funding will come from new industrial taxes.

GLADWIN HILL

Another giant evergreen of Oregon's centuries-old forests falls victim to a lumberjack's saw (left). The environmental well-being of the Pacific Northwest may rely upon the health of its ancient trees (above).

© Tom & Pat Leeson

Virgin Forests Under Fire

by Dean Baker

Chris Maser spends much of his time these days poking around rotting logs in some of Oregon's remaining virgin forests. But examining "fallen trees," as he calls them, is more than an avocation for the U.S. Bureau of Land Management ecologist. Like a surgeon, Maser has his fingers in the heart of a complex, vital life-form: the last great old-growth forest in the Pacific Northwest. And clearly, he is concerned about the future of his patient.

"The fallen tree," says Maser, "is at the crossroads of the forest. It serves a whole different function once it dies. It helps generate new life. People must understand that in a forest, there's no such thing as waste."

Maser is one of several scientists who have spent the past decade attempting to uncover the mysteries of the old-growth forest. Unless some of the nation's attitudes and logging practices

© Harald Sund

change, he warns, the old-growth ecosystem may disappear—and the repercussions for the environment could be disastrous.

Conservationists Versus Loggers

Currently, old growth is the focus of a bitter controversy in the Northwest between conservationists, who are fighting to save the diminishing ecosystem, and loggers, who say that the cutting of the remaining big trees is crucial to the region's economy. "We need to protect jobs," says Lynn Greenwalt, National Wildlife Federation vice president for resources conservation. "But cutting irreplaceable old-growth trees is not the solution. Until we fully understand the ecological significance of these forests, shouldn't we protect what remains of them? If we don't, we may regret it."

Old-growth forests are usually made up of trees more than 200 years old and 40 inches (100 centimeters) or more in diameter. They consist of at least two species of trees—usually Douglas fir and western hemlock—which create a dense, multilayered canopy. The spongy ground in such forests is littered with debris and

fallen trees. "These ancient forests are unlike any other ecosystem in the world," notes federation forester Andy Stahl.

Researchers have found that some of the lush old-growth Douglas fir stands in the western Cascades may support the densest breeding bird populations of any forest system in the country. Because the filtering effect of the debris in old growth stops siltation (the buildup of sediment in rivers and streams), the streams in these forests contain some of the cleanest water in the world—ideal habitat for salmon and trout. And the interaction of life in the woodlands is crucial to the development of new tree life in neighboring forests.

Diminished Acreage

At one time, old-growth forests blanketed some 15 million acres (6 million hectares) in the Pacific Northwest. Some stands included trees 10 feet wide (3 meters), 275 feet (84 meters) tall, and 1,200 years old. In North America, only the coast redwoods and giant sequoias were larger. Because of their size and bulk, old-growth trees represented valuable lumber. During the past century some 12 million acres (4.85 million hectares) of the forests were cleared.

Today the remaining old growth—about 3 million acres (1.2 million hectares)—is found almost entirely on public lands administered by the federal government. Though some of it is protected in national parks and wilderness areas, the vast majority is still available for harvesting. "If current policies remain intact," notes federation attorney Terrence Thatcher, "most of the old growth will be cut within the next two decades."

Cellulose Cemeteries?

Many federal foresters believe it would be wasteful to do otherwise. They tend to take the traditional view that the old forests, with their abundance of decay, are "cellulose cemeteries" that are best replaced with thrifty young stands of fast-growing trees. Why allow valuable wood to decompose on the forest floor?

Chris Maser believes that is where some of the wood belongs. "The value you choose for a tree is the one you see," he points out. "If you think of it in terms of the economics of extinction—which says that if we don't cut the tree down, it's going to rot, and if we don't use it, it goes to waste—then it has no value except in terms of cutting. But if you look at the tree in another way, it has a lot of other values—for

© Chuck Ripper

The ancient stand of Douglas firs depicted above has matured into an "old growth" ecosystem that supports a rich variety of birds, mammals, and plants. Salmon hatch (inset 1) in streams filtered clean by logs and other woody debris. Big brown bats (2) feed on beetles that live in decaying trees. Flying squirrels (3) are prey for the endangered northern spotted owl. The volelike red phenacomys (4) builds lofty nests that are lived in for generations. A dormouse (5) feeds on fungi. At upper left, a goshawk, its short wings adapted for flying in dense forests, hunts for prey.

aesthetics, for clean water, for wildlife, and for genetic value in future trees."

Maser has found that the rotting log plays an important role in natural processes. "I know of no system," he says, "that doesn't replenish itself on the death of some of its components. Our bodies replace our entire complement of cells every seven years. If that didn't happen, we would age rapidly."

Old-Growth Ecosystems

Two years ago, under pressure from conservationists, the federal government and the state resource agencies in the Northwest launched an unprecedented program to learn more about the old-growth forest system.

In 145 stands throughout the Northwest, researchers are probing forests piece by piece—putting down kerosene-smoked plates to capture animal tracks; measuring the flow of water in streams; live-trapping flying squirrels, wood rats, and chipmunks; weighing the amount of debris on the forest floor; putting whole insect communities under the microscope; even analyzing the genetic structure of individual trees.

"We've generated some fantastic data sets," beams Andrew Carey, a wildlife biologist with the U.S. Forest Service. Carey and his associates have discovered that at least 18 creatures prefer—and may depend upon—old growth for breeding and foraging. Some of these animals could become extinct if the remaining old-growth forests are lost to logging. In addition, deer and elk, previously thought to reply only upon openings for browse, have been found to depend on old growth for forage during winter months and for security throughout the year.

Although animals depend on the old trees, the reverse is also true, according to Carey and his associates: the trees depend on the animals. For instance, small mammals such as red-backed voles eat truffles, which are the fruiting bodies of fungi found in rotten wood on old-growth forest floors. These small mammals often travel to areas where young trees grow and excrete the truffles' spores. In a process that scientists have yet to understand fully, the spores grow into fungi that interact with the tiny hairs on tree roots, carrying nutrients and moisture to seedlings. Scientists now know that many other interactions—involving lichens, fungi, insects, small mammals, and carnivores—occur both in the canopy and on the floor of old-growth forests.

Such findings cast doubt on the efficacy of current management programs. Foresters are replacing the old trees with seedlings bred in spe-

© Tom & Pat Leeson

The delicate calypso orchid thrives in the decaying vegetation that carpets the floor of the virgin forests.

cial orchards for fast growth. However, some researchers suspect that these so-called "supertrees" do not have the genetic diversity to survive the climatic extremes that can affect the trees' lives. That, in turn, could greatly affect the region's environmental health in future years.

A herd of Roosevelt elk splashes across Washington's remote Hoh River toward the safety of the dense forest.

© Tom & Pat Leeson

Worried Loggers

Northwest loggers, however, are mostly concerned about the present. "We are harvesting a lot of lumber," says Mike Sullivan, spokesman for the Industrial Forestry Association. "The problem is, we can't make a profit." Predictions of future shortages have caused the price of timber in the region to skyrocket, Sullivan maintains. Old-growth stands are now sold by the federal government for as much as $20,000 per acre. Many timber buyers say they cannot afford to pay that amount. Meanwhile, those companies that rely on federal timber supplies are pushing hard to cut most of the remaining old growth.

"In the past few years, the situation has been very painful for loggers in the Northwest," notes Terence Thatcher. "But we don't think cutting the last remaining old growth will change the problems of high federal deficits, Canadian lumber imports, and high labor costs plaguing the Northwest timber industry. Sooner or later, the transition to a second-growth economy will be complete. The question is, Will there be enough old growth left then to maintain fish and wildlife habitat?"

After two appeals from the National Wildlife Federation, the Forest Service belatedly agreed to prepare a comprehensive environmental impact statement on the potential effects of its old-growth harvesting program—a procedure required by law. The report is due by the end of this year.

Preservation Problems

The analysis will come none too soon, say biologists. Recent research by Russell Lande, a population geneticist at the University of Chicago, found that old-growth harvesting to date may already have jeopardized the survival of one creature, the northern spotted owl. This shy, 20-inch- (50-centimeter)-tall bird, which lives only in old-growth forests, currently numbers about 5,000. Lande calculates that its population is declining at an 8 percent annual rate.

Because the spotted owl needs old growth to survive and is at the top of the food chain, the Forest Service has called it an "indicator species." The bird's health helps reveal the status of the other life throughout the complex ecosystem of the virgin forest.

A Portland forest economist, David Cox, maintains that the owl is too expensive to save: the economic loss of timber in preserving habitat for just 800 birds, he says, would cost $5 billion. The question, however, may be whether we can afford not to save the northern spotted owl and its remaining old-growth habitat.

Recently, Chris Maser returned from Europe, where air pollution appears to be destroying many forests. Maser believes that much of the problem may stem, in part, from forestry practices. For centuries, foresters have tidied up many European forests, keeping the ground clean of life-giving debris. This may have kept such forests from rejuvenating themselves. The result: trees too weak to survive pollution.

"There's a lesson in that," says Maser. "Whenever you simplify a process, you probably cause problems." And as years of study have shown him, the old forests of the Pacific Northwest are anything but simple.

SELECTED READINGS

"Forests are more than trees" by J. D. Hair. *International Wildlife,* September–October 1986.

"Biological diversity: going . . . going . . . ?" by L. Davis. *Science News,* September 27, 1986.

"Deforestation: major threat to ozone?" by J. Raloff. *Science News,* August 23, 1986.

© Tom & Pat Leeson

The marten spends most of its time in the tall trees of the forests, where it stalks smaller mammals and birds.

THE OTHER KIND OF RADIATION

by Nancy Shute

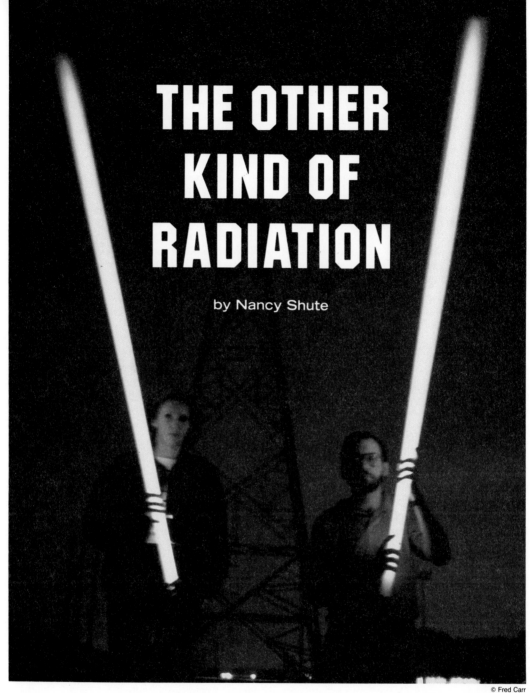

© Fred Carr

Nonionizing radiation emitted by overhead power lines can be strong enough to light fluorescent tubes held far below.

In November 1985, a six-member jury filed into a Texas courtroom and slapped the Houston Lighting and Power Company with more than $25.1 million in punitive damages. The firm's offense: installing high-voltage electrical power lines and towers in the midst of three schools in the suburban Klein Independent School District.

At first the school district only worried students might get hurt climbing the towers. But that all changed when district officials came upon medical reports suggesting a possible link between cancer and the kind of radiation emitted by these transmission lines. That's when they hauled the utility company into court, and won a landmark case.

Cancer from power lines? It sounds like a bad joke. But as the Klein school district discovered, a growing number of scientists and environmental activists see real potential for danger. The cause of their concern: nonionizing electromagnetic radiation. It's an invisible, omnipresent form of energy emitted by power lines and a you-name-it list of modern devices: computer video display terminals (VDTs), microwave ovens, television and radio transmitters, radar, even electric blankets.

The Houston verdict galvanized activists and appalled utility companies. "We felt the jury's judgment was hasty," says Geri Konigsberg of Houston Lighting and Power Company, which is appealing the verdict. "There's no concrete evidence that the lines pose a threat." It's true that no definite link has been discovered between this kind of radiation and cancer. But a growing body of research has raised disturbing questions, disturbing enough for the Houston jury to find in favor of the school district.

Disturbing Evidence

It's long been known that exposure to high doses of nonionizing radiation—above 64.5 milliwatts per square inch, rarely encountered in everyday life—can heat living tissue and cause, for example, burns, cataracts, and sterility. But the big question is: Can this radiation do damage at much lower levels?

There's some evidence that it might. At the first international meeting on VDTs in Stockholm, Sweden, held in May 1986, Swedish researchers presented evidence that radiation similar to that emitted by VDTs (pulsed, very-low-frequency magnetic fields) can cause fetal malformations in mice. The Swedish study is not the first report of potential health risks from relatively low levels of nonionizing radiation. Consider:

A study at the University of Colorado found that women who used electric blankets during the winter had a higher miscarriage rate for those months than nonusers. Normally, miscarriages are evenly distributed through the year, researchers said.

Another finding: Babies who were conceived in the winter by blanket users tended to grow in the womb more slowly—they had longer gestation periods but didn't have a higher birth weight. The researchers, epidemiologist Nancy Wertheimer and her colleague Ed Leeper, are not sure whether these effects come from the blanket's heat, the energy field it emits, or unknown factors other than blanket use.

In another study, Wertheimer compared 344 children who had died of cancers in Denver, Colorado, between 1950 and 1973 with an equal number who hadn't. She found the victims were more likely to have lived near high-current electric lines.

A study by the Maryland Department of Health and Hygiene found an unusually high percentage of electricians, electronics engineers, and utility repairmen among 951 men who died of brain tumors. A similar study from Washington State found that workers exposed to various intense electromagnetic fields were two and a half times more likely to suffer acute leukemia than the general population.

At the Cancer Therapy and Research Center in San Antonio, Texas, Dr. Jerry Phillips showed that electromagnetic fields—like those from power lines—enable human colon cancer cells to grow faster, survive longer.

What does it all mean? "There's no definite proof of carcinogenicity [cancer-causing properties], but there's enough in the way of statistical evidence to arouse concern," says Baylor University cancer specialist Harris Busch, who testified on behalf of the Houston school district. "You have to remember that 50 years ago there was no definitive proof of the carcinogenicity of cigarettes."

Radiation Everywhere

Say "radiation," and most people conjure up nightmarish visions of the Soviet Chernobyl disaster, Three Mile Island, and nuclear war. But electromagnetic radiation—a spectrum of energy that travels in waves—is part of our everyday lives. It includes the sun's visible light and heat-producing infrared radiation. Nuclear energy, a form of ionizing electromagnetic radiation (strong enough to break atoms apart), is at the top of this energy spectrum. The various energy frequencies emitted by electrical lines, VDTs, microwave ovens, or radio and TV transmitters are near the bottom and are called nonionizing radiation. Unlike nuclear energy, they cannot actually change atomic structure.

Although they are all nonionizing, these "everyday" kinds of radiation are as different as apples, oranges, and aardvarks. Example: Research indicates radiation that comes in pulses (like some created by VDTs or radar) may be more biologically active than continuous waves like those from radio and television, says Louis Slesin, publisher of *Microwave News* and *VDT News,* which monitor research in the area. How the waves interact with drugs, chemicals, and the earth's magnetic field can also affect their damage potential.

What About Microwave Ovens?

Since they first came out in the early 1970's, microwave ovens have become the fastest-selling home appliances in America. Almost half of all homes now sport one. And a recent study sponsored by the Campbell Soup Company predicts 70 percent penetration by 1990. These ovens cook by causing the food's water molecules to vibrate and rotate so fast they generate heat—quickly.

Some of the early models emitted too much radiation. So in 1971 the Food and Drug Administration (FDA) established an emission standard for the ovens—6.45 milliwatts per square inch when brand-new, and five times that amount over the life of the oven. The standard is based on known biological effects at certain radiation exposure levels.

Every new oven is required to have two interlocks that cut off power if the door is opened. A monitor system shuts off the oven if the locks fail. The FDA also oversees the manufacturing process and surveys ovens in the field.

End result: Right now, microwave ovens are probably among the safest appliances you can buy. Last year, Consumers Union found microwaves were emitting only half of the FDA's new standard. Thanks to improved design of both ovens and pacemakers, there's no longer concern that microwaves could halt the pacemakers of unsuspecting restaurant patrons.

Despite the good news, it pays to be cautious. An oven can still leak radiation if the interlock system is disarmed, if the seals around the door are damaged, or if the door doesn't close properly. Don Witters, a physicist with the FDA's Center for Devices and Radiological Health, warns: Never operate an oven with a warped door or damaged seals, or when an object is trapped in the door. Also, keep the seals clean.

Not All Bad News

Despite the concern, the findings on nonionizing radiation are not all disturbing. In fact, this radiation offers great potential for good, says neurophysiologist W. Ross Adey of the Veterans Administration Medical Center in Loma Linda, California. He points out that medical science has already harnessed this energy to speed the healing of tissue, broken bones, and surgical wounds, and for Magnetic Resonance Imaging—a highly sensitive diagnostic tool used to obtain pictures from inside the body.

The possible link between cancer and radiation from high-voltage lines may particularly pertain to children.

© Fred Carr

What's troubling is that despite voluminous research, we still know surprisingly little about nonionizing radiation or its hazards.

What Don't We Know?

Broadcasters, utility companies, and the military have disagreed on what levels of nonionizing radiation in its various forms are safe for workers and the public. If studies were to confirm dangers from low-level exposure, tough new standards could cost millions of dollars in preventive measures and lawsuits. Says Arthur Guy, electromagnetics engineer at the University of Washington: "The broadcast industry could be affected very profoundly."

Between 1978 and 1985 the Air Force funded a $5 million general health study at the University of Washington School of Medicine. Rats who were exposed to electromagnetic radiation as part of the study developed a disproportionate number of malignant tumors. But the Air Force downplayed the study because in its view the results were not strong enough to warrant further work.

Dr. Guy, who led the study, disagrees. He terms the findings "provocative," though he says they cannot be cited as evidence of harm until they're repeated. But no one, including the Air Force, has agreed to fund another study. If public pressure were greater, says Guy, perhaps the study's results would be reexamined.

Right now only one nonmilitary federal lab is studying the biological toll of nonionizing radiation—and even that work is being halted. Federal research focusing specifically on VDT safety has also been hurt by budget cuts.

Why such government cutbacks at the very time public concern is growing? "Frankly, we do not have a record of people being harmed," says Richard Tell of the Office of Radiation Programs of the Environmental Protection Agency (EPA). "We have indications from research that we ought to be concerned, but we don't have evidence in the population."

Risk to Pregnant Women?

The news was released by the Swedish occupational safety board. Researchers from Stockholm's Karolinska Institute had found a scary pattern of fetal malformations in pregnant mice exposed to what are called pulsed magnetic fields. The fields were similar to those generated from the sides of VDTs (not the screen). Compared with other mice, the zapped animals produced more deformed fetuses.

The initial report generated such alarm that the Swedish board reviewed it. Their conclusion: The findings were insufficient to justify barring pregnant women from VDT work. But that could change. Full results were formally presented in May, and Dr. Lars-Erik Paulsson, one of the leaders of the Swedish research, says they are "a strong indication that something is happening." He and his colleagues are now conducting a much larger study.

The Swedish study offers some strong evidence of what many suspect: Those ever-present VDTs may pose a health risk. Fears had been prompted earlier by the 1982 results of Drs. José Delgado and Jocelyne Leal in Madrid, Spain, who reported severe malformations in chick embryos also exposed to magnetic fields with some similarities to VDT emissions. This spring, five laboratories around the world, coordinated by the U.S. Office of Naval Research, will attempt to verify the Delgado study using identical magnetic field generators and carefully controlled conditions; it will add more credibility to nonionizing radiation research.

Before the Spanish study, too, there had been controversial reports of clusters of pregnancy problems among VDT workers. Whether these troubles were actually caused by radiation is unconfirmed:

• At Sears, Roebuck and Company in Dallas, Texas, eight of 12 pregnant VDT workers in the computer center experienced problems in one year (1979–1980), with seven miscarriages and one premature infant death.
• Between March 1981 and September 1983, six of 14 pregnant VDT workers at Southern Bell in Atlanta, Georgia, miscarried.
• A British Department of Health and Social Security study reported that 36 percent of VDT-exposed pregnancies between 1974 and 1980 resulted in miscarriage, stillbirth, or malformation, compared with 16 percent of nonexposed pregnancies.

At this point, it's unclear whether such patterns are due to an unknown factor, pure chance, or VDTs. To find out, Dr. Irving J. Selikoff of Mount Sinai Medical Center in New York is launching a major epidemiological survey of VDT use and pregnancy. The four-year study will survey 10,000 VDT users with the help of the Service Employees International Union (SEIU) and 9 to 5, the national association for working women.

Right now there are no national work standards for using VDTs. In fact, a long-planned

Sources of nonionizing radiation are found in nearly every facet of our lives. The radiation from video display terminals (right) is often emitted in pulses, which may be more biologically active than the continuous waves that issue from radios and televisions. Microwave ovens (below) should be well sealed to prevent radiation escape.

Both photos © Cameramann International

epidemiological study by the National Institute for Occupational Safety and Health (NIOSH) has been stalled by budgetary delays.

But under pressure from unions, a number of states—including New Mexico, Wisconsin, and Massachusetts—have issued VDT-use guidelines. The bulk of them center on ergonomic (biotechnological) problems created by the stress of working on VDTs: headaches, back and neck pain, eyestrain, and carpal tunnel syndrome, a painful inflammation of the wrist. Concern over cataracts caused by VDT use has largely dissipated for now because of a lack of substantiated cases.

What Can Be Done?

In the absence of federal standards, how can workers protect themselves? Whether it's a VDT or a home computer, the machine should be shielded, says Bob DeMatteo, safety coordinator for the Ontario Public Service Employees Union in Toronto and author of *Terminal Shock: The Health Hazards of Video Display Terminals*. In front, install a see-through screen called a grounded conductive micromesh filter, designed to weaken low levels of radiation coming from the screen. Terminals that don't have a metal body should be wrapped in a metallized fabric impregnated with copper or nickel and grounded, says DeMatteo.

Back in 1982 the EPA was planning to suggest much stricter guidelines than ANSI's, but did not. Now the EPA says it may make new recommendations, this time for a range of possible levels from ANSI's to one that's 10 times tighter. Some states and local groups have taken up the battle on their own. Connecticut and New Jersey have made the ANSI recommendations enforceable statewide. Massachusetts has its own standard—five times stricter than ANSI's.

In general, there are no quick solutions to the potential risks of nonionizing radiation. Studies of these emissions have been so hampered by political controversy, charges, and countercharges, it's still hard to interpret. But there's reason for hope: The growing pressure for solid answers may finally shift the focus away from rhetoric and toward vital research.

© Terrence Moore/Tom Stack & Associates

Keeping Rivers Wild

by Tony Davis

Man has flung down a great barrier in the path of the turbulent Colorado in Arizona,'' proclaimed the U.S. Bureau of Reclamation during the 1960's. ''It has tamed the wild river—made it servant to man's will.'' The bureau was boasting of Glen Canyon Dam, a 710-foot (216-meter)-high monument in technological prowess, but it could have been talking about any dam in the country. Virtually every major U.S. river has been hitched to a dam, making the regulated river this country's most common riverine habitat.

Many Pros and Cons

The construction of such concrete monoliths as the Hoover Dam on the Colorado River at the Arizona-Nevada border, and the Bonneville Dam on the Columbia River at the Oregon-Washington border, began in the Depression of the 1930's. The federal government promised that in addition to creating construction jobs, the

The Hoover Dam (above) helps provide the arid Southwest with ample water for drinking and irrigation.

dams would control floods, generate electricity, and store water against droughts. Today the public reaps these benefits but is also beginning to recognize the costs. The large dams significantly disrupt fish and plant life downstream and may eventually hurt tourism in the canyons below the dams. The agencies that operate them are facing the heavy costs of modifying the structures to lessen these effects and restore damaged ecosystems.

Consider the Glen Canyon Dam. You could argue that it has done more than any other public-works project to transform the Southwest into the Sunbelt. By storing more water in its reservoir, called Lake Powell, than half the U.S. population consumes in one year, the dam is insurance against droughts. Equally vital for the area's development, the dam's turbines churn out enough electrical power for a city the size of Phoenix. Lake Powell is also a mecca for recreation, drawing 2.2 million visitors a year for boating and other water sports.

But the dam has drowned Glen Canyon, a naturalist's paradise of red sandstone, and environmentalists have nicknamed its reservoir Lake Foul—more in disgust at the loss of the canyon than because of pollution. Now ecologists from national groups such as Friends of the Earth and Friends of the River charge that downstream toward the Grand Canyon National Park, the dam is slowly destroying the delicate web of life along the river. Ecologists have learned that because the dam has lowered the temperature of the water downstream, four native fish species have been wiped out. Recreationists suspect that by holding back sediment that used to replace what natural erosion removed, the dam is slowly destroying beaches that provide camping spots in the Grand Canyon. In 1983 the nearby community watched a flood, caused in part by poor management of the dam, wipe out thousands of trees along the river's banks.

Not all the changes caused by the dam are for the worse. For example, the colder river water that destroyed the native fish nurtures a population of cold-water trout introduced from a blue-ribbon hatchery. By reducing the volume of the river's flow, the dam has allowed trees to grow along the river's banks. Still, concerns are serious enough that the U.S. Bureau of Reclamation, which built and oversees the dam, launched a $4 million study of its effects on the canyon. A team of researchers from five Arizona state and federal agencies and three universities will deliver their results in 1987. If these scientists find merit to the charges, the bureau will almost certainly consider making major changes in the way it operates the dam.

In other parts of the country, dam operators are already implementing changes to keep their rivers healthy. In the South the Tennessee Valley Authority (TVA) is spending about $8 million to retrofit its dams with devices that will increase the river's oxygen level, depleted by the structures, to try to bring back the fish. In the Northwest, where dams generate low-cost electricity for half the region's populations, the Bonneville Power Administration (BPA) is spending up to $30 million a year to modify those dams so that migrating salmon do not get caught in the structures' turbines. (The BPA sells and distributes the power these dams produce, but the Army Corps of Engineers and independent public utilities operate them.) "It took us 80 years to get into this fix," says Sharon Blair, spokeswoman for the BPA in Portland, Oregon. "Who knows how many years we'll need to get out of it?"

Mixed blessing. Colder water in the Colorado River due to damming, while wiping out four native fish species, has allowed the introduction of blue-ribbon trout.

© Kevin Schafer/Tom Stack & Associates

Dams can pose an insurmountable obstacle to the upriver spawning migration of salmon.

A Chilling Effect on Fish

Once you build a dam, what happens over the next decades depends on the dam's purpose and how well its design and operation match the ecology of the river. For example, the location of the dam's intake structures, openings that channel the river's water through the dam, can so adversely affect the river's temperature and oxygen levels downstream that fish will not survive. The Shasta Dam on the Sacramento River near Redding, California, has its intake structures halfway between the river's surface and bottom. In warm, dry years, the river is low and the water from the surface of the heated river flows through the dam. This water, only 2 to 4 degrees warmer than the bottom water, is still warm enough to kill salmon eggs incubating in downstream gravels.

The intake structures of the Glen Canyon Dam are at the bottom of its 468-foot (173-meter)-deep reservoir. All year round, 48° F (8.8° C) water from the chilly bottom of Lake Powell streams through. Before the dam's completion in 1963, the temperature of the water in the hot Arizona sun averaged 75° to 80° F (24° to 27° C) in the summer months. The dam now supports only four species of native warm-water fish compared with eight before the dam went up. The remaining fish depend on the river's warmer tributaries as breeding grounds.

In the Tennessee Valley, where the TVA's 27 dams generate electricity and control floods, operators release water only when the reservoirs reach capacity. This creates a problem known as eutrophication, a biological aging process. In the still water, nutrients, sewage waste, and other improperly treated organic materials react with oxygen, gobbling up the supply needed by the fish. The dam's intakes are at the bottom of the reservoir, where the greatest eutrophication occurs. Thus, the downstream water carries only one part per million of oxygen, even though the fish need five to six parts per million to thrive. This shortage forces the oxygen-starved fish to travel from 1 to 40 miles (1.6 to 64 kilometers) downstream in search of oxygen-rich waters.

Dams also raise unnatural obstacles for fish that spawn in the river and mature in the ocean. For example, the dams' structures slow down the natural speed of the river, especially in reservoirs. The 60-odd dams on the Columbia River affect the progress of young salmon and steelhead trout, which migrate downstream to the ocean on a deadline. Thirty days after the fish begin the journey, their metabolism changes. If they haven't reached the ocean by then, they'll never mature and return to spawn. The reservoirs can increase a fish's typical trip from two weeks to more than six.

A dam's turbine presents the greatest physical danger to fish. Rotating blades, large enough for a human to stand inside, chop up fish. The spinning blades create a partial air vacuum, and the water's pressure changes may be strong enough to stun or knock out smaller fish. Those that do survive offer downstream predators easy targets.

The Drying Riverbeds

By far the biggest change that dams bring to a river's environment results from the fact that they eliminate the natural flooding cycle on which a host of animals and plants depend. In *Impounded Rivers*, Geoffrey Petts notes that willows began to grow downstream from dams on several northern California rivers because the regulated river no longer flooded its banks. The willows encroached on salmon spawning beds, depressing fish populations.

In northeastern British Columbia, the W.A.C. Bennett Dam has altered the natural flood cycle on the Peace River. Because the dam regulates the river's flow, the river no longer floods downstream the way it used to. The victim has been the rich freshwater delta in the 17,000-square-mile (44,030-square-kilometer) Wood Buffalo National Park in Alberta. The delta is in the path of four different North American waterfowl migratory routes, or flyways; it is also home for one of the world's largest herds of wood bison. Yet it has begun drying up because of the lack of flooding. Robert Redhead, the park's chief warden, says a field of sedge meadows that protects the bison and waterfowl is losing ground to willow trees. Bison counts have dropped from 10,000 in the early 1970's to 5,000 today, although Redhead notes that disease has probably taken a toll. If current drying trends persist, Redhead warns, aspens and conifers—denizens of still drier habitats—will move in.

The Glen Canyon Dam has eliminated summertime floods on the Colorado River that once reached 100,000 cubic feet (28,320 cubic meters) per second by restricting flows to no more than 31,000 cubic feet (878 cubic meters) per second. According to researchers at the University of Arizona, this lack of flooding is changing the downstream flora—but not necessarily in negative ways. Tamarisk, acacia, seep and coyote willow, and occasional mesquite trees are sprouting along the river bottom. The trees have drawn four new bird species and sent populations of 30 to 40 others skyrocketing. Yet the low flows have also cut off nourishment to mesquite and acacia on the canyon's old high-water line 250 feet (76.2 meters) above the river.

Yo-yo Fluctuations

By holding back water, the dam also holds back sediment that once restored beaches washed out by natural erosion. Biologist Larry Stevens has predicted that one-third of the remaining beaches will be gone in 15 years and that 90 percent will be gone in 75 years. Another study, by geologists at Northern Arizona University, shows that a gradual, long-term erosion of 25 beaches downstream occurred between 1974 and 1985. Yet still another study of the same beaches, done by two environmental scientists

at the University of Virginia, found little loss to erosion. None of the studies are definitive because they cover only 25 of the canyon's 200-plus beaches. Thus, long-term trends remain uncertain.

Operators of dams that generate electricity raise and lower the river's level according to the public's consumption of power. The operators send high water through the dam's turbines during morning and afternoon peak hours for electricity demand, and send low water—sometimes as little as 3,000 cubic feet (85 cubic meters) per second—during off-peak hours. This system brings in more money to repay the costs of building the dams because there is more power to sell when people want to buy it. The practice also benefits utilities who buy the power, and their customers, who would otherwise have to purchase higher-priced peak power derived from oil or gas. But environmentalists from Friends of the River and Friends of the Earth claim that the yo-yo-like fluctuations in water levels aggravate erosion. "The high water soaks the beaches, and they collapse when the water goes down," says Gaylord Stavely, who is owner of a Flagstaff rafting company.

Tarnished "Jewel" of the Colorado

Dam builders failed to take most of these ecological disruptions into account when they designed the structures. Most dams went up long before 1970, when the National Environmental Policy Act first required environmental impact statements for new major water projects. Dam builders' major mistake was to assume that a dam could serve several functions simultaneously without slighting any of them.

A Bureau of Reclamation pamphlet titled "Lake Powell, Jewel of the Colorado" promised that the Glen Canyon Dam would end both floods and droughts and bring direct or indirect benefits to nearly every U.S. citizen. However, the first two tasks often conflict. A well-operated flood-control dam keeps the water level in the reservoir as low as possible to catch heavy and unexpected runoff. A well-operated water-storage dam is as full as possible to guard against the droughts that haunt the West every few years.

This contradiction became apparent in 1983, when record spring snows melted and streamed into an already full Lake Powell, forcing the bureau to release up to 96,000 cubic feet (2,700 cubic meters) of water per second through the Grand Canyon. The flood took away what the dam had given, wiping out from 16 to 70 percent of four species of trees and from 47 to 100 percent of the nests of three species of birds. The high water did give new life to the aging mesquite and acacia trees above the river: trees that had been going dry for two decades grew several inches (centimeters). It also gave a fresh coat of sand to many of the canyon's beaches, pulling sediment off the river bottom and upper canyon beaches and dumping it on those in the lower canyon. But the new sand proved an unstable gift. One year later, National Park Service studies showed that the new sand had already eroded.

The flood, which caused tens of millions of dollars in property damage to downstream cities and $30 million in damages to the dam itself, brought the bureau a storm of protest. Critics accused the bureau of failing to foresee the problem in time to release water from Glen Canyon and other dams. Critics also accused the bureau of emphasizing water storage at the expense of flood control. Under pressure from state water-resource agencies whose job is to ensure an adequate water supply, the bureau had deliberately kept Lake Powell and other reservoirs full or nearly full, leaving little breathing room.

A year later the Colorado River actually got more spring runoff than in 1983. Yet the snow fell earlier than before, giving the bureau more time to lower the reservoirs. The high water caused virtually no damage, and many Arizona officials praised the bureau for its foresight. Few noticed that the agency's underlying policy of keeping the reservoirs as full as possible had not changed. Although the agency is now far more attuned to the possibility of a flood, officials acknowledge that another high-water year like 1983 could bring the same destructive results.

Ecological Ramifications

Whatever a dam's functions—generating power, storing water, or controlling floods—environmentalists are now arguing that these should not interfere with the river's plant and animal life. However, it is not easy to change the way a dam is operated, since the web of vested interests becomes as complex as the river's ecological relationships.

For example, if the bureau's study proves that the Glen Canyon Dam is indeed eroding the Grand Canyon beaches, operators could reduce the fluctuation in the water releases. The back-

ers of this idea believe that the bureau could obtain the income it needs without running a peak-power operation by raising rates to match those charged by privately held utilities. Although such a move would cut against the grain of federal policy that has prevailed since the Great Depression—that of promoting low-cost hydropower—the idea is not unthinkable. In 1983 a similar scheme proposed for the Hoover Dam lost by 40 votes in the U.S. House of Representatives. Federal officials successfully argued that if they charged market rates, consumers would have to pay higher electric bills.

If the bureau's study shows that the habitat of trees and birds needs to be protected from further destruction, the bureau could store less water behind the dam to guard against future floods. The bureau could especially try to avoid floods in late spring, the peak nesting season. But the states that actually own the river and advise the bureau on how to run the dam are reluctant to allow operators to tilt toward flood control even in the wet season. In the eyes of these states, any water that is released in the name of flood control is wasted.

If the bureau's study supports the idea of bringing back the native fish, the operators could modify the dam's intakes and raise the water temperature. But bureau officials suggest that this could prove counterproductive. If the water gets warmer, the warm-water striped bass introduced years ago to Lake Mead at Hoover Dam might swim upstream and attack the smaller native Grand Canyon fish. "It is a very complex piece of environment down there," says one bureau official. "You can't say modify the temperature and fix everything."

Some scientists question why the government should even bother to protect trees that used to be flooded annually by nature. This issue is especially knotty because floods that hurt the plants on the river bottom help the acacia and mesquite trees above the canyon floor. Moreover, by law the National Park Service must protect the natural environment inside its boundaries. However, thanks to Glen Canyon Dam, little that lies along the riverbanks of the Grand Canyon is truly "natural."

Technologies That Save Fish

Officials at several other dams are already modifying their design and operation to bring back fish populations. When the Bonneville Dam was constructed in the 1930's, scientists thought that salmon and steelhead trout could pass

The Colorado River in 1982 (top). One year later, a flood that environmentalists claim was caused by poor dam management wiped out thousands of trees and shrubs, leaving the river's banks nearly barren (bottom).

Both photos: Ray Turner/US Geological Survey

through the turbines without any problem. According to Dale Evans, chief of the Environmental and Technical Services Division of the National Marine Fisheries Service in Portland, fish losses did not become serious until the 1960's. Before that the river's natural flow far exceeded what the dam's turbines could handle, so water spilled over and around the dams, carrying the fish safely along. During the drought of 1977, the public realized there was a crisis, and Bonneville Power trucked the fish around the dams. Of those left behind in the Snake River (which drains into the Columbia), 98 percent died.

In 1980 fears for the future of the salmon and steelhead trout prompted Congress to pass legislation creating the Northwest Power Planning Council. The council established a water budget program, in which fish and wildlife supporters and hydropower interests negotiate a guaranteed minimum flow to ensure that salmon reach the sea. The council ordered the Bonneville Power Administration to begin the lengthy and expensive process of changing their turbines so they don't act as death traps.

The most promising such modification is fish screens, which divert the fish away from the turbines' dangerous blades. Outside the dam a metal screen forces fish into special intake openings, while inside the dam large wire mesh screens weighing as much as 30 tons (27 metric tons) protect the fish from the turbine blades. The council has ordered the Army Corps of Engineers and three public utility districts to put screens on eight of their dams. Until the screens are in place, the agency is supposed to spill enough water over the dams or truck the fish around to ensure that at least 90 percent survive.

Screens have so far been installed at only five BPA dams. However, the screens installed in 1984 at Bonneville Dam's 10 new turbines do not work, although no one is sure why. One theory is that the currents immediately in front of the dam's powerhouse create an eddy effect, pushing the fish below the screens. The screens are big enough to cover only about the upper third of the 60-foot (18-meter)-deep turbine intake structure. By tracking the fish with sonar, the BPA found that the first screen diverted 25 percent of the fish population instead of the 85 percent they had hoped for. Bonneville was forced to shut down to keep the rest of the fish out of the turbines for two months.

More Fish Spawning

Despite this setback, the council's program has proved successful. In 1985 the council reported that fish populations heading upstream to spawn have increased dramatically since the recovery program began three years ago. Fall chinook salmon and steelhead trout runs at Bonneville and McNary dams on the Oregon-Washington border were at their highest levels since records were first kept in the 1930's.

The Tennessee Valley Authority has also boosted its fish population by modifying its dams. At the Norris Dam on the Clinch River near Knoxville, the TVA installed metallic hub baffles—fan-shaped pieces of pipe that fit at right angles against the holes of the propeller-shaped turbine blades. As the propellers spin, the baffles create negative air pressure, drawing more oxygen into the river. TVA built steel and rock structures called weirs downstream from the dam that back up water and increase river flows immediately below the dam. Such devices help raise the water's oxygen levels.

After two years of using both methods, agency researchers are observing more and greater varieties of the organisms fish eat. Last fall, after Tennessee officials stocked the downstream river with trout, fishers were reportedly catching 0.81 fish an hour. Before the weirs and baffles, they weren't catching anything even though the stream was stocked. The agency has installed similar modifications at a second dam, plans to install them at two more this year, and is studying the possibility of putting them at the TVA's 23 other dams.

Outlook for Dam Building

These experiences deliver a clear message to the current generation of dam builders: It is possible to minimize the downstream impact of a new dam on the fish, plants, and other wildlife. The government's two dam-building agencies, the

At Cowiche Dam on the Naches River in Washington, a fish screen steers fish away from the deathtrap of the turbine's blades.

Both photos: © Bob Tuck

At Washington's Easton Dam (above) and Roza Dam (left), migrating fish climb gently sloping "fish ladders" to reach their spawning grounds upstream.

Bureau of Reclamation and the Army Corps of Engineers, as well as the Federal Energy Regulatory Commission, which licenses the construction of smaller dams used to produce electricity, have taken note of these environmental concerns. But these agencies expect to build few, if any, new dams on the scale of Glen Canyon in the future. Bureau officials point out that good sites already have dams, and those without

them present other drawbacks. Congress has not authorized any new Bureau of Reclamation dams since 1979, and it has approved only five Corps of Engineers dams in the South and East since 1976. In 1983 the TVA instituted a policy of building no more dams because of environmental pressures, and also because federal funds for building dams are drying up. Furthermore, some utilities now have surplus power.

Only the Federal Energy Regulatory Commission foresees a growth in dam construction. It licensed more dams for private and public utilities—81 compared with 75—in 1984 than in 1980. These dams primarily generate electricity and, at less than 15 megawatts (20,000 horsepower), are much, much smaller than any of the dams that the Bureau of Reclamation operates. Yet of 800 hydroelectric dams recently proposed for the four northwestern states, the National Marine Fisheries Service believes that 100 would be so destructive to fish and wildlife that it is ready to go to court to stop their construction.

Whatever the fate of new dams, those that already exist will keep both engineers and environmentalists busy for the foreseeable future. The question now is not how to tame the rivers but how to keep them wild.

Walls of greenery and colorful night lighting on Thums Island in Long Beach harbor conceal what's really there: oil production equipment.

DESIGNER DERRICKS

by David Holmstrom

You're out sailing in Long Beach Harbor, circling one of four small islands in the bay, and wondering what fortunate folk might live in that handsome apartment house rising above the surrounding palm trees. But where are their automobiles? And how do they get to the mainland without a bridge? At close range it dawns on you that these buildings house not people but derricks. This isn't a housing development but an oil development run by Exxon Company, U.S.A., for the city of Long Beach, California.

Now, you are out for a stroll in Los Angeles, California. Here's a high flagstone wall. A neighborhood library? Somewhere, perhaps around the corner, is the front entrance with glass doors, a handrail, and the slot in the wall for returning books overnight. There's a long row of mature, bushy trees near the curb and a neatly trimmed hedge along the wall. Surrounding you at the intersection of Pico and Doheny is a peaceable neighborhood: apartment buildings, modest homes, branch banks, and little shops all blend together in urban compatibility.

The only noise all day is the rush of passing cars. But go around the corner and look for the library entrance and . . . wait a minute. What's this sign saying, "Hard Hat Area?" Beyond the "library" walls there aren't any books or reading tables. Instead there is a very real oil drilling site operated by Occidental Petroleum Company.

And about a mile away, inside a beguiling five-story edifice that looks exactly like an office building (with stairway entrance and glass doors), is Chevron's Packard drilling site. Since 1967 the site has been as much a part of the neighborhood as Olson's Swedish Bakery across the street.

These artfully camouflaged drilling sites, and many others in southern California, quietly and safely produce oil. There are 19 such urban drilling sites in Los Angeles alone. Just about anybody is surprised to learn that within six blocks of Los Angeles City Hall, near bustling Little Tokyo, oil is being produced on a tiny lot about the size of a basketball court.

No Gushers Allowed

Other communities in southern California—Torrance, Huntington Beach, Culver City, Long Beach, Venice, Redondo Beach, Montebello, Sante Fe Springs—also have drilling sites operated by oil companies.

And while it is not uncommon for oil-producing cities to have drilling sites in urban areas, Los Angeles is one of the few to insist that activities there be hidden from public view. Oklahoma City, for instance, has a derrick on its capitol grounds. When the well finally went dry after producing oil (and royalties into the state's treasury) for 50 years, the legislature decided to leave it in place in honor of the state's petroleum heritage. Likewise, in Kilgore, in the heart of the giant east Texas field, a derrick or two have been left standing "because the tourists expect it." But in California, those not accustomed to the presence of petroleum facilities sometimes object.

"The public's concept of drilling for oil," says Jeffrey Druyun, formerly petroleum administrator for the city of Los Angeles, "has been influenced by scenes of black gushers in old Hollywood movies. People have gathered a lot of misconceptions on their own about drilling and production, even though there has never been a major environmental or safety problem at a Los Angeles drilling site."

In Los Angeles, such sites are designed to be unobtrusive and quiet. With stringent approval procedures and constant monitoring, drilling activity in residential or business areas has been going on for years in such a low-key fashion that the public has been scarcely aware of its existence.

In a quick, man-on-the-street poll near the Packard drill site, passersby are asked if they know that the "building" up the street houses an oil drilling rig. Four out of five are unaware of it. One man asks, "Is that the building with the restaurant on top?"

Surprising, perhaps, in a metropolis where petroleum development has been commonplace for almost a century. The search for oil in the rich Los Angeles Basin has never been a modest endeavor as America's need for energy has paralleled its rapid population growth and industrialization. In California, where one out of every 10 motor vehicles in the United States is registered, oil is a vital part of the economy.

And back in the late 1950's, when explosive population growth and new drilling sites started to overlap in southern California, thousands of skeptical residents filled public hearing rooms to object. The people were understandably pugnacious. They sought reassurances from public officials and company engineers that a drilling site next door or down the block would be no uglier than a telephone pole.

"The only people griping," an angry driller was reported to have said at the time, "are the ones who aren't getting any royalties." Because many wells can be drilled from a single location by slanting them out beneath thousands of pieces of property, thousands of property owners receive royalties for their mineral rights.

Industry Need Not Be Ugly

But many residents had genuine concerns. What about noise? Pipelines? Fires? Oily smells? What about the presence of equipment that only an oilman can love? And most of all, "Will we have to look at an ugly oil derrick all the time?"

"Now, over 20 years later," says Jeffrey Druyun, "we know that none of the fears ever materialized. Yet today many people simply ignore the facts or entertain them the way they want."

Los Angeles passed an ordinance in 1963 that permitted core drilling in six districts and required sites to be enclosed, landscaped, and reasonably compatible with the surroundings. "Since 1950 over 300 million barrels of crude oil have been produced by wells within the city of Los Angeles," says Hank F. Ganio, petroleum administrator for Los Angeles. "We wouldn't allow drilling if it wasn't safe."

One of the first urban wells to be camouflaged was on the back lot of the old 20th Century Fox movie lot, now known as Century City. It was simply a derrick wrapped in custom-made, noise-absorbing plastic batting, a sort of unwitting forerunner of Christo, the renowned artist who wraps and ties huge buildings, bridges, and islands in cloth and rope.

So little noise seeped out of the drilling operation that the studio was able to operate a sound stage within 15 feet (4.6 meters) of the derrick. At one time the area at Fox Studios had 29 wells in operation.

Although it is tempting to refer to the enhanced rigs as "designer derricks," such new dressings and shapes did not go unappreciated. A local beautification group in 1965 cited a 161-foot (49-meter)-tall derrick, sheathed in a sky-blue cover and vertical steel fluting, for a beauty award. "Private enterprise," read the award, "is proving that industry need not be ugly."

Behind the camouflage and false fronts are considerable innovations. At the Occidental site at Pico and Doheny, drilling has been done with quiet electric motors. "Everything is accomplished in a confined area, like an offshore rig,"

Only the traffic creates a noisy environment around this dressed-up derrick in Pacolma, California (left). Above, an oil derrick blends in behind the athletic fields at Beverly Hills High School.

says Ron Webb, operation manager for production at Occidental, "and everything is soundproofed. All wellheads are belowground, and there are no gasoline or diesel engines. The L.A. Fire Department inspects the operation at least once a week, sometimes more."

Aside from an occasional workman in a hard hat walking on the sidewalk, there is nothing in view to indicate oil drilling. In a break from tradition, the rig is operated only 12 hours a day instead of around the clock.

At Chevron's Packard site, over 50 wells are in production. Since 1967 over $73 million in royalties has been paid to property owners.

Derrick Longevity

An example of the early camouflaged derricks can still be seen today at the edge of the athletic field at Beverly Hills High School. Owned by Wainoco Oil Corporation, a derrick there, wrapped in gray, tightly fitted pads, is dwarfed by the glass and steel skyscrapers of Century City just behind it. For over 25 years the derrick has withstood rain, wind, heat, and birds. The well has also helped provide around $800,000 a year in royalties to the high school.

Architect Henry Charles Burge designed one of the first camouflaged derricks in 1961 in a ravine near the golf greens on the 145-acre (59-hectare) Hillcrest Country Club in Los Angeles. "It was for Signal Oil," he remembers.

"We took all the protuberances off and wrapped the derrick in fiberglass padding.

"Up at the top we painted it to match the sky on an average day," he says, "a sort of bluish gray which faded to dark green toward the bottom. It's my conviction that the principles of good design can be applied to any structure, a building, a radio tower or a derrick."

In fact, it was Signal Oil and Gas Company that introduced camouflaged wells. In 1956 Signal convinced the oceanfront community of Redondo Beach that six wells could be drilled on three city lots. After a year of heated discussion, the city voted in favor of the project, but demanded a soundproof, odor-free, and virtually invisible operation.

Signal complied. After initial drilling and discovery of oil in commercial quantities, the company buried the "Christmas trees" pumping units, electric motors, and other equipment in a concrete cellar under a paved lot. It looked like a tennis court from the surface. Then Signal sent the crude oil away through a two-way pipeline to a separation center. Tens of thousands of people have passed by this netless tennis court without knowing what was humming just below the surface.

A Case in Point

New designs for derricks may have reached a high-water mark in Long Beach in the 1960's.

When geologists confirmed that the abundant Wilmington field, one of the richest oil deposits in the country, did not stop at the shoreline near Long Beach but extended under the harbor, the state of California arranged with the city of Long Beach to carry out the development. The city as operator contracted with a company named THUMS—a combination of Texaco, Humble (now Exxon), Union, Mobil, and Shell—newly formed to pool resources, drill wells, and produce the Long Beach harbor petroleum.

THUMS's approach was to construct four small offshore islands in the harbor. The Long Beach landscape architecture firm of Linesch and Reynolds was hired to address the problem of how to make the islands look aesthetically pleasing. Having helped with the creation of Disneyland and Busch Gardens, the Linesch and Reynolds solution was the equivalent of making a sweatshirt look like a sport coat.

On the island closest to the shoreline— only 750 feet (230 meters) away—tropical palms, shrubs, and ground cover were planted on the outer-perimeter. This new greenery successfully hid equipment, trucks, and cranes.

The four movable drilling rigs were encased in cylindrical forms and painted in soft pastels, with slightly brighter panels at the upper levels.

The effect, as seen from the shoreline, elicited plenty of sidewalk opinions. From images of launching pads to high-rise towers, to expressions of anger to exclamations of delight, the new islands impressed the citizenry; and for the city of Long Beach, the islands would mean an income of more than $250 million in the coming years.

Municipal Monitoring

"Each Los Angeles site goes through a pretty thorough approval procedure," says Jack Sedwick, an associate zoning administrator for the city. On his desk in city hall, he unfurls two sets of plans for a new Southern California Gas Company drilling site. The proposed facade looks like an apartment building. "Even after the building is constructed, a company has to get permission to modify it in any way."

Despite the track record for safety and the willingness of oil companies to create drilling sites that blend with the neighborhood, opposition exists. For example, Occidental has proposed a California mission–style facade for a drill site in Pacific Palisades. But for over 20 years, the issue has been snarled in the courts.

In Jack Sedwick's office, he points to 16 file boxes full of documents and reports. Each box relates to some aspect of the proposed work at Pacific Palisades.

"I don't know," he shrugs. "It may never be built, but I know that each site we approve in Los Angeles is virtually hand-tailored. And once the site is approved and built, it lives and breathes under a lot of watchful eyes."

Ironically, while urban drilling sites are monitored closely by officials, the general public can't tell one from the local library. And that's the whole idea.

Children frolic down the sidewalk, unaware that a major oil-drilling site sits behind the well-landscaped wall.

A 20th CENTURY NOAH'S ARK

by Maury Bates, Jr.

If it were possible for Bill Blair, president of The Nature Conservancy, to spend a few hours with Noah, they undoubtedly would find a great deal in common. The Bible tells us that Noah gathered two of every living creature into his Ark to save them from a great flood.

In many ways the nonprofit organization that Blair heads is a modern-day Noah's Ark. Its mission is to preserve endangered species of wildlife, plants, trees—and even the microorganisms in the soil and water—through acquiring and protecting property that supports rare representatives of the natural world.

Although Blair and Noah had the same objectives, the scope of their work differs in many respects. Despite the Ark's three decks, Noah must have had quite a job packing so many creatures on a single vessel. By contrast, the Ark that The Nature Conservancy has built over the past 32 years is considerably larger and more diverse than Noah's. The organization has been responsible for the preservation of 2,539,390 acres (1,027,690 hectares) of forests, marshes, prairies, mountains, deserts, and islands in the United States—an area larger than Delaware and Rhode Island combined. The Conservancy has completed almost 4,068 projects since it acquired its first preserve in 1954, and approximately 40 percent of all the preserves are still owned by the Conservancy and managed by staff members or volunteer land stewards. The natural habitats that the Conservancy has not retained were turned over to governmental authorities or private environmental groups after the Conservancy was assured that the rare species on the lands would be properly protected.

A Unique Group

What The Nature Conservancy does is unique among environmental groups. "We are not in business to lobby for environmental legislation, nor to be engaged in environmental lawsuits. There are a lot of organizations that do that," explains Blair. "We can and do work with any person or group, public or private, to acquire the land sheltering species that need protection."

The Conservancy's methods are quietly effective, considering the number of acres and species protected. The organization also could claim to be quietly successful. In 1985 it raised more than $50 million from private sources, including $20 million from corporations. This sizable sum, however, represents only a small fraction of the funds required to complete the protection job in this country alone.

The flood lent a sense of urgency to Noah's work. A different kind of inundation—industrial, housing, and agricultural development—is spurring The Nature Conservancy's activities. "Ironically, just at the time science is beginning to teach us how to use genetic resources in agriculture, medicine, industry, and other ways, the world's gene pools are shrinking rapidly," warns Blair. "In contrast to the past, when the world may have lost one species every millennium, today we are losing at least one species every few hours on the average to development, disease, or other causes," he adds. Because of this accelerating loss, coupled with today's rapid pace of development, the Conservancy has a very short time fuse to save even the small fraction of the natural landscape that needs protection. "The decisions about the future use of the remaining significant pieces of natural land and water in the United States will be made within the next 20 years," says Blair. "Either a group such as ours will have succeeded in protecting the best examples of different kinds of natural habitats, or these areas will have been lost in one way or another."

In case anyone doubts that the extinction of species could have a radical effect on mankind, the Conservancy's scientists can quote a number of significant facts. For example, the world has come to depend on about 15 highly domesticated forms of plants for food. However, there are at least 75,000 edible species, many of which are potentially superior to current crop plants. Production of major crops cannot be maintained or expanded without infusion of fresh genetic material from wild plants. In fact, American farmers need new varieties of wheat at least every 15 years to adapt to changed conditions caused by pests and diseases.

From Deodorants to Paints

The Nature Conservancy scientists also point out that almost half the medical prescriptions contain drugs of organic origin. Many medicines depend on a single plant or animal species for their effectiveness. Various forms of marine life are already serving as the main ingredients of potential anticancer drugs. In industry, compounds from seaweeds alone are used in hundreds of products—from deodorants and paints to building materials and coolants used in oil drilling. "Although wild species are contribut-

The long-billed curlew, living on Conservancy land along the Texas Gulf, migrates to the Arctic to breed.

The Conservancy combined diplomacy and tough dealing in order to save the ecologically important Coachella Valley in California (above). In a South Carolina preserve, bog turtles (right) previously unknown were found.

ing large numbers of ingredients today, they are just the beginning of genetic wonders to come,'' Blair notes. ''The world's wildlife is an invaluable, irreplaceable resource.''

With so little time left for selecting and saving some of the best repositories of nature, the Conservancy's efforts are concentrated on identifying, acquiring, and managing the remaining truly important natural areas. The Conservancy has made much progress on a state-by-state inventory of U.S. wildlife and plants to find the remaining habitats of rare species. Since the late 1970's the inventory has been done principally through ''natural heritage'' inventory programs established by the Conservancy and later turned over to state governments. These inventory processes, now in continuing operation in more than 40 states, have turned up important new information about wildlife. In Ohio, botanists discovered 12 plant species thought to be extinct. Two populations of a bog turtle previously unknown in South Carolina were discovered. In Indiana a plant— the Kankakee mallow—that grows in only five places in the world is being safeguarded as a result of the heritage program.

A Valley in Question

Although the Conservancy's inventories are extensive, no one at the organization suggests that all areas can or should be preserved in their natural condition. ''Obviously, the nation needs land for other purposes,'' says Blair. ''We are interested in identifying the truly top priority areas for preservation.'' Examples of how the Conservancy does this in the framework of compromise and consensus are legion. Recently, representatives of the Conservancy and ten other private and public organizations met to resolve a knotty environmental problem in California's Coachella Valley near Palm Springs. Because of its good winter climate, the valley is being quickly developed, but environmental opposition concerned about its rare oases, sand dunes, and animal and plant life threatened to bring development to a halt. Cooperating with other private conservation groups as well as federal and state bodies that were adamant about preserving the ecosystem, and with developers who wanted to get on with their business, the Conservancy worked out a plan to save 20,000 of the most ecologically important acres worth $20 million. As a result, the conservationists received a perpetually protected ecosystem, and the developers were permitted to proceed in the less environmentally important parts of the valley without fear of legal suits or constraints.

White Elephants

Ecologically interesting land is not the only kind of property for which the Conservancy is searching. In 1981 it came up with the concept of trade lands. Under the program, it invites donations of real estate that do not qualify for preservation, sells the donated properties, and then uses the proceeds to buy important habitats. The Conservancy has acquired and sold an obsolete California winery, a huge mid-city apartment complex, and countless gas stations. Two of the largest gifts under the program were from Consolidation Coal Company, a subsidiary of Conoco.

"Usually we have the experience and expertise to develop creative solutions that can turn white elephants into something useful," says Ray Culter, vice president, Protection Projects. A few years ago a Conservancy member in Huntington, West Virginia, drove past a 100-year-old abandoned factory building in his city and told Culter's group about it. Culter contacted the California-based plastics corporation that owned the building, and learned that the property had been on the market for more than a year, draining corporate funds with the costs of its management, taxes, maintenance, and security. Culter convinced the plastic manufacturer's management that the firm would be better off donating the property to the Conservancy and taking a tax deduction. The Conservancy then enlisted the help of Huntington's Industrial Development Commission. The commission agreed to take over the property while the Conservancy looked for a buyer. As a municipal agency, the commission got the taxes on the property waived and the local police to handle security. After some vigorous marketing, the Conservancy found a buyer—a large supermarket chain looking for a regional warehouse and distribution center. "Everyone benefited," says Culter. "The former owner got rid of a drain on earnings, the city has a new taxpayer and employer, and we are able to use the proceeds to acquire more natural land."

If most of the critical natural habitats in the United States should be gone by the turn of the century as the forecasts indicate, the Conservancy's real estate activities will gradually diminish. "We will be a different kind of organization 10 or 20 years from now," comments Culter. "Instead of bringing land and water under protection, our job will be one of stewardship."

Intelligent Guesses

Blair, Culter, and others at the Conservancy admit that the science of maintaining habitats is in its infancy. "No one has all the answers," admits Blair. "What we now make are intelligent guesses about what is best for wildlife. It's a new science that has evolved only in our lifetime." The Nature Conservancy is using about 25 of its larger preserves as research centers where its staff or scientists from nearby universities can refine their guesses into more solid ecological fact.

The organization also has accelerated its programs for sharing identification and protection methods with other countries. "The need to preserve natural diversity does not stop at the U.S. border," says Blair. "Thousands of plants and animals are unique to one part of the earth or another. We will certainly not be able to carry the load for the whole world, but there are many ways that we can make significant contributions by sharing our techniques."

Surprisingly, most of the land protected by the Conservancy is not off-limits to the public. Even hunting and fishing are permitted on some of the larger preserves. Conservation and use are not opposing objectives when the use is planned so that it does not disrupt the ecology.

"But," Blair continues, "acquiring land for recreation, for its scenic beauty, or for outdoor education is not our prime purpose. Our job is much more basic and crucial. In preserving as many of the world's species as we can, we are assuring that we will be able to provide food, medicine, and an expanding number of genetically based new industries and products for ourselves, for our children, and for generations to come."

Noah would know exactly what Bill Blair is talking about.

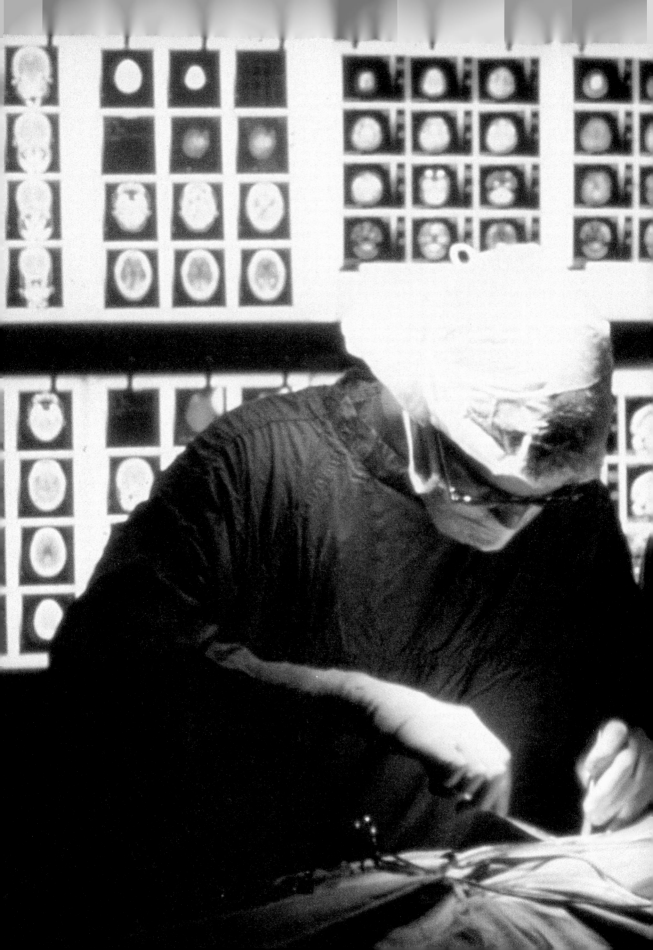

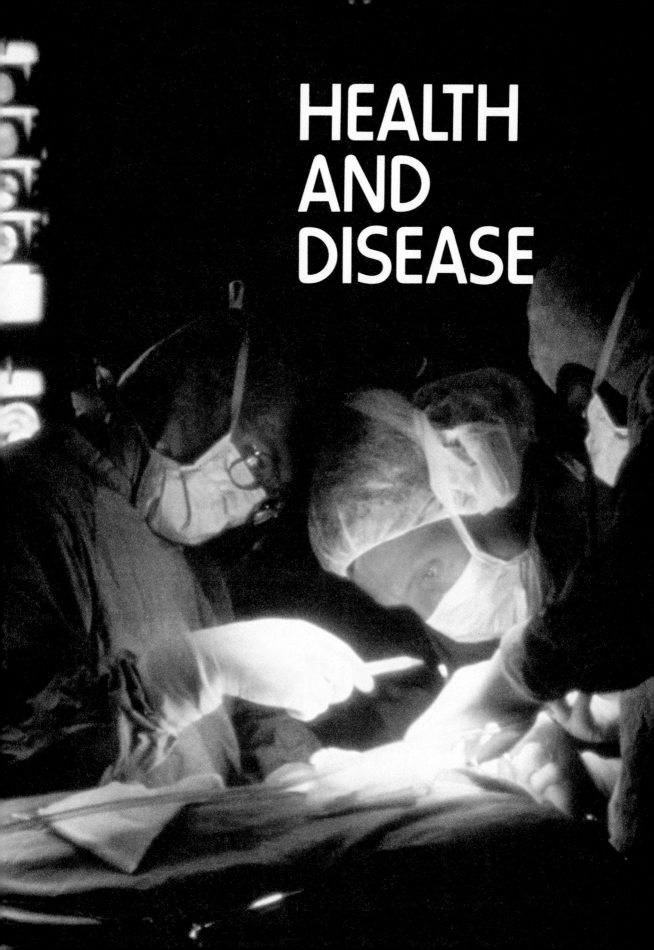

HEALTH
AND
DISEASE

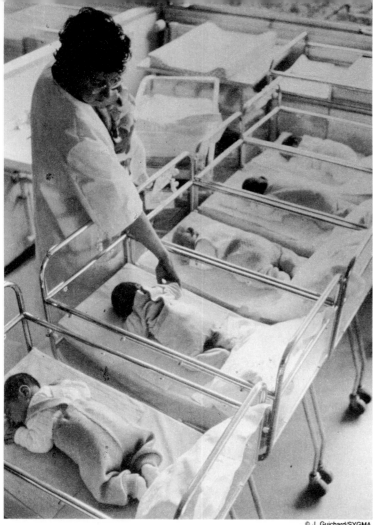

Respiratory ailments have replaced diarrheal diseases as the leading cause of death among infants.

© J. Guichard/SYGMA

REVIEW OF THE YEAR

HEALTH AND DISEASE

Again in 1986, coverage of acquired immune deficiency syndrome—AIDS—dominated medical news. Nonetheless, strides were made toward understanding Alzheimer's disease, doctors succeeded in transforming skeletal muscle into heartlike muscle, and the ailments afflicting high government officials helped enlighten the public as to the nature of a variety of common disorders.

AIDS

As acquired immune deficiency syndrome (AIDS) continued to spread through many countries, numerous public interest groups joined experts

and health leaders in warning that the disease was becoming a health disaster of pandemic proportions, possibly the worst health problem of the century. During the year, scientists learned that AIDS can be caused by at least two viruses belonging to the retrovirus family. One is called HIV-1 (also called HTLV-3 and LAV-1), and the other HIV-2 (also called LAV-2). Swedish scientists were also studying a possible third AIDS virus.

Unless a prevention or therapy is found to halt its spread, AIDS could cause a major catastrophe. An estimated 100,000 people throughout the world have developed AIDS, according to estimates based on the number of cases governments have reported to the World Health Organization (WHO) in Geneva, Switzerland. One million people have AIDS-related disorders, and up to 10 million people are infected with AIDS viruses and are presumably capable of spreading the disease. As many as 100 million people could be infected by 1991, when, according to an analysis of past trends, there will be a total of 270,000 cases in the United States. And in 1991 alone, the number of deaths from AIDS in the United States would be about 54,000, or about the total number of Americans killed in the entire Vietnam War.

The Institute of Medicine of the National Academy of Science charged that serious inadequacies existed in the way the U.S. government had responded to the AIDS epidemic. The institute urged a $2 billion-a-year educational and research effort to avert a further tragedy. The Surgeon General of the U.S. Public Health Service urged parents and schools to discard traditional inhibitions and to begin engaging in "frank, open discussions" with the nation's youth about the hazards of AIDS.

At the same time, WHO began the first coordinated global effort to combat AIDS and called for an annual budget of $1.5 billion by the 1990's to deal with the disease. The budget would be created from new funds and not transfers from other health care projects. The health agency's director, Dr. Halfdan Mahler, stunned many people with a candid public confession that he had not taken the disease seriously enough: "Everything is getting worse and worse in AIDS, and all of us have been underestimating it, and I in particular." Dr. Mahler said, "We stand nakedly in front of a very serious pandemic as mortal as any pandemic there ever has been. I don't know of any greater killer than AIDS, not to speak of its psychological, social, and economic maiming."

Epidemiologists tracking the course of AIDS in the Caribbean nation of Haiti reported that heterosexual intercourse is now the predominant route of the spread of the disease there. The study has shown a striking shift in the Haitian population groups affected by the disease. Originally, most cases were among the groups that have suffered the most in the United States: homosexual or bisexual men, intravenous drug users, and recipients of transfusions or blood products. The existence of AIDS in Haiti was an early clue to the global nature of the disease.

Some African countries that previously denied the existence of AIDS within their borders began to acknowledge its presence. Some governments opened their doors a crack to allow international experts to visit so they can track the spread of the disease closely and give advice about preventive steps. The new openness raised the possibility that researchers may be given greater opportunity to examine some of the most pressing scientific questions about the origins of the disease, its transmission, and the spectrum of viruses that cause it.

There was no further explanation of why the pattern of spread differs so markedly in Africa compared to the rest of the world. In Africa, AIDS seems to be spread primarily by intercourse among heterosexuals, by blood transfusions, and probably by contaminated needles. Elsewhere, AIDS is spread primarily among male homosexuals and intravenous drug users. Although scientists believe that AIDS is a sexually transmitted disease, they do not have a precise biological explanation of how the virus is spread between males and females.

Meanwhile, scientists were puzzled by why Kaposi's sarcoma, the cancer that was one of the original clues to the existence of AIDS, appeared to be declining in its prominence among people with the deadly disease. The proportion of patients with Kaposi's sarcoma when they were diagnosed as having AIDS dropped to 14 percent in 1986 from 34 percent in 1981, when AIDS was first identified. One possible explanation is that there is an unknown factor in addition to the AIDS virus that places homosexual males at risk for Kaposi's sarcoma and that exposure to this cofactor is declining.

A study of a small number of AIDS patients who took a drug called azidothymidine (AZT) found it was the first to show promise against the disease. The initial results were so promising that, for ethical reasons, the researchers who carried out the study stopped giving one-half the participants a dummy pill, or placebo, and replaced it with AZT. However, AZT is not a cure. Because it affects the bone marrow, its toxicity may be a serious problem for many AIDS patients. Scientists urged that AZT be studied for a longer period and that experiments with other drugs be continued until a cure is developed.

In another study, intravenous injections of gamma globulin, a natural blood substance, seem to have lowered the number of certain infections among children with AIDS, but do not cure the AIDS. Fourteen infants with AIDS who were treated with gamma globulin had fewer episodes of fever and infection of the circulatory system than did 27 infants with AIDS who did not receive the therapy. (See also "Seeking an Antidote for AIDS" on page 226.)

ALZHEIMER'S DISEASE

Researchers chipped away at the mysteries of Alzheimer's disease, a dementing disorder that affects an estimated 7 percent of those over the age of 65. Two of the advances reported:

The first involves the prospects of the first diagnostic test. Physicians are handicapped in not having a laboratory test to aid them in diagnosing Alzheimer's disease as they do for many other conditions. Researchers at the Albert Einstein Medical College in the Bronx, New York, reported they had taken a step in that direction by developing an experimental test to detect a protein called A-68 in cerebrospinal fluid. Doctors

A brain tissue sample from a patient with Alzheimer's disease (A) shows the high concentration of A-68 protein (as indicated by black flecks) now found to be characteristic of those suffering from the disease. A similar sample from an elderly person without Alzheimer's (B) has virtually no A-68 protein.

Albert Einstein College of Medicine

can obtain a sample of cerebrospinal fluid by inserting a needle through the skin of the back and guiding it between the vertebral bones—a standard procedure called a spinal tap. The A-68 protein apparently exists in large amounts only in brains destroyed by Alzheimer's disease. However, much work needs to be done to document the test's accuracy and to learn when in the course of the disease the protein first becomes detectable in the cerebrospinal fluid.

The second advance is that encouraging results with an experimental drug, tetrahydroaminoacridine (THA), were reported by doctors in Pasadena, California. THA significantly improved the memories of a small group of Alzheimer's patients and temporarily reduced other symptoms, sometimes dramatically. The findings were in contrast to those of another research team that had not obtained results as favorable in an earlier study. The researchers cautioned that THA would most likely cease to have effects as Alzheimer's disease progresses.

CHILDHOOD DEATH

New surveys and medical data showed that pneumonia and other respiratory infections are now the leading cause of death among infants and small children worldwide, killing perhaps 6.5 million each year. Respiratory infections, which now account for more than 40 percent of children's deaths, have replaced diarrheal diseases as the major killer in the cataloging of children's diseases. As a result, experts believe that major shifts in emphasis are needed to provide more preventive care and more research to better identify the causes of respiratory illness.

MUSCLE

Doctors reported that they had transformed skeletal muscle into heartlike muscle—a feat that medical school professors had said was not possible. The doctors used the technique to allow two dogs to live for several weeks with a fully implanted auxiliary heart without being tethered to a machine and without any wires protruding through their skin. To accomplish the task, the doctors removed a back muscle from each dog and fashioned it into a pump alongside the heart to increase the animal's blood circulation. Eventually the doctors hope they can use the pouch as a partial artificial heart that would avoid the body's rejection of human organs in the case of transplants, help avert the long waits for donor organs, and lessen the chance of formation of clots that develop in mechanical artificial hearts. The research is now on hold, however, while scientists devise an approach to avoid the formation of blood clots that ultimately killed the dogs.

ARTIFICIAL HEART

The two longest-surviving recipients of permanent artificial hearts, William J. Schroeder and Murray P. Haydon, died. The length of their survivals— Mr. Schroeder lived 620 days on a Jarvik-7 heart, while Mr. Haydon lived 488 days—showed that people could live long-term on the plastic and metal device. But the strokes and other complications that Mr. Schroeder and other recipients of permanent artificial hearts suffered impaired the quality of their lives and blunted initial enthusiasm for the heart.

President Reagan receives a call from congressional leaders while still in the hospital recovering from prostate surgery. The publicity surrounding the president's operation helped enlighten the public on the cause, symptoms, and treatment of prostate disorders.

AP/Wide World

MALADIES OF LEADERS

The maladies of three key government leaders focused attention on common as well as unusual conditions.

President Reagan underwent a surgical procedure to relieve symptoms from an enlarged prostate gland. The procedure and condition are called a transurethral prostatectomy and benign prostatic hypertrophy, respectively. The condition is one of the most common among males; about one in three over the age of 65 will need prostate surgery. For Mr. Reagan, it was the second time he had had such an operation; the first was in 1967.

At the same time, the doctors examined the entire length of Mr. Reagan's colon and did CAT scan X rays of his abdomen. They found that there was no evidence of spread of the cancerous polyp that was removed from the beginning section of Mr. Reagan's colon in 1985.

Vice President George Bush had a basal cell skin cancer removed from his face. It is the most common form of cancer, one that an estimated 400,000 Americans develop each year. Unlike most other malignancies, basal cell skin cancers are seldom aggressive. They rarely kill or spread through the body to cause damage elsewhere. Nevertheless, if left untreated, they can be disfiguring and can cause severe local damage, penetrating to underlying nerves and bone. They can be difficult and time-consuming to remove.

William Casey, the director of the Central Intelligence Agency (CIA), was less fortunate. He developed a primary lymphoma of the brain, a form of cancer of the lymph system, from which he died May 6, 1987. Such lymphomas were once diagnosed rarely but are now being identified more frequently. Still, primary lymphomas of the brain make up only 2 percent of primary brain tumors.

ETHICS

The American Medical Association (AMA) said it would be ethical for doctors to withhold all means of life-prolonging medical treatment, including food and water, from patients in irreversible comas even if death was not imminent. The withholding of such therapy should occur only when a patient's coma is beyond doubt irreversible and there are adequate safeguards to confirm the accuracy of the diagnosis. The ruling by the association's judicial council immediately became controversial—hailed by those who thought it would allow more humane care of such patients, and blasted by those who believed it was a form of murder.

LAWRENCE K. ALTMAN, M.D.

225

© James Pozarik/Gamma Liaison

Volunteer groups have sprung up in many cities to provide information about AIDS and assistance to its victims.

SEEKING AN ANTIDOTE FOR AIDS

by Laura Hofstadter

During the spring of 1985, eight-year-old Benjamin Oyler began to experience severe bouts of nausea and diarrhea. "At first, we thought it might be an ulcer," recalled his mother, Christine, but their family physician could find nothing amiss.

As Ben's condition worsened, Chris and her husband, Grant, realized "something was really wrong." Their physician advised them to consult the Children's Hospital at Stanford.

Ben, a hemophiliac, turned out to have AIDS, acquired immune deficiency syndrome. His nausea, diarrhea, and profound weight loss were due to *Cryptosporidium,* a gastrointestinal parasite that causes just one of the multitude of infections to which AID patients are particularly vulnerable.

"We had three hemophiliac sons," Ben's dad recalled recently in an interview at their Carmel, California, home. "We had heard about AIDS . . . but when your own son is sick, you don't think the worst."

Once the diagnosis was made, Ben's parents were faced with the wrenching prospect of watching their son slowly die. "We could feel the doctors mourning along with us. All they could do was treat symptoms. We all knew there wouldn't be a getting-better part," Oyler said.

"It is an extraordinarily difficult situation for patients and families, and also for physicians and nurses," admits Dr. Bertil Glader, the Stanford pediatric hematologist who was Ben's physician. "The diagnosis is a condemnation to dying—nobody yet has survived AIDS."

"But when you have a child with AIDS," Oyler explained, "you don't give up hope. You try to outlast the disease to the point where medicine can catch up with it."

But medicine didn't catch up in time to save Ben. He died July 4, 1986, less than a week after his ninth birthday, at home in his parents' arms.

A New, Deadly Virus

AIDS is presenting medical science with an urgent challenge. "The advent of a new deadly virus was not predictable," points out Stanford pathologist Dr. Edgar Engleman. "We thought we were getting pretty sophisticated in this century—controlling bacterial infections and beginning to come to grips with heart disease and cancer. Suddenly we're faced with a fatal viral infection, and we have to start from scratch."

Medicine is not the only institution challenged by AIDS. The disease is stretching the ethical and moral fabric of society. Extreme, and often irrational, fears about AIDS have surfaced with increasing frequency. Ben was barred from entering third grade at his school because of parents' fears for their children's safety. AIDS patients have lost their jobs, their homes, and have been disowned by their families. And an initiative on the 1986 California ballots would have gone so far as to require county and state officials to report and quarantine all AIDS carriers and patients. The initiative was voted down overwhelmingly.

Although AIDS is an incurable disease, physicians caution that fear and hysteria are not the solution. The antidote to the mounting epidemic, they say, is biomedical research, education, and knowledge that can lead to behavioral change and prevention.

How Does the AIDS Virus Work?

AIDS is caused by a virus that destroys cells in the immune system and in the brain, leaving the sick person defenseless against cancers and countless infections, and susceptible to neurological damage. In many cases there is a lag time of up to five years or more between the onset of infection and the first signs of disease. Twenty to 30 percent of those infected develop the milder form of disease known as AIDS-related complex (ARC) or full-blown AIDS and its accompanying conditions: *Pneumocystis* pneumonia, *Cytomegalovirus* infection, toxoplasmic encephalitis, tuberculosis, dementia, and cancers such as the previously rare malignancy called Kaposi's sarcoma. Due to the protracted lag time, scientists cannot yet say with certainty whether anyone who has been infected will ultimately escape the disease, even though some people seem to remain healthy and symptom-free. Once full-blown AIDS has set in, patients live an average of only three years.

AIDS Transmission

These are sobering facts for people who are infected and admittedly alarming to the population at large. Yet, infected individuals can pass the virus to others in only three ways: through intimate heterosexual or homosexual relations, through exchange of blood, or from an infected mother to her fetus.

It is essential for people to understand that safe sex, such as reducing the number of sexual partners and using condoms, goes a long way toward curbing the spread of AIDS, says immunologist Dr. Dennis McShane. Eliminating intravenous drug use—or at the very least avoiding sharing needles and other drug apparatus—is also critical.

"The risk for becoming infected with the

The AIDS virus, no longer confined to small "high risk" groups, has found victims in the general population.

AIDS virus does not have to do with being a homosexual man or being a member of any group,'' explains Dr. Anthony Fauci of the National Institute of Allergy and Infectious Disease in a recent article. ''The risk for AIDS is a behavior—having sex with someone who is infected or being exposed to blood that is infected.''

Because important facts about its transmission are not fully understood or appreciated by the public, AIDS is gradually spreading from the ''high risk'' groups—male homosexuals and intravenous drug users—into the general population. Although the medical consensus is that there's no need for hysteria, there is also a growing realization that curbing AIDS's incidence may not be possible unless preventive measures become everyone's concern.

''There is no indication that AIDS will diminish soon,'' says Glader. ''It's been projected that in 1991, more people will die of AIDS than will die from car accidents.''

Federal statistics present a glimpse of the future burden of the disease. Since 1981, when AIDS was recognized in the United States, nearly 31,000 people have been diagnosed; by the end of 1986, 18,000 of the victims had died. That year alone, approximately 16,000 cases appeared and 9,000 people died. By 1991— only four years away—more than one-quarter million new cases of AIDS are expected— 3,000 of them children—and a total of 179,000 people will have died. Fifty-four thousand deaths are expected in 1991 alone, approaching the number of U.S. casualties during the entire Vietnam War.

In Africa, where it is believed to have first infected heterosexuals, the AIDS virus may lurk in up to 2 percent of the population. In the United States, 1 million to 1.5 million people are thought to be infected, with as many as 1,000 new exposures occurring every day. The medical costs in 1991 for AIDS are projected to be anywhere from $8 billion to $16 billion.

Although scientists have made headway against the disease, behavioral prevention of AIDS remains the only course until the remaining obstacles to finding a vaccine and a treatment can be overcome.

A Safe Blood Supply

AIDS research passed a first milestone in 1984, when scientists in the United States and France identified the AIDS virus. A second goal was reached after scientists learned that the virus was passed through blood and that high temperatures could kill it. That enabled them to institute heat treatments for the blood components given to hemophiliacs. Another major step came in 1985, when the nation's blood-banking industry adopted an effective screening test to identify infected blood transfusions. Stanford's own blood center had pioneered this work almost two years earlier when it became the nation's first blood bank to screen for potentially infected blood.

''For the time being, the blood supply is much, much safer,'' asserts Engleman, Stanford blood center's medical director. But since there will never be a perfect screening test—an estimated 120 units of tainted blood may slip by each year with the current one—there will probably continue to be a few cases of transfusion-mediated AIDS, he says.

New AIDS viruses bud forth from infected cells. Much medical research now focuses on developing a vaccine that will prevent the mature AIDS virus from binding to a healthy cell and reproducing in it.

CDC

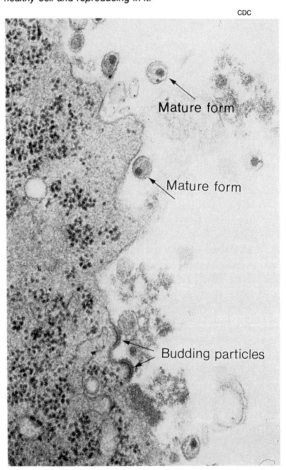

Mature form

Mature form

Budding particles

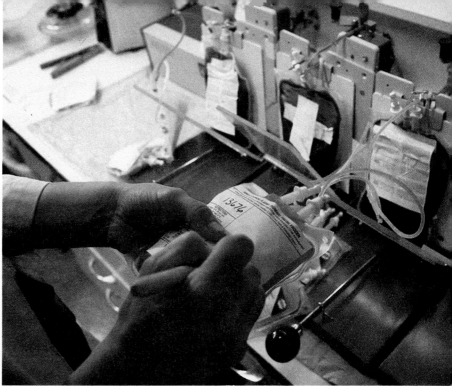

For several years, blood banks have screened all donations to avoid the transmission of AIDS through a transfusion of infected blood.

© Alon Reininger/Contact

More contaminated blood could enter the blood-bank system as the number of cases in heterosexuals continues to rise, Engleman cautions. "Right now, it isn't just the screening test that's slowing the spread," he explains. "It's the fact that people in the high-risk populations have made a conscientious effort to stop donating blood." But as the disease spreads to "low-risk" individuals who don't suspect they are carriers, the problem could grow again.

Engleman's lab and others are working on more sensitive tests that may become commercially available to blood banks within the next two years. More pressing, he explains, is the need to learn more about the AIDS virus and the biology of the disease.

He and associates Jeffrey Lifson, Michael McGrath, and Barry Stein want to know how the virus causes damage. The AIDS virus, they have found, latches onto a specific protein found on helper-T lymphocytes and monocyte macrophages, cells that play a vital role in orchestrating the body's immune defenses. Once the virus latches onto the protein "hook," it then slips inside and commandeers the cell machinery to manufacture more virus particles. To make matters worse, a cell hijacked by the AIDS virus can act like a sponge, sopping up many of its uninfected counterparts to form giant cell conglomerates. These giant cells ulti-

mately die, depleting the immune system of cells it needs to fight disease. This makes the patient vulnerable to the slightest infection.

What Can Be Done?

The ultimate measure against AIDS would be a vaccine. Several Stanford scientists are working toward this goal. Virologist Dr. William Robinson and colleagues are attempting to design a "synthetic-peptide" vaccine. It would consist of a small piece of laboratory-manufactured protein that would mimic the protein coat of an AIDS virus particle. When injected, it would trigger the person's immune defenses to a state of readiness to fight off the actual virus.

The biggest challenge in designing an AIDS vaccine is to make sure it protects against different strains of the virus. David Ludwig, a medical student, and medical microbiologist Dr. Gary Schoolnik are testing an approach that could accomplish this. Their vaccine, based on "anti-idiotype" methods, would interfere with the virus's ability to bind to the protein hooks it uses to invade cells. Since all strains of the virus are thought to invade cells by means of this protein, the vaccine could prevent infection from a variety of differing strains.

However, vaccine researchers are only cautiously optimistic right now. They know that the AIDS virus may be closely related to animal

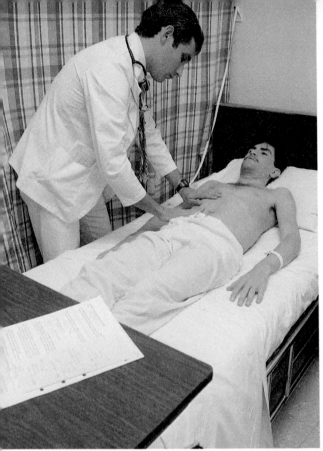

© James Pozarik/Gamma Liaison

Physicians can do little more for AIDS patients than treat symptoms and monitor the progress of the disease.

as many as 1,000 patients. Led by Merigan, Stanford and Kaiser physicians will oversee trials of drugs that may inhibit growth of the AIDS virus. Other institutions will examine drugs that may control the infections and malignancies prevalent in AIDS patients.

Many of the drugs to be tested in the first year of the study act by inhibiting a crucial enzyme—reverse transcriptase—that the AIDS virus uses to reproduce itself. Others may bolster and strengthen the AIDS-weakened immune system. Most physicians are skeptical that any single agent will suffice, Merigan says. One hurdle is the blood-brain barrier—any drug against AIDS will have to be able to get past it in order to reach infected cells in the brain that could otherwise stay sequestered, yet continue to cause damage for years.

Also daunting is the knowledge that the AIDS virus is a retrovirus, a class of viruses that has so far defied drug control. There probably won't ever be a cure for AIDS, Merigan admits, only treatments to suppress symptoms. Even that poses challenges. ''In other diseases such as hepatitis, we have found drugs that can terminate an acute episode. But if you stop therapy, you get a recurrence. The same could very well be true for AIDS,'' he says.

The drug strategy that will eventually subdue AIDS, he adds, will depend on interweaving antiviral medications and immune boosters. Ideally, researchers would like to have a drug that suppresses the virus in infected people who have not yet developed the disease, even though such a drug would have to be taken for the rest of the person's life to continuously muffle the virus.

As if an AIDS vaccine and treatment strategy weren't enough of a challenge, that isn't all that's needed. Scientists also must seek drugs to treat the different infections and malignancies that make AIDS so devastating. Merigan's lab is exploring new drug treatments against *Cytomegalovirus* infection, one prevalent disease associated with AIDS. Stanford oncologist Dr. Sandra Horning leads a study of lymphatic system cancers—Kaposi's sarcoma and lymphomas—in patients with AIDS.

Dr. Jack Remington, infectious disease specialist at Stanford and the Palo Alto Medical Research Foundation, is pursuing new approaches to one of the more deadly AIDS-associated illnesses, toxoplasmosis, a parasitic infection that can affect the brain. Most people are infected with *Toxoplasma* organisms but

lentiviruses, microbes that can incubate in the brain for decades and against which no effective vaccine has yet been devised. Even if scientists can surmount the obstacles, any vaccine against AIDS is still more than five years away, due to the extensive testing that would have to precede its widespread use in people, explains Dr. Thomas Merigan, head of infectious diseases at Stanford. And once it's ready, getting the vaccine to all who need protection will be a monumental task.

Treating AIDS

Then what about people who are already infected? To combat ongoing disease, a vaccine is useless. Effective drugs must be found. In June the National Institute of Allergy and Infectious Disease announced a five-year, $100 million program to test drugs that have shown potential to fight AIDS. Stanford Medical School, in collaboration with the Kaiser Hospital in San Francisco, California, is one of 14 institutions involved in the national study, which may enroll

© Claude Poulet/Gamma Liaison

Screening for AIDS. Some organizations (notably the military) test all personnel for exposure to the AIDS virus.

never become sick because a healthy immune system keeps the parasite at bay. "But AIDS ticks off these little bombshells" in up to 10 percent of AIDS patients, he explains. Without treatment, it leads to death within months.

Remington is searching for diagnostic methods to replace brain biopsy, where brain tissue must be removed in a radically invasive procedure to confirm *Toxoplasma* encephalitis. New drugs he's exploring against toxoplasmosis may possibly replace the effective but sometimes toxic medications currently available. His lab is also studying "biologicals," immune system–bolstering agents that in animal studies have been shown to provide protection against *Toxoplasma* encephalitis.

Concurrent Infections

New work by government scientists suggests that it may take more than the AIDS virus alone to cause the disease—another newly discovered virus may play a role. That there may be an intimate association between AIDS and other diseases has intrigued scientists all along. Remington, for example, is studying a possible link between the *Toxoplasma* organism and the AIDS virus. They are found in the same parts of the brain in AIDS patients, suggesting that they may influence each other in some cause-and-effect way.

Robinson is looking for interactions between the AIDS virus and other organisms, trying to learn why one patient infected with the AIDS virus becomes sick right away while another lives in good health for years. There is circumstantial evidence that people who have several concurrent infections—as is true for many gay men—may develop AIDS more readily than others, Robinson says. His lab team is trying to determine whether the viruses that cause these other infections help stimulate a latent AIDS virus into activity.

Ethical Questions

As researchers around the country are beginning to translate laboratory findings into clinical use, they face a whole range of troubling ethical issues, however. One question is how to test accurately the effectiveness and safety of potential AIDS drugs without temporarily withholding potentially lifesaving treatment. Some researchers have suggested that the traditional method of drug testing—in which half the patient volunteers in a study receive an inert substance (placebo) instead of the test drug—should be thrown aside in evaluating drugs for a uniformly lethal disease such as AIDS. All patients who want experimental drugs should be able to get them, contends Dr. Mathilde Krim, a Columbia University scientist.

But the investigators in Stanford's AIDS treatment evaluation unit believe that imperfectly controlled studies don't give reliable information, and that introducing unproven experimental drugs, even on a "compassionate use" basis, could actually do desperate patients more harm than good. Even if it means denying drugs for now to some patients, "the most important thing is to get the right answer as quickly as possible" to provide the greatest benefit, Robinson says.

Immunologist McShane, who sees many AIDS patients in his practice, raises an equally thorny problem. Now that a screening test for infection by the AIDS virus is available, there is pressure from the frightened public to mass-screen individuals in the high-risk groups. The Centers for Disease Control have recommended that all gay men be tested. Not only would the individual learn about his health status, screening proponents argue, but sexual contacts could then be traced and informed of their risk.

But McShane argues against mass screening in the high-risk groups since there is no treatment available for those who test positive and the test cannot predict who will get sick among those infected. Furthermore, he says, high-risk individuals should follow preventive guidelines, no matter how the test turns out.

"Whether the person is positive or negative, the bottom line is the same," he explains. "If the person's positive, he doesn't want to transmit the disease, so he should follow safe sex practices, like limiting the number of partners and using condoms.

"But if the test is negative," McShane continues, "he wants to make sure he doesn't get the disease. So, the precautions are exactly the same: use safe sex practices, forgo IV drug use, and so on."

The test can be useful in specific cases, he adds, such as for advising a positive hemophiliac or bisexual man not to father children.

But many experts remain reluctant to use the test on a widespread scale because of concerns about constitutional issues such as individual rights and liberties, should the information be misused. Some states, such as Colorado, require mandatory reporting. The results could be used in a discriminatory fashion by insurance companies or employers, McShane argues.

"We have not done testing on many of our hemophiliac patients because from statistical data, we know the likelihood of whether or not they are infected," hematologist Glader notes.

"And because of the political aspects, you're almost better off not knowing."

Widespread testing would lay the groundwork for medically unsound measures such as the quarantine implied in the failed California initiative, McShane says. Most doctors and medical groups, including the California Medical Association, denounced that measure.

Personal Decisions

Prevention can be accomplished only when individuals are well informed, McShane suggests. Echoing an editorial in the *New York Times,* he bemoans the "feeble fight" the federal government has so far mounted against AIDS. "Not nearly enough education has been done except at a grass roots level," he contends. "We must stress over and over again that this is not a disease that can be transmitted through casual contact. But the disease's spread can be slowed or eliminated only if people understand that it's their own decision—the disease is acquired through behavior the individual can control."

At least for now, once individuals become infected, they have relatively little control over the course of their disease. However, a study of AIDS patients at San Francisco General Hospital suggests that patients are making decisions about their medical care, says Dr. Thomas Raffin, codirector of Stanford hospital's intensive care units and chairman of the medical center's ethics committee.

The study found a changing pattern of intensive care unit admissions among AIDS patients with the highly lethal *Pneumocystis* pneumonia. As the number of AIDS patients diagnosed with this condition rose, the number of patients admitted to the intensive care unit dropped, the opposite of what would be expected if the most aggressive treatments were pursued. The explanation appears to be that AIDS patients with only a slim chance of survival are deciding early on in the course of their disease not to be placed on intensive care life support should the choice arise.

And all evidence suggests that at least for the next few years, that agonizing choice will come up more frequently as the AIDS epidemic grows. Researchers are the first to admit they don't have the desperately needed answers yet, but they nevertheless are confident that biomedical science has the tools to proceed. Says Stanford's Engleman: "It's a close race, but I believe we will control this disease with time."

UNSHACKLED FROM DIABETES

by Rob Wechsler

When he was 12 or 13 years old, Bill Lamb made a decision: he wasn't going to let diabetes run his life. The special meals that had been recommended to help keep his blood sugar under control didn't seem to be doing much good, so he forswore them and began eating whatever landed on his plate. Several years later, when partying and hanging around bars became the thing to do, Lamb's doctor told him to stay away from alcohol, but that didn't keep him from going out and having a few beers with the guys; in fact, a couple of brews often helped ease the pain in his legs that was a symptom of diabetic nerve disease. Even knowing how susceptible diabetics are to the hazards of cigarettes didn't faze him: until recently he smoked as much as three or four packs a day. "I didn't want to live my life like some sort of robot," he says. "If living seminormally was going to kill me, so be it."

Lamb was a "brittle" diabetic: the insulin shots he gave himself every day did little to keep his blood sugar levels stable, and he was constantly in fear of "going off the deep end"— passing out. He suffered from episodes of dizziness and anxiety, and once, in junior high, he did pass out during lunch hour. As he got older, the nerve disease in his legs got worse. He was reluctant to take painkillers, because they im-paired the alertness and coordination he needed for his work as an auto mechanic, and he often spent his days in excruciating pain from his ankles to his thighs, and his nights waiting in vain for sleep.

Still, when one of his sisters showed him an article about pancreas transplants, Lamb was skeptical: "Yeah, right, it's Buck Rogers time." But he also knew that someone with his prospects couldn't afford to pass up any opportunity to overcome his disease. On November 4, 1982, after more than six months of deliberating with his family and undergoing comprehensive medical evaluation, Lamb decided to go ahead with the transplant. David Sutherland, a surgeon at the University of Minnesota Hospital, removed a segment of pancreas from Lamb's younger sister, Rita, and grafted it onto Lamb's small intestine. Within a few days his blood sugar control was normal; in a couple of months, his pain was gone; and today, almost four years later, his new pancreas continues to pump out the insulin he needs. At age 34, Bill Lamb can finally sleep peacefully at night.

Juvenile Onset Diabetes

About a million Americans have Type I diabetes, a disease that occurs when the pancreas loses its ability to make insulin. This type, sometimes called juvenile onset diabetes, almost always begins before age 30, whereas Type II diabetes, a more common (10 million sufferers in the U.S.) but less severe form of the disease, usually strikes later in life, predominantly among the obese. The pancreases of Type II victims may continue to make insulin, but their bodies lose the ability to use it effectively. Together, the two types of diabetes kill more Americans than all other diseases except heart disease and cancer.

Type II diabetes can be effectively treated with weight reduction, exercise, diet, and oral drugs; Type I is much more difficult to manage. Since the pancreas of the Type I diabetic makes no insulin, his tissues cannot convert sugar into energy properly. The tissues can survive for some time by burning muscle and fat, but the by-products of this process, ketones and acids, eventually attain dangerous levels in the blood. If those levels aren't reduced, coma or death can result.

Until about 65 years ago, when Canadian researchers isolated insulin, Type I diabetics rarely survived for more than a few months after the symptoms of the disease appeared. Since then, daily injections of the hormone have allowed them to live longer, albeit often with debilitating complications.

While insulin makes the difference between life and death, it can never duplicate the pancreas's ability to pump out insulin on demand. Without this fine-tuning, Lamb says, "your timing is always out of whack. The shots still allow your blood sugar to rise and fall like the tides." And as with the tides, a certain amount of erosion is inevitable. Fluctuations in blood glucose and other substances are thought to be responsible for many of the disorders—eye damage, nerve damage, cardiovascular disease, kidney failure—that strike those with Type I and can lead to death. Even diabetics lucky enough to suffer only minor complications are conditioned by doctors and family to be "realistic" about the future.

Brighter Prospects

Over the past ten years, however, prospects for victims of Type I have brightened considerably. Sutherland's pancreas transplant technique is only one of several controversial new approaches that may finally end the diabetic's dependence on insulin shots. Soon, for example, it may be possible to transplant just the insulin-producing part of the pancreas without

the rest of the organ. Other researchers are seeking ways of preventing the long-term complications of Type I and experimenting with new drugs that would stop the disease before it ever took hold. Their success will depend on advances in the understanding of what causes Type I.

In the Middle Ages the diabetic's high urinary output and his tendency to lose weight no matter how much he ate led doctors to conclude that his body was dissolving and passing out in his urine; in fact, early English physicians referred to the disease as "the pissing evil." Although experiments in the late 19th and early 20th centuries made it clear that diabetes was caused by the pancreas's inability to make insulin, the origin of this deficiency wasn't known. Until recently, many doctors suspected that it was an acute infection, in which a virus invaded the pancreas and abruptly shut down insulin production. One moment a child was fine, it seemed, and the next he had all the classic symptoms.

Frequent injections of insulin help victims of juvenile onset diabetes cope with a malfunctioning pancreas.

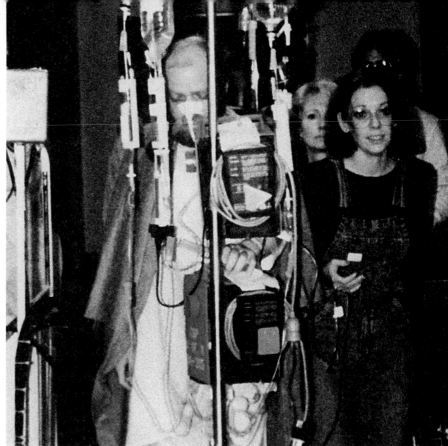

Four days after his 1982 pancreas transplant, Bill Lamb and his donor sister Rita stroll a hospital corridor. The operation involved grafting a section of Rita's healthy pancreas onto her brother's small intestine. Within days, the transplanted tissue was producing levels of insulin high enough to end Bill Lamb's diabetic symptoms.

What Causes Diabetes?

It's now known that Type I actually develops more slowly, and although a virus may be involved, no longer is it thought to be the primary cause. Rather, Type I is regarded as an autoimmune disease, one in which the body's immune defenses turn inward and begin to destroy its cells and tissues—in this case, the beta cells, the insulin producers packed into clumps in the pancreas called the islets of Langerhans. The disease develops only after so many of these cells have been destroyed that the victim no longer produces enough insulin to meet his body's needs.

It's still not clear exactly which component of the immune system kills the beta cells—antibodies and white blood cells called lymphocytes are the main candidates—or whether a combination of agents is involved. But studies have proved that diabetics go through a long period of islet destruction before their insulin levels drop low enough for symptoms to appear.

In a sense, this finding just pushes the question of what causes diabetes one step back—if the immune system is the culprit, what makes it mistake crucial tissues for harmful invaders? While some researchers are looking at various foods and drugs as possible causes, others continue to blame a virus. When a virus infects a person's cells—or even his mother's when she's pregnant with him—his immune system tries to destroy the invaders. But in a diabetic-to-be, if the virus shares some characteristics with the islet cells, the immune system may mistake the islets for viruses and assault them as well. Or perhaps the virus affects the immune system itself, impairing its ability to distinguish native cells from foreign ones, and allowing it to eat away the islets.

Genetic factors are also part of the picture: many victims of Type I have a family history of the disease, and in studies of identical twins, 50 percent of those whose twins had Type I also developed the disease. George Eisenbarth, an immunologist at the Joslin Diabetes Center in Boston, Massachusetts, has studied strains of diabetic rats and mice to determine what genes are involved. He suspects that diabetics are born with abnormalities in a chromosome that plays a role in regulating the immune response. His research in rodents and man indicates that the genetic process may be very complicated, with

HOW THE NON-DIABETIC PANCREAS WORKS

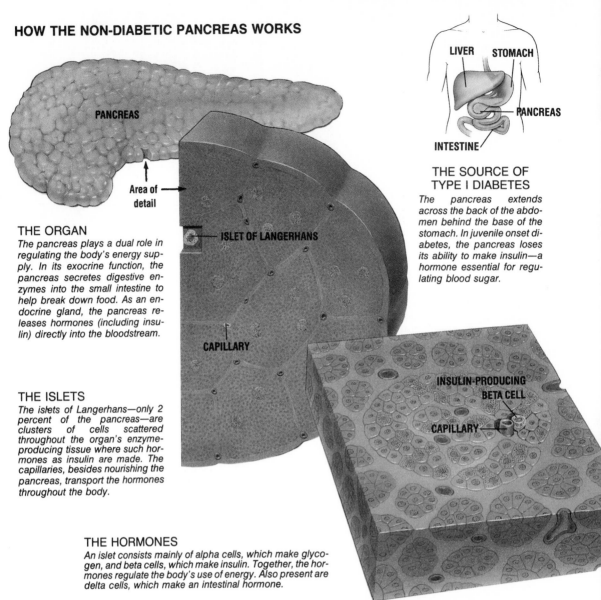

LIVER   STOMACH

PANCREAS

INTESTINE

PANCREAS

Area of detail

ISLET OF LANGERHANS

CAPILLARY

INSULIN-PRODUCING BETA CELL

CAPILLARY

THE ORGAN
The pancreas plays a dual role in regulating the body's energy supply. In its exocrine function, the pancreas secretes digestive enzymes into the small intestine to help break down food. As an endocrine gland, the pancreas releases hormones (including insulin) directly into the bloodstream.

THE ISLETS
The islets of Langerhans—only 2 percent of the pancreas—are clusters of cells scattered throughout the organ's enzyme-producing tissue where such hormones as insulin are made. The capillaries, besides nourishing the pancreas, transport the hormones throughout the body.

THE SOURCE OF TYPE I DIABETES
The pancreas extends across the back of the abdomen behind the base of the stomach. In juvenile onset diabetes, the pancreas loses its ability to make insulin—a hormone essential for regulating blood sugar.

THE HORMONES
An islet consists mainly of alpha cells, which make glycogen, and beta cells, which make insulin. Together, the hormones regulate the body's use of energy. Also present are delta cells, which make an intestinal hormone.

Illustrations: Lewis E. Calver © DISCOVER MAGAZINE 9/86, TIME INC.

---

at least two genes—and possibly more—determining susceptibility to Type I.

Until the culpable genes are tracked down, the best that doctors can do is treat the diabetes when it appears. For Lamb, who is free of pain and no longer what he calls a human pincushion, treatment is impressive enough. He calls Sutherland and his colleagues "the sharpest medical team you're ever going to see. Transplantation up there is second nature. Being something of a gambler, I'd always go where the odds are best, and as far as I'm concerned, that's Minneapolis."

Circumventing Rejection
Indeed, Sutherland and his team are the world leaders in pancreas transplants, having done 151 of the worldwide reported total of 897 as of July 15, 1986. Those statistics are a bit deceptive, however: 22 of Sutherland's patients have even required a third. According to Sutherland, the difficulty with pancreas transplants is an even more formidable version of what led to diabetes in the first place: instead of attacking just the insulin-producing cells, the immune system now sees the entire pancreas as foreign, and wages war on the whole organ.

Inside a beta cell. In the cell nucleus (A), DNA directs the manufacture of an insulin precursor chemical, using energy from the mitochondria (B), the cell's power source. In the Golgi apparatus (C), the insulin precursors are broken down into insulin and encapsulated. The insulin capsule then travels outward (D) to the cell membrane (E). At that point, the capsule fuses with the cell membrane and releases its insulin into the blood.

The only way to thwart this attack is with immunosuppressive drugs, which weaken the rejection response, thus protecting the new organ. But since these drugs suppress the immune system throughout the body, the pancreas transplant presents the diabetic with a tough choice: he has a chance to rid himself of diabetes for life, but he runs an increased risk of infections and cancer—along with such possible side ef-

fects of the drugs as hypertension and kidney damage. And right now immunosuppression is still as much an art as a science; it's almost impossible for doctors to know for sure what doses a particular transplant recipient will need to prevent rejection. Although 90 percent of Sutherland's patients are still alive, less than half of them have had transplants that have lasted more than a year. And when the transplanted pancreas ceases to function, a patient's only way out is to have another one put in or resign himself once again to a life of daily insulin injections.

Lamb is one of the lucky ones. He has shown no signs of rejecting his transplant, and the only evidence he has had of lowered resistance to infection was a cold he got in 1982. But he worries about the long-term effects of the immunosuppressive drugs. Cyclosporine, the main antirejection drug that Sutherland prescribes, has been in use for only about six years, and drug manuals warn that it should be used with extreme caution. Its approval by the Food and Drug Administration (FDA) was based on studies of patients with kidney transplants; although it's legal for diabetics, there's some question about whether it's worth the risks for them.

The way Sutherland uses cyclosporine and other immunosuppressives is one reason he's regarded as a bit of a cowboy by some of his colleagues. One of his critics, Richard Rohrer, is setting up a pancreas transplant program at New England Deaconess Hospital in Boston. Like Sutherland, he's seeking patients who are sick enough to require the operation but not so sick they're unlikely to benefit from it. But while Sutherland tries to do his transplants early, before kidney damage and other complications have set in, Rohrer is warier of the risks of cyclosporine. He has decided to stick to patients who have had (or are having) a kidney transplant; since they're already taking immunosuppressives, the pancreas transplant doesn't represent any increased risk of side effects.

Donor Dilemma

The disagreement between Sutherland and Rohrer centers not so much on the treatment of the transplant recipient as on the selection of the donor. Sutherland does transplant pancreases from cadavers (dead bodies), but he prefers to use those from living donors who are related to the recipient, since genetic similarity lowers the chances of rejection. Pancreas segments from

A MACROPHAGE DESTROYS A BETA CELL

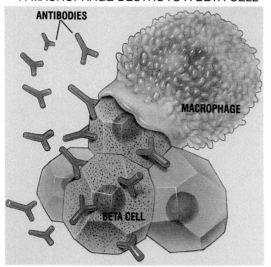

Lewis E. Calver © DISCOVER MAGAZINE 9/86, TIME INC.

In some autoimmune diseases, the body produces antibodies that attack its own tissues. In juvenile diabetes, antibodies (blue) may bind to and destroy beta cells, or else mark them for destruction by macrophages, which engulf them.

live donors have been rejected only 25 percent of the time, compared to 50 percent for cadaver transplants. "All things considered, I'd rather use cadavers," says Sutherland. "But the success of organs from living, related donors argues against that strategy for now."

Rohrer has misgivings about taking part of an organ from a healthy body. First, he says, while the live-donor organs may be less likely to succumb to rejection, in the long run they may not be any better for patients than pancreases from cadavers. A recent study showed that 22 of Sutherland's "best" patients had just as much diabetic retina disease as a group whose transplants had failed.

Then there's the donor to consider. Beyond the usual risks involved in being pumped full of anesthetic, cut open, and having part of one's body removed, the pancreas donor faces special danger. He can survive on half a pancreas provided the rest of his system is healthy, but if the remaining portion of the pancreas is damaged during the operation or thereafter, he has no backup, and could eventually need insulin himself. This may be especially true for relatives of diabetics, who are more vulnerable to the disease. Given the high failure rate of transplants in general and doubt about long-term benefits for the recipient, Rohrer considers the risks to the

donor unacceptable: "A couple of them have gone on to get diabetes, and others have had abnormal glucose tolerance tests. The University of Minnesota is the only place that does live transplants—no one else can justify them ethically."

Lamb contends that most of the people he knows who have had cadaver transplants have had them because members of their families didn't want to be pancreas donors. In his case, as soon as his parents and his three sisters found out about the operation, all of them volunteered to do whatever was needed. Most people who want pancreas transplants aren't so lucky. "It's something that each donor-recipient pair has to wrestle with," Lamb says. "Some of the people I've talked to were gung ho about the operation, but they had relatives who wouldn't donate five bucks, let alone a piece of their body, to see them get better. Coming from a tight-knit family, I find that unconscionable."

Isolating the Islets

A number of researchers are now working on a technique that may eliminate the need for making such a choice. By isolating the islets from a cadaver pancreas and transplanting them without the rest of the organ, they hope to avoid both the ethical question of using living donors and the immune rejection response that has plagued previous transplants. The islets can be harvested in large numbers from cadavers and placed in the abdominal cavity—in the spleen, liver, or kidneys.

There are two obstacles to this approach: first, it's hard to get islets out of a pancreas without destroying them; and second, the only proven way to prevent their rejection is to give the same risky immunosuppressives used for other transplants.

Pathologist Paul Lacy of Washington University in St. Louis has apparently solved the first problem. He had attempted to break down the pancreas with enzymes and scoop out the islets, a technique that works in rats and mice. But when you try this on a human pancreas, all you get is a gooey mess. So he came up with an ingenious solution: he rummaged around in his attic to find an old hand-cranked meat grinder, and began turning pancreas into hamburger before separating out the islets using filters and a centrifuge. "It took months to find the right grind," Lacy says. "It turns out it takes a very coarse grind to avoid destroying the islets. A Cuisinart won't work—we tried it."

Suppressing the immune response to the islets without compromising the rest of the body's defenses has proved to be a more formidable task. Lacy and others believe that much of the response to transplanted islets of Langerhans is switched on by white blood cells from the donor that hitch a ride on them; once the immune system has been primed by these cells, it proceeds to attack the foreign tissue. Remove or inactivate the insidious white blood cells, the theory goes, and the recipient's body won't be incited to attack.

Using a technique based on this theory, Lacy has succeeded in suppressing islet rejection in diabetic rodents. He incubated the islets at room temperature for a week, and then treated them with special antibodies to destroy the white blood cells. When the islets were implanted in rats or mice that were then given small doses of cyclosporine, more than 80 percent of the animals were cured.

So far, Lacy's record with human beings has been less impressive. Of the seven people on whom he and his colleague David Scharp have done islet transplants, six were diabetics, and the new islets functioned in them for only a month or two before they stopped producing insulin. The seventh had chronic pancreatitis, which required removal of her pancreas. Lacy purified the patient's own islets and placed them in a blood vessel in her liver; the islets are still working well a year after the operation.

Lacy thinks that much of the damage to the diabetics' transplanted islets was caused by the action of digestive enzymes from cells that hadn't been purified out, rather than by immune rejection of the islets. He finds encouragement in the fact that the islets functioned at all, if only briefly, and considers the procedure a potentially fruitful one. He now plans to purify the islets more completely, in hopes of thwarting both enzymatic and immunological destruction.

The Polymer Approach

While Lacy has been trying to sneak islets past the body's defenses, physiologist Anthony Sun has adopted a much simpler strategy. Working at the University of Toronto and at nearby Connaught Laboratories, the biotechnology company that introduced insulin commercially in the 1920's, Sun has been able to prevent rejection by coating islets with two polymers, which together form a semipermeable membrane. The membrane allows small molecules like glucose and insulin to pass in and out, but protects the

KILLER CELLS DESTROY BETA CELLS

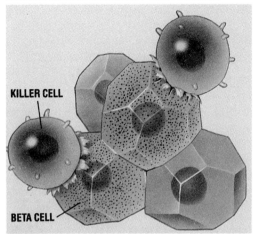

KILLER CELL

BETA CELL

Lewis E. Calver © DISCOVER MAGAZINE 9/86, TIME INC.

The immune system may also have killer cells that destroy normal cells as though they were intruders. In juvenile diabetes, killer cells may see the insulin-producing beta cells as foreign, and thus destroy them.

islets from larger agents like antibodies and white blood cells.

When Sun transplanted the encapsulated islets into rats and mice, they functioned for as long as the animals lived (most died of unrelated causes), and some were recovered for use in another series of transplants. Encapsulated islets are now being tested in dogs and monkeys, and may be available for human trials in the next two or three years.

One obstacle Sun faces is the large number of islets needed for a human transplant. "With rats you can use a few thousand, and the animals will do just fine," he says. "With larger species, such as dogs and people, you need a lot more, about 50 or 100 thousand." Researchers at Connaught are working on a machine that extracts islets from a pancreas more quickly and efficiently than technicians can by hand. They would also like to improve the design of the capsules, possibly by doing the encapsulation in space. They hope to have an opportunity, when shuttle flights resume, to show that coating islets in low gravity produces more nearly spherical capsules that are stronger and less likely to be damaged by surrounding cells.

Islet implantation is without question the wave of the future for treatment of Type I diabetes. The procedure will be far simpler and cheaper than a pancreas transplant, and islets may be a lot easier to obtain than whole or partial organs: they're available not only from cadavers but also from aborted fetuses. Lacy believes that ultimately the best source may be other animals. In theory, human beings can survive on insulin produced by cow or pig islets, since it's very similar to our own. (Much of the insulin now injected by diabetics is from these animals.)

The difficulty with using animal islets is the familiar one of rejection, which is more acute when the transplantation is from one species to another. But Lacy and a number of other researchers have successfully transplanted purified islets from rats to mice, and Sun says there's no reason interspecies transplants of encapsulated islets shouldn't work, since the recipient's immune system doesn't even come in contact with them.

Preventing Diabetes

Impatient with the prospects of treating Type I, some ambitious researchers have shifted their focus to prevention of the disease—particularly to an experimental approach called early immunosuppressive therapy. It emerged from the research that identified diabetes as an autoimmune condition, and works—at least in mice—by halting the disease before complications arise.

For early immunosuppressive therapy to succeed, it's crucial to uncover the markers that announce the disease's onset. Since the diabetes genes haven't been identified, the earliest markers now available to diagnosticians are immune system abnormalities. Unfortunately, the presence of these abnormalities doesn't reliably indicate when diabetes will show up; in some pairs of identical twins, more than a decade elapsed from the time the first twin was diagnosed to the time the second was confirmed as having the disease. In fact, it's possible that some people who show immune system dysfunction will never actually develop Type I.

That restricts "prediction" of the disease to the moment the symptoms appear, and since symptoms may not show up until the autoimmune reaction has destroyed enough beta cells to bring insulin levels close to zero, prevention presents a problem: by the time anything constructive can be done, there may not be any islets to save.

Last year, Eisenbarth and his colleagues at Joslin came up with a way to overcome this difficulty, using an intravenous glucose tolerance test that had been developed for another purpose some 20 years before. When a healthy person has something to eat or drink, his pancreas instantly produces insulin to allow cells to use the nutrients it contains. In the tolerance test, a person at risk for diabetes is given a shot of glucose, and the level of insulin in his blood is monitored over the next three minutes. The slower the insulin levels rise, the fewer beta cells the subject probably has left, and the closer he is to becoming overtly diabetic. "The immune assays tell you something's wrong," Eisenbarth says. "Then the tolerance test tells you the amount of time left until the onset of diabetes. The question remains, With this knowledge, can you now prevent the disease?"

Weighing the Alternatives

In 1984 a team of doctors led by C. R. Stiller and John Dupre at University Hospital in London, Ontario, were able to reverse recently diagnosed diabetes in about half of those that they treated with regular doses of cyclosporine. Eisenbarth and his team are looking at other drugs to see if they have the same effect. But this sort of immunotherapy poses a difficult choice: not all of those who get Type I diabetes go on to suffer the debilitating complications of the disease, and there's no way to tell at the time of diagnosis—when immunotherapy would have to begin—whether the victim will be severely afflicted. Should a 10-year-old child embark upon a lifetime of immunosuppressive drugs when there's a reasonable possibility that daily injections of insulin may be all he'll ever need to live a normal life?

As of now, the only way to apply immunotherapy with minimal risk and still have a chance of preventing diabetes is to use very low doses of the drugs. But tests are already under way using more innocuous drugs and custom-designed compounds that may turn off the autoimmune response to beta cells but leave the rest of the immune system intact. "The field is changing fast," Eisenbarth says. "The only thing we need is better drugs."

Even without those drugs, the lives of a handful of Type I diabetics have already been transformed. Says Bill Lamb: "When I used to go out looking for a job, I'd consider just the salary. 'Take your pension plan and stick it in your ear,' I'd say, because I wasn't going to be around to collect it anyway. But after the transplant you've got to rethink your whole life, because now you've got a shot at becoming old. To find yourself healthy all of a sudden is the weirdest state of being."

a DRUG to FIGHT COCAINE

by Robert Wilbur

© Lawrence Migdale

Illicit use of cocaine has grown at an alarming rate: an estimated 10 percent of Americans have experimented with the drug. Since the long-overdue revelation that cocaine is indeed addictive, much research has focused on ways of easing cocaine withdrawal and overcoming dependence.

Forty-year-old Mark's business was collapsing, and his marriage was headed for the rocks. But a friend had just the thing for him: cocaine. Mark liked it. He liked it so much that he ended up spending as much as $1,000 a week on "Bolivian marching powder." He tried to kick the habit by leaving New York City for a vacation, but he started using cocaine as soon as he returned. Next he entered psychotherapy, but he soon lost confidence in his therapist. With his life crumbling around him and a very expensive habit to support, he finally turned to psychiatrist Jeffrey Rosecan, director of the Cocaine Abuse Treatment and Research Service at Columbia-Presbyterian Medical Center in New York. Rosecan promptly prescribed imipramine, a drug used to treat depression, and two amino acids— L-tryptophan and L-tyrosine. The treatment worked.

For the past several years, psychiatrists have been reporting that antidepressant drugs like imipramine are effective for relieving the craving that drives users back to cocaine. What's more, some of these drugs seem to block cocaine's euphoria (sensation of well-being or elation). The findings, based on a variety of drug treatments, are helping pin down some of cocaine's effects on the brain. But the best news is that drug therapy works when other treatments fail. Mark couldn't stop cocaine on his own or even with counseling. But medications helped him kick his habit, and now he's putting his life back together.

An Addictive Drug

Back in the 1970's, the prevailing opinion, even among prominent psychiatrists, was that cocaine was not addictive. Mark, like many others before him, found out that the assumption was

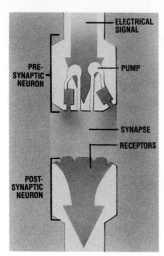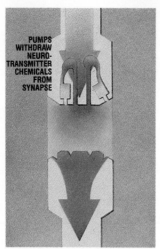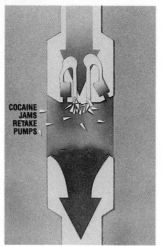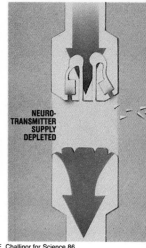

© Mary E. Challinor for Science 86

Cocaine interferes with activity at the synapse—the tiny gap between neurons in the brain—where up to 1,000 electrical signals pass each second. Ordinarily, an electrical signal triggers the release of neurotransmitters (in blue, far left), which convey the impulse across the synapse to receptors on the postsynaptic neuron. The transmission ends when retake pumps (second from left) withdraw the neurotransmitters. Cocaine jams the pumps (third from left), so that neurotransmitters remain in the synapse longer, prolonging neuron stimulation. In chronic cocaine users, the inability to retrieve neurotransmitters (right) may ultimately deplete the brain's overall supply of the chemical.

false. Recent experiments show how dramatically false it was. Roy Wise and Michael Bozarth, both psychologists at Concordia University in Montreal, taught rats to press levers for intravenous cocaine or heroin. They found that it's easy to make rats work very hard for either drug, but a crucial difference emerged between the animals' responses to the two substances.

Rats with unlimited access to heroin remained healthy. "But at the end of week one," says Wise, "most of the rats on cocaine were near death. By the end of three weeks, most of them had died." Cocaine is an appetite suppressant, and by the time of death, the animals on cocaine had lost 40 percent of their original weight. They didn't sleep normally, either, and the combination of impaired sleep and self-starvation made them particularly vulnerable to infections like colds and pneumonia.

In people, too, cocaine suppresses appetite and interferes with sleep. Abusers often take alcohol or sedatives like Valium to "come down" from the intense stimulation of a cocaine high. By the time they seek medical attention, these patients are no longer just cocaine abusers. They end up with a diagnosis of alcoholism or combined drug abuse as well.

Brief Euphoria, Intense Craving

Cocaine hasn't become a media sensation for nothing: one-tenth of the population has tried it, and 4 million to 8 million Americans abuse it,

despite having to pay $100 or more for a single gram. Some of these people find cocaine so intensely euphoric that their entire lives become dominated by the drug. According to Yale University psychiatrist Frank H. Gawin, the driving force behind chronic cocaine abuse is an inability to feel pleasure without the drug. "Cocaine abusers can't get off on the real world," Gawin says. "They have become unable to capture pleasure from everyday experience."

But the short-lived euphoria carries an even higher price than the cost of the drug. Abusers who try to abstain often encounter what seems an insurmountable obstacle: the craving that is the hallmark of addiction. In a preliminary study last year, Gawin and collaborator Herbert D. Kleber reported that desipramine, a drug closely related to imipramine, significantly reduced craving. Patients' cocaine consumption decreased by more than 90 percent after three weeks of treatment. Gawin and Kleber were so encouraged that they now use desipramine routinely for patients who do not respond to a month of psychotherapy, and they are conducting a larger controlled trial that in the next year could deliver the final verdict on desipramine's effectiveness in treating cocaine addiction.

Why Tricyclics Work

Desipramine and imipramine are members of a class of antidepressants called tricyclics. The tricyclics are not habit-forming, but in the brain they have at least one crucial property in common with cocaine. This action affects the way signals are transmitted across the synapse—a tiny, fluid-filled gap between two nerve cells, or neurons.

When a signal electrically stimulates the neuron on the sending side of the synapse, the neuron releases one of several neurotransmitters—chemical messengers that float through the fluid gap until reaching receptors on the receiving, or postsynaptic, neuron. This chemical action restimulates the electrical signal, which sends another message along the postsynaptic nerve. But neurons must then terminate the action of neurotransmitters, or else they would have no way to shut themselves off.

One shutoff mechanism involves an enzyme that degrades neurotransmitters into inactive substances. A second involves the retrieval of neurotransmitters from the synaptic fluid by specialized "pumps." Located in the membrane of the presynaptic neuron, these pumps funnel neurotransmitters back inside the cell. What cocaine and tricyclics have in common is that they both jam the pumps that collect three important neurotransmitters—dopamine, noradrenaline, and serotonin. All three substances are thought to play some role in mood disorders like depression.

In blocking the retrieval pumps, cocaine initially boosts the effect of neurotransmitters by keeping them in the synapse longer, thus prolonging their action on postsynaptic cells. This enhanced neurotransmitter stimulation, in fact, may produce the short-lived euphoria. With repeated cocaine use, neurotransmitters are used up, in effect "wasted" instead of retrieved, which diminishes the brain's overall supply of these chemicals. Many researchers now think that this depletion causes the "crash" that occurs when the high wears off: users feel depressed, anxious, sleepy, and extremely hungry.

The depletion theory is based on clinical observations of the effectiveness of antidepressant drugs. Tricyclics, because they also block neurotransmitter pumps, may be acting in part as a replacement for cocaine. But for reasons not yet clear, antidepressants are not addictive and don't bring about the same overall depletion.

Breaking the Cycle

The tricyclics also act to ameliorate some of cocaine's effects. Prolonged use of cocaine—repeated cycles of euphoria, crashing, and craving—probably brings about changes in the postsynaptic neurons that set hardened users apart from casual "chippers" and "weekend warriors." Specifically, the postsynaptic receptors, as a way of compensating for depletion, become supersensitive to neurotransmitters. Antidepressants, over a period of weeks, appear to decrease this sensitivity.

Dopamine is probably the most important neurotransmitter affected in cocaine abusers, which led Charles A. Dackis, a psychiatrist at Fair Oaks Hospital in Summit, New Jersey, to try an entirely different drug to treat his cocaine patients. He chose bromocriptine, a drug used to relieve the rigidity and tremor of Parkinson's disease, which is linked to a dopamine shortage.

Kicking cocaine. Group therapy is often an effective beginning step toward conquering a serious drug problem.

Bromocriptine stimulates the postsynaptic dopamine receptors, thereby mimicking the action of dopamine. Dackis and his colleagues have treated about 20 cocaine patients so far, the majority of whom experienced reduced craving. "These patients are experts on mood," Dackis notes. "They'll tell you if a drug works or not." The patients may be satisfied, but Wise and behavioral pharmacologist William L. Woolverton at the University of Chicago are worried that it may work a bit too well. Bromocriptine is self-administered by rats and by monkeys—a sign that the animals like it. But so far, there is no conclusive evidence that humans find it worthy of abuse.

How Amino Acids Help

Perhaps the most natural approach to overcoming a depletion has been to feed patients the amino acids for making neurotransmitters. Two have been used with some success: L-tryptophan, which the body uses to make serotonin, and L-tyrosine, the precursor for both dopamine and noradrenaline. L-tryptophan's effect on cocaine abusers is still uncertain, but the evidence is more solid for tyrosine. Pharmacologist Forest Tennant at the University of California in Los Angeles (UCLA) advises less severely addicted patients to use tyrosine alone. Gawin, however, is not convinced that the amino acid relieves craving: "I do think that tyrosine alleviates crash symptoms. When patients crash, they describe feeling intensely hungry, and I think the reason for the hunger is to replace amino acids that have been depleted by cocaine." Medicating for the crash without treating the craving, however, may be like giving an alcoholic relief from his hangovers without attacking the urge to drink.

While antidepressants can reduce craving, their effect on euphoria is not so clear. Ivan K. Goldberg and Harold B. Esecover, psychiatrists at Columbia University College of Physicians and Surgeons, treated their cocaine patients with protriptyline, the most energizing tricyclic. Though very effective against cocaine craving, protriptyline sometimes enhanced the high when patients combined it with cocaine. Reports from Yale University revealed similar results with desipramine.

Preliminary studies with other antidepressants, however, show that some are reliable for blocking cocaine's high. Psychiatrist Rosecan and colleague Donald Klein found that the imipramine and amino acid treatment consistently blocked euphoria. According to Goldberg, so does lithium, the premier drug for treating manic-depressive disease. Goldberg, who has treated patients with lithium, is emphatic about its effectiveness against euphoria: "Lithium is to coke as methadone is to heroin." Both imipramine and lithium affect serotonin in the brain, suggesting that serotonin—as well as dopamine—play a role in cocaine's euphoria.

A Sharp Departure

The use of antidepressants to treat cocaine abuse is still a relatively new approach. The weight of evidence clearly shows that the drugs offer effective help, but clinicians differ in how they use them. According to Tennant, a pioneer in the use of antidepressants to treat cocaine addiction, the vast majority of abusers don't need medication. They can kick the habit by themselves or with the assistance of psychotherapy. He believes that drugs should be reserved for patients like Mark, who try psychotherapy but still can't kick the habit.

At Fair Oaks Hospital, Charles Dackis and his colleagues subscribe to a disciplined treatment philosophy based on the Alcoholics Anonymous approach. The key step, Dackis claims, is for the addict to acknowledge that he is out of control and will do whatever it takes to get well. The psychiatrists demand that their patients abstain from all drugs—not just coke, but alcohol, uppers, downers, and narcotics. They also require that their patients attend self-help groups, first as inpatients and later as outpatients. Dackis uses bromocriptine only for patients with severe cocaine craving.

In contrast to the Fair Oaks approach, Ivan Goldberg uses drug therapy for all of his cocaine-abusing patients, but he points out that drug therapy is not a quick fix. Patients often continue to use cocaine at the start of treatment, and most of them remain on medication for six months to two years. Those with a chronic mood disorder may require permanent drug therapy.

As more specialists adopt the pharmacological approach, new drugs and drug combinations will be tested. It will take time before we possess a complete understanding of cocaine's effects on the brain. Meanwhile, drug therapy marks a sharp departure from older treatments based on individual or group psychotherapy, and it is helping more and more patients to kick a habit that some researchers, like Roy Wise, think is more damaging than heroin.

CRACK: CHEAP, DEADLY COCAINE

Dope peddlers call it the ultimate high. In reality, it is the ultimate downer, resulting in severe addiction and sudden death. It is an inexpensive but exceptionally potent form of cocaine. Its name: crack.

Until the 1970's, cocaine use in the United States was largely limited to snorting the drug's powdered form. Then some people began free-basing. Similar to the South American practice of smoking coca paste (base), free-basing involved "freeing" the cocaine from various salts and cutting agents. This was a hazardous procedure because it required heating a flammable solvent, such as ether. In a widely publicized 1980 incident, comedian Richard Pryor set himself on fire while free-basing.

In contrast, making crack is simple, involving baking soda rather than ether. The end result is a dry beige mass, which dealers break into small chunks called pellets.

Crack usually is smoked in a glass pipe. Its effect is almost immediate, producing a brief but intense high. Within minutes, depression sets in, combined with a craving for another "hit." These sensations result from chemical changes in the brain that were triggered by the cocaine.

The brain's nerve cells depend on substances called neurotransmitters to communicate with one another. Cocaine stimulates the release of neurotransmitters, resulting in the initial euphoria felt by the person. Normally, most of the neurotransmitters return to the nerve cells. But cocaine blocks the return; the neurotransmitters dissipate and break down. The depletion of the cells' supply of neurotransmitters leads to depression and anxiety, which users try to overcome by smoking more crack. This, of course, only aggravates the neurotransmitter deficiency.

Whereas an addiction to snorted cocaine appears to develop only after three or four years of regular use, people can become hooked on crack in weeks or even days. The psychological damage goes beyond depression and yearning for more of the drug. Continued use often results in irritability, sleeplessness, and a paranoid psychosis resembling schizophrenia. Delusions and hallucinations, such as the belief that bugs are crawling over the body, are common.

© A. Tannenbaum/SYGMA

A vial of crack sometimes sells for less than $10.

Smoking crack also can result in shortness of breath and lung damage similar to emphysema. Heart rate and blood pressure increase dramatically, leading in some cases to fatal heart attacks.

The craving for crack suppresses the desire for food, resulting in weight loss and, in severe cases, malnutrition. This was dramatically shown in experiments that allowed rats to have as much cocaine as they wanted. Ignoring food and water, the rats repeatedly pressed a lever that injected cocaine directly into their veins, until they died.

Getting high on crack is significantly cheaper than getting high on powdered cocaine. A pellet sells for $10 or less, making it easily accessible to teenagers as well as adults. But because of its addictive qualities, many users end up spending hundreds of dollars a week on the drug, squandering fortunes or turning to crime to support the habit. "It's the dealer's dream and the user's nightmare," said Dr. Arnold Washton, director of research for the National Cocaine Hotline (800-COCAINE).

Hotline personnel hadn't heard of crack prior to October 1985. Subsequently, intense press coverage of the drug and its devastating effects resulted in increased public and political concern. It remains to be seen if this concern is translated into broad-based, effective programs for preventing the use of crack and other drugs and for treating those who are already addicted.

JENNY TESAR

© Robert Fried

WORKPLACE EPIDEMICS

by Emil J. Bardana, Jr.

Two years ago, something strange happened at the Commerce Building, a state office facility in Salem, Oregon. Over a period of three days, 93 out of roughly 150 employees got sick. Hardest hit were the data processing workers on the basement floor, who, in addition to keeping up with their usual work load, had been scrambling to switch from a card catalog to a computerized system of information retrieval. Eighty-one percent of these workers complained of symptoms as varied as headaches, dizziness, dry throats, sore eyes, metallic taste, disorientation, nausea, burning noses, and fatigue. There were even six reports of fainting and five of convulsions.

Alarmed state officials evacuated the building, fearing that some contaminant was poisoning the workers. Yet, when investigators arrived, they found only that the air was a bit dry (humidity was measured at 34 percent, slightly below the comfort zone) and that the basement had been filled with cigarette smoke when the outbreak began, though the building was extremely well ventilated in general. Moreover, medical evaluations produced no evidence of ill health among the stricken workers. The eight state, local, and private agencies that participated in the investigation concluded that there was simply no apparent cause for what had occurred. The building soon reopened, and the workers reported no further problems.

Reports of outbreaks like this one have become surprisingly common in recent years; they seem to issue daily from schools, homes, hospitals, and office buildings. In fact, it is no exaggeration to speak of a national epidemic:

the number of Americans attributing some ailment to the time they spend in a particular building, usually their place of work, has tripled since the early 1970's. Yet rarely are their complaints linked directly to environmental causes—or even clearly diagnosed. As a result, the rampant phenomenon known as building sickness has never been defined in precise medical terms. Some physicians dismiss it as a symptom of workers' general dissatisfaction, combined with the media's hunger for a good scare story, while others have portrayed it as a full-blown crisis in public health. What is it that so many Americans are suffering from? And how serious is it? The question is worth examining. For whether it is real or imagined, building sickness has become a major drain on the nation's productivity: its annual cost, in absenteeism and investigative resources, now runs to billions of dollars.

Same Old Story?

Work-related medical complaints are nothing new, of course. Hippocrates postulated a connection between people's jobs and their health during the fifth century B.C. and advised his fellow physicians always to consider occupation as a possible factor in disease. That advice was put to good use during the 16th century by Georgius Agricola, a physician living in the Ore Moun-

tains, on what is now the East German–Czechoslovak border. Agricola noted that the local men—most of whom worked in gold and silver mines—all seemed to die young, either of consumption or of disorders later defined as silicosis and lead poisoning.

At the beginning of the 18th century, the Italian physician Bernardino Ramazzini pushed occupational medicine a step further by linking the diseases shared by potters, painters, gilders, glassmakers, and metal diggers to the inhalation of gases and dust. Ramazzini identified other work-related ailments as well, including "baker's asthma"—a respiratory allergy caused by constant exposure to flour dust (he believed that the flour, once inhaled, formed a doughy paste that occluded the respiratory passages). Indeed, all working people seemed to suffer some job-induced malady—even scholars, who, Ramazzini found, developed stiff knees and sluggish bowels from too much sitting and who strained their eyes working by candlelight.

The English surgeon Percival Pott advanced this line of inquiry in 1778, when he demonstrated a high incidence of cancer of the scrotum among chimney sweeps and linked it to the soot that lodged in the skin crevices of their genitalia. But it was not until the late 19th century, with the flowering of the industrial revolution, that occupational health was recognized as

Lack of privacy, poor ventilation, and eyestrain induced by video displays can all add up to an unhealthy workplace.

a serious public issue. A lack of data made it difficult to appreciate the truly appalling death rates in certain industries (many cutlery workers in England were dying of silicosis, then known as grinder's rot, after only five years in the trade), but what could not be conveyed by hard data was conveyed nonetheless—in the fiction of Charles Dickens. Dickens's vivid depictions of mill and factory life awakened the industrialized world to the medical consequences of its newfound prosperity.

During the first half of this century, industrial working conditions were greatly improved in the United States and Europe. Schedules began to reflect the need for sleep, and basic safety measures were adopted in most factories. But a revolution in chemical technology was spawning a new generation of occupational health hazards. Asbestos, for example, which for 2,000 years had been used mainly in lampwicks, became a component of countless manufactured products and, thus, of hundreds of thousands of workers' day-to-day surroundings. The result was a high incidence of asbestosis among the exposed—and, according to a British study conducted in 1947, a 50 percent death rate from lung cancer among those suffering from asbestosis. Meanwhile, the advent of the automobile and the modern highway placed many workers in constant contact with road tar and its potentially carcinogenic component, benzopyrene. And plastics—specifically polyvinyl chloride (PVC), now the most extensively used synthetic material in the world—created an annual demand for 20 million tons of the carcinogen vinyl chloride.

Responding to these developments, specialists in occupational medicine turned their attention to the perils of chemical exposure, and their discoveries led to substantial shifts in public policy. During the 19th century the only recourse open to an injured worker was to bring a common-law action against his employer—an expensive and rarely successful process. But during the early 20th century, Congress passed a series of measures imposing safety standards on employers and mandating compensation to people disabled by their jobs. This trend culminated in 1970, with the passage of the Occupational Safety and Health Act, which created both the National Institute for Occupational Safety and Health (NIOSH) and the Occupational Safety and Health Administration (OSHA).

Now, as the 20th century draws to an end, we find ourselves in the midst of yet another economic revolution—one that has brought the manufacturing sector to its knees, moved millions of would-be factory workers into office buildings to perform services or process information, and spawned yet another generation of occupational health concerns. Few work environments would appear safer than the modern office, its sealed windows and carpeted floors filtering out all the harshness of the outside world. In fact, though, it can harbor an array of pollutants ranging from cancer-causing hydrocarbons and various microbes to radioactive radon gas. The reason is often as simple, or, rather, as complicated, as a lack of ventilation.

The Ventilation Factor

The importance of having fresh air indoors has been recognized since the 18th century, when physicians, armed with a newly acquired understanding of respiration, began linking the death of English sailors to crowded, unventilated steerage cabins on their ships. First to propose a minimum standard for indoor ventilation was the British architect Thomas Tredgold, who declared in 1824 that any enclosed space should receive at least 4 cubic feet (0.11 cubic meter) of fresh air every minute. In 1893 the American physician John Shaw Billings suggested that 30 cubic feet (0.85 cubic meter) a minute would be a more reasonable guideline. His recommendation was accepted formally in 25 states, and it remained in effect for 53 years. But in 1946 the guideline was reduced to 10 cubic feet (0.28 cubic meter) a minute, on the advice of the American Society of Heating, Refrigeration, and Air Conditioning Engineers (ASHRAE). And in 1973, spooked by the impending energy crisis, ASHRAE recommended that minimum ventilation rates be reduced yet again—to just 5 cubic feet (0.14 cubic meter) a minute for each person—to save fuel.

As the inadequacy of this standard became apparent, ASHRAE proposed an entirely new type of guideline, one intended both to encourage energy conservation and to ensure adequate ventilation. The revised standard, adopted in 1981 and still in effect, prescribes different ventilation rates for different spaces, taking into account various special problems. For example, the new rules recommend an air-exchange rate of only 5 cubic feet (0.14 cubic meter) a minute for an office in which smoking is barred but suggest 20 cubic feet (0.57 cubic meter) if

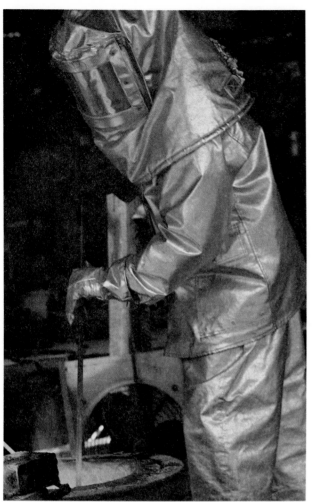

© David & Linda Phillips

smoking is allowed. The comparable figures for a public ballroom are 7 and 35 cubic feet (0.2 to 1 cubic meter) a minute.

No one has complained that these guidelines are inadequate; they are, in fact, the best to date. The problem is that they have never been rigorously enforced. Buildings simply are not inspected for adequate ventilation, as they are for, say, fire safety. As a result, few landlords have any notion of either the actual or the required ventilation rates for their buildings, and no one knows how often the standards are being met. What we do know is that many modern buildings recirculate 80 percent of all indoor air and that the amount of available fresh air often varies widely within a structure. A recent investigation of the Gregory Bateson State Office Building, a modern tower in downtown Sacramento, turned up local ventilation rates ranging from 39 cubic feet (1.1 cubic meters) a minute down to no ventilation at all. Needless to say, many occupants of the building were receiving a grossly inadequate air supply.

The Energy Crisis

The energy crisis also spawned significant changes in construction materials and architectural designs. New insulation products, includ-

Creating a healthier work environment. Protective clothing (left) helps a worker avoid the high heat and fumes associated with bronze casting. Below, methane gas levels in a coal mine are monitored to be certain that the air is safe to breathe.

Bethlehem Steel

ing particleboard that contained formaldehyde and foams made with polyurethane and ureaformaldehyde, were approved for general use, despite their tendency to give off toxic gases and residues. At the same time, new, and noxious, chemical sealants were introduced to stem the loss of heated or cooled air, and, in new office towers, windows that open were eliminated in favor of mechanical ventilation systems. The result, for many buildings considered to be extremely energy-efficient, was an atmosphere two to five times more polluted than even the dirtiest outdoor urban air.

It was amid these dramatic changes in the complexion of the work force, the design of buildings, and the accepted standards for indoor ventilation that the number of building-related health complaints began to surge. Building sickness, or tight-building syndrome, was relatively rare before 1977, but by 1980 it had become a major concern of NIOSH, the Centers for Disease Control, and many state labor and health agencies. And it has since become even more pervasive: between mid-1980 and mid-1981, building-related illnesses accounted for 13 percent of all complaints to NIOSH—a nearly threefold increase over the preceding three-year period. And, unlike work-related hazards of earlier eras, building sickness has shown no social or geographic preferences: the scores of buildings that have come under investigation range from the modest Health Center, in Sandpoint, Idaho, to Manhattan's Rockefeller Center and even—ironically—a Washington, D.C., office of the U.S. Environmental Protection Agency (EPA).

Rarely have investigations of suspect buildings turned up excessive concentrations of any single contaminant, but sensitive monitoring has often uncovered large numbers of toxic substances—ranging from fiberglass, asbestos, and carbon monoxide to phenol, methanol, toluene, xylene, and trichloroethane—in the same building. Thus, even though each contaminant may occur in concentrations 100 or even 1,000 times lower than industrial safety standards would permit, in concert they may still pose substantial risks. Chemists at the Lawrence Berkeley Laboratory at the University of California have hypothesized, for instance, that when a number of hydrocarbons are present in low concentrations, they create a cumulative hazard—especially in buildings whose ventilation systems recirculate 85 percent or more of all indoor air.

Allergic Reactions

As there are similarities of design among many of the buildings that have prompted health complaints, so too are there patterns detected among the complaints themselves. In fact, building sickness generally takes one of five forms, four of which can be linked to a specific type of indoor pollution.

The best-documented of these is allergic alveolitis, a condition characterized by breathlessness and a dry cough along with such flulike symptoms as headaches, malaise, fever, and aching muscles. The long-term effects of allergic alveolitis can include scarring of the lungs, but, because its symptoms are rarely severe, it is often mistaken for a cold. It is, in fact, an inflammatory condition affecting the terminal bronchial tree and the alveoli (tiny air sacs in the lungs) that results from the release of antibodies and sensitized blood lymphocytes to neutralize inhaled organic particles, such as bacteria, fungi, and amoebas. Mild allergic alveolitis is commonly called humidifier fever, for the germs that cause it often dwell in the stagnant water of air conditioners and humidifiers.

An outbreak of this condition can nearly always be linked directly to high levels of airborne microorganisms within a building. While investigating recent complaints about a building managed by the General Services Administration (GSA) in Washington, D.C., NIOSH officials discovered that slime in the building's air-conditioner drain pans was generating more than 83,000 fungi for each 35 cubic feet (1 cubic meter) of air—roughly the level found inside a chicken coop. The GSA has spent more than $500,000 to improve the situation, but problems persist. "We haven't reached final conclusions about what we need to do here," GSA official James Whitlock told *Forbes* magazine. "It's a continuing problem." Fortunately, such cases have been rare.

Another category of building sickness is that of common allergies, such as hay fever or bronchial asthma, that are aggravated by the prevalence of airborne allergens (allergy-inducing substances) within a building. Unlike allergic alveolitis, these conditions are not due entirely to the situation inside a building; they are caused by fungi, mites, dusts, or pollens that occur naturally in the environment but accumulate indoors. Various fungi may, for example, enter a building via the soil surrounding potted office plants and then, because of inadequate ventilation, build up in the indoor air.

The Legionnaires' Disease Outbreak

Just as allergens can flourish in a poorly ventilated building, so can infectious diseases. It is, of course, difficult to know whether conditions in a building are to blame for the rapid spread of an airborne infection; coughs and sneezes may cause a cold or flu epidemic in any shared indoor space. But when a noncontagious disease suddenly sweeps through the population of a building, it usually can be traced to some aspect of the indoor environment. In the summer of 1976, there was an outbreak of respiratory illness at the Bellevue-Stratford Hotel, in Philadelphia, Pennsylvania, where the American Legion was holding a convention. Two hundred twenty-one people contracted a severe form of pneumonia, and 34 of them died. After six months of detective work, investigators from the Centers for Disease Control isolated the responsible germ, which they labeled *Legionella pneumophilia*. The infestation apparently had begun in the Bellevue-Stratford's air-conditioning system, which then circulated the pathogen to the hotel's lobby.

Physicians have now identified at least 20 species of *Legionella* and have linked them to two distinct diseases, which together constitute the third class of building sickness. The pneumonic condition that struck in Philadelphia is the more serious of the two: it usually causes five to six days of coughing, fever, and pneumonia, and, though it often responds to treatment with antibiotics, 15 to 20 percent of all cases have proven fatal. Many of the outbreaks of pneumonic legionellosis reported since 1976 have been linked to aerosols from the stagnant water in shower heads, ice machines, water condensers, and cooling towers atop buildings. In 1985 alone, *Legionella* was associated with outbreaks of respiratory illness at the New York Times Building in Manhattan, and at several Pittsburgh-area hospitals. The second form of legionellosis, known as Pontiac fever, was first described as a building-related condition in 1968, when it attacked 144 workers at a county health department facility in Pontiac, Michigan. This nonpneumonic illness seems to occur under the same circumstances as the pneumonic variety, but its mild, flulike symptoms are more like those of humidifier fever than those of Legionnaires' disease. In fact, Pontiac fever may simply be an allergic reaction to amoebas that have been infected by the *Legionella pneumophilia* bacteria.

The fourth class of building-related sickness, far more common than either variety of legionellosis, consists of rashes, itching, and eye irritations caused by airborne particles of synthetic materials, such as fiberglass insulation. In a recent Portland, Oregon, case, admin-

Infections can spread rapidly at conventions, where thousands of people are crammed together for hours at a time.

© Brad Markel/Gamma Liaison

In many companies the air quality has been improved by permitting smoking only in certain designated areas.

istrative personnel on the 17th floor of a down-town bank building were found to have suffered extensive corneal abrasions after complaining of irritated eyes. The cause of their problem, an investigation found, was that fiberglass insulation particles had been spilling into a ruptured ventilation duct and blowing directly into the workers' offices.

These four classes of building sickness are all fairly easy to diagnose and eliminate—yet together they account for less than half of all building-related health complaints. The majority—fully 60 percent—fall into the category of undiagnosed mucous membrane irritations, such as sneezing, headaches, and soreness of the eyes, nose, and throat. Workers complaining of these symptoms often report that their discomfort increases as the workday progresses, but disappears outside the suspected building. Yet the complaints so closely resemble those associated with hay fever and the common cold that employers are often reluctant to take them seriously. And public health professionals are often no better equipped than employers to determine whether these complaints stem from a building-related problem. If one person is uncomfortable and another is not, which one is better describing the quality of the indoor air? The first person's annoyance may stem mainly from asthma or an allergy. On the other hand,

Disease-control laboratories—still unable to diagnose the majority of cases of "building sickness"—were successful in identifying at least 20 species of bacteria responsible for Legionnaires' disease.

CDC

the second person's lack of annoyance may simply indicate a loss of sensitivity from smoking or disease.

Tobacco Not to Blame

What this means, really, is that the extent to which, and the means by which, buildings are making people sick remain largely open questions. In 1980 the National Academy of Sciences appointed a committee on indoor pollutants, which undertook a major study in the hope of clearing up some of the confusion. The committee's report concluded that workers' health complaints are often the result of poor indoor air quality but that the problem usually has more to do with the activities of the workers themselves—smoking, in particular—than with the building. Tobacco smoke is undeniably a major source of such irritants as carbon monoxide, oxides of nitrogen, aldehydes, aromatic hydrocarbons, and airborne particles. But the data do not support the notion that smoking is the hidden cause of building sickness. NIOSH, the agency responsible for investigating "sick" buildings, has only rarely identified cigarette smoke as a source of the problem. In fact, of the 356 complaints the agency had investigated as of December 1985, only a small percentage could be attributed to cigarette smoke. Investigators linked 19 percent of the cases to other contaminants (whether organic or synthetic) originating inside the building, and 11 percent to the entrapment of outside pollutants. But most cases could not be traced to any particular cause: 11 percent were attributed to "unknown" factors, and another 50 percent simply to "inadequate ventilation."

There is no disputing that indoor air quality has declined in recent decades as a result of our efforts to conserve energy, or that this decline is a factor in the current epidemic. Can it be a mere coincidence that the dramatic increase in building-related health complaints has so closely paralleled the advent of the sealed, energy-efficient building? Simple arithmetic suggests that if the amount of air sealed and recirculated within a building rises from 20 percent to 80 percent, as it typically has in recent decades, the indoor pollution level will quadruple—to the detriment of the occupants. But it seems unlikely that conservation measures alone are to blame for the sick-building phenomenon, or even for the 50 percent of it that NIOSH has attributed to "inadequate ventilation." Too often the affected workers simply

have not been inhaling pollutants in concentrations that would be expected to cause acute symptoms.

All Psychosomatic?

This raises the question of whether building sickness is often a purely psychological phenomenon. Mass psychosomatic illness is not unheard of in the workplace; it is especially common in settings where the work is repetitive and dull and the supervision rigid and authoritarian, where workers are isolated from one another, or work space is extremely cramped. Typically, a number of workers suddenly become ill, complaining that they feel nauseated, dizzy, or overly tired. But medical examinations reveal no underlying pathology (medical cause), and investigation of the building turns up no physical contamination. This is precisely what occurred at the Commerce Building in Salem, Oregon—and at a time when the data processing workers, especially, were under unusual psychological stress.

It is important to keep in mind that these cases, in which an investigation fails to turn up any physical evidence of a building-related ailment, are not exceptions but the rule. Of course, it is possible that they all result from some unidentified toxicant that has infiltrated countless office buildings since 1970. But if that were the case, one would expect at least to find some measurable physical symptom. It seems far more likely that this surge in undiagnosed afflictions reflects a heightened awareness of environmental conditions—that we are in effect worrying ourselves sick over problems we might not have even noticed until recently. Ramazzini's coal miners and Dickens's factory workers would surely have been amused by our concern over indoor air quality.

It is understandable that our perspective on such matters has changed. In recent decades, nuclear and industrial accidents, toxic-waste catastrophes, and the belated discovery of myriad industrial poisons have made us justifiably suspicious of our surroundings. Such suspicion is a good thing to the extent that it makes us more vigilant and less reluctant to question the safety of our working and living conditions. But, to the extent that the sick-building syndrome is an expression of our anxieties, it is a social problem—and not a medical phenomenon at all. In short, for most of America's 50 million office workers, fear is probably the greatest occupational hazard of all.

PAST, PRESENT, AND FUTURE

REVIEW OF THE YEAR

PAST, PRESENT, AND FUTURE

FOOD AND POPULATION

In 1986 the world's population passed the 5 billion mark; the world's food production, at 1,840 million tons (just under last year's record), kept even with it overall. The food stocks to be carried over into 1987 continued to rise as production again outpaced consumption.

The paradox of the increase in the food surplus even when production lags behind population growth is accounted for by the fact that hunger, i.e., inadequate diet, is the result of lack of access to the available food; this access is denied because of inadequate income to grow or buy food. Abnormal food shortages are now expected in 11 countries (seven of them in sub-Saharan Africa), and crop prospects are unfavorable in five.

The major hunger problems are still found in sub-Saharan Africa, although the drought and famine that called world public attention to that region have been largely allayed. Food production in the region grew at nearly 2 percent during the early 1980's, but population continued to rise at about a 2.5 percent rate; this means a decline in food production per capita—the essence of the African food crisis.

World trade in cereal grains, which account for nearly 90 percent of what people consume, will continue to fall off, partly because of better harvests in some importing countries and partly because of the continuing debt burden of many of these countries, which prompts them to reduce their purchases of imported foods. The reduction in trade and the growing reserves have also kept the prices of many food commodities down—a boon to some consumers, but not to producers who rely on export income. One of the groups affected has been U.S. farmers, who have now seen their earlier share of the world market— nearly 50 percent—shrink to just above 30 percent. This reduction in income, which coincides with the highest farm debt on record and very abundant harvests, has been a major cause of the widely reported farm crisis in this country. Many U.S. farmers are in a situation much like indebted Third World countries: as the prices of their products go down, the amounts they must pay on the debts they acquired in the

Photo by Mark Thiessen © National Geographic Society

Alan Walker of Johns Hopkins University holds a cast of a skull from a prehistoric human-related species.

years of high export volume become more and more burdensome—driving many of them out of farming.

Martin M. McLaughlin

ANTHROPOLOGY AND ARCHAEOLOGY

An important new addition to our understanding of the evolution of humans and their early relatives is a skull dating to about 2.5 million years ago discovered near Lake Turkana in Kenya in 1985 but not reported until 1986. The skull belongs to the group designated *Australopithecus boisei,* characterized by a large jaw and rugged skeleton, and represents the oldest of the group found so far. The new discovery, made by a team of American and Kenyan scientists including Alan Walker of Johns Hopkins University and Richard Leakey of the National Museums of Kenya, opens the possibility that *Australopithecus boisei* was not descended from the species *Australopithecus robustus,* as once believed, but rather may have been living in Africa at the same time. If this new idea is correct, then different human-related species may have been living in the same place at the same time during the earlier stages of human evolution.

A French expedition in Brazil has offered new

information concerning the earliest humans in the New World, possibly pushing back the date of their arrival. The archaeological research, carried out in a rock shelter at Rio Piaui in northeastern Brazil, discovered the remains of human activity—not only charcoal from fires, but also paintings on the cave walls. Radiocarbon dating determined the charcoal on the bottom layer of the deposits to be about 32,000 years old. Some scientists are skeptical of these early dates. If the dates prove correct, the rock shelter would be the earliest known human habitation site in the Americas.

The subject of cannibalism has long concerned anthropologists. Recent archaeological research at Fontbrégoua Cave in Provence, southeastern France, has yielded what appears to be evidence of the practice during the Neolithic Period, around 4,000 B.C. Researchers found a pit in the cave containing the skeletal remains of three adults, two children, and one individual of indeterminate age. The bones showed clear traces of having been scraped with stone tools in the same way that nearby bones of sheep, deer, and boar had been scraped when the meat was prepared as food. The human bones had also been broken to extract the marrow. The people who lived in the cave raised sheep and goats, grew wheat and barley, and hunted wild animals. Like other Neolithic peoples, they made pottery and efficient ground-stone axes. This new discovery seems to provide evidence for "dietary cannibalism"—eating of human flesh to supplement nutritional needs—as opposed to "ritual" cannibalism, when the practice was carried out for religious or ritual reasons.

Exploration and research continues on a large number of sunken ships throughout the world. The best known is the *Titanic*, which sank in the North Atlantic in 1912 and was rediscovered in 1985 by a joint American and French expedition.

The ocean liner lies in about 12,000 feet (3,650 meters) of water some 400 miles (645 kilometers) south of Newfoundland. Robert D. Ballard, the expedition leader, provided extraordinary underwater photographs of the ship and its scattered contents taken by the deep-sea submarines exploring the site.

Off the coast of Cape Cod, Massachusetts, Barry Clifford is exploring the pirate ship *Whydah*, which sank in a storm in 1717. The *Whydah* is the only pirate ship to have been identified and salvaged, and the wreck is yielding a rich assemblage of artifacts of the period as well as information about the lives of 18th-century pirates. Clifford discovered the ship in 1982, and in 1985 found the ship's bell with the name *Whydah* on it, confirming its identity. The explorers have already recovered gold and silver objects, plates made of pewter, and cannon from the ship. The ship's crew had a surprisingly international composition.

In the Caribbean, another richly laden ship was found in 1986, following the discovery in 1985 of the treasure ship *Nuestra Señora de Atocha*. The new ship is believed to be the *Nuestra Señora de la Maravilla*, a Spanish galleon that sank in 1656 with its holds full of treasures from the New World bound for Spain. The divers exploring the wreck have recovered gold and silver coins, emeralds, guns with gold inlay, and pottery from Spain and China. The finds suggest that the ship is the *Maravilla*, one of the most richly filled and sought-after vessels of the period. The ship lies some 50 miles (80 kilometers) north of Grand Bahama Island.

These shipwrecks, and others like them, are providing not only extraordinary collections of treasures and daily objects from the past, but also important historical information about trade patterns, ship construction, and the lives of sailors in past centuries.

PETER S. WELLS

The bow and anchor chains of the ocean liner Titanic, *which struck an iceberg and sank on its maiden voyage in 1912. The ship lay undisturbed on the North Atlantic floor until discovered by Robert Ballard and his expedition using deep-sea submarines.*

The Titan City

by Carol Willis

I n October 1925, thousands of New Yorkers viewed an exhibition at the John Wanamaker department store titled "The Titan City, a Pictorial Prophesy of New York, 1926–2026." They saw murals of a spectacular skyscraper metropolis, with colossal setback towers spaced at regular intervals and connected by multilevel transit systems, arcaded sidewalks, and pedestrian bridges at the upper floors. Harmonious future avenues were materialized in miniature along the store's main corridors, where model skyscrapers of fantastic shapes and colors encased the piers, creating a "Grand Canyon of the future."

Urban Optimism of the 1920's

The Titan City typified a new 1920's conception of the urban future—a modern metropolis of high density, advanced technology, and centralized planning. Most prognosticators around the turn of the century had foreseen a metropolis of giant crowding towers—chaotic, congested, and teeming with gadgetry. In the early 1920's, however, these apprehensive projections were replaced by optimistic prophecies of absolute order. Architectural theorists envisioned an ideal city transformed by technology and rationalized by planning. Their visions were quickly embraced by the general public. By the second half of the decade, this city of towers had become the new popular image of the urban future.

American Utopianism had traditionally disdained the city, but these 1920's prophets espoused a new kind of urban optimism. They shared a resolute faith that science and technol-

ogy could solve all social problems and shape the urban future. Armed with the new planning principle of zoning and inspired by advances in engineering, transportation, and construction, they expected to build skyscraper cities that would be everything the contemporary city was not. In his 1930 book *The New World Architecture,* the critic Sheldon Cheney exhorted: "Let the vision be of a city beautiful, with a lift toward the skies; and let it be simple, convenient, sweet-running, airy, and light." He wrote, "Thinking about it, visioning it, will make it come true."

In these schemes, high-rise buildings would house all the necessities of urban life, including businesses, residences, and places of recreation and religion. Giant towers would be widely spaced for light and air. High-speed transportation systems might link their tops. Buildings would shoot up 100 stories and higher, but their modernity lay not so much in their huge scale (many were in fact smaller than those proposed in previous decades) as in their clean lines and simple, sculptural massing and their rejection of traditional ornament.

A Sharp Change

To fully appreciate the radical change represented by these skyscraper-city visions of the 1920's, one need only look back at popular images from the decades just before. Perhaps the most popular and perennial earlier prophecy is one that appeared from 1908 to 1915 in a well-known picture book of New York City landmarks, *King's Views of New York.* Imagining a vista up Broadway in about 1930, this perspective shows a great canyon of motley office blocks. Bridges spring from one rooftop to the next or tunnel through upper floors, and the sky swarms with dirigibles and airplanes. A caption describes this scene as "a weird thought of the frenzied heart of the world in later times, incessantly crowding the possibilities of aerial and inter-terrestrial construction."

The idea of a vertiginous city overtaken by rampant technology was latched onto by many early-20th-century illustrators. Winsor McCay, for example, the creator of "Little Nemo" and other early comic strips, often drew giant agglomerations of teetering towers. Most of the pre-1920's prophets arrived at their conceptions

The pre-1920's book King's Views of New York *had a cluttered vision of how Broadway would look—in 1930.*

Zoning laws enacted by New York City in 1916 sparked an era of creativity in sky-scraper architecture. Some of the design innovations are captured in this sequence of renderings that begins by showing the maximum building mass allowed (left), and evolves the concept through to a practical, stepped-back skyscraper (far right).

simply by enlarging on the present. Their imaginary images were extensions of the contemporary city and its problems, not alternatives.

In the early years of this century, the popular, often pessimistic image of the future city was principally the creation of artists and illustrators; most architects and planners, meanwhile, adhered to an urban ideal modeled on great European cities of the past. In the 1920's, however, architects became the chief oracles of the urban future.

The 1920's were pivotal years for the changing conception of the city. As the historian William Leuchtenburg has noted, "In 1916, Americans still thought to a great extent in terms of nineteenth-century values of decentralization, competition, equality, and agrarian supremacy of the small town. By 1920 the tri-umph of the twentieth century—centralized, industrialized, secularized, and urbanized—while by no means complete, could clearly be foreseen.'' Architects adapted to the age with a growing professionalism in city planning, and embraced the new concept of zoning as a tool with which to control urban growth.

The Effect of Zoning

Indeed, it can be argued that the idea of the city rationalized by planning was a direct outgrowth of the country's first comprehensive zoning law, the New York City statute of 1916. Of particular importance was the "zoning envelope"—a restriction on the maximum legal volume of a tall building requiring that it be stepped back at specified levels. In this formula, some architects discerned the basis for a new aesthetic

Sequence courtesy the Cooper Hewitt Museum, Smithsonian Institution/Art Resource

of simple, sculptural masses and subordinated ornament that they declared both modern and distinctly American. An enlargement of this setback formula also created the "superblock," a giant stepped-back tower rising over a multiblock base. The setback and the superblock suggested a future urban topography of rationally spaced towers.

Early in 1922 the skyscraper architect Harvey Wiley Corbett and the architectural delineator Hugh Ferriss began a theoretical study of the requirements of the New York setback ordinance, and their collaboration spawned a series of articles in which, with escalating optimism, they proclaimed the favorable effects of zoning on skyscraper design and on the future metropolis. Ferriss created renderings in which he gave the legal formula for the setback an almost iconic identity. These drawings were of unparalleled importance in impressing other architects with the power, beauty, and inchoate modernity of unornamented setback towers.

In a 1922 article titled "The New Architecture," Ferriss declared, "We are not contemplating the new architecture of a city—we are contemplating the new architecture of a civilization." Six months later he predicted that within a generation, American cities would be transformed by the zoning laws, and he accompanied his forecasts with fantastic drawings of future urban vistas. Corbett soon began to echo his colleague's optimism. He proclaimed that the "new type of city with its innumerable spires, towers, and domes set back from the cornice line, will provide a fascinating vision, all the novelty and originality in the world brought under a larger scheme."

Fantastic Visualizations

Ferriss and Corbett's 1925 Titan City exhibition was really a summary of many of the professional speculations and pet projects that had occupied the two men for several years. Ferriss's zoning-envelope studies were represented in a series of 12-foot (3.7-meter) monochromatic paintings at the Wanamaker show. Corbett provided the concept behind a series of views of grand avenues and terraced promenades, rendered by the artist Robert Chanler and his staff. The Titan City show also portrayed ideas by other designers. Ferriss's mural of apartments on bridges, for example, was a variation on Raymond Hood's "bridge homes," which had appeared in the *New York Times* earlier that year. Airplane landing platforms built on the roofs of skyscrapers were copied from schematics developed by some of Corbett's students.

In his 1929 book The Metropolis of Tomorrow, *Ferriss advocates well-spaced skyscrapers linked by subway.*

Carol Willis

The Titan City exhibition helped spark a brilliant blossoming of visionary urbanism, and in the later 1920's both professional and public interest in cities of the future reached unprecedented heights. The most frequent approach envisaged a city plan of regularly spaced setback towers, usually connected by aerial highways. A second type clustered skyscrapers in nucleated centers. A third variation featured isolated towers surrounded by open space. The megastructure—an entire city contained within a single building—constituted still another approach.

One particularly regimented version of the orderly avenue of pyramidal towers was proposed by Francisco Mujica in 1929. Mujica, a Mexican archaeologist and architect, believed that the pre-Columbian stepped pyramid offered a native, "Neo-American" precedent suited to the requirements of the New York zoning law. He envisioned regular rows of nearly identical hundred-story setback towers, connected by elevated pedestrian bridges and layered levels of traffic below. Even though Mujica's perspective drawing seems relentlessly rational, his declared motives were idealistic and humanistic. In his book's brief text, he exhorted: "Let us . . . work for the development of the modern city, giving it fully the mechanical and practical stamp of our century, yet not forgetting in our planning that each part of this gigantic human machine has a heart capable of soaring high and loving. . . ."

Apartments on Bridges

A less idealized scheme for nucleated centers of development was proposed in a 1929 project by Raymond Hood called "Manhattan 1950." Hood, who would soon be one of the designers of Rockefeller Center, was already one of the country's most celebrated skyscraper architects. In "Manhattan 1950," he presented a plan for more than 20 tentacular bridges on which would be built luxury apartment towers, each of which might house 10,000 to 50,000 residents.

An entire city within a single giant skyscraper—what today we call a megastructure—was a minor category of speculation during the 1920's. Illustrations of such buildings often appeared in the pages of science fiction magazines. A drawing by Lloyd Wright (the son of Frank), published in the *Los Angeles Examiner* in 1926, depicted a 1,000-foot (300-meter) tower covering 40 acres (16 hectares) at the center of a 20-mile (32-kilometer) square of farms,

Bridge-top apartments in New York City were among the futuristic visions of 1920's architects that never came to pass.

forests, and parks. This structure would contain all the industrial, commercial, and residential requirements for a community of 150,000. Although Wright's schemes owed much to his father's architectural and planning ideas, this drawing was intentionally given a comic-book character that undermined its seriousness in architectural circles.

All these various visionary schemes offered new conceptions of a clean, efficient, rational city, and their images were intoxicated with technology—the attenuated towers, the widespread obsession with high-speed transportation, the aerial perspectives, the dramatic night views radiating man-made light. What was most novel about the super skyscrapers of the 1920's, though, was not their great height, but their simplicity of form and ordered plans. They embodied in a new way the traditional American faith in progress. To most early-20th-century Americans, the word "progress" signified technological and material advancement, but social progress was a corollary. As the historian and social critic Charles Beard put it, people believed that "mankind, by making use of science and invention, can progressively

emancipate itself from plagues, famines, social disasters, and subjugate the material forces of the good life—here and now."

Hollywood's Concept

A Hollywood version of a concept similar to Mujica's was created as a set for the 1930 Fox film *Just Imagine*, which transported audiences to 1980 New York. The set designers constructed a 225- by 75-foot (69- by 23-meter) model of a glittering metropolis in an old army blimp hangar, complete with lofty towers of up to 250 stories, nine levels of multilane traffic systems, personal airplanes, and aerial traffic cops. Built to a scale of one-quarter inch to the foot (about 2 centimeters to the meter), the tallest model represented a building almost 2,000 feet (600 meters) high. In many aspects this set foreshadowed the extravagant models and dioramas created for the 1939 New York World's Fair, particularly the Democracity of Henry Dreyfuss and the Futurama of Norman Bel Geddes.

Many proposals by serious designers rivaled the fantasies of *Just Imagine*. In 1929 the transportation engineer Robert Lafferty pro-

Mexican architect Francisco Mujica's 1929 vision of New York City skyscrapers takes a more symmetrical approach.

posed an elaborate multilevel traffic system that would include a continuous bridge-highway suspended between setback towers called "Station-Pylons." Lafferty argued that "the 6 inch to 8 inch cables, and light strong structure of Airways 200 feet in the air, will cast but little shadow," and that "as this system will minimize noise and vibration, the beauty and attractiveness is obvious." Another traffic engineer, John A. Harriss, put forth a plan for a network of multilane highways stacked six deep across Manhattan.

Harmony and Humanism

In his 1929 book *The Metropolis of Tomorrow,* Hugh Ferriss created the 1920's most complete and compelling vision of the future city. His scheme divided the city into three major zones—Business, Science, and Art—each dominated by a great setback "tower-building" rising 1,000 feet (300 meters) or higher on a base of four to eight full city blocks. Spaced at half-mile (0.8-kilometer) intervals, these "primary centers" were to be built over the intersections of 200-foot (60-meter)-wide avenues and were to serve as "express stops" for the highway system. Secondary centers would be posi-

tioned nearby—for example, at the midpoint between the Art and Business sectors rose the center for the Applied and Industrial Arts, and between Art and Science stood the tower of Philosophy. To Ferriss, this absolute hierarchy signified harmony and humanism. He wrote that this city would be "populated by human beings who value mind and emotion equally with the senses, and have therefore disposed their art, science, and business centers in such a way that all three would participate equally in the government of the city."

The visionary architects' belief in centralized planning coincided with a growing consensus in many areas of American society that planning, and not "rugged individualism," would necessarily be the way of the country's future. Some historians have found the roots of this conviction in the successful mobilization of industry during World War I, the nation's first major attempt at government control over the economy. The historian Ellis Hawley, for example, has argued that the effectiveness of the wartime mobilization offered a model for peacetime management that became a central theme of postwar policy. He breaks with the conventional view of the 1920's as a period of compe-

Hollywood's architectural vision of 1980 New York: the set design for the 1930 science fiction musical Just Imagine.

tition and conservatism, and instead emphasizes the emergence of managerial and bureaucratic institutions that, led by organizational and technical experts, worked together to solve the nation's problems.

The American visionary architects of the 1920's believed that change would be evolutionary, not revolutionary. True sons of their prosperous decade, they saw no conflict between Utopianism and capitalism. If action were to be taken to set rational and reasonable guidelines for future urban growth, they assumed, the irrepressible vitality of the capitalist system would eventually materialize their ambitious designs.

Rejected by Regionalists

These optimistic prophecies were not without their critics. Most of their contemporary detractors concentrated on two points: that the skyscraper cities were inhuman in scale, and that they were economically impracticable. Some viewed them as malignant symbols of capitalist greed. Lewis Mumford, in his review of the Titan City exhibition in *The New Republic,* railed that "innumerable human lives will doubtless be sacrificed to Traffic, Commerce,

and Properly Regulated and Zoned Heights on a scale that will make Moloch seem an agent of charity." Mumford was a leading spokesman of the regionalist movement, advocating comprehensive regionwide planning and a deep ideological commitment to decentralizing cities. Like most regionalists, his chief interest lay not with the collective public good but with the individual home and the neighborhood.

The regionalists, in the end, proved to be the most accurate prognosticators of America's real suburban future. It is easy to see the centralized supercities of the 1920's as authoritarian, oppressive, monotonous, and sterile. Yet the designers of those cities intended exactly the opposite; to them, the vision was democratic, liberating, and hygienic. These dreams of the future skyscraper cities signaled both the demise of the persistent national inferiority complex in the face of European culture and offered, in the New World, a prefiguration of the global future. In assuming that technology could be tamed, the city planned, and the future designed for the benefit of mankind, the visionary architects of the 1920's became the masters of the machine-age metropolis and created America's first modern conception of the city as Utopia.

© Attila Hejja

UNDERSEA CITIES

by Bill Lawren

Two hundred years from now, some astute historian may write that underwaterman was born in a converted houseboat on the river Seine in 1986. There, moored just the other side of the Place de la Concorde and within walking distance of the venerable Paris Opera, sits the *Peniche St. Paul,* the 90-foot (27-meter) houseboat-*cum*-studio of French architect and aquanaut Jacques Rougerie. More than anyone else, he is the man who has thought through—in elaborate detail—the elements of a submarine civilization.

Suboceanic Cityscape

On Rougerie's drafting table is the nucleus of his dream, an underwater village. Its center is a marketplace—a cone-shaped building. Rougerie sees this as an underwater version of the traditional European plaza, the center of small-

town social and economic life. Within its busy confines, explains Rougerie, villagers could exchange gossip, "buy a new pet octopus, or pick up some day labor from the people hanging around."

Clustered around the center are underwater family farms, consisting of a farmhouse; a round, flying-saucer-like main building; and Plexiglas anchored to the ocean floor by a complex system of steel cables. Near each single-family dwelling, there are sheds, garages, pens of fish, and fields of such underwater crops as kelp. All homes are made of concrete resin molded into graceful shapes. Each farm is connected to the rest of the village by a series of tubular, water-filled streets through which residents swim. They feature frequent signs to help undersea commuters find their way. Doorways to the various buildings are in the bottoms of the structures because underwater it requires much less energy to move vertically than horizontally.

Rougerie has thought through all the details. The interiors of all the buildings would be rounded, with no right angles or corners to trap dirt and harbor infection-causing microorganisms. As further precautions against microbes, residents would take daily baths in ultraviolet light and thrice-daily antiseptic showers. Colors used inside would be dark, allowing the eye to wander easily to the large windows and not be "captured" inside by whites or pastels. Moreover, all lighting would be diffuse. ("Point lighting tends to make people aggressive," according to Rougerie.)

The suboceanic citizens would have a staple diet based on domesticated fish and kelp. ("I've got recipes for 30 different kinds of seafood salad," Rougerie says.) It would be supplemented by meats and grains imported from the surface. Seafloor crops would be exported "up" to waiting vessels. Air would be piped in from the surface, at least until artificial gills were perfected. Nonbiodegradable refuse would be sealed in containers and floated to the surface for disposal by oceangoing garbage craft. The considerable power needed to pressurize the interiors of houses and operate desalination plants would be furnished by an ingenious geothermal generator that uses the different water temperatures found layered through the ocean's depths.

"Even as a child," Rougerie explains, "I always had the dream of living under the sea. As I grew up I saw that the two great adventures of this century are the conquest of space and the conquest of the submarine environment. Right now men are able to dive down and look at the fauna for only an hour or so, then they have to come back up to the boat. This is stupid. As an architect I'm trying to create structures so that men can live underwater."

Millennia of Experimentation

The dream of living underwater is at least as old as the pearl divers of Babylon, who, some 5,000 years ago, tried to extend their four-minute bottom time by breathing through hollow reeds. When Jacques Cousteau invented the Aqualung in the late 1940's, that dream became a promising, if distant, reality. By the 1960's it seemed within reach at last. In 1962 a 56-year-old inventor named Edwin Link helped inaugurate the Undersea Age when he spent eight hours submerged off the coast of the French Riviera inside a one-man aluminum cylinder. Link's success emboldened others, and, over the next 15 years, at least 65 different habitats, representing the labors of 17 countries, were built.

A standout was Jacques Cousteau's series of three experiments in which a total of 13 aquanauts and one parrot built fish pens, studied the marine environment, and recorded their physical and psychological reactions over the course of 59 days spent on the ocean floor. Another outstanding effort was the American Tektite II habitat, in which some of the 53 aquanauts lived for a month at a time.

By the mid-1970's the flurry of experiments with underwater living ended, but the aquanauts had made their point: man could live and work successfully in fixed underwater habitats with surprisingly few adverse effects. Medical problems in most cases were minor—the most common being nagging ear infections. Psychological problems were minor as well. After a three- to five-day adjustment period involving sleeplessness and mild depression, most aquanauts settled comfortably and contentedly into their environment. The stresses of confinement were more than balanced by a spirit of adventure. In fact, Tektite aquanauts James Miller and Ian Koblick wrote that "people who have clashed previously on the surface often get along well while on the seafloor."

Aquanauts explore the exterior of the Tektite II underwater habitat, where they live for a month at a time.

The ship above is being purposely sunk to form an artificial reef (left). Soon after, divers discovered schools of fish living within the wreck.

Prototype Habitats

Rougerie hopes to offer others this experience, and, unlike many visionaries, he has done more than dream about it. In the early 1970's he designed and built a submarine habitat, Galithee, large enough to hold five people for as long as three months at depths of up to 195 feet (60 meters). In 1980 several Japanese aquanauts lived there. It was subsequently bought by the Japanese government and put on display in a Rougerie-designed marine pavilion in Osaka. Galithee was followed in 1981 by Hippocampe, a smaller underwater habitat where Rougerie

and French physiologist Bernard Gardette lived for three weeks. Rougerie has also built Aquabubbles—small mobile underwater laboratories that he has used to assemble submarine children's villages—and several varieties of partially submerged vehicles. And his prospectus is overflowing with designs for underwater restaurants, farms, and universities.

"The technology to build submarine villages already exists," Rougerie says. Once started, it will not take long for his dream to become reality. For the most part the village structures would use the same technologies applied to other deep-sea habitats. But some experimenters have already devised ingenious alternatives. Architecturally even more free-wheeling than Rougerie himself is German-born architect Wolf Hilbertz. He has used a process called electrolytic accretion to actually grow submarine structures. His inspiration for the technique came from German attempts in the early 1900's to use electric current to extract gold from seawater. "I read about that as a boy. Apparently it worked, and I soon found out that just about every possible building material can be found dissolved in seawater. So when I became an architect, I decided to try to build like nature did, using natural processes and available materials," says Hilbertz.

During the 1970's Hilbertz adapted the technology by attaching a cathode and anode to chicken wire and submerging it in the ocean. When he passed an electric current through the wire, he found that dissolved matter in the sea-water formed a solid structure. Over the next decade he tinkered with the technology until he developed a strong, lightweight building material he dubbed Seacrete. He has since used Sea-crete to build artificial reefs off St. Croix and is now "accreting" a large spiral structure the size of a room in Galveston Bay. Although he calls it a piece of conceptual art, he says it moves us a little closer to growing not only underwater habitats but startlingly elegant, reeflike submarine cities.

Underwater Resort

Others have already begun to explore the possibility of opening the seafloor to a new generation of aquanauts. Ian Koblick, a veteran of the Tektite projects who has spent more than two months in submarine habitats, is taking a first step. He has refurbished the La Chalupa habitat that he designed and tested in the early 1970's and has outfitted it as a submarine resort hotel. Renamed the Innerspace Resort, it is moored on the seafloor off Key Largo, Florida, and will be accommodating undersea tourists this summer. The six-guest Innerspace, in Koblick's words, will be "very luxurious, like a fancy yacht or customized airplane," and will feature a swimming pool whose bottom opens right into the sea. Even at $250 per person per night, reservations "are already booked way ahead," Koblick says.

Innerspace represents a step in developing an underwater culture, but preparing for a submarine society where people will become residents and not just tourists is a more complex undertaking. Rougerie feels it requires a special sort of individual to maintain the balance and harmony necessary to sustain an underwater civilization. In the peopling of underwater towns, he foresees an exploratory stage in which aquanauts, "like astronauts, will have to be supermen—people who are in extremely good physical condition and extremely strong psychologically." Later, he thinks, the first generation of pioneers could be joined by people who, though still in good physical and psychological shape, would be chosen mostly for specific skills.

Realizing this dream would not take long, Rougerie says. "Given the money, a village could be constructed in two or three years." The project would involve building several villages and then using them as living experiments, watching the physical and psychological reactions of the people sent to live there.

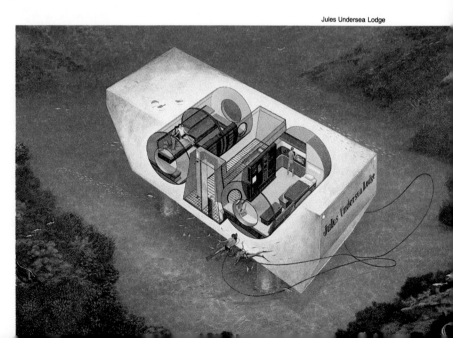

A luxurious vacation spot—30 feet underwater. The recently opened Jules Undersea Lodge offers guests all the amenities of a first-class hotel, plus the opportunity to live among the more than 120 varieties of fish and marine life found in the Florida Keys.

Artificial Gills

The technology to extend man's ability to keep up with the fish is being developed. Perhaps the most spectacular advance is the hemosponge, an artificial gill that works like a fish's, extracting oxygen directly from seawater. In the mid-1970's marine biologists Joseph and Celia Bonaventura, husband-and-wife codirectors of Duke University's Marine Biology Center, decided to mimic the breathing apparatus of the fish. Whereas the human transfers the oxygen he uses from a gas (air) to a liquid (blood), the fish transfers oxygen from one liquid (water) to another (blood). To duplicate that, the Bonaventuras needed a porous material that could retain water and be permeated with a substance that could extract the oxygen and retain it for transfer to a container, where it would be available for breathing.

After several trials, they found a special polyurethane that acted as their sponge. Knowing that blood hemoglobin can withdraw oxygen from water, Joseph Bonaventura experimented first with his own blood and then with fish blood before finally finding success using heme, an oxygen-fixing substance extracted from sheep blood. To free the oxygen from the heme for transfer to a container, the Bonaventuras devised a system that uses an electronic charge.

Right now the most advanced hemosponge can deliver ¼ liter of oxygen per minute, far less than the 2 liters per minute a diver needs. But, says Joseph Bonaventura, it won't take a technological breakthrough to increase oxygen output—"just some engineering, some tinkering." Already the Bonaventuras are thinking big. They believe it is possible to build a sponge that can meet all the oxygen needs of a submarine community of up to 150 people.

Liquid-Breathing Humans?

The next step—one that is vital, says Rougerie—is to create a human whose body and mind are adapted to life in a suboceanic town. In other words, create a fully realized underwater man. Duke University researcher Johannes Kylstra has attempted just that by trying to transform man from an air breather to a liquid breather. During the 1970's and early 1980's, he experimented with filling the lungs of mice, rats, and dogs with a saline solution saturated with oxygen. The animals breathed as long as 43 minutes with no adverse aftereffects. Encouraged, Kylstra filled one lung of a human subject with a similar solution and was gratified

to get the same results. The man breathed comfortably for 47 minutes and suffered no aftereffects once his lung was drained.

Since then, Kylstra has experimented with more promising solutions called fluorocarbon emulsions, which do a more efficient job of retaining oxygen. Although Kylstra sees the technique as limited to such emergency applications as escape from submarines, aquanaut James Miller thinks it could someday be used for routine diving operations as well. One can imagine some future submarine citizen filling his lungs with the appropriate solution and diving outside to swim happily for hours, unencumbered by hardware of any kind.

Once man has settled on the seafloor, nature may take up where technology leaves off. There is already a tantalizing suggestion that the evolution of man's ancestors included a long aquatic phase, holding out the possibility that latent within *Homo sapiens* is the genetic raw material that could engender a sea-dwelling species, *Homo aquaticus*.

The Aquatic Ape

Some of the clues may lie in the Danakil Alps, a particularly forbidding stretch in the backlands of Ethiopia where a series of craggy, almost lunar mountains rise 4,000 feet (1,200 meters) out of a lava and basalt desert. With scrub growth clinging like an afterthought to the few cracks in the rock where moisture can linger, it is the unlikeliest of settings for the emergence of

The polyurethane "hemosponge," a first step toward artificial gills, delivers only ⅛ of a diver's oxygen needs.

© Scott Taylor

what one set of theorists has taken to calling the aquatic ape. Sometime between 2 million and 5 million years ago, advancing seas encroached upon the Danakil Alps and all but isolated them in a swampy marshland. In this region, some believe, lived a small group of australopithecines—the upright apes widely regarded as man's distant ancestor. Separated from their savanna food sources, they survived the only way they could: by spending more and more time hunting for food underwater. Over the next several million years, evolution incorporated the physical capabilities necessary to sustain a partially aquatic life-style. When the seas receded, the australopithecines returned to the savanna and eventually passed their genetic endowment along to *Homo sapiens.*

This theory was originally drawn out by German biologist Max Westenhofer and British marine biologist Sir Alistair Hardy, and later developed by Welsh writer-researcher Elaine Morgan in her book *The Aquatic Ape.* It has been offered to explain a number of curious quirks of the human anatomy. These include our relative hairlessness and well-developed layer of subcutaneous fat. (Both, the theory goes, are of little value in most terrestrial environments but are of value in water. Less hair means less water resistance and faster swimming speed, and the layer of fat offers protection from the cold.) The curiously low placement of the larynx, a potential disadvantage on land because it can impede breathing and swallowing, allows man both to close down his airway and to hold his breath and swallow food while submerged. These features, argues Morgan, are rare among land mammals—virtually unique to primates—but are found routinely among such aquatic mammals as seals, sea lions, and dolphins. Their origin, she thinks, can best be explained by an aquatic phase in human evolution that was realized in the emergence of an aquatic ape.

Hydrodynamic Accommodation

Given a few million years of submarine civilization, evolution might produce a new race of *Homo aquaticus.* Such a man might have the inborn ability to extract oxygen from seawater and to shed carbon dioxide and nitrogen from his body. According to Belgian physician and researcher Mark Verhaegen, a proponent of the aquatic-ape theory, man's neurophysiology might be transformed to function better in a liquid atmosphere: it would change to make such an aquatic species more at ease in the water. His

© Robert Holland/The WaterHouse

Submarine sightseeing. Research aquabubbles allow scientists a panoramic view of the undersea environment.

vision would be diminished, but his hearing would be more acute. Most startling is Verhaegen's image of how the human form might change shape to accommodate the hydrodynamics needed to move swiftly and gracefully through the water. Legs would be reduced and slightly atrophied, but the feet would be broader; and the body would be practically hairless but equipped with more subcutaneous fat. "In other words," he concludes, "more like a seal or a dolphin."

Although Rougerie is sanguine about the idea that we had an aquatic forebear in our evolutionary past or that there may be a newly evolved aquatic human in our future, he does not discount the possibilities. How profoundly man transforms himself into a creature of the seas is a matter future generations will have to decide. As a Jules Verne quotation hanging on Rougerie's wall declares: ANYTHING THAT ONE MAN CAN IMAGINE, ANOTHER MAN CAN REALIZE.

What Happened to the GIANT MAMMALS?

by Anthony J. Stuart

Some 30,000 years ago, both North and South America were home to many spectacularly large mammals such as giant ground sloths, mastodons, and saber-tooth cats. Woolly rhinoceroses, mammoths, and giant deer roamed Eurasia from Britain to eastern Siberia. Down under, fossilized remains of skeletons tell a similar story. The ancient Australian fauna boasted several giant species of kangaroo and a wombatlike marsupial as big as a rhinoceros.

By about 10,000 years ago, however, these and many other marvelous animals had disappeared from most of the globe forever. Left behind were impoverished faunas essentially as we see them today, made up of small- and medium-sized animals with relatively few large forms. Only in Africa did the majority of large mammals known from the late Pleistocene—elephant, black rhinoceros, white rhinoceros, giraffe, cape buffalo, and hippopotamus, among others—manage to survive to the present day. Elephants and rhino also survived in southern Asia.

The extinctions of the late Pleistocene are unique in the geological record in that they affected, with relatively few exceptions, only large terrestrial mammals that weighed more than 88 pounds (40 kilograms). Most smaller terrestrial animals, and marine creatures both large and small, escaped unscathed. Earlier ''mass extinctions'' invariably affected a wide range of both terrestrial and marine organisms. For example, the extinction at the end of the Cretaceous period and the beginning of the Tertiary around 66 million years ago was marked by the disappearance of the dinosaurs on land, the pterosaurs in the air, and icthyosaurs, plesiosaurs, ammonites, and other organisms in the sea.

A Huge Cast of Prehistoric Victims

The disappearance of many large mammals in North America has attracted the most scientific attention. The rich fauna of large mammals in the late Pleistocene included American mastodon, mammoth, four genera of ground sloth, *Glypotherium* (a giant relative of the armadillo), the saber-tooth cat *Smilodon,* and a camel *Camelops*. All subsequently disappeared, together with the lion, now surviving in Africa and southern Asia, and others such as llama, capybara, and tapir, which are still found in South America. Remarkably, horses died out in the New World, where they had originally evolved, and were unknown to the American Indians until the Spanish conquistadors reintroduced them in the 16th century. Both radiocarbon

Prehistoric mammals—all now extinct—include (above, from left) the long-necked camel, two-horned rhinoceros, three-toed horse, giant pig, and the curious clawed Moropus. *Below are the gigantic ground sloth* Megatherium *and two types of armadillolike glyptodonts—the spike-tailed* Doedicurus *and* Glyptodon.

PAST, PRESENT, AND FUTURE **273**

dates and the fossil bones in stratified sequences of sediments show that at least the common species survived until about 10,500 years ago. Many large mammals—such as bison, moose, wapiti (American elk), and caribou (reindeer)—have survived to the present day, but the largest and most spectacular beasts of the North American Pleistocene have gone forever.

Many of the animals that became extinct in North America were lost from South America as well. Mammoths, however, failed to penetrate that far south, and conversely the southern continent in the late Pleistocene still boasted two groups of indigenous ungulates: the bizarre litopterns (represented by *Macrauchenia*, which looked like an elongated, gangling tapir), and the notoungulates ("southern ungulates"), such as the ponderous *Toxodon*. Also present were the giant ground sloth *Megatherium*, as big as an elephant, and the armored, armadillolike *Glyptodon*.

Again, many of the extinct large mammals are known to have lasted until at least about 12,500 to 13,500 years ago, but had entirely gone by 10,000 years ago.

The extinct Australian fauna is especially fascinating, as only one large form, the red kangaroo, occurs on that continent today. Unfortunately, few of the fossil finds are from stratified deposits or have been dated by radiocarbon. Nevertheless, it is clear that the fauna formerly included such exotic beasts as the giant, wombatlike *Diprotodon*; giant kangaroos, including the aptly named *Macropus titan*; *Macropus ferragus*, which stood more than 8.2 feet (2.5 meters) tall; and the short-faced browsers—*Sthenurus* and the gigantic *Procoptodon*, which reached 8.5 feet (2.6 meters) or more. The curious "marsupial lion" *Thylacoleo* probably preyed on kangaroos and wallabies. The few radiocarbon dates obtained so far suggest that most of these animals lasted until perhaps 12,000 years ago, but had succumbed within the next 2,000 years.

Europe was less affected than the three continents so far discussed. But here, too, the extinctions of the late Pleistocene were a remarkable and unprecedented phenomenon. Although there is an enormous amount of work still to do, our knowledge of the European Pleistocene, including its mammals, is better than for any other part of the world. What emerges definitively from the European fossil record is that extinctions were staggered over a long period and mostly occurred earlier than in the Americas. For example, the extinct rhinoceros *Dicerorinus hemitoechus,* known from Last Interglacial deposits to have lived as far north as England some 120,000 years ago, lingered on in Mediterranean Europe well into the succeeding cold period, but appears to have become extinct before 20,000 years ago.

Mammoths, woolly rhino, and spotted hyenas—surviving in Africa—flourished on the open grassy steppe tundra of the last cold period, but had disappeared by about 12,000 years ago. Rather suspect radiocarbon dates suggest that the mammoth may have survived in Russia and Siberia.

The giant deer or so-called "Irish elk" *Megaloceros,* with an antler span of over 9.8 feet (3 meters) in the largest stags, outlived the other extinct species, at least in Western Europe. Its skeletal remains are common in deposits dating from about 10,500 to 12,500 years ago, from which other extinct animals are unknown.

Large mammals that did survive the late Pleistocene extinctions in Europe include the elk or moose, red deer, reindeer, brown bear, and wolf. The aurochs *Bos primigenius,* an inhabitant of Britain during the Last Interglacial, survived 100,000 years of predominant cold farther south in Europe and then returned northward as the climate improved. Although it lived on in the form of domesticated cattle, as a wild species it was exterminated by people in historic times.

The animals of Africa south of the Sahara were, by contrast, hardly touched by the great catastrophe that devastated most of the other continents. The long-horned buffalo *Pelarovis* and the giant hartebeest *Megalotragus* were the only genera to disappear from southern Africa between about 12,000 and 9,500 years ago, and even these may have survived much later elsewhere in the continent.

Extinctions Occurred Rapidly

Another striking feature of the extinctions of the late Pleistocene is that they occurred during what is, geologically speaking, a short span of time. Within broadly 100,000 years, mostly within a few thousand years or perhaps much less, North America lost approximately 33 out of 45 genera (that is, 73 percent) of its large mammals, South America 46 out of 58 (80 percent), Australia 15 out of 16 (94 percent) and Europe 7 out of 23 (30 percent). Africa south of the Sahara escaped much more lightly with per-

Tiny four-toed horses are startled by the appearance of the menacing-looking but harmless six-horned Uitatherium.

haps 2 out of 44 genera (5 percent) becoming extinct. These figures include genera that are totally extinct plus a smaller number that became extinct within a particular area but survived elsewhere.

The fossil record of the Pleistocene shows that these were enormously accelerated rates of extinction. In North America, for example, during most of the Pleistocene (lasting approximately 2 million years), only about one genus, on average, became extinct every 200,000 years. In the late Pleistocene the extinction rate had accelerated to, at the most conservative estimate, one genus per 3,000 years and possibly as high as one per 100 years.

The realization that giant animals inhabited the Earth in the geologically recent past has excited the imagination of successive generations of paleontologists and biologists. Charles Darwin, in the course of his voyage on the ship *Beagle*, excavated the fossil skeletons of a giant ground sloth, the bearlike herbivore *Toxodon*, and other animals at Bahía Blanca in Argentina, and speculated on their demise. In 1876 Alfred Russel Wallace observed that "We live in a zoologically impoverished world, from which all the hugest and fiercest and strangest forms have all disappeared." He added: "It is surely a marvelous fact and one that has hardly been sufficiently dwelt upon, this dying out of so many large Mammalia, not in one place only, but over half the land surface of the globe."

The loss in the late Pleistocene of "so many large Mammalia" is undoubtedly one of the most intriguing mysteries in the history of life on Earth. Researchers are now actively searching for the likely cause or causes of the phenomenon. The debate rages between those who believe that the animals became extinct because they could not cope with the stress caused by climatic changes, and those, notably Paul Martin of the University of Arizona at Tuc-

Arctic adaptation. Woolly mammoths apparently used their turned-in tusks to shovel snow off the plants they fed on.

son, who believe that they were exterminated by human hungers—the hypothesis known as "prehistoric overkill." In either case the large, slow-breeding species are generally supposed to have been the most vulnerable. Epidemic disease has occasionally been suggested as a possible cause, but disease would not wipe out an entire species, nor would it be likely to affect such a wide range of animals over most of the globe.

Is Climate to Blame?

Those researchers who favor a climatic cause for extinctions point to the rapid and profound changes in climate and vegetation that occurred over much of the Earth's surface in the late Pleistocene. About 13,000 years ago the vast open steppe tundras of North America and northern Eurasia began to give way to conifer and broadleaf forests in response to the onset of warmer and wetter conditions. Paradoxically, in Arctic regions a biologically productive vegetation—rich in herbaceous plants that supported herds of mammoths, horses, reindeer, bison, and other animals—was replaced by the relatively barren, often waterlogged tundras of the present day, which support a much more sparse fauna. Elsewhere—in the southwestern U.S.,

for example—the warming at the end of the Pleistocene resulted in the spread of subdesert environments, which also could not support a diverse fauna of large mammals.

Russell Graham of the Illinois State Museum and others consider that during the late Pleistocene, climates in the American Midwest were more equable—that is, with milder winters and cooler summers—than they are today. Extinctions, in this view, were caused by a change to seasonally more extreme climates at the end of the Pleistocene. Dale Guthrie at the University of Alaska, Fairbanks, proposes that before the warming in the late Pleistocene, the world's vegetation was not strongly zoned according to climate as it is today. Instead, he envisages vegetational types distributed in a mosaic pattern, supporting a more diverse collection of mammals. The segregation of plants into marked geographical zones, which is supposed to have occurred rapidly around 11,000 years ago, coupled with the spread of plants with well-developed chemical defenses against being eaten, then led to extinctions on a large scale.

The arguments against the climatic hypothesis are twofold. First, although climatic and accompanying vegetational changes undoubtedly caused major shifts in the geographical distributions of animals as former ranges were denied to them, the same climatic changes should have created equally suitable habitats elsewhere. Many species, large and small, did respond in this way. For example, during much of the last cold period of the Pleistocene, between about 50,000 and 10,000 years ago, reindeer and arctic foxes lived in the south of France. But they retreated to the Arctic when the climate became warmer. In the same way, other Western European members of the cold steppe-tundra fauna, such as saiga antelope and ground squirrels, moved eastward to the grassy steppes of central Asia. Why didn't the mammoths, woolly rhino, and other extinct species similarly respond to climatic change by simply migrating to other suitable areas?

The second difficulty with the climatic hypothesis is that it supposes that there was something very special about the climatic changes that happened at the end of the Pleistocene. Previous changes in climate during the Pleistocene were not accompanied by such episodes of mass extinction. This assertion of uniqueness, moreover, appears to be contradicted by the evidence of past vegetational changes on land, which comes from fossil pollen, preserved in the sediments of lakes and rivers, as well as from cores of deep-sea deposits, which record the waxing and waning of ice sheets. These show that marked fluctuations in climate have been a recurring feature of the past three-quarters of a million years. For much of this long period, it was generally much colder over most of the globe than now. But the prevailing cold was punctuated by relatively short warm phases of some 10,000 to 15,000 years, known as interglacials. The warm period in which we are now living, which began between about 10,000 to 13,000 years ago, appears to be just the latest of these interglacial phases.

David Horton of the Australian Institute of Aboriginal Studies suggests that the Australian extinctions relate to an exceptionally dry climate that occurred approximately 15,000 to 25,000 years ago. As the arid core of the continent expanded, diminishing water supplies on the margins could no longer support the giant marsupials. Although plausible, this hypothesis supposes that no drastic climatic change had occurred previously in the Australian Pleistocene.

The giant Irish elk survived longer than other prehistoric mammals, becoming extinct about 10,000 years ago.

Extinct flesh-eating mammals include the Hyaenodon *(front), which preyed on the plant-eating* Brontotherium *(rear).*

The Overkill Theory

Having found the climatic explanations unconvincing, we now turn hopefully to the more dramatic alternative of prehistoric overkill by human hunters. But here, too, we run into formidable difficulties.

Paul Martin argues that mass extinctions in the New World and Australia coincided closely with the arrival of the first humans in each area. He believes that in the New World from about 11,000 years ago, hunters had a devastating impact on the faunas of the world because the animals had not evolved defensive behavior that would have made them less vulnerable. According to Martin, the same phenomenon occurred much earlier in Australia soon after people arrived about 40,000 years ago. Conversely, the survival of nearly all the African large mammals, and most of the European, can be attributed to long familiarity with humans in these areas. In both Africa and Europe, the modern form of *Homo sapiens* with Upper Paleolithic stone and bone artifacts appeared about 35,000 to 40,000 years ago, while the record of earlier forms of *Homo* goes back much further.

The archaeological evidence, and what we know of such hunters as the North American Indians and the Australian aborigines, suggests that Upper Paleolithic peoples would have lived in small, scattered communities, subsisting by gathering food and hunting. They probably killed the animals with spears or other weapons, sometimes driving them into traps, natural or artificial. It is difficult to imagine how a few hunters, with what is to us a primitive level of technology, could have exterminated numerous species of large mammals. The density of human populations began to increase 10,000 years ago with the advent of farming and the civilization that it made possible. Only within the past few centuries have large-scale destruction of habitat and the use of firearms caused or threatened the extinction of many species.

Another problem with the theory of prehistoric overkill is that modern hunters concentrate on the smaller, less dangerous, and most abundant animals. In the archaeological record, too, remains of horses, reindeer, and other smaller animals predominate in Upper Paleolithic sites in Europe. The formidable mammoth and woolly rhino—both of which later became extinct—are scarce from several sites in eastern Europe. These sites are widely quoted as examples of an economy based on mammoth hunting, but there is no definite evidence that people killed these animals.

Yet on oceanic islands that people colonized in recent times, human activity has caused major extinctions. In New Zealand, humans first arrived about A.D. 1000. They had exterminated the several species of indigenous giant flightless birds—the maos—sometime after A.D. 1600. On Madagascar, several giant lemurs, the "elephant bird" *Aepyornis*, and other species had probably nearly all gone by about A.D. 1000, although here there is some evidence for much later survival of a few large species. Humans probably settled on this island in A.D. 500. In both areas, extensive destruction of habitats, combined with hunting in a restricted geographical area, apparently caused the extinctions.

The Blitzkrieg Hypothesis

An early criticism of the overkill hypothesis was that human artifacts are rarely found among the remains of extinct animals in the New World. Usually there is little evidence that the extinct animals were ever hunted. Even more remarkable, in Australia the bones of extinct marsupials have so far never been found in the same layers of sediment that have yielded artifacts. In response to this anomaly, Martin advanced his "blitzkrieg" hypothesis. He proposes that the impact of human hunters on the previously unmolested faunas in both the New World and Australia was so swift and devastating as to leave little evidence behind.

The blitzkrieg hypothesis, however, is apparently flatly contradicted by the Australian evidence, which indicates that there was a period of about 30,000 years when the humans and giant marsupials coexisted. Here Martin questions the validity of the radiocarbon dates on the bones of the extinct animals. His explanation for extinct animals and artifacts not being found together is simply that people and extinct animals coexisted for only a brief period after humans first came to the continent. Moreover, a major, but staggered, wave of extinction occurred in Europe, where conditions for blitzkrieg were absent.

What's the Answer?

In attempting to distinguish between the rival hypotheses or climatic environmental change versus overkill, we need to look carefully at the geological record of the late Pleistocene. If climate was the cause, then extinctions should correspond closely in time with climatic change. If, on the other hand, extinctions were caused by prehistoric people, either by their first appearance in an area or as a result of a major innovation in hunting technology, then perhaps we cannot reliably predict how this would register in the fossil record. The more recent extinctions in Madagascar and New Zealand, however, occurred many hundreds of years after colonization by humans. In my view, there remains much room for controversy because we lack reliably dated and stratified fossil material. Only more work in all parts of the world will provide the firm body of data that will allow us to choose between conflicting hypotheses.

Yet, despite insufficient information and the many problems that beset the overkill hypothesis, the circumstantial evidence that humans were somehow responsible for the mass

Painting by Charles R. Knight, © National Geographic Society

Mass extinctions of giant mammals may have coincided with the abrupt appearance of prehistoric hunters.

extinctions of the late Pleistocene is compelling. It is the appearance or immigration of anatomically modern *Homo sapiens,* with Upper Palaeolithic technology, that is the one obviously new phenomenon in the late Pleistocene throughout the world. In many areas, certainly in Europe and North America, populations of animals may have already been under stress due to climatic changes, and therefore especially vulnerable to pressure from hunting.

Are we, then, as a species already burdened with the "original sin" of having exterminated many large and wonderful animals in remote prehistory? This disturbing possibility at least serves to emphasize our moral responsibility to conserve what we have left today. Whatever the answer may prove to be, it is difficult to disagree with W. S. Gilbert, who commented, albeit in a different context, that "Man is Nature's sole mistake."

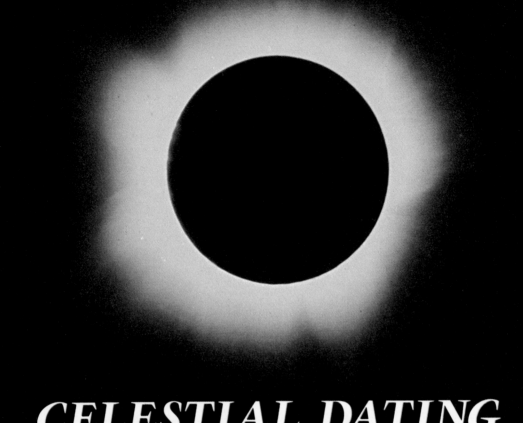

Wards Science/Photo Researchers

CELESTIAL DATING

by F. Richard Stephenson

Xerxes, emperor of Persia, was murdered on or about August 6, 465 B.C. On October 1, 331 B.C., Alexander the Great and his Macedonians crushed the Persian armies under Darius III in the battle of Gaugamela, in today's Iraq. Saladin, leader of the Moslem armies, took the city of Ascalon (Ashqelon, in what is now Israel) from the Crusaders after a fierce battle on September 4, 1187. And on October 2, he took Jerusalem.

How do historians know these dates, sometimes to the hour? Or are such statements about major events merely inspired guesses about the remote past?

From the earliest times, saga singers and, later, the first historians were interested in fixing the dates of events; the problem was how to do it. The ancient Greeks often marked dates by stating who the archon, or chief magistrate, was in a given year. Thus the record shows that the Peloponnesian Wars between the Greek city-states of Athens and Sparta began in 431 B.C.

when Pythodorus was archon of Athens, and that a Carthaginian attack on Sicily was mounted "in the year when Hieromemnon was archon of Athens."

Since archons were elected annually and since the Greeks knew each archon from the seventh century B.C. on, they were quickly able to calculate the year a historical event occurred. We can do so as well—not from the seventh century, but from about 500 B.C. on, thanks to a list covering 200 years, from 500 to 300 B.C., compiled by the Greek historian Diodorus of Sicily. Also preserved into modern times were similar lists, such as one of Roman consuls, that date events after 300 B.C.

The time of such celestial events as eclipses (above) and comets can be accurately predicted for the future and precisely pinpointed in the past. Ancient writers who associated celestial events with historical occurrences inadvertently provided modern historians with a foolproof method of assigning dates to many significant occasions.

Tracking Events with Calendars

However, the dates of archons before about 500 B.C. are uncertain, and even the post-500 dates may yield the year when an event occurred but may not allow us to fix the exact day of its occurrence. Eventually, various peoples—Egyptians, Babylonians, Chinese, Greeks, Hebrews, Hindus, Romans—developed calendars to suit their needs. Their aims were both religious and practical: to keep track of various ceremonies and as an aid to agriculture. To be useful, a calendar had to keep pace with the seasons and match the solar year of about 365¼ days.

Most civilizations divided the year into 12 months, but there are actually about 12⅓ lunar months in a solar year. Therefore, the calendar makers either divided the year into 12 artificial months, which did not keep track of the moon (as is the case with our modern calendar), or they used 12 lunar months and every three years or so added an extra month so the year always began during the same season.

Civilizations with a strong astronomical tradition—for instance, the Babylonians and the Chinese—preferred to keep track of the moon, whereas more practical peoples—such as the Egyptians and Romans—employed artificial months, that is, months that had nothing to do with the moon. In more recent times there have been a whole string of calendars—the Julian, the Moslem, the Mayan, and the Gregorian, to mention a few. None of these follows the solar

year exactly, although the Gregorian calendar closely approximates it. The Moslem calendar is unique in world history, for it is exclusively lunar. A year consists of 12 months of 29 or 30 days, so that the beginning of the year continually moves through the seasons, coming back to its starting point every 33 years.

The problem faced by modern historians is how to deal with the inaccuracies of those ancient calendars. Apart from the major difficulty of trying to fix the year when an event occurred, it is often hard to determine the time of year. This is especially true for the old Roman calendar, which, before the time of Julius Caesar, arbitrarily changed the length of the month. In 190 B.C. the start of the year was 117 days in error, but by 168 the discrepancy had fallen to 72 days, rising again to 90 days in

Many ancient people developed strong astonomical traditions. The disc of Phaestos (right) from the Minoan civilization of ancient Crete may be an early form of calendar. Below, a Babylonian tablet records the intervals between new moons of a 25-month period from 103 to 101 B.C.

Right: Art Resource; Below, British Museum

On his fourth voyage to the New World, Columbus, knowing a lunar eclipse was about to occur, coerced food from the natives by threatening to make the Moon disappear forever. Once the eclipse began, the Indians agreed to supply food. Modern astronomers have now pinpointed the eclipse to February 29, 1504, shortly after 6 p.m.

46 B.C. Hence it is not surprising that a modern historian often finds it impossible to determine exactly what day in our modern calendar an ancient event took place.

Computerizing Celestial Events

Until recently, in such cases the historian was at a loss. But the ability of today's historian to fix with exactitude the occurrence of such major celestial events as eclipses and to tie these to ancient accounts has opened up enormous possibilities in historical dating. For example, several ancient Greek poets, such as Archilochus (in the seventh century B.C.) and Pindar (fifth century B.C.), mention eclipses in their writings, frequently using vivid imagery. When they tie these accounts to major events, the references provide us with a means of dating.

Astronomical dating is by no means a new idea, however, and it was particularly in vogue during the 19th century. But historians then were able to make only rough calculations as to when eclipses and the like occurred. Today computer programs make the remarkably complex calculations needed to compute the rapid and irregular motion of the moon in its monthly orbit around the earth, and historians can produce reasonably accurate pictures of what ancient skies were like.

This process requires approximately 1,000 numerical terms for each eclipse. Moreover, even the earth's daily rotation cannot be relied on as a timekeeper. Studies of some accurately dated ancient and medieval eclipse records, principally those in which the observers made careful estimates of the time of day or night, reveal that the length of the day is gradually increasing. Although the rate of increase—about one-fiftieth of a second every 1,000 years—may seem trifling, in the million or so days that have elapsed since the earliest reliable astronomical records (700 B.C.), the earth has lost several hours compared with an ideal clock that would keep perfect time, neither gaining nor losing. The above-mentioned loss is produced largely by the tides and must be carefully allowed for if there is more than one eclipse, to ensure that the correct one is identified.

The Importance of Eclipses

Eclipses of the sun and moon have the greatest value in ancient chronology since by medieval times, dating was often fairly securely established. Nevertheless, there are several notable exceptions. A total eclipse was seen in the 12th century by Saladin on one of his campaigns against the Crusaders. Imad-ed-din, Saladin's chief secretary, reported that the eclipse took place when Saladin's army was crossing the Orontes River (in Syria). He wrote, "The Earth was in darkness and the stars shone clear in the midday sky." Imad-ed-din gives the correct lunar month (Ramadan), but the year of the Hegira (the flight of Muhammad from Mecca to Medina in 622) is in error. This corresponds to A.D. 1175, but we can show that the eclipse took place on April 11 the following year.

Like many other eclipses in medieval times, this one was noted elsewhere. The Christian chronicler Michael the Syrian independently observed the same event in Antioch, giving the exact date. He wrote: "The Sun was totally obscured: night fell and the stars appeared . . . . this was a sad and terrifying sight which caused many people to lament with weeping; the sheep, oxen, and horses crowded together in terror. The darkness lasted for two hours; afterwards the light returned." Two hours may be an overestimate for the duration of a total eclipse, but not infrequently, observers were so shocked by the sudden darkness that they lost all sense of time.

Eleven years later, on the day that the Crusaders surrendered the city of Ascalon to Saladin, there was another large eclipse that fixes the date of this event precisely. Saladin had already captured in rapid succession several other important Christian strongholds. The computed date of the eclipse is Friday, September 4, 1187. Although the obscuration of the sun was only partial, 91 percent of the sun would have been covered at 2:20 P.M. The eclipse would have been significant enough to be regarded as an omen of disaster. Worse was to follow, for within a month, on October 2, Jerusalem itself was also taken by the Moslems.

Even if an eclipse was not associated with an important ancient event, it could still provide a useful check on the chronology of the period. Such is the case for the Peloponnesian Wars, which lasted 27 years. The contemporary historian Thucydides, in his history of the wars, noted three eclipses: two of the sun and one of the moon. In each case he gave only the year of the wars and the season. The dates are: first year, summer (a very large partial solar obscuration in which stars became visible); eighth year, early summer (a partial eclipse of the sun); and 19th year, summer (a lunar eclipse). The calculated dates of these eclipses are August 3, 431 B.C.; March 21, 424; and August 27, 413. These dates confirm that the general chronology of this early period is very reliable. In particular, the eclipse of 431 B.C. reached a magnitude of 87 percent at Athens, which would have made Venus visible by day.

Dating the Death of Xerxes

The Persian emperor Xerxes, who reigned between 486 and 465 B.C., is perhaps best known for his unsuccessful invasion of Greece in 480.

In a famous Crusades battle, Richard the Lion-Hearted fights for possession of Jerusalem against the Moslem leader Saladin. A solar eclipse, now dated to September 4, 1187, had presaged Saladin's initial victory over the Christians.

The Granger Collection

Giraudon/Art Resource

Comets also held supernatural significance in earlier times. Above, the Bayeux tapestry depicts Comet Halley's passage just prior to the Norman conquest of England in 1066. At right, the Italian painter Giotto incorporated a comet into his famous nativity scene.

Scala/Art Resource

His campaign there was marked by the battles of Thermopylae and Salamis—familiar names to students of ancient history. When his mile-long bridge of boats across the Hellespont (Dardanelles) was twice washed away by a storm, he is said to have had the sea scourged with 300 lashes by his soldiers. Fifteen years later, Xerxes was murdered—either by his son or by members of his court in the Persian capital of Persepolis. How do we know these dates are accurate when we're not even sure of the year of Xerxes' birth (about 519 B.C.)? His death is accurately fixed by one of the Babylonian astronomical texts in the British Museum. A year or so ago, these clay tablets attracted much attention when they were found to contain early references to Halley's comet.

One of these broken tablets, measuring only about four square inches, gives a list of lunar eclipses at 18-year intervals—a lunar period well known to the Babylonians. This was compiled by Babylonian astronomers from observations made between 609 and 465 B.C. Near the end of this list, between two eclipse reports in the same year, we find the following statement: "Lunar month V, day 14 [?], Xerxes was murdered by his son." The sign for the day of the month is unfortunately damaged and could be anything from 14 to 18; the year is not

given at all. Nevertheless, using the lunar eclipse observations, we can establish a narrow range of dates with considerable confidence. Although the year is not provided, it can be readily deduced from the 18-year Babylonian sequence of lunar eclipses at 465 B.C.

However, even if the year had been known only approximately, it could still have been dated by the two eclipses that were reported at about the same time. The first of these occurred when the moon was in the constellation of Sagittarius, and the second on the 14th day of the eighth lunar month. For many years both before and after 465 B.C., we find no such combination of eclipses; it can be found only in 465 itself. The calculated dates of the two eclipses are thus June 5 and November 30 in that year. These dates enable us to determine that the fifth lunar month began on July 22 in 465. Hence we can conclude that Xerxes was murdered sometime between August 4 and 8 in 465 B.C.

The Persian dynasty came to an end with the death of Darius III, following his defeat by Alexander the Great at Gaugamela in 331. It is recorded that Darius fled from the field of the battle—his second ignominious escape from a conflict with Alexander. Greek historians such as Arrian and Plutarch record an eclipse of the moon occurring 11 nights before the battle. This was described as total or very nearly so. The year is definitely known (by the archonship of Aristophanes in Athens), and corresponds to 331 B.C. In any case, the only large eclipse of the moon visible in western Asia at about that time took place on September 20, 331. This fixes the date of the battle, an important event in the history of Alexander's conquests, as October 1.

Eclipse at Sea

One of the most intriguing of ancient eclipse observations was made at sea in the fourth century B.C. by Agathocles, who had set himself up as tyrant of Syracuse some years before. The most detailed record is provided by Diodorus, who gives the year as the archonship of Hieromemnon in Athens (310 B.C.). Just before the time of the eclipse, Agathocles and his fleet of 60 ships were blockaded in Syracuse harbor by the Carthaginians. They managed to escape in the confusion when some grain ships arrived. Diodorus continued: ''They gained unhoped for safety as night closed in. On the next day there was such an eclipse of the Sun that utter darkness set in and the stars were seen everywhere. Thus Agathocles' men, believing that the prodigy portended misfortune for them, fell into even greater anxiety about the future.''

Five days later, Agathocles landed near Carthage, where he proceeded to attack his enemies' homeland with considerable success. The date of the eclipse—August 15 in 310 B.C.—is absolutely certain, and it can be further computed that it occurred at about 8:00 A.M.

It has long been a puzzle whether Agatho-cles sailed to the north or the south of Sicily after escaping from Syracuse. Thanks, however, to contemporary computer technique, we now know that the track of a total eclipse passed to the north of Syracuse, so it seems likely that Agathocles sailed through the Strait of Messina and around the northern coast of Sicily before heading toward Africa.

A final example is a lunar eclipse that preceded the death of King Herod the Great, who was king of Judea when Christ was born. The most detailed historical source for this period is the Jewish history written by Josephus toward the end of the first century A.D. He wrote: ''As for the other Matthias who had stirred up the sedition, he [Herod] had him burnt alive along with some of his companions. And on that same night there was an eclipse of the Moon. But Herod's illness became more and more severe. . . .'' The actual date of Herod's death is uncertain. On historical grounds, it may be fixed in the very last years before the Christian era. The lunar eclipse that best fits the historical circumstances is that of March 13 in 4 B.C.

The Gregorian Calendar

Fortunately for historians living in the year 3000, much less effort will be required to decode the precise day when events in our era have occurred. Lunar calendars are still in use for religious purposes (for example, to determine the date of Easter), but for civil needs, the use of a solar calendar, independent of the moon, has become almost worldwide. This is the Gregorian calendar, introduced by Pope Gregory XIII in the late 16th century. Under the guidance of the Jesuit astronomer Christopher Clavius, the new scheme was designed to replace the less accurate Julian calendar and was first adopted in October 1582.

The Gregorian calendar is a very good approximation of the solar year of 365.2422 days. Every year that is divisible by 4 is a leap year—apart from those century years that are not divisible by 400. Thus, A.D. 1700, 1800, and 1900 were not leap years, but 2000 will be. It is easy to see that in a 400-year period, there are 146,097 days ($400 \times 365 + 97$), making the average length of the year 365.2425 days. Hence, compared with a truly solar calendar, over about 3,000 years the Gregorian calendar is in error by only about one day. Very small further refinements to our modern calendar have been proposed, but are not likely to be put into effect during our lifetime.

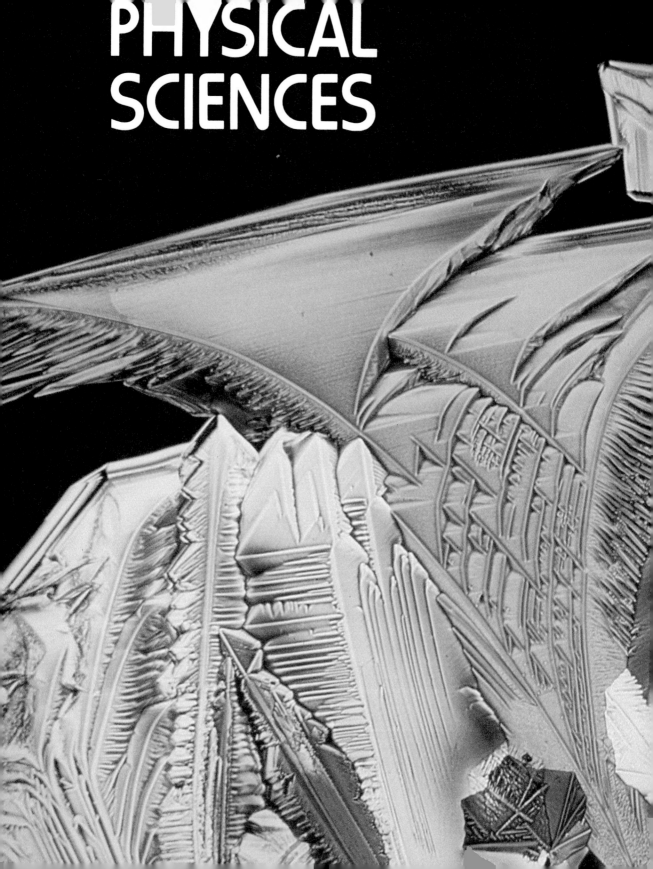

PHYSICAL
SCIENCES

For closer study of atomic nuclei, physicists use particle accelerators to raise elementary particles to velocities, or energy levels, high enough to penetrate and break apart the nuclei.

Photo Cern

REVIEW
OF THE
YEAR

PHYSICAL SCIENCES

PHYSICS

Analysis of data derived from a 1980 experiment performed at the European Center for Nuclear Research (CERN) laboratory in Geneva, Switzerland, disclosed evidence for the existence of three new subatomic particles, dubbed U^+, U^0, and U^-. The particles, with masses of about 3.1 BeV (billion electron volts)—about three times that of a proton—decay into a combination of a lambda hyperon, an antiproton, and pions.

Reanalysis of experiments performed in Hungary in the early 20th century to test the law of gravity by measuring the attraction between the earth and various materials yielded evidence for the presence of a fifth fundamental physical force. (The other four forces are gravity, electromagnetism, and the strong and weak subatomic forces.) The fifth force—considered a kind of negative gravity—is a repulsive force carried by hyperphotons, according to Dr. Ephraim Fischbach. Dr. Fischbach also found evidence linking the fifth force to electromagnetism and the weak force. If true, an important step in the theoretical unification of all physical forces—the so-called Grand Unification Theory (GUT)—may have been made. Later in the year, critics of the fifth force proposal suggested that convection currents could have exerted forces on the weights suspended from

the balance used by the Hungarian researcher during his original work. This, rather than hyperphotons, they claimed, could have been the source of the observations noted by Dr. Fischbach.

Physicists at the Fermi National Accelerator Laboratory in Batavia, Illinois, succeeded in slamming together a proton and antiproton of energies nearly three times larger than any other laboratory has reached. The collision of the 800-BeV proton with an equally energetic antiproton in the Fermi tevatron was an important test run of the equipment, which will be used to study rare particles, such as W and Z particles, that appear only once in màny thousands of such collisions.

Fusion research got a boost when scientists at AT&T Bell Laboratories in New Jersey developed a lanthanum-barium–copper oxide alloy that might become superconducting (lose all resistance to electric current) at 50° above absolute zero with further refinement, and in the future, at as high as 77° above absolute zero. This easing of the temperature requirement for achieving superconductivity (which normally requires much lower, more difficult to reach temperatures) could have enormous implications for the generation, storage, and transmission of electricity, and the generation of fusion energy. It could also lead to substantial cost reductions in the construction of a proposed superconducting atom smasher with a 60-mile (96-kilometer) acceleration ring.

New data suggest that neutrinos are slightly magnetic. If true, this would be a revolutionary discovery that would force a reevaluation of many theories of particle physics. The theory, which is not endorsed by all physicists, is based on the observation that, like low-energy cosmic rays, neutrinos seem to be deflected by magnetic fields, such as those emitted from the sun during peak solar activity. The data, obtained by Raymond Davis of the University of Pennsylvania, also suggest that neutrinos might decay into another particle, the majoron.

CHEMISTRY

In 1986 chemists succeeded in devising new methods for both combining and separating atoms and molecules. These methods hold promise for new purification and manufacturing technologies.

Researchers produced a new form of composite material consisting of alkali-salt-crystal "storage boxes" that entrap "guest molecules" within their matrices. The process, patented by Josef Michl of the University of Texas at Austin, permits chemists to study, under controlled conditions, such molecules as naphthalene trapped within cesium iodide crystals. The new process is important because older techniques required the use of frozen gases to trap molecules for study, and thus restricted chemists from running high-temperature experiments, which would have vaporized the gases. Michl plans to devise a way to isolate guest molecules from each other within crystals in order to be able to study their photochemical properties.

In another development that promises to improve chemical technology, chemists discovered that certain organic compounds that are bound to isotopes of the same atom differ in their affinity for electrons. An isotope-enrichment technique that exploits this difference was developed by Gerald R. Stevenson and his co-workers at Illinois State University in Normal. The technique can be used for enriching radioactive material, and some medical products manufacturers are also looking into the practical uses of the technique.

In another unexpected discovery, Soviet scientists announced that a compressed mixture of tetrazole and sodium tetrazolate burns with a liquid flame. Researchers at the Byelorussian State University in Minsk reported that when cylinders of the mixture are ignited with a red-hot wire, an initial molten layer forms on the surface and gives off gaseous combustion products. A glowing, liquid ball forms, and enlarges as it skims across the surface. After cooling, the ball hardens into a light-gray, porous bead containing sodium carbonate and complex nitrogen-carbon compounds. The scientists suggested that, since substances remain in the combustion zone for a long time, relatively slow chemical processes, such as polymerization, might take place in a liquid-flame reactor.

Chemists in the United States used magnetic fields to align molecules of polymers quickly and efficiently. Samuel I. Stupp of the University of

Illinois at Urbana-Champaign and his colleagues added paramagnetic organometallic compounds, such as copper complexes, to liquid crystal polymers, such as aromatic polyester. The organometallic compounds insert themselves into the loosely organized polymer chain or attach to the chain's backbone. When the mixture is placed in a magnetic field, the paramagnetic additives interact with the field, pulling the polymer molecules into line. Upon solidification, the pattern is locked into place. The technique, which can increase a material's electrical conductivity in one direction and alter its mechanical properties, might become a useful, efficient means for strengthening thin plastic films used as coatings.

Magnetism associated with chemical reactions that cause corrosion was detected for the first time. A superconducting quantum interference device (SQUID) magnetometer detected magnetic fields generated by the electrochemical reactions that occur during erosion of metal. The magnetic field repeatedly changed directions during corrosion. Such small magnetic field fluctuations might indicate changes in the process of corrosion. In the future, this measurement technique might be useful in the remote detection of corrosion on hidden structures, such as oil rigs and artificial implants in humans.

Modified quartz crystals were used to detect minute quantities of the pesticide parathion in the air, and may be used in the future to detect airborne cocaine, morphine, and heroin. George G. Guilbault of the University of New Orleans coated the surface of quartz crystals with antibodies to parathion, and then set the crystals vibrating with an electric current. As molecules of the pesticide latched onto the antibodies, the crystals grew heavier, altering the frequency of the vibrations. This is the first time such work has been done with substances in the gas phase.

Different teams of researchers each developed a way to modify hemoglobin, the oxygen-carrying molecule of red blood cells, to make it more efficient at giving up oxygen to tissues. Workers at the University of Cincinnati Medical Center bound phytic acid, in place of the natural molecule DPG, to hemoglobin, by altering the blood cell membrane to permit phytic acid to enter. Workers at Columbia University's College of Physicians and Surgeons in New York City incorporated an analogue of vitamin B_6 onto hemoglobin molecules isolated from red blood cells. Such chemical modifications of hemoglobin promise to improve treatments for a variety of conditions, including heart attacks and strokes, that are caused by a reduced flow of blood to tissues. Isolated hemoglobin might be added to the blood of emergency victims, or used to oxygenate organ transplants during shipment.

MARC KUSINITZ

Flavors: MORE THAN A MATTER OF Taste

by Ellen Ruppel Shell

Charles Wiener's laboratory seems, at first encounter, to be a rather sterile place, with the usual array of spotless glass tubing, stainless-steel sinks, and row after row of tightly stoppered bottles all lit by a glaring slash of neon. But upon entering the lab, one is immediately struck by an aroma that is totally at odds with the setting—the earthy smell of roasted peanuts punctuated with the undertones of just-ripe bananas all wrapped in an overlay of blueberry jam. There is not a morsel of food in sight.

"Try some," Wiener urges, spooning up something thick and purple from a clear-glass jar. One hesitates—this is, after all, a laboratory, not grandmother's kitchen. But Wiener, a robust and jovial man, insists and the glop is duly ingested. It is delicious. "I think that is the best blueberry flavor that's ever been made," he says, beaming triumphantly. "And there's not a scrap of blueberry in it."

Wiener is a flavorist, one of about 100 experts nationwide who are entrusted with creating the thousands of flavors that go into our food, drink, cigarettes, mouthwash, and toothpaste. Like all flavorists, he has the nose of a bloodhound and the tastes of an oenophile (wine lover). He also has a Ph.D. in biochemistry. He got into the business, he says, simply because he loves to eat. That was 15 years ago. Today he is head flavorist at International Flavors & Fragrances Inc. (IFF), the largest producer of flavorings in the world.

Becoming a flavorist is nothing like becoming a doctor or plumber or teacher. For one thing, few have ever heard of the specialty. It is not and cannot be taught in school. Flavorists must have an acute sense of taste and smell, a flair for the artistic, and a technical inclination. Most begin their careers doing something unexotic like organic chemistry. Wiener got his start at an oil company, where he worked on wax formulations. An advertisement in a professional journal alerted him to the field of flavorings and sent him, Ph.D. and all, scurrying to apprentice himself to Ernest Pollack, now retired but still considered one of the foremost flavorists in the world. Five years later he emerged a full-fledged flavorist.

"A lot of flavorists never mature; they are technicians rather than artists," flavorist Wiener says. "There are only a handful of people in the world who can create flavors from scratch, and many of them are retired. It's something of a dying art."

Wiener's windowless basement laboratory is stocked floor to ceiling with hundreds of potions and powders that he likens to the colors on an artist's palette. There is jasmine and rose oil from Bulgaria, cold-pressed lime oil from Sicily, blue chamomile oil from Morocco, cassia oil from China. There are roots, leaves, dried berries, and seeds from every corner of the globe. It would seem that alchemy is practiced here, and in a sense it is. For creating flavors is no mere matter of squeezing a little juice from, say, a raspberry or mashing its pulp into a seedy essence. Flavors are delicate, elusive things that seem almost to evaporate with handling. The trick is to tease out from the hundreds of compounds that make up a raspberry those few precious elements that are essential to its flavor, then concentrate these compounds into a sample with a good deal more zest than that found in the natural berry.

At Monell Chemical Senses Center, arriving researchers draw inspiration from the sculptured nose and mouth.

By trapping and analyzing food aromas, scientists hope to discover the chemicals responsible for flavor.

No Machine Can Judge Flavor

"Nature has a way of decoying its secrets with unnecessary ingredients," Wiener says, chuckling. Coffee, for instance, contains more than 800 different chemical compounds which may contribute to its flavor, and yet only a fraction are absolutely essential to its characteristic flavor. To identify the essential flavor compounds in a food, chemists use a gas chromatograph, a machine that separates the food into its basic chemical constituents. But no machine can make judgments about which of these hundreds of chemicals contribute to the food's flavor—this is where the artistry comes in. Each of the chemicals is either smelled or tasted by the flavorist to determine whether it is crucial to the food's distinctive flavor. Those chemicals that are deemed critical are then precisely recombined into a facsimile of the natural flavor.

Identifying all of these essential flavor compounds can, in some cases, be like trying to track down a particular grain of sand on a broad stretch of beach. Some flavor chemicals occur in such small concentrations—parts per trillion—that they cannot be detected in laboratory samples. To detect these tiny concentrations of flavor particles, scientists must sort through thousands of pounds of material. To do this they go on location—to jam, coffee, or chocolate factories where tons of fruit and beans are processed every day. They rig up enormous contraptions to capture the aroma of the roasting beans or steaming berries, which they then analyze in hopes of discovering the tiny traces of chemicals that are so important to the distinctive flavors of the foods.

They do not always succeed—there are no widely accepted artificial coffee or chocolate flavors, nor are there good synthetic substitutes for strawberry or roasted meat. These foods are the Holy Grail of the flavor industry. Their flavor is not characterized by one or two or even half a dozen compounds, but by an orchestra of substances that, acting in concert, create an irreproducible (so far) chemical symphony. Some taste experts theorize that it is the very complexity of these flavors that makes them so appealing: the bitter/sweet taste of chocolate and the sour/sweet taste of strawberry, combined with their multitude of olfactory notes, make them enduring favorites.

But these foods are the exception. Most flavors have been characterized and mimicked so precisely in the laboratory that it has become nearly impossible to distinguish the fabricated from the original, says IFF research director Ira Katz. And some very popular flavors do not even exist outside of their synthetic renditions because they have no natural counterparts at all. For example, cola nuts taste nothing like the soft drink that bears their name. Cola flavor is a purely synthetic construct of natural ingredients—a "fantasy flavor," in the words of Katz. Were it not for the ingenuity of the legendary Southern pharmacist who whipped up the first batch of Coca-Cola 100 years ago, cola flavor might not exist.

Entirely New Flavors a Rarity

But the invention of entirely novel flavors like cola and Dr Pepper is extremely rare. Most of the work done by the flavor industry involves not the creation of new flavors but the duplication of established ones to suit the world's millions of different tastes. Hungarians like the flavor of paprika, while Indonesians enjoy the taste of the fruit of the durian tree, a prickly fruit whose smell, to the Western nose, inspires the unfortunate impression of expired skunk. Latin Americans like the nutty flavor of cashew, and Indians favor ghee, the flavor of clarified butter, sometimes from yak or buffalo milk.

"Orange is by far the most favored taste internationally," says Al Clausi, senior vice president and chief research officer of the General Foods Corporation, one of the largest food manufacturers in the world. "But there are some unique flavors preferred in certain regions of the world. For example, there is a flavor in Peru called *chicha morada*—it's very hard to describe, and Peru is the only country that I know of that sells it. In Mexico there's 'Jamaica,' a flower extract with a sort of tropical-fruit flavor that's very popular in beverages and gelatin desserts."

But while every culture has its favorites, flavor preference is not a genetically inherited characteristic. Several scientists around the world have devoted their careers to studying how taste preferences are acquired, and some have done at least part of their work at Monell Chemical Senses Center. This is a research institution that is loosely affiliated with the University of Pennsylvania.

Located on four floors of a rather stodgy office building that sits squarely across the Schuylkill River from downtown Philadelphia, Monell would be completely undistinguished were it not for the enormous gilded sculpture of a human nose and mouth that perches just in front of its entrance. Inside, the main order of business is made immediately obvious by a pervasive series of odors wafting through the halls. The smell varies with the particular floor and hallway one happens to be walking through, but the overall olfactory effect is that of a large cage in which a family of not entirely hygienic hamsters is baking chocolate chip cookies.

Inborn Taste Preferences

Gary Beauchamp, a psychologist and associate at Monell, has neither pets nor cookies in his office, though he does have an enormous photograph of a guinea pig on his door. Through studies of these animals and of humans, he has learned a great deal about taste acquisition. People, he says, are born with only a few taste prejudices—for example, a preference for sweet and a dislike of bitter. There is a very good reason for this. In the wild, sweet plants are generally nutritious while bitter ones are often poisonous, so a built-in sweet preference and bitter aversion has helped the species survive. But there is little evidence that children are born with any other inherent preferences. In fact, humans and most other animals are neophobic about food—they distrust and dislike any food

until they have grown accustomed to it. Sheer experience has made many parents painfully aware of this phenomenon; that first loving spoonful of cereal shoveled into junior's mouth is often returned less lovingly and far more emphatically into the dead center of mother's eye. But the clever parent quickly learns to disguise new foods in old, familiar ones. Sweet foods like applesauce make particularly effective carriers for small bits of, say, strained peas. The infant's natural predilection for sweet will override its distrust of the new food, and the amount of sweet taste can be slowly diminished until the baby will, in some lucky cases, actually eat strained peas straight.

When discussing flavor preferences, researchers emphasize that it is important to explain how taste and olfaction (the sense of smell) relate to flavor. Some scientists believe that humans can distinguish only four tastes: salt, sweet, bitter, and sour. Our experience of food relies not on the taste buds alone but on a combination of taste, smell, and tactile and temperature perception.

Children tend to adopt the food preferences of their parents, not because they inherit them but simply because they are exposed to the foods that their parents eat. A vivid example of this is the yen for chili peppers exhibited in young children in Mexico. These peppers contain capsaicin, an irritant. Capsaicin causes pain in the mouth, and the feeling of burning heat. Small children of every descent wisely avoid eating chili peppers and anything else that causes them pain. But at about the age of five or six, Mexican youngsters begin to like the effect and start piling their tortillas with the fiery veg-

Children adopt the taste preferences of their parents through exposure to the foods their parents like to eat.

etable. This, researchers say, is a prime illustration of flavor preferences as learned behavior. No one is born with a taste for pain; we have to learn to love it.

"Humans can learn to like anything—that's why we are such a successful species," says Jeannette Desor, an experimental psychologist who trained at Monell, Yale, and Cornell and who now works as a research scientist for General Foods. "You can drop humans anywhere and they'll thrive—only the rat does as well. But we do acquire preferences for things that we are exposed to, and by the time we are adults, these preferences can be quite strong."

The food industry is well aware of how difficult it is to change long-entrenched flavor preferences—some who have tried say that people will more willingly change marriage partners than eating habits. Americans, for example, are very fond of meat, a costly item in the world market basket. Soy products, which are widely favored in the Orient, can be equally nourishing and are a lot cheaper to produce than meat. But when the food industry first introduced soy burgers into this country more than a decade ago, they failed miserably. Soybean flavor has been difficult to sell here, but recent sales of new soy-protein products, such as frozen desserts, have been brisk.

To monitor products aimed at the "public taste," major food manufacturers carefully se-

Research suggests that people change marriage partners more readily than long-entrenched eating habits.

lect and train professionals to sample and describe new products before they are brought to the open market. Lydia Ohan, a junior scientist at General Foods, trained for three months to learn to differentiate between smoky and musty coffee and to distinguish ten variations on the theme of orange gelatin. Unlike flavorists, these individuals are not selected for an extraordinary sense of taste or smell. Their job is to represent the general public, to react to a product the way the majority of consumers would, but to learn to describe their reactions precisely. "It's something like learning a foreign language," Ohan says. "We don't say what our preferences are—we are used like analytic instruments to compare each food to an accepted standard and judge how close it comes to that standard." If it is determined that a particular segment of the American public likes its coffee mild and mellow, coffee geared toward that market doesn't leave the factory until the taster judges it to be mild and mellow. Only then is the coffee ready for market testing, at which time volunteers from outside the company are asked whether they like the taste.

American Tastes a Moving Target

American tastes have become something of a moving target in the past 15 years, and food companies are scrambling to keep up with them. In the late 1950's and early 1960's, consumers wanted easy-to-prepare foods that would fill their families' stomachs without breaking their budgets. In the post-Sputnik era, the public's awe of technology translated into a trust in synthesized foods. Not many people worried about artificial flavorings or colors, and the biggest sellers included ground-beef extenders, macaroni-and-cheese mixes, instant mashed potatoes, and an array of other food products that never had any pretense of being "natural." Those days are gone.

"More Americans than ever believe that they truly are what they eat," says General Foods' Al Clausi. "They want freshness, lightness and, most of all, they want naturalness. This pull from the market place has pushed science."

While American consumers have grown leery of artificial flavorings, their experience with artificially flavored foods has caused them to demand a lot of taste. They won't accept an "all-natural" soda with only a faint hint of cherries, or an ice cream vaguely reminiscent of bananas. They want a big, robust taste, but without the chemicals—and this poses an enormous challenge to the flavor scientist.

"Most natural flavors simply do not stack up to their best synthetic counterparts," says Clausi. "In blind tests, people almost invariably prefer synthetic flavors because natural flavors lose some of their characteristic taste when they are extracted from their source by heat or other methods."

So while people believe they want natural flavors, they often actually prefer synthetic ones. Robert A. Kluter, a senior food technologist at the U.S. Army Research and Development Center in Natick, Massachusetts, has tested the taste preference of military personnel for more than 15 years. He says that most recruits prefer diluted orange juice concentrate to the fresh-squeezed variety and would rather have an artificially flavored fast-food shake and burger than a carefully seasoned stew. "In the past ten years or so, I've seen a change in what young people say they prefer," he says. "They want food with much more flavor—more spicy and smoked foods, more zestiness." For this reason, Tabasco pepper sauce is now standard issue for soldiers out in the field. Kluter says the soldiers pour it on everything—from their morning eggs to their evening chipped beef. The object, he explains, is to fill the mouth with lots of flavor, even to the point of pain.

Reluctant Chewers

"Many overweight Americans tend not to expend a lot of energy in chewing food," explains Susan Schiffman, a professor of psychology at Duke University Medical Center and a leading taste researcher. "They tend to want the biggest possible 'taste' impact with the least amount of energy output." This means they want a lot of flavor, but aren't always willing to work for it by either cooking, seasoning, or even chewing food carefully. "Fast food is popular because it takes very little energy to consume and the high fat content carries flavor," Schiffman says.

Food products have traditionally provided high flavor impact through the magic of organic chemistry. This is not a recent phenomenon—late-19th-century scientists worked out schemes to chemically create cheap synthetic versions of costly spices like cinnamon, clove, and vanilla. Before these chemical formulations were worked out and perfected, the major source of flavoring was the simple extraction of essential oils from foods. But this is a very expensive and time-consuming process—it takes 4,400

Characteristic aromas captured and condensed in products give the food a greatly heightened taste impact.

pounds (2,000 kilograms) of cocoa beans, for example, to get less than an ounce (28 grams) of cocoa oil. But recent advances in biotechnology have made it possible to derive "natural" flavors using methods that would no doubt leave Mother Nature dumbfounded.

One long-established approach is to get microorganisms such as mold, yeast, and bacteria to churn out the flavors as waste products. Fermentation is one well-established version of this technique; yeast converts sugar to alcohol and carbon dioxide, thereby changing grape juice into wine. Cheese is aged in a similar, albeit less direct, fashion: mold feeds on the milk, producing enzymes that change a relatively flavorless mass into a creamy Camembert or Cheddar.

Scientists are now using different techniques to induce microorganisms to produce the chemical building blocks of flavors. Milton Manowitz, vice president of research and development of Givaudan Corporation, a Swiss-based flavor and fragrance manufacturer, says that the components of many meat flavors can be formed by microorganisms growing in a soup of natural products unrelated to meat. "This technique is rather expensive, but it is desirable because it is a natural process," according to Manowitz.

Of course, getting the flavor directly from the fruit or vegetable would be even more desirable. The song lyric "The eggplant that ate Chicago" comes to mind when scientists describe just how they plan to engineer "super" produce for use in the flavoring of other foods. But this image is quickly dispelled by the assurance that these fruits and vegetables will not be superbig but superflavored—so flavorful, in fact, that they will have too much taste to be eaten as they are.

DNAP Corporation, a firm that specializes in agricultural biotechnology, is at the cutting edge of fruit and vegetable design. Research manager Robert Whitaker says that a supertomato has already been designed for use in the making of soup and purees. To get this supertomato, DNAP scientists use tissue-culture techniques, which entail growing many plants from the body cells of a single plant. This saves the time it normally takes plants to reproduce and allows scientists to select certain desired characteristics—in this case, strong flavor—without having to worry about variation induced by the crossbreeding of plants.

"We'd also like to get plant cells in culture

With low-salt soups suffering a dismal market failure, the search goes on for an acceptable salt substitute.

to make flavors, just like bacteria in culture can produce antibiotics," Whitaker says. "But trying to pin down the genes that code for flavors is very, very difficult. Flavors are multichemical—if a flavor contains 200 different chemicals, it would take at least 200 genes to reproduce it, more likely a multiple of 200. The genetics of flavor is very complex."

Trapping Odors That Go Out the Chimney

But not all natural flavors need be the product of such exotic technologies. One tried-and-true method is to trap flavors as they literally go out the chimney. "Ever go by a bakery and take a deep breath?" asks Warren Wong, technical director at Firmenich, an international flavor company based in Princeton, New Jersey. "Or smell the exhaust coming out of a candy factory?" Those odors, he says, can be captured and condensed from these processes and used as flavor bases for products such as bread.

Ironically, the flavor that industry is most eager to mimic is cheap and widely available in its natural state, as well as a cinch to produce in the laboratory. That flavor (or taste, as it is more correctly called, since it has no smell) is salt—a taste that, according to Monell psychologist Gary Beauchamp, humans develop a preference for by the age of four months. The problem is that sodium, one of table salt's two components, has been implicated as a contributor to high blood pressure, and the surgeon general recommends that most Americans cut back on it. But we like salty taste and are loath to give it up. Low-salt soups, put on the market several years ago, proved a dismal failure.

"Soup companies would like to offer consumers something other than salty water; they do not want people getting high blood pressure, but people by their very nature like the taste of salt," Beauchamp says.

Finding an acceptable sodium-free salt substitute has been difficult partly because scientists are not even sure how humans perceive the salt taste. For years it's been known that salt perceptors on the tongue's surface pick up and transmit salt sensation. But scientists at several research institutions recently discovered that the sodium in salt is not just passively perceived on the surface of the tongue, but is also transported by special channels through the membrane and into the body of cells on the tongue.

"This is the first breakthrough we've had in understanding the taste reception of salt," says General Foods' Jeannette Desor. "Once

In the food industry, flavorists work in the lab while companies keep track of the ever-changing public tastes.

we have a clear understanding of the entire process of how salt is perceived, we might then be able to find a new way to synthesize a perfect substitute.''

Morley R. Kare, director of Monell, says that many questions of taste are still unresolved because the science is so new. ''This field is very backward,'' he says. ''We don't really understand the mechanism of taste, partly because there are so few scientists working in the field and partly because the questions themselves are so tough.''

Taste and Aging

One of the biggest and most damaging misconceptions, Kare says, is that the sense of taste fades with age. ''If you're healthy and active, your tastes don't really change,'' he says. ''Taste buds regenerate about every 10 or 11 days; the elderly lose a few, but not enough to matter. Go to a meeting of any wine-and-food society, and you'll see an awful lot of old people who haven't lost their sense of taste.''

Duke researcher Susan Schiffman says that the elderly do lose some sense of taste, but more of their sensory loss is due to a decreased sense of smell. To combat this, Schiffman has worked with the flavor industry to create a number of powders and sprays that enhance the flavor of various foods.

''Thirty percent of the elderly experience nutritional difficulties,'' Schiffman says. ''They don't get enough vitamins, minerals, or calories.'' But foods sprinkled with tuna, olive oil, tomato, or mashed-potato flavor spark elderly appetites and encourage them to eat a better balance of foods. These flavorings are not yet commercially available, Schiffman says, because industry hesitates to target any product specifically to older customers. ''The problem is that a 72-year-old shopper will look at a product like this and will say to himself, 'Oh, something for my mother,' '' Schiffman laughs. ''Nobody likes to think of himself as old.''

Regardless of the findings and breakthroughs of psychologists, chemists, and flavorists, industry can only respond to, not dictate, public demand. And what the American public wants now, says William F. Zick, vice president for marketing in the flavor division of International Flavors & Fragrances, is a salt-free salt flavor, a fat-free fat flavor, and a no-calorie sweetener that tastes just like sugar. We'd also like a no-alcohol beverage with all the punch of good whiskey, and a no-tar, no-nicotine cigarette just like the real McCoy. ''It would be nice to have a really good chocolate flavor, too,'' Zick says wistfully. The world's flavorists have their work cut out for them.

SELECTED READINGS

''A philosophy of taste'' by J. Preuss. *New York Times Magazine*, June 22, 1986.

''A minute on the lips . . .'' by K. Freifeld. *Forbes*, June 16, 1986.

''The unsweet tooth'' by J. Meer. *Psychology Today*, October 1985.

© Erika Stone

WATER · The Most
Essential Nutrient

No chart will tell you exactly how much you need, but you cannot survive without it. In fact, while you can live without most vitamins and minerals for extended periods of time, just a few days without this nutrient will surely result in death. The nutrient, of course, is water, that colorless, calorieless compound of hydrogen and oxygen that virtually every cell in the body needs to survive. Even tissues that are not thought of as "watery" contain large amounts of this substance. Water makes up about three-fourths of the brain and muscles, for instance. And bone, which is seemingly dry, is more than one-fifth water. Overall, water accounts for about half to two-thirds of the body makeup. Put another way, we each have about 40 to 50 quarts (38 to 48 liters), enough to fill more than a couple of sinks. Men contain more than women because they have proportionately less fat, and lean tissue holds more water than fat tissue.

A discussion of the role of water as a nutrient could easily fill a book. One of water's many essential tasks is to carry nutrients and oxygen to all parts of the body through the blood and the lymphatic system. In addition, it plays an important part in maintaining body temperature; the heat released when we lose water via the evaporation of perspiration helps keep the body cool. Water also removes metabolic waste by way of urine and sweat, lubricates the joints, surrounds and protects an unborn child, gives "form" to the cells, and serves as the medium for thousands of life-supporting chemical reactions that constantly take place within us.

The Role of Thirst

The average adult consumes, and excretes, about 2½ to 3 quarts (2.4 to 2.8 liters) of water a day. People who live in hot climates or whose jobs or hobbies involve strenuous physical activity require more. Thirst is generally a good indicator of when the body needs to replenish its water supply. This supply is regulated by the sodium concentration of the blood; when the sodium (or salt) level of blood rises, "receptors" in the brain's hypothalamus trigger the thirst sensation. In addition, "thirsty" blood draws water from the salivary glands, making the mouth feel dry.

Although thirst goes a long way in ensuring that we have enough water, it is not a perfect mechanism. It is quite possible that a person will drink enough fluids to quench his dry or parched throat but not enough to put back into his body what he needs. That is the reason people are advised to drink six to eight 8-ounce glasses of fluids a day, thirsty or not. This recommendation has special implications for the elderly, for there is evidence that senior citizens are less likely to feel thirsty when their bodies require water. People on high-protein diets also have to take in more water than they thirst for—perhaps eight to 10 glasses a day—so the kidneys will have enough to flush out the waste products of protein metabolism. Drinking past the point of thirst also reduces the risk of dehydration for those who live in extremely hot climates as well as for athletes and laborers who sweat excessively. Under ordinary circumstances, drinking more water than you need can't hurt. It's almost impossible to take in too much, because the body is efficient at getting rid of what it doesn't need.

Water Sources

Most of the water we take in comes from beverages, including juice, milk, and soft drinks. Alcoholic beverages as well as tea and coffee also supply water, but because they are diuretics, they increase water output and can actually raise water needs.

Although we get most of our water from liquids, solid foods also contribute significantly to our daily intake. Most fruits are more than 80 percent water, and even foods that aren't "juicy" or "moist" supply us with large amounts. Water makes up 60 percent of cooked lean beef, for instance, while bread is a third water and butter is roughly 15 percent water. Nothing is more surely water, however, than water itself. But is all water the same? Yes and no.

Although water is always two parts hydrogen to one part oxygen, its composition also depends on where it comes from and how it's processed. It can be hard or soft, carbonated or still, "natural" or "modified." The source of the water may be buried deep within the earth's surface or may be a reservoir or pond. In addition, water has varying amounts of bacteria and contaminants like arsenic and lead. And water suppliers may choose whether or not to add fluoride and/or other substances.

Another distinction, one that is taking on greater importance for a growing number of people in the United States, is whether the water is bottled or from the tap. Concern over the contamination of some municipal water supplies,

along with a belief that bottled water is somehow more healthful (and chic) than tap water, are leading some people away from their faucets and toward the "prepackaged" varieties of nature's thirst quencher. Whether bottled water is really better for you than tap water, however, is open to debate. Either way, there are often differences between the two that bear examination.

From the Faucet

Public water systems provide 90 percent of the U.S. population with drinking water. Close to half of our municipal tap water comes from surface water, such as rivers and streams. The rest comes from groundwater, including wells, springs, and aquifers—porous rock, sand, or gravel that is fed by rain and snow. In some areas the water is naturally hard—that is, it contains comparatively high concentrations of minerals, notably calcium and magnesium. Soft water has higher levels of sodium. Your water utility should be able to tell you just how hard or soft your water is.

Many people prefer soft water for a number of reasons. It makes soap lather better and leaves less of a ring around the tub. Hard water, on the other hand, doesn't get clothes as clean and causes the teakettle to build up a residue of rocklike crystals after a while. Some municipalities—and individuals—soften their water by

Thirsty or not, joggers and other athletes should drink plenty of water to replace fluid lost to perspiration.

© Jim Anderson/Woodfin Camp

© Paula Kobylarz

Questionable water quality has led some people to use bottled instead of tap water for internal consumption.

date back to 1500 B.C. And a Sanskrit quotation from as early as 2000 B.C. talks about appropriate methods for filtering water.

Concern for the purity of drinking water remains high today. The composition of water that comes out of the tap is strictly regulated by the Environmental Protection Agency (EPA) under the provisions of the Safe Drinking Water Act of 1974—a law that sets minimum national standards for drinking-water quality. One of the agency's requirements is that tap water must be treated, if necessary, to prevent contamination from bacteria. That ensures against outbreaks of waterborne diseases such as cholera, typhoid, and dysentery.

Much of the tap water in the U.S. is disinfected with chlorine. (Chlorine levels tend to be higher in summer—one reason tap water may taste better in winter.) Although chlorine kills many bacteria effectively, it has been found to react with organic compounds to form what are known as trihalomethanes, which are suspected of causing cancer or genetic mutations that promote cancer. For that reason, the level of trihalomethanes in municipal drinking water is restricted by the EPA. It may not exceed 100 parts per billion (0.10 milligram per liter of water). At that level and below, scientists believe, water is perfectly safe for human consumption.

The EPA has also set limits for many other contaminants that are found in drinking water. These include mercury, nitrate, and silver as well as pesticides and radioactivity. Responsibility for monitoring the levels of contaminants in water falls to the water utilities. The utilities, in turn, must periodically report the quality of the water supply to the state (or, in some cases, federal) government. If the water is deemed unsafe to drink at any point, consumers must receive notification through the media and be given instructions on the necessary precautions to take. Rochester, New York, is a case in point. Residents there had to boil their water or buy bottled water for several weeks because of low-level bacterial contamination found in the city's water system.

To avoid incidents like the one in Rochester and further ensure that our water remains safe, Congress has recently passed several amendments to the Safe Drinking Water Act that will become effective over the next few years. These amendments contain several provisions for better protection of our groundwater resources, which are becoming increasingly threatened by leaking underground storage

removing calcium and magnesium, both essential nutrients, and adding sodium in what is known as an ion-exchange process. From a nutritional standpoint, this practice has its drawbacks. For one thing, our average diet is quite high in sodium, and although the levels of sodium in most water supplies don't add much, we certainly don't need any more. In addition, soft water may pick up undesirable metals, like lead and cadmium, from pipes.

It is thought that hard water may help prevent cardiovascular disease; communities where water is hard tend to have a lower incidence of heart attack than areas in which the water is soft. To be sure, the evidence is inconclusive, since many other factors may be coming into play here. Nonetheless, people who use home water softeners might consider attaching their softening equipment to the hot water line only and stick with cold water for drinking and cooking.

Beyond Hard and Soft

Along with differences in mineral concentration, tap water has varying levels of heavy metals, microorganisms, and organic compounds, all of which must be filtered out (or, in the case of microorganisms, killed by disinfection) to the point that they do not endanger human health. The filtering process is nothing new; man has been "cleaning" his drinking water for thousands of years. Pictures of water-clarifying apparatus have been found on Egyptian walls that

© Jim Howard/FPG

Carefully regulated amounts of chlorine are used to disinfect much of the public water supply in the U.S. For public swimming pools, even higher levels of chlorine are needed to kill bacteria and algae that can contaminate water.

tanks, faulty septic systems, landfills, oil and gas exploration, and other industrial practices. They also include stricter criteria for disinfection and filtration.

Strictly enforced regulations for filtration will help remove a number of impurities, including a microorganism, *Giardia lamblia,* that has been plaguing our water with increasing frequency. Over the past 15 years, this one-celled parasite has made its way into water supplies from Colorado to Massachusetts and has caused outbreaks of giardiasis, a waterborne disease characterized by diarrhea, abdominal cramps, bloating, flatulence, and fatigue. Improved filtration should render giardiasis extinct.

The Fluoride Factor

It has been over 40 years since Grand Rapids, Michigan, became the first town to fluoridate its water supply. Since then, it has been well established that fluoride helps strengthen the teeth and prevent cavities, and fluoridation is now endorsed by several organizations, including the American Dental Association and the American Medical Association. Yet almost 40 percent of our tap water remains unfluoridated or does not have enough fluoride to fight tooth decay effectively. Why?

According to Harald Loe, D.D.S., director of the National Institute of Dental Health, there is a lack of public funding. Moreover, misguided antifluoridation activists, some of whom claim that fluoride promotes cancer and sickle cell anemia as well as AIDS, have succeeded in persuading local government agencies and voters in many areas to reject fluoridation.

It is true that dental fluorosis, a harmless, if somewhat unsightly, mottling of the teeth, appears in communities where the naturally occurring fluoride level in the water is more than 2 parts per million. But fluoride is added to water in lower concentrations, and children who live in areas where the water is fluoridated do, in fact, have many fewer cavities than children whose water is not fluoridated.

To find out whether your tap water is fluoridated, you can contact your local water department or the state board of health. Based on the amount of fluoride in your supply, your dentist should be able to tell you if your child needs fluoride supplements and in what doses. The American Dental Association currently recommends that youngsters who live in areas where the fluoride concentration is less than 0.7 part per million should receive fluoride supplementation from birth until they are 13 years old.

If your water comes from a private well, you'll want to have it analyzed for fluoride levels by a laboratory. Private wells, incidentally, are not protected by the Safe Drinking Water Act. Therefore, people who own their own wells should, at the very least, test for bacteria, which their local health department may do for free. Local health officials or a professional engineer should also be able to tell you which other laboratory tests are appropriate. (Living near a particular type of industry, for instance, might call for analysis for a particular contaminant.)

Bottled Becomes a Big Business

Why would someone pay the same price for a gallon of bottled water as for a gallon of gasoline when tap water is practically free and almost always safe to drink? The answer, in part, is because no matter how vigilant the efforts of the EPA, isolated instances of tainted tap water do occur. That happened several years ago, when two wells in Woburn, Massachusetts, were found to be contaminated by toxic waste. Many people are convinced that the incidence of leukemia in 12 children there can be linked to the unclean water.

Such cases have no doubt helped spur the remarkable growth of the bottled-water industry. Sales of bottled water increased 300 percent from 1975 to 1985, says the International Bot-

tled Water Association, an industry trade group. Americans drank close to $1 billion worth in just 1985 alone. Almost one out of 17 people now drink bottled water regularly, and in southern California, the number is one out of three. California actually accounts for almost half of the bottled-water consumption in the entire United States.

Of course, a major issue to consider with bottled water—barring the occasional contamination of municipal water supplies—is whether it is really better for you than tap water. Certainly, it may very well taste better than what comes out of your faucet. That's because much of our tap water is disinfected with chlorine, while most bottled-water companies kill bacteria with ozone, and ozone does not give water the aftertaste or smell of chlorinated water that some people find offensive. (The reason it is not used in municipal supplies is that it is not as stable as chlorine over the long term and cannot guard against the recontamination of water in pipes.)

As for nutritional quality, although members of the International Bottled Water Association cannot, by law, make any health claims per se, they do their best to convince consumers that bottled water has special properties that contribute to good health. Evian natural springwater, for instance, has a full-page magazine advertisement in which it shows two men and a woman

Trendy "water bars" have sprung up around the country that cater to the tastes of the bottled-water connoisseur.

Bottled Water Glossary

Minimum standards for the quality of bottled drinking water are set by the Food and Drug Administration (FDA) and match the standards for municipal water supplies set by the EPA. Standards aside, however, understanding terms used for the different types of bottled water may be confusing. The following may help:

• *Natural water* is water that has been unmodified by minerals.

• *Naturally sparkling water* has enough carbon dioxide to be bubbly without the introduction of "foreign" outside chemicals. The term *sparkling water,* on the other hand, means that the water was made effervescent by injection of carbon dioxide from an outside source.

• *Springwater* naturally flows out of the earth at a particular spot and is bottled at or near its source. Like natural water, says the International Bottled Water Association, it is not altered by the addition or deletion of minerals.

• *Drinking water* is usually noncarbonated, or still. It is generally used as an alternative to tap water instead of as a substitute for soft drinks and cocktails. Over 90 percent of the bottled water in the U.S. is used as drinking water. (And the source

may well be a municipal water supply).

• *Purified water* has been demineralized. Purified water that is vaporized and recondensed is *distilled* water.

• *Mineral water* is an imprecise term, since with the exception of distilled and purified water, all water has minerals. The FDA has no "standard of identity." The International Bottled Water Association, however, which represents over 80 percent of the sales of bottled water in the U.S., says that mineral water "contains not less than 500 parts per million total dissolved solids." Minerals, incidentally, are what give water its taste. The more minerals, the "stronger" the taste.

• *Seltzer* is usually tap water that is injected with carbon dioxide and contains no added salts.

• *Club soda* is also artificially carbonated, but it contains added salts and minerals. Neither seltzer, club soda, nor naturally sparkling water is regulated by the FDA as "bottled water." They are viewed, instead (along with soft drinks such as cola), as soda water. As such, manufacturers of these products may add up to 0.02 percent caffeine and 0.5 percent alcohol by weight.

with lean, muscular bodies. The caption reads: "Evian, with its unique balance of calcium and magnesium, gets into your body faster than other waters to rid your system of impurities and replace the fluids you lose during a workout. With no sugar, salt, or chemicals."

While it's true that a liter of Evian has 78 milligrams of calcium and 24 milligrams of magnesium, there is nothing particularly special about that "balance." Furthermore, all drinking water "gets into your body fast" to flush out impurities and replace lost fluids. Municipal water supplies never contain sugar, and a number of them have very little salt. Finally, chemicals added to public drinking water via disinfection or filtration make it safer, not less healthful. That's not to say that Evian doesn't taste good or that it's not good for you, but there is no proof that it is nutritionally superior to standard tap water.

The same applies to bottled waters that claim "no calories or artificial flavorings." No tap water has any calories, and the only artificial "flavorings" in municipal supplies may be some added minerals. The bottom line is that no scientific evidence exists to support the notion that bottled water is somehow more healthful than tap.

When all is said and done, then, the decision to buy bottled water should not be influenced so much by health concerns as by cost, taste, and aesthetic preferences. To be sure, it is certainly better for one's health to opt for a before-dinner sparkling mineral water than a martini, as many people are now doing. But in truth, all types of water make the best thirst quencher, all serve well as our most essential nutrient, and all contribute to better athletic performance. "To your health" applies to drinking water across the board.

© George W. Gardner/Stock Boston

Nice News About **NOISE**

by Denise Allen Zwicker

To you, it might be the music playing (full blast) on your neighbor's stereo. To your neighbor, it might be the tinkling of your favorite wind chimes.

To an office worker, noise might be a coworker's loud telephone conversations. To a parent, it might be the cacophony of children's voices mingled with the incessant chatter from the television.

In many cases, one person's noise is another's music. But certain sounds are noise to all of us. Jet engines, chain saws, and gunfire are a few examples. Listening to them is uncomfortable and irritating. Worse, they can damage our hearing beyond repair.

Noise as a Stressor

How people react to noise is manifested in many ways. In New York City, for instance, a group of parents whose children attend a school near urban train tracks have sued the city's Transit Authority, saying their children's learning has been hampered by the noisy passing trains.

Also in New York, a man has taken legal action against his neighbor's children, claiming that their ball playing and noise outbursts in front of his home hastened his wife's death from cancer. A Dutch study of the medical problems of people living near Amsterdam's Schiphol Airport has found that people in the noisiest areas seek medical help much more frequently than people in the quieter areas. The incidence of high blood pressure in the noisiest area is 72 percent higher than in the quietest area.

We know that noise can cause hearing loss. But it also is considered a stressor, and therefore may play a role in other health problems as well.

According to Dr. Hans Selye, president of the International Institute of Stress in Montreal, Quebec, noise induces a three-stage response by

Noise control in action. A far-reaching ordinance in Denver, Colorado, limits the noise level of a truck or automobile with a gross vehicle weight (GVW) less than 10,000 pounds to an 80-decibel weighted sound pressure (dbA). For heavier vehicles, the maximum is 88 dbA.

our bodies: alarm, resistance, and exhaustion. During the alarm stage, blood-pressure and blood-sugar levels rise, releasing energy. As the noise continues, your body begins to resist, and finally, in the third stage, becomes exhausted. This state of exhaustion, says Selye, can leave you prone to stress-related problems such as ulcers and can lower your resistance to colds and flu.

In one study, monkeys exposed to daylong tapes of average urban noises developed higher blood pressure. And several studies of school-children in high-noise areas seem to indicate noise-induced problems. A 1978 study even reported that pregnant women disturbed by over-head airplanes were more likely to give birth to children with birth defects.

Is Noise the Culprit?

"But there's a problem when we talk about the nonauditory effects of noise, because they also have their roots in non-noise-related conditions," says Dr. David M. Lipscomb, director of the Noise Research Lab at the University of Tennessee Department of Audiology. "So many influences bear on our physical and mental health that it's difficult to focus on the noise problem alone.

"For instance, I just moved into a home with barking, baying dogs nearby. I know what their clamor is doing to me, but I can't quantify it. You've probably had the same experience when someone comes blasting up a hill on a noisy motorcycle. You know what's happening to your attitude, but laboratory workers are having a terrible time trying to quantify it."

Until the data are in, you may have a hard time convincing your noisy neighbor to pay for your headache medication. But you can start working now to reduce your exposure to noise—and perhaps live a calmer, healthier, longer life.

How Much Is Too Much?

The intensity of sound is measured in decibels (abbreviated db). The decibel scale is logarithmic: for each 3-decibel increase, the intensity of the sound doubles. Thus, if you leave a quiet office (40 db) and go home to use a power saw (100 db), you've increased your noise exposure 500,000 times.

Noises of 120 db (an overhead jet, a loud home stereo, a turbine generator) cause hearing discomfort for most people. Noises above 140 db (a gunshot blast, a toy cap pistol, a rocket launching pad) can cause actual pain and even hearing damage.

The Occupational Safety and Health Administration (OSHA) limits workers' noise exposure to no more than a 90-db average during an eight-hour workday. Subways, a motorcycle 25 feet away, and a loud shout are examples of 80-db sounds.

The trouble is, no such regulations govern our private lives. A food blender (88 db), for example, is louder than a diesel truck (84 db). Yet how many cooks wear earplugs when they whip up a dip? A power mower is louder than a rock drill, and a chain saw is louder than a scraper-loader. But how many of us wear earplugs while we mow our lawns or trim a tree?

The corporate community is concerned. "At Exxon, we've had hearing-conservation programs for employees for more than 35

Sounds of summer? A young sunbather seems disturbed by the inharmonious blare of a beachful of boom boxes.

Protection from noise begins at home. Users of loud yard tools should shield their ears to guard their hearing.

Hearing Loss Is Gradual

Most of us don't think about hearing conservation until it's too late—when we've already suffered a serious hearing loss. That's because, in most cases, hearing loss is gradual and painless.

"When you put your hand on a hot burner, you know immediately that you've made a mistake. But hearing loss is generally painless—and so gradual that it may be weeks, months, years, even decades before you notice a hearing loss," says Lipscomb.

"One of the best demonstrations of the gradual nature of hearing loss would be to follow a young couple from the time they get married until, say, their 40th wedding anniversary," says Richards.

"Without their knowing it, I'd like to go in and mark the volume knobs on their stereo and TV," he says. "Let's say they like to go dancing to loud music and they own a motorboat and go waterskiing. And let's say they both work in factories or plants where they're exposed to a fair amount of noise.

"What I'd like to do is go back in 40 years and check the volume controls on their stereo and TV. They may not have noticed it, but chances are those volumes would be quite a bit higher than they were 40 years earlier."

Hearing Loss

Hearing loss occurs when noise damages and eventually kills the sensory cells (called hair cells) in our inner ears. No one knows exactly how noise damages these cells—only that the damage is progressive. Like footsteps treading on grass day after day, noise, over a long

years," says Jack Richards, medical administrator for Exxon Company, U.S.A. "We make sure our people protect their hearing on the job.

"But what we can't control is what they do to their hearing off the job," he continues. "The same person who is conscientious about on-the-job hearing conservation may leave here and spend hours at a shooting range or a rock concert or using power tools without hearing protection.

"Actually, all of us are guilty," Richards adds. "We'll wear safety glasses and steel-toed shoes and earplugs on the job, then go home and put on our shorts and a pair of thongs to mow the yard."

The headgear of aircraft carrier crews, besides muting outside noise, incorporates radios for easy communication.

period, can damage and finally kill the hair cells of the inner ear.

Since the hair cells "specialize" in certain frequencies, most hearing loss is specific rather than general. That is, we lose the ability to hear certain frequencies—usually high frequencies, like the sound of a violin or a child's high-pitched voice.

Most of us think of hearing loss as an inevitable part of aging. Hearing lost at high frequencies (a condition called presbycusis) is most common in older people. However, some evidence suggests that presbycusis could be the result, not of aging, but of a lifetime of hearing damage. If that's true, we can help stop it.

The key is in education. And many of the warnings fall on unbelieving ears.

The Headphone Factor

In the late 1960's, for example, Dr. Lipscomb tested thousands of young people (sixth grade to college freshmen) and reported an alarming trend toward high-frequency hearing loss. Although most of the hearing impairments were not serious, Lipscomb says the results suggest that this generation of young people will encounter much more serious hearing problems in their middle years than have their parents and grandparents.

Although it has been more than 15 years since he reported those findings, Lipscomb says he has no reason to believe the situation has improved. Today's young people may experience even greater damage, he says, due to the widespread use of headphones to direct high-volume music directly into their ears. Eventually, hearing will be affected.

A child undergoes a hearing test. Some companies perform similar tests on employees who work in noisy areas.

"Tests on the volumes being played—when the headphones are taken off the users' ears under actual listening conditions—show that they're often running at 110, 115, 120 decibels, which is several thousand times louder than we consider the potential danger level."

But let's not place all the blame on loud music. Airplanes, trucks, and—yes—refineries and drilling rigs can damage our hearing, too. The nice news is that companies have done, and continue to do, something about it.

For example, modifications to jet engines have greatly reduced airport noise levels in the past decade. The same is true of trucks and automotive tires. "Traffic noise, especially, is much better today than it was 10 to 12 years ago,"

In the line of duty, police will likely lack the hearing protection they are required to wear during night firing practice.

says Lipscomb. "There have been dramatic reductions in the noise output of trucks, and many formerly noisy vehicles are being muffled."

One Company's Efforts

Among the companies participating in noise-reduction efforts is Exxon, which requires low noise levels in trucks and other equipment. It's part of the company's approach to hearing conservation, which it divides into five parts:

- Noise identification and measurement,
- Noise reduction or elimination,
- Administrative controls,
- Personal hearing protection, and
- Audiometric testing.

"The first step in the program is for our industrial hygienists to identify potential noise-hazard areas and measure the noise levels to determine if they are high enough to cause hearing loss in our employees," says Robert Diakun, director of industrial hygiene. "We take detailed measurements of the equipment itself to pinpoint the noise sources.

"The second step is to reduce or eliminate the noise—by buying quieter machines in the first place or dampening the noise enclosures," he continues. "Sometimes, excessive noise is caused by malfunctioning equipment. Perhaps a repair job or a better maintenance program is called for.

"Of course, not every noise problem can be eliminated with engineering controls. For example, an enclosure could cause heat buildup and create a fire hazard. In those cases, we go to the third step—administrative controls. The most important of these are our educational programs on hearing conservation. Another example is setting up work patterns that reduce workers' exposure to noise. We also use warning signs in noisy areas.

"The fourth step is the use of personal hearing protection—earplugs or earmuffs," Diakun says. "But hearing protection doesn't do a bit of good if it isn't worn—or is worn improperly." And that, unfortunately, is a problem with some employees.

"Believe it or not, we've had some employees tell us that hearing protection is for sissies—that their ears are 'tough enough' to handle the noise," notes Richards. "And we hear other excuses all the time, too.

"People will tell us they can't remember to wear hearing protection, even though we have signs posted everywhere. Or they'll say it's uncomfortable, which it's not if the plugs or muffs are fitted and worn correctly," he continues.

"Another argument we get is that hearing protection isn't safe because it prevents them from hearing fellow workers or warning signals. But this just isn't true. Properly designed hearing protection works like sunglasses: it blocks out the extraneous noise, but still allows you to hear specific sounds."

The fifth part of Exxon's hearing conservation program is audiometric testing. All employees who work in noise-hazard areas must have their hearing tested before they begin working in that area and every year thereafter. Test results are available to employees, and, if even a slight hearing loss is detected, the employee and his or her supervisor receives a written notice, along with explicit instructions on how to prevent further losses.

Hearing Conservation at Home

Most of the same components that make up Exxon's hearing conservation program have been included in recent government regulations for worker safety. And you can apply the same practices to the noise you encounter in your private life.

First, think about the noises in your home and leisure activities. In some cases, you may be able to reduce or eliminate excessive noise—by buying quieter home appliances or investing in heavy drapes to muffle outside noises.

Next on your agenda is reducing your exposure to excessive noise—by giving your ears regular rests from noisy activities.

For a few dollars, you can invest in a pair of earplugs or earmuffs to wear when you use power tools, go hunting, or ride a motorcycle.

And, finally, you can include a hearing test in your regular physical exam.

Make Some Noise

But what about the noise that isn't "yours" to regulate? What can you do about excessive noise in your neighborhood and community?

Actually, quite a lot, says one woman who should know. Dr. Arline L. Bronzaft, a New York City psychology professor, has studied the effect of noise on learning, and chairs the noise committee of the Council on the Environment of New York City. She's successfully lobbied for noise reduction in one of the noisiest cities in the country.

All it takes to get something done is, ironically, enough people, making enough noise.

© Dick Luria/Photo Researchers

MEASURING: *An ancient art refined*   by Benedict A. Leerburger

Counting, weighing, recording temperature, tracking time—measuring: common occurrences that we too often take for granted. For most of us, the need to measure to an ultrafine degree is rarely required. But for many, the growing pace of technology has been matched by an increasing need for precision measurements. Missiles rendezvousing in space, for example, require exact timing and a precise measurement of distances. A chemist may be required to measure one part in a million; a physicist must know the exact speed and temperature of a spinning electron within a cyclotron. Available technology can measure the weight of a human body, single electron, or the moon.

The problem of weighing an object, be it a sack of gold, the earth, or a microbe, has been with man for thousands of years. Weights and measures were among the earliest tools invented by man. Primitive societies needed basic measures for many tasks: constructing dwellings,
making clothes, or bartering food. Man turned first to parts of his body and his natural surroundings for measuring instruments. Early Babylonian and Egyptian records and the Bible indicate that length was first measured with the forearm, hand, or finger. Time was measured by the periods of the sun, moon, and other heavenly bodies.

Ancient Methods

The first scales, dating from roughly 2500 B.C., were the weights and balances of the pre-Aryan civilization of northern India used by goldsmiths, jewelers, and temple priests to weigh gold dust. Most of these weights were highly polished stone. Each nation devised its own standard of weights, usually in the form of polished blocks or hard stone or carved figures, like the "resting duck" of the Assyrians or the "boar's head" of Mesopotamia. Wherever these early weights have been unearthed, close by were some artifacts of gold.

When it was necessary to compare the capacities of containers such as gourds or clay vessels, they were filled with plant seeds, which were then counted to measure the volumes. The "carat," for example, now a unit of weight for gems, derives from the carob seed. As various civilizations grew, each maintained its own set of measurement standards, coining terms still used today to define weight, distance, and time. Such terms as "digit," "palm," and "span" were derived from parts of the body.

Roman contributions include the use of the number 12 as a base. (We still divide our "foot" into 12 inches.) The twelve divisions of the Roman "pes," or foot, were called *unciae*. Our words "inch" and "ounce" are both derived from that Latin word. The "yard" as a measure of length was first used by early Saxon kings. They wore a sash or girdle around their waist that could be removed and used as a convenient measuring device. The word "yard" comes from the Saxon word *gierd*, meaning girth, or the measure of a person's waist.

In England under Edward I, the legal unit of measurement was the "iron ulna." This, by royal decree, was the distance of three feet. Later, Edward II broke the standard down to the "inch," or one thirty-sixth part of an ulna. It was further ordained that "three grains of barley, dry and round, make an inch." And, following the Romans, "12 inches make a foot; three feet make an ulna; 5½ ulna make a perch; and 40 perches in length and four perches in breadth make an acre." This figure was arrived at simply by measuring how much land a yoke of oxen could plow in a day. Obviously, this all depended on the country, the oxen, and the time of year. In Scotland, Ireland, and several English counties today, an acre still differs according to local customs. In the United States an acre is legally defined at 160 square rods. But what is a rod? Now it is defined as a linear measure equal to 5.03 meters. Back in 1575, an English publication defined the rod as "the total length of the left feet of the first 16 men as they come from Church on Sunday morning."

The French Experience

Perhaps the first precision standard was the common poppy seed. In the 1700's it was found that the "inch" (the length of 3 barleycorns) could be further subdivided. Each barleycorn equaled four poppy seeds, and each poppy seed "equaled 12 human hairs." Unfortunately, no common standard existed. In France, nearly ev-

More than 5,000 years ago the ancient Assyrians used this "resting duck" sculpture as a standard of weight.

ery city and province had its own system of weights and measures. Even in present-day Marseilles, some shops still use the so-called Marseilles system despite national laws enforcing the metric system.

At one time, France used a decimal metric system imposed on the nation by the French Republican Convention in 1790. The system—based on an inaccurate breakdown of metric decimal fractions of the quarter meridian running through Paris—caused nothing but confusion. Months were divided into three periods of 10 days each. Days were divided into 10 hours of 100 minutes, each containing 100 seconds. At the end of each year, five days called *jours sans-culottides* were left over. The law was so strictly regulated, it was a crime to sell any commodity by the dozen—you had to buy 10 or 20. The system caused such problems that on August 1, 1793, all scientific academies were closed and the weights and measures committee abolished. The following year the principal member of the committee, famed chemist Antoine Lavoisier, was sent to the guillotine.

For decades, countries throughout the world used various local standards. Then, in the late 19th century, a series of worldwide conferences, culminating with the international 1875 Convention of the Meter, finally formalized the now-familiar metric system. The meter was defined as a standard equaling one ten-millionth of the distance from the North Pole to the equator along the meridian of the earth running near Dunkerque, France, and Barcelona, Spain—equivalent to approximately 39.37 inches. An actual "standard" metric stick, located in Sèvres, France, is still used to verify and recheck existing measuring devices. The metric unit of mass—the gram—was defined as one cubic centimeter of water at its temperature of maximum density.

Spectral Lines

With the advance of both science and technology, the need to redefine the metric standards became obvious. In 1870 the Scottish physicist James Clerk Maxwell suggested that standards of length, time, and mass be based "on the physical constants of atoms and molecules rather than arbitrary standards, such as the distance between two scratch marks on a bar of metal." The discovery of atomic spectral lines made Maxwell's suggestion possible. Since each element has a specific, measurable wavelength, it became possible not only to identify substances by a spectroscopic analysis of their wavelength, but also to use the wavelength of a substance as a standard. The wavelength of an atom does not vary with temperature or pressure, and is therefore a true constant, unlike the platinum-iridium bar formerly used as a metric standard, which may vary due to environmental factors.

Following the discovery of atomic spectral lines, physicists sought to develop methods to measure wavelengths with great precision. In 1881 American physicist Albert A. Michelson invented an instrument called an optical interferometer that could measure the effects on the speed of light produced by the motion of the earth through space. He later adapted his interferometer to compare the length of the standard meter bar with the wavelength of the element cadmium. Inadvertently, Michelson's work in measuring the velocity of light led to another constant—the speed of light itself.

For decades the standard meter was the length of the platinum-iridium bar stored in a safe at the Bureau International Des Poids et Mesures (BIPM) in Sèvres, France, just outside Paris. In 1960, following the suggestion of Maxwell nearly a century earlier, the standard meter was based on a "physical constant"—1,650,763.73 times the wavelength of the radiation emitted at a specific energy level of krypton-86. In 1983 the Conférence Générale des Poids et Mesures redefined the meter again, this time in terms of the velocity of light. The current standard meter is thus "the length of the path traveled by light in a vacuum during a time

US Department of Commerce

Alone among units, the kilogram is still defined by a physical object: a cylinder of platinum-iridium alloy.

interval of 1/299,792,458 of a second." This new standard is more accurate than the previous. More important, it is a standard obtainable in any advanced physics laboratory.

The standard for mass presents another problem. Like the metric stick, a solid block of metal has served as the standard kilogram for close to a century. Specifically, a kilogram is defined as the mass of a cylinder of the alloy platinum-iridium measuring 39 millimeters in both height and diameter. Since 1889 the actual physical standard has been stored in the safe at the BIPM. A duplicate in the custody of the National Bureau of Standards (NBS) in Gaithersburg, Maryland, serves as the mass standard for the United States.

Measuring Time

Deciding upon a standard for measuring time was simplified early in this century when it was realized that a natural oscillator such as an atom or a molecule would provide a timing device whose frequency was both stable and readily reproducible. The standard today is based upon the hyperfine transition in which the spins of the outermost electron of the cesium atom and the cesium nucleus change their relative orientation. The international standard for the second is the duration of 9,192,631,770 periods of the radiation corresponding to the transition between the two hyperfine levels of the ground state of the cesium-133 atom.

The base unit for measuring temperature is the Kelvin, named after the British physicist William Kelvin. It was discovered experimentally that all gases, when their temperature is reduced, contract at such a rate that their volume would be zero at a temperature of $-273.16°$ Celsius. The Kelvin temperature scale begins at this low point and maintains the same size of a degree as the Celsius scale. Thus, $0°$ K, the lowest possible temperature, is known as absolute zero. As a standard, the Kelvin is defined as a "unit of thermodynamic temperature: 1/273.16 of the thermodynamic temperature of the triple point of water."

The mole, or gram-molecular-weight, another SI unit, is a chemical measure used to define a quantity of particles of any type equal to a constant known as Avogadro's number. As a standard, Avogadro's number is defined as 6.02252×10^{23}. A mole of carbon, for example, contains as many elementary entities as there are atoms in 0.012 kilogram of carbon-12.

The SI unit used to measure the intensity of light is known as the candela. The rather complex standard is defined as "the luminous intensity, in a given direction, of a source that emits monochromatic [one color of] radiation of frequency 540×10^{12} hertz, and that has a radiant direction of 1/683 watt per steradian." According to Dr. Barry N. Taylor, chief of the electricity division at the NBS Center for Basic Standards, "We're just concerned with realizing that definition, which is the least accurate of all standards, but adequate for measurement of luminous intensity."

In addition to the various mechanical units, the basic SI electrical unit is the ampere. It is defined as "the constant current that, if maintained in two, straight parallel conductors of infinite length and negligible circular cross section, and placed one meter apart in a vacuum, would produce between the conductors a force equal to 2×10^{-7} newton per meter of length." Taylor notes that while the definition will remain the same, "We're trying to improve its realization by a factor of 50 to 100 with new absolute-ampere experiments."

Quartz Crystals

With the rapid growth in technology, the need to measure to closer and closer tolerances has increased. Although electronic scales have become commonplace, the familiar balance scale is today more sophisticated, more delicate, and more accurate than ever before. For measuring distance, both light and sound waves are used. For example, the moon's distance from the earth was accurately recorded by bouncing a laser beam off the moon's surface. By marking the time it took for the beam of light to travel to and from the moon, it was possible to compute an exact distance. Quartz crystals that vibrate at a constant and known frequency have changed timekeeping. Until the 1960's a balance wheel and escapement mechanism were the principal parts in every watch and clock. Now, with quartz watches, we can measure time more accurately and less expensively than ever before. And, as technology continues to demand more exacting tolerances, our international standards will keep abreast of the changes.

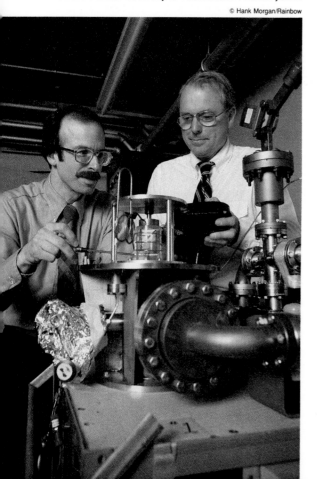

By measuring the vibrations of cesium atoms, atomic clocks maintain accuracy to 4 seconds in 1 million years.

© Hank Morgan/Rainbow

THE 1986 NOBEL PRIZES
Physics and Chemistry

by Elaine Pascoe

Work that has expanded scientists' knowledge of the world at molecular and atomic levels brought Nobel prizes to six researchers in 1986. The prize in physics was awarded to Dr. Ernst Ruska, the German scientist who invented the electron microscope in the early 1930's, and to Dr. Gerd Binnig of West Germany and Dr. Heinrich Rohrer of Switzerland, who developed the scanning tunneling microscope in 1981. The chemistry award was shared by three scientists—Dr. Dudley R. Herschbach of Harvard University, Dr. Yuan T. Lee of the University of California at Berkeley, and Dr. John C. Polyani of the University of Toronto—for work that led to a clear understanding of how chemical reactions occur.

German scientist Dr. Ernst Ruska won a Nobel Prize for his invention of the electron microscope.

AP/World Wide

The Prize in Physics

The electron microscope developed by Ruska—honored by the Nobel committee as "one of the most important inventions of this century"—has been used to examine metals, viruses, and proteins, among other structures, opening up wide new avenues of study in both biology and medicine.

In a single leap, the electron microscope overcame the inherent limitation of conventional light microscopes. Since the images viewed through such microscopes are formed when light bounces off the surface of the object under view, no feature smaller than the wavelength of the light (about 2,999 times the diameter of a typical atom) can be detected.

Ruska's work began in the 1920's, after several scientists had shown that electrons, like light, move in waves—and that the lengths of these waves can be as much as 100,000 times shorter than the typical wavelengths of light. Using magnetic coils, Ruska found that he could focus an electron beam in the same way that an optical lens focuses a light beam. By 1933 he had produced an electron microscope that could reveal details smaller than those visible using light microscopes.

Over the following years, many refinements were made by Ruska and others to the basic design. In early models the electron beam penetrated a thinly sliced specimen; disturbances in the electrons as the beam passed through were recorded. Later versions recorded electrons bouncing off the surface of the specimen. Present-day electron microscopes can resolve details as small as 1 angstrom (2.5 billionths of an inch).

The scanning tunneling microscope works on an entirely different principle: rather than bombarding the subject with a beam of electrons or light, it traces the surface with a stylus, in the same way that a phonograph needle plays a recording. The Nobel committee noted that the device, which was developed at an International Business Machines (IBM) laboratory in Zurich,

IBM

Drs. Heinrich Rohrer (left) and Gerd Binnig were recognized for developing the scanning tunneling microscope, which has extraordinary resolution.

although still in its infancy, has already opened up "entirely new fields . . . for the study of the structure of matter."

The tip of the microscope's stylus—a single atom—rides across the specimen surface on a thin blanket of electrons produced by a low electrical current. In the "tunneling" effect, the thickness of the electron blanket varies with the level of the current. By keeping the current constant, the stylus can be made to ride at a steady level within two atomic diameters of the surface. The movements of the stylus are fed into a computer, which produces a detailed map of the specimen.

Scanning tunneling microscopes have been developed with a horizontal resolution of 2 angstroms (5 billionths of an inch) and a vertical resolution of 0.1 angstrom (0.25 billionth of an inch), permitting even the electron bonds between atoms to be revealed. Although its initial use has been in the field of semiconductor research, the device also holds promise for other fields. Unlike the electron microscope, which requires a vacuum, it can view objects in their natural state, even underwater. Picking up on the idea, other researchers suggest that the technology may even be adapted to print circuit lines on microchips.

Ernst Ruska, who received half of the

$290,000 Nobel award, was born on December 25, 1906, in Heidelberg. He studied at the Technical University of Munich and the Technical University of Berlin, where he began his research into electron beams. He continued the work as a researcher for the Siemens Company and, after World War II, as director of the Institute for Electron Microscopy at the Fritz Haber Institute in West Berlin. He retired from active research in 1972.

Heinrich Rohrer, born June 6, 1933, in Switzerland, studied at the Federal Institute of Technology in Zurich. He began work at the IBM laboratory in 1963, and in 1978 was joined by Gerd Binnig.

Gerd Binnig, born July 20, 1947, in Frankfurt, studied at Johann Wolfgang Goethe University and earned a doctorate in physics and superconductivity.

The Prize in Chemistry

For years, scientists dealt with static models of chemical molecules—understandably, since such molecules could be studied only at rest. This all changed when Herschbach, Lee, and Polyani, working in the 1950's and 1960's, developed ways of revealing how chemical reactions take place and how energy flows during the reactions. Reaction dynamics, as the area of study is known, also bears on specific areas, such as depletion of the ozone layer in the atmosphere and the control of chemical reactions in industry.

Herschbach, working at the Lawrence Berkeley Laboratory and at Harvard, took a page from particle physics and developed a new method of studying chemical reactions: he sent beams of different types of molecules on a collision course inside a vacuum, and then measured the angular distribution and velocity of the products of the reactions that took place when they met. In the late 1960's, he was joined by Lee, who refined the technique and developed a sensitive mass spectrometer to analyze the reaction products in greater detail.

The method has yielded a wealth of information. For example, in an early experiment, beams of potassium atoms and methyl iodide were used to produce potassium iodide. By measuring the distribution of the potassium iodide molecules as a function of angle, Herschbach showed that the product is formed only when a potassium atom strikes the iodide end of a methyl iodide molecule at a certain angle. Work with other substances has shown similar patterns of distribution. The research has also revealed that temporary reaction complexes created during molecular collisions sometimes survive a surprisingly long time.

Polyani, meanwhile, worked in the area of chemiluminescence, developing a method of measuring and analyzing the weak infrared radiation emitted as newly formed molecules shed excess energy after a collision. Using an infrared spectrometer, he showed, for example, that a newly formed hydrogen chloride molecule emerged from the reaction rotating and vibrating vigorously, and shed energy in a shower of infrared photons. Using the infrared emissions as clues to the energy states of molecules, he was able to map the flow of energy as bonds break and form during this and other chemical reactions. The work was central to the development of powerful chemical lasers.

Dudley R. Herschbach, born in San Jose, California, in 1932, studied at Stanford University, where he earned a bachelor's degree in mathematics and a master's degree in chemistry. He earned a doctorate in chemical physics at Harvard and, after teaching briefly at Berkeley, returned to join the Harvard faculty in 1963.

Yuan T. Lee, born in Taiwan in 1936, became an American citizen in 1974. He studied at Taiwanese universities and at the University of California at Berkeley, earning his doctorate in 1963. He began working with Herschbach while doing postdoctoral studies at Harvard, and he later taught at the University of Chicago before returning to Berkeley in 1974.

John C. Polyani was born in Berlin in 1929 but spent most of his childhood in England, where he earned a doctorate from Manchester University in 1952. He took a position with Canada's National Research Council soon after, and in 1956 joined the faculty of the University of Toronto. His father, Michael Polyani, a noted researcher, helped create the transition state theory of chemical reactions in the 1930's.

The 1986 Nobel Prize for Chemistry was shared by three scientists who pioneered the field of reaction dynamics—the study of how chemical reactions take place and how energy flows during the reactions. The winners are (clockwise from right) Dudley R. Herschbach, John C. Polyani, and Yuan T. Lee.

T. Campion/SYGMA

Above and below: AP/Wide World

TECHNOLOGY

© François Duhamel/SYGMA

The two-passenger Voyager *became the first aircraft to fly nonstop around the world without a single refueling.*

REVIEW OF THE YEAR

TECHNOLOGY

Computer advances again took center stage in the technology arena during 1986. Unlike past years, many of the breakthroughs in 1986 focused on specialized applications and markets geared exclusively to the consumer, rather than innovations apt to have industry-wide impact. Overshadowing many of 1986's technological achievements was the spectacular global circling of the *Voyager* aircraft at year's end.

THE *VOYAGER* FLIGHT

On December 23, 1986, *Voyager,* an experimental aircraft piloted by Richard G. Rutan and Jeana Yeager, landed at Edwards Air Force Base, California, after a 25,012-mile (40,250-kilometer), nine-day, nonstop flight on a single fill-up of gas. The craft, built almost entirely of stiffened paper and plastic components, weighs 2,680 pounds (1,215 kilograms) empty, but is designed to carry nearly 9,000 pounds (4,100 kilograms) of aviation gasoline—some 1,500 gallons (6,820 liters). The two-person crew ride in a cramped cabin only 7.5 feet (2.3 meters) in length and 2 feet (0.6 meters) wide. The crew's compartment is bordered by a pair of external fuel tanks each attached to a single 111-foot (34-meter) long wing much like a pair of canoe outriggers. A rear-mounted, 110-horsepower (82-kilowatt), liquid-cooled engine permits *Voyager* to cruise at speeds of 80 to 100 miles (125 to 160 kilometers) per hour.

The crude craft, which incorporates a radical aeronautical design and advanced structural materials, was designed and built without any federal funding at an estimated cost of $550,000 by the copilot's brother, Burt Rutan, president of the Rutan Aircraft Factory, Mojave, California. According to Rutan, "It's a very strong airframe with efficient wings that permit tremendous endurance. I can imagine that at the end of the century, very large cargo aircraft and unpiloted military reconnaissance drones might look like the *Voyager.*"

DIGITAL TAPE CASSETTES

With the rapid acceptance of the compact disk (CD), several Japanese manufacturers, including Akai and Sony, announced the 1987 introduction of the next generation of high-quality micro sound reproduction systems for home use: the digital audiotape (DAT for short). The DAT works on the identical principle as the CD. During recording, sounds are converted to a series of numbers— digital images—that are stored on a compact disk or DAT. During playback the digital data are computer-converted back to their original sound and amplified through a conventional sound system. Unlike records or audiotapes, digital disks and DATs do not wear out. Since digital images are read by a laser with no direct contact with a needle or recording head, their sound quality also is considered far cleaner and purer.

The new DAT cassettes look like miniature videocassettes. They are slightly thicker than the familiar audiocassette but about one-third smaller. The playback units, however, are only one-quarter the size of an audiotape cassette deck—about the size of a pack of cigarettes. The cost of a DAT playback deck is more expensive than an audio deck: the cheapest sells for about $250. Unlike CDs, which cannot be used to copy live music or other recorded tapes, the DAT is similar to the versatile audiocassette deck and is able to rerecord and play back sounds.

MACHINES THAT OBEY VOICE COMMANDS

To solve the problem of taking your eyes off the road when dialing a mobile telephone, AT&T introduced its 1680 cellular telephone that recognizes voice patterns. After preprogramming up to 20 names, one can just pick up the car phone and say, for example, "Christopher," and within seconds be on the line to Christopher. The price: $1,750. Telephones that respond to voice patterns are not the only new machines that "listen." Dr. Richard A. Foulds, director of the Department of Rehabilitation Medicine at Tufts University, developed a robot that is keyed to an individual's vocal patterns. Designed for those unable to use their hands, the robot responds to vocal commands and dials a push-button phone by depressing keys on a small telephone switchboard. The robot costs about $6,000. A vocal-recognition microcomputer invented by a Frenchwoman, Martine Kempf, stores set commands such as "left," "right," "up," "down," etc. By repeating a command three times, the 5-pound (2.2-kilogram), shoe-box-size device, dubbed Katalavox, can direct a motorized wheelchair or control the precise movements of a surgical microscope.

COMPUTER ADDS COLOR TO OLD MOVIES

Before the advent of the color film process, hundreds of movie classics were produced in "black and white." Even after the introduction of movies in color, many producers, either for economic or artistic considerations, produced a myriad of superior black-and-white films. Now, with increased consumer demand for color movies, particularly for presentation on television, a new process has been developed to add color to old black-and-white films. The process, developed independently by two competing firms, Vidcolor Image, Inc., Toronto, Ontario, and Color Systems Technology of Los Angeles, California, has been applied to such classics as *Yankee Doodle Dandy, Topper, It's a Wonderful Life, The Maltese Falcon,* a selection of Laurel and Hardy features, and the early TV show *"The Honeymooners."*

Coloring must be done on a frame-by-frame basis. First, an electronic scanner breaks each frame into an array of 525,000 dots called *pixels*. An art director determines a specific color for every subject on the screen, and a computer does the rest by assigning one of 4,096 increments of color to each pixel on every frame. The process costs more than $200,000 for a standard black-and-white movie.

AIDING ART RESTORATION

A technique developed by physicist John Asmus of the University of California in San Diego uses a computer to assist in cleaning and art restoration. A transparent color photograph of a painting is analyzed by a computer, which then reproduces the image in digital form. This computerized form of image enhancement led to the discovery that Leonardo da Vinci's *Mona Lisa* wore pearls around her neck that were painted over. Art historians are unsure whether the pearls were originally painted by Leonardo or a later "artist" who tried to improve upon the master's genius.

BENEDICT A. LEERBURGER

Adding color to old movies has met with success, despite protests that the films are degraded artistically. Below, a scene from a Laurel and Hardy film, Way Out West, *as it appeared in black and white and after colorization (right).*

Photos: Courtesy Hal Roach Studios

Chunnel for the Channel

by John Free

Colorful British and French flags bedecked city hall in the French city of Lille in early 1986. Schoolchildren waved tiny flags, and bands played the *Marseillaise* and *God Save the Queen* before French President François Mitterrand called it "a grandiose vision of the future." British Prime Minister Margaret Thatcher, although not fluent in French, dubbed it *passionnant*—exciting. It should be exciting; it's been delayed more than 200 years.

"It" is something that was set in motion by an agreement, signed in Lille, between the French and British: the construction of the Chunnel—a tunnel under the English Channel—to link the countries.

The Chunnel project oozes superlatives. It

The 22-mile-long tubes beneath the English Channel will link Calais, France, with Dover, England.

© Scott MacNeill

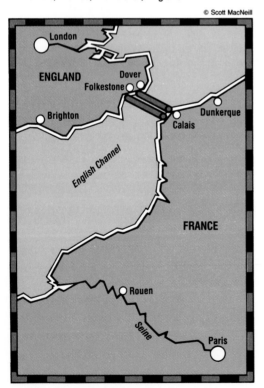

will be the largest civil engineering project in the history of Western Europe. Thousands of workers will support some of the world's most advanced tunnel-boring technology to push three parallel tunnels the 31 miles (50 kilometers) from Cheriton, in Kent, England, to Frethun, in northern France. Work is slated to begin this year. The first paying customers should zip between England and France in 1993. Following the announcement, I visited London to learn more about this frequently delayed project.

The most remarkable thing about the Chunnel is that the countries now seem serious about building it. Perhaps the earliest tunnel proposal came from French engineer Nicolas Desmaret in 1753. Napoleon resurrected the idea in 1802. In the 1870's, British and French companies began drilling shafts from opposite sides, then quit. The idea surfaced again in 1907, 1916, 1924, 1930, and the early 1960's. An article in July 1960 outlined plans. That project, actually started in the 1970's, halted when the British pulled out, saying it would cost too much.

Why This Time?

So why will it work this time? Says Bill Shakespeare, a publicist for the British group promoting the project: "We're convinced the political will to build it exists. The reality of the traffic buildup across the channel forces a solution of some kind on both governments."

The numbers bear him out. Surveys estimate that cross-channel traffic will double by the year 2000. That would far exceed the capacity of present cross-channel ferries, which are subject to delays from weather and labor conflicts. The chunnel will initially handle 1,000 vehicles an hour. Its maximum capacity is four times that—enough to handle traffic well into the 21st century.

Other reasons to expect success: Technology is available to do the job, and planning is exhaustive at the Channel Tunnel Group and its French partner, France Manche, a privately

© Scott MacNeill

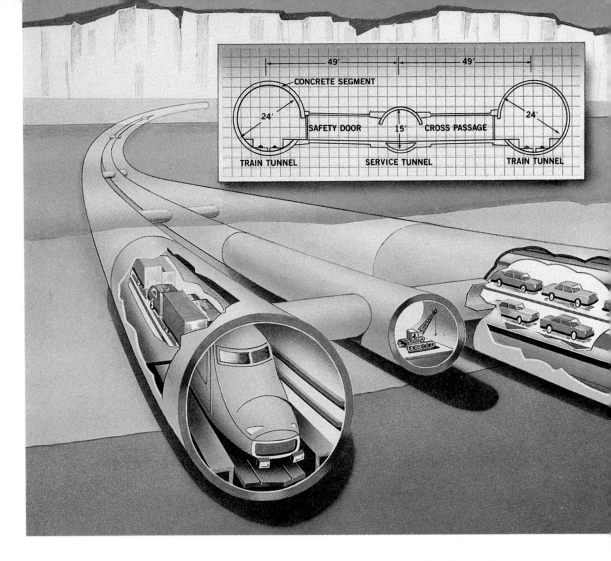

Electric shuttle trains will transport passenger cars, trucks, and buses underneath the English Channel. The service-ventilation tunnel will run between the two train tunnels (above). Final tests are being performed to ensure that the planned tunnel size is adequate to accommodate the swaying motion of a variety of train sizes. Most of the tunnel will be bored through chalk marl, a soft rock impervious to water. On the French side (below), where the tunnel passes through fractured chalk beds, a grouting technique will be used to form a series of protective cones to reinforce the tunnel walls.

© Walter Hortens

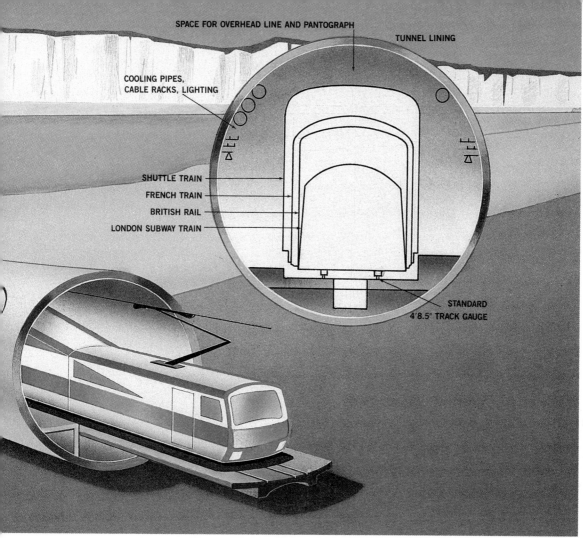

SPACE FOR OVERHEAD LINE AND PANTOGRAPH

TUNNEL LINING

COOLING PIPES, CABLE RACKS, LIGHTING

SHUTTLE TRAIN
FRENCH TRAIN
BRITISH RAIL
LONDON SUBWAY TRAIN

STANDARD 4'8.5" TRACK GAUGE

© Walter Hortens

funded consortium selected for the project. To uncover details about their scheme, I first visited Michael Gordon, managing director of the Channel Tunnel Group, at his temporary offices in a trim central-London house.

"The costs of our construction are fairly predictable," says the Cambridge-educated mechanical engineer, showing me drawings and summaries of proposals that fill a long bookshelf. "It's conventional tunneling through a medium that is well known and well researched."

Chunnel Specifics

The project calls for two 31-mile (50-kilometer)-long, 24-foot (7.3-meter)-diameter train tunnels with a 15-foot (4.6-meter)-diameter service tunnel between them. Every 1,125 feet (343 meters), the three shafts will be connected with cross-links. "You can walk through to the ser-

vice tunnel," says Gordon. "These cross-links are necessary for security in case you have a breakdown or fire."

The train tunnels are 31 miles (50 kilometers) long but will cross the channel at its narrowest point, 22 miles (35 kilometers) from shore to shore. They will be carved through a chalk layer about 130 feet (40 meters) below the channel floor. Double-deck shuttle trains for passenger cars and other shuttles for trucks and buses will cross the channel in 30 minutes—at speeds up to 100 miles (161 kilometers) per hour.

Although technology planned for the privately financed project is conventional and engineers know the geology, no one expects the job to be easy. Most of the work will be done by giant moles—tunnel-boring machines with circular cutting faces the size of the tunnel being bored. The giant cutter heads, driven by up to

2,400 horsepower (150 kilowatts), push dozens of carbon-steel discs against the tunnel face with up to 50,000 pounds (22,680 kilograms) of pressure. Fortunately, most of the path planned for the Chunnel project is through a chalk-clay material. "It's an ideal material," says Gordon. "It's easy to bore through and almost impervious to water."

Because the chalk-clay substance is almost waterproof, the workers will not have to pressurize the tunnel. "What we're going to do," explains senior engineer Colin Kirkland, "is drive the 15-foot (4.6-meter) pilot, or service, tunnel several kilometers ahead of the other tubes. About every 150 feet (46 meters) we'll stop and probe ahead another 100 feet (30 meters) to find out if there are any areas likely to cause problems." If faults are detected, holes will be bored into the rock and injected with a cementlike grout to seal, strengthen, and reinforce the area ahead. "At the same time we'll drive a fan of holes from the pilot tunnel into the path of the other two tunnels and similarly study the ground and pretreat it where necessary," says Kirkland.

As the tunneling machines advance, the cylindrical hole left behind will be lined with either concrete or cast iron, depending on conditions.

Pressure Shields

Drilling problems for the French are more complex. Unlike the British, they must tunnel through water-filled fractured layers of rock to reach the chalk-clay tunneling layer below. Says Jean Renault, director general of the French construction team: "We have a good idea of what we're going to meet and have planned our methods accordingly." The first part of this strategy is to use a different kind of tunnel-boring machine. The French have been negotiating with Japan's Kawasaki to obtain machines with full-face pressure shields. These machines develop a powerful localized pressure with a slurry or other materials to counteract water pressure at the drilling face.

How do you ensure that French and British workers starting 31 miles (50 kilometers) from each other will meet in the middle of the channel? Lasers will play a key role from start to finish, said project engineers I talked with. The trick is to lay out survey lines across the channel above ground, then use these to align lasers that help steer the drilling machines.

Because a laser beam is perfectly straight and spreads very little over a great distance, it has become a useful tool for guiding tunnel-drilling machines. Normally, the drill operator watched where a laser beam falls in front of the tunneling machine after it passes through a set of cross hairs in the rear. The operator keeps the beam centered by adjusting support legs as drilling progresses.

But clouds of dust and strong vibrations make this centering job tough. So automatic-steering systems have been developed in which the guiding laser beam hits a light-sensitive panel of photodiodes. A microcomputer in the system then calculates the machine's position to within a few inches (centimeters) and makes necessary corrections. "With lasers," says John Taberner, engineering director of the British tunnel group, "you can have a tolerance of, say, two centimeters [0.8 inch] whether you're going 1 mile [1.6 kilometers] or 10 miles [16 kilometers]."

Tunnels for Cars?

One unresolved problem of the project involves drive-through automobile tunnels. The current plans do not call for any; all vehicles travel on special shuttle trains. But the agreement between the British and French governments says that the tunnel group must build a car tunnel before the year 2000 or lose its monopoly.

Whether that can be done is uncertain. The tunnel group studied a drive-through tunnel and concluded that—at least for now—it isn't feasible. There are two reasons. First: "A road tunnel with sufficient safety for two lanes must be in excess of 33 feet [10 meters] in diameter," says Kirkland. But the chalk tunneling layer thins near the center and the French side, so tunnel walls may not have enough structural support overhead, or be too close to the soft clay layer below.

Second, technology cannot yet overcome the smog caused by vehicles moving at slow speeds for safety. "You would have to have massive injections of air into the tunnel that would result in winds of some 70 miles [112 kilometers] per hour," explains Gordon.

Still, the tunnel group plans to probe the thickness of the chalk layer as the Chunnel is built to see whether it could support 33-foot (10-meter) car tunnels. "We would also pretreat the ground as we go through this time," says Taberner. "Then the decision to build a road tunnel could be made later on the basis of available traffic."

PERSONAL ROBOTS
OF TOMORROW by Mike Higgins

Robots are now beginning to follow computers from the workplace into the home. In 1975 personal computers began to spread outside the ranks of the talented hobbyist and into the mainstream of our lives. Now it's time for personal robots to make the same move.

Robots can already be used to entertain young children. Their entertainment value for older children and adults, however, is for the most part limited to the intellectual challenge of programming them. But future robots will be complete home-entertainment centers, able to sing and dance and tell jokes, as well as control all your electronic entertainment equipment—TV, radio, stereo, computer games, and telephone.

Your robot will either have its entertainment equipment built in or be connected to it electronically. Just tell your robot you would

© Ellis Herwig/Taurus

An educational robot holds the attention of a group of kindergarten students by playing a learning game with them.

like to see the news, and it will turn on the TV, search its data base for a station carrying news at that particular time of day, and tune it in. Do you have a sudden impulse to listen to Tchaikovsky's *1812* Overture at high volume? Just tell the robot, and it will select the right compact disc, switch on the stereo, turn up the volume, and let it rip!

Computer games and wireless telephone can easily be built into the robot. All you'll have to do is call the robot to have these functions brought to you wherever you are. No more running out of the bathroom, dripping wet, to pick up the phone. Let the phone come to you. And if you don't want to take the call, have the robot take a message.

Robotic Educators

After entertainment, education is the next easiest application for a personal robot. After all, robots have one of the attributes a teacher needs most—infinite patience. Robots are capable of repeating the same material over and over again, day after day if necessary, without ever becoming tired, bored, or frustrated.

Using principles developed for computer-aided instruction, robots can adjust the pace of their delivery to each student's ability to learn. Tests can be administered and scored automatically, with automatic repetition of any material that the student has failed to absorb.

Perhaps the greatest value of robots in education is their ability to motivate even the most jaded students. With robots in the classroom and at home, our educational system may begin to recover some of the effectiveness it seems to have lost in recent years.

Other Complex Tasks

Entertainment and educational applications are relatively easy to build into personal robots, because, for these applications, the interface between the robot and the real world is not very complex. Tasks requiring the robot to act as a companion, security guard, or servant are more difficult because of the many complex interactions necessary. But some of the applications that we can only talk about today will almost certainly become part of our everyday lives in the near future.

Personal robots could be the solution to the growing problem of caring for our elderly population. As more and more people pass retirement age and begin to need assistance in taking care of their daily needs, our social systems for helping the aged are becoming strained. Instead of dedicating one young and healthy individual to look after one elderly or infirm person, we could use robots to perform 90 percent of the fetching and carrying chores these people sometimes cannot manage themselves.

Similarly, as an increasing number of people find themselves faced with a choice between career advancement and caring for a child, personal robots can help out. Obviously, a robot will not be able to do all the things a parent does, but at least the robot can perform some of the more mundane functions, giving parents more time to spend pursuing a career.

With advances in artificial intelligence and expert systems software, robots will eventually be able to learn, to reason, and to make decisions. This will greatly enhance their usefulness to us. It is not unreasonable to foresee an "artificial personality" to go with the artificial intelligence, making robots even more practical as mechanical pets and companions. The Heath Hero Jr. robot already possesses the first traces of an artificial personality.

Personal robots will definitely become sophisticated enough to perform basic household chores in the very near future. One of the first applications will surely be vacuuming floors. With improved manual dexterity and visual acuity, more complicated tasks such as dishwasher loading should not be too far behind.

The Sociology of Robots

As personal robots begin to be more sophisticated and intelligent, we will have to answer some questions that have never come up before. It's only a matter of time before concerned citizens' groups spring up to demand civil rights for robots. "Turning off a robot's power supply is a

At home, personal robots will also double as entertainment centers (above). And it's only a matter of time before robots become regular shoppers at the local supermarket (left).

In the home of the future, mundane household chores like vacuuming will be relegated to the "domestic" robot.

form of murder," they might say. Robots will be seen as "mechanical slaves," and a small but determined minority can be expected to fight for "robot emancipation."

While liberal extremists are trying to give robots their freedom, conservative extremists may well wage a war against the incursion of "mechanical monsters" into areas where only humans should be allowed. Personal robots that look and act like people may be viewed as "evil" or "unnatural" creations that should be banned. On top of all this, people who stand to lose their jobs to robots may resort to violence and vandalism.

Some people, on the other hand, may decide that robots are so much easier to get along with than people that they will refuse to interact with people anymore. We may need "robot-abuse" clinics, just as we already have drug- and alcohol-abuse clinics.

Personal robots could also be used for objectionable purposes. There's always one in a crowd who takes a good thing to excess, and this could be a potential problem area once personal robots become widely available.

The most obviously undesirable application of robots is their use in criminal activities. Again, it's only a matter of time before the first personal robot rolls into a bank and says, "Fill this bag with money or I'll blow this place up."

Special methods will have to be developed to combat crimes involving the use of robots.

Eventually we will need an entirely new body of law to deal with robots. There will be conflicts over liability for accidental damage, responsibility for deliberate damage, and regulations specifying where robots are allowed to go and where they may be banned. Robots will undoubtedly give rise to enough legal problems to start a lucrative new legal specialty.

The Super-Robot

New combinations of microprocessor and biogenetic technology may lead to computers based on living cells instead of silicon. If successful, such new technology could increase the power and capacity of today's microcomputers by several orders of magnitude. Ultimately a robot built with such a powerful electronic "brain" could become a "super-robot," able to converse in ordinary English (and other languages), including dialects and slang.

Such a super-robot could have senses equal to ours in the range of physical quantities we can detect, and extending into regions we are unable to sense directly, such as ultrasonic sound and infrared and ultraviolet light. With suitably advanced arms and legs and sophisticated artificial intelligence, the super-robot could do virtually all our manual labor for us.

The super-robot could take care of all the housework, look after the children (or the grandparents), and cater to all our entertainment needs. It could be an accomplished musician, a first-class dancer, and a star actor. With a sufficiently humanlike appearance, the super-robot could become a sexual surrogate—some women have even suggested this application of personal robots as a way of ridding themselves forever of troublesome boyfriends. And some people might even want to marry a robot!

The super-robot need not be limited to manual labor. With the equivalent of an entire reference library stored in its memory, the super-robot could go into the consulting business, solving complex problems or diagnosing rare diseases. This is not just wishful thinking—systems programmed with the combined knowledge and experience of the world's top medical specialists can already outperform human doctors in cases involving difficult diagnoses.

The Self-aware Robot

The most significant question facing us as we consider the potential power of personal robots is this: Can robots ever become self-aware? For-

Robots hold great potential for the disabled. Seeing-eye robots could become invaluable to the blind.

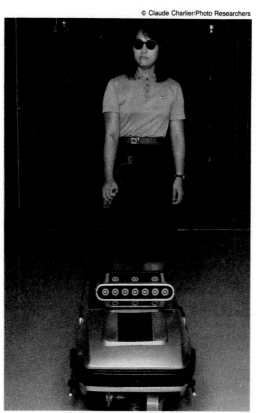

© Claude Charlier/Photo Researchers

get, for the moment, the technical difficulties involved in building the super-robot. Just assume for the sake of argument that it can be done (a reasonable assumption in view of our technological progress since the beginning of this century). What would be the implications of our ability to create a self-aware super-robot? What if the super-robot not only became self-aware, but decided it wanted to run its own life without a bunch of humans always telling it what to do?

Suppose the super-robot decided it didn't want to spend the rest of its "life" cleaning the house and taking care of the kids. In the case of a self-aware super-robot, civil rights questions would certainly not be out of order. We may find ourselves obliged to protect the super-robot from total and irreversible loss of power (life), to free it from slave labor (liberty), and allow it to choose how it spends its time (the pursuit of happiness).

These philosophical and ethical questions are very real, regardless of any personal opinions about whether or not the super-robot will ever evolve. In fact, the best answer to the old question of "What are personal robots good for?" may be that they will make us think about the very nature of life itself and our place in the universe.

Are we trapped in the ultimate irony of working feverishly to design our own replacements as the highest form of evolution on the planet? Should we burn all robot builders at the stake as punishment for treason against the entire human race?

Let's address the second question first. It would be futile to ban the building of robots, because they can be built in a basement by anyone with a few simple tools and a basic familiarity with mechanics and microcomputer technology. As to the first question, Isaac Asimov (the man who invented the fictional equivalent of the personal robot 40 years ago) believes future artificial intelligence will be so different from human intelligence that the two will never compete. Asimov's story *The Bicentennial Man* tells of a robot with capabilities similar to our "super-robot." The robot in the story becomes self-aware and develops a single, overriding ambition: to become as much like a human as possible.

No one knows how the real-life super-robot story will end. But it seems likely that, one day in the distant future, we will have an opportunity to find out.

The 10,000 mph AIRLINER

by Gene Bylinsky

Around the country, wind tunnels are rumbling, computers whirring, construction workers expanding test buildings. From the National Aeronautics and Space Administration's (NASA's) Langley Research Center in Virginia and Edwards Air Force Base in southern California to the design centers at Boeing in Seattle and Pratt & Whitney in West Palm Beach, Florida, scientists and engineers are burning with an excitement not seen since the heady days of the Apollo program that put men on the moon. Many aeronautical designers are postponing retirement, and hundreds of others are trying to get into the act. Ron Samborsky, project manager at Aerojet TechSystems in Sacramento, California, a subcontractor, echoes the experience at participating companies, laboratories, and research centers: "Hardly a day goes by without a request from someone to be transferred to this program. I wish I could take them all."

The cause of the excitement: hypersonic flight, which by most definitions begins around 3,800 miles (6,000 kilometers) per hour. Achieving it, many experts believe, will launch a revolution in military and civilian aircraft as far-reaching as the one the jet engine produced. If their promise turns into reality, these so-called aerospace planes will come in a variety of sizes, shapes, and functions. They will reach unheard-of speeds: some will zoom into orbit at 18,000 miles (29,000 kilometers) per hour, 25 times the speed of sound, and crease the edge of space 350,000 feet (107,000 meters) above the earth. That's nearly ten times as fast and more than three times as high as an airplane has ever flown.

The earliest experimental aerospace plane, the X-30, could fly as soon as 1993. But the version of greatest interest to the jet-lagged traveler is the passenger-carrying Orient Express, so named because it could cross the Pacific nonstop in two hours, would cruise at up to 10,000 miles (16,000 kilometers) per hour, or about Mach 14 (Mach 1 is the speed of sound, 760 miles [1,225 kilometers] per hour at sea level), and have a range of 8,000 miles (13,000 kilometers). The British-French Concorde, by contrast, is downright sluggish and short-legged, with a speed of just 1,350 miles (2,175 kilometers) per hour and a range of 3,800 miles (6,100 kilometers).

High Cruising Altitude

Putting the world's major cities in easy touch with each other—New York to London in just over an hour, Paris to Sydney in about three hours—the Orient Express will take off with a roar not much different from that of today's jetliners. But its climbing angle will be steeper, pushing passengers back in their seats and subjecting them to pressure not unlike that felt by the driver of a hot sports car flooring it from a standing start. Does that mean that a grandmother or someone with heart disease could not fly aboard this dream machine? Not at all, according to experts.

At the cruising altitude of 100,000 feet (30,500 meters), twice that of the Concorde, passengers will have no sensation of speed, since they will be too far above clouds and geographical features to perceive the plane's motion. Designers may sacrifice such niceties as individual windows to save weight, substituting small liquid crystal screens connected to external closed-circuit TV cameras. A single large viewing window might be installed as a concession, however. Through it the passengers could see, say, the California coast from San Francisco Bay to San Diego and, above, layers of the earth's atmosphere shading from blue into the deep black of space.

One thing will probably remain unchanged. Says former test pilot A. Scott Crossfield, 65, who made 30 flights into the stratosphere aboard the X-15 rocket plane: "You have breakfast in New York and tomorrow night's supper in Peking because you have

The hypersonic Orient Express (above), still in the planning stage, will cross the Pacific Ocean nonstop in two hours. Below, the X-30 aerospace plane, which could fly as soon as 1993, will take off horizontally from an ordinary runway.

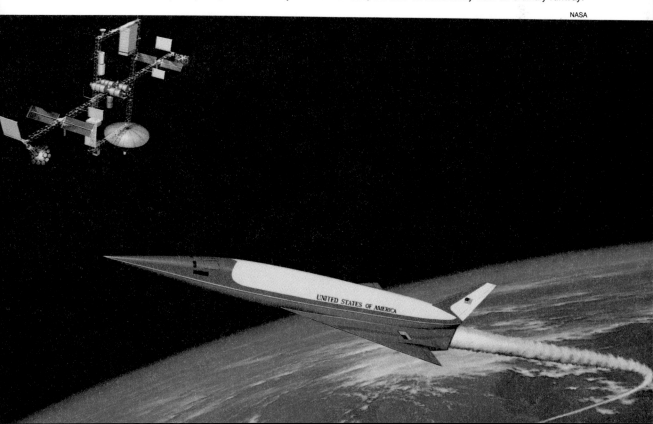

crossed the international date line. You fly back and have tonight's supper in New York. Meanwhile, your bags go to Rio.''

Whether the Orient Express ever flies will depend on the success of the National Aerospace Plane Program, which is gathering speed. The first hypersonic plane, the X-30, would be about the size of a DC-9 airliner and a third as large as the Orient Express. Seven years from now, if the schedule holds, two test pilots will take off from a conventional runway in the X-30 and zoom to about 200,000 feet (61,000 meters) at 18,000 miles (29,000 kilometers) per hour. Novel air-breathing engines will carry it to that lofty plateau. Then rocket engines using conventional liquid hydrogen and liquid oxygen fuels would ignite, sending the X-30 into orbit. After completing its mission in space, it would reenter the atmosphere just as the shuttle does and land on an ordinary runway.

New Technologies Arising

In the complex flight, the X-30 will serve as the test bed for a whole new flock of different hypersonic aircraft. To make them possible, government labs and commercial aerospace and engine companies are rapidly developing a sunburst of new technologies: propulsion systems, materials that will withstand the searing heat of those mind-boggling speeds, and airframes that combine, in effect, a huge flying thermos bottle containing supercold hydrogen that will both cool the plane's surfaces (some heated to 5,000° F [2,760° C], half as hot as the surface of the sun) and fuel its furnace of an engine.

First will come a full-fledged orbiting aerospace plane based on the X-30. Such a craft could serve as a successor to the space shuttle and a truck to haul components of the Strategic Defense Initiative (SDI), or ''Star Wars,'' into orbit. The aerospace plane could cut the cost of flights to orbit to a tenth of those of the shuttle. At some distant date it could even be used as a civilian transport, taking passengers on pleasure trips to space station hostels like the futuristic Howard Johnson's in *2001: A Space Odyssey.*

The second version of the aerospace plane could become a potent new U.S. weapon. Capable of zipping along near the top of the atmosphere at speeds approaching 18,000 miles (29,000 kilometers) per hour, it would be the most elusive spy plane ever built, or a fast-response fighter-bomber that could fly anywhere on earth in about two hours. Fleets of such military craft could be airborne by the end

of the century—just 13 years from now. Reflecting the importance the military places on the aerospace plane, the Defense Department is picking up 80 percent of the development tab for the X-30, NASA the remaining 20 percent.

Finally the civilian Orient Express would emerge, possibly leapfrogging any successor to the supersonic Concorde. It would actually be technically simpler to build than the earlier planes, since it would not need to reach orbit or fly faster than 10,000 miles (16,100 kilometers) per hour. The Orient Express will be designed and produced not by the government but by aircraft builders such as Boeing, Lockheed, and McDonnell Douglas, which are already conducting preliminary studies. Development could start years before any military aerospace plane flies. A propulsion system that works at those lower speeds could be peeled off along the way to perfecting more complex engines for an orbital aerospace plane.

First, though, comes the awesome challenge of building the X-30, the test vehicle for the combination orbiter–hypersonic airplane. ''The danger we face is promising too much,'' says Robert M. Williams, 42, director of the program and an intense aerodynamicist at the Pentagon's Defense Advanced Research Projects Agency (DARPA). His deputy, Air Force Brigadier General Kenneth E. Staten, 47, echoes his boss: ''We know there are risks. There will be disappointments, setbacks, even failures.''

Some critics feel that the aerospace plane managers may have bitten off too big a slice of an untried high-tech cake. Willis M. Hawkins, 72, a retired senior vice president of Lockheed and now a consultant to the company, suggests that the aerospace plane could come a cropper because the requirement that it attain orbit will add severe weight and propulsion problems. A veteran of Lockheed's fabled Skunk Works, where such remarkable spy planes as the U-2 and the SR-71 Blackbird were developed, Hawkins would have been happier if program managers had settled for a hypersonic plane that did not have to reach orbit.

Sonic Boom Muffled

The idea of an aerospace plane is not new. In the early 1950's the U.S. Air Force experimented with various programs, including Dynasoar, a shuttlelike craft that would have been rocketed into space to return like an airplane. The closest anyone came was the X-15. Dropped from be-

Technology related to that of the Orient Express *and the X-30 will be used in aircraft now being designed for the U.S. Air Force. Above, the Advanced Tactical Fighter (ATF) will be highly maneuverable at supersonic cruising speeds. The F-15E fighter jet at left will excel at low-altitude strikes and night missions.*

neath the wing of an airborne B-52 bomber, it made 250 flights, briefly attaining hypersonic speeds approaching 4,500 miles (7,240 kilometers) per hour and flying as high as 354,000 feet (107,900 meters). The Air Force had plans to turn the X-15 into an orbiter, but the shift to earth-to-orbit rocket-based space exploration in the 1960's put all those aviation developments on the shelf for more than 25 years. The fastest, highest-flying airplane today—the Air Force's

SR-71 Blackbird spy plane, which reaches speeds of 2,100 miles (3,380 kilometers) per hour and altitudes of 80,000 feet (129,000 meters)—is now 25 years old.

The Concorde first flew in the late 1960's; the U.S. plan to build a bigger, faster SST died in 1971 because of concern about ear-shattering sonic booms and potential damage to the ozone layer in the atmosphere that protects life on earth against cosmic radiation. (The Concorde

Computer simulations of aircraft design help engineers determine areas most affected by stress from air pressure.

flies below the ozone layer. Its sonic booms have confined it to over-the-ocean routes, making it a technological, but not a commercial, success.)

Because the Orient Express would fly so high and so fast, its sonic booms would be muffled to the point where they would become mere sonic peeps. It would soar above the ozone layer; since it would burn a mix of hydrogen and atmospheric oxygen as fuel, with water vapor as the end product, it would not damage the atmosphere.

Active Cooling at Mach 25

The aerospace plane was resurrected in its present form by DARPA's Bob Williams. In 1982 he was investigating the use of hypersonic propulsion for missiles and became curious about how high an airplane could fly using an air-breathing engine. Since no one knew the answer, Williams recruited an expert in propulsion and a specialist in materials. He even had a computer wizard run simulations for him. A little drama ensued once Williams began egging on the computer expert to fly faster and faster.

"I'm up to Mach 12, but it's getting awfully hot—this thing looks like it's going to melt," he warned Williams at one point. Williams told him to cool things off by flying higher, where the air is thinner and creates less friction. The computer model started getting too hot even at a higher altitude, but Williams reassured the man that he could go still faster since DARPA was developing advanced materials to cope with that kind of heat.

When the man reported that he had pushed even the new materials to their limit, Williams told him to try active cooling. Williams foresaw a double benefit: the hydrogen fuel, the most efficient available, would be pumped around parts of the aerospace plane to cool it—and the fuel would burn still more efficiently when heated. "There was a long silence for about two weeks," Williams recalls. "Finally, about 12:30 or 1 o'clock one night, I get this phone call: 'All right, damn it, Williams, I've been up for a whole 24 hours running this thing. I'm at Mach 25 and 200,000 feet. What do you want now?' I said, 'Nothing more—we're there. We're at orbital speed.' "

© John Madere

A mockup of the engine for the aerospace plane is set in a wind tunnel for simulated exposure to hypersonic speed.

In 1984 Williams got a go-ahead for the program along with funds for some critical experiments, mainly in propulsion and materials. He assembled a small team of specialists from the Air Force, NASA, and the Navy. (The Navy, responsible for keeping track of what goes on in the oceans, is interested in the aerospace plane's surveillance capabilities.) The team worked secretly under the code name Copper Canyon.

Project Gearing Up

Reviewing the work last year, DARPA decided that the program merited a big expansion. It presented the project to top officials of the agencies involved, including the Star Wars program. "It met with incredible support in all quarters," says Williams. "It was as if this had been a dream of a lot of people. Each agency was willing to offer up funds from its own budget to apply toward this program. Shortly after that, the president spoke about the program and it took off like a shooting star." He adds: "Now I have to make good on all those claims."

In April 1986, the National Aerospace Plane Program awarded about $450 million in initial contracts. After about three years the Pentagon and NASA will decide whether progress justifies building the X-30. To make sure it does, Williams zooms around the country with evangelical zeal. Says an executive at one contractor company: "I think of Bob Williams as a male Joan of Arc. You know, the Lord came down and touched this guy on the top of the head and said to him, 'Baby, go and make hypersonics real.' And he's doing it."

To do it will require what Williams describes as "bringing the technological might of the U.S. to bear on one of the most engrossing technological challenges this country has ever faced." He'll need every ounce of that might, because much of what the aerospace plane will have to do is unusual or even unique. For one thing, while the fastest aircraft today merely push air molecules out of the way, the aerospace plane will go so fast that it will literally tear the molecules apart. The molecular fragments will heat the plane's skin to the point where it will act as a catalyst, producing new molecular combinations that could damage the skin.

The aerospace plane builders' biggest challenge, the propulsion system, must operate at a stunning variety of speeds under varying flight conditions. It will probably consist of a number of different engines, each switched on as needed. To allow conventional takeoff, the aerospace plane must be equipped with an air-breathing engine, most likely a turbojet similar to those on passenger airliners. To push the plane beyond Mach 2 (1,520 miles, or 2,446 kilometers, per hour), a simple ramjet engine will take over. A ramjet contains no whirling turbines, only a cone-shaped structure facing the onrushing air, which it compresses, or "rams," and slows down for burning.

But the ramjet is limited to both ends of the speed scale: it cannot gather enough air to work efficiently at subsonic speeds, and it becomes inefficient again at Mach 5 (3,500 miles, or 5,630 kilometers, per hour). At that point a supersonic combustion ramjet—"scramjet," for short—must take over. ("Supersonic" refers to the speed of air through the engine.) The scramjet is the most elegantly simple of all air-breathing engines: it's merely an elongated box with some angled struts inside to slow down the incoming air, and a combustion area in the back into which fuel is injected. The trick is to ignite the fuel-air mixture quickly as it rushes through the scramjet. Model scramjets have been tested in NASA wind tunnels and elsewhere up to Mach 20, but never in flight. Computer projec-

tions do show, however, that the scramjet will work at the aerospace plane's intended top speed of Mach 25.

Supercomputer Simulation

What gives the aerospace plane designers a lot of confidence right now is their rapidly evolving ability to use supercomputers to simulate the effects of air pressure and heat on a hypothetical airframe. Scientists can now "fly" the aerospace plane inside a computer—not quite as well as real-life flight, but nonetheless allowing designers to try out a large number of configurations under varying conditions.

For the skin to survive stresses never before encountered in sustained flight, designers are banking on man's increasing ability to fashion specialized materials. Those now under development include new alloys produced by so-called rapid solidifications technology, which uses astounding cooling rates of up to 1 million degrees Fahrenheit per second to make materials with such desirable properties as light weight, great strength, and heat resistance. The abrupt cooling realigns the atoms in ways that do not occur under ordinary conditions. Another promising technology: composites, which join at least two different materials such as carbon filaments and a metal matrix to yield a unique set of useful characteristics.

But even the best of today's materials can withstand temperatures no higher than about 2,800° F (1,540° C)—not good enough for the aerospace plane. Its needle-sharp nose, along with the leading edges of its wings and tail, will be exposed to the greatest air resistance. It was this problem that led Williams to think of using supercooled hydrogen to soak up the heat.

Using hydrogen for fuel introduces new challenges on the ground, although the danger of fire is less than with conventional fuels because its ignition temperature of 1,085° F (585° C) is twice that of aviation-grade kerosene. NASA studies show less hazard to the crew, passengers, and the immediate surroundings from crash-generated fire in a hydrogen-fueled aircraft than in one powered by conventional hydrocarbon fuels. NASA has learned how to handle supercold hydrogen in space launches.

Economic Viability

For civilian flight, proponents of the Orient Express make the surprising claim that a 300- to 500-seat hypersonic airliner could be not only

An early model of a hypersonic aircraft is prepared by a technician for simulated high-altitude exposure.

© John Madere

more successful commercially than the Concorde but as profitable as subsonic aircraft like the Boeing 747. The Air Force has studied the economics of a hydrogen-fueled Orient Express that would fly at speeds between 4,500 and 9,000 miles (7,240 and 14,480 kilometers) per hour. The study found that direct operating costs per flight could be competitive with current subsonic aircraft. That conclusion assumes a fast turnaround, although the Orient Express could be so hot an hour after landing that it would need a liquid nitrogen bath to cool it off for ground maintenance.

The conclusion also rests on the much shorter flight times for the Orient Express—about two hours from New York to Tokyo, versus 14 hours on a 747—as well as the need for only one crew for the run. "You can really get a day's work out of it," says Benjamin Lightfoot, Northwest Airlines' vice president for maintenance and engineering. He has calculated that in less than 24 hours, an Orient Express could fly twice across the Atlantic and four times across the Pacific—a total of 27,600 miles (44,410 kilometers), or the equivalent of more than once around the earth.

Obviously the economic viability of the Orient Express will depend on growth in long-distance passenger traffic as well as still uncertain development and production costs. By the end of this century, McDonnell Douglas expects air traffic between the U.S. and the Pacific rim countries—Japan, China, South Korea, Singapore, among others—to soar from the present 6 million passengers a year to more than 30 million, making the Pacific the world's busiest air travel corridor. No one knows yet how much an Orient Express will cost the airlines, although some authorities have speculated that the price would be $200 million to $300 million per plane (versus about $100 million for a 747). Lightfoot says an airline probably couldn't get away with charging more than 10 to 15 percent more than present-day fares for hypersonic flight.

The probable development cost of the first two X-30s, plus an earthbound test model, is known, however: about $3 billion. This is not a high price for entry into a new arena of flight. The Concorde precedent suggests that if the U.S. doesn't build the aerospace plane, others will. Research is already under way in Britain, West Germany, Japan, and most likely the Soviet Union, which has always had a strong tradition in aviation. The British want to build a craft that will go directly into orbit, like the

© John Madere

Molten metal drawn from huge vats is rapidly solidified at cooling rates up to 1,000,000° F per second. The result: specialized lightweight alloys of extraordinary strength and heat resistance for the aircraft's skin.

U.S. version. The West Germans are pushing a two-stage vehicle that would piggyback a small space shuttle high into the atmosphere and launch it into orbit from there; the first stage could also serve as a basis for developing a hypersonic transport. Lightfoot fears that the Japanese may try to beat the U.S. into the potentially lucrative market for an Orient Express.

Bob Williams and General Staten claim that Americans could do the job best because they are the world's best engineers. That is doubtless a chauvinistic exaggeration, but Americans have shown themselves to be the world's best aeronautical engineers. Says General Staten: "The aerospace plane is very much in the American personality. It's the kind of thing we've done before. It stimulates the pioneer in all of us."

Standing up to
EARTHQUAKES by James R. Chiles

The Latinoamericana Tower stands undamaged amid the devastation of the 1985 Mexico City earthquake.

On September 19, 1985, the most disastrous earthquake in North American history struck Mexico City. More than 20,000 people were killed after a layer of wet clay amplified a distant temblor (earthquake) and set downtown buildings rocking. Hundreds of the buildings collapsed, crushing or trapping their inhabitants. But it could have been far worse. Thousands more buildings stood, including the landmark Latinoamericana Tower.

That 43-story tower (designed in part by an engineering professor from the United States and built in 1954) has now been through two serious earthquakes with no damage of any consequence. Decades of observation of the effects of earthquakes lie behind the fact that engineers now know how to build structures able to resist quakes so strong they would throw people off their feet. A lot of that engineering development was done in the United States, particularly in California.

California gets practically all the notoriety for earthquakes in the United States, but it doesn't get all the shocks; states generating major quakes have included Massachusetts, South Carolina, Missouri, Alaska, Nevada, Texas, Utah, Arizona, and Washington. However, the United States has been remarkably fortunate: in all our history, earthquake fatalities have totaled fewer than 2,000. By contrast, tremors worldwide claimed about 300,000 lives in 1976 alone.

Sparse population is largely responsible for the low U.S. death toll. Disaster planners estimate that one powerful quake in a megalopolis would still claim thousands of lives. The San Andreas fault is due to unleash a terrific quake in the Los Angeles area sometime in the next several decades. When it comes, it will be an unforgiving test of how well constructed our new buildings are, and how many dangerous old buildings we've removed. It will give us the measure of our earthquake engineering, a science that, for the most part, we have had to learn the hard way.

The San Francisco Earthquake

The United States and Japan are the world leaders in earthquake engineering, but the serious work of preparing for quakes began only in 1933. The famous slip of the San Andreas fault near San Francisco on April 18, 1906—our best-known earthquake—cost 700 lives, but it produced more interest in guarding against postquake fires than in preventing building collapse.

Many large structures came through the San Francisco quake (8.3 on the Richter scale) with little or no damage; of 52 major buildings downtown (the tallest was 19 stories), all but six survived. The bigger buildings endured because of designs intended to make them resistant to strong winds—some of their steel frames had

Many buildings that survived the tremors of the 1906 San Francisco earthquake fell victim to the fire that followed.

The reflecting pool of Wright's earthquake-proof Imperial Hotel in Tokyo doubled as a fire-fighting reservoir.

been stiffened with masonry fillings. The masonry absorbed a lot of excess energy and kept the steel from bending.

The biggest destroyer in San Francisco was fire. Flames from heating and cooking devices caught hold in the wreckage of innumerable houses and small buildings. Fire fighters couldn't keep up because the earthquake had crippled the water system. Hundreds of pipes broke where the distribution system crossed soft, filled-in ground, sapping the whole system's pressure. Fire engines rapidly emptied cisterns buried under the street intersections, and the fire burned for three days and leveled 500 city blocks. By 1912 San Francisco had completed a second, independent, high-pressure water system specifically for fire fighting, which it maintains scrupulously to this day. The city also made arrangements to close off pipes broken by earthquakes and installed more water cisterns.

For the next two decades, there was little interest anywhere in this country in preventing earthquake damage to buildings. One engineer hired by the San Francisco chapter of the Economic Society of America even argued that California was peculiarly resistant to earthquakes, because deep sedimentary deposits in the state's valleys would act like giant shock absorbers. Meanwhile, horrendous death tolls after earthquakes in Italy (1908) and Japan (1923) spurred action in those countries to toughen building

requirements. Tokyo slapped a 100-foot (30-meter) maximum on all buildings after 1923 and kept it for the next 40 years.

The Imperial Hotel Survives

Because of its regular quakes, Japan provided a brisk business for American designers and engineers interested in the problem. The architect Frank Lloyd Wright became world-famous after his Imperial Hotel survived the 1923 Tokyo earthquake and fire. A few years later, American architects and engineers designed the massive Mitsui Bank in Tokyo to resist earthquakes.

Wright's hotel went against the popular earthquake-engineering wisdom of the time, which favored simple, strongly braced, heavy buildings built on rock or firm ground. The foundation of the Imperial floated on short piles driven into a shallow layer of firm soil atop a shaky layer of mud. Wright segmented his hotel into 12 sections that could move independently. He tapered the reinforced concrete walls so that the upper sections were much lighter than the bottom ones. Anticipating the fire that would follow any large quake, he insisted on a pond in the courtyard as a fire-fighting reservoir.

But other major buildings besides the Imperial Hotel survived the Tokyo disaster, and no simple lessons emerged. Back in the States, knowledge remained unsettled. The main reason was that no one even knew what the ground did during an earthquake. No recording instruments were in place in quake-prone areas, and, in fact, standard seismographs were too delicate to remain functioning when exposed to shocks strong enough to damage buildings. Although architects and engineers had learned that buildings had their own peculiar frequencies to which they would vibrate when agitated, designers needed to know the frequency of ground waves during powerful quakes, because if the quake's frequency happened to match, a resonance could be set up. Just as a fine crystal goblet will break when exposed to a critical note, a building might rock gently, then violently, until it collapsed. Lacking the instruments to study ground motion, researchers sent out thousands of postcards to Californians and asked them to report on any quakes. They went to graveyards and recorded the fall of the headstones. One man sent in a drawing of the scratches his gas stove had left on his kitchen floor during a quake; it was one of the best records available.

The Long Beach Experience

In 1932 the U.S. Coast and Geodetic Survey began installing "strong-motion" seismographs capable of catching an earthquake's wild signature. Then, one year later, a near disaster

The 1933 quake that tilted a steeple of this Long Beach church led to stricter building codes in California.

Culver Pictures

brought real earthquake engineering to the United States. Just before six in the evening on March 10, 1933, a Richter 6.3 earthquake centered in the ocean not far from Long Beach, near Los Angeles, killed 120—most of them struck in the streets by falling stone, brick, and glass. An uproar was caused by evidence that thousands more would have died had the quake come a few hours earlier—when schools were in session.

Of the 42 major masonry buildings in the Long Beach school system, 38 were unusable after the quake, and nearly half were total losses. In Los Angeles, tens of thousands of schoolchildren had to attend classes in tents and bungalows for the next two years, and about a fifth of the schools required demolition. The collapsed schools had typically been cheaply built with walls of unreinforced brick or hollow tile supporting wood roofs. One writer called them "the most shocking collection of death traps that ever disgraced a great metropolis."

Just as hazardous as unreinforced masonry walls were the parapets and stone decorations on buildings. Tremors shook these through roofs or onto the streets, where they exploded like fragmentation bombs. The poor performance by school and commercial buildings prompted the passage of state laws requiring inspectors to oversee school construction. The laws also mandated that new buildings, and schools in particular, had to be capable of handling sideways pushes equaling as much as 10 percent of the total weight. One new Los Angeles school met that requirement with brick walls heavily laced by steel, and floors and a roof of reinforced concrete.

The lateral-load requirement was not a very sophisticated way of preventing damage—an earthquake is not comparable to a giant hand pushing on a wall in a steady way—but it was good enough. In the San Fernando earthquake of 1971, these post-1933 schools would all remain standing.

Measuring Resonating Frequency

Several of the strong-motion seismographs installed by the U.S. Coast and Geodetic Survey the year before the Long Beach quake lay close enough to the epicenter to produce usable charts. These tracings, the first ever, showed high accelerations and fast vibrations at the outset, tapering off to one or two seconds between much gentler shocks. Researchers at the Massachusetts Institute of Technology (MIT) pounced

A shaking table, guided by bumps on the wheel at right, helped engineers of the 1930's mimic earthquakes.

on these tracings. They rigged a hydraulic-powered platform to reproduce the motions, and tested model buildings on the platform. At a similar Stanford lab, models went onto a heavy wheeled cart that was struck by a half-ton pendulum and shaken by an off-balance flywheel to re-create the quake.

In 1934 the same Stanford mechanical-engineering laboratory produced a portable real-building shaker, and the Geodetic Survey used it in the ensuing years to measure the resonating frequencies of dozens of actual buildings, dams, and bridges. Bolted to something substantial in these structures, the machine would impart a lurching, back-and-forth motion to the building. The operator would start at a high frequency and work his way down to the lower ranges; with the help of seismographs installed around the structure, he could find its critical frequency. A typical medium-sized building might resonate at one to two seconds per cycle. Sometimes the building shook so much—a few fractions of an inch—that the operator could tell the frequency by the rattling of windows.

This information gave designers feedback on exactly how the height and stiffness of a building affected its frequency (generally speaking, the taller or more flexible a building, the lower its frequency). It also allowed them to check for damage after an earthquake. If the resonating frequency of a building was lower after a quake, damage was the most likely explanation, because cracks to a building's frame make it more flexible.

The popular press called them "earthquake machines," but that wasn't quite the case. They didn't have enough power to simulate the extreme forces of an earthquake, so still more raw information on actual earthquake ground motion was needed. Seismologists didn't have long to wait. When an earthquake measuring 7.1 on the Richter scale rattled California's Imperial Valley in May 1940, a strong-motion seismograph was already at work in the southern town of El Centro. The graph showed a maximum sideways acceleration one-third the force of gravity. "For many years afterward, it was the strongest motion ever recorded," says Professor George Housner of the California Institute of Technology (Cal Tech). "It was treated by some as the maximum possible." In fact, engineers who thought even the El Centro graphs understated the dangers and tried to design seismographs still more stoutly "were fired or had very few jobs," recalls engineering geologist James Slosson of Los Angeles.

The Effect of Topography

They were vindicated later. A Parkfield, California, earthquake in 1966 registered one-half of gravity horizontally, and then came the San Fernando quake of 1971 (maximum 1.25 gravities horizontally) and another Imperial Valley quake in 1979 (a peak of 1.75 gravities vertically). These peaks were most likely shock waves amplified by unusual topography, but it was clear that the 1940 El Centro record had been no ceiling at all.

Meanwhile, quakes in Mexico City (1957), Japan (1964), and Alaska (1964) taught that soil conditions could make shock waves much more dangerous than acceleration peaks might indicate. In Mexico City the problem was the soft, wet soil under the business district. It vibrated at just the right frequency to set small towers rocking violently. In Niigata, Japan, vibration made the sandy soil liquefy, and apartment buildings tilted crazily. In Anchorage the quake caused large areas of soil to slump and crack.

Extra Margin of Ductility

The complete collapse of some modern buildings in Anchorage and serious structural damage to others suggested that frames might need more emergency reserves of strength than the old code had required. This extra margin would come from a concept engineers call "ductility." Seismic building codes first recognized it in the 1950's.

A frame of steel or reinforced concrete can always absorb a limited amount of energy and return to its original shape, like a spring. That's nonductile behavior. But that frame can absorb a great deal more energy by permanently bending or cracking. If you can design the frame so it will remain standing after that damage, that's a ductile-frame building.

Two years after the Alaska earthquake, Los Angeles changed its seismic-design code to allow more ductile design and, as a gesture of confidence, removed the 13-story height limit. The first tall building to take advantage of this opportunity was the 210-foot (64-meter) Sheraton-Universal Hotel, which used a reinforced-concrete frame. The engineers provided vertical columns stronger than the horizontal beams, inserted weak points halfway down the beams and columns to absorb damage, and put extra-strong connections between them to ensure that the frame wouldn't fold up under the shocks like a card table.

Floors and Bridges

The 1971 San Fernando earthquake also dealt a severe blow to a 50-year-old concept called the "soft story"—the idea that a flexible floor near the base of a building could absorb ground motion and prevent the top floors from whipping around like a sapling in a storm. Architects liked the concept because it allowed them to leave out heavy, windowless walls on the first floor and put in bright, street-facing shops. Many buildings that had used a soft-story design collapsed in the 1971 quake.

What really turned engineers against the idea, recalls Professor Housner of Cal Tech, were results from strong-motion seismographs placed in buildings before the 1971 shocks. "For the first time," he says, "we recorded in many buildings the shaking at the base and the vibration of the building itself at roof, basement, and mid-height. Suddenly the picture became very clear, and a lot of misconceptions were swept away."

Researchers believe a flexible lower story can in fact increase the motion of upper floors. Furthermore, according to Henry J. Degenkolb, a San Francisco structural engineer, "in any building with a change of stiffness from floor to floor, you get a concentration of stress."

The 1971 San Fernando quake held still other, more painful lessons. All 15 bridges at the intersection of Interstates 5 and 210 sustained damage ranging from cracks to total collapse. A total of 62 bridges needed repair or replacement afterward. The most common problems were nonductile concrete columns and poor or nonexistent ties, which allowed long roadway ramps to separate at the hinges. That prompted the state's highway department to change the standards for new bridges and examine 13,000 pre-1971 bridges. One-tenth of them have recently been strengthened.

Nonstructural Damage

Another conclusion from 1971 was that it's not enough for a building to survive. About half the dollar loss came from nonstructural damage—to facades, interior walls, and equipment—and for some buildings it far exceeded the cost of structural damage. Nearly 10,000 customers lost phone service when tons of automatic switching equipment fell over. In the Los Angeles metropolitan area, the massive counterweights of almost 700 elevators shook loose from their guide rails, and some crashed through the roofs of cabs moving in the other direction. The quake knocked the emergency generators at Olive View Hospital in Sylmar, California, from their spring mounts; life-support machines in the intensive care unit winked out, and two patients died.

The first solution was to screw everything down more tightly and design automatic locking devices to prevent runaway elevator counterweights. Another approach, called base isolation, aims to reduce damage by mounting entire buildings on rubber feet.

The idea of insulating structures from ground vibrations goes back many years; the Japanese have long known that placing their houses' foundations on smooth boulders would allow them to slide around harmlessly. John Milne, a professor at Tokyo's Imperial College of Engineering at the turn of the century, once built a lighthouse on ball bearings. And a 1947 addition to a Sears, Roebuck store in Los Angeles used two layers of roller bearings to separate the old from the new construction.

The laser light flashing over Hollister, California, measures minute changes in the terrain near an active fault.

Building on Bearings

But anything on rolling bearings has to be restrained from wandering; base-isolation research now concentrates on laminated steel-and-rubber blocks. For several decades, heavy rubber mounts have been used to support highway bridge sections, allowing them to safely change length during temperature swings. Rubber pads have also insulated dozens of London buildings from subway-train vibrations. A school built in Skopje, Yugoslavia, in 1969 was the first building to use rubber pads for seismic protection; the Foothills Communities Law and Justice Center in San Bernardino is the only building in this country that relies on them for that purpose. The four-story Foothills building sits on 98 round pads made of interleaved rubber and steel sheets. Each pad is the size of a small coffee table.

James Kelly, an engineering professor at the University of California at Berkeley and a co-designer of the Foothills bearings, says the bearings are substitutes for a ductile frame and should provide better protection. He adds, though, ''You don't need it for very tall buildings, and you probably couldn't use it on them,

either.'' Tall buildings need tension connections to restrain them from capsizing during an earthquake, and rubber bearings don't provide much tensile strength. Whether they become common on shorter buildings will depend on the performance of the existing few. ''Base isolation is like religion—some believe it and some don't,'' says Mete Sozen of the University of Illinois. ''I don't have that religion.''

Shake Tables

Even more visionary are two seismic-protection schemes proposed by American researchers. One plan, by a group of University of Southern California (USC) faculty members, proposes using large tanks of compressed air. Jets of the air released from a building's upper stories would act like thrusters to oppose quake-induced motions. The other idea, called active control, was developed at the State University of New York at Buffalo (SUNYAB). It would use computer-controlled hydraulics to tighten or loosen steel cables on selected floors of a building, thereby counteracting oscillations caused by winds or earthquakes. Professor Tsu Soong of SUNYAB admits that the machinery sounds hard to maintain, but adds, "It can be tested periodically to see that everything works. I don't think that's a problem."

One of the tools used by an earthquake engineer like Soong is a modern shake table. A typical table is supported on a cushion of air while large hydraulic cylinders shove it all over the compass and up and down. Scale models mounted on the platform register what a full-scale building might do in a similar situation. The earthquake laboratory of the University of California at Berkeley recently finished a five-year project that used its 20- by 20-foot (6.1- by 6.1-meter) shake table to cross-check parallel experiments taking place at an extraordinary facility in Tsukuba, Japan, called the Large Size Structure Laboratory. While Berkeley worked with scale models of both a reinforced concrete and a steel-framed building, the Japanese tested the same two types, but at life size, using hydraulic cylinders anchored to a massive wall nearby. Computers controlled the cylinders, forcing the same distortions that an earthquake would cause. Everything took place in ultra-slow motion: the cylinders moved a few fractions of an inch, then paused as the computers recalculated the next step. One 30-second earthquake required ten days to run but provided highly detailed data, says Robert Hanson, a technical coordinator for the American team.

An Earthquake Is the Only Real Test

For a long time to come, though, nothing will beat a real earthquake for showing what works and what doesn't. The 1985 Mexico City disaster provided the severest test ever of large modern buildings. Damage was concentrated in only a small portion of the city's area, but for buildings having a resonating frequency near two seconds, it was a terrible ordeal. A layer of lake-bed sediments took the fading shocks from a Richter 8.1 quake 200 miles (320 kilometers) away and amplified them into a motion that rocked the ground 16 inches (40 centimeters) back and forth every two seconds. In less than a minute, more than 700 buildings sustained severe damage; about a third of them collapsed.

"I think it has confirmed our understanding of structural response," says Professor Sozen, who led a seven-member team of U.S. earthquake investigators at Mexico City. "A few changes in the seismic code will come out of it, but nothing dramatic." His advice for American cities exposed to infrequent but powerful earthquakes: Be prepared to dig out the

© James Sugar/Black Star

Modern versions of the shake table vibrate scale models of buildings to evaluate their earthquake resistance.

survivors very quickly. Of the 20,000 to 30,000 people killed in the Mexican quake, four out of five died because rescuers couldn't get to them in time.

Unfortunately, Sozen admits, there's no likelihood of earthquake-proofing cities like Memphis, Tennessee, to the degree that California cities have been—though that city is exposed to powerful quakes of the type generated at nearby New Madrid, Missouri, in 1811. "It would take billions of dollars and many years," he says, and the citizens won't support it because quakes in that region are so rare.

The economics of quakeproofing aside, it's clear that in the past half-century, we've learned an enormous amount about how to make our structures stand up to the strongest earthquakes. We may never tame earthquakes, but we're well on the way toward subduing our buildings—and they are the real killers.

WILDLIFE

An animal control warden tries to capture a 12-foot alligator that had been napping on a highway near Pascagoula, Mississippi. Across the South, once-rare alligators have multiplied to the point that the U.S. Fish and Wildlife Service has declared them secure throughout their North American range.

© Jerry Moulder

REVIEW
OF THE
YEAR

WILDLIFE

Habitat is still the name of the game for wildlife. As long as plenty of living space exists for birds, mammals, fish, and other wildlife, species will thrive. But when the pressures of urbanization and intensive agriculture intrude on natural habitats, wildlife strategies must expand to meet the challenge by developing such programs as specific, species-by-species rescue operations to supplement broad habitat preservation efforts.

SPECIES-SPECIFIC RESCUE

One such program involves taking animals from areas where they are plentiful and reintroducing them into areas where they are scarce. Two dozen caribou trucked 1,200 miles (1,930 kilometers) from Newfoundland to Maine now form the nucleus of a new herd in that state. Fifty trumpeter swan eggs were flown to Minnesota from Alaska to augment earlier restoration efforts. Seven red wolves, the first North American land mammals to be reintroduced to nature after becoming extinct in the wild, were flown from a Tacoma, Washington, zoo to North Carolina, where they will be released—more than 80 years after they disappeared from the East.

One mainstay of wildlife rescue programs— the Endangered Species Act—is threatened with extinction. Since its enactment in 1973, this legislation has focused attention on the plight of species whose very existence are threatened. Now this keystone act faces endangerment, as the U.S. Congress debates whether or not to renew the law.

HABITAT DESTRUCTION

Ironically, the debate in the U.S. comes at a time when scientists worldwide are warning that a mass extinction of species is occurring right now. The biggest threat appears to be the destruction of the world's rain forests. But even in the United States, estuaries continue being filled, wetlands drained, rivers channelized, and irreplaceable forests cleared. Some species on the road to eradication are not yet even known to science. Although some observers feel that creatures with names like furbish lousewort are not worth saving, history has proven otherwise. Among the many plants and animals with growing importance to the survival of people is, for instance, the Madagascar periwinkle, from which comes vincristine, a treatment for some human cancers.

Since many U.S. bird species winter in the tropical rain forests of Central and South America, tropical deforestation threatens scores of the songbirds Americans commonly think of as their own. The U.S. should therefore assume a leading role in reducing wildlife habitat destruction throughout the Western Hemisphere, before species of songbirds, sea turtles, birds of prey, whales, and other migratory wildlife disappear forever.

Some wildlife species adjust well to changing environments. Raccoon flourish in recently urbanized areas where the food (mainly garbage) is abundant. Canada geese thrive—and often fail to fly south for the winter—because of water and food available near suburban ponds, lakes, and golf courses. In the farm belt, white-tailed deer are doing so well they have become pests, eating corn, apples, and other crops. In fact, whitetail numbers have swelled from 500,000 around 1900 to 15 million today, according to the U.S. Fish and Wildlife Service. Over the same period, elks have increased fivefold, from 100,000 to 500,000; pronghorn populations have climbed from 13,000 to 750,000; and the number of wild turkeys has grown from 31,000 to 2.5 million today. And only six years after the top of the Mount St. Helens volcano blew off, a herd of 500 Roosevelt elk was thriving on its denuded slopes.

ENDANGERED SPECIES

In its annual report on the state of wildlife in the United States, the National Audubon Society stated that several wildlife species are in danger of extinction and many others are threatened. Two species—Kemp's ridley sea turtle (see page 362) and the sage grouse—could disappear at any time. Others in trouble include the woodland caribou, spotted owl, and the hooded warbler.

The sole remaining dusky seaside sparrow was crossbred with related species to keep its gene pool alive. The species became extinct when the bird died June 16, 1987.

© Paul W. Sykes, Jr., US Fish & Wildlife Service

One of the more stunning success stories of recent years is the American alligator. In deep trouble during the 1960's, the alligator has now regained healthy populations throughout its 10-state range. In South Carolina alone, the alligator population is 16 times greater than its level just one decade ago. This remarkable comeback was accomplished simply by halting all alligator killing.

Other species require more direct assistance to survive. The U.S. Forest Service, for example, unveiled a plan to help 1,250 pairs of spotted owls survive in the old-growth timbers of national forests in the Pacific Northwest.

In the state of Washington, a small private hatchery is attempting to reestablish a spawning run of king salmon. Farther south, the California Nature Conservancy acquired a $25 million, 13,000-acre (5,260-hectare) desert preserve to protect the Coachella Valley fringe-toed lizard.

Status reports on other, more familiar species bring both good news and bad: only 1 percent of the red-cockaded woodpecker's original habitat remains, and that small amount declines by 13 percent per year. Only about 475 pairs of piping plover, a shy shorebird, were reported by the Fish and Wildlife Service last year.

Bureaucratic ado continues to brew over efforts to save the last California condors. Plans presently call for captive breeding of all living condors, with hopes to release them in the wild once a larger population is achieved. But just a few birds remain in the wild, and the successful breeding of the two dozen individuals in captivity remains in question. Similarly, the wild populations of the extremely rare black-footed ferret are being captured for captive breeding programs in a desperate attempt to save the species. The last representative of the most endangered species in the United States—the dusky seaside sparrow—died June 16, 1987.

On the brighter side, the endangered gray wolf seems to be making a slow but steady comeback in the Rocky Mountains. The National Park Service reports a dramatic increase in grizzly bear cubs born in Yellowstone National Park; scientists there spotted 23 females with 43 newborn cubs, almost double the number of previous years. Bald eagles are also making a comeback in the United States. Thanks to tough antishooting laws and the ban of DDT and some other pesticides, the 1986 bald eagle population in the lower 48 states was double the total of the early 1970's. And the ivory-billed woodpecker, last seen in the U.S. during the 1950's, has been spotted in a remote mountainous forest in Cuba.

Except for overharvesting, notably of ocean fish, and direct poisoning, the basic problem of wildlife species in trouble is that their living space has been altered or taken away.

BOB STROHM

© Michael S. Quinton

STALKING THE GREAT GRAY OWL

by Mark Nelson

Last year about 3 million visitors marveled at the "crown jewels" of California's Yosemite National Park—the majesty of Half Dome and El Capitan, and the cascading beauty of Bridalveil and Yosemite falls.

One of the park's greatest natural treasures, however, remains largely unknown and mostly hidden. Its colors blend with the firs and sugar pines; its nocturnal movements fan the sky with a bold silence.

This mysterious, almost mystical creature is the great gray owl—the rarest owl in the state and, with a wingspan of more than 5 feet (1.5 meters), among the largest owls in the world.

Nicknamed the "Phantom of the Northern Forest" because of its reclusive personality, this magnificent bird teeters on the brink of extinction in California. Only about 50 great gray owls have been detected recently in the state,

and about 24 of them inhabit meadows in the tree-studded ridges of Yosemite. Although never a common bird here, there were an estimated 325 in California about 150 years ago.

Yosemite is the southernmost location in the world for great grays, which are thought to have come from central Canada and the northern United States.

Learning the Great Gray's Habits

Since this owl thrives elsewhere in North America (especially in the wild boreal forests of central Canada), as well as in coniferous forests in northern Europe and Asia, its gradual demise in California is somewhat mysterious.

Great gray owl with young (above). Rather than nest, these owls just settle in broken-off tops of dead trees.

Through funding provided by the Chevron Corporation and the U.S. National Park Service, biologists affiliated with the University of California at Davis have begun a four-year study at Yosemite to find some answers about the great gray—one of the world's least-researched birds.

Armed with ornithological expertise and high-tech tracking gear, the researchers are trudging through the backwoods and meadows of Yosemite to study all aspects of the great gray—its daily and nightly routines, foraging habits, hunting strategies, mating and breeding behaviors, and day roosting locations, as well as its reactions to the presence of another species, man.

Through their work the researchers initially hope to determine whether or not National Park Service proposals for more campsites, cross-country skiing trails, and parking lots could further endanger the already precarious existence of the great gray owl at Yosemite. Moreover, their findings could help to substantiate theories on why the owl's overall numbers have fallen throughout northern California.

"There's a definite danger that the bird could become extinct in California," says Jon Winter, the senior project researcher. "The great gray owl is scarce enough inside Yosemite, where the environment is relatively pristine. It's nearly impossible to locate the owl elsewhere in California, which suggests that it has been harmed by environmental disturbances."

Diminishing Presence

Winter—who has tracked the great gray owl for 20 years, and who wrote a master's thesis about its diminishing presence in California—suspects several major factors have contributed to the owl's decline here. First, logging that provided wood for the mining camps during the California Gold Rush in the 1800's began to alter much of the owl's natural habitat.

During this century, Winter believes the great gray's stamping grounds have been damaged by timber harvesting and grazing activities on U.S. Forest Service land. Before 1977 it was standard practice in federal timber sales to remove all dead snags (tree remains), which the owls use for their nests. Grazing could have reduced the abundance of meadow mice and pocket gophers, which the owls depend on for their food. By 1980 the great gray was listed as an endangered species in California.

Meanwhile, Yosemite remains a kind of

Chevron Corporation

Electronic hide-and-seek. Biologist Jon Winter relies on high-tech tracking equipment to monitor great gray owls fitted with special-frequency transmitters. Only about 50 great gray owls are known to survive in California.

Photos: © Michael S. Quinton

The neutral coloration of the great gray owl blends in with almost any background, including a favorite bathing spot (above). Even when silhouetted against a deep blue sky (right), only the piercing yellow eyes of the great gray readily distinguish the owl from its perching place.

oasis for the owl in California, a refuge with proper habitat, ample prey, and a minimum of environmental intrusions. Even there, finding and following the great gray owl can test the most dedicated biologist's patience.

Sloshing through a soggy meadow in pursuit of a particularly evasive owl one crisp morning, Winter remarks, ''You can really run yourself into the ground chasing these birds. There's a lot of painstaking research we must perform to get accurate information on their life-styles—checking their day roosts, tracking their movements, looking for droppings, and gathering the pellets [regurgitated wads of feathers and bones that can't be digested] of their prey around the edges of the meadows.''

Stooping to pick up a fresh pellet, Winter examines it, puts it into a plastic bag, and adds, ''Pellets tell us a lot about dietary habits. You could say there is a method in the madness.''

Silent and Sharp-sighted

Researchers are at a great disadvantage when tracking this owl. A great gray perched high on a branch is nearly invisible because its brownish-gray feathers look like tree bark. And when the owl glides overhead, it even can be missed in daylight because its movements do not make a sound.

This owl also is blessed with extraordinary eyesight (up to 1 million times better than a human's at night) and hearing (up to 100 times

better and immensely more accurate than a human's). Great grays hunt mostly by pinpointing sounds so precisely that when they dive-bomb, they can snatch prey burrowed nearly two feet under snow.

Such sensory talents make it virtually impossible to sneak up on a great gray. Consequently, the researchers rely on technology, which was purchased in part with Chevron funds. Winter and a handful of graduate students trapped six great grays in Yosemite last year and fitted them with custom-made transmitters, which are harnessed to the birds in mini-backpacks.

The transmitters emit special-frequency signals that can be detected by a hand-carried antenna attached to a receiver. This tracking procedure, called biotelemetry, is widely used in varying forms to monitor such wild creatures as caribou, condors, deer, mountain lions, whales, and sea turtles.

Winter says even the state-of-the-art equipment can be frustrating at times because the signals can bounce off rocks, trees, and hillsides, making it difficult to zero in on the bird.

Flights of Fancy

During a recent expedition, Winter, accompanied by research assistant Sue Skiff, this writer, and Chevron photographer Dennis Harding, trekked about 5 miles (8 kilometers) through the hilly forests of Crane Flat (it's not all flat) in pursuit of an elusive owl appropriately nicknamed Houdini. With the receiver beeping erratically, that owl led us on a zigzag path of electronic hide-and-seek, exhausting everyone without even offering a glimpse of his magnificent self. At dusk our efforts finally were rewarded when we came upon two juvenile owls hunting in a large meadow. The strenuous hike was worth it. Close up, you notice the owl's intense yellow eyes set in a humanlike face. Its swift and riveting glance makes it seem as if this raptor (bird of prey) can peer right through you.

The researchers also have erected a "blind," or platform, about 120 feet up a sugar pine with a clear view into a nest about 50 feet (36 meters) away. Great grays do not build nests like most other birds; they simply settle down in the rotted, broken-off tops of large, dead trees.

The researchers usually perch in the blind at night and use a light-intensifier scope to observe the type and amount of food delivered by the male to the female and their owlets.

The research sometimes follows unexpected flights of fancy. For instance, at Crane Flat, one of two main areas where the birds live (the other is along Glacier Point Road near Badger Pass), Winter says it appears that some hanky-panky might be going on among these usually monogamous birds.

Only one couple, Houdini and Madonna, is known to inhabit Crane Flat. However, a second female, which Winter has named Desiree, recently has entered the picture. Madonna hasn't made a fuss, which is unusual for the highly territorial birds. "We don't know what this means," says Winter. "Perhaps there's a skewed sex ratio—not enough males to go around."

Labor of Love

Despite some of the work's daily drudgery, it's obvious this project is a labor of love. "After all the years I've been in this business, I'm not impressed with birds very often. But when I saw a great gray swoop down in a deadfall from 100 feet [30 meters] with its talons outstretched, not making a sound, I was very impressed," says Dr. Charles van Riper III, who wrote the grant proposal and is overseeing this project.

To Winter, the great gray has a mystical quality. "Something about it pulls at your imagination. It conjures up an image of an animal inextricably linked with a pristine, wild world. Throughout history there's been a curiosity about owls. It's partially because they're nocturnal and mysterious, and partially because their faces are so humanlike they remind us of ourselves."

When asked why people should care about the near extinction of a bird few will ever see, Winter turned philosophical. "We shouldn't have isolationist attitudes. We can no longer afford them. Why care about the sperm whale or a starving family in Africa? It's because we live in a global community.

"Birds are good monitors of environmental integrity," Winter continues. "If an environment is deteriorating so badly that birds have trouble living there, then it's a clear symptom that something is seriously wrong. There's no reason we can't coexist with the great gray owl if we treat it with respect."

A hungry great gray owl keeps an eye on its next meal. With its extraordinary vision and hearing, the owl can spot potential prey at great distances and, in a matter of seconds, silently swoop down on its victim and make the kill.

TEXOTIC WILDLIFE

by Robert F. Jones

Strange things are happening in Texas. You might almost say it's a zoo down there.

• In the mesquite thickets of the Hill Country in the central part of the state, a cowpoke rides out to feed the stock—not Santa Gertrudis or Hereford steers, but beisa oryxes, rapier-horned antelope fierce enough to kill lions and men in their native sub-Saharan Africa.

• Among the live oak groves nearby, a surly Texas longhorn looks menacingly at a dark sika deer from Japan as they contest a mouthful of alfalfa. European fallow deer, the bucks with wide palmated antlers, stand by nervously, hoping to snatch a bite for themselves.

• On a game plain as stark as any in South Africa, bristly snouted white-tailed gnu gallop insanely by a flock of Armenian red sheep, while in the foreground an aoudad from the Atlas Mountains of Morocco bullies its way past a pair of hungry blue-legged ostriches to nip a handful of corn from the front seat of a battered ranch truck. Awaiting its turn is a timid young Nile lechwe from the famine-stricken Sudan.

• In the dense cedar woods along the headwaters of the Nueces River, a gawky nilgai from India emerges from cover to head for a feeding station; beyond it come wild Rio Grande turkeys, European mouflon sheep, Indian black buck, and American white-tailed deer. Nearby a young African eland grazes. At the click of a camera shutter, the nilgai flees, muscles bulging huge beneath the gunmetal blue of its hide. The others follow their sentinel, and soon only wet, dark eyes peer from the shrubbery—American, Asian, African, European, all equally wild, equally hungry, and now equally Texan.

A Haven in Texas

What's going on here? Well, it's the Invasion of the Exotics—or "Texotics," as some Lone Star chauvinists would have it. They're the five dozen species of nonnative animals, many of them threatened or endangered in their home-

© Susan Gibler

Putting on the feedbag. Four Grevy's zebras, a species threatened with extinction in its native Africa, line up for dinner in an unlikely new setting—a Texas ranch.

lands, that now share a home on the range with the deer and the antelope. Since 1930, when the enormous King Ranch in south Texas began importing nilgai, 370 Texas ranches—most of them in the Hill Country—have added exotics to the mix of beef cattle, horses, sheep, and goats that are the traditional mainstays of the state's herding economy. Today, as the cattle market buckles under the sledgehammer blows of high feed prices and a national dietary shift away from red meat, game ranching can, for some ranchers, spell the difference between marginal success and a foreclosed mortgage.

"If we ran only domestic stock on our 50,000 acres [20,235 hectares]," says Harvey Goff, wildlife manager of the 106-year-old YO Ranch 100 miles (160 kilometers) north of San Antonio, "we'd realize six or seven dollars an acre. With exotics added to our beef, horses, sheep, and Angora goats, we earn 10 dollars."

A 1984 census of exotics conducted by the Texas Department of Parks and Wildlife showed 120,201 nonnative game animals in the Lone Star State, representing 59 species. By contrast, the state's herd of native white-tailed deer numbers about 3.7 million—largest in the nation and by some estimates fully a fifth of all the whitetails in the world. But whitetails, like all native Texas game, can be hunted only during the two-month season decreed by the state. Exotics are considered private property—like livestock—and can be hunted at any time. The animals themselves, after, in many cases, dozens of generations roaming free on the Texas hills, feel wildly at home there.

But not all Texotics are there to be hunted. Many ranchers take pride in providing new habitats for species threatened with oblivion on their native grounds. Experiments are under way with the African rhinoceros, whose extinction is imminent because of heavy poaching (an 18-inch [46-centimeter] rhino horn can bring up to $30,000 from the aphrodisiac industry in Asia or from entrepreneurs in Yemen who use them for dagger handles). But rhinos are fence busters—and ferocious to boot—so they must be kept penned. As a result, most of those imported to Texas have died.

Greater success has been achieved with the Père David's deer, a swamp dweller about the size of a small American elk. Père David's deer

WILDLIFE **355**

had died out in its native China, but zoo specimens in England kept the gene pool alive, and now the species thrives on half a dozen Texas ranches. Other creatures on the brink of extinction that have a second chance in these surroundings include the scimitar-horned oryx (from war-torn Chad), the addax (from the Sahara), Indian barasingh deer, Persian gazelles, red sheep, Nile lechwes, and the mountain nyala from Ethiopia.

In fact, only six of the Texotics species are hunted regularly for profit. Most abundant and therefore the most popular quarry is the axis deer of India and Sri Lanka. Slightly bigger than most whitetails, it has a beautifully spotted russet coat and three-pronged antlers that can sweep to nearly 3 feet (1 meter) in length. There were 38,035 axis deer by the last count—nearly a third of the Texotics total. Black buck, 18,789 of them, are next most abundant, followed by 15,394 nilgais (rarely hunted because of their small horns). Aoudads (14,651), fallow deer (10,507), and sikas (7,956) round out the top six. The remaining 14,869 animals—"superexotics"—comprise fully 53 species, including everything from the endangered black rhino to small but spectacular herds of giraffes.

Breeding Controversy

Nobody shoots giraffes anymore, not even in Texas. Yet you can find a head mount of a bull giraffe in the showroom of Woodbury's studio in Ingram, Texas, which does most of the taxidermy work for the YO. Jimmy Dieringer, 29, the protégé of a legendary taxidermist and sculptor named Lloyd Woodbury, explains that 10 giraffes owned by Texas A & M died of the cold three winters ago on the Mecom Ranch in South Texas, where they were being held pending the construction of the $1.5 million Wildlife and Exotic Animal Center to be associated with the university's College of Veterinary Medicine. Dieringer and Woodbury raced to the Mecom Ranch as fast as they could, but managed to salvage only giraffe skin. Yet the mount they produced, which dominates their elegant studio, is a masterwork of the taxidermist's art.

As might be anticipated, the Texotics phenomenon has bred almost as many opponents as the animals it has saved. Some ecologists argue that any tampering with nature is anathema. They point to the introduction of starlings, house sparrows, carp, and rats to North America as examples of the import taking over the habitat of native species.

Texas Parks and Wildlife biologists fear that such exotics as axis deer and aoudads will ultimately outcompete native deer for forage and perhaps damage rangeland used by cattle, sheep, and goats. Biologists William E. Armstrong and Donnie E. Harmel fenced six sikas and six whitetails on 96 acres (39 hectares) in the Hill Country's Kerr Wildlife Management Area. In another 96-acre (39-hectare) pasture were six whitetails with no competition. After nine years, there were 62 sikas in the first pasture but no whitetails at all. In the other pasture the original six whitetails had increased to 14.

"Our range could be in a lot of trouble," says Armstrong. "We need to go in there and correct the situation. The exotics are here. They're a fact of life. There is no reason we cannot have axis or sika, but we cannot have them in the numbers people want. Landowners will have to make a conscious decision about how many of each animal they will have."

Many of the earlier introductions—from Chinese ring-necked pheasant, Eurasian chukar partridge and their Hungarian cousins to German brown trout—have benefited both the economy and the quality of American life. But until the introduction of Texotics half a century ago and their rapid escalation in the past decade, few mammalian imports had been tried. (The European or "Russian" boar was one that took.) Today, in Texas at least, the exotics have established a hoofhold unique in North America. To get a feeling for what they mean—or might bode for the future—photographer Bill Eppridge and I spent two and a half weeks hunting and photographing Texotics on a variety of Hill Country ranches. This is what we saw and felt.

Safari—Texan Style

Buttery's Ranch, better known as the Bar-O, near Llano in the northern reaches of the Hill Country, is a rugged sprawl of cactus-spiked plains and granite outcroppings cut through with sand rivers reminiscent of East Africa. Oaks and mesquite stud the plains like Texas versions of African baobab and acacia trees, and conceal herds of game far spookier than anything Eppridge or I had seen in our African travels. Apart from the small-bodied but big-antlered whitetails that flag from every thicket, there are aoudads, axises, sikas, fallow deer, and mouflon sheep. The mouflon, originally from the islands of Corsica and Sardinia but now established throughout central and southern Europe,

Top: © Susan Gibler; Bottom: © Bill Eppridge/Sports Illustrated

At home on the range. A giraffe explores its Texas surroundings (above). Frequent feedings and a lack of predators almost guarantees survival. At right, an Orinoco goose stays one step ahead of a pair of red deer.

is among the smallest of the world's wild sheep. But like most of its cousins, it is fast, wily, and as keen-sighted as a man with 10-power binoculars, and it prefers to hang out in rugged, ankle-busting country.

We chose to begin our Texas safari at the Bar-O because of the presence there of Finn Aagaard. Aagaard, 54, is a former white hunter and outfitter from Kenya, where I've made five safaris, and Eppridge, two. Hard of hearing because of years of proximity to big-bore gunfire, Aagaard left Kenya with his family (wife Berit; sons Erik, 16, and Harald, 14; and daughter Marit, 10) after a ban on hunting went into effect there nine years ago. Kenya-born, of Norwegian parents, he had grown up on a plantation near Nairobi, in what used to be magnificent game country. "Texas isn't quite the same," he says laconically, "but then nothing is. Not even Kenya today."

The Aagaards live in an echoing, 100-year-old "dog trot" ranch house—the architectural style, typical of the Hill Country, takes its name from the long center hallway dividing living and sleeping quarters—surrounded by a wire fence festooned with age-whitened antlers. A long, dark trophy hall is hung with horns and hides, some of them from Aagaard's safari days in Kenya. The skull of a cattle-killing lion Aagaard shot on his father's land rests on the mantel below the gleaming black 42-inch (107-centimeter) horns of a Cape buffalo. "Not especially big," he admits, "but I took it entirely on my own. No trackers, no skinners, no help at all. I'm rather proud of it, I suppose."

That, of course, is the rub in guided hunts. A guide or professional hunter takes care of the best part of the hunt: learning the country, locating the good animals, taking you to where they might be found, and telling you if the one in your binoculars is worth stalking. In Texas they call such an animal a "shooter." Aagaard allows only "fair chase" hunting on his territory—no shooting from the open windows of trucks, as too many "road hunters" do.

Aoudad Stalking

That morning I learned that aoudads—strange animals with back-curving horns, long throat beards, "chaps" of long hair on their feet, and amber eyes with the horizontally slotted pupils common to members of the sheep family—are unique to the rocky slopes of the northern Sahara mountain ranges, from Morocco clear across to Eritrea on the Red Sea. The moment they see, smell, or hear something new, they head for the rocks. But they don't necessarily stop when they get there, sometimes continuing for 5 miles (8 kilometers) or more from their starting point. Fast and surefooted, they pay little heed to cattle fences, sliding under them at full speed like base runners hitting second. Aagaard says that even the 8-foot (2.4-meter) wire-mesh game fences, built at a cost of $10,000 per mile on many Texotic ranches, cannot hold aoudads. "They don't jump them; they tunnel under," he says. "Damned clever, the old Barbary sheep."

The following day, cold and rainy, we managed to stalk within shooting range of three good-sized rams. But Aagaard hadn't seen them as we came up toward the live oak they huddled under for shelter, and he couldn't hear my worried whisper of warning. When he raised his head a bit too high over the brush we were using for cover, the sheep upped their tails and buck-

Old meets new in Texas. These feeding longhorn cattle seem puzzled when a courageous sika deer from Japan tries to horn its way in for a bit of food.

© Bill Eppridge/Sports Illustrated

The gemsbok—a South African antelope of much-diminished numbers—has already borne young in its adopted home.

eted madly off. Later Eppridge stalked to within 100 yards (91 meters) of a sizable band of ewes and young rams, using the sun at his back to dazzle them as he shot pictures. Aoudads do not hear as acutely as they see or smell, but even at that they started at every click of Eppridge's shutter. So we learned it was possible to hunt close enough on foot to shoot aoudads either with gun or camera, but the stalking had been every bit as tricky as it was in Africa.

Roaming the YO

"There's an old Texas saying," drawls Harvey Goff. "It's easier to pick a tourist than a bale of cotton." He lofts a squirt of tobacco juice into the weighted spittoon on the dashboard of his "office"—a battered Chevy half-ton the color of masticated Red Man—and squints at the passing countryside. Goff has been the wildlife manager of the YO Ranch for the past 16 years, and is thus the man in charge of providing shooters for the ranch's hunting clients. But his comment is less cynical than it sounds.

Back in 1900 the YO totaled 550,000 acres (222,585 hectares). Today it's down to one-eleventh that size, and only by combining a hunting program with traditional stock raising can it survive.

In the 1950's the YO began its exotic ranching, under the leadership of Charles Schreiner III— or "Three," as he's more familiarly known. The grandson of the Alsatian immigrant who founded the ranch in 1880, he is a stocky, round-faced man with a grizzled mustache who looks like a hammered-down Hemingway. Three wears a weathered white Stetson, collects Colt pistols, and knows more Texas history than most university professors. His gun collection and library—secured behind an ancient Wells Fargo vault door—occupy a wing of the big stone house that sits on a knoll above a plain teeming with game. A Gatling gun dominates the center of the room. During the Bicentennial 10 years ago, Three got hold of some clips loaded with blanks. He wheeled the ancient weapon out onto the patio and cut loose with a few clattering bursts in celebration of America. The game below hardly looked up.

Less than one-eighth of the YO ranch is devoted to exotics. This area is under "high fence," i.e., barriers tall and strong enough to contain wild game. The fences cordon off "pastures" ranging in size from 300 to 3,000 acres (120 to 1,200 hectares). Most of the 6,000 exotics on the ranch are now many generations removed from their zoo-stock progenitors and

© Howard Castleberry/Sports Illustrated

Texan Tom Mantzel, owner of the Fossil Rim Wildlife Ranch, pets one of his prize acquisitions—a black rhino.

Redneck is a mature male Masai ostrich as fierce as the warrior tribe he's named for. No sooner had we entered the pasture where he lives with a flock of South American rheas and Australian emus (along with zebras, giraffes, beisa oryxes, and other mammals), than Redneck charged the truck, pecking viciously at the side mirrors and Murff's hand, which was full of corn. At one point, Redneck pecked a dent into Eppridge's 300-millimeter lens, then kicked the truck with a resounding whump that left a deep, foot-long crease. "Put a helmet and pads on that rascal and he'd be the new Ray Guy," said Murff. "They can kill you with a kick." Getting out of truck to open the gate so that we could leave the pasture was a tactical problem solved only by luring Redneck far away with more corn, rushing out to open the gate, then driving through it like A. J. Foyt. As we slammed the gate behind us, the big ostrich was charging with blood in its eye. "I'd like to be the one who shoots that bastard when the time comes," Murff said. "But there's a waiting list. And ol' Three's at the head of it."

We followed a truck driven by a hand named Fibber McGehee. Fibber was tranquilizer-darting small whitetail spike bucks for transfer to another pasture. Usually exotics ranchers resort to tranquilizer darts only after other methods fail, preferring to lure animals they want to move into new pastures with feed or trapping them under big drop nets. Dosages must be delicately measured for high-strung game, and a milligram too much succinylcholine chloride can kill. But McGehee has darted some 6,000 deer and antelope in his 15 years on the YO and lost only 50, Goff later told us.

One Final Stop

Our final stop was the Auerhahn Ranch, a 1,700-acre (688-hectare) spread of hilly parkland near Boerne, just north of San Antonio. It's owned by Bob and Betty Kelso. He's a retired lieutenant colonel of armor cavalry; she's president of the Exotic Wildlife Association, a nationwide group that is trying to impose order on the burgeoning exotics business. The ranch is named for the German version of the capercaillie, the largest of the Eurasian grouse, although the Kelsos have more than 70 species of exotic birds on the ranch.

Ranch foreman Ronnie Shackleford, 35, is a shambling, wide-grinning transplant from Oklahoma who sounds and even looks like a younger, bearded Slim Pickens. We toured the

thus every bit as wild as any in nature. Only 5 percent of these "naturals" are killed by hunters each year.

Fierce Redneck

Our guide on the YO was Jim Murff, 40, a lanky cowpoke with the slow, sly wit of Owen Wister's Virginian. Munching ice cubes from a Styrofoam cup, Murff (no one uses his first name) showed us the sights. There was Sammy, an aoudad, who climbed into Murff's lap for a handout of corn; Watusi, a huge red and white Ankole bull from Central Africa with horns three times as thick as a longhorn's but with as big a span; a herd of Livingstone's eland, bigger than most beef cattle but capable of jumping a game fence if spooked. Then there was Redneck. "Just keep your hands inside the truck," Murff warned. "This bastard bites."

ranch for two days in his pickup. In one pasture were four greater kudu, one a magnificent bull with spiral horns in excess of 50 inches (127 centimeters). In another were five sable antelope, tall, powerful animals with rich, almost black coats marked with ivory white. One is a pettable three-year-old cow named Suzy, but the bull, kept separate from his congeners except for the presence of a submissive mate, is another story. "That guy's a killer," said Shackleford. "Last year we put a young bull in with him, his son actually. He drove a horn clear through his chest. We found the young-'un stiff in the pasture next mornin'." I looked at the back-sweeping horns. The sable stared back, narrow-eyed, waiting. It put me in mind of a story Goff told at the YO. A hand on another Hill Country ranch a few years ago went out to feed the herd of beisa oryxes. He didn't come back. Two days later they found him dead, still on the horns of the oryx cow that had killed him.

Both Goff and Shackleford feel it's downright stupid, if not indeed fatal, to treat these exotics like gentle spin-offs from "Wild Kingdom." "I wish television would do a special on how cruel nature can be," Betty Kelso says. "They should show what it's like when a flock of wild ducks turns on one of its weaker members and pecks it to death. Nature is marvelous—powerful, complex, magnificent as the planet itself—but it's not all sweetness and light."

The pride of the Auerhahn is its herd of 13 Père David's deer. Betty Kelso acquired the nucleus of the herd from a Missouri rancher in 1982 after he had been unable to get them to reproduce. She learned that the stags—two of them—had been kept separate from the eight hinds (females), putting only one in with them during the rut. She gambled and put them all in together. It paid off. The stags battled mightily during the rut, and the competition turned on the winner's reproductive urge. Roaring and rutting for two weeks straight (during which he lost 100 pounds [45 kilograms]), the "harem master" who had won the initial battle finally wore himself out. Then the loser took over for another two weeks. This went on for six weeks straight, and fawns were soon on the way. The deer are doing so well that the Kelsos have volunteered under the aegis of the International Union for Conservation of Nature and Natural Resources to help reintroduce Père David's deer to China.

© Bill Eppridge/Sports Illustrated

Roundup time at the YO Ranch. Lariat-wielding cowboy Jim Murff gets set to lasso a tiny beisa oryx.

A Magical Combination

For good or ill, the Texotics invasion is here to stay. Just how far it expands remains for the ranchers and wildlife biologists—in concert, we hope—to decide. But there is certainly something splendid, almost magical, about the juxtaposition of these odd, elegant creatures with the Texas landscape. Leaving the Hill Country—reluctantly—I thought suddenly of Finn Aagaard's 10-year-old daughter, Marit. Born in Kenya, now learning to talk with a Texas drawl, living in the midst of animals most Americans have never even heard of, she dreams not of aoudads or axises, nilgais, or nylas, but of—unicorns. She draws them, collects them in the form of stuffed toys, charms, even a snowfall paperweight with a unicorn inside, given her by one of her dad's hunting clients. The desire for the exotic lies deep in all of us.

The Riddle
of the
Ridleys

by Robert W. Willett, Jr.

The tide is going out for a little-known denizen of the salty seas known as Kemp's ridley sea turtle. Where tens of thousands of these homely sea creatures once swam the Gulf of Mexico and Atlantic Ocean, now just hundreds remain. In fact, *Lepidochelys kempii*—the scientific name for Kemp's ridley turtles—would probably be extinct today were it not for emergency measures taken by the governments of the United States and Mexico; the active involvement of volunteers, especially a group known as HEART (Help Endangered Animals Ridley Turtles); and financial support from the corporate community, including such companies as Exxon, for programs aiming at solving the riddle of the ridley's life cycle.

Less of a riddle is the reason for the precipitous decline in the ridley population. For decades, it was the defenseless victim of organized predation by human turtle fanciers. Declared an endangered species by the United States government in 1973 and protected since then, ridleys are no longer harvested as food, but many still suffocate when caught accidentally in shrimpers' trawls. In some parts of the world, ridleys are killed for the neck hide, from which a fine leather can be made.

Annual Mating Ritual

The Kemp's ridley sea turtle might not be in such trouble if not for its habit of laying its eggs on only one known nesting beach, an isolated strip of shoreline along Mexico's Gulf coast. Bales of ridleys gather offshore there in the spring to await a windy, rainy day. When conditions are right, the females come ashore to lay their eggs. In an earlier time as many as 40,000 female turtles would haul out on the beach in a single day; today fewer than a thousand participate in the annual ritual during an entire mating season that extends from April through July.

Leaving the surf, the mother turtle pushes her horny snout repeatedly into the wet sand, seeking something that tells her that she has arrived at the proper place to lay her eggs. From waterline to the dunes, she continues testing the sand with her nose. Only the Kemp's ridley and its cousin, the olive ridley, have this habit. Scientists think the characteristic taste and odor of the beach of its birth somehow become imprinted on a hatchling, enabling it to return to that spot years later.

On a sandy beach along Mexico's Gulf coast, ridley hatchlings emerge from their eggs (below), only to begin a perilous race for survival down to the water (left).

When satisfied that she has found just the right spot among the dunes, the female ridley excavates a bell-shaped chamber in the sand, backs into it, and lays approximately 100 leathery, golf-ball-sized, golden-hued eggs. This done, she fills in the hole, tamps down the sand with her flippers and by a rocking motion of her body, and returns to the sea, leaving behind her offspring to hatch by themselves in the warmth of the Mexican sun. Some 50 to 60 days later, little ridleys dig out of their sandy nest and scramble down to the surf.

High Mortality Rate

Few make it. In the days when the ridleys were numerous at Rancho Nuevo, coyotes would gather in huge packs to dig up and eat the eggs. Skunks and raccoon would join in. On hatching, the remaining silver-dollar-sized infants would run a gauntlet of hungry seabirds and ghost crabs only to fall prey to waiting fish upon entering the Gulf. Yet the species could have survived these losses were it not for overharvesting by human egg gatherers who used to haul huge loads of turtle eggs to market.

Nesting ridleys had declined to the low thousands when the Mexican government decided to act in the mid-1960's. They literally sent in the marines to protect the beach at Rancho Nuevo. Now, although no egg gathering is permitted and there are few coyotes, there are nonetheless many fewer eggs over which to stand guard.

Three-Phase Program

To help the species recover, the Mexican *Instituto Nacional de Pesca* (INP) and several U.S. agencies mounted a program in 1978 that provided for increased protection for the ridley, research on its life cycle, and the establishment of a second nesting site on Padre Island National Seashore near Corpus Christi, Texas. Robert King, biologist at the National Park Service (NPS) field station on Padre, explains that scientists hope to use the turtle's imprinting behavior to expand its nesting range. But station biologists aren't sure exactly how the sensing mechanism works. "It might be the chemical composition of the water on beach sand, the exact position of the sun at that spot, or something else in the environment," King says. Also unknown is just how imprinting takes place. "It may happen while the hatchling is still in the egg, crawling up through the sand after breaking out of the egg, crawling down to the beach, or upon entering the water," King points out. To cover all possibilities, biologists conduct a three-phase program.

A volunteer gathers tiny ridley turtles just after they hatch (left). Her inert plastic gloves prevent the turtles from imprinting the scent of her skin. The ridleys are allowed to briefly crawl on the beach and enter the surf, thereby imprinting the sand and water of that particular beach, before being scooped up in inert plastic nets (below). The captured ridleys are then carefully maintained in plastic buckets for their first year. After one year (right), the turtles—now large enough to fend for themselves—are released into the Gulf of Mexico.

In Mexico, biologists of INP, the U.S. Fish and Wildlife Service (FWS), and the Gladys Porter Zoo of Brownsville, Texas, gather eggs at the moment the turtles lay them, collecting them in plastic bags so that they never touch Rancho Nuevo sand. Some 2,000 eggs are swiftly packed in sand brought from Padre Island in Styrofoam boxes and stored at a facility run by the INP. The Gladys Porter Zoo coordinates the Mexican phase and transports the eggs to Padre Island by private aircraft.

At Padre Island, summer interns, supported by grants from companies such as Exxon Company, U.S.A., receive and care for the eggs under the direction of scientists with the NPS. As the tiny ridleys hatch, interns wearing inert (nonreactive) plastic gloves carry them to the beach, where they are released. Orienting themselves with the aid of the sun, the ridleys scurry to the surf. But they are allowed just 20 seconds in the water. Then volunteer workers catch the hatchlings in nets of inert plastic mesh. The turtles are placed in plastic boxes on a bed of urethane foam saturated with seawater and returned to the field station for weighing and measuring. From there they go by truck to the National Marine Fisheries Service (NMFS).

Fed Through Donations

For a year the little turtles live in plastic buckets that have been perforated to permit seawater to flow through. They are fed a modified trout food developed for use at a green sea turtle farm in the Cayman Islands. The food is bought with donations, largely from schoolchildren, to HEART. The organization is a special committee of the Piney Woods Wildlife Society, a

nature club of North Harris County College. HEART raises money by publicizing the plight of the ridley among school groups and conservation organizations. Carole Allen, founder and chairwoman of HEART, explains that everyone finds baby turtles particularly appealing. "To feed a turtle for a year takes about $4," she says. Every person making a donation of $4 or more gets his or her name posted on the bulletin board at the NMFS Galveston lab.

In a year at Galveston, the young ridleys grow to the size of small dinner plates and are large enough to fend off most predators. Dr. Charles Caillouet, chief of the Life Studies Division of the NMFS laboratory, is in charge of this phase of the program, which is called Head Start. "We add 1,500 or so one-year-olds to the Gulf of Mexico each year," he says. Through 1985, 9,258 ridleys have been reared, tagged, and released, more than 10 times the number of adult females that are now coming ashore to lay eggs at Rancho Nuevo. Caillouet hopes that by helping the young turtles through their first high-risk year, Head Start will contribute to an increase in population numbers necessary for survival of the species.

Wide Dispersion

In preparation for joining the rest of the turtle world, a yearling is first tagged on a flipper with a metal alloy tag stamped with a code number and a return address. It is hoped that anyone finding or catching the animal will note its size, tag number, date, and place of capture and send this information to the NMFS at Miami, Florida. The tag should not be removed, as it is the only means of identifying a Head Start Kemp's ridley. The tagged turtle should be returned to the water unharmed so that its future move-

ments might be learned. Data gathered from tag reports also help biologists learn travel patterns and survival rates. Very young ridleys seem to vanish for a year, possibly hiding in the bays and estuaries of Texas and Louisiana. Many slightly older ridleys are found in the Gulf, but also as far north as the coast of New England, apparently swept there by the Gulf Stream. The smallest and most aggressive of the sea turtles, a few wander as far from home as the coast of Europe, Morocco, and the Azores. Regardless of where they have been, sexually mature ridleys are found only in the Gulf of Mexico.

The Success of Imprinting

Leaving Galveston, the young turtles go for a ride on the *Point Baker,* a U.S. Coast Guard cutter, or on the *Longhorn,* a University of Texas research vessel, and are released off Padre Island near the hatch site. If imprinting works as it is supposed to, here is where surviving females will return some six to 13 years later to reproduce themselves. The success of imprinting is not certain, however. Some scientists suggest that young turtles may simply follow older ones to the nesting site and memorize its location. They note that less memory is required for a turtle to return every one or two years than for it to recall the site after an absence of six to 13 years preceding sexual maturity. If turtles indeed follow the leader, then the attempt to imprint turtles on Padre Island will have failed.

Nevertheless, the Head Start program is favored, in part because it offers hope—if imprinting is the correct answer, the Kemp's ridley sea turtle may yet survive—but also because the experiment is the only way to solve the reproduction riddle.

Invariably the turtle biologists and volunteers are asked why they go to so much trouble and expense to save what others might consider an insignificant sea creature whose presence or absence would seem to matter little in the grand scheme of things. There are several answers. One suggests that the turtle is part of the web of nature and may well serve a significant purpose as yet undetected. A practical reason is that the ridley is sensitive to the level of pollution in the ocean, and its health may serve as an indicator of environmental quality. But most ridley fans favor Caillouet's belief: "We are not this planet's only species," he emphasizes. "When we contribute to the survival of another species, in a way, we enhance our own environment and the probability of our own survival."

© Jack Couffer/Bruce Coleman Inc.

Red-tailed hawks have set up residence in many city parks, where they help control the squirrel and rat populations.

BRINGING WILDLIFE BACK *to the* CITY

by Robert S. Dorney

Peregrine falcons circling overhead in downtown Boston, wild dogs roaming the streets of the Bronx in small packs of twos or threes, coyotes raiding garbage in suburban Los Angeles and eating pets—these are stories that grab headlines and evoke fear and fascination in the hearts of many urban dwellers. But such episodes are only part of a larger, far more interesting story: the growing presence of wildlife in our cities, and the expanding realization that cities can be consciously designed to encourage desirable species of wildlife to live there. After all, why should the urban environment be perceived as a place to escape from, a towering brick and concrete edifice hostile to nature?

Some animals, of course, will always be unwelcome in the urban environment. Rats, pigeons, and cockroaches have flourished amid the garbage and debris of city life for centuries, bringing with them disease and unpleasant associations. Some of the newcomers to urban life are equally unwelcome; no one particularly enjoys the sight of coyotes and stray dogs foraging for food in suburban and urban habitats. These animals also introduce the threat of rabies and bite injuries, particularly to young children.

Valuable Assets

As urban development continues to devour rural habitats in the United States and Canada, however, other animals are beginning to make their homes in the complex urban ecosystem. And many of these animals offer a pleasing dimension to life in the big city. Urbanites know that spring has arrived when they hear cardinals whistling in the trees that line their streets.

Many people also find pleasure in the wild ducks that increasingly make their homes in public parks, and in the hawks and owls that have begun to roost in a few city parks. Such animals do not threaten the human population and, in fact, are admired for their attractive appearance, interesting behavior, and tendency to prey on unwanted species such as rats and pigeons. Such desirable wildlife can also improve the economic worth of the areas in which they settle. A recent study in Ontario showed that a housing development designed to fit into the natural landscape and attract certain kinds of wildlife actually brought its developer higher profits than a comparable development designed with no thought to natural landscaping.

Given these aesthetic and economic benefits, developers and city planners should design their projects to attract desirable and possibly endangered forms of wildlife to the city. At the same time, renovations and new construction should be designed to deter undesirable species such as pigeons, starlings, and rats. To achieve these goals, developers, landscape architects, civil engineers, naturalists, and city planners must work closely with wildlife biologists and ecologists. Through deliberate planning and design, cities can become places where people and wildlife commingle in harmony.

"Sloughs of Despond"

One would think that our European ancestors would have automatically built an awareness of nature into the design of Western civilization's first cities and towns. But as history and artifacts reveal, early cities were built according to a rigid format to defend the populace from military threat and to capitalize on the economic benefits of trade. European cities certainly did not originate as places of luxury and leisure. Indeed, the wealthy feudal lords of the Middle Ages lived outside the cities on their country manors; only the poor and burgeoning middle class lived in town. As European cities grew rapidly without planning or design, they became known as places of filth and disease. City dwellers simply hurled their garbage onto streets already littered with the manure of horses and cattle. Rats and disease ran rampant.

Jonathan Swift captured the unsavory image of the city in an 18th-century poem in which he describes the results of a London rainstorm:

Sweepings from the butchers' stalls, dung, guts, blood.

Drowned puppies, stinking sprats, all drenched in mud,

Dead cats, and turnip tops, come tumbling down the flood.

Over the centuries, other writers and poets have only reinforced that image. Boccaccio, an Italian Renaissance author, wrote in *The Decameron* of ladies and gentlemen escaping to a pastoral Shangri-la far from the cities' plague and stench where they could idle away the time with music and story.

Indeed, until the 20th century, our cities were "sloughs of despond," in John Bunyan's words, and some still are. But today, more than ever before, the leading cities of the world are culturally dynamic and revitalized hubs of activity that attract increasing numbers of people as residents, workers, and tourists. At least 80 percent of all North Americans live in suburban or urban environments, and even many of those who live in the country rely on the city for economic and cultural sustenance.

As a result, the quality of life in cities has become increasingly important, and they are no longer perceived as places to escape from. At the same time, many species of wildlife, their natural habitats under pressure from suburban development, have begun to adapt to life in the city or on its fringe. For both these reasons, urban wildlife and its effect on city life have begun to attract the attention of biologists and ecologists. In the past 15 years, in fact, a new discipline called urban ecology has been created, and an increasing number of biologists,

In Boston's cleaned-up Charles River, goldfish discarded by students have become food for cormorants.

© Frank Revi

landscape architects, foresters, and biogeographers have discovered that urban wildlife is a topic worthy of study.

The Urban Ecosystem

It is surprising how much green area there is in a typical city. In Waterloo, Ontario, one of the few cities in the world whose biological surface has been mapped, 35 percent of the city's area is in active agricultural use, 9 percent is growing weeds as abandoned agricultural land, 25 percent is in suburban grass and trees, 13 percent is in natural forest, and 3 percent is in city parks. Thus, about 85 percent of Waterloo is "green," with agriculture an unexpectedly strong land use in the outlying area just inside the city boundary. These statistics seem typical for North American cities with populations of around 70,000. Many larger cities also have suburban areas and agricultural fields, giving them a similarly high percentage of green areas.

Even some cities in countries known for high urban densities have extensive green areas. Satellite photos show that Japan's Chiba City, with a population of 800,000 and lying on the east side of Tokyo Bay, has 22 percent of its area in forestland, 52 percent in agricultural land, 3 percent in marshland, and only 23 percent in actual buildings. Thus there is precedent for even large cities retaining the 100- to 250-acre (40- to 100-hectare) blocks required to sustain the high complement of woodland birds typically found in rural areas.

To better understand the urban ecosystem, my colleagues and I at the University of Waterloo have divided it into three mappable areas. The core is the built-up city zone that contains residential high rises, offices, and industrial buildings as well as lower-density suburban housing. Lying outside this core but often still within the city boundary is the urban fringe zone, which contains rural land slated for development. Beyond that is the urban shadow zone, the outer area of the urban complex that workers commute to and from daily.

Although essentially rural with small towns and villages, this third zone contains commercial farms as well as "hobby" farms, gravel pits, waste dumps, scenic river valleys, and airports. In essence, it is a mix of the old rural landscape with the new suburban "station-wagon set." In large metropolitan areas, the core city may be completely built up, with the urban fringe and urban shadow located around nearby satellite cities.

These three urban zones provide a range of opportunities for different wildlife species. In the urban fringe, woodchucks and seed-eating bird species flourish in agricultural fields and hedgerows—much to the dismay of serious farmers. In the abandoned fields that ring both the urban fringe and shadow zones, pheasant, woodchucks, field mice, rabbit, raccoon, possums, chipmunks, and deer can be found. Since hawks and owls feed on field mice and cottontail rabbit, they can also be found in these zones. Many bird species, generally between 15 and 25 different types, frequent suburban areas with older trees, flowers, and grass.

Some Species Undesirable

In the city zone itself reside such traditionally undesirable species as rats, pigeons, English sparrows, and starlings. Like pigeons, starlings and English sparrows are largely considered pests; they befoul buildings and grounds, and noisily congregate on winter roosts. Most urban dwellers are also not particularly happy about such Johnny-come-latelies as raccoon, "wild" dogs, and coyotes.

Raccoon actually pose a serious health

threat in the United States by bringing rabies into cities. Although rabid raccoon do not usually bite people, they do transmit the disease to pet dogs who roam the same urban and suburban terrain. Dogs, in turn, transmit rabies to humans, particularly young children.

Three types of dog populations now live in a typical city: dogs owned by residents, dogs who are abandoned and become strays, and feral (wild) dogs who are the offspring of strays. Contrary to popular belief, pet dogs are the canines most likely to attack and bite young children. They are less afraid of humans than are stray or wild dogs, and they are more likely to defend their perceived territories.

Stray dogs usually find shelter in areas of high human density—in abandoned cars and even in the hallways and common areas of occupied buildings. Feral or wild dogs are more common in areas of low human occupancy, such as the decaying sections of larger cities where there is food, cover, and little effort to control animals. Alan Beck of the University of Pennsylvania has reported packs of wild dogs roaming the streets of St. Louis, Missouri, and deserted areas of Baltimore, Maryland. Both stray and wild dogs feed on the dumps and trash cans that proliferate in urban areas, fouling sidewalks and killing trees and plants with their digging and urine.

Skyscraper Cliffs

By contrast, many urbanites are enthralled by such newcomers as the owls and hawks that spend their winters in public parks, and by the peregrine falcons that now breed and nest successfully in cities such as Boston, Baltimore, and such Canadian cities as Calgary, Edmonton, Montreal, and Toronto. Ecologists have deliberately released peregrine falcons, an endangered species, into many North American cities to save the birds from extinction. The tops of modern skyscrapers turn out to be a rough facsimile of peregrines' traditional home: the rocky cliff ledges of North America. These birds also serve a very useful function: they feed on starlings and pigeons.

In contrast, the red-tailed hawk has made its own way into downtown Boston, attracted by the plentiful supply of squirrels and rodents in the Boston Common and Public Garden. Some hawks now spend the winter in Boston, migrating north when spring finally arrives. Owls have also been observed in Boston-area parks in the fall and winter.

Certain kinds of wildlife move among all three urban zones, tying them together into a complex, interdependent ecosystem. For instance, in the fall, hundreds of starlings roost downtown at night but fly many miles into the urban shadow to feed on waste grain from commercial farms. Mallard and Canada geese loafing in urban ponds by day will make morning and late-afternoon flights to feed on the same waste grain.

The Gull-hatching Index

The urban ecosystem often affects wildlife in unprecedented ways. For example, in most major cities, afternoon air rises over the downtown

Raccoons, thriving on a plentiful supply of garbage, are a less-than-welcome addition to the urban wildlife scene.

area as the mass of buildings warms the area. Such heat islands carry insects up over the city from adjacent parkland, providing food for the nighthawks and chimney swifts that careen back and forth over the urban center. The nighthawks used to build their nests and roosting habitats in flat prairie areas, and the chimney swifts nested in the hollow trees of forests. But as forest and prairie land disappeared and the birds found insects available in cities, these birds began to nest on the flat roofs of buildings and in abandoned chimneys. These two attractive species are now more common in North American cities than in rural areas.

Similarly, in Tucson, Arizona, urban development of desert areas—with the resulting increase in weeds and grassy areas as residents create lawns—has attracted Inca doves and other unusual bird species from the surrounding desert.

In the urban shadow zone, landfills increasingly provide a steady food supply for gulls. The gulls commonly nest on islands at sea or on those created by dredging and filling harbors. These gulls fly substantial distances daily to feed on outlying landfills, and their populations have increased considerably with the rise of cities. If nothing else, the "gull-hatching index," or GHI, might be a valuable indicator of economic activity for the gullible economist.

Unwanted Imports

Many cities are also home to species that have either escaped from captivity or were deliberately released into the urban environment—not always with desirable results. Perhaps the best-known example of this was the release of starlings in New York City's Central Park in 1890 by sentimental literary buffs trying to establish European birds mentioned by Shakespeare. Although the nightingale, released at the same time, did not survive, the starlings have become one of our more successful urban birds, and a distinct nuisance.

More recently the Monk's parakeet and canary-winged parakeet, imported as pets from South America in the 1960's, have become successful colonists in Miami and Tampa. Hundreds of these exotic fruit-eating birds have invaded rural areas in southern Florida, damaging mango, avocado, and orange groves. Citrus growers have been forced to bring in trappers to capture these birds and give them back to pet stores. In Boston, schools of goldfish are making their home in the increasingly clean waters of the Charles River. Dumped there by departing college students, the goldfish have recently been discovered by cormorants, seabirds that are also showing up in growing numbers around the Charles River basin.

Saving Animals While Saving Money

The aesthetic reasons for attracting wildlife to the city are obvious. Most people would also consider attempts to help endangered species adapt to urban life a worthy social goal. Nonetheless, many urban developers, politicians, and planners view efforts to design with nature in mind as a "frill," and they are hesitant to

The problem of stray and wild dogs roaming city streets is largely the fault of people who abandon their pets.

include such details in their plans for new projects. After all, custom landscape designs and environmental consultants only raise the cost of a project, and developers often say they have no evidence that these extra costs will be offset by higher profits down the road. Solid evidence of economic benefits from large-scale urban projects does remain scarce. However, my colleagues and I have found that natural landscaping and design can increase the overall value of suburban housing developments.

In the 1960's the city of Waterloo, Ontario, approved two mixed-density private housing developments, each about 450 acres (180 hectares) in size. In the development known as Beechwood, a civil engineer and a landscape architect worked together to incorporate natural valleys and upland woodlots into the area's overall design. The developers laid out lots, roads, driveways, and service lines so as to retain the wooded areas and preserve the trees in each home's backyard.

The developers of the other parcel, known as Lakeshore Village, made no effort to save trees throughout the lots, nor did they seek professional landscape, architectural, or environmental advice. Instead, they preserved one large wetland forest as public parkland to meet the city's minimum requirements for open space. The stream that ran behind some lots was converted into a straight engineered ditch for storm drainage.

Because the Beechwood development retained natural wooded areas, bird populations remained diverse and plentiful. We counted 31 different species of birds—including kingfishers, mallard, cardinals, and chipping sparrows—in a single area of the development. We found that this bird population has as high a diversity as nearby rural woodlots but almost three times the density. The shrubs, lawns, and bird feeders that have now replaced cornfields and pastures presumably provide better nesting and wintering habitat for many species.

In Lakeshore Village, by contrast, both the number of birds and their diversity have plummeted since the development was built. We counted only 12 to 18 different bird species, and found that many of the native populations had been replaced by starlings and English sparrows—not exactly the most popular birds.

More important from a developer's point of view was the marked difference in profits that resulted from the two projects. The costs per acre for Beechwood were $18,687; those for

© Roy Morsch/Bruce Coleman Inc.

Penthouse for peregrines. Falcons feel at home atop a New York City skyscraper because its sheer drops resemble the cliff ledges of the falcon's natural habitat.

Lakeshore, $17,625. Moreover, the net profit per acre for Beechwood was $15,945; that for Lakewood, $10,295. Although the Beechwood developers experienced higher up-front costs because of their careful landscape design, higher charges for routing utility lines, and construction of a community recreation center, their profits were one-third higher in the end because homeowners clearly preferred Beechwood over Lakeshore Village. The Beechwood housing development is one example of how builders can profit from designing open space and preserving trees around homes to attract desirable species. Studies have also shown that lots with trees preserved in natural arrangements have a higher market value than those without trees.

Drawing in the Wildlife

Homeowners and developers can use other strategies to attract wildlife as well. Many bird species prefer specific types of plants for nesting and feeding. Hummingbirds like red flowered plants that provide them with nectar; song sparrows require at least a tenth of an acre of shrubs, trees, and lawns to nest successfully. Butterfly bush, also called by its Latin name *Buddleia*, can attract swallowtail butterflies to feed. Milkweeds, including butterfly weed, attract mon-

Architectural design encouraged the barnacle goose above to visit a condominium development in Miami, Florida. At right, an eagle, perched atop a chimney, enjoys the relative safety of the urbanized Connecticut coastline.

© D.P. Hershkowitz/Bruce Coleman Inc.

© Peter Fraboni

arch butterflies. Wood nesting boxes hung in quiet treed areas can attract house wrens.

Some forms of urban architectural design inadvertently discourage desirable forms of animals, particularly birds. For instance, migrating birds often perceive the reflecting windows on skyscrapers as actually being the sky, and thus fly into the glass, killing themselves. Installing venetian blinds in those windows is a good way to warn the birds about the glass. Bright floodlights on towers that confuse migrating birds and bring about their death through collision and exhaustion can be dimmed after 10 o'clock at night to reduce such losses.

Minimizing the Unwanted

Designers can also minimize habitats used by undesirable animals while renovating and constructing buildings. For instance, developers building high rises should avoid installing cornices and deep windowsills, which attract pigeons. In older historic buildings, where niches cannot be removed, wire protection, removal of nests, or the use of chemical repellents may be required.

Signs placed flush with building surfaces can discourage the presence of English sparrows in winter, since signs placed slightly off buildings offer the birds warm shelter. Open overhangs and laundry vents can also be ideal places for starlings to nest. Closing these overhangs by adding soffits to box in the eaves, requiring that all new buildings have boxed-in eaves, and covering vents with screen can help reduce starlings' breeding sites.

Planners can also control undesirable species by designing habitats that encourage desirable animals to compete for the same food supply. For example, urban landscape architects could plant blocks of oaks, hickories, and red maples in parks and on institutional sites to attract gray squirrels. Since squirrels scavenge food scraps, high squirrel populations should put a brake on rat populations wherever the two species overlap, such as in schoolyards, zoos, and park pavilions.

In most cities, animal-rescue squads attempt to keep down the number of stray or wild dogs by capturing and eventually killing them. However, the people who have the most effective long-term control over the urban stray population are the dog owners of the city. Wild or stray dogs do not reproduce well in an urban environment—their mortality rate is simply too high. Instead, their numbers are continually fed by abandoned or runaway pets. If urban pet owners themselves were more conscientious about supervising their dogs, the stray population now found in some cities would eventually disappear.

Considering Wildlife in the Design Process

The ecological information for this type of careful planning is already available, amassed over the past two decades by biologists and ecologists who specialize in urban wildlife. However, it is not always accessible to the developers, landscape architects, city planners, and civil engineers who make the important decisions about urban design. Many of the engineering firms in the United States and Canada continue to do urban landscaping without the benefit of advice from wildlife specialists, and it is rare to find city planners who have expertise in wildlife ecology.

There are a number of solutions to this problem. First, architecture and engineering schools must do a better job of teaching their students about the biological dynamics of landscape and the monetary advantages of planning for urban wildlife. Second, city planners and engineering firms must seek out the advice of wildlife biologists on urban projects. About 5,000 full- and part-time environmental consultants now practice in North America. Although these people spend most of their time assessing the environmental impacts of roads, power plants, and waste-management plants, they could apply these skills to urban environmental design. Many small consulting firms can combine advice on managing soil erosion, woodlots, urban wildlife, and water quality.

Third, computer models could identify the specific components of a habitat—the type of plants and size of plantings—required to attract different wildlife species. These models could then be made accessible to working landscape architects and engineers. Urban designers already use similar models for managing traffic, noise, trees, and surface water. A wildlife model would simply add to the designer's tools by predicting the wildlife that would inhabit various land-use configurations.

Environmental Reports

A few cities now require developers to include wildlife studies in their environmental reports before approving subdivisions and allowing builders to convert rural land to urban. For instance, Mississauga, Ontario, a wealthy suburb of Toronto, requires that all developers submit a plan detailing the size and scope of wooded areas to be preserved in a new development. The plan must also outline the type of vegetation planned for individual lots and open spaces. Municipal officials must approve this plan before the developers can even submit the overall subdivision plan. Municipalities throughout the United States and Canada would do well to imitate this type of approval process if they want to preserve wildlife and enhance the aesthetic value of their communities.

Some municipal officials have already recognized the value of preserving natural urban areas as part of large-scale revitalization projects. In Ontario, for instance, local officials have reclaimed waterfront parkland among Lake Ontario by creating small grassy areas along the shore with excavated fill. Local residents use these jutting miniparks, lined with stone to prevent erosion, to launch small boats, and to fish, swim, and otherwise enjoy the ducks, geese, and other forms of wildlife that have flocked to these areas.

Urbanites interested in attracting wildlife to their backyards, porches, and terraces can consult a number of organizations for advice. The National Wildlife Federation in Washington, D.C., provides a kit that includes information on plants attractive to wildlife, blueprints for bird feeders and birdhouses, and beneficial designs for backyard pools, among other features. More books on natural gardening, which incorporates native trees, shrubs, and herbs in natural assemblages into front- and backyard areas, are being published each year. Natural gardening techniques shelter the house and thus save energy costs, reduce maintenance costs, enhance privacy, and encourage wildlife, improving the aesthetic environment. More and more homeowners in North America are beginning to realize that landscaping for small urban lots (one-fifth of an acre or so) can have a naturalistic as well as a decorative focus.

Designing with nature in mind, as opposed to just bulldozing it, favors property owners, other urban dwellers, and developers alike. If nuisance species can be controlled through architectural design, and special plantings and nesting structures can be created in parks and backyard gardens, a better fit between humans and nature is achievable in our cities.

SELECTED READINGS

"Urban wildlife populations: a look at downtown, uptown, and suburban residents" by R. S. Dorney. *Smithsonian Institution Symposium Proceedings—Wildlife Survivors in the Human Niche,* forthcoming.

City Form and Natural Process by M. Hough. Van Nostrand Reinhold Company, 1984.

The Granite Garden: Urban Nature and Human Design by A. W. Spirn. Basic Books, 1984.

The BIG SLEEP

by Alan Pistorius

Before the coming of man on earth, Itsayaya, the coyote, called a great council of the animals. Among the weighty issues they decided was the duration of day and night. Hahats, the bear, argued for five years of day followed by five years of night, which would give them all time for a really good sleep. "That's fine for you, you huge fat bear," retorted Matskoy, the chipmunk, "but little animals like me couldn't eat enough to last that long." Matskoy argued for the status quo, a divided 24-hour regimen.

Itsayaya set up a contest to settle the matter, and Matskoy prevailed. The incensed Ha-

hats seized Matskoy and raked his back with his claws (which is how the chipmunk got his stripes), and Itsayaya, feeling sorry for the thwarted bear, granted him a special dispensation: "Henceforth, Hahats, you do not have to wake up every morning like the rest of us . . . . You may find a cave and sleep through the long cold winters," said the coyote.

Thus goes a legend of the Nez Percé Indians, who were struck, as their more scientific successors have been, by the bear's long hibernation. The bear figures prominently in the scanty folklore of winter sleep. That is not surprising considering that hibernation is an essentially invisible activity and that only the bear—a large animal with atypically accessible den sites (caves, hollow trees, even top-of-the-ground nests)—was likely to be caught at it by primitive man.

Science, of course, has been more systematic in its investigation of hibernating animals. Even as you read this article, research biologists around the world are bending over inert furry forms in dark/cold, light/cold, dark/warm, and light/warm lab vaults, measuring oxygen consumption, graphing heartbeats, snipping away at glands, injecting exotic fluids, and removing blood serum.

What Is Hibernation?

Oddly, however, although we have learned a great deal about hibernation in recent years, we lack an accepted definition of what it is, and, hence, we aren't agreed on which animals hibernate and which do not. One could argue that Hahats the bear does not hibernate while Matskoy the chipmunk does. One could also argue that both do or that neither does. Why the confusion?

In part it comes from the opposition of terminological "loose constructionists" and "strict constructionists" among biologists interested in hibernation. If one defines hibernation as "periodic dormancy," then the Earth is knee-deep in hibernators, which include everything from protozoans and earthworms, to frogs and snakes, to anteaters and trees. Seasonal dormancy is a widespread response to environmental stress, and it appears in a number of guises, often with identifying names. The "resting" state in insects, called *diapause*, is usually seasonal, but it may—as in the case of periodic

cicadas—last for years. We are also familiar with winter dormancy in *ectotherms* (the old, misleading term was "cold-blooded" animals) such as frogs, salamanders, and snakes. For the most part, ectotherms enter and leave dormancy in direct response to environmental temperatures.

Other instances of periodic dormancy are not so familiar. In many regions, particularly arid ones, some animals regularly retreat underground and remain dormant in summer in response to too much heat and too little water. That state is called *estivation*. In extreme and unpredictable environmental conditions like drought or flood where seasonal dormancy won't protect animals, some have evolved the ability to initiate periods of temporary dormancy quickly and at any time of year. That trick is called *retraherence*. Other creatures are

The dormouse (right) is one of the few mammals that exhibits classic, or "deep," hibernation. By contrast, the Eastern chipmunk (below) is a "shallow" hibernator, breaking up its winter sleep with active periods.

A fertilized female yellowjacket hibernates under tree bark. If it survives the winter, the female will found a new colony and be its queen. Males and sterile females, neither of which hibernate, die each year from the cold.

bears are "light sleepers." By contrast, classic small hibernators appear to be barely alive when in torpor. Researchers can—and, boys being boys, occasionally do—play catch with torpid specimens in labs. It's never a good idea to play anything with dormant bears. Lynn Rogers, an experienced black-bear researcher in Minnesota, has crawled into many occupied winter dens wielding a rectal thermometer—and has often come out faster than he went in.

While dormant bears neither eat, drink, defecate, nor urinate, the chipmunk may do all of them, particularly eat. It stores food not in the form of fat, but rather as burrow caches. With nuts and seeds at the ready, Matskoy is likely to be warm and active much of the winter. Chipmunks may, like bears, even leave their burrows and walk about on mild winter days. Strict constructionists of hibernation refer to those mammals—and others, including raccoon and skunks—as "shallow" hibernators.

Classic, or "deep," hibernation is exhibited by relatively few creatures: many rodents (from the size of dormice and jumping mice up to marmots), many bats, a few of the *Insectivora* (notably hedgehogs), and a couple of birds of the goatsucker family. The familiar woodchuck is a typical mammalian "deep" hibernator. Having spent the summer working up a good layer of fat over the shoulders, back, and rump (probably in somebody's garden), it seals its burrow entrance with a soil plug and curls into a ball in its vegetation-lined hibernation chamber. Starting from ordinary sleep, it drops by stages into torpor, in which condition its normal heart rate of 75 to 175 beats per minute (depending on activity) falls to 4 or 6, its respiration rate from 15 or 20 breaths per minute to 2 or 3, and its body temperature from 99° F (37° C) to less than half that figure, or a few degrees above typical winter burrow temperatures.

A Mixed Blessing

The physiology of torpor is amazing. The torpid animal's basic metabolic rate drops by 90 percent or more, as does its brain's electrical activity. Blood-vessel constriction reduces blood flow to the animal's posterior. Most of its internal organs, including the digestive tract, all but shut down. Perhaps the most remarkable aspect of torpor is that brain and heart activity continue at the low body temperatures of torpid animals, which are far below lethal levels for other endotherms.

Torpor is a mixed blessing for its practitio-

capable of regular, but brief, periods of torpor. Many hummingbirds, for example, especially montane (mountain) species, fall torpid at night, rewarming in the morning.

For the strict constructionist, hibernation is what is left of periodic dormancy when you subtract all of the above. A hibernator, then, is an *endotherm* ("warm-blooded" animal) that undergoes extended periods of cold-season dormancy marked by deep metabolic depression and from which it can arouse itself using self-generated heat. So, are our friends Hahats and Matskoy hibernators or are they pretenders? They satisfy our definition, but purists quibble. The kicker for bears is body temperature, which drops during winter lethargy only from about 100° F (37° C) to about 90° F (32° C). It would take forever to cool a bear-sized body, and to rewarm it would be energetically extravagant. Because of its size, the bear is able to put on enough fat to maintain its body temperature at a fairly high level all winter. As a consequence,

ner. Presumably hibernation evolved in response to the double whammy with which a cold season hits an animal—an increasing fuel demand (to maintain body temperature) and a decreasing fuel supply. Torpor's major benefit is energy conservation through metabolic depression, but there are other benefits. Some parasites succumb to the cold body temperatures of their torpid hosts. Deep hibernation—a state approaching suspended animation—may even extend the animal's life. At any rate, lab tests with Turkish hamsters show that the greater the part of the year spent hibernating, the longer the individual lived. The down side of torpor is that systems on hold don't do their normal repair work. Immune systems slow to a crawl; cell-building and DNA synthesis are greatly reduced. Bone and eye tissues have been shown to deteriorate. And what about body wastes?

Periodic Arousal

Those problems may explain the purpose of what biologists call "periodic arousal." Hibernation is not a long winter's sleep but rather a series of bouts of torpor interrupted by arousals. Dormant periods are typically shorter early and late in the hibernation season and vary in length in midseason from a week or two to more than a month in some bats. Arousals may represent an emergency response having to do with chemical imbalances produced during low-level metabolism, an expression of endothermic rhythmicity, or both.

Not surprisingly, arousal is the mirror image of falling into torpor. Heart rate, blood pressure, and respiration rate soar at the beginning of arousal, while the increase in body temperature—starting in the anterior part of the body—lags behind. In the typical hibernator, arousal is initially powered by brown adipose tissue ("BAT" or "brown fat" for short), a specialized fat designed to produce heat rather than power muscle contraction. Midway through arousal, muscular shivering—powered by ordinary white fat—may take over to finish the waking process.

The time required to complete the rewarming process and the length of an arousal bout are correlated to body size. A midsized hibernator, like the golden-mantled ground squirrel, requires about two hours to warm fully and will remain active for ten or eleven hours. As a descriptive term, however, "active" is little short of imposture. Two researchers monitoring arousal behavior found that aroused squirrels spent 93 percent of their warm time curled in hibernation posture and most of the rest in perfunctory grooming and bedding arrangement. Presumably the real work was going on inside the animals: cell replication, tissue repair, restoration of chemical balance.

However inactive hibernators are while warm, the process of arousal is costly. On the order of 75 to 90 percent of all energy expenditure and weight loss experienced during hibernation occurs during those relatively brief intervals of arousal. It is the cost of arousal in terms of animals' energy that makes winter visits to bat caves so destructive. Disturbances that cause just a few extra arousals during the course of a winter may result in the death of large numbers of the hibernating bats.

Biological Clock

Like migration—another complicated and costly strategy for defeating winter—hibernation is triggered by an innate *circannual* (meaning approximately yearly) biological clock. Ground squirrels will enter torpor on schedule despite radically inappropriate temperatures. Woodchucks transported to Australia reset their clocks to Southern Hemisphere seasons within two years. Again, as in the case of migration, the circannual clock is wound and fine-tuned by environmental cues.

Research suggests that different animals "immerge"—enter their dens prior to hiberna-

Deep sleeper. The Belding ground squirrel can even be handled while hibernating without risk of awakening it.

© Alan French

tion—in response to a wide variety of positive and negative stimuli. Some species apparently need to experience a certain degree and duration of cold. Some will immerge when water is available but food is not, and some vice versa. Researchers found that they could induce torpor in the garden dormouse at any season by feeding it a diet lacking protein.

Most of our temperate-zone hibernators retreat to their *hibernacula* (the den, burrow, or other hibernation chamber) in autumn, but not all. Gail Michener, a researcher at the University of Lethbridge, Alberta, has spent years studying immergence and emergence schedules of Richardson's ground squirrels living in the southern Prairie Provinces of Canada. Michener concludes that these animals fatten as soon as possible and immerge as soon as they are fat enough. Adult males, whose family responsibilities end with mating, enter hibernation as early as June to sleep away summer and autumn as well as winter. Adult females cannot fatten until the costs in energy of gestation and lactation have been made good; they bed down in late July and August. Last of all to immerge are the juvenile ground squirrels, which must grow up (more than half of the ground squirrel young succumb during their first winter, and undersized young have little chance of survival) before fattening. They immerge in September and early October. That schedule—males before females before young—applies for the same reasons to many hibernators, including our common little brown bat, but typically the lag times are measured in days or weeks rather than months.

Emergence Patterns

Biologist Alan French of the State University of New York at Binghamton found that Belding's ground squirrels emerge in the same order. Adult males terminate hibernation abruptly and arbitrarily regardless of the weather. They tunnel up through the snowpack and spar with one another as their sperm matures and they await the emergence of females. The latter, meanwhile, arouse more and more frequently from hibernation as the season advances, and once or twice during each late-season arousal period, they run up their tunnels to assess the soil-plug temperature. (Researchers found they could stimulate early emergence by warming the plug with a heat pad.) A couple of weeks after the males emerge, the adult females terminate hibernation, emerge, and are bred within days.

Yearlings emerge last, when food is beginning to appear.

For a much larger hibernator like a marmot, the major constraint affecting time of emergence is not one of available energy but of time. The marmot has adequate fat reserves to survive a foodless mating season, and it must get on with its relatively protracted reproductive cycle so that the young can mature before their first immergence. Both male and female marmots end hibernation arbitrarily and early, taking a chance on the weather to get on with breeding.

Most hibernating species of bats have evolved an ingenious means of maximizing the reproductive use of their active season. They mate during the fall and occasionally during arousal in the hibernaculum. Live sperm is stored in the uterus, and ovulation and fertilization commence in spring immediately after the females terminate hibernation. Several species of bear have pushed that strategy one step further. Our North American black bear, among others, gives birth in the midst of winter lethargy. The cubs begin their prolonged development with an ideal mother—one, that is, who is always there and always obliging. They nurse and sleep, nurse and sleep (they do not fall torpid), and emerge in spring having already increased their birth weight tenfold at the expense of mother's hibernation fat.

Hibernation Versus Sleep

How did hibernation originate? We don't know. Until very recently, hibernation was thought to be an anachronism, a harkening back to the inability of ectotherms to thermoregulate from within. But hibernators do thermoregulate—their thermostats are not turned off but rather are set just high enough to keep their "pipes" from freezing. Contemporary researchers suspect that hibernation is a highly adaptive process that may have evolved from sleep, with which it shares a number of traits. Indeed, it has been theorized that sleep itself may have evolved not primarily as a restorative but as a means of conserving energy during recurrent short periods when food was unavailable or difficult to find.

The physiological mechanisms controlling hibernation are difficult to isolate, but laboratory research has made great strides in recent years in discovering how those mechanisms work. The primary regulator is almost certainly that part of the brain known as the *hypothala-*

Little brown bats—shown in a typical hibernating cluster—lose up to 35 percent of their body weight while asleep.

mus, which is known to control—probably through the release of message-carrying neurochemicals—temperature regulation, appetite, water retention, and sleep.

The Hibernation Trigger

What researchers would dearly love to isolate is the "hibernation trigger" (HT), a substance whose power was dramatically demonstrated by an experiment in which blood serum from hibernating woodchucks was injected into rhesus monkeys (which don't, of course, hibernate). The injections depressed the monkeys' appetites, heart rates, and body temperatures for several weeks, during which period they sat about as if anesthetized. Thought to be a chemohormone, HT apparently bonds to the blood protein albumin. It seems to work like an opiate. Indeed, ground squirrels that became addicted to morphine when *euthermic* (warm and metabolizing normally) proved immune to the drug when torpid, suggesting that HT occupies and hence blocks morphine's attack sites in the brain.

The search for HT is not entirely a quest of disinterested science. A host of potential benefactors wait in the wings, hoping the agent can be isolated and synthesized. The medical industry is first on the list. As Robert Myers of the University of North Carolina puts it, HT is believed to contain "factors that are ideal as antihypertensives, anesthetics, analgesics, and antiobesity agents." Organ transplants and other surgical operations would be easier and less dangerous if performed on torpid subjects. The fact that some kinds of tumors cease to grow during hibernation and that radiation is less damaging to torpid than to warm tissues suggests applications in cancer therapy.

Although it is difficult to imagine how human beings could be kept alive at the body temperatures and metabolic levels that sustain torpid ground squirrels, the National Aeronautics and Space Administration (NASA) is also interested in the physiology of hibernation. What a boon dormancy would be to astronauts in long-distance space shots, odysseys during which a craft might be absent from earth for decades. Not only would on-board hibernation solve the difficult psychological problems of boredom and isolation, it might also slow the astronauts' aging. And, of course, spacecraft engineering would be revolutionized by a solution to the problem of how to build a craft big enough to stockpile huge quantities of food and drink, not to mention clean laundry, toiletries, and the myriad other sundries daily consumed by euthermic man.

IN MEMORIAM

ABBETT, ROBERT W. (83), U.S. engineer who directed major port development projects in the United States and in more than 50 other countries. A founding partner of the New York architectural and engineering firm of Tippetts-Abbett-McCarty-Stratton, he also designed the Broadway Bridge over the Harlem River and the Roosevelt Island Bridge in New York City; d. New York, NY, April 7.

BARNABY, RALPH S. (93), U.S. glider pilot and Navy captain. His feats included breaking, in 1929, the world soaring record of 9 minutes, 45 seconds set by the Wright brothers in 1911. He also flew to a safe landing from a glider that had been carried to an altitude of 3,000 feet (900 meters) by a dirigible (in 1930), and tested an experimental seaplane glider for the Navy (in 1943). He was awarded the Air Medal in 1946 and retired in 1947; d. Philadelphia, PA, May 14.

BEHRENS, WILLIAM W., JR. (63), U.S. oceanographer and Navy vice admiral who was among the most decorated officers of flag rank. He served on submarine patrols in World War II, commanded four submarines from 1953 to 1963, and commanded the amphibious force of the Seventh Fleet from 1967 to 1969, during the Vietnam War. He also served as a deputy assistant secretary of state and an advisor to the Atomic Energy Commission, and in 1970 he was named Oceanographer of the Navy. He retired in 1974, taught marine science at the University of Florida, and in 1978 became director of the Florida Institute of Oceanography; d. St. Petersburg, FL, Jan. 21.

BENESCH, REINHOLD (67), U.S. biochemist known for his studies of the mechanisms by which hemoglobin transports oxygen through the blood to body tissues. Born in Poland, he emigrated to England and later became a naturalized U.S. citizen. With his wife, Dr. Ruth Erica Benesch, he conducted studies at Columbia University that led to the discovery of an organic phosphorous compound that loosens the bonds between hemoglobin and oxygen, permitting the oxygen to be delivered to the tissues. He was a professor of biochemistry at Columbia and was also associated with the Woods Hole Oceanographic Institution; d. New York, NY, Dec. 30.

BETTERTON, JESSE O., JR. (65), U.S. metallurgist whose work produced the purest single titanium crystal ever obtained. He began his career with Dow Chemical Company in 1942 but left to pursue a doctorate under Sir William Hume-Rothery at Oxford University in England. On his return to the U.S. in 1950, he joined the Oak Ridge National Laboratory, where he was a group leader in the metals and ceramics division until 1968. From then until his retirement in 1981, he taught at the University of New Orleans, where he worked on the ultrapurification of metals; d. Evergreen, CO, Jan. 20.

BING, R. H. (71), U.S. mathematician known for his work in topology. A professor at the University of Texas, he was a former president of the Mathematical Association of America and of the American Mathematical Society, as well as a past member of the National Science Board; d. Austin, TX, April 28.

BONESTELL, CHESLEY (98), U.S. artist known for his realistic portrayals of space themes. He illustrated the 1949 book *The Conquest of Space* (Wernher von Braun and Willy Ley), as well as other books and space-related articles in *Life, Look,* and other magazines. His work also appeared in science fiction films, notably *When Worlds Collide* and *Destination Moon;* d. Carmel, CA, June 11.

BRODE, ROBERT B. (85), U.S. physicist who worked on the development of the atomic bomb. He led a research team that developed the proximity fuse for the bomb, and later taught physics at the University of California at Berkeley. He was among 12 scientists who, in 1950, urged the U.S. government

to promise never to use the bomb first in warfare; d. Berkeley, CA, Feb. 19.

BUEDING, ERNEST (75), U.S. scientist who developed drug treatments for two potentially fatal tropical diseases: hookworm and schistosomiasis. He modified an existing drug to develop amoscanate, which kills the parasites responsible for these diseases. He also developed the drug oltipraz, which reduces the effects of certain carcinogens; d. Baltimore, MD, April 18.

DASSAULT, MARCEL (94), French aircraft manufacturer whose designs for civil and military planes made him a major figure in the aviation world. Born Marcel Bloch, he developed his first successful aircraft company after World War I. When it was nationalized in 1936, he promptly founded another. He was imprisoned in a Nazi concentration camp during World War II but survived to rebuild his company. Among his most famous designs were the Mystère and Mirage fighter planes. His business was again nationalized in 1981, but he remained involved. One of the richest men in France, he also took part in several publishing and film ventures and held a seat in the French Parliament almost continually from 1981; d. Paris, France, April 18.

DENG JIAXIAN (62), Chinese scientist who helped develop China's atomic and hydrogen bombs. He was educated in China and in the United States, where he received a doctorate in physics in 1948; d. July 29.

ESPENSCHIED, LLOYD (97), U.S. electrical engineer who was a co-inventor of the coaxial cable that made television transmission possible. A member of the technical staff at Bell Laboratories, he took part in radiotelephone experiments in 1915 that first transmitted the human voice overseas. In 1929 he developed the coaxial cable with Herman A. Affel. He also developed the radio altimeter, a precursor of radar, in 1936, and he held more than 100 patents in communications; d. Holmdel, NJ, June 21.

EWING, GIFFORD C. (82), U.S. oceanographer whose research into the use of satellites and remote sensing devices was important to ship and submarine operations. A Navy captain during World War II, he conducted his research at the Scripps Institute of Oceanography in La Jolla, California (1948–66), and the Woods Hole Oceanographic Institution (1966–74). He received several awards, including the Medaille Albert Premier; d. La Jolla, CA, Dec. 10.

FIELD, HENRY (83), U.S. anthropologist who advised two presidents and was known for his work in the Middle East. Among his discoveries at Kish, an ancient city near the Euphrates River, was a 3,000-year-old wheel, the oldest known. This and other finds led him to the view that the area was the "nursery" of civilization; he also uncovered evidence of a flood that he said could have been the deluge described in the Bible. He was an adviser to Franklin D. Roosevelt and Harry S. Truman and was associated with Harvard University and the University of Miami; d. Miami, FL, Jan. 4.

FLESCH, RUDOLF (75), U.S. authority on reading and writing whose well-known book *Why Johnny Can't Read* blamed rising illiteracy on teaching methods. He criticized educators for teaching children to read by recognizing whole words, rather than the sounds of the letters (phonics). Born in Austria, he became a U.S. citizen in 1944 and was the author of more than 15 books; d. Dobbs Ferry, NY, Oct. 5.

GORO, FRITZ (85), German-born U.S. photographer credited with developing the technique of microphotography. After emigrating to the United States in 1936, he worked for most of his career with *Life* and *Scientific American* magazines, covering the major scientific developments of the World War II and postwar eras; d. Chappaqua, NY, Dec. 14.

GUNDERSEN, ALF (87), U.S. surgeon who developed a now common technique for prostate surgery. President of the Gundersen Clinic, founded by his father in LaCrosse, Wisconsin, he introduced transurethral prostatic surgery, in which enlarged prostate tissue is removed without an incision. He received a Knight of the Order of St. Olaf medal in 1984; d. LaCrosse, WI, June 1.

HALLOCK, ROBERT L. (88), U.S. inventor who developed the disposable vacuum cleaner bag, the lever-handled ice cube tray, and other household and industrial items. His more than 30 patents included one for the Gripnail, which can be driven into steel girders as if they were wood. He was the author of *Inventing for Fun and Profit;* d. Boston, MA, Sept. 2.

HANFMANN, GEORGE M. A. (74), Russian-born U.S. archaeologist known for his work at Sardis, an ancient city in western Turkey that was once the capital of Lydia. He directed a Harvard-Cornell expedition at the site from 1958 to 1976, unearthing a marble-paved shopping street, evidence of gold refineries, and a synagogue dating from the A.D. 200's. Hanfmann also taught at Harvard and was curator of ancient art at the university's Fogg Art Museum. He wrote or coauthored more than 350 books and articles, including many on the Sardis discoveries; d. Cambridge, MA, March 13.

HOFFMAN, BANESH (79), British-born U.S. mathematician and physicist who was a colleague of Albert Einstein and an outspoken critic of standardized tests. He worked with Einstein at the Institute for Advanced Study in the 1930's and later published a biography, *Albert Einstein, Creator and Rebel* (1972). His other books included *The Tyranny of Testing* (1962), which criticized multiple-choice tests as inadequate measures of knowledge. He was on the faculty of Queens College for most of his career; d. Queens, NY, Aug. 5.

HUGHES, JOSEPH M. F. (81), U.S. psychiatrist and neurologist who was known for his work with reading problems. A professor of neurology at the University of Pennsylvania, he conducted research that clarified the role of emotions in reducing reading ability. He also researched electroshock treatments; d. Bucks County, PA, June 23.

HURST, GEORGE (59), U.S. inventor and automotive engineer who developed the "jaws of life" rescue device and several innovations for high-performance vehicles. Founder of Hurst Performance Products Co. in Pennsylvania, he invented the rescue tool in the 1960's as a way of saving race drivers involved in crashes; it was later adopted by police departments and other agencies. His other inventions included the four-speed transmission linkage; d. Redlands, CA, May 13.

HYNEK, J. ALLEN (75), U.S. astrophysicist known for his research into UFOs. His 20-year involvement with the Air Force UFO research project began in 1948, while teaching at Ohio State University. He later founded the Center for UFO Studies and continued his research into unexplained sightings. In the 1950's he directed the satellite tracking program at the Smithsonian Astrophysical Observatory; he then joined the faculty of Northwestern University in Illinois, where for 18 years he taught astronomy and directed the Dearborn Observatory. His books include *The UFO Experience* (1972), in which he coined the phrase "close encounters of the third kind" to refer to human meetings with aliens. He later had a cameo role in the 1977 movie that took its title from that phrase; d. Scottsdale, AZ, April 27.

JACUZZI, CANDIDO (83), Italian-born U.S. inventor who developed the whirlpool bath that bears his name. In the early 1900's, his family established a machine shop near Berkeley, CA, that made airplanes and aircraft parts. Jacuzzi designed and built the whirlpool bath—basically a pump that could be used in a bathtub—in 1949 for his 15-month-old son, who suffered from rheumatoid arthritis. He began to market the pump in the early 1950's, and it was followed by Jacuzzi spas; d. Scottsdale, AZ, Oct. 7.

JERVIS, GEORGE AMEDE (82), Italian-born U.S. psychiatrist who was the first to establish the link between biochemistry and genetics in mental retardation. He was director of research at the Joseph P. Kennedy Foundation (1962–71) and of the Institute for Basic Research of the New York State Office of Mental Retardation and Developmental Disabilities (1967–73). Through his research, he identified the enzyme deficiency that causes the genetic disorder phenylketonuria, which can lead to severe mental retardation; d. Stony Point, NY, June 5.

KLATSKIN, GERALD (75), U.S. physician who developed liver biopsy techniques. He performed the first liver biopsy (1947) and became known for studies that related clinical features of the liver to abnormalities. A graduate of Cornell University, he taught at Yale; d. Hamden, CT, March 27.

LEHNINGER, ALBERT L. (69), U.S. biochemist who pioneered in the field of bioenergetics, which deals with the way nutrients are converted to usable forms by the body. A professor at Johns Hopkins University and other schools, he wrote *Biochemistry,* an important text on the subject. He was elected to the National Academy of Sciences in 1956 and was a past president of the American Society of Biological Engineers; d. Baltimore, MD, March 4.

LIBBY, LEONA MARSHALL (67), U.S. nuclear scientist who was the only woman and one of the youngest members of the Manhattan Project, which developed the atomic bomb. She worked on Enrico Fermi's first nuclear reactor and taught at the University of California at Los Angeles, New York University, and other schools. She was also associated with the Brookhaven National Laboratory and Los Alamos National Laboratory; d. Santa Monica, CA, Nov. 10.

LIPMANN, FRITZ ALBERT (87), German-born U.S. biochemist who was a co-winner of the Nobel Prize in Physiology or Medicine in 1953. He shared the prize with Sir Adolph Krebs of Britain for the discovery of coenzyme A, a body chemical that helps convert fatty acids, steroids, amino acids, and hemoglobins into energy. A professor at Harvard and, later, Rockefeller University, he was awarded the National Medal of Science in 1966; d. Poughkeepsie, NY, July 24.

LIVINGOOD, JOHN J. (83), U.S. nuclear physicist who was the first to use a particle accelerator to artificially produce a radioactive isotope (bismuth 210). As a research assistant with Ernest O. Lawrence at the University of California in Berkeley, he was involved in the design and construction of the first cyclotron and used it to produce the isotope in 1936; d. Hinsdale, IL, July 21.

LOEWY, RAYMOND (92), French-born U.S. industrial designer known as the "father of streamlining." His first major design, made in 1929 for the Gestetner duplicating machine, had a profound influence. He later founded his own company and put his distinctive mark on dinnerware, sewing machines, appliances, and countless other items, including logos for the U.S. Postal Service and several major firms, the interiors of Lever House in New York City, supermarkets, passenger liners, and the Studebaker Starliner (1953) and Avanti (1961). His autobiography is *Never Leave Well Enough Alone* (1953); d. Monte Carlo, Monaco, July 14.

MARKHAM, BERYL (83), British aviatrix who was the first to fly solo across the Atlantic from east to west. She was raised in Kenya and learned to fly there, becoming a bush pilot for safari groups and for Baron von Blixen (the husband of Isak Dinesen). She made her historic flight in 1936, leaving from Abingdon Royal Air Force field in Britain and landing in Nova Scotia. Later she published a memoir, *West with the Night* (1942), and was a consultant for Hollywood films; d. Nairobi, Kenya, Aug. 3.

MENARD, H. WILLIAM (75), U.S. geologist whose work became the foundation for the theory of plate tectonics. One of the first geologists to use the aqualung to study the seafloor, he made 25 expeditions and discovered the chain of undersea mountains that runs from Hawaii northward; the Mendocino Escarpment, a great submarine cliff off the California coast;

and fracture zones parallel to the escarpment in the eastern North Pacific. The finds led to the plate tectonics theory, which says that the continents and ocean basins are in constant motion. A professor at the Scripps Institute of Oceanography, Menard wrote six books, including *The Ocean of Truth,* and was awarded the Bowie Medal by the American Geophysical Union; d. Feb. 9.

MILLER, CARL S. (73), Canadian-born U.S. chemist who invented thermography, the duplicating process that was the forerunner of modern copying systems. The process, which used heat-sensitive paper, was introduced by Minnesota Mining and Manufacturing (the present-day 3M Company) in 1950 with the Thermo-Fax copier and was popular until the mid-1960's; d. St. Paul, MN, April 15.

MUELLER, JAMES I. (69), U.S. ceramics engineer who helped develop the ceramic tiles used as heat shields on U.S. space shuttles. A faculty member at the University of Washington since 1949, he led a research team that tested the tiles' ability to withstand temperatures up to 2,600° F (1,425° C); d. Seattle, WA, April 2.

MULLIKEN, ROBERT S. (90), U.S. chemist and physicist who won the Nobel Prize for Chemistry in 1966 for his studies of the chemical bonds that hold atoms together in molecules. He focused on studies of electrons and on quantum theory, and his work was considered the foundation of modern theories of molecular structure. He taught at the University of Chicago and was elected to the National Academy of Sciences at 32, in 1928. He also coordinated several projects connected with the development of the atomic bomb; d. Arlington, VA, Oct. 31.

MYCIELSKI, JERZY (56), Polish physicist known for his work in semiconductors. He headed the solid-state-theory group at the University of Warsaw and, in addition to his own contributions to semiconductor research, was an important figure in Polish scientific circles. He also explored problems in mathematics and economics and was a member of several international committees; d. Warsaw, Poland, Feb. 10.

NUNN, WILLIAM D., JR. (43), U.S. biochemist who studied genetic and molecular biologic aspects of the regulation of fatty acid metabolism. He was a consultant to the National Institutes of Health and a professor at the University of California at Irvine; d. Irvine, CA, July 1.

NYSWANDER, MARIE (67), U.S. psychiatrist who pioneered in the use of methadone as a treatment for heroin addicts. She was introduced to the problem of drug addiction while serving with the Public Health Service and continued to treat addicts when she entered private practice in New York City in the 1950's, doing much of her work from a storefront clinic in Harlem. The methadone treatments were initiated in the 1960's after research by Nyswander and her husband, Vincent P. Dole, showed their success. She was the author of *The Drug Addict as Patient* (1959) and served on many advisory boards; d. New York, NY, April 20.

PAPANIN, IVAN D. (91), Soviet explorer who commanded his country's first ice-floe research station (1937–38). With three others, he spent nine months on the ice floe, which drifted from the North Pole to a point near southeastern Greenland. The research ended with a dramatic rescue after the floe threatened to break up, and he received the title Hero of the Soviet Union. Papanin also held several high posts in government and science and received a second Hero of the Soviet Union title in 1940, when he led an expedition to rescue the icebreaker *Georgi Sedov,* which had been trapped in Arctic ice for 28 months; d. Moscow, USSR, Jan. 30.

PERKINS, E. MARLIN (81), U.S. zoologist who was familiar to millions as the television host of "Wild Kingdom" and "Marlin Perkins' Zoo Parade." His first program appeared in 1945 on local television in Chicago, where he was curator of the Lincoln Park Zoo; "Zoo Parade" aired nationally four years later. In "Wild Kingdom," which first appeared in 1963, he and his assistants covered the globe in search of animals, often stressing concern for endangered species. He continued as

host of the program until 1985, and was also curator of the St. Louis Zoo and the author of four books on his experiences; d. St. Louis, MO, June 14.

SCHROEDER, WILLIAM J. (54), the longest-surviving recipient of a permanent artificial heart. A retired federal worker, he received a Jarvik-7 artificial heart at Humana Hospital–Audubon in Louisville on Nov. 25, 1984, and survived 620 days despite several strokes. In 1985 he was twice able to leave the hospital for a specially equipped apartment nearby, but he returned after suffering another stroke in November of that year; d. Louisville, KY, Aug. 6.

SEMYONOV, NIKOLAI B. (90), Soviet chemist whose research into chemical chain reactions made him a co-winner of the 1956 Nobel Prize in Chemistry. Much of his research dealt with explosion processes. He worked at the Physical Technical Institute in Leningrad and later headed the Soviet Academy of Science's Institute of Chemical Sciences, and he was the recipient of numerous awards from the Soviet government; d. Sept. 25.

SLOAN, LAWRENCE WELLS (89), U.S. physician who was a specialist in diseases of the thyroid gland. He was on the teaching staff of Columbia-Presbyterian Medical Center and was a former president of the American Thyroid Association; d. Hightstown, NJ, April 29.

TAUSSIG, HELEN BROOKE (78), U.S. physician who helped develop the "blue baby" operation, which saved the lives of thousands of children born with heart defects. She devised the technique at Johns Hopkins in the 1940's with Alfred Blalock, after using fluoroscopy to study congenital heart malformations. She was also among the first to study the effects of the drug Thalidomide and to warn of its potential for birth defects; d. Chester County, PA, May 20.

WELLS, EDWARD C. (75), U.S. aeronautical engineer whose designs included the wing for the B-17 bomber. He joined the Boeing Company in 1931 and played an important role in the design of every Boeing plane from the late 1930's through his retirement in the 1970's. He was awarded the Lawrence Sperry Award of the Institute of Aeronautical Scientists in 1942; d. Bellevue, WA, July 1.

WIENS, JACOB H. (75), U.S. nuclear physicist who worked on the Manhattan Project in World War II. He taught at the College of San Mateo in California for 31 years and held patents in the fields of radio, television, and aerial photography; d. Magalia, CA, Jan 24.

WINTROBE, MAXWELL M. (85), Austrian-born U.S. physician who was known for his studies of blood disorders. He developed the hematocrit, a device that measures the quantity and concentration of red blood cells and is used to diagnose anemia. He also researched blood-related cancers and the effects of diet on blood. From 1943 to 1966, he headed the Department of Medicine at the University of Utah; d. Salt Lake City, UT, Dec. 9.

ZACHARIAS, JERROLD R. (81), U.S. physicist and educator who revolutionized high school science education with the theory that students could be inspired by fundamental concepts and hands-on experiments rather than formal problems. In World War II, he helped develop radar and also worked on the atomic bomb project; later, as director of the Laboratory of Nuclear Science at Massachusetts Institute of Technology, he developed the first atomic clock. His focus on education began in the 1950's, when he helped develop a new high school science curriculum as head of the Physical Science Study Committee; d. Belmont, MA, Sept. 9.

ZARISKI, OSCAR (86), Russian-born U.S. mathematician known as a leading algebraic geometrist. He taught at Johns Hopkins, the University of Illinois, and Harvard, where he was chairman of the Department of Mathematics from 1958 to 1960. He received the National Medal of Science in 1965 and published four volumes of collected works; d. Brookline, MA, July 4.

INDEX